MW00785800

THE
LLEWELLYN
COMPLETE BOOK
OF
PSYCHIC
EMPOWERMENT

CARL LLEWELLYN WESCHCKE is Chairman of Llewellyn Worldwide, Ltd., one of the oldest and largest publishers of New Age, Metaphysical, Self-Help, and Spirituality books in the world. He has a Bachelor of Science degree in Business Administration (Babson), studied Law (La-Salle Extension University), advanced academic work toward a doctorate in Philosophy (University of Minnesota), has a certificate in clinical hypnosis, and honorary recognitions in divinity and magical philosophy.

He is a lifelong student of a broad range of Metaphysical, Spiritual, and Psychological subjects, and variously studied with the Rosicrucian Order and the Society of the Inner Light. After corresponding with Gerald Gardner and several of his associates in the late 1950s and early 1960s, he became known for holding the "Weschcke Documents," including a carbon copy of Gardner's own Book of Shadows.

He is a former Wiccan High Priest, and played a leading role in the rise of Wicca and Neo-Paganism during the 1960s and 1970s. Author Donald Michael Kraig has referred to him as "the Father of the New Age" because of his early and aggressive public sponsorship of new understanding of old occult subjects. In the fall of 1973, Weschcke helped organize the Council of American Witches and became its chairperson. Weschcke rightfully prides himself on having drafted "The Thirteen Principles of Belief" Statement, one of the cornerstones of modern Wicca. This document went on to be incorporated into the US Army's handbook for chaplains.

While no longer active in the Craft, he retains ties to the Wiccan and Neo-Pagan communities through Llewellyn. He was also, for a time, Grandmaster of Aurum Solis, an international magical order founded in Great Britain in 1897. He withdrew from the order in 1991, and is not actively affiliated with any group at the present time.

Still actively associated with Llewellyn, he is devoting more time to studies and practical research in parapsychology, quantum theory, Kabbalah, self-hypnosis, psychology, Tantra, Taoism, Tarot, Astrology, Shamanism, Wicca, Magick, and World Spirituality. He is also actively writing, and has coauthored three books with Dr. Joe Slate *(Psychic Empowerment for Everyone, Self-Empowerment through Self-Hypnosis,* and *Self-Empowerment & Your Subconscious Mind)* and a new edition with commentary of *The Compete Magick Curriculum of the Secret Order G∴B∴G∴,* originally authored by Louis Culling in 1969. He and Dr. Slate are planning several more coauthored projects.

Joe H. Slate holds a Ph.D. from the University of Alabama, with post-doctoral studies at the University of California. Dr. Slate was appointed Professor Emeritus in 1992, after having served as Professor of Psychology, Head of the Division of Behavioral Sciences, and Director of Institutional Effectiveness at Athens State University in Alabama. He is an Honorary Professor at Montevallo University and former Adjunct Professor at Forest Institute of Professional Psychology. Dr. Slate is a licensed psychologist and member of the American Psychological Association. He is listed in the National Register of Health Service Providers in Psychology and the Prescribing Psychologist's Register.

As head of Athens State University Psychology Department and Director of Institutional Effectiveness, he established the University's parapsychology research laboratory and introduced experimental parapsychology, biofeedback, hypnosis, and self-hypnosis into the instructional and research programs. His research includes projects for the US Army Missile Research and Development Command, the Parapsychology Foundation of New York, and numerous private sources. He is founder of the International Parapsychology Research Institute and Foundation (PRIF) which, in addition to sponsoring research, has endowed a scholarship program in perpetuity at Athens State University.

His official research topics have included: Rejuvenation, health and fitness, the human aura, psychotherapy, reincarnation, precognition, retrocognition, telepathy, clairvoyance, psychokinesis, objectology, numerology, astral projection, sand reading, crystal gazing, dowsing, dreams, the wrinkled sheet, table tipping, discarnate interactions, psychic vampires, hypnosis, self-hypnosis, age regression, past-life regression, the afterlife, preexistence, the peak experience, natural resources, learning, problem solving, and the subconscious, to list but a few.

He established the Dr. Joe H. and Rachel Slate Scholarship at the University of Alabama (Tuscaloosa), and the Dr. Joe H. and Rachel Slate Scholarship for the Arts at Athens State University. Each scholarship exists in perpetuity and is awarded annually to students who need financial assistance.

Dr. Slate has appeared on several radio and television shows, including *Strange Universe*, the *History Channel*, and *Sightings*.

TO WRITE TO THE AUTHORS

If you wish to contact the authors or would like more information about this book, please write to the authors in care of Llewellyn Worldwide and we will forward your request. The authors and publisher appreciate hearing from you and learning of your enjoyment of this book and how it has helped you. Llewellyn Worldwide cannot guarantee that every letter written to the authors can be answered, but all will be forwarded. Please write to:

Carl Llewellyn Weschcke and Joe H. Slate, Ph.D.
℅ Llewellyn Worldwide
2143 Wooddale Drive
Woodbury, MN 55125-2989

Please enclose a self-addressed stamped envelope for reply,
or $1.00 to cover costs. If outside U.S.A., enclose
international postal reply coupon.

Many of Llewellyn's authors have websites with additional information and resources. For more information, please visit our website at
http://www.llewellyn.com.

THE
LLEWELLYN
COMPLETE BOOK
OF
PSYCHIC
EMPOWERMENT

A Compendium of Tools & Techniques for Growth & Transformation

CARL LLEWELLYN WESCHCKE
JOE H. SLATE, PH.D.

Llewellyn Publications
Woodbury, Minnesota

FIRST EDITION
First Printing, 2011

Cover art © iStockphoto.com/Ryan Lindsay
Cover design by Lisa Novak
Editing by Connie Hill
Interior illustrations by the Llewellyn Art Department
Photograph of Gerald Gardner compliments of Raymond Buckland
Photograph on page 350 by Joe Slate
The Decanates of the Zodiac on page 468 from *The New Golden Dawn Ritual Tarot* by Chic Cicero and Sandra Tabitha Cicero, redrawn with permission

Llewellyn Publications is a registered trademark of Llewellyn Worldwide Ltd.

Library of Congress Cataloging-in-Publication Data
Weschcke, Carl Llewellyn, 1930–
   The Llewellyn complete book of psychic empowerment : a compendium of tools & techniques for growth & transformation / Carl Llewellyn Weschcke, Joe H. Slate. — 1st ed.
      p.   cm. — (Psychic empowerment series)
   Includes bibliographical references and index.
   ISBN 978-0-7387-2709-7
1. Psychic ability. 2. Success—Psychic aspects. I. Slate, Joe H. II. Title.
   BF1031.W4175   2009
   133.8—dc22   2011011842

Llewellyn Worldwide Ltd. does not participate in, endorse, or have any authority or responsibility concerning private business transactions between our authors and the public.
   All mail addressed to the author is forwarded but the publisher cannot, unless specifically instructed by the author, give out an address or phone number.
   Any Internet references contained in this work are current at publication time, but the publisher cannot guarantee that a specific location will continue to be maintained. Please refer to the publisher's website for links to authors' websites and other sources.

Llewellyn Publications
A Division of Llewellyn Worldwide Ltd.
2143 Wooddale Drive
Woodbury, MN 55125-2989
www.llewellyn.com

Printed in the United States of America

ABOUT LLEWELLYN'S "PSYCHIC EMPOWERMENT" SERIES

We all, to some extent, suffer from the illusion of *powerlessness*. Many of us live from day to day feeling that "something important" is missing, or that we are victims of circumstances that make success impossible.

From childhood on, we experience situations beyond our control. We may learn from our parents that "we just can't do anything about it." In schools we may learn about powers beyond our own. In churches we learn of a "greater power," but we that it may be no help in our personal affairs. As adults, we may learn that our employer is unable to meet all our needs, and even our government is limited from providing all we ask of it.

But let's look at "personal power" from another angle, and refer to it as "success." We all want to be successful in social and athletic endeavors, in education and training, employment and career, in marriage and parenting and having the home we desire, participating in our community, attaining financial security, enjoying health and long life, and—ultimately—in feelings of personal accomplishment, personal worth, and spiritual wholeness.

Success is really what life is all about. It's how we may be measured after we depart mortal life. Success happens from *inside out!* Real success is *what you can take with you.*

The secret to success is really no secret at all. Just ask any successful person. The "secret" is really a universal truth that belongs to each and every human being on the planet. Success begins in the Mind and the greatest barrier to success is the illusion of helplessness and powerlessness—that you have no choices in life.

The good news is that you possess the power—inside yourself now—to sweep illusions from your mind and use your mind for what it was intended: to lift human consciousness to a higher level and make this world a better place for you and your children.

HOW IS THIS DONE?

That's where Llewellyn's *Psychic Empowerment* and *Self-Empowerment* books come in. Techniques and tools are available to activate your inner resources and create exciting new potentials in your life. Some techniques specifically involve psychic empowerment—developing your innate psychic powers into psychic skills that are integrated into your Conscious Wholeness.

Psychic empowerment techniques and tools directly engage your undeveloped and ignored subconscious powers and integrate them into the conscious mind. Whether a simple affirmation or a complex empowering procedure, each technique embodies a firm regard for the divine spark of greatness existing in everyone.

Your psychic faculties are standing behind an inner door of consciousness. With their development, you *become more than you are.* With the techniques presented in this book, you can open the door and enjoy a success beyond your wildest dreams.

When you are self-empowered, Success is your destiny.

WE ARE BEING CHALLENGED

A major challenge facing us today is to demystify the so-called *paranormal*, which will explain its nature and unleash its empowering potentials. The psychic experience, whether voluntary or involuntary, is always empowerment driven. Discovering its capacity for empowerment requires attention to the psychic event and understanding its significance.

A major focus of this book is on workable programs designed to promote psychic empowerment through the development of our psychic potentials. As a growth process, psychic empowerment requires the exploration and practice of many approaches to discover those that work best for us individually. Some of the programs presented in this book are designed to promote a general state of psychic readiness, whereas others are structured to activate specific psychic faculties. Each program is unique and can be practiced independently of other programs; however, they share three common features: self-discovery, commitment, and investment.

Only through psychic channels can we meet some of the world's most pressing needs. World peace, for example, must eventually flow not from the destructive wizardry of futuristic war technology, but from the positive power of raised global consciousness, and a firm commitment to global harmony.

Our self-empowerment rests largely on our willingness to master the tools and techniques required to develop our higher potentials and integrate them into our lives. By personally experiencing the psychic nature of our existence, we come to know our psychic side and the empowering potential of psychic phenomena. The psychic experience is an important and convincing teacher, because it validates the essential nature of our existence and connects us to the inner, knowing part of the self.

The full actualization of our psychic potential requires diligence in acquiring essential tools and techniques. This book provides the resources to establish you firmly on your

JOURNEY OF A LIFETIME

ANNOTATED TABLE OF CONTENTS

Your authors have chosen to provide a detailed, or annotated, Table of Contents and we want to tell you why.

Because we anticipate this book being extensively used as a combination Reference and Practical Textbook—one that we hope you will not merely refer to often but will use as a practical guide to all of the Tools and Techniques of Psychic Empowerment—we wrote these chapter descriptions to serve as a concise introduction to each subject.

At the same time, rather than create an encyclopedia by adding many more chapters, we chose the subjects carefully to serve as a master foundation for you to build your own Self-Empowerment program of personal development and experiments.

These introductions carefully follow the construction of each chapter and then provide a quick sequential reference to the included content.

We have also provided a Master List of the Charts, Tables, Programs and Procedures, and a List of Illustrations and Photographs so you can quickly find or refer back to particular information regardless of its chapter location.

We hope that you will find this book to be as exciting as it is useful; that it will open doors and windows revealing new worlds of mind and spirit; and that it will inspire a revolutionary movement of mental and spiritual innovation to move beyond present concepts of conflict and limitation. We live at a turning point in human history as alone and together we take the next steps in our evolution and the realization of the first global civilization.

What is "Psychic Empowerment"? That's what you're going to read about in this book, but it's not just one thing but many. There are many subjects we can group under "Psychic" and we can ask many questions about what we mean by "Empowerment."

But, we can't just define "Psychic" by the many subjects it encompasses (some of which are listed below) any more than we can comfortably define as "Physical" by listing all the subjects from Astronomy (and Astrology) to Hatha Yoga and Zoology that the physical world encompasses. And the same is true of words (and worlds) like "Mental" and "Spiritual."

The reality is that each person has physical aspects and psychic aspects, as well as mental and spiritual. You have a physical body, you have a mind, and most people believe they have a soul or spirit. The reality is that you also have innate psychic powers and attributes, but they are often underdeveloped because we have a primarily material viewpoint of the world we live in.

This book is giving you a new perspective, and it is also providing you with the means to develop your psychic powers and attributes. And we're going to show you that, in doing so, you are going *to become more than you are*—you are going to grow and develop into the whole person you are intended to be.

For each chapter described here in the Table of Content, we're going to list some interesting statistics taken from Amazon and Google, but for this Foreword there really isn't one specific subject to relate to, so we're just going to give a broad selection of the same information. If you walk into a bookstore and look for books related to Psychic Empowerment, you are going to end up in the New Age section. *New Age* is a bookstore category for books also classified under "Body, Mind, and Spirit" or "Metaphysical," and sometimes "Self-Help." It includes Astrology and Witchcraft, Parapsychology and Hypnosis, Magick and Spell-casting, and a whole lot of other subjects.

Contents include: The "New Age" is Real!; Dr. Joe H. Slate, Pioneering Parapsychologist; If Everyone is Psychic…; To Become More Than You Are; Four Major Empowering Principles; Demystifying the Paranormal; Discover a New World of Your Own; Mind over Matter—Every Day; Tomorrow as Probability; But What about Astrology, and Palmistry?

Amazon lists 102,836 titles for New Age, 26 for Psychic Empowerment, 8,940 for Paranormal, 93,264 for Body, Mind, and Spirit, 9,193 for Parapsychology, 17,159 for Astrology, 19,515 for Occult, 18,084 for Metaphysics, 3,409 for Wicca, and 7,805 for Witchcraft.

Google lists 186,000,000 results for New Age, 2,410,000 for Psychic Empowerment, 19,500,000 for Paranormal, 6,670,000 for Body, Mind, and Spirit, 983,000 for Parapsychology, 43,000,000 for Astrology, 8,980,000 for Occult, 7,800,000 for Metaphysics, 3,210,000 for Wicca, and 7,420,000 for Witchcraft.

There's nothing very accurate about these numbers because the subjects themselves are not well defined and include duplications from related (in the eye of the programmer) subjects. But numbers are interesting. There are 29,603 Astronomy titles on Amazon, 338,426 Psychology titles, 9,165 for Quantum Physics, and 49,534 for Ghosts.

Psychic empowerment, rather than a theoretical possibility, is a measurable though complex process of personal evolvement. Using the tools and techniques presented in this book, you can accelerate that process by accessing your dormant inner potentials and activating them to enrich the quality of your life.

This book goes beyond the mere presentation of information and beliefs about psychic phenomena by offering rational explanations of the "unexplained" and focusing on the personal benefits of the psychic experience. It explores a host of psychic tools and formulates effective techniques for applying them. It systematically develops *the psychic empowerment perspective* by focusing on our inner potentials and our ability to develop and apply them.

Presented at the end of the book is a "Journey of Your Lifetime" Development Program, which organizes the seminal concepts of psychic empowerment into an accelerated, step-by-step program for the systematic development of your psychic potentials.

You are, by nature, psychic. The central theme of this book is the development of *psychic empowerment through practice and firsthand experience.* Psychic empowerment is a continuous process of growth and self-discovery. In the empowered state, you can achieve your loftiest goals and improve the quality of your life.

Equipped with knowledge and related skills, you can at last take full command of the forces—both within and beyond—that affect your life. You can accelerate learning, improve memory, increase creativity, solve complex problems, overcome debilitating fears, promote better health and fitness, break unwanted habits, and even slow the aging process. On a larger scale, you can contribute to the greater good and make the world a better place for present and future generations.

Contents include: Empowerment Possibilities of Psychic Knowledge; Threefold Premise of Psychic Empowerment; The Psychic Empowerment Perspective; Four Empowering Principles; The Psychic Empowerment Hierarchy; Psychic Empowerment Programs; Self-discovery, Commitment, Investment; Guidelines to Psychic Empowerment.

CHAPTER ONE—EXTRASENSORY PERCEPTION:
OUT OF THE LAB INTO THE REAL WORLD... 11

Extrasensory perception (ESP) is knowledge of or response to events, conditions, or situations—past, present, or future—independently of known sensory mechanisms or processes. While not yet fully understood, ESP is one of our most valuable channels for experiencing the inner and outer realities of our existence. Bypassing ordinary sensory functions, it can directly engage realities that are otherwise unavailable to us.

In its capacity to send and receive both thoughts and feelings through *telepathy*, ESP can expand our communication capacities, promote productive interactions, and provide information, often from a great distance, otherwise unavailable to us. In its capacity to perceive spatially distant realities through *clairvoyance*, ESP can dramatically expand our world of awareness and uncover critical sources of new knowledge and power. In its capacity to perceive the future through *precognition,* ESP can provide advanced awareness that equips us to prepare for future events and, in some instances, to influence or prevent them altogether.

Contents include: Empowering Effects of Psychic Knowledge; The Developmental Nature of ESP; Factor X; Becoming Psychically Empowered; Positive Self-Talk; Psychic Empowerment Through Self-Talk—Telepathy, Precognition, Clairvoyance; The Power of Mental Imagery; Mental Imagery and the Palm Viewing Exercise; The Finger Interlock Technique; Extrasensory Interactions with the Spirit Realm; ESP and the Dream Experience; Beyond Dreaming.

Amazon lists 793 titles for Extrasensory Perception. Google lists 223,000 results for Extrasensory Perception.

CHAPTER TWO—ASTRAL PROJECTION &
THE OUT-OF-BODY EXPERIENCE 23

Astral projection is the greatest adventure in consciousness we can have while still living in our physical body. It offers proof that being within the physical body is necessary to know, to feel, to love, to live, and to fulfill the great plan of growing and evolving to *become more than we are*. We are beings of consciousness sometimes inhabiting physical bodies that we can learn to leave at will, to travel in time and space, and tap into memory archives and knowledge banks even greater than those of Internet search engines. Going outside of the physically limited brain consciousness enables the soul traveler to enter the heaven worlds, meet and communicate with deceased loved ones, receive guidance from spiritual counselors, and even to intervene in the physical world, often healing the body of disease.

Contents include: What is Astral Projection? The Astral Body and the Astral Plane; Macrocosm and Microcosm; Mathematical Measurement Prefixes and their Meanings; Vibration Ranges of Different Phenomena; Infrasonic to Very Low Frequency (VLF) Waves, Magnetism and Gravity; Physical Senses—in Vibrations per Second; Brain Waves in Vibrations per Second; Earth's Schumann Resonant Frequency; Electromagnetic Spectrum, Longer Waves; Super high frequencies (SHF)—Microwaves; Infrared, Heat; Visible Light (visible to human *physical* sight); Ultraviolet; Spirit Light (visible to human, *psychic,* sight); Gamma and Cosmic Rays; Seven Planes of Solar System and Seven Levels of the Human Structure; Physical and Etheric Planes and Bodies; Astral Plane and Body; Mental Plane and Body and Causal Body; Buddhic Plane and Body; Atmic Plane and Body; Monadic Plane and Monad; Adic Level and Divine Spark; Levels of Consciousness, Soul and Spirit, and the Whole Person; The Evolutionary Plan of the Psyche; A New Way of Thinking; Inducing the Out-of-Body Experience; the Copper Penny; Destination Control; Home Territory; Eye-Blink Procedure; Astral Flight.

Amazon lists 711 Astral Projection titles, 284 for Astral Travel, 67 for Astral Sex, and 487 for Out-of-Body Experience. Google lists 993,000 results for Astral Projection, 638,000 for Astral Travel, and 1,060,000 for Astral Sex.

CHAPTER THREE—AURAS: SEEING & READING WHAT CAN'T BE HIDDEN 47

The human aura is a developmental, life-sustaining energy force that surrounds, penetrates, vitalizes, and characterizes every human being, animal, entity, and object. It has shape, form, and color that reveals consciousness, health, character and substance. This chapter shows how to see, read, and interpret the aura, including your own.

Contents include: What is an Aura? Of What Value is the Aura? Man vs. Machine; Seeing the Aura Instructions; To See Your Own Aura; More than One Aura; Colors in the Aura; Chakra Names, Colors, Associated Planets, and Tattwas; Aura: Interpretation of Colors, Their Intensity, and Their Location; Interpreting the Aura; Magical Mirror of the Universe; Sphere of Sensation; Functions of the Aura System; Self-Perception and Cosmic Centering Procedure; The Aura Self-Massage Procedure.

Amazon lists 6,159 Aura titles. Google lists 104,000,000 results.

CHAPTER FOUR—THE CHAKRA SYSTEM: SPINNING WHEELS OF PSYCHIC POWER 65

Chakras are not physically real but are the energy "transformers" between the physical and the nonphysical, and are vital to body, mind, and spirit. They are located on the surface of the Etheric Double but have subtle connections with certain glands and nerve complexes in the physical body and particular energy centers in the astral body. The Etheric Double is created in advance of birth and functions as a matrix for the developing physical body. No matter the cause, diseases first show up in the astral body, flow down into the Etheric Double, and then manifest in the physical body. This is why etheric or "energy healing" can be so effective through the hands of a competent healer acting *early* in the disease process. Once disease manifests in the physical body, physical treatments are usually necessary but can be supplemented from the ether/energy level as well.

Contents include: Out-of-Body Chakras—Location, Color, and Function; The Etheric Double; Physical Matter Exists in Seven Orders of Density; Functions of the Four

States of Etheric Matter; Energies: *Fohat, Kundalini, Prana;* Primal Energies of the Universe; The Chakras; The Primary Chakra System; Grounding Exercise; The Base Chakra *(Muladhara)* Correspondences; Appreciation Exercise; Energy Flows from Sacral Chakra; The Sacral Chakra *(Svadhisthana)* Correspondences; Self-Control Exercise; The Solar Plexus *(Manipura)* Correspondences; The Love Exercise; Heart Chakra *(Anahata)* Correspondences; Self-truth Exercise; Throat Chakra *(Vishuddha)* Correspondences; Seeing Divinity Exercise; Brow Chakra *(Ajna)* Correspondences; Self-Surrender Exercise; Crown Chakra *(Sahasrara)* Correspondences; The Nature of Psychic Development; Chakra Development Exercises; Kundalini Rising; Nine Main Siddhis; Eight Primary Siddhis; Ten Secondary Siddhis; Five Siddhis of Yoga and Meditation.

Amazon lists 4,335 Chakra titles. Google lists 6,540,000 results.

Clairvoyance is a psychic technique traditionally defined as the perception of tangible objects, current events, or existing conditions not present to the physical senses, but nevertheless having objective reality. Unlike sensory perception, clairvoyance requires no stimulation of sensory mechanisms, and is not subject to the limitations of conventional sensory experience. The spontaneous clairvoyant experience usually provides the means to action.

Complementing inner-clairvoyance as a source of personal insight and power are our clairvoyant interactions with the spirit realm, which often manifests its presence through sensory channels. Frequently, dreams provide the channel for clairvoyant knowledge. Dream mechanisms promote a subconscious transfer of information to conscious awareness. Common among the dream's clairvoyant functions is the delivery of information concerning urgent situations.

Meditation exercises that focus on creative imagery seem particularly conducive to clairvoyant empowerment. The third eye, a chakra thought to be connected to the pituitary gland and associated with clairvoyance, appears particularly responsive to meditation strategies that engage the mind's imagery powers. The Third Eye Exercise given here was specifically designed to develop that faculty.

Contents include: Inner-clairvoyance; Clairvoyance and the Spirit Realm; Clairvoyance and Dreams; Clairvoyant Strategies; Third Eye Exercise.

Amazon lists 2,645 Clairvoyance titles. Google lists 1,890,000 results.

Remote Viewing is the purported ability to gather information about a distant or unseen target by means of extrasensory perception. Typically, a remote viewer is expected to give information about an object that is hidden from physical view and separated at some distance. Several programs sponsored by the CIA, US Army, the Air Force, and others actively explored distant clairvoyance and astral projection during the Cold War between the old Soviet Union and the United States.

Contents include: Remote Viewing and the Cold War; Astral Projection or Clairvoyance; Methods for Remote Viewing; Astral Projection Program; Clairvoyance Program; Programming for Remote Vision.

Amazon lists 157 Remote Viewing titles. Google lists 3,350,000 results.

Dreams are always purposeful and empowerment driven. They are, however, often cloaked in symbolism or other forms of disguise, thus challenging us to discover their meanings and apply them. Paradoxically, the absence of transparency in the meanings of dreams actually increases their empowerment potential. By nature we place higher value on new knowledge requiring effort and involvement. Knowledge too easily acquired is often cast aside as unworthy of serious consideration.

Although dreams have been with us forever, only in recent years have we developed effective dream empowerment programs connecting us to the enormous resources of the subconscious. With new understanding of dreams as expressions of the subconscious, a new dream technology is clearly emerging. As Shakespeare noted, "We are the stuff as dreams are made on, and our little life is rounded with a sleep!" The typical dream experience is energized by not only our subconscious motives but new growth possibilities as well. By accurately interpreting our dreams, we can increase awareness of our subconscious resources and activate totally new growth processes. Self-enlightenment and self-empowerment become the twofold goal of dream interpretation.

Advanced dream intervention programs have been developed in the laboratory setting and are now available for use by everyone in solving personal problems, accelerating learning, overcoming blockages, improving memory, slowing aging, increasing creativity, activating out-of-body travel, and interacting with the spirit realm. Dreams deliver new insights for solving complex problems. Aside from their problem-solving functions, dreams are often psychic in nature. Almost everyone recalls having a precognitive dream that later came true, or a clairvoyant dream that expanded awareness of an existing situation or condition, often at a distant setting. Aside from these, telepathic dreams in which messages are sent and received between dreamers are not uncommon.

Contents include: Dreams are Always Purposeful and Empowerment Driven; The Nature of Dreams; Dream Interpretation Guidelines; Dream Intervention Programs; The Finger Spread; Solar Plexus Rest; Arm Lift Technique; Pre-sleep Meditation; and a concise Dream Symbols Dictionary.

Amazon list 2,065 Dream Interpretation titles. Google lists 3,330,000 results

A cardinal principle of psychic empowerment holds that psychic potentials exist in everyone and can be developed through appropriate programs. Common to those programs are the following three essentials. *Motivation*: Given motivation, you become goal oriented and focused in your pursuit of psychic empowerment. *Learning*: Through your exploration of various psychic concepts, exercises, and development programs, you will discover the knowledge that's essential to your psychic growth and development. *Practice*: The necessity.

In developing your psychic potentials, there is no substitute for practice. Through practice using various exercises and programs, you will discover the tools and techniques that work best for you. Through continued practice, you will develop your psychic powers to their peak.

Contents include: Essentials for Discovery and Development of Psychic Powers; Conscious vs. Subconscious; General Psychic Development; The X Position; Mind/Body Interactions; Telepathy, Clairvoyance, and Precognition: Exercises for Growth; Psychic Balance and Attunement Technique; Empowerment-at-Once Procedure.

Amazon lists 6,179 ESP titles. Google lists 68,600,000 (many of these have nothing to do with Extrasensory Perception but rather a guitar company of that name).

Rituals are basic to civilized life, and many of them have their foundations in magical theory and come down to us through mythic origins. Most rituals mark turning points in life and are, in essence, "initiations" aiding in our transformation from onestate or status into another state or status. Other rituals are celebrations that express the natural rhythms of life and of the seasons. Without these rituals, we would lose attunement to the stages of life and of nature.

Other rituals are esoteric, as in Masonry, Organized Religion, and Magickal groups, and involve the arousal and direction of psychic forces for particular purposes, often transformative psychologically and spiritually. These rituals, knowingly or not, employ hypnosis and utilize established symbols and substances to infuse special energies into the process.

Most rituals can be practiced solitary and involve self-hypnosis. The lack of group energy is compensated for with particular exercises drawing upon the unlimited power of the Cosmos. Gerald Gardner and the Eight Paths to the Center are discussed in detail, along with the principles of Shamanism. The principles of hypnosis and self-hypnosis are given, along with the practices of invocation and evocation.

Contents include: Rhythm and Pattern in Ritual; Esoteric Rituals; Hypnosis; Hypnosis in Ritual Settings; Conscious Participation in Group Rituals; Self-Hypnosis; Prayer and Spells; The Magic of Faith; Extra-Consciousness; Shamanic Techniques and Experiences, and The Eight Paths to the Center in Witchcraft; Programming for Self-Directed Rituals and Self-Hypnosis; *The Principles of Induction;* Belief and acceptance; *Induction Aids;* Security and confidence; The Right Time; *The Key Steps in the Induction process:* Preparation; The Relaxation Process; Invoking your Sub-Conscious Mind; Script for Developing your ESP and PK Potentials; Script for Interacting with Spirit Guides; Script for Developing your Mediumistic Powers; Script for Discovering Higher Planes of Power.

Amazon lists 78,350 Magic titles (5,142 for Magick), 26,615 for Ritual, and 2,151 for Shamanism. Google lists 271,000,000 results for Magic, 2,980,000 for Magick, 34,000,000 for Ritual, and 1,540,000 for Shamanism.

The ability to perceive the future independently of presently known predictive circumstances exists to some degree in everyone. The future is not fixed but exists only in varying degrees of probabilities, ever dependent on past and present realities. Personal consciousness interacts with those future probabilities to generate a *mind/future interaction* that not only "sees" the future but influences it, bringing about desired change.

By developing our ability to interact with the time continuum, we can not only access the future through precognition but dip into the past through retrocognition. While the past can't be changed, increased knowledge of that dimension can alter our perceptions of the present and empower us to more effectively shape the future.

Precognitive awareness is activated deliberately through certain procedures and techniques, some of which were developed in the controlled laboratory setting. To deny our capacity to experience the future through precognition is to eliminate one of the most important gateways to new knowledge, growth, and power. Fortunately, procedures are now available to develop our precognitive capacities and apply them as personal empowerment resources.

Hypnotic age progression has demonstrated unusual effectiveness in identifying future events of both personal and global significance. The program uses self-hypnosis to induce the trance state, during which awareness flows with ease along the time continuum until it is arrested either voluntarily or spontaneously to engage areas that command special attention. This approach is especially effective in identifying future happenings that can be either prevented or minimized through appropriate intervention measures. Crises related to business and personal concerns are particularly receptive to this approach.

Contents include: Precognition and the Subconscious; Precognitive Role of the Subconscious; The Precognitive Reality Slip; Empowerment at its Peak; Precognition and Psychic Empowerment; Precognitive Development; Future Probe Program; The Future Screen Program; The Doors to the Future Program; Precognitive Review Program; Hypnotic Age Progression.

Amazon lists 2,129 titles. Google lists 405,000 results.

CHAPTER ELEVEN—PSYCHOKINESIS: A HOLISTIC VIEW: MIND OVER MATTER—EVERY DAY

PK is the ability to move or influence physical objects without physical intervention. From a holistic perspective, it becomes increasing conceivable that the teleportation of materials and matter to distant destinations is a reasonable reality awaiting our discovery and poised for unfoldment.

Within our definition of PK is the assumed capacity of PK to influence not only external conditions but also physiology, including the most critical systems and organ functions. The capacity of PK to intervene physiologically has been dramatically illustrated in the biofeedback setting, where increased awareness of biological processes led to the ability to mentally control them, including blood pressure, muscular tension, migraine and tension headaches, heart rate, and brainwave patterns. Given these powers of the mind over the body, PK interventions that promote wellness and healing become reasonable possibilities.

Aside from these, lab studies offered convincing evidence of the capacity of PK to slow the aging process, and in some instances to literally reverse the effects of aging.

Contents include: PK in the Laboratory; Reality PK; The Deliberate Induction of PK; Stages of Induced PK; PK Bombardment Drill; PK and Wellness; Mind-Body Interaction for Wellness; The Wellness Activation Program; PK and Rejuvenation; PK Rejuvenation Principles; Rejuvenation PK Program.

Amazon lists 193 titles. Google lists 238,000 results.

Our past-life experiences remain forever with us for a purpose. But rather than being automatically available to us at the beginning of each lifetime, they challenge us to retrieve them and discover their relevance for ourselves. Only then can we integrate them into our present lifetime. It's through concentrated effort and self-discovery that we learn and grow. It's then that knowledge of the past becomes power for the present. It's then that we uncover totally new potentials to be realized and enjoyed. Once we discover them, our past-life achievements in particular can build feelings of worth and well-being. We become less constricted in our self-identity and more at one with the universe.

The most effective self-hypnosis program for past-life enlightenment is called Past-life Corridor, which uses a combination of age-regression and past-life regression. The procedure introduces the concept of a Past-life Corridor of many doors with each door representing a past lifetime. Additional programs explore preexistence and life-between-lives.

Knowing that you do live forever and are constantly growing and learning—forever becoming more than you are—gives significant meaning and justification to life.

Contents include: The Multiple Dimensions of Personal Existence; Interacting with the Subconscious; Self-hypnosis and Past-life Regression; Past-life Regression Self-hypnosis Procedures; EM/RC and Past-life Corridor Regression Program; Sleep Intervention Program; Preexistence and Life-Between-Lives; Exploring Preexistence; Life between Lifetimes; Benefits of Preexistence Regression; Past-life Regression and ESP.

Amazon lists 4,416 Reincarnation and 73 Past Lives Regression titles. Google lists 4,410,000 results for Reincarnation and 898,000 for Past Lives Regression.

A picture may be worth a thousand words as stated in an ancient Chinese proverb quoted again and again. A specifically created drawing of a particular thing or idea may be worth many thousands of words in clarifying our understanding of it. A sigil may be worth more than words because it is a magical formula charged with energy to do a certain kind of work.

As you will see, the "modern" form of sigil magick is very similar to the practice of self-hypnosis involving specific goals expressed in affirmation form. Both sigil magick and traditional self-hypnosis are a kind of programming to mobilize the resources of the subconscious mind to accomplish your objectives.

Contents include: What are Sigils? Traditional Sigils; The Rose Matrix for Sigil Magick; The Modern Sigil; Sigils in Practical Magick; Sigils and Thoughtforms; Principles of Sigil Magick; Magick in Theory

Amazon lists 383 titles. Google lists 147,000 results.

Telepathy is communication without physical limitations and surpassing even the most advanced communication technology. It includes not only the sending and receiving of thought messages but the emotions and motives underlying them. It can even include the transference of positive energy.

All social interactions include a spontaneous telepathic component that can promote productive interactions by enriching the communication process. In the group setting, the communication process as well as the productiveness of the group can be strongly influenced by telepathic interactions.

The sender in the communication system has two major functions: first, formulating the message in some appropriate encoded form, notably imagery, words, symbols or a combination of these, and second, sending the encoded message. The receiver in the communication system likewise has two major functions: first, receiving the encoded message and second, decoding it.

Similar to self-hypnosis, inner-telepathy empowers us to command the complex, ongoing interactions within the self. One of the most common examples is *self-talk* with thought messages subsequently dispersed throughout the self-system or to selected inner targets. Self-talk combined with mental imagery is especially effective in generating creative ideas.

Global telepathy is based on the premise that we can psychically generate global interactions that affect global conditions and bring forth global change.

Contents include: Telepathy Explained; Telepathic Initiative Program; Telepathic Activation Procedure; Two-part Composite Telepathic Procedure; Global Telepathy.

Amazon lists 2,857 titles. Google lists 1,970,000 results.

Chapter Fifteen—Visualization: The Key to Empowering Your Imagination

To imagine is to create. The imagination (image-plus-action) is our faculty that puts an image into action. To act upon an image is to turn it into reality. The essential element for successful Creative Visualization is *emotion*. Effective visualization is the key to empowering your imagination to "make real the unreal." To imagine and to visualize is to move from past into future, which becomes the present. "Present" in time, and a "present" (i.e., a gift) to you.

The image in the imagination was visualized—created wholly out of "mind stuff" which can become the seed or matrix or core of energy that becomes converted into matter to enter the world of reality. To enable that process to happen, the visualized image attracts energy and matter that become the thing visualized through any of a variety of processes.

The "power of attraction" uses creative visualization to activate opportunities to bring fulfillment to your desires and accomplish your goals in life. Know what you want, be specific without limiting the opportunity to access the reality by which it can be accomplished, find the picture or symbol to represent your desire or goal, empower it with emotion, see it in your imagination, and "put yourself in the picture" so that the opportunity comes to you. Your ability to effectively visualize turns your imagination into a **psychic power tool** for use in psychic work as well as in all forms of magical application, active meditation, astral travel, Qabalistic pathworking, the development of clairvoyance, remote viewing, symbol "doorways" to access specific areas of the astral world, activating archetypal powers, the assumption of god forms, entering mythic worlds, and much more.

Contents include: What's the Difference? Creative Visualization; The Power of Attraction; Visualization as a Technique; Are there Practical Applications? Making the Imagined Image as "Real" as REAL; Cultivating Visualization.

Amazon lists 4,903 titles. Google lists 17,500,000 results.

An important technique of psychic empowerment is to adopt certain objects as "tools" for indirect means to access our inner psychic potentials and promote their development. These psychic tools are material objects purposefully applied to connect us to sources of psychic power within the self. We call the study of these tangible tools and the techniques associated with them "objectology."

Psychic empowerment tools and techniques are valuable, not only in stimulating our psychic functions and promoting their development, but also in research designed to explore and better understand the world of psychic phenomena. Through the use of tangible objects, we can develop techniques and assemble objective data that can be statistically analyzed for significance and relevance to the psychic experience. The application of dowsing rods, for example, can yield specific data regarding natural subterranean resources which can be analyzed for accuracy. Likewise, the pendulum when appropriately applied can provide a wealth of data in a quantified form that can be treated statistically. ESP cards are often used by researchers to gather objective data related to various psychic faculties and provide comparisons of psychic abilities among individuals. Many of our conclusions concerning the nature of psychic phenomena are based on the results of studies that applied tangible objects under appropriately controlled, scientific conditions.

Amazon lists no titles. Google lists 2,150 results.

The pyramid, along with the circle, square, triangle, etc. is one of the basic geometric shapes fundamental to the universe, and through our creative imagination it connects us to the energies of the material world. As an archetypal symbol it is used in Masonic and Esoteric programs to align the psyche with basic philosophical concepts.

Inside the Great Pyramid are passageways and chambers historically used in mystical practices while a schematic representation of the interior is used to describe divisions of human consciousness.

A popular view of pyramid power centers on the inherent empowering properties of the design itself along with its inspiring, balancing, preserving, and rejuvenating properties. When the pyramid is oriented with one side accurately aligned to one of the four cardinal points of the compass, its positive potentials are activated. For most personal applications, the pyramid's empowerment potentials are expanded through appropriate affirmations.

Ascending the Pyramid is a practical psychic empowerment meditation exercise used in relation to goal setting. When used in meditation, pyramidal imagery increases the effectiveness of empowering affirmations.

Contents include: A Universal Symbol of Power and Mystery; Divisions of Human Consciousness; Basic Geometric Shapes Fundamental to the Universe; Possible Healing Properties; The Pyramid's Applications as an Empowerment Tool; Pyramidal Strategies; Ascending the Pyramid Meditation Strategy; Benefits of the Ascending Imagery.

Amazon lists 17,572 Pyramid titles. Google lists 26,100,000 results for Pyramid.

Crystal gazing is one of the most widely known techniques to stimulate inner psychic functions and expand psychic awareness. Through the centuries, crystal gazing, or , has been used to probe the unknown; and, in recent years, it has been incorporated into a variety of self-empowerment strategies designed to open new vistas of psychic understanding and knowledge.

Crystal Gazing enables the discovery and transfer of specific knowledge found in the subconsciousness to the conscious mind as needed or on demand, or as required in certain telepathic communications. As a meditation technique, crystal gazing will often produce profound personal insight as well as highly relevant psychic knowledge.

For both precognition and retrocognition, crystal gazing functions in two important modes: forward and reverse. In its forward mode, the technique transports awareness into the future to target selected events, while in its reverse mode, it projects awareness to unknown past events or experiences.

Aside from its relevance in stimulating various psychic functions, crystal gazing has been successfully applied as a stress management, meditation, and general self-empowerment technique.

Contents include: Stimulating Psychic Functions; The Mind's Imagery and Concentration Powers; Positioning the Crystal Ball; Crystal Gazing Facilitates Transfer from Subconscious to Conscious Awareness; The Function of Focal Points; Crystal Gazing Procedures; Crystal Gazing as Meditation Aid.

Amazon lists 167 titles. Google lists 192,000 results.

"Dowsing is the exercise of a human faculty, which allows one to obtain information in a manner beyond the scope and power of the standard human physical senses of sight, sound, touch, etc."

Dowsing rods and pendulums are simply external tools of the psychic mind. As "antennae" of mind and body, dowsing instruments stimulate a host of sensory and extrasensory receptors for gathering a vast amount of information. As the psychic mind develops, so does our capacity for dowsing.

As a technique for gathering information, dowsing has been successfully applied to science and technology, business and industry, forensics, and the military. Valuable subterranean resources including oil, coal, water, minerals, and natural gas have been located through dowsing. In industrial settings, dowsing has been effective in locating buried cables, water, gas lines, and valuable resources. There is some evidence that dowsing may have valuable diagnostic potential when applied to the human body.

We share energy and consciousness with the Earth and ourselves at both the physical and more subtle levels known as etheric and astral. It is within our personal consciousness—our subconscious and conscious minds—that we can make the fine attunements that can channel specific information useful in practical and beneficial applications. The greatest value of dowsing with the pendulum is communication between the subconscious mind and the conscious mind, and actually going beyond to the universal consciousness in which all memories and all knowledge resides.

The pendulum can accurately explore our inner motives, abilities, interests, and potentials. As a probe of external realities, the pendulum can tap distant sources of psychic insight and connect us to a vast wealth of empowering psychic knowledge.

Contents include: Dowsing is a Respected Profession; Dowsing and the Magnetic Field; Energy and Consciousness; Test it Yourself; You Have the Power; It All Starts at the Beginning; An Ancient Practice Renewed; Channels of Communication accessing Subconscious Knowledge; How to Dowse with Rods and Sticks; Dowsing's Many Practical Applications; Dowsing as a Diagnostic Aid; American Dowsing Society Website; Dowsing with the Pendulum; Detecting Gender; Alphabet and Number Charts; Pendulum Prospecting with Maps; Pendulum Power—Pendulum Magic; Detailed Instructions for both Dowsing and Pendulum Work; Taking the Next Step.

Amazon lists 653 Dowsing and 2,847 Pendulum titles. Google lists 600,000 results for Dowsing and 10,900,000 for Pendulum.

CHAPTER TWENTY—GEOMANCY: WHAT THE EARTH TELLS YOU

Geomancy is an Earth-based divination system providing a *picture* of the immediate environmental influences on the question at hand. Psychologist Carl Jung called it "terrestrial astrology," following the West Nigerian practice of creating the astrological chart by counting pebbles to arrive at ones and twos to produce a chart read like a horoscope.

All divinatory systems connect the Conscious Mind to the Subconscious and thence to the Universal Consciousness to provide a map of the Unconscious at that moment. Psychic Empowerment depends on our abilities to consciously "channel" our questions to these *lower* realms and to refer the answers to our *awakened consciousness* for their analysis and application. While it can be used to gain some insight and alternative views of events, it will primarily relate to the personal state of awareness rather than the fully objective "outside" world.

While geomancy is shamanic in origin, the common form of European geomancy is derived from ancient Arabic and Roman practices combined with astrology and the Greek doctrine of the four elements. The sixteen geomantic signs (four rows of dots or lines) represent all possible basic combinations of the elements. Each of the seven traditional planets is associated with two geomantic signs, the remaining two signs being associated with the nodes of the moon. Zodiacal symbols are assigned to the geomantic signs associated with the planets according to each planet's zodiacal rulership. From its simple origins, it has evolved into a complex operation working at subconscious levels.

While some practitioners simply put dots on paper, proceeding from right to left, and then count them, the better method is to use a box of clean sand and a common pencil as a stylus. Marks are made, and counted, and the process repeated to complete the forms which are then interpreted according to established rules extended through intuition and psychic insight.

Contents include: An Earth-Based Divination System; A Picture of Earth Energy Influences; Terrestrial Astrology; Communication Disguised in Symbols and Strange

Words; Geomancy's Evolution from Simple to Complex; the Flow of Earth Energies; Miniature Sand Box; Sixteen Tetragrams; Four Mothers; A Map of the Unconscious at the Moment; Necessity of a Geomantic Journal; History and Origins; Hermes Trismegistus; The Golden Dawn; Practice of Geomancy; The Question is the "Need to Know"; The Shield; Four Daughters; Four Nieces; Two Witnesses; The Judge; Geomantic House Meanings; Techniques of Consultation; Geomantic Attributions (Tables); Reconciler; Signification of the Houses; The Geomantic Map; Geomantic House Meanings; Geomantic-Astrological Rules of Planets in Signs; Geomantic Steps in Divination; Geomantic Golden Dawn Ritual of Operation.

Amazon lists 218 titles. Google lists 380,000 results.

Handwriting refers only to *writing* and only rarely to hand *printing*. Your writing sample is most likely to be a note taken at a meeting or as a summary of a phone or other conversation; the more spontaneous it was the better. Your analysis starts with simple observation and your impressions: *Is it orderly, neat, messy, unbalanced, heavy?* Write down your impressions. *Does the writing appear fluid or rigid, natural or stilted? Is it balanced and symmetrical? Is the use of white space harmonious? Does the writing feel rhythmic?* Write your impressions. As you notice different factors that seem unusual, write the same thing yourself (even if you wrote the note originally) and see how it feels.

Handwriting analysts break the handwriting into zones. Zones are the portions occupying the main area of the writing, and then those above and below, and are viewed symbolically for the energies expended in particular areas of the writer's life. All references are to noncapitalized letters. The *Upper Zone* identifies with the superconscious mind—the mental, spiritual, political, and intangible areas of life. The *Middle Zone* identifies with the conscious mind—the mundane matters of daily life, social relationships, and conscious choices.

The *Lower Zone* identifies with the subconscious mind—the basic biological drives and desires, sex and sensuality, sports and material matters of money, and consumer comforts.

Baseline Slant reflects the writer's emotional state and the extremes of optimism or pessimism. Letter Slant relates to the writer's emotional direction and degree of emotional control. Letter Size projects the writer's self-importance and claim to space. Pressure relates to the intensity and depth of feeling. Connecting Strokes reveal the writer's attitude toward others. Letter Spacing reveals the writer's expression: introversion, extroversion, repression. Word Spacing reveals the writer's degree of contact with the immediate environment. Line Spacing reveals the writer's sense of direction and order. Margins reveal the writer's relationship to the world as expressed in economy, consistency, tolerance, desire for esteem, and urge for acceptance. Letter Formations can reflect considerable character tendencies, but vary considerably even within a single writing sample.

The signature is still commonly used to legally affirm a contract, to transfer funds with a bank check, and to confirm or acknowledge the details of a report. While most of the rules of handwriting analysis can be applied to the written signature, it is necessary to consider that the personal signature is often deliberately created as a public representation of the self.

The pronoun "I" is most commonly used in statements of affirmation, promise, and commitment, and often used in self-hypnosis.

Contents include: The Two Powers of Divination; Understanding the Circumstances of the Moment to Determine a Course of Beneficial Actions for "Fortune Building"; Handwriting as a Method of Communication and Recording; Scientific Method of Character Study; Forensic Aid in Criminal Investigations; Relationship Probabilities; Handwriting Today; Graphotherapy—Changing Handwriting for Self-Improvement; Main Elements of Handwriting Analysis; Connecting Strokes; What Letter Spacing Reveals; The Meaning of Margins; What Letter Formations Reveal; What the Handwritten Signature Has to Say; The Personal Pronoun "I" and the Private You.

Amazon lists 635 Handwriting Analysis titles. Google lists 552,000 results.

CHAPTER TWENTY-TWO—THE I CHING: WHEN THE MOMENT IS RIGHT

"Chinese Thought" is concerned with Virtue and Correct Conduct, and divination is performed to determine the right course of action. The *I Ching* is not a fortune-telling system but a way to examine the *nature of the moment* to determine right conduct. "Correct Conduct" is not always the most personally beneficial action but it is the *right thing to do*—ethically, practically, and "spiritually" in the cosmic scheme of things.

In all things, "timing is the key to success" and when the moment changes, so will its nature. When the moment is right, the "rainbow bridge" connects heaven and earth, placing the forces of Yin and Yang in perfect balance. Such balance becomes the foundation for right action. The premise of the *I Ching* is that all things—past, present, and future—are interrelated, and constantly changing and transforming. The past is in the present, for the past is the present's base and influence. The seeds of the future are in the present, and the future's roots are in the past. However, even though all things are constantly changing, a given moment in time may be isolated and its unique characteristics determined.

Carl Jung called this the "synchronistic concept" of the universe. Since the exact parameters of a moment occur only once, this becomes *legible* by means of the hexagram form. As the moment is, so do the thrown sticks or coins or dice or shuffled cards fall because they have the quality of that moment alone, a visible summation of all things past and present. The function of divination is to understand past and present in order to foresee the future, drawing from the unconscious to the conscious mind whatever is needed to understand the question asked and provide its solution.

The eight basic trigrams symbolize all that is knowable, spiritually and physically. The trigrams are symbols of all that is in the midst of a state of change and are true representations of life itself. Your trigram throw is yours alone. Yang and Yin lines compose a trigram based on the triune Principle of Body, Mind, and Soul. The bottom line is the body and automatic emotions. The middle line is the thinking man, mind, and intellect. The top line is the soul, spirit, and one's intuitive wisdom.

There is one Great Key, and only one to the interpretation of each of the sixty-four hexagrams in relation to any question. This Key is the right comprehension of the meaning of each of the eight trigrams, plus the special implications of the trigram's position in the hexagram, upper or lower. By placing yourself in touch with the flow of universal energies through the random draw, you will find your place in the scheme of things—at this moment. The *I Ching* is not so much predictive as revealing of your circumstance if you continue to follow the path you are on. The interpretation will suggest ways to realign yourself with the deeper harmony.

Contents include: From Unity Comes Duality—Yin and Yang; Yin and Yang Manifest in a Trinity—the Trigram; All Things are Interrelated, Constantly Changing and Transforming; Jung's "Synchronistic Concept"; How It Works—The Eight Basic Trigrams Symbolize All that is Knowable, and Represent Life Itself; When "the Moment is Right"; Body, Mind, and Soul in the Trigram; Three Great Principles of Activity, Substance, and Form; Putting the Question; Casting the Yi Hexagram; Casting by Coins; I Ching 64-Card Deck; Chess Method of Casting; The Dice Method; Interpretive Guide

Amazon lists 1,843 titles. Google lists 4,280,000 results.

Spirits have been with us from the beginning of anything we know about humanity. Their presence is recorded in the sacred literature of all peoples and in their mythologies as well. They are in the Jewish and Christian Bible, in our folklore, and part of religious history studies and paranormal research. Spirits are an intimate experience in African-Spiritist based religions of Santeria, Macumba, Voudoun, and others prominent in the African-American and Hispanic cultures of the United States, the Caribbean, and Latin America.

The modern renaissance started with rapping sounds in 1848 in the Fox family home in Hydesville, NY. The two young sisters started communicating with the spirit making the rappings and news of this brought reporters and observers from New York City and more distant places. Among the observers were H. P. Blavatsky, who later founded the Theosophical Society and Spiritualism as religion, and the subject of psychical research dominated public interest.

Laboratory research at Athens State University and elsewhere has demonstrated and measured a range of phenomena associated with Spirit presence and communication, including out-of-body experiences, psychokinesis, and hauntings, and has verified the history behind such spirit appearances. Included in ASU research projects was the astral body of one person sharing the physical body of another person.

Research refutes the lore and claims of negative experiences and harm from spirit communication and finds only positive benefit. Experimentation included table tipping and séance, leading to the development of programs developing "the medium within."

The deeper our understanding of spirit communications, the deeper our understanding of ourselves and the spiritual nature of our existence. Although we are mind, body, and spirit, without the spirit we would not exist. Only the spirit is forever. It's the spirit that gives meaning to our existence and direction to our strivings as soul beings.

Contents include: A Little History; Parapsychology and Metaphysics; The New Age of Spirit; Spirituality in the Laboratory; Spirituality and the Out-of-body Experience; Out-of-One's-Own-Body-and-Into-the-Body-of-Another; The Nature of Spiritual Communication; The Down Side of the Other Side: Fact or Fiction; The Medium Within; Tools and Techniques; Table Tipping; Table Tipping Applications; The Séance; Spirit Communication for just One or Two; Automatic Writing; Dream Symbols and Meanings; Prophets as Channels of God; Spirits and Spirits.

Amazon lists 2,406 titles. Google lists 3,330,000 results.

Runic Divination and Runic Magick work reliably and reveal a well-structured cosmology and esoteric psychology comparable to the Qabalah. However, the Northern Tradition's World Tree is not directly compatible with the Qabalah's "Tree of Life." Each provides complex structures for organizing human experience and perceptions of the workings of the universe. Individual components of each system can find a correspondence in the other, but they are not always identical.

The Runes are little-understood images used in Divination and Magick. The word itself means "secret," and secret they are until personally activated by the user. Their origin is ancient and prehistoric, coming to us through verbal tradition, song, and poetry. They are part of the Nordic and German pagan traditions, and like all ancient religions were ruthlessly suppressed by the Roman Catholic Church and then further repressed and lost as modern culture denigrated the Pagan past.

It is as symbols that the runes are significant. Some symbols are historical in origin, associated with an event and used as a "sign of affiliation," and have come to embody specific "magical powers" related to religious functions of blessings and acceptance into the faith. Other symbols originated as signs but have taken on many associations that evoke feelings, remind us of historical events, and represent arguments and debates. Other symbols represent archetypal functions, perceptions, and events such as those in Tarot Cards, and yet others like those of the I Ching that represent the flow of life processes. These symbols—astrological, alchemical, religious, magical, etc.—are "loaded" with meanings that are in turn specifically informative or that evoke feelings and awaken intuition.

Other symbols, like the Runes that have mythic origins, are *occult formulae* for working the Cosmic Forces as perceived by their shamanic discoverer, and actually embody psychic, magical, and spiritual powers, energy processes, and movement that seem as if they were *self-evolved* or "channeled" from a higher consciousness.

The wizards who used the runes for magical purposes regarded themselves as blood kin to Odin, the Nordic god who was popularly accredited with inventing the runic alphabet. As we have seen, they were basically followers of the shamanistic tradition, which is one of the oldest, if not the oldest, religious belief systems known to humanity...

Michael Howard believes that the Runes are so ancient and so fundamental—*so loaded with intrinsic power*—that their modern usage will turn the user into a kind of shaman. The "father-god" of the Norse people was himself a shaman and everything about the Northern tradition is shamanic. Their study will involve more than a "dictionary of meanings" and will require some immersion into the world of their gods and goddesses, into their practical magick, and a feeling for their poetry.

In the creation myth, we first see two opposing forces coming from opposite directions, and then their synthesis in the center. It was this that established the two basic principles of Duality and Trinity that permeate every aspect of the Northern Tradition.

Later, in the three families of the Runes, we see this same conflict between inner and outer forces, and then their synthesis in a third family. Such is the nature of the cosmos and the psyche—opposition and then synthesis—repeated again and again in higher levels of growth and development, of evolution and progress.

Contents include: The Source of Divination and Magic; The Role of Myth and History; Background to the Nordic Creation Myth; The Myth: Fire and Ice; The Nature of the Norse Universe; Ragnarok, End of the World; Discovery of the Runes; Norse Gods, Goddesses, and Other Supernatural Beings: Their Lore, Powers, and Influence; The Lesser Beings, Aspects of Soul and Personality; Runes, Their Meanings and Correspondences; The Outer Life; The Inner Life; Relationship and Synthesis; Runic Divination—Techniques of Reading and Consultation; Runes and Their Basic Meanings; Runecasting Techniques and Layouts, Step-by-Step; Living the Tradition; Runic Magick; Rune Magick Glossary of Words and Concepts; After the Coming of Christianity?

Amazon lists 2,734 titles. Google lists 7,660,000 results.

The desert sands seem forever, yet record the transiting passage of men and events, whether of footprints or monuments. A box of sand, like one used in Geomancy, can hold an impression of a palm that can be read as a simple recording of a "psychic moment," or as a palm print by the rules of palmistry.

As a *direct impression*, it's like a physical and psychic photograph that can be read both from simple objective observations of depth, pressure, finger spread, and details that uniquely reflect the feelings of the person in 3-D, and with the subjective impression to be felt and intuited before the moment passes.

Contents include: Instructions for Making and Reading the Hand Print in Sand.

Amazon lists 121 titles. Google lists 25,100,000 results.

Along with astrology, the tarot is one of the most important and powerful systems of Self-Empowerment in the Western Tradition, and indeed—like astrology—it has passed beyond cultural limitation and become global and universal in acceptance and application. However, unlike astrology, the tarot is powered by the imagination to enable the user to soar beyond Earth and the solar system to all the dimensions of the universe.

Your cards are rich in symbols, the language of the Unconscious, illustrated to express—through specified colors, images, and actions—archetypal powers derived from the Tree of Life. That a picture is "worth a thousand words" is a gross understatement. The colorful images speak directly to our emotional and mental selves. Even without the specific descriptions and interpretations that come later, you will find that you already "know" a great deal. It is better, initially, to learn by actually experiencing the cards in action.

The "secret" to all systems of divination starts with establishing rules and definitions to guide your interpretations of cards drawn in response to your well-defined questions. The first step is to define your question(s) as specifically as possible—even as questions asking for a "yes" or "no" answer—even though your answers will be much more extensive than that. With experience, your questions may become more general and expansive, while your answers will actually become more specific in application to your personal situation.

The cards of the Minor Arcana present to us the vibrations of Number, Color, and Element—that is, the plane on which number and color function. Thus, in the Ten of Pentacles we have the number Ten and tertiary colors, citrine, olive, and russet, working in *Malkuth*, the material plane. Whereas in the Ten of Wands we have the number Ten and the tertiaries working in pure energy. In these cards, the Sephirah is indicated by the coloring of the clouds; the plane by the coloring of the symbols.

The Tarot's greatest use is as a magickal implement which can bring spiritual attainment to one who studies it. This is because each Tarot card is an astral mirror of the human mind. Meditating on specific cards helps tune the student in to different aspects of his/ her own mind establishing a communication link between the conscious and the subconscious… (The New Golden Dawn Ritual Tarot, by Chic and Sandra Tabatha Cicero)

We must live *whole* lives—learning to use the *whole* of our consciousness—and not limit ourselves by the hereditary divisions. We are entering into a new age of evolutionary opportunity that is calling forth responses that once were relegated to "special studies" like shamans, priests, and other class distinctions. You have all the powers and abilities that enable you to function at a "whole" level—but you must develop those innate psychic powers that open the channels between conscious and subconscious minds and thus enable what we call the "Superconscious mind" that completes the structure we call "Self-Empowerment."

The Tarot is much more than a Divinatory System. That's just the beginning journey. The Tarot can be used in Dream Interpretation, Meditation, Pathworking, Astral Travel, and a complete program of self-development and Self-Empowerment, growing into the Whole Person of our Destiny.

Pathworkings are journeys, almost like magical train trips, from one station through exotic landscapes to another station. The goal is to follow all the paths in reverse, starting with the thirty-second, called "the Universe," that runs from the station named *Malkuth* to the one named *Yesod*. Each magical trip on the paths—working in reverse—is progressive in training your mental skills (concentration, visualization, memory recall) and developing your psychic abilities (astral travel, clairvoyance, constructive imagination) while expanding and integrating your growing knowledge. And, like any journey, the more you travel each one, the more you will expand your horizons as you observe and experience the scenery and inner world inhabitants, gaining knowledge that can be turned to practical benefit.

The pertinent cards of the Minor Arcana establish different "platforms" or levels for each station, while the Major Arcana card assigned to the path is your ticket and passport for the particular journey. The more you know about the Tree of Life and the correspondences to the Sephiroth and Paths, the richer your trip will be. It is like moving up from an economy class to higher luxury classes with better accommodations and more interesting traveling companions.

There has been a special interest in using Tarot Cards as an "astral doorway" in a manner less complex than pathworking, but still based on the same concept that the card becomes a "key" to a specific area of the astral world. Rather than a journey from station to station, it is comparable to traveling to a single destination, and then passing through a doorway composed of the card and sightseeing at that single destination, and then turning around and exiting through that same door back to this world to come back home.

The trained imagination, which also means that it is controlled by the conscious mind, is *the creative power of the mind.* And that which is imagined is experienced in the astral world. Pathworking, astral doorways, and meditation, are exercises of the creative imagination just as are creative art, design, music, literature, inventions, scientific breakthroughs, and the ability to visualize.

Without the creative imagination, innovation would not happen. Without the creative imagination, humanity would exist only as animals on a planet on which the predator large animals would be the victors.

Pathworking, meditation, astral travel, and all magical and creative work are exercises of a controlled and guided imagination. Think about it, and pick a card to work with. Let it act as a doorway, but keep to the images and ideas that are associated specifically with that card. Record your experience, and compare it with the information provided. The more you practice, the more rewarding will be your experience and your ability to employ the trained imagination in your material world as well as your astral world.

Contents include: History and Myth; Gypsies, Mystics and Occultists; Hebrew Letters and the Tree of Life; Symbols, Images, and Qabalistic Correspondences; From Jung to the Golden Dawn: Divination and Magick, Meditation, and Astral Travel; Archetypes, The Major Arcana and the Paths on the Tree of Life; The Minor Arcana and the Sephiroth; Four Worlds, Colors, and Numbers; Brief Meanings of the Major Arcana, Also Called the 22 Keys—from Fool to Universe; the Four Suits and the Four Elements; The Four Worlds and the Four Divisions of the Soul; Your own Birthday Card from the Tarot; Meanings of the Minor Arcana and the Court Cards; Divination: Your Path to the Future; Concise, Single-sentence Meanings You Can Remember; First Steps, and Rules; Significator and Spreads; On the Signification and Dignity of the Cards; Clairvoyance and Intuition; Meditation: Your Path to Inner Worlds; Dream Work; Pathworking: Your Path to Inner Growth; Astral Travel: Your Path to Inner Awareness; Ritual Magick: Your Path to Power; Alternative Realities: Your Path to Revelation; The Whole Person We Are Destined to Become.

Amazon lists seventy-two Tarot Book-only titles, 191 book and deck sets, and 742 card decks. Google lists 796,000 Tarot Book and 208,000 Tarot Deck results.

Chapter Twenty-seven—Tea Leaf & Coffee Grounds Reading: May Your Cup Brimeth Over

Your simple teacup can "brimeth over" with information about your present situation and answers to your carefully phrased questions. *How is this possible?* Because everything is available in your subconscious mind and Tea Leaf Reading, like other forms of divination, can call up the exact information you need. But you must understand the subconscious mind stores information in symbols rather than words, so we have to relate to those symbols in our reading and turn them into a story.

The patterns found in wet tea leaves often clearly show recognizable images and symbols, but other times we must use the imagination to "fill in the blanks" to arrive at a definable picture, and then create an individualized interpretation or solution to a posed question. As you progress, you will more often use the imagination to trigger the subconscious mind rather than depending on a dictionary definition.

It's this expansion of awareness, using the imagination calling to the subconscious mind and feeling the intuitive response that helps open your psychic abilities. That's what we are really after—using this simple tool to bring you Psychic Empowerment.

People use tea leaf reading to understand a current situation and to forecast the future, and the practice will help "train" your imagination to develop your psychic skills and intuition.

Coffee Ground Reading: Coffee ground reading is a relatively new concept to the Western world, but is an old practice still surviving in the Middle East and the countries surrounding the Mediterranean Sea. Basically, reading coffee grounds is similar to tea leaf reading and starts with the preparation of a cup of coffee intended for reading, one cup at a time.

Contents include: Tea Leaves and Meaningful Images; Your Aura—An Information Interchange; Every Cell of Your Body Stores ALL Your Personal Information; "Channeling" and "Trance"; You are a Free Spirit; The Equipment You Need; And How to Do It; Asking the Question; What You Can Learn; Dictionary of Common Tea Leaf Symbols; Preparation for Coffee Ground Reading.

Amazon lists fifty-two titles for Tea Leaf Reading and three for Coffee Ground Reading. Google lists 310,000 results for Tea Leaf Reading and 1,090,000 for Coffee Ground Reading.

Chapter Twenty-eight—The Wrinkled Sheet: Anything can work because the Power is in You, not the Thing

The Wrinkled Sheet, like Sand Reading (Chapter Twenty-five), demonstrates an important point: the Psychic Tool need not be something with a long history and established lore about its use *because the "power" is not in the thing, i.e. the tool, but in the psyche of the reader.* Anything, old or new, simple or complex, inexpensive or expensive, natural or manufactured, etc. can be adapted for use in a psychic reading.

What is important is that the reader sees the "thing" to be a *tool* and remembers that a tool is an extension of the body and of the psyche. In almost every situation involving a tool, the selected instrument is a *multiplier* of the physical or psychic strength of the user, just as is a hammer, shovel, pen, or computer.

Examining the process of adapting an ordinary object into a Tool of Psychic Empowerment may reveal something of the nature of psychic development and the capacity of the psyche to extend itself into the environment to meet its own goals or fulfill its needs.

In the divinatory process, the key step is to establish rules that will become the vocabulary of interpretation. While it helps if there is a seeming natural correlation between the defining rule and something about the object being used as a tool—for example, calling the most prominent line in the palm the "life line"—but the real importance comes with the psychic (subconscious) feeling of correctness to the meanings so assigned.

Even with the arbitrary choice of the divinatory tool, we will find signs and symbols that resonate with long-established "intuitions" that will work with the new tool as well as with other "established" tools.

Before a reading is undertaken, the important question should be carefully formulated and expressed.

Generally the "thing" is then given a charge of energy, preferably by the person for whom the reading is being given. Cards are shuffled, dice are shaken, sand is carefully raked and smoothed, and the paper sheet is deliberately crumpled. With these principles and rules established, you can see how it is that "anything" can be substituted for the "real thing" in psychic divination. Just the same, those tools like the Tarot or Runes or the I Ching that do have a long history and established literature also have a *hereditary* power that is truly valuable and helpful to the reader.

The avenues for exploring the mind, like the mind itself, are endless. The wrinkled sheet technique, like sand reading, provides in symbolic form a representation of the innermost self. Its intricate complexity parallels the complexity of the human psyche, and when appropriately interpreted, provides yet another valuable source of psychic insight. In our continuing struggle for wisdom and understanding, the wrinkled sheet can offer critical raw material for activating the creative, inquiring mind.

The exquisitely complex wrinkled sheet effectively engages its counterpart, the exquisitely complex mind, in an interaction that is both challenging and empowering. The greater our psychic skills, the more easily we can make that subjective leap into psychic space.

Contents include: Any "Thing," Old or New, Can Be Used as a Tool in Psychic Reading; An Extension of Body and Psyche; Rules and the Vocabulary of Interpretation; A "Charge" of Energy; It is *Personal Action* that Sets the Psychic Imprint; The Capacity of the Object to Activate Psychic Insight; Seeing the Whole, and the Part; Seeing Patterns, with Open Awareness for their Potential Meanings; Principles of Pattern Interpretation.

Amazon lists no titles. Google lists 3,130,000 results but not the kind of sheet we're talking about!

Self-Empowerment does begin with Psychic Empowerment! It is the "Next Step" in the Great Work of our evolutionary development, and is bringing the innate psychic powers resident in the lower unconscious into the light of the conscious mind. It is the necessary *Next Step* in the integration of the Lower Self with the Higher Self in the Whole Person. Self-Empowerment *empowers* the Whole Person to comprehend the world we live within so that we may live intelligently and responsibly with our human family and other species in the home we all share.

Psychic Empowerment is not the only Next Step in our evolutionary journey being thrust upon us in the most critical moment in human history, but it is vital to our understanding the ramifications and necessity of other scientific, technological, economic, social, and medical innovations that must be made to adjust for new environmental and geopolitical realities challenging our survival.

Psychic powers are not new, but their open "availability" is. Since any historic recording began—including mythical and religious—certain select people have exercised clairvoyance, far-seeing, astral projection, psychokinesis, telepathy, and precognition. These few people became priests and prophets, advisors to kings, and adored saints. They were separated from the general population, enjoying power and prestige, while establishing a hierarchy of students learning their "secrets" under controls that were more "political" than ethical.

Science has changed *Belief* into certainty, and *Secrets* are replaced with knowledge, practical techniques and tools, and pertinent applications.

Psychic skills are as important to successful living as other physical and mental skills and through systemic integration programs of heightened conscious awareness, meditation, and self-hypnosis, your psychic powers become as "normal" and familiar as logical analysis, creative thinking, ethical judgment, and communal responsibility.

As scientists of the psyche—whether we are called psychologists, parapsychologists, or metaphysicians—we recognize that we can only see one part of the picture. Physical scientists—in particular physicists, biologists, and astronomers—see another part of the picture, while quantum physicists are beginning to see the unifying field where those parts come together in the Big Picture. As we work together, a more complete picture emerges and we learn that consciousness itself is pervasive in every dimension of the universe.

The metaphysical universe is divided into "worlds" (or planes)—Physical (which includes the Etheric), Astral, Mental, and Spiritual (which also includes several "higher" planes. Each plane has a vibratory range that is distinct to the "substance" of that world (See Chapter Two). All things, living and nonliving, have counterparts in the astral and other worlds, so to confine the discussion to the human, we each have astral, mental, and spiritual bodies, and an in-between etheric body that is really the energy part of the physical body. It is within the etheric body that we can locate the chakras, meridians, and other of the "esoteric" organs and energy pathways important in the alternative systems.

While the substance of each world and each body is distinctive, consciousness is pervasive and only requires an appropriate means of perception and expression in each world.

Humanity is on a journey moving beyond the frontiers of past times, calling upon each and every one of us to individually move beyond past beliefs about personal limits to become more than we are, and accept the greater responsibilities that our growth and development require. It's a journey comparable to that leading to the founding of the American Republic and the first lunar landing. But it's a pioneering journey that only you can make—no government funding needed, no expensive equipment required, no strenuous physical preparation necessary. For you, it is not only a journey, it is also an adventure and it is personal development that benefits all of humanity.

Contents include: The Next Step; Self-Empowerment Begins with Psychic Empowerment; The Empowering Potentials of Psychic Empowerment; No More Secrets! Unlimited Power Within; Windows of the Mind, Doors to Soul; I Am Not the Brain; the Brain Is Not Me; The "Higher" Unconscious; Seeing the Bigger Picture; Levels of Conscious, Soul, and Spirit, and the Whole Person; The Evolutionary Plan of the Psyche.

Amazon lists 989 titles for Self-mpowerment and 21,602 for the Great Work (although most deal with "work"). Google lists 1,980,000 Self-Empowerment and 318,000,000 Great Work results.

Successful Hypnosis is a goal-related state of altered consciousness in which attention can be productively focused on specific goals. All hypnosis involves acceptance and participation by the subject—thus, *all hypnosis is self-hypnosis* and is possible for everyone. With the subject in control and using the proven techniques of self-hypnosis, goals are more efficiently accomplished and self-hypnosis becomes a true method of self-help applied to the needs and interests of the self-hypnotist, including such *quality-of-life goals* as weight control, self-healing, substance abuse, slowing aging, pain control, rejuvenation, overcoming fears, accelerated learning, memory improvement, accessing past lives, astral projection, and promoting psychic development. *Successful goals focus on possibilities, not limitations.*

Self-hypnosis is an indispensable gateway to self-empowerment. It provides ready access to the highest sources of power, both within you and beyond. Once equipped with the programs presented in this chapter, you can seize with confidence the splendor of the moment and the challenges of the future. Each built-in part of your being—psychic, healer, educator, therapist, creator, rejuvenator, and hypnotist—is then poised to ensure your destiny for endless greatness.

You may also discover that the sound of your voice increases the effectiveness of your suggestions. Throughout the session, addressing oneself as "I" rather than "you" typically facilitates successful hypnosis by more effectively engaging the subconscious. Likewise, the so-called "I am" approach tends to promote successful induction as well as application.

Contents include: The Subconscious as a Storehouse of Power; The Hypnotist as Facilitator; The Best Hypnotist is the Self-Hypnotist; Self-hypnosis Essentials; Four Essentials for Effective Self-hypnosis; I AM Statement; Inducing and Applying Self-hypnosis; The Solar Plexus Program; Knee-press Program for Progressive Relaxation and Induction; Peripheral Glow Program; Cosmic Power Program; Empowering Properties through Color.

Amazon lists 5,690 titles for Hypnosis, 2,351 for Self-Hypnosis, 937 for Self-Hypnosis Audio CDs, and 12 DVDs. Google lists 9,650,000 Hypnosis and 1,570,000 Self-Hypnosis results.

Hypnosis, self-hypnosis, and meditation are all associated with special mental states that facilitate positive personality changes and connect with higher dimensions of the psyche.

Like Self-Hypnosis, meditation is mostly self-administered and can be applied entirely for physical, emotional, and mental benefits. From a Body/Mind ("BM") perspective meditation is a non-drug way to lower stress levels, relax any area of the body, reduce blood pressure levels, calm the emotions, and clear the mind.

Mantra meditation, mostly associated with Hinduism and Buddhism, is by far the best-known form of meditation. Each mantra, while having similar physical and mental effects, will also produce different emotional feelings and induce unique spiritual effects identified with the particular tradition and the words or names used. Phrases containing "God Names" are especially powerful, as you would expect.

Mantra meditation is common in other traditions as well. The wisdom of the Kabbalah and its core symbol, the Tree of Life, is the foundation of Western metaphysics and *invisibly* of the whole of Western science and philosophy. With it, we have the means to understand and relate to the body of the Universe and Man and the Soul of Man and the Universe.

While there are individual Hebrew mantras, the premier form of meditation is found in the practices of "Pathworking." These are imaginative journeys or *guided meditations* following the twenty-two paths between the ten Sephiroth which should be understood as the "God Forces" behind the universe. Because pathworking is a visual exercise, it needs visual focus and the images of the Tarot Trumps are among the most productive for this purpose, and often serve to frame the vision that ensues.

Pathworking has been described as *the art of clairvoyantly investigating the Paths of the Tree of Life.* The technique was largely developed by adepts of the Golden Dawn and Aurum Solis but has become a comprehensive meditative system outside the magical orders. Once the meditator has passively followed the guided meditation, he should then attempt to retread the Paths *out-of-body* following certain ritual techniques involving visualized symbols, performing certain gestures and vibrating Divine Names.

Just as the individual Tarot Arcanum communicates particular information and *energies,* so do the individual Hebrew letters. The twenty-two letters of the Hebrew alphabet are profound realities embodying primal spiritual forces that are, in effect, the "building blocks of Creation." Hebrew is called a "flame language" and each letter appears to be shaped out of *flames* that can channel forces connecting Heaven with Earth in special ways. Because of the belief that these letters (the forces embodied therein) predated Creation, the letters themselves and the order and manner in which they are utilized are of crucial significance, and their properly pronounced sounds transformative. Hebrew chants (mantras) were designed as special formulas able to arouse spiritual forces.

Contents include: Body/Mind (BM) Relaxation; Tension and Release to Aid Physical Relaxation; Mantra Meditation; Meditation vs. Self-Hypnosis; "Personal" vs. "Traditional"; "Trance" and a "Focused State of Consciousness"; the "Words; The "Goal"; Concentration; Mindfulness; *Transcendent Mindfulness;* Mantras in Hinduism and Buddhism; Sanskrit Pronunciation Guide; Judaism; Hebrew and Christian Mantras; The Tetragrammaton; The Middle Pillar Exercise; Christian Mantras and Prayers; The Open Dialogue.

Amazon lists 44,243 titles. Google lists 30,900,000 results.

APPENDIX A—JOURNEY OF A LIFETIME: A PROGRAM FOR ACTUALIZING YOUR PSYCHIC POWERS 569

It's a program designed to activate your psychic powers and initiate a psychic-empowered lifestyle with totally new growth possibilities. It's a do-it-yourself Journey based on the premise that the best psychic growth specialist exists within yourself—the Journey empowers you to connect to that specialist. It organizes the concepts of psychic empowerment into a plan that progresses from positive self-affirmations to step-by-step psychic development techniques, all of which you can do for yourself. Included in the Journey are totally new approaches that embrace the whole person in a growth process extending far beyond the completion of the step-by-step exercises presented in the program.

Psychic development is a natural and continuous process so that even sporadic and experimental involvement will yield positive results—but the full realization of your psychic potentials needs a more organized approach that recognizes your inherent capacity to access and activate your growth resources. The results will be a mental, physical, and spiritual state of empowerment that transcends the demands of even the most difficult life situation.

The exercises that follow are designed to initiate a Journey with life-changing possibilities for self-discovery, growth, and power. Through this Journey of a Lifetime, you will discover that the possibilities are unlimited when you tap into the powers within!

Exercise One: Promoting Growth Readiness and Expectations of Success
The psychic-empowerment goal for this introductory exercise is twofold: first, to generate a state of psychic growth readiness and second, to promote powerful expectations of success.

Exercise Two: Picture Recall
The purpose of this second exercise is to build the visualization skills required to access your inner potentials and apply them toward achieving your personal goals.

Exercise Three: The Blank Sheet
The Blank Sheet is designed to further exercise your visualization skills and empower you to use them to achieve your stated goals. This exercise is especially effective in activating your psychic faculties.

Exercise Four: Becoming Balanced and Attuned
The goal of this exercise is to achieve an empowered state of mental, physical, and spiritual balance and attunement. Once you are wholly balanced and attuned, you are at your peak empowerment—nothing is beyond your reach. In that empowered state, you can achieve your loftiest goals. You can solve your most difficult problems and overcome all barriers to your success.

Exercise Five: The Four A's of Psychic Empowerment
Everyone is psychic, but developing and effectively applying your psychic powers requires recognition of your psychic potentials and a commitment to actualize them. This exercise is based on the four A's of psychic empowerment: Awareness, Appreciation, Actualization, and Application.

Exercise Six: Becoming Altruistically Empowered
Altruism is the pinnacle of mental, physical, and spiritual empowerment. Possibly nothing is more empowering than acts of kindness toward others, including persons and animals alike.

The Journey of a Lifetime is an endless adventure with unlimited possibilities for growth, self-discovery, and fulfillment. It's a journey of necessity as well as of opportunity. Without growth, we come to a dead end; with continuous growth, our potential is infinite.

LIST OF ILLUSTRATIONS AND PHOTOGRAPHS

LIST OF CHARTS, TABLES, PROGRAMS, PROCEDURES AND EXERCISES

FOREWORD

By
Carl Llewellyn Weschcke

THE BOOK YOU HAVE IN YOUR HANDS
IS DESTINED TO BE A MODERN CLASSIC

I say this with the certainty of a half-century experience publishing "New Age" and paranormal books, and as a keen observer of trends. *New Age* is a sometimes abused term, and some readers may not appreciate a solid book written primarily by a well-respected and distinguished academic and pioneering scientist in the field of parapsychology being shelved alongside titles that others may think a little "weird."

Let's talk about this a bit. *New Age* is a bookstore category for books also classified under "Body, Mind, and Spirit" or "Metaphysical," and sometimes "Self-Help." The primary base for this was developed by the Book Industry Study Group (BISG) to facilitate computer-generated purchasing and sales data for book retailers and publishers. Whether the book's subject is parapsychology, paranormal phenomena, psychic powers, psychic celebrities, psychic people, or hypnotism, shamanism, astrology, ritual magick, Wicca, Spiritualism, etc., it is going to be shelved where the larger bookstores and chain stores know their customers will be browsing and buying these topics. Smaller specialty stores do shelve their books under the individual subjects most interesting to their customers, often in more expansive collections than usual in the larger stores.

The New Age, like any other category, has all sorts of books, and the Psychic or Paranormal subject area has different authors writing on matters as diverse as mass-market pop culture to very scientific research and exposition. Some writers will be happy to tell you about their celebrity clients and their own interesting lives from babyhood on, and about their successful forecasts of personal and world events, while others have stories of encounters with ghosts and hauntings, and there are many 'how-to' books on such consciousness-expanding *techniques* as astral projection and aura reading and such awareness-extending *tools* as pendulums and Tarot cards. At the other end of the spectrum, most books classified under *parapsychology* and the *paranormal* will often present exciting research backed with statistics, surveys, and cross references to quantum physics, physiology, and other sciences. More and more of these are books that are exciting adventures based on solid scientific research and personal experience in developing practical applications pertinent to today's needs and challenges.

Sometimes—as in any category—some books *are* "weird." But I have learned to value every book as potentially the 'right book' for a given person at a particular time, even though it may not be a book I would choose for myself or want to recommend. A good bookstore is like a democracy in which every person can find his or her niche and discover just the right book. And, in the case of a metaphysical specialty store, you will often find expert personnel who can honestly advise the customer regarding book choices.

Books are among the foundations of modern civilization and our freedom of speech and our access to books is equal in importance to quality education and the welfare of every person and child.

Beyond these concerns, I consider the subject area of the *psychic world* AND *parapsychology and the paranormal* to be of extreme importance, and it is the growing awareness of these broader dimensions of both the inner and outer worlds that has driven the public interest in these subjects to an all-time high. All you have to do is scan television programming, listen to nighttime radio, leaf through popular magazines, and visit the shelves of your local bookstore to view serious studies along with fictional and real life experiences of the psychic and paranormal.

THE "NEW AGE" IS REAL!

Why? I believe the New Age to be real! It may only be a marketing concept for certain book retailers, but during the last half of the twentieth century there was a general awakening of human consciousness and expansion of awareness that is constantly accelerating in response to personal interest and experience, and the influence of the World Wide Web. Dimensions of consciousness, accessible knowledge, scales of communication, and worldwide awareness have opened up, along with the increasing acceptance of individual responsibility for local and global well-being—environmental, economic, health, and peace among nations.

Why? Because we are growing toward increased wholeness and *becoming more than we are!* We are evolving because of an innate human characteristic within us from the beginning of our being. And we are turning innate, undeveloped psychic and mental powers into consciously controlled and useful skills. We are expanding into the undeveloped potentials of the human mind—from utilizing a theoretical 10 percent of our mental capacity toward using more and more of the remaining 90 percent.

Almost all of this undeveloped potential is variously labeled *psychic* and *mental* and *spiritual.* Learning about these powers and attributes, developing them, and bringing them under conscious control, is what this book is about.

DR. JOE H. SLATE, PIONEERING PARAPSYCHOLOGIST

Dr. Joe H. Slate, coauthor of this book, is a distinguished and prolific writer of more than twenty books on parapsychology, psychic empowerment, and self-empowerment. He is the retired chairman of the psychology department at Athens State University in northern Alabama, a practicing clinical psychologist, and a respected researcher and founder of the International Parapsychological Research Foundation. He established an experimental laboratory and conducted research projects funded by the US Army, the Parapsychology Foundation of New York, and numerous private sources. He introduced parapsychology into the university curriculum, a first for the state of Alabama, and nearly the first in any academic environment. The foundation continues to promote parapsychology through its education, research, and scholarship programs.

Dr. Slate believes that everyone is psychic, and he challenges each of us to develop and use our own psychic potentials to help ourselves and others to a better life. He writes: "Everyone is psychic. The challenge is to develop your psychic potentials, not only to promote your own growth, but to help others as well. A major goal of my work in education, research, and writing has been to make psychic empowerment readily available to everyone."

IF EVERYONE IS PSYCHIC…

If everyone is psychic, why do we need to develop our "psychic potential? Why can't we just perceive the future, see and read auras, project out-of-body, see and understand the chakras, interpret our dreams, move objects at will, remember past lives, find water or minerals or lost objects by dowsing or using a pendulum, speak with spirits, read palms and Tarot cards, etc.? Why can't we see our own health problems and heal ourselves and others?

Well, why can't you (and I'm fairly sure you can't) lift thousand-pound weights, run a hundred meters in ten seconds, jump more than ten feet, and other record-breaking feats? *Because you have not trained to do so.* You haven't developed the muscles to do so. You don't have the skills. But, at least in theory, you could. At least in theory, you can develop the strength, the skills, the know-how to fulfill the highest goals you can imagine.

We don't have to set the goals so high in our psychic empowerment, but the principle is the same. Some people are born stronger and faster than others; some people train and exercise to become champions. Some people run as a regular discipline for better health and others work out at the local gym or with home equipment. Those people become physically empowered. You can become psychically empowered. Just as physical empowerment is beneficial so is psychic empowerment.

Physical empowerment is hard work; psychic empowerment is a lot easier, but both are accomplished by doing. Practice makes perfect, but we don't have to seek perfection to gain personal and practical benefits through psychic practices.

You are born with physical muscles and you are born with psychic "muscles" too, only they are not really muscles but innate powers. These psychic powers, just like physical muscles, need to be exercised in order to develop them. And just as physical tools can multiply and direct the application of muscular power to various constructive tasks—some for just the fun of it as in sports and games—so do we have psychic tools that we can apply in different ways to various tasks, and some just for the fun of it.

In this book, you will learn about your psychic powers, learn various psychic techniques for their development and application, and also explore various psychic tools that can multiply and give direction to your growing skills. You will learn how to benefit from those skills, and you will learn how to enjoy them.

Through experiencing these techniques you will have a greater appreciation for human unity. We are all able to develop these "technologies of the sacred" rather than believe they are reserved just for a spiritual elite. As you explore the many tools that extend your psychic awareness, you will also see and appreciate human diversity and ingenuity. Everywhere people have discovered and developed ways to explore their energetic connections to the external and the *internal* worlds, and the role of the subconscious mind to relate to those energies and bring their revelations into the conscious mind.

Modern studies are not merely *popularizing* paranormal "discoveries," but are making them real and personal—neither limited to laboratory or church, nor to people called "weird" or "unusual"—and part of everyday life. We realize it is not just some guy on television who can read minds or just some woman born a medium who can see ghosts and communicate with Spirit.

TO BECOME MORE THAN YOU ARE

Anyone can do these things if they are willing to make the effort. And there is more benefit to doing so than what happens in those stories. To grow, and to "become more than you are" is your destiny, but it requires effort on your part. I can only tell you that it's worth it. To grow in every dimension of your being is to expand your opportunities for joy and success in all you do.

What makes *this book a classic?* It is what it is. It is a book based on solid research and experimentation, with personal experiences that both fascinate and demonstrate the validity of the psychic techniques and tools described, *and* a complete and practical compilation of the tools and techniques that empower *you* to develop your own innate psychic powers into genuine skills that will change your world for the better.

This is a book that will continue to be your resource in growth and development toward the wholeness that is not only your birthright but the fulfillment of your life purpose—*becoming more than you are.* Your life, and how you continue to learn and grow, is the very means to the continued evolution of the human genome and the matrix of human consciousness.

This book will continue to be a companion that will inspire you and constantly open new doors and opportunities for your evolving psyche.

As Dr. Slate has written, the traditional focus on the mysterious side of psychic phenomena is now giving way to logical explanations and practical strategies to access valuable knowledge to promote the quality of human life. We normally experience our world through sensory-based perceptions that are cognitively organized, a process dependent on limited biological mechanisms. Psychic experiences, on the other hand, reach beyond ordinary sensory and cognitive functions to augment sensory experience, expanding awareness and acquiring new knowledge. Examples are telepathy, precognition, clairvoyance, out-of-body experiences, and spiritual phenomena. Taken together, these phenomena suggest four major empowering principles:

FOUR MAJOR EMPOWERING PRINCIPLES

1. The essence of our existence transcends biological or physical experience alone.
2. With the conventionally prescribed limits of human experience removed, the potentials for human growth and knowledge are significantly expanded.
3. We can dramatically increase our scope and store of knowledge by developing our psychic capacities.
4. Psychic self-empowerment and self-fulfillment are reasonable expectations for everyone.

DEMYSTIFYING THE PARANORMAL

Our challenge is to demystify the so-called paranormal, explain its nature, and unleash its empowering potentials. The psychic experience, whether voluntary or involuntary, is always empowering. To unleash that power requires awareness of the psychic event and understanding its significance to us. Many of our dreams are psychic and potentially empowering, but benefiting from the dream requires first recalling the dream, then understanding its message, and, in some instances, acting upon it. The problem-solving dream challenges us by providing, in disguise, the raw material we need for a solution. Discovering the solution requires imagination and diligence in unraveling the dream, interpreting its symbols, and creatively applying its message.

But in demystifying the world of the paranormal, we lose none of its magic, none of its adventure, none of its capacity to awaken us to the glory and beauty of the greater universe that now unfolds for us. Each technique we learn—even without fully exploring all its potential—opens another door, adds another layer, to our own greater self. We grow through our psychic exploration and through the applications of these techniques and tools described in this book.

Of course, as large as this book is, we have only touched the surface while hinting at more to come. The human capacity to uncover new mysteries and invent new tools to aid in making our lives richer is amazing. Just look at the table of contents and note the various techniques and tools we do explore with you—from Astral Projection to Visualization, and from Ascending the Pyramid to the simplicity of the Wrinkled Sheet—and then turn to the glossary where we describe many more techniques and tools.

What I want to point out is that many proven tools of divination that have come down to us from earlier times—some with mythic origins reaching very far into ancient times—are only tools that extend your own innate divinatory ability. The power is within you, not the tools. As you look at the many tools and methods described in the glossary—from Aeromancy to Xylomancy—let your imagination soar. The truth is that "any old thing" can become a divinatory tool so long as you establish *rules* and provide a method of *observation* or of *finger manipulation*. From observing the shape of clouds to crumpling a sheet of paper, the power is yours to understand the phenomena and events of life around you and to answer your questions on those circumstances affecting you directly and to forecast the probable future in matters of your concern.

You have the power.

And as you explore the different techniques of psychic application, the excitement of life's adventure will grow and fascinate you. Here is one example of what is forthcoming as you read this book:

DISCOVER A NEW WORLD OF YOUR OWN

Can you imagine living in a world that is for the most part uncharted and undeveloped? Imagine the hidden resources and abundant possibilities existing beyond the limited zone of your present awareness. You could, of course, choose to live your lifetime in the familiar but constricted zone of that planet, or you could choose to boldly explore its unknown regions and uncover its hidden resources. As an explorer, you know of course that you could encounter the unexpected. But given what you already know about the planet, your confidence will only build as you uncover its hidden side and experience the rich rewards of your new discoveries.

Interestingly, such a largely unknown planet does indeed exist, not at some distant, faraway place, but as an essential part of yourself. We call it your subconscious, that vast world of possibilities within. Like the call of an unknown planet beckoning discovery, your subconscious at this moment beckons your interactions. It reveals its existence in a variety of ways, including such spontaneous channels as dreams, intuitive awareness, déjà vu, precognitive impressions, and flashes of insight and creativity. That "other country" within reaches forth with persistence in its efforts to reveal its treasures and enrich your life with expanded knowledge, awareness, and power.

—JOE H. SLATE, *REINCARNATION AND PAST LIVES REGRESSION* (CHAPTER 13)

MIND OVER MATTER—EVERY DAY

What Dr. Slate and other pioneer researchers—and people everywhere—have done is to take their discoveries and insights out of the laboratory and show that all these powers and skills are within us and have always been there for us to develop and use. And many do and have done so for a long time, but without the understanding and practical application know-how that modern research gives us.

The Psychic World is no longer restricted to the few lucky enough to have developed native talent at an early age, or to have been taught by a skilled elder. It is no longer shrouded in mystery and glamour and practiced by the exclusive few.

Your mind gives you the power to learn and develop your own powers and to master skills that bring you new opportunities and control over your life. Read the chapter on Psychokinesis and marvel at the potential of your own "mind power."

TOMORROW AS PROBABILITY

Read the chapter on Precognition, and you will have a new foundation for understanding the real potential for not merely "seeing the future," but for "shaping the future" through the revelations of quantum theory regarding probabilities and the role of *intention* in moving the probable to the actual.

Science has moved beyond the old "clockwork" mechanical concept of the universe to one based on energy and consciousness. Through consciousness you and the universe are united, but you are gifted with the power of mind and you will have the ability to bend probabilities to reflect your choices.

It may seem "magical," and it is indeed the real foundation of a magical universe, but the reality is that the universe has always been magical and spiritual in nature. But human beings had lost that vision of reality and then we saw the spirit and life being taken out of the natural world, leaving us today with the threat of an abused and lifeless planet.

BUT, WHAT ABOUT ASTROLOGY, PALMISTRY, AND NUMEROLOGY?

Some readers will wonder why we do not include Astrology and Palmistry as tools of divination. My answer is that we don't consider them as primarily psychic but rather properly called "scientific."

Astrology is "astronomy brought down to earth," employing astronomical measurements of planetary positions and mathematical calculations of their relationships to one another and to the birth place and time of the person (or event) for whom a horoscope is calculated. The interpretations are based on thousands of years and many millions of actual cases.

The value of astrology is in its analysis of planetary energies to bring about self-knowledge and self-understanding, and to foresee particular periods of opportunity and challenge during your lifetime. Astrology is also beneficial in its analysis of relationships from this energetic perspective, and foreseeing the potentials for conflict or support in the planetary movements for each person in the relationship.

Yes, the interpretative and counseling ability of the astrologer or individual working with his own chart is enhanced by his psychic skills, but that is outside the scope of astrological study per se.

The same is true of palmistry, likewise based on thousands of years of observation and many millions of cases. The technique is largely scientific, and can be enhanced through careful measurement and analysis of the lines and figures in the palm, the knuckles and back of the hand, the shape of hands, fingers and fingernails, lines on the wrists, and may even include scars, venous circulation, skin tone, and more.

As with astrology, the interpretative and counseling ability of the palmist or individual working with his own hand or palm print can be enhanced by his psychic skills, but that is outside the scope of palmistry study.

Numerology opens a more challenging question than with either astrology or palmistry. While it appears easy and even scientific and mathematical on the surface, that simplicity is deceptive. Numerology is really part of the very complex study of the Kabbalah and its vast system of correspondences related to the Tree of Life glyph, and like astrology and palmistry, the Kabbalistic tradition is many thousands of years old.

There are numerological systems in other than Western cultures, but I've not made a study of them and cannot comment on them.

Most popular systems of numerology are based on an arbitrary code of assigning number values to the letters making up your name, but—unlike Hebrew where the number value of each letter is based on the vibratory sound of the letter—the English system seems, *to me,* lacking in a logical foundation. Obviously, others disagree, and an argument can be made that numerology, like any other predictive system, can be a structure for communication between the subconscious and conscious minds.

And, where popular numerology analyzes the birth time, I would rather use astrology.

Still, I may respect what others have to say without my personal endorsement for its practice. Don't necessarily let that deter you from its study. I have strong respect for every technique and tool of analysis and prediction. And I have respect for my "elders"—numerology has been practiced for a long time by many people who have found it useful.

Regardless of personal preference or disagreement with any of the developmental techniques and divinatory tools, the real point is that all offer paths to psychic empowerment, and psychic empowerment is a personal growth strategy that gives you more control over your life and greater ability to succeed in every aspect of your life. It's really a life work, and one that should occupy the rest of your life.

Dr. Slate is fond of reminding each of us that, "the best is yet to come!" It is what you will do with this book that is the very engine of tomorrow's greatness for all of the Earth's children.

Yes, the best is yet to come!
Carl Llewellyn Weschcke

Preface

By
Joe H. Slate, Ph.D.

This jointly authored book introduces the contributions of Carl Llewellyn Weschcke to the revised version of my earlier book, *Psychic Empowerment* (1995). This book is, however, far more than simply a revised and expanded version of an earlier work. Woven throughout the book are the advanced threads of psychic empowerment that only Carl Weschcke can provide. As the universally acclaimed Father of the New Age, he is rapidly gaining recognition as the Father of Psychic Empowerment, a title he has earned many times over through his writing and contributions to the publishing world. His unparalleled success as founder and now as chairman of Llewellyn Worldwide is a testament to his commitment to make psychic empowerment an attainable reality for everyone. I am indeed honored to be his coauthor in this effort to achieve that important goal.

We now know that psychic empowerment, rather than being a theoretical possibility, is a measurable, though complex, process of personal evolvement. Using the tools and techniques presented in this book, you can accelerate that process by accessing your dormant inner potentials and activating them to enrich the quality of your life. Beyond that, you can become the master builder of an endless *tower of power* to the great beyond, a tower that connects you to the far reaches of the cosmos and the entire powers underlying it. Built of the finest materials—those found in your own being—the tower of power can become your empowerment connection to the boundless resources of the great beyond. It's a tower that brings you into balance and constant attunement to the universe.

This book goes beyond the mere presentation of information and beliefs about psychic phenomena by offering rational explanations of the "unexplained" and focusing on the personal benefits of the psychic experience. It explores a host of psychic tools and formulates effective techniques for applying them. It systematically develops *the psychic empowerment perspective* by focusing on our inner potentials and our ability to develop and apply them.

This book holds steadfastly to the belief that every individual is a person of incomparable worth, endowed with the potential for greatness. It explores a host of psychic tools and develops effective techniques for applying them. Presented at the end of the book is a "Journey of a Lifetime" Development Program, which organizes the seminal concepts of psychic empowerment into an accelerated, step-by-step program for the systematic development of your psychic potentials.

While the centerpiece of this book is personal empowerment, we recognize the critical importance of global empowerment. Global empowerment must begin somewhere. Becoming personally empowered can be seen as the first step toward empowering the globe and making the world a better place for present and future generations. In its exploration of the essential concepts, this book attempts to strike a reasonable balance between scientific objectivity and practical application. The inner sources of power perceive the existence of other planes. While they may remain largely unknown, they are nonetheless receptive. This power recognizes the complexity of our makeup as mental, physical, and spiritual beings and the capacity of each to influence the other. The pinnacle of psychic empowerment is the promotion of our personal evolvement while contributing to the greater good. Accepting the task of making this world a better place for present and future generations is a major goal of this book.

Joe H. Slate, Ph.D.

Introduction
The Nature of Psychic Empowerment
Joe H. Slate, Ph.D.

Psychic empowerment is for everyone. Once empowered, you can overcome all barriers to your growth and turn even the most difficult problems into exciting new growth opportunities. You'll discover that fear, insecurity, inferiority, and doubt all yield to the empowered self. Now as never before, you can make empowerment a reality in your life.

Knowledge is power, and psychic knowledge is power at its peak. Psychic knowledge is relevant mentally, physically, psychically, and spiritually as well as culturally and globally. It has relevance even on a universal and multiuniversal scale. Here are but a few examples of the empowerment possibilities of psychic knowledge:

EMPOWERMENT POSSIBILITIES OF PSYCHIC KNOWLEDGE

- It can expand your awareness and increase your understanding of your existence as a life force being.
- It can unveil new dimensions of reality and facilitate empowering interactions with them.
- It can generate mental, physical, and spiritual attunement and balance.
- It can enrich your social interactions and promote your career success.
- It can bring you into a state of harmony with other dimensions and higher planes of power.
- It can promote your development of the skills required to achieve your personal goals.
- It can reveal the endless nature of your existence as an evolving soul.

- It can promote global peace and suggest solutions to global problems, such as reckless depletion of natural resources and disregard for threatened or endangered species.
- It can dispel the myths that are often associated with the paranormal.

The central theme of this book is the development of *psychic empowerment through practice and firsthand experience.* You are, by nature, psychic. You possess an array of psychic potentials, many of which are often expressed effortlessly or spontaneously. Others, however, exist in hidden or dormant form. They require effort not only to uncover them, but even more importantly, to develop them. That being said, acquiring relevant knowledge and mastering strategies that apply it become the overarching essentials of psychic empowerment and the focus of this book.

Equipped with knowledge and related skills, you can at last take full command of the forces—both within and beyond—that affect your life. In that empowered state, you can achieve your loftiest goals and improve the quality of your life. More specifically, you can accelerate learning, improve memory, increase creativity, solve complex problems, overcome debilitating fears, promote better health and fitness, break unwanted habits, and even slow the aging process. On a larger scale, you can contribute to the greater good and make the world a better place for present and future generations. Although some of these goals may seem at first unattainable, you will discover that they are all within your reach when you become psychically empowered.

Psychic empowerment, rather than a dormant, inactive state, is a continuous process of growth, discovery, and personal fulfillment. It can activate an interaction within that promotes the full unfoldment of your potentials. It's a dynamic process that helps ensure an unshakable foundation for personal fulfillment and success. Should that process for some reason become thwarted or blocked, atrophy and decline could set in. Although greatness is your destiny, fulfilling that destiny requires our best efforts. I'm a firm believer that the best is yet to come, but with one caveat: we must do whatever we can to make it happen. When psychically empowered, you can "dream the impossible dream" and make it a reality in your life. A major goal of this book is to inspire that all-important effort.

Psychic empowerment as presented in this book is a hopeful, optimistic concept that recognizes both the complexity of the human experience and the incomparable worth of each individual. It emphasizes the emerging self as the major determinant of individual growth and success. The limitations of heredity and the adverse effects of cultural or any other environmental influences yield to the psychically empowered self and its capacity to overcome all growth barriers. Once fully empowered, there remains neither space nor need for alibis.

People differ and times change. Multiple forces—internal and external, conscious and subconscious—constantly interact to influence our behavior. When psychically empowered, you can take command of the complex forces that affect your life. Through the concepts and strategies presented in this book, you can become the master architect of your destiny. Beginning now, you can add meaning, happiness, success, and power to your life.

Psychic empowerment is a continuous process of growth and self-discovery. When we are psychically empowered, we become increasingly aware of the boundless power within ourselves and the unlimited possibilities and opportunities around us and beyond. Through psychic empowerment, we can unleash vast inner sources of new growth potential and achieve new levels of personal fulfillment. We can lift consciousness to a higher plane and discover totally new meaning to our lives.

The concept of psychic empowerment is based on a threefold premise:

THREEFOLD PREMISE OF PSYCHIC EMPOWERMENT

1. Within each of us is an abundance of untapped power and underdeveloped potential.

2. We can independently access and activate these inner resources to empower our lives.

3. Through that empowering process, we can literally create an upward spiral of personal growth that empowers us to achieve our personal goals while contributing to the greater good.

Almost everyone recalls some form of empowering psychic experience. Common examples are dreams that came true, intuitions that proved accurate, or simple experiences of déjà vu. Psychic experiences are so common among so many people that we no longer consider them paranormal or extraordinary. Yet, questions concerning the nature of psychic phenomena persist, primarily because psychic experiences seem to lie outside our conventional explanations of human behavior. Furthermore, psychic phenomena are typically spontaneous, and do not readily lend themselves to objective analysis and empirical study. Precognitive dreams are reported by about three-fourths of all college students, but research efforts to generate and verify them in the laboratory have not been fully successful. Similarly, fleeting spontaneous glimpses of past-life experiences among both children and adults are common, but verifying them is a difficult needle to thread. Along another line, telepathic communication occurs so frequently that many of us consider it a normal part of our daily interactions, but laboratory efforts to demonstrate telepathy, even among individuals who report it as a common occurrence, have not consistently validated the phenomenon. Nevertheless, the documented instances of precognition, telepathy, and other forms of psychic phenomena, both in the laboratory and in everyday life, are so numerous that, when viewed objectively, they leave little room for doubt that these events do indeed occur.

The evolving body of evidence for psychic phenomena demands a careful reexamination of our thinking and a restructuring of our traditional views about human life and experience. The fact that the mind seems capable of experiencing realities beyond the known limits of sensory perception challenges our conventional systems and raises new questions about the nature of reality and human existence itself.

Critical to our personal development and better understanding of ourselves is an open but vigilant mind that can objectively assess and accommodate new knowledge, even though it may contradict our old ways of thinking. Our personal empowerment requires exposure to diverse opinions and contradictory ideas. The results include a constant flow of new knowledge that, when seriously considered and integrated into the self system, becomes liberating and empowering, but when arbitrarily rejected, becomes constricting and disempowering. It reasonably follows that a recognition of knowledge from many sources is essential in our struggle for self-understanding and full self-empowerment.

THE PSYCHIC EMPOWERMENT PERSPECTIVE

Knowledge is power, and knowledge of psychic origin is power in its highest and purest form. While the most convincing evidence of that power continues to be personal experience, the traditional and at times sensational focus on the paranormal is finally giving way to objective observation and controlled experimentation. The result is an emergent emphasis on logical explanations and practical programs to access valuable knowledge and promote the quality of human life, while at the same time contributing to global needs.

We experience our world through sensory mechanisms and sensory-based perceptions that are cognitively organized, a process that is dependent on biological mechanisms. Psychic experience, on the other hand, reaches beyond known sensory and cognitive functions, thus augmenting sensory experience, while suggesting totally new alternatives for expanding awareness and acquiring knowledge. Examples of these are telepathy, precognition and retrocognition, clairvoyance, out-of-body experiences, and discarnate survival phenomena, to mention but a few. Taken together, these phenomena suggest four major empowering principles:

FOUR EMPOWERING PRINCIPLES

1. The essence of our existence transcends biological or physical experience alone.

2. With the conventionally prescribed limits of human experience removed, the potentials for human growth and knowledge are significantly expanded.

3. We can dramatically increase our scope and store of knowledge by developing our psychic capacities.

4. Psychic self-empowerment and self-fulfillment are reasonable expectations for everyone.

A major challenge facing us today is a riveting, demystifying probe of the so-called paranormal that will explain its nature and unleash its empowering potentials. The psychic experience, whether voluntary or involuntary, is always empowerment driven. Discovering its capacity for empowerment requires attention to the psychic event and understanding its significance. For example, many of our dreams are psychic and potentially empowering, but benefiting from the dream requires first recalling the dream, then understanding its message, and, in some instances, acting upon it. The problem-solving dream challenges us by providing, often in disguise, the raw material we need for a solution. Discovering the solution requires imagination and diligence in unraveling the dream, interpreting its symbols, and creatively applying its message.

The empowering effects of the psychic experience can be profound and enduring. They often involve the critical issues of our existence and our ultimate destiny. To disregard such phenomena, or to shrug them off as inconsequential, is to negate their empowering capacity to promote our growth and expand our range of knowledge and experience.

THE PSYCHIC EMPOWERMENT HIERARCHY

When we are psychically empowered, our multiple faculties function in a dynamic hierarchy that is constantly evolving and rearranging itself. Those abilities required for immediate coping spontaneously rise within the hierarchy to assume an appropriate place of prominence, thereby meeting our empowerment needs of the moment. Those abilities not in immediate demand descend in the hierarchy, but remain in reserve for future use as needed. In other words, our inner faculties are placed "online" within a psychic system that is responsive to our empowerment needs, even those we do not consciously anticipate. This precognitive feature of the hierarchical system is a major characteristic of the psychically empowered individual. When initiative is required, the hierarchical system activates it. When courage is needed, the empowerment hierarchy delivers it. When creativity is demanded, the hierarchy reorganizes to generate it. When such practical skills as problem solving or analytical evaluation are called for, the empowerment hierarchy shifts its order to effectively access them. In situations involving danger, the empowerment hierarchy creates a shield of protection, and delivers the power needed to cope effectively with threatening situations. The resources required for wellness, stress management, habit control, and personal enrichment exist within a hierarchy that is responsive to the empowered self's multiple, changing demands.

Although our empowerment hierarchy functions spontaneously, at times it requires deliberate activation to meet certain situational demands or personal growth needs. When psychically empowered, we can access the hierarchical system and call forth specific inner resources at will. Achieving that empowered state demands mastery of many psychic empowerment tools and techniques.

PSYCHIC EMPOWERMENT PROGRAMS

A major focus of this book is on workable programs designed to promote psychic empowerment through the development of our psychic potentials. As a growth process, psychic empowerment requires the exploration and practice of many approaches to discover those that work best for us individually. Some of the programs presented in this book are designed to promote a general state of psychic readiness, whereas others are structured to activate specific psychic faculties. Each program is unique and can be practiced independently of other programs; however, they share three common features: self-discovery, commitment, and investment.

Self-discovery

Psychic self-empowerment is possible only when we discover our inner psychic potentials and responsibly liberate them to work for ourselves and others. In undiscovered form, our psychic faculties seek expression and recognition through numerous indirect channels. They stand at the door of consciousness and knock, but they do not intrude—they make no forced entries. Sadly, to reject these psychic overtures is to close the door to self-discovery and a vast wealth of empowering possibilities.

Commitment

Through commitment to develop our psychic side, we liberate ourselves to achieve the highest levels of self-enlightenment and fulfillment. With unlimited psychic resources at our command, we can shape our own destiny while contributing to the common good. Only through psychic channels can we meet some of the world's most pressing needs. World peace, for example, must eventually flow not from the destructive wizardry of futuristic war technology, but from the positive power of raised global consciousness, and a firm commitment to global harmony.

Investment

Developing our psychic resources demands personal investment in the pursuit of new knowledge and psychic fulfillment. Although some psychic activity will occur effortlessly or spontaneously, the full actualization of our psychic potential requires diligence in acquiring essential tools and techniques. Even the psychically gifted find that hard work is essential in fine-tuning their skills. Fortunately, a very modest investment in the psychic realm will often yield a generous payoff. The inner, knowing part of the self appears constantly poised to reward even a nominal probe of its empowering capacity.

The programs of psychic empowerment developed in this book are anchored in a clear recognition of the dignity and incomparable worth of all human beings. Whether a simple affirmation of power or a complex empowering procedure, each program embodies a firm regard for the divine spark of greatness existing in everyone. Among the most empowering techniques known are affirmations such as:

I am a person of incomparable worth.
Success is my destiny.
I am empowered.

These affirmations, when combined with visualization that crystallizes positive thought energy into reality, can build an empowered state of mind, body, and spirit that simply cannot fail.

From a global perspective, psychic empowerment suggests new approaches for promoting a higher plane of global actualization. Global issues such as poverty, homelessness, crime, hunger, human and animal suffering, and war are vital concerns of the psychically empowered. These problems require a firm commitment of our resources and energies toward making the world a better place. The abuse of human and animal rights, inequality in educational and economic opportunities, environmental pollution, loss of species, and reckless exploitation of the Earth's resources demand our involvement, because our globe and the survival of future generations are now at risk.

Our self-empowerment rests largely on our willingness to master the tools and techniques required to develop our higher potentials and integrate them into our lives. By personally experiencing the psychic nature of our existence, we come to know our psychic side and the empowering potential of psychic phenomena. The psychic experience is an important and convincing teacher, because it validates the essential nature of our existence and connects us to the inner, knowing part of the self. It can advance us to a new level of self-understanding and appreciation of life as an exciting, endless journey of growth and discovery.

The psychic empowerment concepts and programs presented in this book recognize the sources of ultimate power as residing within the self. Delegated power, whatever its origin, becomes real power only when internalized, integrated, and finally validated by the self. Likewise, such concepts as Universal Power, Cosmic Oneness, and Divine Power become personally empowering only when experienced as realities by the responsive, choosing self. In becoming self-empowered, there can be no substitute for personal autonomy and choice. Within each of us is the capacity to change the present and shape the future. When we are self-empowered, we are the sole architects of our destiny.

As you master the tools and techniques found throughout this book, here are a few guidelines that will help keep you on track:

GUIDELINES TO PSYCHIC EMPOWERMENT

1. Reinvent yourself by changing your thinking as needed. Replace old limiting views with awareness of unlimited possibilities for growth, abundance, and happiness. Generate powerful expectations of success.

2. Let your mind, body, and spirit work together. Keep them aligned and in harmony with each other.

3. Stay connected to your subconscious. Embrace your subconscious resources and use them to achieve your personal goals.

4. Find ways of contributing daily to the greater good.

5. Take time out as needed. A brief relaxation break can renew the mind, body, and spirit.

6. Keep in mind that you are a divine being with a divine purpose. Because you are divine, your existence is endless and your destiny is success.

7. Let the baggage of fear and self-doubt dissolve away.

8. Remind yourself that you are empowered with unlimited potential.

9. Embrace life as an endless journey filled with opportunity.

10. Become connected to the afterlife realm and its abundance of resources, including ministering spirit guides, helpers, and growth specialists.

11. Commit yourself to successfully mastering the essential tools and techniques of psychic empowerment.

PART ONE
Consciousness-Expanding Techniques for Psychic Development

1

EXTRASENSORY PERCEPTION
Out of the Lab into the Real World

Extrasensory perception (ESP) can be defined as the knowledge of or response to events, conditions, or situations, whether past, present, or future, independently of our known sensory mechanisms or processes. While its dynamics are not yet fully understood, ESP as a goal-oriented phenomenon is one of our most valuable channels for experiencing the inner and outer realities of our existence. Through bypassing ordinary sensory functions, it can directly engage realities that are otherwise unavailable to us.

Although often dismissed as a chance occurrence or something other than psychic, ESP is a valid and highly common phenomenon that is experienced from time to time by almost everyone. Among the common examples are *telepathy, clairvoyance, precognition,* and *retrocognition,* each of which can expand our world of awareness. In its capacity to send and receive both thoughts and feelings through *telepathy,* ESP can expand our communication capacities, promote productive interactions, and provide information, often from a great distance, that's otherwise unavailable to us. In its capacity to perceive spatially distant realities through *clairvoyance,* ESP can dramatically expand our world of awareness and uncover critical sources of new knowledge and power. In its capacity to perceive the future through *precognition,* ESP can provide advanced awareness that equips us to prepare for future events and, in some instances, to influence or prevent them altogether. While some future events exist as fixed, unalterable destinies, others exist as probabilities that are subject to our intervention. Through precognition, you can become empowered to eliminate the negative probabilities while accentuating the positive. Given precognitive knowledge, you can generate a powerful expectancy of success that literally transforms probabilities into realities. You can thus literally create the future of your choice.

Complementing the capacity of ESP to tap into the future through precognition is its capacity to tap into the past through *retrocognition.* In that role, ESP expands our awareness of relevant past events and experiences, including those of past-life origin. The result can be a "peak experience" that resolves conflicts, reduces anxiety, and extinguishes, often instantly, such conditions as phobias, obsessions, and compulsions. While effective programs have been developed to retrieve past-life experiences related to present-life conditions, the spontaneous retrocognition of past-life experiences has shown equally effective results. That possibility was illustrated by a biology teacher whose fear of germs combined with a hand-washing compulsion seriously interrupted her career. Finally, while working in her lab after class, she experienced a clear image of herself in a past life with an injured hand that was seriously swollen and infected. She knew instantly that the image was past-life related. Equipped with past-life knowledge, she also knew instantly that her fear of germs and the accompanying hand-washing compulsion were at last under her control. Amazingly, both conditions vanished instantly.

The wide diversity of the retrocognition experience is illustrated by its common use in the criminal justice setting, where it has been known to uncover critical evidence required for solving crimes. Interestingly, such evidence when experienced by investigative psychics is usually attributed to ESP, but when experienced by crime investigators it is often explained as a "lucky hunch" or simply intuition.

When we add to these multiple functions the capacity of ESP to interact with other dimensions of reality, the empowerment potentials of this phenomenon become almost without limits. Psychic interactions with the spirit dimension clearly illustrate the spiritual side of ESP along with the spiritual nature of our being as evolving souls. Like other forms of ESP, interactions with the departed as well as spiritual guides and other growth specialists can occur spontaneously ,or they can be initiated deliberately through a variety of techniques that include table tipping, automatic writing, and the séance, to list but a few. The wide-ranging rewards that accompany these interactions are clear manifestations of the spirit realm as a present dimension that welcomes our search for knowledge and understanding.

You've heard it before: *Knowledge is power, and knowledge of psychic origin is power in its purest form.* Psychic knowledge is power typically available from no other source. Given psychic knowledge, you can unleash vast inner reserves of power required to achieve new heights of personal fulfillment. You can become empowered to enrich your life, achieve your most difficult personal goals, and shape your own future. Here are some other examples.

EMPOWERING EFFECTS OF PSYCHIC KNOWLEDGE

- Psychic knowledge in its various forms can enrich your life with a deeper understanding of yourself and the purpose of your existence.

- Telepathy, believed to be the most common form of ESP, can increase your ability to communicate effectively and generate more positive social interactions.

- Clairvoyance can increase your awareness of distant realities that have important relevance to your present life situation.

- Precognition can help you to avert misfortune and muster the resources required to cope more effectively with formidable situations.

- ESP can provide information critical to effective problem solving and planning.

- ESP can facilitate creativity.

- Psychic insight can overcome all barriers to personal growth and success.

- Psychic insight can generate totally new feelings of personal worth and well-being.

- ESP can connect you to the highest realms of enlightenment and power.

- On a very broad scale, psychic insight can equip us to take command of global conditions and empower us to initiate positive global change.

Admittedly, we do not know all there is to know about ESP. We do know, however, that the ESP potential exists to some extent in everyone, and in animals as well. Furthermore, there are proven tools and techniques, many of them developed in the controlled lab setting, through which you can develop that potential. Discovering your psychic potentials and developing them to their fullest is the overarching theme of this book.

THE DEVELOPMENTAL NATURE OF ESP

The psychic potential is an integral part of your total being. It's not a matter of "You either have it or you don't." It is critical to your development as an evolving soul. It remains, however, up to you to develop it—no one can do it for you. Very early on, numerous lab studies at Athens State University were designed to investigate the developmental nature of ESP as well as other forms of psychic phenomena, including psychokinesis (PK) and mediumistic interactions. Three critical factors—motivation, practice, and experience—were found to be the keys to success in developing one's psychic potentials.

Those early studies revealed a distribution of ESP in the general population in which everyone was found to be psychic to some extent. Subjects scoring in the high range for one form of ESP, whether telepathy, precognition, or clairvoyance, typically scored in the high range for other forms, a finding that suggested the presence of a general factor, which we called *Factor X*. Typically, persons with a high Factor X showed a bright, expansive aura (that energy system enveloping the physical body—see Chapter Three) with a high degree of symmetry and balance as indicated by repeated electrophotographs of the aura in a highly controlled experimental setting. Interesting, our studies found that techniques designed to attune and balance the aura system were also effective in accelerating the psychic development of our subjects, including those with a low Factor X.

Aside from controlled laboratory measurements, among the best indicators of psychic potential are the spontaneous manifestations of ESP in daily life. Our studies found that a high frequency of ESP in daily life tended to be an excellent predictor of high performance on controlled laboratory tests of ESP, but with one exception: Practicing clairvoyants who claimed high psychic skills did not always perform well on laboratory tests, a finding suggesting that clairvoyance functions best in the informal social context rather than in the structured lab setting.

Although ESP is considered a normal and vital part of everyday life, it is all too often suppressed or denied expression. In its suppressed or dormant form, the psychic potential becomes like a butterfly trapped in a bottle. Immobilized, it offers only a constricted view of its beauty and power. With its wings creased, it seeks release and struggles for freedom. When finally liberated, it unfolds it wings with unparalleled grace and ascends in magnificent splendor. Like the majestic butterfly, our psychic potential, once liberated through motivation, practice, and experience, becomes able to soar in a brilliant unfoldment of power that enriches the quality of our lives.

BECOMING PSYCHICALLY EMPOWERED

Psychic empowerment, rather than a dormant state of power, is a dynamic, on-going process of psychic growth and self-development. Nothing is more important to that process than commitment and experience. Numerous programs have been developed, many of them focusing on specific psychic functions, to promote psychic empowerment. Among the common and most highly effective elements of these programs are positive self-talk and mental imagery.

Positive Self-Talk

Positive self-talk can be seen as a form of inner telepathy in which your own messages, whether silent or vocal, target specific psychic faculties, not only to stimulate their development but to focus them on specific goals. Self-talk can be initiated in an instant in almost any life situation. In unexpectedly stressful or demanding situations, the simple message, "I am self-confident, secure, and in command," can induce a secure, empowered state that ensures your complete success.

The effectiveness of self-talk can be dramatically increased through practice in which you listen to your own voice messages and allow them to be absorbed within. Keep in mind that the sound of your own voice is a convincing, energizing force. Although positive self-talk can be initiated at almost any time or place, a quiet, peaceful state of mind can increase the effectiveness of the technique. Before falling asleep and immediately upon awakening are excellent times to practice self-talk.

Following are a few examples of empowering self-talk related to the development of specific psychic faculties. You can increase the effectiveness of these examples by adding to them your own self-talk messages in your own words. You can also add more highly specific messages that target your designated goals. Keep in mind that visualization significantly increases the power of self-talk. When combined with relevant self-talk, a mental picture is worth ten thousand words.

PSYCHIC EMPOWERMENT THROUGH SELF-TALK

Telepathy: *Through telepathy, I have immediate access to the most advanced communication system known. I can use that system at any moment to communicate and interact with others. My telepathic powers are now unlocked and activated to enrich and empower my life.*

Precognition: *The future is now at my command. I can probe it at will to gain knowledge and increase awareness. My precognitive powers are like giant antennae that tap into the future. All the information I need is now available to me. Armed with precognitive insight, I am empowered to change the present and shape the future. My precognitive powers are now unlocked and activated to enrich and empower my life.*

Clairvoyance: *Through clairvoyance, I can dissolve the boundaries of my existence and transcend all the limitations of sensation and space. Clairvoyance is the information vehicle that connects me to all I need to know. I am now receptive to clairvoyant knowledge, and I will use it wisely. My clairvoyant powers are now unlocked and activated to enrich and empower my life.*

Our studies of positive self-talk showed it can be effectively used by both individuals and groups. In the controlled lab setting, subjects who practiced appropriate self-talk immediately before testing performed significantly better on a variety of ESP tests. The simple self-affirmation, "I now unlock the psychic abilities within myself," when presented immediately before tests using ESP cards, resulted in a significant improvement over previous scores. As a footnote, the possibility of the "practice effect" was ruled out by comparisons with a control group that did not use positive self-talk.

The application of positive self-talk, aside from its value in promoting ESP, is also effective in promoting other forms of psychic phenomena, including out-of-body travel and interactions with other dimensions of power, among them the discarnate realm. The simple self-affirmation, especially when presented audibly, "I am now ready to travel outside my body," can set the stage for successful travel to designated destinations. Similarly, the simple self-affirmation, again when presented audibly, "I am now ready to interact with the spirit realm," can facilitate engagement of that realm in a profoundly meaningful interaction, whether practiced by individuals or groups.

Positive self-talk is not limited to the activation and development of your psychic powers. You can adapt it to meet the demands of any situation or to promote achievement of any personal goal. For instance, you can use positive self-talk to build the skills required to solve complex personal problems, increase feelings of personal worth and well-being, facilitate achievement of personal goals, enrich social relationships, promote career success, and improve performance on any task. Students have used positive self-talk before and during course evaluations to improve their test performance; teachers have used it to improve classroom interactions and increase teaching effectiveness; attorneys have used it sharpen their skill before and during court sessions; and artists have used it to increase creativity and improve the quality of their works, to list but a few of the possibilities. The performance of a group of college students enrolled in remedial algebra rapidly improved with the introduction of positive group self-talk at the beginning of each class session. Among the self-talk affirmations were: *I have decided to develop my math skills. Nothing can stop me now. My math potentials are now free to unfold.*

THE POWER OF MENTAL IMAGERY

As already noted, the power of self-talk can be dramatically expanded through relevant mental imagery. Mental imagery gives added substance to verbal messages while literally increasing the capacity of your subconscious mind to target its resources on your designated goals.

Mental imagery is an acquired cognitive skill. In developing your imagery skills, you are acquiring the language of your subconscious mind. Through imagery combined with self-talk, you can successfully interact with your subconscious resources and even expand them. You can awaken your dormant resources and exercise them in ways that enrich your life with new potentials for growth and success. With the powers of your subconscious mind at your command through a combination of self-talk and imagery, literally nothing is impossible for you. You can take command of your life to achieve your highest goals, whether mental, physical, or spiritual. Happiness, health and fitness, and success, to list but a few, are all available to you through self-talk and mental imagery. You can energize your biological systems and even influence brain activity to rejuvenate and recreate yourself. You can increase the length and quality of your life by protecting and fortifying your innermost energy system.

You can initiate an upward growth spiral that promotes continuous renewal of the mind, body, and spirit through your combined use of self-talk and mental imagery.

The Palm Viewing Exercise: Among the most effective techniques for developing you imagery powers is the simple Palm Viewing Exercise. The complexity of mind, body, and spirit interactions seeks simplicity in manifesting and activating them. The Palm Viewing Exercise was developed in our lab to meet that goal. Your hands are the antennae of the body to the universe. By focusing on them you can develop your imagery skills and use them to communicate with your subconscious mind as well as the sources of power beyond. At Step 5, which is optional, you can state a personal goal, visualize it, and affirm your complete success in achieving it. Your goal can range from developing your ESP powers to mastering a particular skill or, at another level, breaking an unwanted habit or even reversing the effects of aging. Here's the simple procedure.

MENTAL IMAGERY AND THE PALM VIEWING EXERCISE

Step 1. Take a few moments to view the palm of either hand, paying particular attention to its lines and unique patterns, such as crosses, triangles, stars, and squares.

Step 2. Close your eyes and create a mental picture of your palm. Focus your attention again on its unique characteristics, including lines and patterns.

Step 3. Again view your palm and note its specific lines and patterns. Notice the characteristics you may have missed in the mental picture you generated in Step 2.

Step 4. Close your eyes and once again picture your palm in full and complete detail. Before opening your eyes, affirm: *Imagery is the language of my subconscious mind. Through imagery and the self-talk that accompanies it, I can unlock the powers within myself and use them to emrich my life with abundance and complete success.*

Step 5 (Optional). State a personal goal and visualize it as an unfolding reality while affirming your complete success in achieving it. Again, *simplicity rules!* If, for instance, your goal is rejuvenation, visualize yourself at your youthful prime while affirming: *This is the true me.* On the other hand, if your goal is to break the smoking habit, visualize yourself being offered a cigarette while affirming: *No, I am a nonsmoker.*

This simple technique can be used almost anywhere. With practice, you will be amazed at its effectiveness.

The Finger Interlock Technique

The Finger Interlock Technique: Another highly effective technique for developing your mental imagery powers is the Finger Interlock Technique. This simple technique developed in our labs, however, goes far beyond its imagery application. It generates a relaxed, empowered state while enveloping the body with a bubble of powerful, protective energy called "the halo effect," a phenomenon illustrated in our labs using electrophotographic techniques.

As illustrated in the Palm Viewing Exercise, *complexity seeks simplicity*. The complexities of the subconscious mind, including its multifaceted, dynamic, and intricate functions, are receptive not only to imagery and empowering affirmation but to simple gestures as well. From the Freudian perspective, a simple, unintentional slip of the tongue or gesture can have profound implications for uncovering hidden motives and repressed experiences. Unlike an unintentional Freudian cue, the Finger Interlock, though a simple gesture, has profound implications from the psychic empowerment perspective. Here's the simple technique.

THE FINGER INTERLOCK TECHNIQUE

Step 1. Take in a few deep breaths, exhaling slowly. Focus only on your breathing as your mind becomes increasingly passive.

Step 2. Join the thumb and middle finger of each hand to form two circles.

Step 3. Bring the hands together to form interlocking circles.

Step 4. Relax your hands while holding the interlock gesture. Visualize the gesture while affirming, *I am now fully empowered.*

Given even limited practice of this simple four-step technique, the finger inter-lock gesture can be used almost anywhere for instant self-empowerment. You can even use it with your hands behind your back. You can use it during a speech to improve communication or to instantly extinguish stage fright. You can use it during job interviews, tests, or any stressful situation to induce a relaxed, self-confident state. In situations involving threat or danger, you can use it to erect a protective field of powerful energy around your full body to ward off any invasive force, including that of the so-called *energy vampire*. The Finger Interlock is an essential technique for anyone seeking a more fully empowered state of mind, body, and spirit.

EXTRASENSORY INTERACTIONS WITH THE SPIRIT REALM

There is an emerging body of evidence that ESP, rather than an unexplained exten-sion of sensory perception, is a fine-tuned manifestation of the nonbiological or spiritual nature of our being. As such, ESP often includes interactions with the spirit realm. Psychic interactions with spirit guides and helpers, as well as departed loved ones, friends, and in many instances animals, can be critical sources of comfort and enlightenment regarding the nature of the afterlife as well as our on-going develop-ment in this dimension as evolving souls. Our interactions with the afterlife realm in a situation involving the transition of a loved one is especially empowering in that it provides reassurance of life beyond death while promoting a rapid recovery from loss by fulfilling two very basic human needs—our need to remain in touch with the departed and their need to remain in touch with us. Those needs are especially great in situations involving sudden, unexpected death.

Our interactions with the spirit realm can include a complex combination of both sensory and extrasensory perception. For instance, a collectively perceived orb of en-ergy or an apparition that can be photographed suggests a tangible manifestation of a nontangible or spiritual reality, a phenomenon sometimes called *materialization*. Similarly, sensory perception of an aroma or sound associated with a spirit entity can become the tangible precursor of an interaction that can include the exchange of in-formation with a spirit entity, along with the transfer of energy that can be mentally comforting and physically healing in nature. That phenomenon was illustrated on the campus of Athens State University where a green iridescent orb of energy periodically appeared for many years on the second floor of Brown Hall, a historic Greek Revival structure which once served as the campus infirmary. Our controlled on-site studies of the orb, which included both individual and group interactions with it, revealed a variety of healing and rejuvenating qualities. Even very brief physical contacts with the orb consistently reduced pain while apparently accelerating the healing process, par-ticularly for sports injuries, findings suggesting that the orb functioned as a physical manifestation of a spiritual presence for the express purpose of transferring healing energy. Unfortunately, during an extensive renovation of the building, the orb vanished, never to be seen again.

ESP AND THE DREAM EXPERIENCE

Many of our psychic faculties, including various forms of ESP, appear to exist as subconscious processes that are receptive to our efforts to activate them through such tools and techniques as hypnosis, meditation, automatic writing, dowsing, crystal gazing, quartz crystal programming, and a host of empowering interactions with nature. Yet another highly effective channel for psychic enlightenment of subconscious origin is the dream experience.

Dreams, while often cloaked in symbolism and disguises, are one of our most important sources of precognition. Almost everyone can recall a dream experience that later came true. Precognitive dreams often identify a future event with important relevance to the present. A graduate student majoring in clinical psychology reported a vivid dream experience in which he viewed a man dressed in black with tattoos of chains on his wrists. A few days later he attended a campus lecture on the widespread exploitation of children around the world. At the end of the program, the lecturer, a man dressed in black exactly as seen in his recent dream, raised his arms to reveal tattoos of chains on his wrists, a bold statement of his commitment to break the chains of child abuse which included the expanding sex-trade of children in his country. The student, moved by the fulfillment of the dream experience, became an active participant in a global initiative to expose the blatant practice and bring it to an end.

Another instance of the precognitive role of dreams was illustrated by an artist who used the dream experience to generate creative ideas for his paintings. His technique used mental imagery of a blank canvas immediately before falling asleep accompanied by the autosuggestion that, during sleep, pictures of future paintings would appear vividly on the screen. Immediately upon awakening, he recorded the dream experience in detail, including sketches of the dream's artistic content. With the introduction of precognitive dreaming, his artwork took on a creative edge totally unlike that of his past works. His paintings today are in great demand as major works of art.

Aside from precognition, dreams are often clairvoyant in nature. In that role, dreams can provide critical information related to distant, unseen realities. They can reveal the exact location of lost objects as well as missing persons and animals. Troubled by the disappearance of her dog companion, a student assisting in our dream research program experienced a vivid dream of the dog's exact location. Following a leg injury, the dog had sought safe haven under a nearby abandoned building. Armed with clairvoyant insight, the student promptly retrieved the dog, which soon fully recovered.

Though it may seem at first farfetched, certain sleep techniques have been developed in the experimental lab setting to induce clairvoyant dreaming and use the experience for military purposes such as the inspection of classified documents and listening in on sensitive conferences and conversations. The results of these studies, while raising certain ethical questions, suggest the interesting possibility that sleep techniques designed to induce clairvoyant dreaming may also give rise to out-of-body travel to targeted destinations.

Beyond Dreaming

You can facilitate psychic dreaming, whether clairvoyant or precognitive, through a simple technique called Beyond Dreaming. Developed in the lab setting, Beyond Dreaming specifies a certain goal and then focuses the dream experience upon it. Beyond Dreaming not only promotes psychic dreaming, it activates the subconscious resources required for successful achievement of your stated goals. Beyond Dreaming generates a powerful anticipation of success so essential to the achievement of both personal and career goals. Beyond that, the dream can literally unleash the subconscious resources required for your complete success. Here's the technique:

BEYOND DREAMING TECHNIQUE

Step 1. Formulate your goal and record it in your dream journal. Remind yourself that your dreams are sources not only of psychic enlightenment related to your stated goals; they can also connect you to the subconscious sources of power required for successful goal achievement.

Step 2. During the drowsy state preceding sleep, review your goal, which can range from very general to highly specific. Remind yourself that your dreams will become channels for information and power required to achieve your goal. Further remind yourself that upon awakening, you will have full recall of the dream experience.

Step 3. As your dreams unfold, flow effortlessly with them while intervening as needed to focus them on your stated goal.

Step 4. Upon awakening, record your dream experiences in your dream journal.

Step 5. Take time to reflect on your dreams and their relevance to your stated goals while keeping in mind that dream messages are often symbolic in nature.

In a later chapter, we will further explore the dream experience as a doorway to the subconscious mind. We will examine the problem-solving dream, the significance of dream symbols, and develop ways of "dreaming true."

SUMMARY

Our goal in this chapter was twofold: to increase our knowledge of ESP and to master the skills related to that remarkable phenomenon. That goal is relevant not only to ESP, but to psychic empowerment in general. Given the knowledge and skills presented in this chapter, you are well on your way to a state of a fully empowered mind, body, and spirit. If we are serious in our pursuit of psychic empowerment, we can settle for nothing less.

Given the multiple functions of ESP, the empowerment potentials of this phenomenon become almost without limits.

SOURCES AND RECOMMENDED READING

Melita Denning and Osborne Phillips, *Practical Guide to Psychic Powers: Awaken Your Sixth Sense* (Llewellyn, 2000).

William Hewitt, *Psychic Development for Beginners: An Easy Guide to Developing and Releasing Your Psychic Abilities* (Llewellyn, 1996).

Joe H. Slate and Carl Llewellyn Weschcke, *Psychic Empowerment for Everyone: You Have the Power, Learn to Use It* (Llewellyn, 2009).

Joe H. Slate and Carl Llewellyn Weschcke, *Self-Empowerment & Your Subconscious Mind: Your Unlimited Resource for Health, Success, Long Life & Spiritual Attainment* (Llewellyn, 2010).

2

ASTRAL PROJECTION & THE OUT-OF-BODY EXPERIENCE

Out-of-body experiences (OBEs) at once reveal the true nature and greatest possibilities of our being. You can travel to a dimension where the effects of aging, injury, disappointment, and depression are replaced by the best the universe has to offer. A place where the painful residue of past-life issues is wiped clean. Through astral projection, anxieties associated with past-life trauma, empowerment issues, and ill health are effectively eliminated. You will finally discover new meaning to your existence as a conscious, enduring energy force in the universe.

—JOE H. SLATE, *ASTRAL PROJECTION AND PSYCHIC EMPOWERMENT*

Perhaps no psychic experience is as exciting as that of temporarily and voluntarily leaving the physical body to travel to distant locations and other dimensions. And there is probably no other psychic experience as challenging to our familiar beliefs in the mortality and limitations of the physical body. Astral projection is the greatest adventure in consciousness we can have while still living in our physical body. It also offers present proof that being within the physical body is necessary to know, to feel, to love, to live, and to fulfill the great plan of growing and evolving to become more than we are.

We are beings of consciousness, sometimes inhabiting physical bodies that we can learn to leave at will, to travel in time and space, and tap into memory archives and knowledge banks beyond that are even greater than those of Internet search engines. Going outside of the physically limited brain consciousness enables the soul traveler to enter the heaven worlds, meet and communicate with deceased loved ones, receive guidance from spiritual counselors, and even to intervene in the physical world, often healing the body of disease.

To go out of the body allows you to rise to the level of your own soul.

Astral Projection

While a belief in the human soul is common to most cultures, modern westerners have been taught that consciousness is a function of the brain, and upon the death of the brain, consciousness as we know it is snuffed out. Some people are taught that on some future *Resurrection Day* the dead will arise with full memories and consciousness of the single life they enjoyed (or suffered) while inhabiting that risen body. Supposedly it is their soul that remembers, but *where was the soul all that time between death and resurrection?* And if consciousness is a function of the brain, *how can consciousness with its memories reappear when the brain has decayed?*

To experience consciousness separate from the body is to know that your life is eternal and the physical body's death is not the end but just another beginning. Experiencing life beyond the body brings appreciation for life in the body and understanding of its purpose. Being no longer bound to this one physical body opens doors to new opportunities of growth and development with vision from the highest perspective.

WHAT IS ASTRAL PROJECTION?

We're going to explore several avenues to adequately answer the question, but we'll start with one that will provide us with several directions for our effort:

> *ASTRAL PROJECTION is the act of separating the astral body from the physical body. This happens normally as part of the sleep process, typically when one has reached the deepest dream level. One of the goals in Wiccan/Witchcraft practice is to be fully aware of the astral projection experience. This is called conscious astral projection.*
>
> *Through conscious astral projection, one can recall events that take place during astral journeys. The astral body can be employed by the conscious mind to explore not only various places on earth, but also different realms within other dimensions. Conscious projection of the astral body is obtained through deep meditative states. Some people leave the physical body through the solar plexus area, while others exit from the third eye or simply find themselves suddenly looking down at their physical body. Traveling while in the astral state can be accomplished by such methods as dream-like flight or through visualizing the place one wishes to visit.*
>
> —RAVEN GRIMASSI, *ENCYCLOPEDIA OF WICCA & WITCHCRAFT*

The most important word for us in this definition is "conscious." Many people do have spontaneous "out-of-body experiences" (the generally preferred term among paranormal investigators), while many more have dream experiences that "seem real" and may be "lucid dreams" (which we will discuss later). *Conscious astral projection is undertaken with intent to achieve specific results.*

Conscious astral projection allows us to not only explore physical places, but to see them from a larger perspective that often provides details including psychometric knowledge of their history, the discovery of lost objects, and even intuitive knowledge of health and other problems of people seen.

Conscious astral projection also allows us to travel through space and time to explore the universe, but—more importantly—to explore the astral plane and better understand the astral dimension of our own psyche.

THE ASTRAL BODY AND THE ASTRAL PLANE

Our definition has already introduced us to the astral body, but hasn't explained it, and to do so we have also to discuss the astral and other planes and bodies.

Everything has "substance," even your feelings, thoughts, and highest aspirations. Your physical body is made up of physical substance taken from the physical plane. An "upper" part of the physical plane is called the etheric subplane, from which substance your etheric body, or more properly "etheric double"—also called your "energy body"—is made. This double or duplicate of the physical body is also known as the *Doppelganger* in German.

In the next chapter, focusing on the aura, we will discuss more about the etheric double and the chakra system. The etheric double can also be projected, in part, from the physical body and it is with the etheric double and its energies that certain psychokinetic phenomena can be accomplished. This can include distant healing, the actual movement of objects, and even forms of sexual contact. Etheric projection is not part of our discussion in this book but etheric energy and substance is involved in many of the psychic tools and techniques that are discussed.

In Chapter Three we will actually be discussing the etheric, astral, mental, and spiritual bodies in relation to the layers of the aura.

Our ordinary experience and our education has led us to believe that the only *substance* is physical, but both ancient wisdom and modern quantum science say that everything that exists has substance, so we must accept this principle and realize that even thoughts and feeling are "substantial"—consisting of substance. But these are not physical substance but astral and mental substance.

When metaphysicians and psychics, and even a growing number of parapsychologists and other scientists, speak of planes or worlds—physical/etheric, astral, mental, and spiritual—they are recognizing the existence of different kinds of substance. These substances are distinguished by distinct ranges of vibration.

Everything that exists "vibrates." And our perceptions are uniquely *tuned in* to specific ranges of vibration that we sense with our appropriate organs—physical as well as psychic—although these psychic organs are different in structure and nature than the physical ones. Nevertheless, some psychic perceptions combine the physical organ with one of the chakras—which we can call "psychic" or etheric organs.

"Vibration" refers to movement and "vibrations" are measured by their frequency per second. Touch, sound, odor, taste, and sight are each characterized by particular ranges of vibrations and all phenomena perceived by these senses occur within defined ranges of vibration.

The following table is scientific and speculative. It is also visibly incomplete and begs reader input. Its intention is to provide a structure for our understanding of the position of the Whole Person within the Whole Universe, inclusive of all that lies outside of our physical perception.

MATHEMATICAL MEASUREMENT PREFIXES AND THEIR MEANINGS

nano- means	**n** 10^{-9} or 0.000000001 (minus 8 zeros = milliardth)
micro-	**u** 10^{-6} or 0.000001 (minus 5 zeros = millionth)
milli-	***m*** 10^{-3} or 0.001 (minus 2 zeros = thousandth)
centi-	**c** 10^{-2} or 0.01 (minus 1 zero = hundredth)
deci-	**d** 10^{-1} or 0.1 (no zeros = tenth)
	10^{0} or 1
deca-	**d** 10^{1} or 1 zero = ten
hecto-	**h** 10^{2} or 100 (2 zeros = hundred)
kilo-	**k** 10^{3} or 1,000 (3 zeros = thousand)
mega-	**M** 10^{6} or 1,000,000 (6 zeros = million)
giga-	**G** 10^{9} or 1,000,000,000 (9 zeros = billion)
tera-	**T** 10^{12} or 1,000,000,000,000 (12 zeros = trillion)
peta-	**P** 10^{15} or 1,000,000,000,000,000 (15 zeros)
exa-	**E** 10^{18} or 1,000,000,000,000,000,000 (18 zeros)
zeta-	**Z** 10^{21} (21 zeros)
yotta-	**Y** 10^{24} (24 zeros)
yocto-	y 10^{24} (minus 14 zeros = quadrillionth)
zepta-	**z** 10^{21} (minus 21 zeros = trillardth)
atto-	**a** 10^{18} (minus 18 zeros = trillionth)
femto-	**f** 10^{15} (minus 15 zeros = billiardth)
pico-	**p** 10^{12} (minus 12 zeros = trillionth)

Frequency (approx. Vibrations, Beats, Waves, Cycles, or Hertz (Hz) per Second)

VIBRATION RANGES OF DIFFERENT PHENOMENA

Infrasonic to Very Low Frequency (VLF) Waves, Magnetism and Gravity:
(measured in **G** Gauss (not a prefix)10^{-2} or minus 2 zeros to 100 Hz)

Certain Paranormal senses and phenomena, including levitation:

.00000	.0000	.000	.00	0 gauss
ESP	Dowsing	Black	Gravity	Magnetic
	Field	Streams*	Field	Field

*Described as "harmful earth rays" studied by members of the Institute of Electrical and Electronics Engineers in John Keel's *The Eighth Tower*.

Physical Senses—in vibrations per second:

Touch	2 to 16
Hearing	(from 16 in infants) 20 to 28,000
	Infrasonic Base Treble Ultrasonic
Taste	
Smell	
Sight	370 THz to 750 THz
	Infrared Red Violet Ultraviolet

Brain Waves in vibrations per second (Hertz):

Delta	1 to 3
Theta	4 to 7
Alpha	8 to 13
Beta	14 to 28

Earth's Schumann Resonant Frequency: **7.8 Hertz**

Electromagnetic Spectrum, longer waves: in Hertz:

Electric Power & AC Motors	60 to 100
Very Low Frequency Radio	3 KHz to 300 KHz
Radio, AM	540 KHz to 1630 KHz
Radio, Shortwave Broadcast	5.95 MHz to 26.1 MHz
Very High Frequency (VHF)	30 MHz to 300 MHz
Television, Band I	54 MHz to 88 MHz
FM Radio, Band II	88 MHz to 174 MHz
Television, Band III	174 MHz to 216 MHz
Ultra High Frequency (UHF)	300 MHz to 3000 MHz
Television, Bands IV & V, Channels 14-70	470 MHz to 806 MHz

Super High Frequencies (SHF)—Microwaves: **3 GHz to 30 GHz**

Infrared, Heat   **300 GHz to 430 GHz**

Visible Light (visible to human, *physical,* sight): 430 THz to 750 THz

Red	400 to 484 THz
Orange	484 to 508 THz
Yellow	508 to 526 THz
Green	526 to 606 THz
Cyan	606 to 630 THz
Blue	631 to 668 THz
Violet	668 to 789 THz

Ultraviolet	**1.62 PHz to 30 PHz**
Spirit Light (visible to human, *psychic,* sight)	**300 GHz to 40 PHz**
X-Ray	**30 PHz to 30 EHz**
Gamma Rays	**30 EHz to 3000 EHz**
Cosmic Rays	10^{20} **to** 10^{21}

Includes levels of Psychic Projections, and of Soul Essence

SEVEN PLANES OF THE SOLAR SYSTEM AND SEVEN LEVELS OF THE HUMAN STRUCTURE

Physical Plane:

Solid	)	**Physical Body**: vehicle of thought,
Liquid	)	feeling, awareness,
Gaseous	)	and action in the physical world.

Etheric	)	**Etheric Double**: connecting link between
Super-etheric	)	the inner and outer man, the container of
Subatomic	)	vital energy *(prana)* received physically
Atomic	)	from the sun and superphysically from the
		spiritual sun.

Adapted from Powell: The Etheric Double

Astral Plane:	)	**Astral Body**: vehicle of desire, emotion.
(Seven subplanes)	)	

Mental Plane: *Rupa*	)	**Mental Body**: vehicle of the formal mind
(Lower four subplanes)	)	and instrument of concrete thought.

Arupa	)	**Causal Body**, or higher mental body: vehicle of the abstract mind of the threefold Spiritual Self, the Augoides or Ego.
(Higher three	)	
subplanes)	)	
Buddhic Plane	)	**Buddhic Body**: vehicle of spiritual intuitiveness; Soul
	)	
Atmic Plane	)	**Atmic Body**: vehicle of the spiritual will; Spirit
(aka Nirvanic)	)	
Monadic Plane	)	**Monad**: the Dweller in the Innermost
(aka Paranirvanic)	)	
Adi (aka Manapara-nirvanic)	)	**Divine Spark**

Note: The names for the Seven Planes and the Seven Levels are not universally adhered to, but the overall concept of the invisible structure of man and universe is important to understanding the potentials of Astral Projection.

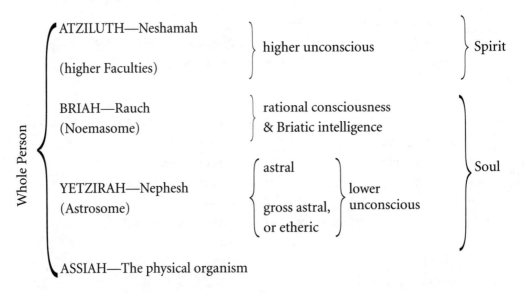

Levels of Consciousness, Soul, and Spirit, and the Whole Person
(This diagram, and the following diagram on page 31, Denning and Phillips, 2005)

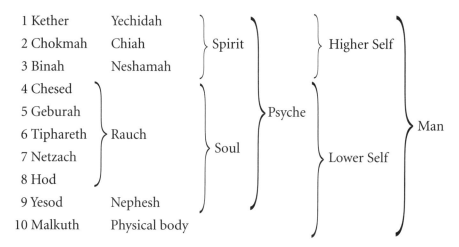

The Evolutionary Plan of the Psyche

No single view of either Macrocosm (the Universe as a whole) and the Microcosm (the Human as a whole) can comprehend all there is. A Qabalistic approach provides another perspective.

Action on the physical plane/world requires a physical body. We are misled in believing that thoughts and emotions and aspirations all arise from the physical brain and have no substance of their own or any need for bodies. Instead, we do have an astral body, a mental body, and a spiritual body. And, actually, there are still higher planes and bodies, but they are not pertinent to our subject in this book.

Just as we act, feel, think, and aspire while centered in the physical body, so can we act, feel, think, and aspire when we are centered in the astral body, or in the mental body, or in the spiritual body. Yet, each body has particular limitations and particular abilities. In the physical body, you cannot *think* yourself to a different location, but in the astral body you can. In the astral body, you cannot reach out and move a physical object as you can with your physical hand. (Actually, you can—using your mind—by projecting an astral hand, and using special techniques that bring etheric substance—which is a higher vibratory part of the physical—into the astral body, but these techniques usually require training and discipline, as in certain practices of yoga, the martial arts, shamanism, and forms of African and Western magick.)

What you can learn to do is to center your consciousness in the astral body, and use it as a *vehicle,* just as you normally use the physical body as a vehicle for your conscious mind. Think of it as a vehicle made of a different kind of substance and using a different kind of fuel.

A NEW WAY OF THINKING

The mind, and especially your conscious mind, enables you to center your consciousness in one or another of these vehicles. And that's the purpose of this chapter. It's a big subject, and there are hundreds of books written about techniques of astral projection, astral travel, soul travel, traveling in the spirit vision, and other terms, but it really boils down to a simple formula: Belief, Knowledge, and a Goal. *Belief* that you can do it based on case studies showing that others are doing it; *Knowledge* of techniques of how to do it; and a *Goal* of where you want to go or what you want to accomplish.

Yes, there are spontaneous out-of-body experiences. Some of these are induced as an escape from physical pain or as the astral body is projected when the physical body is unconscious and perhaps in trauma from an accident. Others are induced in religious and shamanic ceremonies accompanied by drumming, ecstatic dancing, chanting, fasting, sensory deprivation, meditation, and prayer. And many occur during sleep but are rarely consciously perceived and remembered—*although you can train yourself to do so.*

For our purposes, for the purpose of psychic empowerment, it is essential that we learn to consciously induce the out-of-body experience, and consciously determine what we are going to do through it. As pointed out in Chapter One, there are three critical factors in this and other psychic work: *motivation, practice,* and *experience.* These are the keys to success in developing your psychic potentials.

Beneath all the techniques and tools we are exploring in this book is one fundamental point: Human Consciousness, directed by the Conscious Mind, knows of no limits other than those imposed by unawareness, fear, false or biased teachings of science and religion, and that imposed by the simple belief that you cannot become more than you are.

No matter how it is framed, the truth is that we barely and rarely use even a tenth of our potential. The capacity is there and the undeveloped powers are intrinsic to our nature, but like almost everything else, those intrinsic powers have to be developed into reliable skills through experiment and practice.

The *Lucid Dream* is one example of a relatively common experience that can be extended by simply becoming aware that you are actually dreaming a situation and then taking *conscious* control of the dream. Usually a lucid dream involves the dreamer in a situation that suddenly appears *lucid:* unusually real—often glowing in light and marked by brighter colors, feelings of intensity, and other factors that clearly let you know that it's not an ordinary dream. Unfortunately, this can also include nightmares.

This very knowledge of lucid dreaming should be sufficient for you to determine—affirming as you prepare for sleep: *In a lucid dream, I will become consciously aware that it is a dream and will take control of its content.* The lucid dream is a self-created *astral drama,* an imagined reality structured of astral substance. It is *yours* to direct as if you were the director of a stage play. But unlike a stage play, where the script is fully created, you can now rewrite and direct your astral drama to fit your own *conscious* objectives.

Once again, we have important factors that stand out: conscious control (or intent) and astral substance. The astral world is real, but of a different substance of a much higher vibratory nature than the physical world. Our astral body is composed of this substance just as our physical body is composed of physical substance of a much lower vibratory nature. Another point that must be recognized is that there is no hard demarcation of the astral from the physical—they coexist, but the astral extends in space in ways that the physical seems not to do. In reality, even "empty" space contains some physical matter, but not sufficient to sustain physical life, while the astral body can travel in space at least within our solar system. "Visitors" from beyond our system have to employ mental or spiritual bodies, which are not as readily employed by the average person as is the astral.

TO REITERATE

Because of the importance of Belief, Knowledge, and Goal to the successful accomplishment of conscious astral projection, we're going to review the basics.

Reports of the out-of-body experience (OBE) commonly describe the phenomenon as *enlightening, profound, spectacular,* and *empowering.* Out-of-body experiences—also called "astral projections" or "astral travels"—are states of awareness encompassing a conscious awareness of being in a spatial location away from the physical body. The out-of-body concept assumes a duality of human nature, and the existence of an extrabiological consciousness or astral double. OBEs further assume the capacity of the extrabiological to disengage the physical body, and in that disengaged or out-of-body state, to travel consciously to experience distant or other dimensional realities.

OBEs can occur both in the normal state of awareness and in altered states such as sleep, hypnosis, and meditation. The out-of-body state itself could be considered an altered state distinctly unlike other states of consciousness in that it is usually accompanied by a profound awareness of separateness from the physical body. Although sometimes described as dreamlike, OBEs appear to be expressions of the disengaged extrabiological state rather than simply the products of sleep. Furthermore, the OBE subject often chooses a destination and brings back clear, conscious recall of the experience.

In recent years, the out-of-body experience has become the subject of increased interest and speculation, not only because of numerous reports of the phenomenon, but also because of an emerging recognition of its potentially empowering value.

One view considers the sleep experience itself to be an out-of-body state in which, as we sleep, the nonphysical or extrabiological double hovers over the physical body. The experience of falling asleep could involve literally a "rising out of the body" with the astral body drifting away from the physical body. Supportive of that perspective is the fact that drifting into sleep is often accompanied by sensations of being borne aloft, or of flowing away from the physical body. Any sudden disruption of that drifting astral experience seems to result in an unpleasant "falling" or "jolting" reentry.

This view further holds that sleep, as an out-of-body state of projected consciousness, is highly conducive to out-of-body travel; but actual out-of-body travel occurs only when the projected astral body moves to a spatially distant location to experience other realities. In contrast, the typical dream experience, which often includes symbolism and distortion, is more likely an expression of the subconscious. On the other hand, dreams of drifting over terrain and vividly experiencing other realities that are free of distortion can be explained as astral travel, rather than subconscious manifestations or other dream products.

Notwithstanding the many reports and mounting evidence supporting OBEs, conventional science remains reluctant to accept the existing data. This is in part due to the elusive and subjective nature of the experience and the often inconclusive results of OBE research. These problems, along with the admittedly biased views of many researchers, have constricted research efforts, and in some instances shrouded the topic with undue mystery. Not surprisingly then, many individuals who experience the phenomenon reject it outright, or anxiously question its normality.

For many people, however, the out-of-body experience is profoundly meaningful. A psychologist recalled an out-of-body experience that may have literally saved her life. Prior to a serious automobile accident, she experienced troubling, recurring dreams in which her car overturned several times. When the accident finally occurred, she spontaneously entered the out-of-body state, during which she watched her car from above as it overturned several times down an embankment, exactly as seen in her dreams. She walked away from the accident without injury, and attributed her escape to the out-of-body experience, which gave her physical protection at a time of great danger.

Typically absent in the out-of-body state are experiences of pain and distress or physical and mental limitations. Furthermore, OBEs, as empowering phenomena, have reportedly accelerated recovery from certain physical and mental impairments. Of particular interest are reports that impairments associated with damage to the central nervous system are absent in the astral body during OBEs. This was illustrated by an athlete, partially paralyzed by a spinal injury, who reported frequent OBEs during which he functioned normally and experienced no discomfort. He attributed his remarkable recovery to OBEs that enabled him to exercise his body mentally while stimulating the damaged regions of his nervous system. In a similar instance, a stroke patient confined to a wheelchair reported OBEs in which the astral body functioned normally. She attributed her recovery to the mental exercise provided by her recurring OBEs. She saw the OBEs as stimulating healing and literally repairing the specific brain areas damaged by the stroke.

In another instance, a policeman, partially paralyzed by an injury sustained in the line of duty, reported daily OBEs in which he experienced no impairment of astral body functions. He valued the out-of-body experiences for their enrichment and motivational benefits, as well as their actual physical effects in accelerating his eventual recovery. The physical benefits of OBEs are further illustrated by the reports of a young executive who suffered from tinnitus, a persistent and distressing ringing in the ears that often impaired his ability to concentrate. He discovered that upon entering the induced, out-of-body state, the ringing in his ears abruptly ceased. Upon his return to the body, the ringing resumed, but with less intensity. He began practicing OBEs daily as a means of relieving the ringing. Eventually, the ringing that had plagued him for years permanently ceased.

Although spontaneous OBEs are often associated with normal, everyday activities, they can also occur under conditions that are intensely stressful. For instance, a prisoner of war, while being interrogated by his captors and subjected to excruciating pain, experienced the spontaneous sensation of drifting away from his physical body. Free from pain in that projected state, he saw his physical body lying apparently lifeless on the floor. He recalled the out-of-body experience as profoundly empowering, because it enabled him to cope with otherwise intolerable pain; perhaps even more importantly, it strengthened his will to live. He attributed his survival and eventual escape to the empowering effects of the out-of-body experience.

There is some evidence of psychokinesis (PK) during the out-of-body state. The capacity of the mind in the out-of-body state to influence external events seems to be enhanced in dangerous accident or near-accident situations, typically for the purpose of preventing injury. This concept, "out-of-body PK," was illustrated by an equestrienne who, upon being thrown from her horse, immediately entered the out-of-body state, and while viewing her fall from a distance, slowed the fall and cushioned the impact, thereby escaping the fall uninjured. In a somewhat similar instance, a student spontaneously entered the out-of-body state upon losing his balance when stepping from his shower. While viewing his fall from overhead, he mentally directed his body away from the dangerous edge of the tiled shower opening, preventing a possibly serious injury. These instances of spontaneous out-of-body PK reflect the mind's psychic vigilance, and its remarkable capacity for immediate, powerful intervention when needed.

OBEs are often valued as a source of personal pleasure, as illustrated by a writer and her husband whose careers required frequent travel and lengthy separations. Both were skilled at out-of-body travel, so they decided to use OBEs as a vehicle for intimacy. They designated certain times and places for their out-of-body rendezvous during periods of separation. They insisted that these out-of-body intimacies were highly gratifying, both emotionally and physically. For this application of OBEs, they noted that "my place or yours" could be anywhere in the universe, from the exotic Orient to the enchanted Caribbean, or even some distant planet among the stars.

Among other reported applications of the out-of-body experience is its usefulness as a search strategy for locating lost objects and missing persons. In one celebrated case, a psychic's out-of-body search accurately located a plane crash in a remote mountainous region. Similarly, a parcel of narcotics known to have been dropped somewhere on an island was located through a consulting psychic's out-of-body search. Even lost animals have been located through this search strategy. A physician whose cat had strayed reported a spontaneous out-of-body experience during sleep, in which she successfully located the lost animal. Scanning the neighborhood from above, she saw the cat sitting on the steps of a vacant building several blocks from her residence. She awakened in the night, drove to the abandoned building, and found the cat on the steps exactly as seen in her out-of-body search.

OBEs are often viewed as expressions of our spiritual side. Possibly one of the most profound implications of OBEs concerns survival of bodily death and the permanence of our conscious being. If personal identity remains intact in the state of temporary astral disengagement from the physical body, it could be argued that following bodily death and the resultant permanent disengagement from the physical body, nonbiological consciousness and identity would likewise survive. Supporting that argument are numerous accounts of near-death experiences (NDEs) during which meaningful out-of-body interactions with other dimensions occurred. Many of these accounts detail active participation in distant realities and significant interactions with others who had successfully completed the transition to the other side.

NDEs can be so profoundly meaningful that perceptions of life and death are permanently altered by the experience. That phenomenon was illustrated by a clinical psychologist who reported a near-death experience following a cardiac arrest, during which he was guided by an angelic presence to a place of indescribable beauty. He recalled entering a garden and recognizing his deceased mother waving happily to him from a distance. He was then gently guided back to his physical body. The experience was so intensely meaningful that the psychologist's beliefs about life and death were deeply affected.

OBEs, like other forms of psychic phenomena, are inherently empowering because they expand our capacities to experience realities beyond the scope of biological mechanisms alone. Some of these realities, like the superintelligent part of our being, are within ourselves, and some exist as distant physical environments. Others appear to exist as higher planes, or as dimensions quite unlike the familiar realities we have come to know through the channels of our physical senses.

Possibly our most valuable empowerment faculty is our capacity to transcend the physical world and experience realities of a higher spiritual plane. Many OBEs and more specifically NDEs clearly reflect that empowering, transcending part of our being. Subsequent to the near-death event, death is often seen not as an end of existence and awareness, but as a transition to a higher plane of enriched experience. For many who encounter near-death, life after death is clearly confirmed not as some meaningless state of nothingness, but as continued, conscious, purposeful, and exciting existence.

Basic to human nature is the need to experience meaning beyond that possible through sensory perception and biological experience. Philosophers and theologians address that human search for significance, but resolving the issues and discovering the meanings of life demand personal investment and self-involvement. Only when we are committed to probe the mysteries of our being can we know the deeper meanings of life and death, reality and experience, and finally, the full scope of existence itself. Because it disengages the biological body and frees consciousness to soar, the out-of-body state provides a valuable vehicle for exploring the unknown and discovering hidden realities. OBEs often reveal the missing conceptual link between ultimate concerns such as mortality and immortality, existence and nonexistence, being and nonbeing, and the physical and the spiritual. OBEs are often so penetrating that they give clear substance to our hopes for permanence and firm confidence in our spiritual destiny.

As noted previously, OBEs are different from other forms of psychic phenomena because they require a separation of two human systems: the biological and the extrabiological or astral. This concept, the "two-component disengagement principle," views the extrabiological as the embodiment of consciousness with the capacities to think, perceive, learn, feel, and grow. As the vehicle for an indestructible entity, the extrabiological becomes our energizing life force, the essential element and core of existence itself. It is not surprising that OBEs are often more meaningful than experience that is limited to sensory stimulation and perception. The out-of-body state effectively subdues the biological inhibitors of experience and sheds biological baggage to allow conscious awareness to flow freely.

The two-component disengagement principle holds that the physical body is the instrument of the psychic mind. As such, our physical system is endowed with certain empowering capacities—sensory, autonomic, defensive, and regulatory systems—that facilitate our functioning in the physical world. However, the seat of our human powers, both physical and mental, is not the physical body, but the mind. Our limited physical capacities are transcended by the unlimited powers of our inner being. The two-component disengagement view explains why human experience continues in uninhibited and even enriched form in the out-of-body state.

Transcendant experiences during OBEs often do not translate well to our familiar consciousness, since neither our biological systems nor our language reference is sufficiently equipped to permit such a translation. However, with continued experience, we become more adept in such translations—often in the poetic and symbolic form of mystical literature. Reading such writings from this higher perspective allows a deeper and greater understanding and appreciation.

Exceedingly complex mental processes and a wide range of rich emotions characterize many OBEs. Furthermore, sensory-like functions such as sight, hearing, taste, and smell continue in the out-of-body state. A host of pleasurable emotions including joy, contentment, peace, and serenity typically occur, while experiences of sadness, fear, anxiety, and distress are absent. Individuals who are inexperienced in out-of-body travel will occasionally report some apprehension upon first entering the induced out-of-body state; but with even limited practice, almost all subjects describe the experience as enlightening, liberating, and personally rewarding.

INDUCING THE OUT-OF-BODY EXPERIENCE

Several strategies have been developed to induce the out-of-body state and to facilitate out-of-body travel. We will start, however, with an exercise preliminary to actual out-of-body work. This is called "The Copper Penny," and is adapted from Donald Tyson's *The Magician's Workbook*. This same practice is useful in developing your clairvoyant sight by stimulating your brow chakra while involving the mechanisms of physical sight. It trains your psychic sight.

THE COPPER PENNY

Step 1. Secure a copper penny and clean it thoroughly.

Step 2. Lie on your back with your head slightly elevated, arms at your sides and your feet about six inches apart.

Step 3. Using your right hand, press the penny on your forehead between your eyes and slightly above. (Actually, for your amusement, you will find that the penny will adhere to this spot until you remove it, even if you walk around.)

Step 4. Tense and relax your body parts, starting with your left leg, then your right leg, left arm, right arm, working your way up the body to your eyes and forehead.

Step 5. Be aware of your consciousness separate from your body, and then imagine yourself floating gently in a boat on a slowly moving river.

Step 6. Focus your attention upon an imagined red spot *inside* your forehead beneath the penny. Concentrate on the red dot, seeing it floating in space against a dark background like the great disk of a setting sun. Imagine it becoming larger and larger, filling all your field of vision.

Step 7. Feel yourself as a point of consciousness in the void, without a body. Feel yourself rising up and floating toward the great red dot and then gently pass through its center as through an open doorway. You are surrounded by warm, glowing redness.

Step 8. Float within this nurturing redness. Enjoy the sensation of drifting weightlessness. Hold the awareness of yourself as a separate consciousness, free of the physical body.

Step 9. Become aware that you now are in your astral body with the red glow shining through your closed astral eyes.

Step 10. Open your astral eyes without opening your physical eyes and contemplate a clear blue sky surrounding you on all sides. You may or may not see things, but if you do merely note the details without reaction.

Step 11. Close your astral eyes and again perceive the cheerful red glow all around you. Feel your point of consciousness sink gently backwards until the red light around you again becomes a large red disk in front of your mental sight. Watch the red disk shrink to a red dot on a dark background.

Step 12. Feel the weight of the penny on your forehead, and remove it with your left hand and set it on the floor beside you.

Step 13. Gently press your palms against your face so that you feel the heels of your palms in the hollows of your closed physical eyes. Slide your hands downward, open your eyes, stretch, and get up.

This exercise can be used to initiate astral visions and astral journeys. The contact of the penny actually stimulates the brow chakra, while the red dot acts as a doorway through the brow chakra, the psychic center that controls astral sight.

Because sleep appears particularly conducive to out-of-body travel, a procedure called "Destination Control" was devised to promote OBEs during the sleep state.

DESTINATION CONTROL

Step 1. *Mental Intent.* The objective for out-of-body travel is determined, and the intent to travel out-of-body is clearly formulated. The destination can be either specified or left indefinite, depending on your goals.

Step 2. *Pre sleep Affirmation.* This step is designed to pave the way for out-of-body travel through affirmations presented to the inner self just prior to falling asleep. To delay sleep while affirmations are presented, the Finger-Spread Technique is recommended. The technique requires simply spreading the fingers of either hand, and then holding the tense-spread position. Suggested affirmations to induce OBEs are:

> *As I sleep, I can leave my body at will to travel wherever I wish.*
> *I will remain in control, and I will be protected as I travel.*
> *My out-of-body experiences will enrich and empower my life.*
> *I will return to my body at any moment I decide to do so.*
> *I am now ready to travel out of my body.*

For unspecified destinations, the Destination Control procedure is ended here by slowly relaxing the hand and allowing sleep to ensue. For specific destinations, however, the finger-spread position is maintained during the two remaining steps.

Step 3. *Destination Control Imagery.* This step guides the out-of-body experience to a specified destination by allowing a clear mental image of that destination to emerge and become absorbed as fully as possible. If the destination is unfamiliar, imagery of its location on a globe or map is effective in promoting travel.

Step 4. *Imagery/OBE Fusion.* This final step actually initiates the out-of-body travel experience. As the finger spread is ended by slowly relaxing the fingers, images of the physical body at rest are fused with awareness of floating away from the body and being guided to the desired destination.

OBEs during sleep have reportedly engaged interactions with discarnate dimensions, including visits with historical figures or famous personalities who had made the transition. A student reportedly experienced an out-of-body visit with Albert Einstein, who presented an array of complicated formulas and calculations to him. Upon awakening, the student immediately recorded Einstein's lecture conclusions in his dream journal as follows: "As you can readily see from our calculations, the form of time as we know it in this place is symptomatically caused by the dominant energy of this plane known as light and can be nonexistent or different on other planes determined by the dominant and subdominant energy forms."

Another student, enrolled in an OBE seminar, reported traveling out-of-body during sleep to a distant Alabama coastal city, and visiting a friend whom she had not seen in several years. During the visit she noted yellow appliances, white tie-back curtains, and a fresh arrangement of red tulips on the counter in her friend's newly decorated kitchen. A phone call the following morning verified the details of the out-of-body visit. Perhaps with more study and refinement of strategies that evoke OBEs during sleep, the empowerment potential of this phenomenon for increasing awareness will become recognized more fully.

Another simple practice involving the sleep technique can be given the name of "Home Territory."

HOME TERRITORY

This will be conducted before sleep, but otherwise will loosely follow the steps outlined previously.

The intention here is to project into the familiar surroundings of home and neighborhood, and to limit the projections to these familiar places as you familiarize yourself with the nature of the astral world. An important part of this technique is to learn to observe without adding subjective feelings to the experience.

Step 1. Before sleep, pick an object in a room other than your sleeping area. Pick up the object and study it from all angles. Practice visualizing the object in great detail.

Step 2. Then go to sleep continuing that visualization, and you should project to the object and in your astral body repeat the process of studying the astral counterpart of the physical object.

As an extension of this experience, learn to project to a known person (not a child) and observe the person in his or her environment. This will allow you to subsequently verify your observation and refine your ability to remain objective.

Another variation of "Home Territory" was recommended by Ophiel, an early writer in this field, in his classic *The Art & Practice of Astral Projection.* Here the idea is to pick an area in the home that you can study in detail in order to visualize it likewise in complete detail. An ideal situation would involve a hallway from your bedroom or practice area that leads to another room. Once you have mastered the detail and can duplicate it in your visualization, make it your intention to do so in your astral body. Whether with the physical body asleep or totally relaxed in a semi-trance, feel yourself in your astral body moving along the hallway and into the target room, all the while noting each of the details you previously studied.

A highly effective technique, previously described in *Beyond Reincarnation* by Joe H. Slate, Ph.D., is the *astral projection* strategy called Eye Blink Procedure, which utilizes eye blinks and innovative orientation techniques designed to induce the out-of-body state and facilitate travel to either physical or nonphysical destinations. The procedure, which is based on the research of Gene Chamberlain of the Parapsychology Research Institute and Foundation (PRIF) and tested in their labs, incorporates remote viewing as a practice exercise into a procedure designed to induce astral projection. Astral projection and remote viewing are similar in that they both provide information concerning spatially distant realities. They are different, however, in that astral projection, unlike remote viewing, incorporates disengagement of the astral body from the physical and usually includes a much wider range of experiences. Once you have developed your remote viewing abilities, astral projection is much easier to master.

It is important to read the entire procedure before starting. The steps are well defined and easy to follow. Here's the procedure.

EYE BLINK PROCEDURE

Step 1. *The Setting*. Select a safe, quiet area that facilitates walking among a variety of items, such as tables, chairs, sofas, appliances, and plants. The typical home setting with living room, dining room, family room, and kitchen connected provides an excellent situation. If a large area is unavailable, a single room or office with space for walking around furnishings is sufficient. The setting should include a comfortable recliner or couch for use during astral projection. Select the specific path you will follow while walking, preferably a circular route that includes a variety of things to view.

Step 2. *Physically Walking*. Walk slowly through the path you selected, paying special attention to what you see on either side.

Step 3. *Viewing and Eye Blink*. After walking through your selected area several times, stop and pick a well-defined object, such as a lamp or vase. Gaze at the object for a few seconds and then snap your eyes shut. Rather than closing them slowly, snap them as you would if blinking. Think of taking a snapshot of the item with your eyes. With your eyes closed, you will note that the afterimage of the object will remain briefly. When the image disappears, open your eyes and repeat the exercise. You will note that when you first start this process, the image may turn negative. This will change with practice.

Step 4. *Forming Mental Impressions*. As you continue to practice Step 3, you will notice that the afterimage of the selected object stays with you longer. As the duration of the image increases, you will note that a mental impression of the image remains for a few moments even after the image itself fades. Developing this awareness requires practice, possibly for several minutes. Test your effectiveness by turning your head to see if the mental impression remains. When the impression of the image remains, you are ready to go on to the next step.

Step 5. *Walking and Eye Blink.* Resume walking around the area you selected as your chosen path. As you continue to walk, repetitively snap your eyes shut for about a second and then open them for about a second while always facing forward. Carefully adjust your eye-blink rate and step so as not to stumble or collide with anything. Upon beginning this routine you will probably see the images in your mind's eye as stationary. After several times around and possibly more than one session, you will notice that when your eyes are shut, the items continue to move so that your eyes can be closed longer before the movement stops. You will know you have this mastered when the objects you envisioned are adjacent to you when you open your eyes.

Step 6. *Mental Walking.* Having mastered Step 5, find a comfortable place to recline or lie down with your legs uncrossed and your hands resting at your sides. As you relax, make the entire trip mentally with your eyes closed. While mentally walking through your selected space, pay special attention to the familiar details along your pathway. Observe them from different viewpoints as you sense yourself walking among them.

Step 7. *Remote Viewing.* As you remain relaxed with your eyes closed, select a familiar distant place and view it remotely. Pay particular attention to the specific details of the distant setting you are viewing. Take plenty of time for the setting to emerge in full detail.

Step 8. *Astral Projection.* Having remotely viewed a distant setting, you are now ready to travel out of body. With your eyes remaining closed, mentally walk around your selected path once more. View in detail the setting as you move among its furnishings. As you continue this mental exercise, you will begin to sense yourself literally walking out-of-body through the room, maneuvering among pieces of furniture and noticing objects in even greater detail. You will then sense that you can travel out-of-body beyond the room to experience first-hand other surroundings, including the place you remotely viewed in Step 7. You are now ready to walk out the door and travel to that place. Take plenty of time to travel to that place, and once there, add to your awareness such sensations as hearing and touch. Remain in that place long enough to get a full sense of your presence there.

Step 9. *Distant Travel.* You can now travel to places you have not physically been before. Note your sense of freedom and control. By intent alone, you can travel in any direction to any location you choose. Your destination can include both physical and spiritual realities. You can travel to familiar distant settings or to places totally unknown to you. You can observe others, including other astral travelers, and possibly interact with them. You can engage the spirit realm, again by intent alone. You can interact with your spirit guides and other entities in the spirit realm. You can experience the magnificent beauty of that dimension and the empowerment resources it offers.

Step 10. *The Return*. To return to your physical body and reengage it, give yourself permission to first return to the familiar setting you visited earlier, and from there to your physical body at rest. Allow plenty of time for yourself to slip into your body, fully re-engaging it. When you notice such sensations as breathing, heart rate, and weight, you will know you are back in your body.

Step 11. *Resolution and Verification*. Take a few moments to reflect on your out-of-body experiences. Explore the relevance of the experiences, particularly your visitations to the spirit realm. Verify as far as possible that what you experienced during astral travel was accurate.

Other strategies have been designed to facilitate the out-of-body experience during the normal waking state. "Astral Flight" is an OBE-induction procedure that uses physical relaxation along with astral imagery.

ASTRAL FLIGHT

Step 1. *Preliminary Considerations*. A relaxed, semi-prone, or reclining position is recommended for a period of approximately thirty minutes, during which there must be absolutely no distractions.

Step 2. *Physical Relaxation*. Induce deep physical relaxation by mentally scanning the body, identifying areas of tension, and progressively relaxing specific muscle groups. The procedure is facilitated by slowed breathing and peaceful imagery, along with empowering affirmations such as:

> *I am tranquil and serene; I am secure and in control;*
> *I am now fully empowered to travel out-of-body.*

Step 3. *Astral Imagery*. A progression of images engages the out-of-body state and directs the travel experience. First, images of the body at rest are formed, with particular attention focused on specific regions of the body, the position of the body, and the physical setting. Next, mental images of consciousness are generated as a radiant light form separating from the body and drifting upward. Finally, conscious awareness is centered in the rising light form, which is then mentally enveloped in a transparent sphere and directed to float outward to probe distant realities, as the biological body remains at rest. A silver cord is envisioned connecting the enveloped light form of consciousness to the physical body.

Step 4. *The Return*. The out-of-body experience ends with the simple intent to return to the physical body, and imagery of the enveloping sphere dissolving as the light form of consciousness reenters the body. The procedure is concluded by a brief period of peaceful reflection and introspection.

Education, forensics, espionage, and psychotherapy are among the emerging frontiers of contemporary interest in OBEs. In the educational setting, the out-of-body technique has been experimentally applied as a motivational and skills-development strategy. An interesting example of that application was a college art class that used out-of-body travel to gather artistic ideas. Similarly, a college drama group used the technique as a strategy for improving acting skills. The out-of-body experience in these academic situations tended to release the flow of creative energy and improve the quality of creative expression.

The application of OBEs in forensics has centered primarily on the investigative effort. The technique has been particularly useful as a strategy for locating missing persons and gathering criminal evidence. Although this application remains speculative and experimental, the cumulative instances of success suggest many possibilities for this technique as a valuable investigative tool.

A potentially darker side of OBEs is their intelligence gathering and espionage applications. The out-of-body technique has intriguing potential for acquiring classified data and monitoring secret military and research activities. Out-of-body experts reportedly have been used routinely by some governments for scientific research and intelligence purposes. Through her out-of-body experiences, a physicist with extraordinary psychic skills reportedly assembled a wealth of important scientific data depicting highly advanced technology. Notwithstanding many troublesome ethical issues, governments of the future will, in all probability, continue to explore out-of-body strategies for espionage and research purposes.

Only recently have we begun serious consideration of the therapeutic applications of the out-of-body experience. In instances of severe mental distress, therapeutically managed OBEs can facilitate a more rapid recovery, particularly from disorders such as clinical depression and debilitating stress. A patient undergoing treatment for depression reported that, in the out-of-body state, "I was my old self again." The experience gave him the essential therapeutic support he needed to affirm his potential for complete recovery. Along a similar line, OBEs are sometimes instrumental in promoting recovery from grief. A businessman reported an unusual out-of-body experience in which he visited his recently deceased father in a dimension he described as "filled with light." He embraced his father and at that moment recalled, "I felt complete peace."

SUMMARY

A better understanding of the out-of-body state, its purposes, and its experiences is important because the phenomenon not only offers new explanations of behavior, it also suggests new frontiers of experience and self-empowerment possibilities. In transcending biological limitations, OBEs can effectively engage a liberated state of freedom from biological baggage, thus suggesting unlimited expression of nonbiological being. With the physical barriers removed and our mental faculties permitted unrestricted expression, it is not surprising that heightened psychic functions often characterize the out-of-body state.

The new insight and expanded awareness resulting from OBEs can increase our knowledge base, while at the same time inspiring and motivating us to overcome growth barriers and achieve new levels of self-fulfillment. The out-of-body experience can suggest solutions to personal problems and provide strategic withdrawal from painful realities, during which we can muster our empowering resources. Perhaps most importantly, OBEs can increase our understanding of our selves and the nature of our existence in the universe.

OBEs are reflections of our claim to permanence in the universe as a conscious entity, and the absolute survival of our personal identity beyond mere biological existence. To experience the out-of-body state is to experience, although in limited and emblematic form, the transition to a liberated and empowered state of discarnate enrichment. The underlying message of the out-of-body state is the conclusion: *I am immortal.*

SOURCES AND RECOMMENDED READING

Melita Denning and Osborne Philips, *The Sword & the Serpent* (Llewellyn, 2005).

Raven Grimassi, *Encyclopedia of Wicca & Witchcraft* (Llewellyn, 2000).

John A. Keel, *The Eighth Tower* (Dutton, 1975).

Ophiel, *The Art & Practice of Astral Projection* (Weiser, 1974).

Joe H. Slate, *Astral Projection and Psychic Empowerment* (Llewellyn, 1998).

Donald Tyson, *The Magician's Workbook* (Llewellyn, 2001).

3

AURAS: SEEING & READING WHAT CAN'T BE HIDDEN

The human aura is a developmental, life-sustaining energy force that characterizes every human being. Without it, we could not exist.

—JOE H. SLATE, *AURA ENERGY FOR HEALTH, HEALING & BALANCE*

Before we discuss what an aura actually is, we should really consider as fact that you have your own aura and so do all humans, all living creatures (animal, fish, vegetable, insect, cell, amoebae), and even inanimate objects (rocks, computers, automobiles, your home). Some aura visionaries say that they see auras around angels, archangels, elementals, and other astral and spiritual entities.

The point is that everything in our universe has an aura—including planets and their satellites, stars and their solar systems, galaxies, and, for all we know, the universe itself. It is also true that *belief* is the major stepping stone toward *becoming more than you are* and thus to become psychically empowered as your innate psychic powers become awakened and trained psychic skills.

Auras originate from the energy that is within everything, whether animate, inanimate, or spiritual. The complexity of an aura is not limited to its energy source but is an embodiment of that basic energy of the singular unit plus the energies of its composition (organs, cells, blood, and the chakra system found in higher level beings) and the active consciousness of the unit.

Everything has some level of awareness as a function of that consciousness, even if it is incapable of expressing it in any recognizable way. However, the aura will reflect its interaction with other entities—retreating from or reaching out toward an approaching human or animal.

WHAT IS AN AURA?

We can now attempt to define what an aura really is. A traditional definition taken from *The Watkins Dictionary of Magic* by Nevill Drury says it is:

> ... *the psychic-energy field that surrounds both animate and inanimate bodies. The aura can be dull or brightly coloured, and psychics ... interpret the condition or state of the person or object according to the energy vibrations. Bright red, for example, indicates anger; yellow, strong intellectual powers; and purple, spirituality ... Theosophists distinguish five auras: the health aura, the vital aura, the karmic aura, the character aura, and the aura of spiritual nature.*

Dr. Shafica Karadulla described three types of force field clairvoyantly observed about the human body: 1) a *vital field* reflecting the physical body's health; 2) an *emotional field* reflecting the individual's feelings; and 3) a *mental field* reflecting mental activity.

In early Christian literature, the term *aureole* was used for the whole-body aura, and *nimbus* or *halo* for the aura around the head, or crown chakra. In the more modern magical tradition, the Hermetic Order of the Golden Dawn refers to the aura as the *Sphere of Sensation* and describes it as "an etheric structure filled with astral energies and serving as the 'magical mirror of the universe,' in which all objects of perception and all inner activities of thought and feeling are reflected."

Because an aura is not normally seen, unaided, by physical sight, we need to also establish what it is not.

It is not a mere reflection, or *bounce-off*, of bright light off an object. This can often be seen as a kind of glow around people and objects under bright sunlight, and is sometimes misunderstood as the aura. However, this glow can be helpful in learning to see that aura because your awareness of it helps stimulate *Ajna*—the "brow chakra—which Robert Bruce (1990), believes to be the actual psychic organ for seeing the aura. We'll discuss this more later.

Neither is the aura the electromagnetic *biofield* of the living body. Again, however, by extending your awareness through *feeling* this biofield, you are initiating the process that can help activate true auric perception. We often feel this living energy when close to a person with whom we have empathy, and we likewise feel it around animals, plants, and trees. Cultivating your sensitivity to these radiant energy fields will extend your capacity for other levels of perception. Especially when walking in a natural wooded area or a garden rich in flora, you can accept the opportunity to open your senses, not merely with the familiar sights and sounds, but to the smells and the invisible energies of the vegetation and perhaps even to the nonphysical presences of elemental nature spirits, devas, and other consciousnesses that are part of the great planetary being we lightly refer to as "Mother Nature."

In summary, the aura is a manifestation of a person's (or other unit's) energy *and consciousness* that can be seen by developing the psychic sensitivity of the brow chakra working in conjunction with the normal physical sight's visual apparatus extended in *peripheral* vision. We will get further into that process later.

It is also important to refer back to Nevill Drury's mention of the five auras described by Theosophists: health, vital, karmic, character, and spiritual. Other people give them different names, but when you become adept at seeing the human aura, you will become aware of these divisions, and perhaps others. You will also note variations between people as to how far the auric field extends beyond the body—from a fraction of an inch for the close-in, vital or etheric aura to many feet for a more energetic and developed human. Some have claimed that the spiritual aura of the Buddha extended hundreds of feet.

Size also varies under various conditions—from repose to extreme activity, and also enlarges in sunlight. Public speakers, who often absorb energy from audiences or congregation—have auras that sometimes reach out to encompass the whole group. During sexual orgasm the aura expands. Feelings of love toward another person will extend to enfold that person. And couples often show a blended aura.

OF WHAT VALUE IS THE AURA?

The aura is a reflection of your energies, together and at different levels. Thus, perceiving the health aura provides the perceiver with the means to determine the health status and even—for an experienced reader with medical training—a means for diagnosis and perception of progress or lack of progress in treatment of diseases.

For any medical practitioner, the ability to see *inside* the health factors revealed by the aura should be of immense value. This would be especially relevant in the case of energy work such as acupuncture, Reiki, chakra balancing, Rolfing, massage, etc., where seeing the immediate effect of the therapy could be extremely helpful.

Damage to muscles is shown as holes in the etheric aura which disappear as healing takes place.

Mark Smith, in *Auras: See Them in Only 60 Seconds!*, writes that people practicing various professions have distinctive auras, and young people with similar auras can be guided in their career choices to making wise educational decisions.

Many aura visionaries also claim the ability to tell if a person is lying. If the aura is constantly shifting in reflection of one's energies, then it is equally true that the aura would reflect emotions and emotional stress, just as a lie detector machine does. But, by seeing color changes and fluctuations in the different auric fields, the aura visionary would perceive subtleties beyond the capacity of a lie detecting machine, and with experience would gain advanced skills allowing a far greater understanding of what may be behind those fluctuations and subtle changes in color.

There have been examples where the stress shown by the lie detector involved misunderstanding of the question being asked—whether because of the educational level of the subject (the person who is being read) or language problems or fear of retribution or still other factors that could be of considerable pertinence.

MAN VS. MACHINE

Just as there are lie detector machines and other mechanical and electrical *tools* for measuring stress or the various electrical functioning in the physical body (muscles and nerves), so there have been inventions of aura goggles, aura cameras, the special uses of dowsing rods and the pendulum, and other aids to see or measure the human aura.

In 1908, Dr. Walter Kilner invented an aura goggle involving a screen of dicyanin, by which he could perceive the ultraviolet part of the field around the body that he termed "The Human Atmosphere" in a book of that title he published in 1911. A revised edition titled *The Human Aura* was published in 1920 and is still available.

In 1939, Semyon Kirlian, a Russian scientist, developed Kirlian photography, which reveals an energy discharge around fingers, plant leaves, or other living forms. Rather than photographing the actual aura, the Kirlian photograph shows a corona discharge occurring when the subject is placed on a film upon a metal plate charged with high-voltage electricity. Dr. Thelma Moss, Dr. Joe H. Slate and his students and researchers at Athens (Alabama) State University, and others have done valuable research showing specific variations of the high radiation corona discharge under varying conditions including the Kirlian photograph as an alternative to the lie detector.

Another Russian scientist, Dr. Konstantin Korotkov, developed a variation of the Kirlian photograph using glass electrodes creating a pulsed electrical field to detect stress levels in preventive medicine. This technology led to the creation of the Gas Discharge Visualization (GDV) camera to photograph energy fields at the quantum level, enabling the user to observe the real-time effectiveness of medical treatments. The GDV camera is now certified as a medical instrument and is used in Russian hospitals and among medical professionals. One of the particular uses has been to identify plants and flowers useful in treating human health needs.

As a result of GDV technology, there is a new perception of the body as a web of energies that also extend beyond its borders to intercommunicate with its environment, including other humans, plants, animals, and the energy fields of the planet. In addition, Dr. Korotkov and his associates experimentally confirmed the esoteric concept that there is a kind of collective intelligence or spirit relating to a garden of vegetation, a forest grove or garden, and even of humanity as a whole and of the Earth Being. (Peterson, n.d.)

Other variations of the aura camera as a biofeedback device can be found online.

The machine as a diagnostic device and even machines for the treatment of various conditions are a sign of the modern age, and many do have genuine uses. But, there probably never will be a real substitute for the trained and experienced practitioner or aura visionary. The human mind, and all its powers drawn from the innate psychic powers of the subconscious mind, is infinite in its capacities.

In learning to see and read (interpret) the human aura, you not only gain a valuable skill for aura analysis and health diagnosis *but you extend your own aura in your own psychic development as you broadly expand your awareness into more dimensions.*

SEEING THE AURA

Mark Smith says that anyone can learn to see auras in only sixty seconds. And it is in this initial seeing that you will build confidence and accumulate experience, gradually extending what you see from the simple to the more complex. In his book, *Auras: See Them in Only 60 Seconds!,* he breaks this instruction down into a few easy steps:

AURA SEEING INSTRUCTIONS

Step 1. Stand the subject eighteen inches to two feet in front of a bare white wall. Avoid walls with colors or patterns. Joe Slate in his *Aura Energy for Health, Healing & Balance* suggests that you place a small shiny object such as a thumbtack or adhesive dot on the wall a few inches to the upper left or right of the subject.

Step 2. Use indirect lighting—natural ambient daylight, if possible. Avoid fluorescent light or direct sunlight.

Step 3. View the subject from at least ten feet away.

Step 4. Ask the subject to relax, breathe deeply, and rock gently from side to side with hands unclasped at his or her side.

Step 5. Look past the subject's head and shoulders, and focus on the wall behind.

Step 6. Avoid looking at the subject, concentrating instead on the texture of the wall or the shiny object behind him or her, *using your peripheral rather than direct vision.*

Step 7. As you look past the outline of the body, you will see a band of fuzzy light around the subject, about one-quarter inch to one-half inch in depth. This is the *etheric* aura.

Step 8. Continue to look past the outline of the body, and you should see the subject as if he or she is illuminated from behind, sometimes with a bright yellow or silver color. One side might glow more strongly or slowly pulsate. Auras rarely are uniform.

Step 9. As you progress you will soon see a second, larger band of light three inches to two feet around the body. This is the *astral* aura. It is usually darker and more diffuse than the etheric.

Step 10. Joe Slate says that once you see the aura, you should shift your attention from the shiny object to the aura and observe its various characteristics. Should the aura begin to fade away, shift your focus back to the shiny object, and repeat the procedure.

An additional helpful technique in using your eyes' peripheral vision is to also *feel* that you are seeing with your brow chakra. Just feel a sensation between your eyes and slightly above. Likewise, it is sometimes helpful to center your attention (not focus) on the brow of the subject while still gazing past the subject. Dr. Jonn Mumford recommends that you press a shiny copper penny over the brow chakra—it will normally adhere to the skin—as a way to increase your psychic sensitivity.

Another technique used to stimulate the brow chakra and your psychic perception is to use the Yogic practice of *tratak,* essentially staring at a particular object until the eyes water, and then closing the eyes to see an afterimage, or looking at a white surface for the afterimage. More effective yet is to perform tratak on small pieces of colored paper in the primary colors and then seeing the complementary color in the afterimage. Even better is to use *Tattwa Cards,* which are composites of two complementary colors into a single image of the Tattwas that represents the primary elemental forces operating throughout the universe. These practices directly stimulate the brow chakra and train your ability to visualize and imagine an image in specific detail. Such visualization is also used in the technique of "astral doorways" that we will discuss later in relation to the tarot cards.

TO SEE YOUR OWN AURA

1. Stand in front of a mirror at least eighteen inches away, farther if possible.
2. Place yourself with a white or neutral color surface visible in the mirror behind you.
3. Relax, breathe deeply, and sway gently from side to side.
4. Focus on the texture of the surface on the wall behind you. Again, a shiny object such as a thumbtack placed strategically on the wall can facilitate the process.
5. As you stare past the outline of your head and shoulders, you will see the envelope of light around your body move with you as you rock gently.
6. Remember to breathe normally.
7. Lighting should be subdued, neither too bright nor too dark.

8. Color of clothing is unimportant, although Robert Bruce says the colors have their own aura and can skew the observation. Nudity, or neutral colors, will avoid such distortion when viewing the aura about the body.

As mentioned previously, there are health opportunities in daily viewing of your own aura. Try to do it on a regular basis, perhaps even as you are getting ready for the day or preparing for bed in the evening.

Some people experience more difficulties than others in seeing the aura, particularly their own. Sometimes it is helpful to close your eyes and visualize an aura about your head and shoulders, or of the body as a whole if viewing in a full-length mirror, and then attempt to hold that visual image when you open your eyes.

Visualization is a powerful stimulus to the psychic faculty.

Going back to the principle of "Belief" in achieving psychic empowerment, we can say that we are learning to perceive through extended awareness, going beyond the limits of the physical senses. Yet, it is also pertinent to accept the concept that our psychic senses do often utilize the same mechanisms as those involved with seeing, hearing, smelling, tasting, and feeling.

Belief based only on past experience or narrow education can be very limiting as can be demonstrated in the story of the Spanish Conquistadors landing on the shores of Patagonia near the southern end of South America. The story says that the natives saw the Spaniards suddenly appear in their rowboats approaching them, but they could not see the Spanish galleons anchored out at sea *because they had no experience of such large sailing ships.* Only, with great effort, with squinted eyes, did the tribal shaman finally see those very large ships. And once he could see, then slowly others could see them as well.

It is by moving beyond limited beliefs that we open the doors of perception to greater realities just beyond self-imposed horizons and barriers that previously prevent us from growing in wholeness, that otherwise prevent us from *becoming more than we are!*

MORE THAN ONE AURA

As quoted earlier in Nevill Drury's definition of the aura, Theosophists and others describe five auras—*the health aura, the vital aura, the karmic aura, the character aura, and the aura of spiritual nature.*

All of these have been given various alternative names by different authorities, and all of these are part of the total aura that you can sense more or less as layers of the aura. Yet, they are different and they are manifestations of different aspects of our total selves. For the main part, these different auras are functions of what we also refer to as the *subtle bodies:* Etheric, Astral, Lower Mental, Higher Mental, and Spiritual.

We divided the Mental into Lower and Higher, and in truth that division can be applied to the others, with the exception of the Etheric Body (or more properly, the "Etheric Double"), which can be said to be the "higher" aspect of the physical body. The Etheric Double is commonly referred to as the *Energy Body,* and that's one reason for its closeness to the physical—radiating only a quarter to a full inch from the surface of the physical body—and for its particular characteristic of looking like *needles,* or "energy lines," seen by the experienced aura visionary.

It is the energy or health aspect of the etheric double that is of such considerable importance in diagnosis and continued observation, whether by a health professional working with clients or your own observation aided by a mirror. It can also be observed without aid by looking at your hands, but the larger view of head and shoulders or of the full body is obviously more revealing.

Primarily it is the energetic appearance that is of importance. The shape of the energy lines—straight and strong, or bent and weak—and the distance that the aura radiates outward from the physical body are indicative of physical vitality. Obviously, with increased experience and analysis your expertise will improve, and new aspects of what this aura means will become part of your understanding.

The next band out beyond the etheric/health aura is a manifestation of the astral body, and it is that which provides most of the colors that are perceived. While there is reference to this as the "vital" body, that is only a part of its expression, and really could be defined as part of the *lower* astral. Examined together with the health aura, this vital aura reveals still more of the broader complex that we now often refer to as Mind/Body.

To better understand this, and the aura as a whole, really means a broader study of the astral body, beyond the present purpose of this book, which is to introduce you to the aura's role among the techniques of psychic empowerment.

The astral body is also the emotional body, but even more, it and the astral *plane* are a *transition zone* for energies and thoughts on their way toward physical manifestation. When the clairvoyant speaks of "shadows of things to come," he or she is seeing forthcoming events "casting their shadows before them" (from Plutark's *Lives*). Everything moves through the astral before it becomes physically manifest. It is this that forms the basis for clairvoyance, premonitions, and precognition. And it is this that allows us the opportunity not only to see the probable future, *but to alter it!* It's like seeing a log rushing down a fast-moving river, and being able to divert it into a pool of still water.

The mental body and the mental aura is still another layer, or possibly two layers—although none of these "layers" are sharply defined, but simply blend into each other as the total aura.

A greater division of the visible aura relates to the location of the chakras, but more simply to positions above the head, around the head, around the throat, heart, solar plexus, genitals, and base of the spine. And some aura visionaries can make distinctions in the aura as the feet meet the earth and unite with the energies and aura of the earth itself.

And, finally, there is the spiritual aura and the spirit body, which is more of potential interest than of practical concern.

COLORS IN THE AURA

Colors have meaning. They are vibrations in the visible spectrum. And their locations are in direct relation to the major chakras while their vibrancy, shades, and extent is in relation to the activity of the particular chakra. The following table shows the approximate location on the physical body, the generally accepted name from the Hindu system, the primary color of the chakra, the corresponding planetary energy, and the corresponding Sephirah (sphere) on the Kabbalistic Tree of Life. For the five lower chakras, we also give the associated Tattwa and primary Element. These are of interest mainly for your deeper study and practical exercises involving meditation and visualization.

CHAKRA NAMES, COLORS, ASSOCIATED PLANETS, AND TATTWAS

Crown: Sahasrara, color violet, associated planet (none), Sephirah Kether.

Brow: Ajna, color indigo, associated planet moon, Sephiroth Chokmah and Binah.

Throat: Vishuddha, color blue, associated planet Mercury, Sephirah Daath, associated Tattwa *Akasha,* symbol of the element of Spirit.

Heart: Anahata, color green, associated planet Sun or Venus, Sephirah Tiphareth, associated Tattwa *Vayu,* symbol of the element of Air.

Solar plexus: or "Navel Chakra," located below the navel, *Manipura,* color yellow, associated planet Mars, Sephirah (none suggested), associated Tattwa *Tejas,* symbol of the element of Fire.

Genital area: or "Sacral Chakra," *Svadhisthana,* color orange, associated planet Jupiter or moon, Sephirah Yesod, associated Tattwa *Apas,* symbol of the element of Water.

Base of spine: or "Root Chakra," *Muladhara,* color red, associated planet Saturn, Sephirah Malkuth, associated Tattwa *Prithivi,* symbol of the element of Earth.

AURA: INTERPRETATION OF COLORS,
THEIR INTENSITY, AND THEIR LOCATION

Blue: Throat Chakra—Religious (but not limited by doctrine). Light blue is associated with balance, tranquility, self-insight, flexibility, optimism, and empathy for others. Deep blue is associated with mental alertness, sharpwittedness, and emotional control. Dullness of blue anywhere in the aura is associated with negative stress, pessimism, despondency, and insecurity (feeling blue), whereas dark, dingy blue may indicate suicidal tendencies.

Brown: Strong interests in the earth and natural resources, along with personality traits of practicality, stability, and independence. Brown is also characteristic of such professionals as geologists, ecologists, archaeologists, and landscape and construction workers. Brown in the aura is commonly indicative of outdoor interests such as hiking, skiing, mountain climbing, and hunting, as well as physical fitness.

Gold: Advanced spirituality. People with gold in the aura are charismatic and able to handle large-scale projects, but they usually attain their successes later in life.

Gray: Usually a transient color that can foreshadow illness, adversity, and even death. Small areas of gray can signify health problems in relation to their location.

Green: Heart Chakra—Love, affinity with Nature, often a natural healer. Bright green signifies healing energy, self-actualization, and raised consciousness, particularly concerning global conditions. Bright green is typical for health care professionals and environmentalists. The auras of psychic healers are usually iridescent, a feature not often found in the auras of other health care professionals. Dull green is associated with envy (green with envy), inner conflict, personal unfulfillment, and resistance to change. A very dull green with shades of gray is often a precursor of serious adversity, personal catastrophe, or physical illness. Associated with healing energy.

Indigo: Brow Chakra—Intuition, nurturing. See also purple, as indigo and purple are sometimes difficult to distinguish from one another. Associated with spiritual awareness.

Orange: Genital or Sacral Chakra—Social extroverts who typically pursue careers requiring considerable social interaction, such as politics and sales. They are independent, competitive, and possess strong persuasive skills. Discoloration in the orange aura is associated with impatience, egotism, emotional instability, and a low tolerance for frustration. Associated with emotional energy.

Pink: The color of youth, longevity, rejuvenation, sensitivity, humanitarianism, ideal-ism, and talent. Typically, older people with an abundance of pink in their auras have achieved prominence in their careers through hard work, have moderate political views, and are interested in the arts and such matters as historical preser-vation. Associated with affection.

Purple: Associated with philosophy and abstract interests, purple is often predomi-nant in the auras of ministers, philosophers, and theoreticians. People with purple in their auras value intuitive knowledge, often possess superior verbal skills, and command respect from their peers. Wealth often comes easily to them and they settle into comfortable careers in which they can pursue personal interests.

Red: Base of Spine or Root Chakra—Vitality, sensuality, physical energy, impulsive behavior, strong emotion, outbursts of anger (seeing red), the need for excitement, adventure, and risktaking. While flashes of red in the aura (anger) are usually transient, more permanent strands of red woven into the aura may be indicative of violent and uncontrolled aggressive impulses. Areas of red are not uncommon among male college students active in contact sports and similarly in professional athletes in competitive sports. Red can also relate to leadership, responsibility, drive, and charisma. Associated with sexual energy.

Silver: While rarely seen, people with silver in their auras are often full of grand but impractical ideas, more characteristic of dreamers than doers.

Violet: Crown Chakra—Advanced spirituality and psychic skills. People with a lot of violet in their auras sometime exhibit an offputting air of superiority and are often involved in metaphysical pursuits.

White: Not commonly seen, but indicative of purity, self-effacement, and being peace-loving.

Yellow: Solar Plexus—Intellect, mental power, creativity, strong personality. The brightness of the yellow is associated with intelligence, while the expansiveness of the color is associated with social competence and dependability. Bright yellow around the head is associated with abstract thinking, problem solving, and verbal skills, while bright yellow around the shoulders and chest is associated with supe-rior eye-hand coordination and mechanical skills. Dullness and constriction in the predominantly yellow aura may indicate stressful conditions and difficulties in social interactions. Associated with mental energy.

INTERPRETING THE AURA

Since the aura is directly perceived only through our psychic vision, or *clairvoyance*, the interpretation of it is more subjective than objective and builds upon the personal experience of the observer.

The main factors to consider are:

1. The various fields about the body reflecting the etheric, astral, mental, and spiritual bodies or *sheaths*.

2. The levels of the body corresponding to the location of the chakras.

3. The colors and their clarity, brightness, and intensity.

4. The presence of irregularities and patterns such as blockages, holes, depressions or bulges, blotches, streaks, fluctuations, fissures, points of light or darkness, streams and clusters of energy, tentacles, arcs, agitation, symmetry, and balance.

5. In some auras, there will be geometric figures.

6. The size of each of the fields as distance out from the physical body.

7. The overall structure, which Dr. Slate refers to as the unique *signature* of the individual.

8. The observer's *feeling* or psychic impressions.

While some specific observations can be augmented with the use of dowsing rods and pendulums as well as the hands in sensing the aura, the aura visionary, or reader, should attempt to start with basic observations of the above factors, and then slowly perceive the complexity of the overall aura in which the following elements are important considerations:

- Streams of Energy. These can occur in a variety of formations and colors anywhere in the aura. They can radiate outward as brilliant streamers or meander about in a network of energy. Any blockage to these streams should be noted in relation to the color and location.

- Clusters of Energy. These intense concentrations of colorful energy can occur anywhere in the aura and typically are in response to specific empowerment needs. Color and location should be noted.

- Points of Light. These are associated with powerful forces intervening to empower the individual's life, and can signify a spiritual presence such as a guide or angel. Intensity and location should be noted.

- Points of Darkness. These may signify an attack on the aura, possibly—in rare instances—an actual psychic attack or involuntary psychic vampirism, but more often as points of severe weakness or injury.

- Voids. Larger than points, voids are inactive areas with little or no energy that often reveal psychological factors such as discouragement, feelings of hopelessness, depersonalization, detachment, etc.

- Agitation. Appearing as churning turbulence accompanied by discoloration, they suggest fractured relationships, insecurity, fear, excessive anxiety, unresolved conflicts, and when localized may indicate the site of chronic pain.

- Symmetry. This signals a healthy, harmonious mind, body, and spirit able to accommodate change and opportunities as new learning experiences.

- Fissures. These are breaks and tears with jagged and irregular edges and are usually gray in color. They originate in the outer layers of the aura as the result of psychic injury—often from early childhood or past-life experiences. They may be indicative of physical or emotional abuse and often appear in the auras of battered women. The effects of past-life experiences survive and are reflected in the aura.

- Tentacles. These extend outward from the aura's external boundary and are often associated with immaturity and dependency needs—a reaching out for support. They are frequently found in the auras of people who look for instant gratification, or who make selfish and unreasonable demands on others. Too, they are found in the auras of pseudointellectuals, self-anointed "scholars" who specialize in debunking views contrary to their own. Tentacles are often associated with psychic vampirism in which the tentacle reaches from one aura to another.

- Arcs. Arcs connect the upper regions of two auras in close and satisfying social interaction and will sometimes lead to a literal merging of the two auras.

- Geometric Forms. Geometric forms can occur anywhere in the aura as specialized concentrations of energy originating either within the subject or from an external force.

  - Spheres. Like other aura signature forms, the color and location offer clues to its energizing role. For example, a bright yellow sphere in the upper region of the aura is associated with intellectual enrichment. A bright green sphere indicates healing energy being applied in the physical body at that location.

  - Pyramids. Psychics often have a bright pyramid of energy in the upper regions of the aura, sometimes directly overhead.

- Sheath. A large, shieldlike ring of intensely bright energy may enclose the entire aura as a protective boundary.

- Asymmetrical globs, often smoky in coloration, tend to constrict the aura and suppress its energies.

Interpretation of the aura should not be based on strict *rules* following these listings of colors, brightness, size, shapes, and so forth, but rather a holistic synthesis characterized by the aura visionary's empathy with the subject—even when viewing one's own aura. While details count toward the whole, we must never let the details overwhelm the whole in our interpretation.

MAGICAL MIRROR OF THE UNIVERSE
SPHERE OF SENSATION

Both of these are expressions used in reference to the human aura in esoteric literature and magical practice. Both are descriptive of magical perspectives relating to practices for self-development, psychic empowerment, and personal growth. The etheric aura is the immediate sphere of sensation, and the aura as a whole is the magical mirror of the universe, reflecting the interaction between personal energies and those from the cosmos.

For many years, these practices were secret and reserved to members of esoteric orders like the famous Hermetic Order of the Golden Dawn. In recent years, those practices have been made available in book after book, and esoteric terms and concepts have been translated from Latin, Greek, and Hebrew words and convoluted language into common and familiar terminology. The subjects involved have moved from lodge rooms and folk magic into scientific laboratories verifying the reality of the aura, the various subtle bodies, and the techniques and tools with which we can apply them ourselves.

Yes, there is more to the aura than reading the colors. It is not fixed at birth, but is a continuous expression of all that is going on in your body, mind, and spirit. It receives input from *inside* your whole system, and from *outside* environmental sources that include social, climatic, and even cosmic forces that are in constant interplay with our individuality.

In his most comprehensive book, *Aura Energy for Health, Healing & Balance*, Dr. Slate outlined the multiple roles of the aura system:

FUNCTIONS OF THE AURA SYSTEM

- It is a highly complex system that generates energy and sustains us mentally, physically, and spiritually.

- It is a sensitive yet dynamic force that encodes the totality of our individuality and connects us to the cosmic origins of our existence.

- It is an evolving chronicle of our past, present, and future.

- It is an interactive link between our innermost self and the external environment, including the aura systems of others.

- It is a repository of abundant resources with potential to enrich our lives.

- It is an interactive phenomenon receptive to our intervention and empowerment efforts.

- At any given moment, it is a weathervane of our personal development.

- The more we learn about the aura, the better we understand ourselves.

In summary, the aura is your own personal mirror, not only of health but of character, emotional strength, mentality, and spirituality. The aura can be strengthened, massaged, healed, enlarged, shaped, and charged with specific energies and energy forms for direct interaction with other entities. The aura is your personal psychic self-defense system. The aura is part of you that reaches out to touch and embrace a loved one. The aura is your shield against invasive sales, advertising, and propaganda attempting to persuade you into decisions against your own best interests. (Of course, there is no substitute for rational and informed thinking, and plain common sense, but your auric shield is your first line of defense.)

As an aura visionary you have the ability to actively engage with your own aura for self-improvement and self-empowerment, psychic empowerment, and spiritual growth. The psychic skills you develop in viewing and interpreting your own aura are the critical foundation for the next step in personal empowerment: *deliberately interacting with the aura system, activating its capacities, and using its resources.*

There are two basic techniques that we can employ, both of which can be adapted and expanded for specific applications.

SELF-PERCEPTION AND COSMIC CENTERING PROCEDURE

1. Set aside approximately thirty minutes in a space where you will be comfortable and not likely to be interrupted.

2. Close your eyes and physically relax with a few slow and deep breaths. Now, feeling deeply relaxed, mentally scan your physical body from head to feet. Identify and release any accumulations of muscular tension. Take three deep breaths, exhaling slowly, and then affirm to yourself: *I am now fully relaxed.*

3. Focus your inner awareness on your aura's inner core—the center of energy you feel in your deepest, innermost being. Visualize it as a luminous inner core situated in your solar plexus. Let your imagination and your feelings

guide you to this. Think of it as an energy powerhouse, radiating abundant energy that fuels your total being—mental, physical, and spiritual.

4. Visualize your aura and mentally scan it from above your head to just below your feet. Note the sensations and impressions that accompany this aura scan.

5. Still visualizing your aura, contemplate first the full aura and then focus on specific areas and characteristics. Allow insights to emerge either as impressions or images.

6. Internalize the experience, taking a *mental snapshot* of your aura and file it away in your mind for future reference.

7. With your thoughts turned inward, sense the energy emanating from this inner core and permeating your total being. Visualize your body enveloped in a radiant glow. Affirm to yourself: *I am infused with powerful, radiant energy.*

8. Envision the distance center of the cosmos as a brilliant core of powerful energy. Think of it as the powerhouse that fuels the universe. Focus your full attention on its limitless power.

9. Visualize a powerful channel of bright light connecting the luminous core of your inner being to the brilliant core of the outer cosmos. Let yourself become fully infused with pure cosmic energy. Affirm to yourself: *I am attuned to the cosmos and empowered with abundant cosmic energy. I am fully energized and balanced mentally, physically, and spiritually.*

10. Conclude the procedure by again viewing your aura and noting any changes in coloration and intensity. Again take a mental snapshot of your aura, and compare it with an earlier snapshot, noting any particular changes in colorization and intensity from the earlier snapshot.

Note: It is always desirable to summarize your experience in a personal journal.

THE AURA SELF-MASSAGE PROCEDURE

The concept of self-empowerment is based on a simple premise: Positive interactions with the self can be enlightening, energizing and empowering. We can deliberately generate positive thought messages that build self-confidence and self-worth. We can create mental images that empower us to achieve personal and career goals. We can create powerful mind/body interaction to promote better health and fitness. Aura self-massage procedures can be adapted to many specific goals. The following is for self-healing.

Step 1. *Physical Relaxation*. Assume a comfortable seated or reclining position, and take a few deep breaths, exhaling slowly. Mentally scan your body from your head downward, pausing at points of tension to relax every fiber, joint, and tendon. Envision relaxation as soft light accompanying the scan, slowly illuminating the entire body. Let relaxation soak into the body's innermost regions to permeate every organ and system.

Step 2. *Inner Energy Infusion.* With your physical body fully relaxed, envision the bright inner core of your aura system in your solar plexus region. Sense the pulsating energy emanating from there spreading throughout your body.

Step 3. *Solar Plexus Aura Massage.* Rub your hands gently together until they feel vibrant and tingly, and then—without touching the body, the hands just an inch or so above the surface—massage the aura in the solar plexus region with gentle circular motions as you envision healing energy spreading outward in all directions. Follow the circular massage with vertical motions to spread the healing energy evenly to the upper and lower body. Then use wide circular motions as you envision each organ and system of your body becoming infused with bright shining energy. Envision your circulatory system aglow with healing energy, dispersing it into every fiber of your body. Feel the infusion process reach its highest point, and then affirm: *The healing power within myself is now permeating my whole body with healing energy.*

This does not require that you know every organ and system as if you were studying anatomy. It is belief and intent that you are treating every organ and system that counts. Think of those you know in the background of your vision while focusing your intent to heal.)

Step 4. *Cosmic Energy Infusion.* Visualize the cosmic center as a brilliant sphere of pure energy radiating immeasurable power to sustain the universe and think of your hands as antennae receiving that energy. Lift your hands, palms turned upward, and visualize streams of energy entering your hands from the cosmic center and merging with energies from your own energy system.

Step 5. *Cosmic Aura Massage.* As you visualize the powerful union of energies at the core of your aura system, spread bright cosmic healing energy throughout the body by repeating the solar plexus massage in Step 3 above. Sense and visualize the vibrant renewal process in your body.

Step 6. *Focused Massage.* Focus on any particular areas, organs, or system, and aura massage in slow, circular motions. Envision the target becoming infused with luminous healing energy.

Step 7. *Concluding Affirmations.* Conclude the procedure, as with other procedures, with relevant affirmations such as: *I am attuned mentally, physically, and spiritually to the highest sources of power. My total being is filled to overflowing with power energizing me with health and vitality. I am empowered by awareness of the cosmic origin of my very existence and knowledge of the supreme power within myself.*

By simply extending Step 4 above, we can deliberately access higher spiritual dimensions and engage deeply meaningful interactions with spirit guides and angels. With experience and experimentation with these two techniques, you can adapt them to many goals.

The human aura is a powerful resource. By developing the skills required to intervene into its functions and direct its energies, you can attain your highest level of personal empowerment.

SOURCES AND RECOMMENDED READING

Robert Bruce, "Training to see auras," 1990, astraldynamics.com.

Melita Denning and Osborne Phillips, *Practical Guide to Psychic Self-Defense: Strengthen Your Aura* (Llewellyn, 2001).

Nevill Drury, *The Watkins Dictionary of Magic* (Watkins, 2005).

John Michael Greer, *The New Encyclopedia of the Occult* (Llewellyn, 2003).

Jonn Mumford, *Chakra & Kundalini Workbook: Psycho-Spiritual Techniques for Health, Rejuvenation, Psychic Powers & Self-Realization* (Llewellyn, 1997).

Paula Peterson, Interview of Dr. Konstantin Korotkov, *Spirit of Maat,* Vol. 3, No. 1.

Plutark's *Lives,* multiple editions.

Joe H. Slate, *Aura Energy for Health, Healing & Balance* (Llewellyn, 1999).

Joe H. Slate, *Psychic Vampires: Protection from Energy Predators & Parasites* (Llewellyn, 2002).

Mark Smith, *Auras: See Them in Only 60 Seconds!* (Llewellyn, 1997).

4

The Chakra System

Spinning Wheels of Psychic Power

*Humankind has always been aware of the existence of certain vital areas
in the human body. The use to which the esoteric knowledge
of these nerve zones was put varied from civilization to civilization.*

—JONN MUMFORD, *A CHAKRA & KUNDALINI WORKBOOK*

The Chakra System is one of the more challenging psychic technologies to write about and one of the most important for us to explore and incorporate into our understanding of how psychic power works and how it affects the most fundamental structure of the Whole Person.

The first major challenge comes about because of our innate desire to perceive things from only the physical perspective and ***the truth is that chakras are not physically real!***

Yes, there are physical body correlates that some writers have attempted to *define* the chakras with particular endocrine glands and nerve ganglia, but these are misleading for the simple reason that chakras are psychic centers without *any* direct physical connections, but are located on the surface of the etheric double *over* areas associated with these body parts.

The second major challenge comes about because the chakras are not really singular but form a system with energies in constant movement and interchange. Many of the things we will be listing in tables and descriptions of the individual chakras are fluid, not static. The colors listed, for example, are often *shades* that change and merge, and that change in brightness as well.

At the same time, our first table serves to show basic relationships that are important to perceiving them as a system. Another table shows a major interchange of energies that is continuous but fluctuating. The paragraph descriptions are extremely important for the purpose of meditations that will be part of the developmental process described later.

As mentioned, the chakras are located *on the surface* of the etheric double, but there are corresponding chakras located *within* the astral body, projecting energies to the etheric chakras. The etheric double is composed of subtle matter and energies, forming a duplicate of the physical body extending about a quarter inch beyond the body's outer skin.

> *At the inner core of each one of us spin seven wheel-like energy centers called chakras. Swirling intersections of vital life forces, each chakra reflects an aspect of consciousness essential to our lives. Together the seven chakras form a system for modeling that consciousness that enables us to better see ourselves—in mind, body, behavior, and culture. The system is a valuable tool for personal and planetary growth.*
>
> *Chakras are centers of activity for the reception, assimilation, and transmission of life energies. As all our action and understanding arise from and return to points within ourselves, our chakras, as core centers, form the coordinating network of our complicated mind/body system. From instinctual behavior to consciously planned strategies, from emotions to artistic creations, the chakras are the master programs that govern our lives, loves, learning and illumination.*
>
> —ANODEA JUDITH, *WHEELS OF LIFE:*
> *A USER'S GUIDE TO THE CHAKRA SYSTEM*

Actually, there are more than seven chakras, according to Benjamin Walker, but it is the seven major chakras following the path of the spinal column that together form the vital system that brings life to the physical body in the form of energies from the sun through the air we breathe and the food we eat, in the form of the life force we call *prana*. It is these seven that are of fundamental importance to our psychic development.

> *... there are eighty-eight thousand chakras in the human body. Each one forms a focus from which a number of nadis or subtle channels branch out connecting up with one or more areas of the physical body. A complete knowledge of all the chakras and their ramifications is impossible, but there are alleged to be specialists in sri-vidya who are able, for instance, to cure a toothache by messaging one of the ribs, or ease asthma by gently pressing a point behind the ears. Such knowledge of the chakra points is handed down as a family secret, and their efficacy has frequently been attested.*
>
> —BENJAMIN WALKER, *THE HINDU WORLD*

Walker lists twenty-three additional chakras that connect with points activating the sense of locality, acquisitiveness, the sense of order, the sense of veneration, the sense of aesthetics, the sense of time, the sense of quantity, body heat, and the sense of protection, the sense of purpose, the sense of dependence, the sense of faith, the sense of domesticity, the sense of color, the sense of shape, the sense of solitariness, the sense of interiorness, self-respect, pride and affection, dreams, hallucinations and illusions, altruism, compassion, magnanimity, patience, and sincerity.

Cyndi Dale in *New Chakra Healing* describes five "out-of-body" chakras that connect to the physical body but are not located within it. She writes: "They are the chakras through which magic is wrought, imagination becomes real, humanity receives salvation. They are the chakras which exchange elemental and celestial energies." The following is paraphrased from Dale's book.

OUT-OF-BODY CHAKRAS: LOCATION, COLOR AND FUNCTION

- The Eighth Chakra is located about 1½ inches above the head, is colored silver or ultraviolet, and contains our personal Akashic Records—all our memories. Thus it is the source of all past knowledge, our karmic memory, with access to other dimensions and times. In addition, it includes the decisions made by the soul before our current birth.

- The Ninth (Soul) Chakra is located an arm's length above the head, is colored gold or infrared, and contains programming of the soul and self. It contains symbols, patterns, and archetypes that function like chromosomes in the design of the physical body, that mold a life to meet the soul's goals, and to channel energy from the Divine Source to bring change at the soul level.

- The Tenth (Grounding) Chakra is located 1½ to 4 feet below foot level, is colored earthy—citrine, brown, russet, olive green, limestone yellow and obsidian, and contains the four elements (fire, earth, air, water). To be grounded means to be fully in our physical bodies and fully attached to the earth and thus able to function in this life. Contrary to many metaphysical ideas that suggest that the body is a hindrance to spiritual growth, the truth is exactly the opposite. The body is our foundation, without which our life lacks focus, stability, and actual ability to progress with psychic empowerment.

- The Eleventh Chakra is located in the palms of both hands and the soles of both feet, is colored pink, and contains the ability to transmute physical energy into psychic energy, and vice versa. It provides energy through our hands and feet to deal with the dangers and opportunities of physical life.

• The Twelfth Chakra is actually a system of thirty-two "access" points located both within the physical body and beyond in its aura, which connect us to natural forces and particular archetypes.

Some of the seeming confusion between the various authorities' attributes to the major chakras most likely originates with one of the nearby lesser chakras. In some older texts there was a crossover in descriptions for the Heart and Solar Plexus chakras. In addition to the various major and lesser chakras listed so far, there is a major center described in relation to Kundalini called *Bindu* located at the top and back of the head.

THE ETHERIC DOUBLE

The reality is that the etheric double is, in fact, part of the physical body when seen from an energetic perspective. That's why we prefer to call it the "double" rather than a "body" as we do when referring to the astral, mental, and other bodies forming the complex of the individual *system* manifesting through the physical body.

At the same time, it is important to understand that it is through the chakra system that the etheric double manages the nature, composition, and consciousness of the whole person.

Programmed by astral intelligence, the etheric double is created in advance of birth out of etheric matter from the mother's body, and then acts as a matrix for the developing physical body acting under the influence of "karma" from previous lives and the determined purpose of the current life.

Essential to the life of the physical body, its immediate function is to receive and distribute *prana* emanating from the sun. Not being an actual body like the physical body or the astral body, its consciousness is primarily that of our triune mind: the conscious mind *bordered* by the subconscious mind and superconscious mind. These *borders* are likewise fluid: contents of the subconscious mind move into the conscious mind, and those from the conscious mind slip into the subconscious mind.

The etheric double of the body is systemic in that an "etheric envelope" develops around every particle of matter, liquid, or gas making up the physical body. In other words, the "body" is actually dual in nature, characterized by two distinct functions. In the simplest perspective, the physical body acts in the physical world, and the etheric double—acting in the "etheric world"—interchanges energy and information from the astral body and plane with the physical body and plane.

Physical reality is made up of seven kinds of material, each distinguished by a frequency range of "vibrations" that determine its state. All seven of these states coexist in every physical structure—animate or inanimate—from the minutest bacteria to the immense planets and suns of our universe.

In the case of the human body and its etheric double, the following chart should be helpful:

PHYSICAL MATTER EXISTS IN SEVEN ORDERS OF DENSITY

Atomic	)	
Sub-Atomic	)	Etheric Double
Super-Etheric	)	
Etheric	)	
Gaseous	)	
Liquid	)	Physical Body
Solid	)	

Adapted from Powell: *The Etheric Double*

When we speak of the physical body we must—so long as it is alive—understand that we have both a physical structure composed of the three recognized states of physical matter—solids, liquids, and gases—and its etheric double composed of four states of subtle matter: etheric, super-etheric, sub-atomic and atomic.

FUNCTIONS OF THE FOUR STATES OF ETHERIC MATTER

1. Atomic   The medium thought, transmitted "brain to brain"
2. Sub-Atomic   The medium of the "finer forms of electricity"
3. Super-Etheric   The medium of light
4. Etheric   The medium of sound and "ordinary current electricity"

Adapted from Powell: *The Etheric Double*

Unfortunately, these names and concepts are somewhat ambiguous and reflect the earlier historic time when their use first became established. Don't let it scare you that you are composed of atomic matter any more than you worry about being composed of liquids and gases. You're still on solid ground!

The appearance of the etheric double is a luminous kind of pale violet gray. It is the unconscious source of much spiritualist séance phenomena, including raps, knocks, and other sounds, ectoplasm and materialization, and levitation of objects and sometimes even of people. It is especially involved with energy healing, magnetic healing, and in mesmerism.

No matter the cause, diseases first show up in the astral body, flow down into the etheric double, and then manifest in the physical body. This is why etheric or "energy healing" can be so effective through the hands of a competent healer acting *early* in the disease process. Once disease manifests in the physical body, physical treatments are usually necessary but can be supplemented from the ether/energy level as well.

The Etheric Double develops within itself the chakras that enable the person to perceive the etheric world and etheric phenomena separately from the physical world. Both etheric matter and prana are subject to the human will, and can be shaped into a shield against germs and psychic vampirism and into temporary "bodies" of thought-created familiars and etheric vehicles for angels, spirits, and other entities brought to visible appearance in magical operations.

Just as the physical body digests incoming materials and then excretes waste products, so does the etheric double use up the pranic material received from food, air, and the astral centers, and discharges them as waste through the breath and pores of the skin. Some of that etheric waste radiates outward from the lower part of the body through the pores and can be perceived clairvoyantly in a kind of *exhausted* green and orange-red colors. Other waste radiates in dark blue and violet from the top of the head.

However, as psychic development proceeds, the orange-red rays increasingly are discharged also from the top of the head as a fiery cascade often pictured in paintings of saints and true initiates.

ENERGIES: FOHAT, KUNDALINI, PRANA

There are three primary energies, or forces, that are important to our understanding that we live in an energy-manifested world. These are first described by their Sanskrit names and the basic Hindu or Theosophical concepts concerning their meanings:

PRIMAL ENERGIES OF THE UNIVERSE

Fohat: The primary Cosmic Energy fundamental to the universe.

Kundalini (the Coiled One): Also called "the Serpent Fire," it is located in the base of the Spine chakra.

Prana (Breathe forth): The life force emanating from the sun as vitality absorbed from the air we breathe and the food we eat.

These three forces are fundamental and have their own functions throughout the universe at all levels.

Fohat

Fohat manifests as universal physical forces: motion, gravity, electricity, magnetism, sound, heat, chemical reactions, radiation, etc. These physical forces are convertible, one into another.

Prana

Prana manifests as universal life force, breathing life into being and breathing out in the fundamental rhythm we experience as life and death, and life again. It is the energy that gives life to the body and all its parts, providing structure, and holding the physical molecules and cells together as organs and in relationship to each other.

Prana exists at all levels and *animates* all the bodies composing the whole person. Astral and physical prana create nerve-matter. Cells develop into nerve fiber, and prana pulsates through these fibers. It is by means of the etheric double that prana runs along the nerves of the body to carry both external impact and motor force from within.

Prana is also one of the seven elements—Prana, Manas (mind), Ether, Fire, Air, Water, and Earth—corresponding to seven regions of the universe. In Hebrew Kabbalism, Nephesh (the Psyche) is Prana combined with Kama (Love), together making the vital spark that is the "breath of life."

Kundalini

Kundalini manifests as a transforming force centered in the Base Chakra, operating within the body and driving evolution, desire, sex drive, growth, and individual development. It exists on all planes in seven degrees of force.

Bringing astral experiences into conscious (physical brain) awareness requires some arousal of kundalini and its movement through other chakras, whether deliberately or spontaneously.

THE CHAKRAS

Chakras have no physical reality. They are vortexes of consciousness forming a kind of "management system" that transforms energies to meet the needs of the evolving body-mind-spirit complex operating as a human entity.

The chakras are located on the *surface* of the etheric double, varying in size from about two to six inches and each with a different function distinguished by colors. The colors are manifestations of energies at different vibratory rates. They have two functions: 1) to absorb and distribute prana to the etheric and thence to the physical body to keep it alive; and 2) *to bring down into physical consciousness whatever may be present in the corresponding astral center.*

These corresponding centers are *within* the astral body, and likewise in the mental and spiritual bodies. In other words, the chakra system exists at every level of the composite human person, but with functions that vary at each level.

Our primary interest is at the etheric level, and to a lesser extent with the astral and mental levels. It is at the physical, etheric, astral, and mental levels that we consciously function, and where—*through the conscious mind*—we understand the chakra functions and undertake their development. The goal, as in all esoteric practice, is to accelerate our development, or evolution, in a controlled manner extending over lifetimes.

Without such practice, their development varies: when undeveloped, they glow dully and the etheric particles move sluggishly; when developed, the chakras glow brightly and pulsate with activity.

The practical and more immediate benefit is that such development turns innate psychic powers into reliable and expert psychic skills.

It is claimed that in addition to the seven primary chakras, there are three lower chakras only used by black magicians (Powell, 1925).

The following chart is a simplification of the primary chakra system.

THE PRIMARY CHAKRA SYSTEM						
No.	Common Name or Petals	Sanskrit Name	Location [1]	Color [2]	Spokes Associated	Gland[3]
1	Base	*Muladhara*	Base of Spine[4]	Red	4	Ovaries, Testicles
2	Sacral	*Svadhisthana*	Over Spleen	Orange	6	Pancreas
3	Solar Plexus	*Manipura*	Over Navel	Yellow	10	Adrenals
4	Heart	*Anahata*	Over Heart	Green	12	Thymus
5	Throat	*Vishuddha*	Throat	Blue	16	Thyroid
6	Brow	*Ajna*	Brow	Indigo	96 [5]	Pituitary
7	Crown	*Sahasrara*	Top of Head	Violet	960 + 12 [6]	Pineal

1. These are the most commonly assigned locations, but authorities differ. Instead of the Solar Plexus, Theosophists identify it with the spleen, others with the navel.

2. These are the most commonly assigned colors, but authorities differ.

3. Again, there are disagreements among authorities. Remember that there is no direct physical connection between the etheric chakras and the physical body.

4. Between anus and perineum.

5. Commonly, this is given as two, but it is really two "wings" of 48 each.

6. Most commonly, it is identified as a thousand-petaled lotus. The crown chakra has 960 spokes plus another 12 in its center which is gleaming white with gold at its core.

1. THE BASE CHAKRA (MULADHARA)

Sometimes called the "root" chakra, it is located at the base of the spine and is concerned with survival and procreation. It is important for health and vitality, and keeping a person *grounded*. This chakra is fiery red and has four spokes, often represented as the elemental quadrants separated by an equal-armed cross image. Its function in both the etheric double and astral body is the seat of the kundalini transforming force. Its subtle force is called *Prithivi,* the prana of earth, and is concerned with cohesion, the energy of smell, and the action of the feet.

It receives orange, dark red, and dark purple prana from the sacral center, along with the primary force from the astral energizing the sex organs and the blood. As psychic development progresses, the dark purple energy rises to the brain as pale violet to quicken spirituality, the orange energy becomes yellow to intensify the intellect, and the dark red becomes crimson to stimulate affection.

Grounding Exercise

Imagine your spine extending deep into the ground like a root, and imagine any excessive stress running down and dissipating into the earth. Then imagine you are drawing up healing energies from the earth, strengthening your whole body.

1. Base Chakra (Muladhara) Correspondences

Alchemical Planet: Saturn

Alchemical Element: Lead

Tattva: Prithivi (Earth)

Animal: Bull, elephant, ox

Basic Drive: Security

Tattva Color: Yellow

Body Function: Elimination

Chakra Color: Red

Tattva Form: Square

Element: Earth

Gemstone: Ruby, garnet, lodestone

Tattva Sense: Smell

Gland: Adrenals

God-form, Egyptian: Geb

God-form, Hindu: Bala Brahma (Child God)

God-form, Greek: Gaia, Demeter

Goddess-form, Hindu: Dakini (Security)

Incense: Cedar

Location: Base of spine

Order of Chakra Unfoldment: 1st

Yogic Planet: Saturn

Part of Body: Between anus and genitals

Psychological Attribute: Solidarity

Bija Mantra: LuNG, LuM (3)

Psychic Power: Pain control, psychometry, dowsing, telekinesis

Sense: Smell

Spinal Joint: 1st, 2nd, 3rd

Spinal Location: 4th Sacral

Tarot Key: XXI, The World

Tree of Life Sephiroth: Malkuth

Yantra (internal): Blue Square

Tarot Suit: Pentacles

 Yellow

2. THE SACRAL CHAKRA (SVADHISTHANA)

The Sacral Center is located a few inches below the navel. It is concerned with self-protection and initiates the release of sex hormones, stimulating the sex drive and attraction to the opposite sex. This chakra is orange-red in color, radiant and sun-like. Its primary function is to absorb vitality from the atmosphere and distribute the component atoms charged with specialized prana to the various parts of the body through its six spokes. Its subtle force is called *Apas*, the prana of water, and is concerned with contraction, the energy of taste, and the action of the hand.

It also receives a primary force from the corresponding astral center, giving the astral body the power to travel consciously.

Appreciation Exercise

The Sacral Chakra is pleasure driven, and seeking pleasure can easily become obsessive and even compulsive. Slow down, and realize pleasure is always available—you don't have to chase after it. Sacral Chakra magnetism will eventually bring it to you—so much so that you will need to exercise discrimination rather than let it dominate you.

ENERGY FLOWS FROM SACRAL CHAKRA

Physical location of chakra	Spokes	Appearance	Vitality Received from Location	Vitality Sent to Location	Region Vitalized	Function of Astral Center	Function of Etheric Center
Over Base of Spine	4	Fiery orange-red	Orange and red with some dark purple from Sacral Center		Sex organs, blood for heat of body	Seat of kundalini. Kundalini vivifies each Center in turn.	Seat of kundalini, kundalini vivifies each Center in turn.
Over Spleen	6	Sun-like		Indigo to Crown center. Violet-blue to Throat center. Yellow to Heart. Green to Solar Plexus. Rose-red to Nervous System. Orange-red with some dark purple to Base of Spine center		Vitalizes Astral Body.	Vitalizes physical body. Memory of astral journeys
Over Navel	10	Shades of red and green	Green, from Sacral Center		Solar plexus, liver, kidneys, intestines, and abdomen generally	Feelings; sensitivity.	Feeling astral influences
Over Heart	12	Glowing gold	Yellow from Sacral Center	Yellow to Blood, Brain, and Middle of Crown	Heart	Comprehension of Astral Vibrations	Consciousness of others' feelings.

ENERGY FLOWS FROM SACRAL CHAKRA (CONTINUED)

Physical location of chakra	Spokes	Appearance	Vitality Received from Location	Vitality Sent to Location	Region vitalized	Function of Astral Center	Function of Etheric Center
In front of the Throat	16	Gleaming bluish silver	Violet-blue from Sacral Center	Dark blue to lower and central part of brain.		Hearing	Clairaudience Etheric & astral hearing
In front of the Brow	96	Half, rose with yellow; Half, with purplish blue				Sight	Clairvoyance. Magnification.
Above Crown of head	960 12	Outer part gives chromatic effects; Center part gleams white with gold				Perfects, and completes faculties	Continuity of Consciousness.

With development, the Base of Spine Center vitalizes the brain with these ray changes through the Spinal Column:

Orange-red becomes yellow and stimulates intellect.

Dark red becomes crimson and stimulates affection.

Dark purple becomes pale violet and stimulates spirituality.

It is claimed that there are three lower centers that are used only by "black magicians."

2. Sacral Chakra (Svadhisthana) Correspondences

Alchemical Planet: Mars, Pluto

Alchemical Element: Iron

Tattva: Apas (Water)

Animal: Crocodile

Basic Drive: Pleasure

Tattva Color: White (Silver)

Body Function: Sexuality, Pleasure

Chakra Color: Orange

Tattva Form: Crescent

Element: Water

Gemstone: Coral

Tattvic Sense: Taste

Gland: Pancreas

Goddess-form, Egyptian: Tefnut

Goddess-form, Hindu: Rakini (Sexuality)

God-form, Hindu: Vishnu (Preserver)

God-form, Greek: Pan, Diana

Incense: Orris, gardenia, damiana

Location: Over the spleen

Order of Chakra Unfoldment: 3rd

Yogic Planet: Sun

Part of Body: Genitals, kidney, bladder, circulatory system

Psychological Attribute: Flexibility, equanimity

Psychic Power: Empathy, psychic diagnosis

Sense: Taste

Bija Mantra: VuNG, VuM (4)

Spinal Joint: 7th

Spinal Location: 1st Lumbar

Tarot Key: XIX, The Sun

Tree of Life Sephiroth: Yesod

Yantra (internal): Black Crescent

Tarot Suit: Cups

 White (Silver)

3. THE SOLAR PLEXUS CHAKRA (MANIPURA)

The Solar Plexus Chakra is located a few inches above the navel. It is concerned with empathy and stimulates the release of the adrenal hormones responsible for our fight-or-flight response to threat. This chakra is colored yellow. It receives its primary force from the corresponding astral center and the yellow ray from the sacral chakra, and distributes it in ten directions through its ten spokes. The function of the etheric chakra is feeling and emotion, while that of its astral correspondence is sensitivity to astral influences. Its subtle force is called *Tejas,* the prana of fire, and is concerned with expansion, the energy of color and form, the energy of sight, and the action of the anus.

The etheric chakra gives awareness of the feelings of others and the astral center gives comprehension of astral vibrations. It distributes the yellow ray both to the blood and to the brain and crown chakra. Meditation on this chakra is said to bring freedom from pain and disease.

Self-control Exercise

The Solar Plexus is your power center from which you assert yourself in the world. But you can be power-driven to the point of an obsession to dominate everyone and everything around you. Don't! Any obsession brings frustration. Use your common sense, and learn the art of cooperation.

3. Solar Plexus (manipura) correspondences

Alchemical Planet: Jupiter, Sun

Alchemical Element: Tin

Tattva: Tejas (Fire)

Animal: Ram

Basic Drive: Pleasure

Tattva Color: Red

Body Function: Digestion

Chakra Color: Yellow

Tattva Form: Crescent

Element: Fire

Gemstone: Amber, topaz

Tattvic Sense: Taste

Gland: Adrenals

Goddess-form, Egyptian: Tefnut

Goddess-form, Hindu: Lakini (Authority)

God-form, Hindu: Braddha-Rudra

God-form, Greek: Apollo, Athena

Incense: Carnation, cinnamon

Location: Over navel

Order of Chakra Unfoldment: 4th

Yogic Planet: Sun

Part of Body: Solar Plexus, Navel

Psychological Attributes: Power, passion, energy

Psychic Power: Empathy, psychic diagnossi

Sense: Sight

Bija Mantra: RuNG, RuM (4)

Spinal Joint: 7th

Spinal Location: 1st Lumbar

Tarot Key: XVI, The Tower

Tree of Life Sephiroth: Hod, Netzach

Yantra (internal): Green inverse triangle

Tarot Suit: Wands

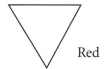 Red

4. THE HEART CHAKRA (ANAHATA)

The Heart Chakra is located, appropriately enough, over the heart. It is the energy center of the body and is concerned with healing of self and others. This chakra is a rich forest-green, has twelve spokes, and is associated with the thymus gland responsible for our immune system fighting infections. Its subtle force is called *Vayu*, the prana of air, and it is concerned with movement, the energy of touch, and the action of the penis.

Love Exercise

"Love" in the lower three chakras is need based. You grasp for more sex, more pleasure, more power, and can never have enough. Love from the Heart Chakra is not need based, nor is it limited to any one person or things. Let yourself love without restraint, seeing the beauty around you where before you saw limitation. With such unconditional love, you will become an attractor of all the love and abundance you can ever handle.

4. Heart Chakra (anahata) correspondences

Alchemical Planet: Sun, Venus

Alchemical Element: Gold

Tattva: Vayu (Air)

Animal: Birds, Deer

Basic Drive: Love

Tattvic Color: Blue

Body Function: Respiration

Chakra Color: Green

Tattva Form: Hexagram

Element: Air

Gemstone: Rose quartz, Emerald

Tattvic Sense: Touch

Gland: Thymus

Goddess-form, Hindu: Kakani[1]

Goddess-form: Greek: Aphrodite, Pan

God-form, Egyptian: Maat

God-form, Hindu: Ishana Rudra (Devotion)

Incense: Lavender, Jasmine

Location: Over Heart

Order of Chakra Unfoldment: 2nd

Yogic Planet: Jupiter

Part of Body: Lungs

Psychological Attribute: Compassion, tolerance

Psychic Power: Hands-on Healing

Sense: Touch

Bija Mantra: LuNG LuM (1)

Spinal Joint: 26th

Spinal Location: 8th Cervical

Tarot Key: X, The Wheel of Fortune

Tree of Life Sephiroth: Tiphareth

Yantra (internal): Red Hexagram

Tarot Suit: Swords

 Blue

5. THE THROAT CHAKRA (VISHUDDHA)

The Throat Chakra is located over the throat and is, as you would guess, involved in speech—particularly inspired speech. This chakra is a silvery sky-blue, has sixteen spokes, and is associated with the thyroid gland. It receives the primary force from the corresponding astral center and the violet-blue ray from the sacral center, which divides into a light blue ray to vivify the throat center and the speech function, and distributes the dark blue and violet ray to the upper part of the brain and the outer part of the crown chakra, giving spiritual thought and emotion, and the dark blue ray to the lower and central part of the brain, stimulating thought power. The function of the etheric chakra is etheric and astral hearing and that of the astral center gives astral hearing or clairaudience. Its subtle force is called *Akasha*, the prana of ether, and is concerned with space, the energy of hearing, and the action of the mouth.

Self-truth Exercise

The Throat chakra is about inspired speech. But, much of the time, inspiration is about creativity, and as such it may not always be from your own truth center. Your need is to discover and express your true beliefs and true understanding. Do not speak to hear your own voice; do not overwhelm conversations with your constant prattle; do not let your words speak lies even to you. Discover your own truth, and speak on its behalf.

5. Throat Chakra (vishuddha) correspondences

Alchemical Planet: Venus, Jupiter

Alchemical Element: Copper

Tattva: Akasha (Ether, Spirit)

Animal: Bull, Lion, Elephant

Basic Drive: Creativity

Tattva Color: Blue-Violet

Body Function: Speech

Chakra Color: Bright Blue

Tattva Form: Oval

Element: Spirit (Ethyr)

Gemstone: Turquoise

Tattva Sense: Hearing

Gland: Thyroid, Parathyroids

Goddess-form, Celtic: Brigit

Goddess-form, Hindu: Shakini (Knowledge)

God-form, Egyptian: Seshat

God-form, Hindu: Pancha-Vaktra (5-faced Shiva)

God-form, Greek: Hermes

Incense: Frankincense

Location: Throat

Order of Chakra Unfoldment: 5th

Yogic Planet: Venus

Part of Body: Neck, shoulders, arms, hands

Psychological Attributes: Communication, Empathy

Psychic Power: Channeling, clairaudience, telepathy

Bija Mantra: HuNG HuM

Spinal Joint: 31st

Spinal Location: 3rd Cervical

Sense: Hearing

Tarot Key: III, The Empress

Tree of Life Sephirah: Chesed & Geburah

Yantra (internal): White oval

 Blue Violet (Black)

6. THE BROW CHAKRA (AJNA)

Also known as "the Third Eye," "the Eye of Horus," "the Horn of the Unicorn," and "the Command Center," the brow chakra is located on the brow, above the eyes. This chakra is indigo blue in color and has ninety-six spokes divided into two winglike halves of forty-eight spokes each—one wing is rose and yellow, the other wing is a purplish blue. It is associated with the pineal gland and with intuition. The function of the etheric center is clairvoyance and of the corresponding astral center is sight. Its power is that of imagination and its need is to find meaning in life. Its subtle force is called *Manas* connecting with mental energies.

The Third Eye is "under construction" as its "lens" is located in the aura just in front of the Brow Chakra. During meditation, focus on this point to facilitate this development and the Theta level of consciousness. Meditate on the Brow Chakra for inspiration and an understanding of your purpose in life. Development of this Chakra allows you to remember your out-of-body experiences.

Seeing Divinity Exercise

Seeing "Divinity" in all things has nothing to do with religion per se, or even with belief in God (or Goddess). It is seeing the creative force behind all manifestation everywhere, in all things, in all people, in all beings. It's the realization that divinity is there, even when there are disasters, when people do terrible things during terrible illnesses, and the most malicious crimes. It is also believing that in "witnessing" the divine, you can assert your own love, your own will, your own belief in goodness into reality. Believe in the "Plan" guiding all evolution, in yourself "becoming more than you are," and truly realize that you are an evolving Star.

6. Brow Chakra (ajna) correspondences

Alchemical Planet: Moon

Alchemical Element: Silver

Tattva: Manas (Mind)

Animal: Owl

Basic Drive: Transcendence

Tattva Color: Half, rose with yellow; half, purplish blue

Body Function: Sight, consciousness

Chakra Color: Indigo, with purplish blue

Element: Light, mind

Gemstone: Quartz, lapis lazuli

Tattva form: Winged globe

Gland: Pituitary

Goddess-form, Egyptian: Isis

Goddess-form, Hindu: Hakini (insight)

God-form, Greek: Apollo

God-form, Hindu: Shiva-Shakti (Male and female in union)

Tattva Sense: Mind

Incense: Saffron, mugwort

Location: Brow

Order of Chakra Unfoldment: 6th

Part of Body: Eyes

Sense: Mind, Awareness

Yogic Planet: Moon

Psychic Power: Clairvoyance, precognition, remote viewing, aura reading

Seed Syllable/Number: AuM (0)

Psychological Attribute: Logical thinking

Sense: Awareness

Spinal Joint: 32nd

Spinal Location: 1st Cervical

Tarot Key: II, The High Priestess

Tree of Life Sephirah: Chokmah and Binah

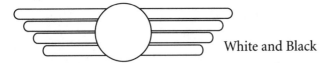 White and Black

7. THE CROWN CHAKRA (SAHASRARA)

The crown chakra has 960 spokes plus another twelve in its center which is gleaming white with gold at its core within the violet vortex. In addition to receiving the primary force from the corresponding astral center, it receives violet from the throat center and yellow from the heart center. It is associated with the pituitary gland. The function of the etheric center is to give continuity of consciousness, and that of the astral is to perfect and complete the faculties.

The development of etheric center enables the person to leave the physical body and return to it in full consciousness.

In some people, the astral chakras corresponding to the brow and crown etheric chakras converge upon the pituitary body, while in others the brow chakra is attached to the pituitary while the crown chakra is slanted to coincide with the pineal.

Self-surrender Exercise

"Not my will but thy will" has been taught in all religions and all self-transcending programs. It's the true secret of "Letting Go." *But, what does it really mean?* It does not mean surrender *of* self but merger of self *with* the divine everywhere. It means to feel what you only saw in the "Seeing Divinity" exercise. It truly means *becoming more than you are* through becoming one with the All. You can do this anytime, anywhere. It's being open to the experience that may take the form of actual "enlightenment," where you are filled with Light. It may take the form of experiencing oneness with the flow of universal energy. You may feel oneness with total Love. You may see "the Face of God" while knowing that the image is only in your imagination, while the reality is real in knowing the Creative Power that is everywhere for all time.

7. Crown Chakra (sahasrara) correspondences

Alchemical Planet: Mercury, Uranus

Alchemical Element: Mercury

Tattva: Bindu (a dot)

Animal: None

Basic Drive: Union

Tattva Color: Clear

Body Function: Superconsciousness

Chakra Color: Violet

Tattva Form: Rose seen from above

Element: Thought

Gemstone: Diamond

Tattva Sense: Higher Self

Gland: Pineal

Goddess-form, Hindu: Maha Shakti (Union)

God-form, Egyptian: Nut

God-form, Hindu: Brahma Vishnu (Inner teacher)

God-form, Greek: Zeus

Incense: Lotus, gotu kola

Location: Crown of Head

Order of Chakra Unfoldment: 7th

Yogic Planet: Mercury, Uranus

Part of Body: Cerebral cortex, central nervous system

Psychological state: Bliss Seed Syllable/Number: H(0)

Psychic Power: Astral projection, prophecy

Sense: the Divine Connection

Spinal Joint: 33rd

Spinal Location: None

Tarot Key: I, The Magician

Tree of Life Sephiroth: Kether

  Red

THE NATURE OF PSYCHIC DEVELOPMENT

In some people, psychic development is spontaneous and perhaps a carry-over from previous lives. More generally, development follows a pattern not unlike that of other skills: First, there is interest in a subject, followed by study, and then some kind of implementation of practice or exercise. If a person wants to be a better swimmer, he or she learns about the muscles involved, about the techniques involved in particular kinds of swimming, and then adopts particular forms of developmental exercise followed by practice, practice, practice.

Psychic development is similar. But the muscles involved are psychic—actually the chakras, individually and as the whole chakra system.

The particular forms of developmental exercise involve meditation and visualization. And the practice involves the application of techniques and the use of "tools" such as described in the second part of this book.

The meditation and visualization exercises that we will describe are dependent upon knowledge of the chakras themselves in many ways involving appearance, structure, color, function, and various symbolic associations and attributions. In addition, further exercises will involve the chakra system as a whole, sometimes referred to as "balancing." And, always, there is the matter of focusing energies.

CHAKRA DEVELOPMENT EXERCISES

The exercises given here do not take much effort, but their value is increased to the extent that you do any of them regularly, and better yet, that you add to them. In the previous section, we provided you with information about Hindu deities, the Sanskrit names, tarot cards, alchemical factors, etc. You can add to those lists by reference to the books listed at the end of this chapter.

Their value is in adding to and personalizing the information about each chakra for your use in meditation. Of course, the most important of these factors are location and color, and for later use the order of unfoldment. But, depending on your interests, you can add to your meditation with any of the other factors described.

Another point to bear in mind, always, is that the chakras do not function in isolation from one another but are part of a *system* of energy flowing between them and between the etheric chakras and the corresponding astral centers.

First Series

The first series is certainly the easiest, and yet its value is significant. These are adapted from David Pond's excellent book, *Chakras for Beginners.*

Base Chakra

Take a deep breath, and as you exhale, imagine a beam of white light moving from above your Crown chakra down to your Base chakra. Inhale and hold your breath while imagining the white light filling the base of your spine, and that light turning deep red. Exhale while keeping that vision, and then inhale and hold it again while you feel yourself becoming filled with the qualities of energy, strength, courage, and passion for life. Exhale and see the red glow and the qualities dissipate to the world. Repeat a couple of times.

Sacral Chakra

Take a deep breath, and as you exhale, imagine a beam of white light moving from above your Crown chakra down to your Base chakra. Inhale and see the white light rise to fill your sacral area and, as you comfortably hold your breath, see that light turning deep orange. Exhale while keeping that vision and then inhale and hold it again while you feel yourself becoming filled with the qualities of magnetism, sensuality, vitality, vigor, and the ability to attract all you need. Feel yourself alive and alert. Exhale and see the orange glow and the qualities dissipate to the world. Repeat a couple of times.

Solar Plexus Chakra

Take a deep breath, and as you exhale, imagine a beam of white light moving from above your Crown chakra down to your Base chakra. Inhale and see the white light rise to fill your solar plexus area and, as you comfortably hold your breath, see that light turning bright yellow. Exhale while keeping that vision and then inhale and hold it again while you feel yourself becoming filled with the qualities of independence, personal power, clarity, and the ability to assert your personal values. Feel yourself alive and alert. Exhale and see the yellow glow and the qualities dissipate to the world. Repeat a couple of times.

Heart Chakra

Take a deep breath, and as you exhale, imagine a beam of white light moving from above your Crown chakra down to your Base chakra. Inhale and see the white light rise to fill your heart area and, as you comfortably hold your breath, see that light turning a rich sky-blue. Exhale while keeping that vision and then inhale and hold it again while you feel yourself becoming filled with the qualities of awareness and self-worth. Feel yourself alive and alert. Exhale and see the blue glow and the qualities dissipate to the world. Repeat a couple of times.

Throat Chakra

Take a deep breath, and as you exhale, imagine a beam of white light moving from above your Crown chakra down to your Base chakra. Inhale and see the white light rise to fill your throat area and, as you comfortably hold your breath, see that light turning to a bright sky-blue. Exhale while keeping that vision and then inhale and hold it again while you feel yourself becoming filled with the qualities of inspiration, creativity, and the ability to express your personal truth. Feel yourself liberated and self-expressive. Exhale and see the blue glow and the qualities dissipate to the world. Repeat a couple of times.

Brow Chakra

Take a deep breath, and as you exhale, imagine a beam of white light moving from above your Crown chakra down to your Base chakra. Inhale and see the white light rise to fill your brow area and, as you comfortably hold your breath, see that light turning to a bright indigo-blue. Exhale while keeping that vision and then inhale and hold it again while you feel yourself becoming filled with the qualities of clear vision and awareness of both physical and etheric levels around you, and the ability to see from a higher spiritual perspective. Feel yourself more understanding of the world around you. Exhale and see the indigo glow and the qualities dissipate to the world. Repeat a couple of times.

Crown Chakra

Take a deep breath, and as you exhale, imagine a beam of white light moving from above your Crown chakra down to your Base chakra. Inhale and see the white light rise to fill your crown area and, as you comfortably hold your breath, see that light turning to a bright violet. Exhale while keeping that vision and then inhale and hold it again while you feel yourself becoming filled with the qualities of total awareness and oneness with all creation, and the ability to feel the divine presence in all things. Feel yourself to be part of the meaning of life and know you have a role to play in the Great Plan of continuing evolution. Exhale and see the violet glow and the qualities dissipate to the world. Repeat a couple of times.

Second Series

The second series will seem like the easiest of all—at first. It can turn out to be most productive if you make the effort of doing additional research to adapt it to your own interests.

In the section on Chakras we gave you basic information on each chakra, but you can make extensive additions to this using both the references listed at the end of this chapter and the many more books and DVDs that are available.

You should use this information as the foundation for meditations on each chakra to the point of feeling internal awareness of each one. While meditating, you may chant the Bija Mantra using a rather deep guttural voice, leaving the last part of the sound (the last two upper-case letters) to linger in the roof of the mouth and then fade away.

Third Series

This is the "graduate" level of chakra meditation as it should incorporate all you have experienced thus far.

For each chakra, we have provided a simple black and white drawing. Colored Chakra cards are available, but your imagination can provide all the color you need.

Do one chakra meditation daily, starting with the base/earth and progressing through throat/spirit. Yes, just five chakras at first. Ideally you should begin on the first Monday of a month and finish on Friday. Then do not do these meditations on Saturday and Sunday. Continue this pattern for four weeks.

Looking at the table of correspondences for the Base Chakra we gave you earlier (as duplicated here just for this chakra to demonstrate the process) take the information on the element (Earth), the Tattva form (Square), the Tattva color (Yellow), Location (Base of spine), the Bija Mantra (LuNG), and the Psychological attribute (Solidarity).

1. Base Chakra (Muladhara) Correspondences

Alchemical Planet: Saturn

Alchemical Element: Lead

Tattva: Prithivi (Earth)

Animal: Bull, elephant, ox

Basic Drive: Security

Tattva color: **Yellow**

Body Function: Elimination

Chakra Color: Red

Tattva Form: **Square**

Element: **Earth**

Gemstone: Ruby, garnet, lodestone

Tattva Sense: Smell

Gland: Ovaries, Testicles

Goddess-form, Hindu: Dakini (Security)

God-form, Egyptian: Geb

God-form, Hindu: Bela Brahma (Child God)

God-form, Greek: Gaia, Demeter

Incense: Cedar

Location: **Base of spine**

Order of Chakra Unfoldment: 1st

Yogic Planet: Saturn

Part of Body: Between anus and genitals

Psychological Attribute: **Solidarity**

Bija Mantra: **LuNG**, LuM (3)

Psychic Power: Pain control, psychometry, dowsing, telekinesis

Sense: Smell

Spinal Joint: 1st, 2nd, 3rd

Spinal Location: 4th Sacral

Tarot Key: XXI, World

Tree of Life Sephiroth: Malkuth

Yantra (internal): Blue Square

Tarot Suit: Pentacles

 yellow

Settled into meditation, imagine the form (Square), make it become the color (Yellow), feel its location (Base of Spine) and its psychological attribute (Solidarity), and hold the vision and feelings while chanting aloud the Bija mantra (LuNG) in a deep guttural voice that starts back in your throat, moves forward along the roof of your mouth, and then projects outward to the universe.

Continue the meditation for five to fifteen minutes, continuing to chant.

The next day repeat the procedure for No. 2 Sacral Chakra, and then on through No. 5, to finish on a Friday.

The next month, starting again on a Monday—unless you can devote four weekends in a row to the exercise—first work with No. 6 Brow Chakra and then on the second day work with No. 7, the Crown Chakra, with one variation from the established process. Instead of visualizing the whole form in one color, try to imagine the rose with a dense center of white and gold, surrounded by a wreath of petals vibrant with ever-changing chromatic effects.

After you have mastered the entire process, find time to go through all seven chakras from Base through Crown in one continuous exercise, feeling each merging upward from one to the next.

There's much more you can do extending this third program of exercises, but it's really beyond the scope of this book. However, what we have been doing is working at the etheric level. Once you have mastered the program, let your awareness expand as you ascend through the chakras and begin to consciously connect with the corresponding astral centers, and then to the mental, and spiritual centers. Once you start this process your intuition (Higher Self) will be your guide.

Remember that it is a consciousness-based process and not a physically based one, although there may be physical effects. It's a lifelong process of growth and psychic development.

KUNDALINI RISING

Earlier we defined Kundalini as a *transforming force* centered in the Base Chakra and operating within the body driving evolution, desire, sex drive, growth, and individual development. More simply put, it is the consciousness driven life force that makes us alive but that *can also make us more alive and may be involved in controlled instant healing in specific application.*

Kundalini, the *Serpent Fire,* is generally imaged as a serpent coiled at the base of the spine until it is "awakened." Then the serpent becomes erect like a cobra ready to attack, and moves up the spine to the crown chakra, energizing each chakra as it proceeds. However, there are two kinds of kundalini movement: (1) kundalini "awakens" and moves during sexual orgasm, other experiences of physical and emotional ecstasy, and even during crowd excitement at sports events, political rallies, and religious evangelism. (2) Kundalini is awakened and rises in a prescribed and directed manner to transform the chakras through which it moves.

Look back at our definition of kundalini as a *transforming force.* We are born with this force coiled at its "home base." **Doesn't that say that *we are born to be transformed?***

Throughout history, people have experienced such transformation, and are known as great healers, yogic and occult masters, mystics, miracle workers, religious prophets, and great spiritual teachers. *Born with the potential for transformation, they realized their potential.* This potential for transformation has been with us from the beginning as intrinsic to the Great Plan of personal growth and development, of *becoming more than you are.*

Many times this transformation occurs in the course of lives devoted to great causes, but it is also known that the rise of the Kundalini force can itself be undertaken as a course of development through various methods of yogic postures and movement, prayer and devotion, meditation and visualization, prolonged shamanic practices, emotional clearing and catharsis, and even of just "letting go" of predetermined concepts so that *Fate happens.*

Since this is a book on Psychic Empowerment, we are looking for ways to change potential to manifest reality by accelerating the natural evolutional unfoldment.

However, it can be said that there is a preferred order of unfoldment from Base Chakra to the Solar Plexus to the Heart Chakra to the Sacral Chakra to the Throat

Chakra to the Brow Chakra to the Crown Chakra. In other words, instead of the standard numbered sequence, it becomes 1-3-4-2-5-6-7.

But, let's not look for *magical formulas* where none may provide the answers we are looking for. There probably has been more myth written about Kundalini Rising than about the stories of Shangri-la, the hidden masters of the universe, and the fountain of youth. We are warned of great dangers if Kundalini is not raised in the right manner, which only your personal guru can determine clairvoyantly. Stories are told of people burned in spontaneous human combustion, of others driven mad or of men turned into sex-driven perverts. And, of course, nearly all these stories are told of men as if women don't have kundalini at all.

In this book we are interested in the development of our innate psychic powers into dependable psychic skills, but the student of Tantric Yoga is warned against developing psychic powers as these are a diversion from the main goal of liberation from this world of manifestation. At best, the Yoga masters see the *siddhis* (the Sanskrit word for perfection and psychic powers) as distractions and even as "temptations" leading the student from the true path. We see them as powers progressively developing to complete the potentials of the Whole Person.

Wikipedia gives a long list of siddhis, *which are also psychic powers or skills*, which we have condensed:

NINE MAIN SIDDHIS

Parkaya Pravesha: One's soul entering into the body of some other person or animal or bird. Through this knowledge even a dead body can be brought to life.

Haadi Vidya: A person feels neither hunger nor thirst, and can remain without eating food or drinking water for several days at a stretch.

Kaadi Vidya: A person is not affected by change of seasons, i.e. by summer, winter, rain, etc. A person shall not feel cold even if he sits in the snow-laden mountains, and shall not feel hot even if he sits in the fire.

Vayu Gaman: A person can become capable of flying in the skies and traveling from one place to another in just a few seconds.

Madalasa Vidya: A person becomes capable of increasing or decreasing the size of his body according to his wish.

Kanakdhara: One can acquire immense and unlimited wealth through this Siddhi.

Prakya Sadhana: Through this a yogic master can direct his disciple to take birth from the womb of a woman who is childless or cannot bear children.

Surya Vigyan: Using it, one substance can be transformed into another through the medium of sun rays.

EIGHT PRIMARY SIDDHIS

Anima: Reducing one's body even to the size of an atom.

Mahima: Expanding one's body to an infinitely large size.

Garima: Becoming infinitely heavy.

Laghima: Becoming almost weightless.

Prāpti: Having unrestricted access to all places.

Prakamya: Realizing whatever one desires.

Istva: Possessing absolute lordship.

Vaśtva: The power to subjugate all.

TEN SECONDARY SIDDHIS

anūarmi-mattvam: Being undisturbed by hunger, thirst, and other bodily disturbances.

dūra-śravaṇa: Hearing things far away.

dūra-darśanam: Seeing things far away.

manaḥ-javah: Moving the body wherever thought goes, i.e. teleportation.

kāma-rūpam: Assuming any form desired.

para-kāya praveśanam: Entering the bodies of others.

sva-chanda mṛtyuh: Dying when one desires.

devānām saha krīḍā anudarśanam: Witnessing and participating in the pastimes of beautiful supernatural women.

yathā saṅkalpa saṁsiddhiḥ: Perfect accomplishment of one's determination.

ājñā apratihatā gatiḥ: Orders or commands being unimpeded.

FIVE SIDDHIS OF YOGA AND MEDITATION

tri-kāla-jñatvam: Knowing the past, present and future.

advandvam: Tolerance of heat, cold, and other dualities.

para citta ādi abhijñatā: Knowing the minds of others.

agni arka ambu viṣa ādīnām pratiṣṭambhaḥ: Checking the influence of fire, sun, water, poison, and so on.

aparājayah: Remaining unconquered by others.

All these siddhis can be developed through various programs of postures, movements, and meditation, but they also appear spontaneously in the course of spiritual development and can be attained in a deliberate program of meditation. For readers wishing to explore this further, we recommend Swami Satyananda Saraswati's *Kundalini Tantra.*

Kundalini is the life force everywhere present in not only all the chakras, but everywhere in the physical body, the etheric double, the astral and mental bodies, and everywhere there is life. It rises of its own accord from the base chakra, and in and through other chakras during times of excitement, exhilaration, and ecstasy, and also during meditation, artistic expression, creativity, scientific exploration, deep prayer, absorption in beautiful music, scenery, and even the excitement of a thunderstorm.

You may wish to devote your life to a program of kundalini Yoga, but if you instead choose to live fully and continue your growth to becoming a Whole Person, Kundalini will be there to help energize your path. Set your goals high enough, and Kundalini will follow and process your transformation in the natural course of your life.

SOURCES AND RECOMMENDED READING

Cyndi Dale, *The Subtle Body: An Encyclopedia of Your Energetic Anatomy* (Sounds True, 2009).

Douglas De Long, *Ancient Teachings for Beginners* (Llewellyn, 2000).

John Greer, *Encyclopedia of the Occult* (Llewellyn, 2003).

David Hulse, *The Eastern Mysteries* (Llewellyn, 1993).

Anodea Judith, *Wheels of Life: A User's Guide to the Chakra System* (Llewellyn, 1987).

Jonn Mumford, *A Chakra & Kundalini Workbook* (Llewellyn, 1994, 1997).

Genevieve Lewis Paulson, *Kundalini and the Chakras* (Llewellyn, 1991).

David Pond, *Chakras for Beginners* (Llewellyn, 1999).

A. E. Powell, *The Etheric Double* (Theosophical, 1925).

Israel Regardie, edited by Chic and Sandra Tabatha Cicero, *The Middle Pillar: The Balance Between Mind and Magic* (Llewellyn, 1998).

Swami Satyananda Saraswati, *Kundalini Tantra* (Bihar School of Yoga, 1985).

Benjamin Walker, *The Hindu World* (Praeger, 1968).

Bill Whitcomb, *The Magician's Companion: A Practical Guide & Encyclopedic Guide to Magical & Religious Symbolism* (Llewellyn, 1993).

5

CLAIRVOYANCE
Seeing Beyond Your Nose

Because it was declared beautiful, beautiful it was, and beautiful it is now.

—BRIAN BENTLEY

Clairvoyance is a psychic technique traditionally defined as the perception of tangible objects, current events, or existing conditions not present to the physical senses, but nevertheless having objective reality. Unlike telepathy, clairvoyance functions independently of another mind, except in instances of collective clairvoyance, in which the clairvoyant faculties of two or more persons are combined to preternaturally perceive existing realities. Unlike sensory perception, clairvoyance requires no stimulation of sensory mechanisms, and is not subject to the limitations of conventional sensory experience.

But, clairvoyance is far more than just the perception of realities not otherwise available to sensory awareness. It includes the attentive organization and practical application of those realities. For instance, the clairvoyant location of a missing animal can include detailed information regarding the animal's physical condition, along with the most effective rescue approach. In the criminal justice setting, psychic clairvoyants have been known to provide crucial investigative information, including the location of missing weapons and physical descriptions of the perpetrators of a crime along with the motives underlying the crime. At another level, clairvoyance can uncover important information relevant to a vast range of life circumstances and strivings, including personal relationships, health conditions, and career decisions.

Clairvoyance is possibly the most intricate and advanced form of ESP, demonstrating the wondrous capacity of the human mind to expand its own field of awareness to encompass limitless realities. It is the *ne plus ultra* of psychic experience. It can bring the earth into panoramic view, and link us to the infinite expanse of the universe. As with the development of all our psychic powers, clairvoyant enhancement enriches our vision of the cosmos to become a vivid and exciting playground for the psychic mind.

The underlying dynamics of clairvoyance are complex and not yet fully understood. They appear to be distinctly unlike those of either telepathy or precognition. In the absence of the influence of another mind, the sources of clairvoyant knowledge must lie within the self or in some external condition or energy source. The bulk of clairvoyant insight probably engages both sources, but we "see through a glass darkly" in our efforts to explain this remarkable and potentially empowering phenomenon.

Through spontaneous clairvoyance, you can acquire information available from no other source. In some instances, it can involve matters of life-and-death significance. For instance, a college instructor discovered through spontaneous clairvoyance the location of her young son who had wandered into the wilderness during a family camping trip. Following an exhaustive search as darkness fell, the instructor was guided by what seemed to be an unseen force to a bridge that crossed a rushing stream approximately a mile from the camp. As she approached the bridge, a detailed image of the child huddled under the bridge appeared before her. The child was promptly found unharmed, exactly as seen in the clairvoyant image.

Clairvoyance can also be deliberately initiated, but whether spontaneous or deliberately induced, it is almost always purpose driven. It can target a particular happening and provide critical information regarding surrounding circumstances. For instance, the parents of an Air Force pilot stationed in the Pacific were awakened in the night by a loud sound not unlike that of a jet plane exploding in mid-air. Sleepless for the remainder of the night, they experienced together the comforting presence of their son. Upon later being notified of their son's death in a collision with another Air Force jet over the Pacific, they again experienced his presence. The clairvoyant experience at the time of the crash seemed specifically designed to prepare them for the loss of their son.

Even animals have been known to experience clairvoyance. In the above instance, the Air Force pilot's dog companion that had been left behind in the care of his parents reacted with fright at the exploding sound, though none of the neighborhood residents reported hearing the noise. The dog remained restless throughout the night and the following day.

Like dogs, cat companions have also been known to experience clairvoyance, which can involve emergency situations. In a rather remarkable instance of apparent clairvoyant insight, a cat led a child's mother to an underground storm pit where the child and a playmate had become accidentally locked inside on a hot summer afternoon. The cat, a longtime family household pet called Sailor, first commanded the mother's attention by repeatedly clawing at a door leading to the outside. Once outside, he led her directly to the storm pit. The pit, with limited air circulation, could have posed serious danger for anyone trapped inside.

The deliberate induction of clairvoyance through specialized tools includes dowsing, crystal gazing, automatic writing, the pendulum, and the pyramid, to mention but a few. The fact that tangible objects are often instrumental in initiating clairvoyance suggests that it may not be altogether self-contained. Beyond simply providing the point of focus often considered critical to many psychic functions, some tangible objects seem to provide the conditions for mental interactions that extend beyond inner processes alone. The mind becomes engaged in a complex exchange, which can generate profound psychic insight.

In a remarkable example of dowsing as a clairvoyant technique, a skilled dowser used metal rods to identify the exact location of a mercury-contaminated stream flowing under a northern Alabama town. Upon discovering the noxious stream through dowsing, the ninety-two-year-old dowser with a long history of successful dowsing drove a metal stake into the ground and then expertly tapped upon it with a hammer to relocate the stream. Follow-up tests revealed the effectiveness of his procedures. The use of tools and techniques designed to induce clairvoyance is further discussed in a later chapter.

Specific clairvoyant data is often accessed through the deliberate use of related physical objects. Psychometry is the clairvoyant application of relevant objects to gain highly specific psychic information. A clairvoyant, for instance, located a teen runaway through information gained by holding the teen's bracelet. Psychometry also includes the clairvoyant use of nonpersonal but relevant aids to locate missing articles. A psychometry study group used a map of a shopping mall to locate a lost ring. A floor plan provided the framework required by another study group to locate a valuable antique brooch. The combined impressions of the group pinpointed the brooch's exact location: inside an old baby shoe stored in the bottom drawer of a bedroom chest.

Occasionally, the object spontaneously invokes the clairvoyant faculty, and functions as the essential channel for the clairvoyant message. A mother, whose son was injured in a random, late-night shooting in a distant city, awakened at the exact hour of the shooting to the sound of a sports trophy crashing to the floor in her son's vacant bedroom. She immediately sensed danger involving her son. In another instance, a student, distraught over the death of her grandmother, reported a dream in which her grandmother appeared with a yellow rose and the message, "This rose is especially for you. I send it with happiness and love." A few days later, she received a beautiful yellow rose from her grandmother's sister with the message, "This rose is especially for you. I send it with happiness and love." Although the dream experience could be interpreted as precognitive, the student saw it as a clear clairvoyant manifestation of her grandmother's successful transition, which was confirmed by the gift of the yellow rose.

INNER-CLAIRVOYANCE

Whether spontaneous or deliberately activated, clairvoyance is always purposeful and empowerment driven. When focused outward, clairvoyance can reveal important physical realities not otherwise available to conscious awareness. When focused inward, clairvoyance can reveal important nonphysical realities that are also hidden from conscious awareness. It can discover psychological growth blockages and reveal ways of dissolving them. It can target subconscious conflicts and repressions and alleviate the anxiety generated by them. Inner-clairvoyance is, in fact, among the self's most powerful therapeutic techniques. We now know that the best therapist, like the best psychic, exists within the developing self. Inner-clairvoyance is among that therapist's most effective tools. Major therapeutic breakthroughs are almost always inner-clairvoyantly driven.

Inner-clairvoyance can access the vast subconscious storehouse of past experience, including that of distant past-life origin. In that role, clairvoyance remains, by definition, the perception of distant realities not otherwise available to sensory awareness. Furthermore, it includes, as with other forms of clairvoyance, the attentive organization and practical application of those realities. Given past-life enlightenment through inner-clairvoyance, you can awaken past-life memories and energize them with empowerment possibilities. Through inner-clairvoyance, past-life baggage becomes a present-life growth resource.

CLAIRVOYANCE AND THE SPIRIT REALM

Complementing inner-clairvoyance as a source of personal insight and power are our clairvoyant interactions with the spirit realm. Rather than a distant, inaccessible dimension, the spirit realm is a present, though nonphysical, reality not typically available to sensory awareness. It does, however, often manifest its presence through sensory channels. Examples include sensory perceptions of both sights and sounds that can announce a spirit presence. Often collectively perceived by two or more persons, sensory manifestations of spiritual realities offer convincing evidence of the existence of the afterlife realm. When we add to these the extrasensory clairvoyant interactions, whether experienced inwardly or turned outward to embrace the spirit realm, our existence as endless souls is clearly confirmed.

At a deeply personal level, clairvoyant interactions with the spirit realm can provide important spiritual insight, including increased awareness of personal spirit guides and growth specialists. Through clairvoyance as a spiritual phenomenon, you can interact with them as sources of knowledge and power. They can provide guidance in clarifying your personal goals and promoting your success in achieving them.

As a spiritual phenomenon, clairvoyance can become our best source of attunement and balance, both of which are critical to our spiritual growth and fulfillment.

CLAIRVOYANCE AND DREAMS

Frequently, the dream experience provides the channel for clairvoyant knowledge. Clairvoyant insight, like precognitive awareness, often seems to reside in the subconscious. Dream mechanisms logically could promote a subconscious transfer of information to conscious awareness. Common among the dream's clairvoyant functions is the delivery of information concerning urgent situations. A building contractor's dream, for instance, identified a critical error in the blueprints of a building under construction. An attorney's dream identified the exact location of an important legal document that had been lost. Unexplained synchronicity is sometimes observed in clairvoyant dreams, particularly among individuals who are closely associated or related. Two brothers, eighteen and twenty-one years of age, reported simultaneously dreaming of their parents' involvement in a serious train accident. Their dreams, according to their report, vividly detailed the accident at the exact time of the event.

The clairvoyant dream will often provide clues concerning its psychic significance. Among frequently reported clues are the immediate awakening of the sleeping subject upon conclusion of the dream, the vivid physical sensations accompanying the dream experience, and the convincing, often urgent nature of the dream. The clairvoyant dream can generate a strong motivational state to either act upon the dream or to investigate its psychic significance.

Clairvoyant dreams, like precognitive dreams, have been known to occur in a series that guides the dreamer, often symbolically, and monitors the dreamer's progress. This form of clairvoyant dreaming is usually characterized by a central theme and a succession of related events. Transitional life situations and personal crises tend to precipitate the serial clairvoyant dream. Its goal is empowerment through personal insight. Once recognized and understood, such dreams can provide important therapeutic support and guide the growth or recovery process. This was illustrated by a college student who was undergoing therapy to resolve the trauma of sexual abuse during childhood. His series of clairvoyant dreams provided a weathervane of his progress from social withdrawal to rewarding interpersonal relationships. The dreams further provided the essential support required for overcoming the painful trauma. The serial clairvoyant dream is yet another manifestation of the skilled therapist existing within each of us. Our inner-therapist, like our inner-teacher, probes our world of experience with persistence and a singular purpose: the full empowerment of the self.

CLAIRVOYANT STRATEGIES

The clairvoyant faculty frequently engages our most advanced mental faculties, including our creative imagery powers. These powers can translate clairvoyant impressions into images that depict meaningful realities. Not surprisingly then, exercises designed to develop clairvoyant skills are usually more effective when they emphasize activities that promote creative imagery, such as sculpting, drawing, painting, and other forms of creative work or play.

Meditation exercises that focus on creative imagery seem particularly conducive to clairvoyant empowerment. The third eye, a chakra thought to be connected to the pituitary gland and associated with clairvoyance, appears particularly responsive to meditation strategies that engage the mind's imagery powers. The following exercise was specifically designed to develop that faculty.

THIRD EYE EXERCISE

Step 1. Induce a relaxed state using such techniques as body scan, relaxing imagery, and slowed breathing.

Step 2. With eyes closed, envision a smooth, glasslike plane void of disruptive structures.

Step 3. Imagine a myriad of glowing, geometric structures—spheres, obelisks, cubes, pyramids—as they rise above the plane.

Step 4. Focus on the structures and allow images to emerge as if projected on their surfaces.

Step 5. From among the various images, select a particularly relevant one and allow a progressive, spontaneous unfolding of new images.

Step 6. Mentally create a dominant structure to function as a clairvoyant screen, and project upon it the critical elements of a current situation for which additional information is sought. Allow new information to unfold on the screen as clairvoyant images.

Step 7. Conclude the exercise with positive affirmations of clairvoyant empowerment.

This exercise has demonstrated particular usefulness in locating missing items, as illustrated by a college student who used the procedure to find a lost sorority pin. During Step 6 of the exercise, she erected a mental pyramid on the plane and projected an image of the pin on its surface. Almost instantly, the pin became surrounded by images that revealed its exact location: inside a candy tin stored in a desk. In a more dramatic application, a twin, who was separated from her sister in childhood, projected the image of her sister on a sphere she had mentally erected on the plane. A map of Canada first appeared on the sphere, then a close-up of British Columbia, and finally a close-up of Vancouver. She eventually reunited with her sister, who had been living in Vancouver for more than twenty years.

Certain strategies for inducing the precognitive dream can be readily adapted to accommodate clairvoyant dreaming. The finger-spread procedure can be applied to delay sleep while clairvoyant autosuggestions are presented. Affirmations such as those that follow are usually sufficient to promote clairvoyant dreaming.

My clairvoyant powers will be activated as I sleep.

My inner psychic powers will generate the insight I need as I sleep.

These general affirmations can be supplemented with specific statements to access solutions and detailed clairvoyant information.

Clairvoyance, like other forms of ESP, improves with practice. Practice in meditation designed to enhance the mind's creative capacities is particularly valuable, because it builds the basic skills underlying not only clairvoyance, but many other psychic faculties as well. Our surroundings also provide practice opportunities for developing clairvoyant skills. Effective activities involve familiar materials and everyday situations. Excellent practice exercises include guessing the time before checking, pulling a book from a shelf and guessing its total number of pages, and guessing the amount of change in your pocket or purse. With practice, these simple activities can strengthen clairvoyant skills and the capacity to initiate clairvoyance at will.

Occasionally clairvoyant data are revealed rather amusingly in reverse or other disguised form. In one instance of clairvoyant reversal, the 382 total pages of a book were clairvoyantly discerned as 283 pages. In a group practice session, the name "Peru," written on a concealed card, was clairvoyantly perceived by the group as "Urep," clearly a psychic impression in reverse form, but mistakenly interpreted as signifying Europe.

SUMMARY

Clairvoyance is our claim to oneness with the world in the here and now. Expanded awareness through clairvoyance empowers us with an unlimited width, breadth, and depth of knowledge, which reveals what we otherwise cannot see, as it enriches our lives with new ideas and creative solutions. Equally important as these profound revelations are the simple joys of the clairvoyant experience itself, such as that felt in the discovery of a lost possession or the sudden "Ah ha!" of clairvoyant insight.

Whatever the nature of its expression, clairvoyance is empowerment in highly practical form: It can provide the critical information we need to solve our most pressing problems and achieve our loftiest goals. Clairvoyance is so basic to the empowered life that, without it, we often grope in darkness, out of touch with critical sources of psychic enlightenment.

SOURCES AND RECOMMENDED READING

Cyndi Dale, *Everyday Clairvoyant* (Llewellyn, 2010).

Debra Lynne Katz, *Extraordinary Psychic: Proven Techniques to Master Your Natural Psychic Abilities* (Llewellyn, 2008).

Debra Lynne Katz, *You Are Psychic* (Llewellyn, 2004).

6

REMOTE VIEWING
*Psychic Research or "Voodoo Warfare"**

Remote Viewing is the purported ability to gather information about a distant or unseen target by means of extra-sensory perception. Typically a remote viewer is expected to give information about an object that is hidden from physical view and separated at some distance. The term was introduced by physicists turned parapsychologists, Russell Targ and Harold Puthoff in 1974.

REMOTE VIEWING AND THE COLD WAR

The modern history of Remote Viewing started during the Cold War between the Soviet Union and the Western Allies that existed from the end of World War II in 1945 to the collapse of the Soviet Union in 1991.

While there was never a direct military confrontation between the two sides, there was constant competition through military and economic aid to various satellite states associated with each side, conventional force deployments facing each other, various proxy wars, espionage, the nuclear arms race, sometimes outrageous propaganda, and then such indirect competition as technological competition and the Space Race.

The Cold War was in reality a "War of Ideas." And the American intelligence agency, the CIA, funded many projects to counter the Communist appeal among the intellectuals in Europe and the developing world. The Soviets were more centered on technological competition and were the first to develop long-range intercontinental ballistic missiles (August 1957) capable of reaching the continental United States. In October of the same year, they launched the first Earth satellite, Sputnik, inaugurating the Space Race that culminated in the Apollo moon landings, which astronaut Frank Borman

---

* A phrase used by columnist Jack Anderson's associate, Ron McRae, quoted in *Psychic Powers.*

later described as "just a battle in the Cold War" with superior spaceflight rockets indicating superior ICBMs.

Since there was no openness between the two sides, separated not merely by the Iron Curtain but by ideology taking on a nearly religious bellicosity, there was a constant flow of rumor and deceit, conspiratorial allegations, false news stories, and mutual paranoia that latched on to every kind of mystery—UFOs and Aliens, Crop Circles and Weird Weather, stories of Abominable Snowmen and Bigfoot, Pyramid Energies and Psychic Healing—to variously insinuate the superiority of the two conflicting political systems.

Many articles were published and conferences organized under the pretense of stimulating the intellectual communities while hiding the actual psychic research being carried on mostly in Russia and the United States.

In 1952, the CIA was already calling for government sponsored psychic research, but in 1960 the psychic arms race heated when it was reported that the United States was successfully conducting telepathy exchanges between a man at a Duke University laboratory and a man submerged at sea aboard the nuclear-power submarine, *Nautilus*. This led to the Soviet approval of a special study of telepathy at the Russian University of Leningrad.

Then, in the mid-1960s, freelance journalists Sheila Ostrander and Lynn Schroeder (*Psychic Discoveries Behind the Iron Curtain*) reported increasing evidence of Soviet psychic research and claimed that the United States was "fifty years behind the Russians in psychic research," setting off the US response through funding of psychic research at Stanford in a program called "Scanate."

In 1972, physicist Harold Puthoff tested psychic Ingo Swann's remote viewing ability at Stanford Research Institute (SRI), and the experiment quickly resulted in a visit from two employees of the CIA's Directorate of Science and Technology, leading to a $50,000 CIA-sponsored project. The initial CIA-funded project was later renewed and expanded. A number of CIA officials—including John McMahon, then the head of the Office of Technical Service and later the Agency's deputy director—became strong supporters of the program.

In a 1974 program, Harold Puthoff and Dr. Bonnar Cox of the Stanford Research Institute in Menlo Park, California were to drive aimlessly about for thirty minutes and then were to stop at a spontaneous, unplanned destination. A man in an electrically shielded room in SRI's engineering sciences building would then describe the scene where the two had stopped.

The man, Pat Price, a retired police commissioner of Burbank, California, even before the thirty minutes was up, proceeded for twenty minutes to tell physicist Russell Targ about the scenes he was seeing while Puthoff and Cox were still driving, and then predicted where they would stop and accurately described that scene. Targ and Puthoff continued their remote viewing experiments with Pat Price and psychic Ingo Swann for ten more years at SRI with similar positive results.

In addition to their mainstream scientific research on quantum mechanics and laser physics, Russell Targ and Hal Puthoff initiated several studies of the paranormal with funding from the Parapsychology Foundation and the Institute of Noetic Sciences.

When the CIA dropped its sponsorship, it was picked up by the Air Force, and then in 1979 the Army's Intelligence and Security Command was ordered to develop its own program. First it evaluated research in the Soviet Union and China, and concluded that their programs were better funded and supported than US research.

Next, Stanford continued its research in remote viewing, with the famous result of Pat Price's description of a big crane at a Soviet nuclear research facility, followed by a description of a new class of a strategic submarine and the location of a downed Soviet bomber in Africa.

One problem encountered in this research was the seeming unreliability. One day, the viewer's abilities would be "on," but another day they would be "off." At SRI, Ingo Swann and Hal Puthoff developed a remote-viewing training program meant to enable any individual with a suitable background to produce useful data. A number of military officers and civilians were trained and formed a military remote-viewing unit based at Fort Meade, Maryland.

At its peak, the Stargate Project was a twenty-million-dollar program before it was terminated in 1995.

In December 1980, Lt. Col. John B. Alexander, writing in *Military Review*, the professional journal of the United States Army, stated that "there are weapons systems that operate on the power of the mind and whose lethal capacity has already been demonstrated." In the same article, he further discussed "the ability to transmit disease over distance and said that illness or death had been successfully induced in lower organisms such as flies and frogs." (*Psychic Powers*, 1987.)

In response to this article, nationally syndicated columnist Jack Anderson reported that the United States was using psychics "to spy on the Soviets by projecting their minds outside their bodies" and that "the CIA was considering deploying 'psychic shields' to protect American secrets from the Soviets." Ron McRae, Anderson's associate, ridiculed this as "Voodoo Warfare."

Currently, we can only speculate about military involvement in any form of psychic research in the United States or in other countries. With the rise of the Fundamentalist Far Right, it is doubtful that any Republican and perhaps many Democrat politicians are going to endorse and support "the Occult" in any form, whether as the science of parapsychology or as the natural psychic power of any healthy person.

ASTRAL PROJECTION OR CLAIRVOYANCE

As paranormal researchers, we are confronted by the apparent fact that remote viewing is not, itself, a natural psychic power. But neither are we able to determine exactly what it is.

The natural powers closest to the phenomena of the remote viewing experience are astral projection and clairvoyance. Whether it is one or the other, or both, seems to be a matter of choice by the viewer, or even as may be activated by the techniques of its employment.

In reports over the years where remote viewing has occurred, it has been associated with magical and shamanic rituals seemingly involving astral projection, and also with cases involving hypnosis or self-hypnosis and meditation seemingly suggestive of clairvoyance.

Dr. Slate's work with students at Athens State University validates the either/or conclusion as perfectly viable.

The studies include controlled lab research as well as informal classroom instructional exercises. Some of the studies were case studies of students who seemed to have mastered remote viewing. One student, in particular, believed that she traveled out of body accompanied by her personal spirit guide named Jeremy. She believed that her guide was a past-life mentor who led her out of Germany and to safety during World War II.

Another student, also highly proficient in remote viewing, believed it was a function of the third eye. She activated that function by simply relaxing and touching her forehead, and maintaining the touch for the duration of remote viewing.

Both students, participating in controlled situations involving the viewing of an oil painting in another campus building, were successful in identifying its three essential elements.

Students enrolled in Experimental Parapsychology varied in their remote viewing skills, depending on the programs used. Among the most effective was a progressive relaxation program with included suggestions of a "subconscious" link to other selected realities. Using that approach, a location is selected and visualized. Detailed mental images are then allowed to appear.

In one remarkable example, fourteen out of thirty-two college students enrolled successfully identified an animal (a frog) concealed in a box at a biology laboratory located in another campus building. Upon their arrival out-of-body at the designated site, the yellow box was located by fourteen students, but viewing its concealed contents required another phenomenon: clairvoyance, which was experienced by only eight of the fourteen successful students. It must be noted that three of the fourteen successful students reportedly identified the frog in the box through the sound it made.

It is Dr. Slate's opinion that remote viewing can involve clairvoyance, out-of-body travel, or combinations of both. Some of his most successful research subjects first entered the out-of-body state, and while in that state viewed the distant reality but did not travel to it. In that state, they gave highly detailed and accurate information of a distant reality. Other students felt they entered a spiritually liberated state in which they had access to new information as needed—the information came typically in imagery form. Yet other subjects explained the experience as a manifestation of self-contained higher mental functions that exist to some degree in everyone. These findings and views reaffirm the concept that any phenomenon (like any act of behavior) can have multiple explanations; furthermore, the more complex the phenomenon, the more varied the explanations.

METHODS FOR REMOTE VIEWING

Preparation:

For any method of self-induced remote viewing, preparation is necessary. Simply arrange for a period of one hour or more of uninterrupted time in a comfortable room where you will not be disturbed by noise, people, and phone calls. Keep the body comfortably warm. Adopt a position most conducive to physical relaxation. A recliner is recommended.

Practice any form of relaxation that has proven effective for you in the past. The essential elements of a relaxation program include:

- A posture or position that you will be comfortable in for an hour or more.

- A light covering providing sufficient warmth for the inactive body.

- Breathing that is slow and regular, proceeding from a series of deep breaths to the resumption of a natural rhythm.

- Deliberate relaxation of the body. This may effectively include progressive relaxation from feet to head, or it may involve "tensing and relaxing" muscle groups progressing from left foot up to groin, and then right foot up to groin, then the groin and abdominal areas, up through stomach and chest, then the left hand up to the shoulder followed by the right hand up to the shoulder, and then particular attention on the shoulders themselves, the neck, and the facial and back of the skull muscles.

- As desired, this can be followed by self-hypnosis procedures leading toward either astral projection or clairvoyance.

- In any case, let the procedure end in either natural sleep or a deliberate "return" of progressive awakening, comfortable stretching, and a few moments to record your experience.

ASTRAL PROJECTION PROGRAM

There are numerous programs for astral projection induction, including those in Chapter Two. One method well suited for work with Remote Viewing was developed by Ophiel, an early writer in this field, in his classic *The Art & Practice of Astral Projection*.

Here the idea is to pick an area in the home that you can study in detail in order to visualize it likewise in complete detail. An ideal situation would involve a hallway from your bedroom or practice area that leads to another room. Once you have mastered the detail and can duplicate it in your visualization, make it your intention to do so in your astral body. Whether with the physical body asleep or totally relaxed in a semi-trance, feel yourself in your astral body moving along the hallway and into the target room, all the while noting each of the details you previously studied.

The preliminary work is exceedingly important, and attention to the details will get you used to the feeling of consciousness outside of the physical body, *but* with the same intensity of focus that is possible with your physical senses. We refer to Sight, Smell, Taste, Hearing, and Touch as *physical* senses, but they are actually *etheric* (see Chapter Two) senses using physical organs.

Another way to understand this is to remember that sensation is an energy phenomenon involving energy pulsing at different vibratory rates ranging from the slowest at physical touch to the highest with physical sight, with hearing, taste and smell in between.

Ophiel's basic method was to combine actual physical sensations with visualized images of himself moving along a specific route with stops at six stations along the route where he had placed particular objects or painted symbols, some distinctive odors (herb, essential oil, perfume), perhaps different colored lamps and maybe bells, each with a distinctive sound. He didn't include foods in the program.

The procedure is to walk the route, carefully noting everything about it, especially the sides and not just what lies before you—see the color and feel the carpet (you could intensify the experience barefoot), shades and patterns (and even feel) of wallpaper, furniture (recalling any memories associated with an heirloom chair, for example), doors, etc. and then stopping at each station to pick up and examine each of the six objects or symbols, smell each of the different odors, note the different colored lamps, note the sounds of the bells when they are struck, and so on. Note your feelings about any permanent feature of the route, such as that family heirloom chair, an unusual picture on the wall, and so on.

The point is to completely familiarize yourself with every detail of the route, especially those singular items at the six stations.

Don't gloss over the details, but initially spend at least fifteen minutes at each station memorizing every sensation—touch, color, sound, and smell—and reliving every memory and feeling involving furniture and pictures along the route. Then go back over the route in your imagination and again note every detail.

No, that's not the end. With the imagined details fresh in your memory, physically go back over the route and carefully note what you missed and add it to your remembered imagery. Then reverse the route and do the same thing backwards. Repeat the complete procedure—forward and then backward—several times until you make no mistakes.

It's tedious but important. When you succeed in it, you will never regret this intense training program.

After several days of this walking memorization, go to bed and then imagine rising up in your visualized body, slowly walking the same route and repeating your examination of all those details, and returning and lowering your visualized image back in your bed. Go to sleep.

What you are doing is learning to travel in consciousness. Don't concern yourself with the concept of "bodies" at this point.

Every night, repeat your visualized trip, and every morning check your memory against the actual physical details. Note every failure and correct it. The Astral World is the world of fantasy, and you are learning to separate the real from the unreal, as Theosophists teach. Your control over the imagined image will give you control over astral imagery in contrast to fantasy.

You can embellish your training if you have dreams of physical details in your home, and then correct those dream details against the real thing.

Now, if possible, move on to greater challenges by laying out an outdoor route with all its natural distractions, and learn to make your visualized trip ignoring distractions—whether fantasized or actually experienced in the astral dimension. Later, learn to pay attention to those distractions but without emotional response.

Even within your home, you can practice with more variety by extending your nightly visualized trip into rooms you are familiar with but where you have not intensely studied the details as in your first work. Learn to navigate around unexpected obstructions, such as a chair that has been moved from its proper place. Note details in your visualized trip such as magazines or books, unopened mail, children's toys, unwashed dishes, etc., and then check them against reality the next morning.

Astral projection and remote viewing are similar in that they both provide information concerning spatially distant realities. They are different, however, in that astral projection, unlike clairvoyant remote viewing, incorporates disengagement of the astral body from the physical and usually includes a much wider range of experiences.

Remote viewing by means of astral projection offers much greater opportunity for observing details and being able to move into unexpected places. Try to project to places you plan to visit in the near future—such as a vacation spot, or a business trip to another city. Gather information about the location from books and the Web to give you the means to target and focus on the area, but expect to encounter the unexpected—a road detour, a new building, a street fair, store window displays—go to museums or viewing sites, and other variations that will interest you.

Record it all in your journal, and then check your astral travel with the actual physical travel, and try to find explanations for any variations. Perhaps that road detour has ended, the street fair is over, new fashions have appeared in the window displays, the museum has rotated its showing, and weather events have changed the scenes from the viewing platform. Like President Reagan, *Trust but Verify.* Trust your vision, but verify with real observation.

While your remote viewing skills may never be employed in spying on foreign military sites, learn to consider verification a significant part of your learning process whenever it's possible to do so.

CLAIRVOYANCE PROGRAM

Repeat the preparation program of relaxation, and then refer to the chapter on Chakras and repeat the third series exercise for the Brow Chakra. Keeping your physical eyes closed, visualize the image of the Winged Globe firmly in your mind's eye, reach up and touch your brow with your index and middle fingers at that point above and between your eyes where the "Third Eye" is located, and feel that your inner vision is now open.

Keeping your joined two fingers in contact with the Third Eye, visualize anything that links you to the location desired. Calmly let images appear in your vision.

Either of the above procedures could be used with voice guidance or hypnosis with a second person.

PROGRAMMING FOR REMOTE VISION

Before you proceed with either astral projection or clairvoyance techniques, determine your goal—the location for your remote vision using whatever knowledge you can bring together. That may be as little as the name of a person residing there, the longitude and latitude, the physical address, a photograph or an image, etc., along with an approximation of what you anticipate seeing there.

In other words, if you think of yourself as a "psychic spy" for the military, what is it that you are looking for at that site? If you were there physically, what would you do, what would you want to discover, what information do you want to bring back from your trip?

What are your goals? You could be checking on the health of a relative. You might be visiting the site of a future sales call. You may want to check out a vacation destination. You may be viewing the road ahead for a driving trip.

The better your preparation, the more likely your success.

SOURCES AND RECOMMENDED READING

Ophiel, *The Art & Practice of Astral Projection* (Weiser, 1974).

Sheila Ostrander and Lynn Schroeder, *Psychic Discoveries Behind the Iron Curtain* (Random House, 1971).

Joe H. Slate, *Astral Projection and Psychic Empowerment* (Llewellyn, 1997).

Joe H. Slate, *Beyond Reincarnation: Experience Your Past Lives & Lives Between Lives* (Llewellyn, 2005).

Joe H. Slate, *Psychic Phenomena: New Principles, Techniques and Applications* (McFarland, 1988).

Psychic Powers, "Mysteries of the Unknown" series, (Time-Life, 1987).

7

DREAM INTERPRETATION & INTERVENTION

*Dreams can promote enlightenment and activate a host of inner
resources, including our psychic faculties.
Becoming psychically empowered depends largely on a clear
understanding of the capacity of dreams to enrich our
lives mentally, physically, and spiritually.*

—JOE H. SLATE, *PSYCHIC EMPOWERMENT FOR EVERYONE*

DREAMS ARE ALWAYS PURPOSEFUL AND EMPOWERMENT DRIVEN

They are, however, often cloaked in symbolism or other forms of disguise, thus challenging us to discover their meanings and apply them. Paradoxically, the absence of transparency in the meanings of dreams actually increases the dream's empowerment potential. We, by nature, tend to place higher value on new knowledge that requires greater effort and involvement. Knowledge, if too easily acquired, is often cast aside as either irrelevant or unworthy of serious consideration.

Although dreams have captured the interest of cultures over the centuries, only in recent years have we developed effective dream empowerment programs that connect us to the enormous wealth of resources existing in the subconscious. Because of advances in our understanding of dreams as expressions of the subconscious, a new dream technology is clearly emerging—its beneficiaries will be everyone who invests in the liberating and empowering possibilities of dreams.

THE NATURE OF DREAMS

We now know that the very essence of our existence is often reflected in our dreams. Our understanding of the dream experience thus becomes a critical component of our personal development and empowerment. As Shakespeare noted, "We are the stuff as dreams are made on, and our little life is rounded with a sleep!" The typical dream experience is energized by not only our subconscious motives but new growth possibilities as well. By accurately interpreting our dreams, we can increase awareness of our subconscious resources and activate totally new growth processes. Self-enlightenment and self-empowerment thus become the twofold goal of dream interpretation.

Because everyone dreams, there exists in each of us a valuable spontaneous process that requires no training or skill. Benefiting optimally from that process, however, does require skill, including the ability to not only interpret the dream but in some instances, actually initiate new dream experiences that target specially designated goals. As we'll see later in this chapter, advanced dream intervention programs have been developed in the laboratory setting and are now available for use by everyone in meeting such goals as solving personal problems, accelerating learning, overcoming growth blockages, improving memory, slowing aging, increasing creativity, activating out-of-body travel, and generating interactions with the spirit realm, to list but a few.

Even in the absence of dream intervention efforts, dreams often spontaneously activate totally new growth potentials that enable us to achieve otherwise unattainable goals. It's as though the subconscious mind often senses our needs and purposefully uses the dream experience to fulfill them. That possibility, however, requires attentiveness to the dream and receptivity to its message, a twofold process illustrated by an art student who experienced what she called "creative blockage" in her ability to generate creative ideas for her paintings. Following a lengthy interval of frustrating blockage, she experienced a colorful dream in which she viewed an exhibition of her paintings that consisted of totally new creations. Upon awakening, the paintings remained vividly detailed in her mind. She went to work at once to create the paintings that, when later entered in an exhibit, received excellent reviews by art critics. The breakthrough dream experience, by her report, proved to be "a turning point" that unleashed totally new artistic potential.

Further reflecting the power of spontaneous dreaming are the many accounts of its therapeutic benefits. A college student with profound feelings of inferiority reported a vivid dream experience in which he was awarded a certificate of recognition for his contributions to the college's community services program. The dream experience proved precognitive in nature—a few weeks later at the school's honors and awards event, he received the prestigious award to the enthusiastic applause of students, faculty, and community leaders. The precognitive dream and the recognition it predicted extinguished once and for all the feelings of inferiority that had plagued him since early childhood.

In another instance of the therapeutic benefits of dreaming, a student with an exaggerated fear of water experienced a progressive series of dreams that included first walking along a beach, then wading in water, and finally swimming. Upon later visiting the beach with friends, she experienced for the first time a total absence of fear of water. The dream experience, in her words, "opened a new door of growth and freedom." Through her receptiveness to the series of dreams, she extinguished a fear that had limited her life since childhood.

Inherent in the dream experience are its problem-solving functions. Dreams can spontaneously deliver new insight and stimulate the specific mental functions required for solving complex problems. That function, of course, requires attentiveness to the dream message and reflecting upon it. The problem-solving capacity of dreams was dramatically illustrated by a chemical engineer whose dream revealed the missing component in a new solid-fuel booster rocket being developed for use in space launches. The engineer, who had experimented with a variety of booster rocket fuels in a controlled experimental setting, reportedly omitted a critical ingredient that was detailed in the dream experience. With the addition of that component, he developed an innovative formula that was considered a major achievement in rocket science.

Aside from their problem-solving functions, dreams are often psychic in nature. Almost everyone recalls having a precognitive dream that later came true, or a clairvoyant dream that expanded awareness of an existing situation or condition, often at a distant setting. Aside from these, telepathic dreams in which messages are sent and received between dreamers are not uncommon. The psychic nature of dreaming was dramatically illustrated by a student who observed during dreaming an early-morning multivehicle accident on the street she typically took to her school. The next morning, she took a different route. Upon arriving at school, she was informed of the accident, which occurred exactly as detailed in her dream.

Our discussion of the nature of dreams would be incomplete in the absence of dreams as important sources of past-life knowledge. The past-life regression dream can tap into past-life experiences stored in the subconscious and deliver them to full conscious awareness. Existing within the subconscious is an advanced inner therapist that seems to know what past-life knowledge is important to retrieve and when to retrieve it. Through the dream experience, that therapist within each of us can uncover past-life experiences that are important to us at the moment. Knowledge is power, and therapeutic knowledge of past-life origin is among the highest and most powerful forms of knowledge. While past-life regression through self-hypnosis can retrieve relevant past-life experiences, the dream experience, when at the command of the therapist within, is unsurpassed in its capacity to deliver knowledge with therapeutic potential beyond all limits. It's up to each of us, however, to listen to the messages of that therapist. Once understood, the past-life regression dream can provide the insight required to resolve deep-seated conflicts, phobias, and a variety of other conditions of past-life origin.

The therapeutic power of dreams was pointedly illustrated by a college student who was constantly hounded by her fear of trunks. Adding to the intensity of the fear was its irrational nature. She carefully avoided all situations that might expose her to trunks. Finally, in a highly lucid dream, she experienced becoming entrapped in a trunk in a past life. She had climbed into the trunk as a child when the lid accidentally slammed shut. Awakening immediately from the dream, she knew at last the origin of her fear. Given that knowledge, her fear of trunks, no longer a mystery, soon vanished, a clear example of the therapeutic power of past-life knowledge.

Here are a few other examples that illustrate the empowering possibilities of dreams:

- A student nearing completion of her degree in business administration experienced a series of recurring dreams that suggested a financial crisis involving the company where she worked as a student intern. In each dream, a stream flowed under the company's central office building and emerged on the other side carrying away large sums of money. Finally, she shared the dreams with a company administrator who, upon investigating the company's financial affairs, discovered serious financial mismanagement. The company took corrective action that, according to the administrator, may have saved the company from financial failure.

- In another career-related dream experience, a graduate student nearing completion of her doctorate in psychology experienced a vivid dream of visiting the campus of a distant university. In the dream, which had features suggesting out-of-body travel, she first viewed the campus from overhead and then entered the building that housed the psychology department. In her follow-up of the dream experience, she discovered that a psychology faculty position in psychology had recently become available at the university. She promptly applied for the position and was accepted. In her words, the clairvoyant dream with its possible out-of-body component "opened a door of opportunity at the opportune moment."

- A high school teacher with a long history of anxiety and fear related to trees avoided any contact or association with trees. He was especially fearful when under a tree. It was through a highly vivid dream that he discovered the apparent source of his anxiety. In the dream, which he considered past-life related, he was critically injured when a massive limb fell from the tree under which he was sitting. Armed at last with a rational explanation, he experienced complete liberation from his long history of fear related to trees. By his account, awareness of the source of his distress was alone sufficient to fully extinguish it.

- A couple whose fragile relationship was progressively deteriorating experienced together the same dream: that of holding hands while walking along a familiar nature trail. Although the effect of the so-called *companion dreaming* was itself rewarding, they decided to put into practice what they considered to be "the therapeutic prescription of their dreams"—they initiated daily *companion walks* along the trail. The results were immediate and profound. They are convinced that companion dreaming combined with companion walks both saved and enriched their relationship, yet another example of the therapeutic excellence of the subconscious as manifested through the dream experience.

- A psychologist who sustained a severe head injury that required emergency surgery experienced soon after surgery a two-phase dream, the first being that of a combat situation in which he was under gunfire and surrounded by dangerous explosions in a nighttime setting. In the dream's second phase which had elements suggesting a near-death experience, he viewed at a distance an open door with rays of bright light streaming through it. Beyond the door was a magnificent display of multicolored planes far more beautiful than anything he had ever seen before. Upon approaching the door, he saw slowly appearing in the doorway a glowing figure with arms outstretched, as if to welcome him should he decide to enter. Pausing within steps of the door, he knew that he could either enter the door or he could turn away from it—the choice was his. Then slowly forming in his mind were thoughts of family, friends, and close associates, along with tasks underway and goals yet to be achieved. As these thoughts flooded his mind, the figure at the door gently faded and the door slowly closed, thus ending the dream. Following the experience, his recovery was rapid and complete. He is today a practicing psychologist, parapsychology researcher, and coauthor of this book (Slate).

DREAM INTERPRETION

Some dreams require no analysis. Their meanings are clear and their empowering effects are immediate. Others, however, possess elements of disguise including but not limited to symbolism, along with such mechanisms as antithesis and condensation. In antithesis, the dream's object, action, or event represents its direct opposite. For instance, a dream of accomplishment can represent failure, whereas a dream of loss can represent gain. Symbolically, an open door can represent a new opportunity, but in antithesis, it can represent the absence of opportunity. In condensation, the dream presents large bodies of information in a highly condensed form. For instance, a book can represent a body of knowledge, and opening the book can represent your progress in mastering that knowledge. Traveling can represent your life's journey and your progress in achieving your life's goals.

The purpose of disguise in dreaming varies. It can be simply a subconscious mechanism designed to protect sleep, or it can be used by the subconscious to challenge us to unravel the disguise and discover for ourselves the dream's true meaning. Clearly, the greater your understanding of your dreams, the more empowered you become. Here are a few guidelines that will assist you in discovering the true meaning of your dreams.

DREAM INTERPRETATION GUIDELINES

- Keep a daily dream journal. Simply recording your dreams in a journal immediately upon awakening can improve your memory of the dream experience and increase your understanding of its relevance.

- Reflecting on your dreams can increase your understanding of them. Audibly recalling the dream's essential elements can increase your understanding of the dream. The sound of your own voice can clarify the dream's underlying message and magnify its empowerment potential.

- Keep in mind that your dream messages are intended for you, the dreamer. They are for your personal enlightenment and empowerment.

- While references abound that can be useful resources toward interpreting your dreams, you alone are your best dream analyst. You know yourself better than anyone else. Through your dreams, your subconscious manifests itself in ways designed to increase your understanding of yourself and your existence in the universe.

- Use free association to determine the meaning of symbols used in the dream experience. Audibly state the symbol and allow a word, image, or condition to spontaneously come to mind. For instance, if the dream includes a bridge, simply say, "Bridge" and take a moment for a response to emerge. Through free association, you can build your own dream dictionary.

DREAM INTERVENTION

The empowerment potential of dreaming can be optimized through dream intervention programs that specifically target designated goals. Effective dream intervention programs based on laboratory research are now available to accelerate learning, improve memory, increase creativity, promote career success, and slow aging, to list but a few. Aside from these, there is abundant evidence that dream intervention programs can effectively retrieve experiences of past-life origin as well as preview future happenings of present relevance. Our lab studies also offered convincing evidence that dream intervention efforts can facilitate interactions with the spirit realm and facilitate out-of-body travel, including travel to specifically designated locations.

Fortunately, the dream state as well as the subconscious mind with its abundant resources is receptive to our intervention efforts. The subconscious mind, not unlike the spirit realm, persistently invites you to explore it and experience its powers. Dream intervention techniques are among our best ways of doing just that.

DREAM INTERVENTION PROGRAMS

Each of the dream intervention programs that follow is goal-related and thus requires a clear designation of your goal prior to sleep. Each program is sufficiently general in nature that you can adapt it to a wide range of specific goals. Certain programs were specifically designed, however, to meet particular goals. Through practice and experience, you will discover the programs that work best for you and your stated goals.

Each program is initiated during the relaxed state prior to sleep by a restatement of your goal and a clear affirmation in the first person of your complete success in achieving it through dream intervention. As drowsiness deepens, again restate your goal using the "I am" principle when possible. Examples are *I am committed…, I am determined…,* and *I am succeeding.* Follow your affirmations with imagery of your success in achieving your stated goal.

Certain dream intervention programs can be seen as essentially "hypnagogic arrest," since they can delay the hypnotic-like state that immediately precedes sleep. Suggestions presented during that state are believed to function as hypnotic suggestions and are thus effective independent of dream intervention efforts. But when combined with dream intervention efforts, their empowerment potentials are magnified.

Following are four dream intervention programs developed in our labs. Common to each program is recognition of the potential of dreams to connect us to the subconscious sources of enlightenment and power. For each program, it's important upon awakening to take a few moments to reflect on the dream experiences and record them in your dream journal.

THE FINGER SPREAD

This program is especially recommended for goals related to health, fitness, and rejuvenation. It is highly effective in managing weight, breaking unwanted habits, slowing aging, and even reversing the physical signs of aging.

To initiate the program, upon becoming drowsy, spread the fingers of either hand and hold the spread position as you state your goal in the first person, using the

"I am" principle accompanied by visualization of your success. As drowsiness deepens, slowly relax your fingers while reminding yourself that all the resources required for your success are now within your reach. Dream experiences using this approach often include images of yourself at your youthful prime or in a peak state of health and fitness. Upon awakening, review your goal and again affirm your progress in achieving it.

Aside from goals related to health, fitness, and rejuvenation, this program is also recommended as a way to accelerate learning, improve memory, and stimulate creativity. It has been highly effective in accelerating mastery of new languages. Artists have used this program to generate dreams in which creative materials and ideas unfold, often upon canvas. Musicians have used this program to generate dreams in which creative musical compositions unfold as either sound or sheet music with both notes and words. Writers likewise report having used this approach to generate creative ideas for their works.

With practice of this program, you can use the finger-spread gesture as a post-intervention cue to fully activate the effects of the program.

SOLAR PLEXUS REST

The Solar Plexus Rest has shown remarkable effectiveness as a dream intervention program. It is especially recommended for activities that require precision and advanced technical skills.

To begin this exercise, rest either hand on your solar plexus as you sense relaxation spreading throughout your body. State your goal and affirm your success in achieving it. Sense the almost instant balancing effect of this approach as you become increasingly aware of your subconscious resources related to your goal. Visualize yourself having achieved your stated goal. As drowsiness deepens, you can continue to rest your hand on your solar plexus, or if you prefer, you can assume another relaxed position. Upon awakening, again rest your hand on your solar plexus as you sense the empowering effects of this program. This approach is especially recommended for goals related to interactions with the spirit realm. Often precognitive awareness of the future will emerge during dreaming using this approach.

You can use the simple gesture of your hand resting briefly on your solar plexus as a postintervention cue to initiate in an instant the full effects of this program.

ARM LIFT TECHNIQUE

This technique is preferred especially for generating motivation and promoting academic and career success. It's initiated upon becoming drowsy by lifting either arm and holding it in a slightly raised position as you state your goal and affirm your success in achieving it. Visualize your goal as a reality poised for unfoldment. Affirm that as you sleep your dreams will tap into the subconscious resources required for your success.

College students who have used this program often experience increased motivation and marked improvement in their academic performance. In their dreams, they often experience rewarding classroom activities in which they are confident and capable. This approach when practiced before course evaluations tends to reduce test anxiety and stimulate recall and problem solving. Briefly lifting the arm to a slightly raised position can effectively reactivate at any time the empowering effects of this program.

PRE-SLEEP MEDITATION

This meditation exercise, when practiced immediately preceding sleep, is designed to reduce tension and promote a mental, physical, and spiritual state of balance and attunement prior to sleep. It is based on the premise that balance and attunement work together to promote healthful sleep, insightful dreaming, and renewal. The exercise combines rhythmic breathing, relaxation, visualization, and positive affirmation. Here's the procedure:

Step 1. While resting comfortably prior to sleep, take in a few deep breaths, exhaling slowly while clearing your mind of all clutter.

Step 2. While breathing slowly and rhythmically with your eyes closed, mentally scan your body from your forehead downward. Take plenty of time for relaxation to soak deep within your body.

Step 3. Visualize a peaceful, relaxing scene, perhaps a mountain stream, a sunset at sea, or a still moonlit cove. Affirm: "I am balanced and attuned, at peace with the world and the universe."

Step 4. As you slip into restful sleep, affirm: "I am open to the messages of my dreams. My dreams are a source of enlightenment, power, and peace."

Step 5. Allow restful sleep to ensue.

These are only a few of the many dream intervention approaches that promote healthful sleep as well as quality of life. Beginning now, you can use your dreams as empowering resources that enrich your life and open new gateways for growth and self-discovery.

CONCLUSION

If music is the language of the universe, dreaming is the language of the subconscious. Mastering that language is one of life's great challenges. A deeper understanding of your dreams can accelerate your growth and open totally new doors of understanding.

The subconscious knows, and through your dreams, you can get to know your subconscious. Beyond that, you can discover new meaning to your existence—past, present, and future. You can become more fully aware of "the whole person that you are."

DREAM SYMBOLS DICTIONARY

The interpretative significance of a dream symbol depends on a number of factors—among them, the nature of the dream itself, and the dreamer's personal characteristics, past experiences, and prevailing life circumstances. Despite these influencing variables, the meanings of many dream symbols appear to be reasonably stable. The purpose of this short dictionary is not to constrict the potential meanings of dreams, but to expand the interpretative possibilities of dream symbols, and to illustrate the potential value of dreams in promoting our personal insight and growth.

abyss: Emptiness or the unknown. "Falling into an abyss" suggests despair and feelings of hopelessness.

accident: The unexpected; loss of innocence or opportunity. Accidents suggest the importance of planning, foresight, caution, and critical assessment of current circumstances.

acrobat: Free, uninhibited, playful, and happy.

animal: The characteristics typically attributed to certain animals are often symbolized by the animal. The dove will often symbolize peace; the cat, independence; the dog, friendliness; and the bear, aggression. A dream of a struggle with an animal can symbolize a threatening impulse, whereas a dream of stroking a pet can represent our need to nurture.

auditorium: The social self. An empty auditorium can represent constricted social interests, whereas a crowded auditorium suggests a need for social interaction.

avalanche: Urgency, future adversity, a need for immediate action.

badge: Courage, honor, or striving for integrity.

banner: Future achievement, success, or unexpected recognition.

barn: Practicality, basic needs, or a simple lifestyle.

bird: Aspiration, drive for self-fulfillment, or the human spirit. A specific bird can represent a particular characteristic or preferred course of action. The eagle symbolizes power and suggests dominance; the sparrow, a carefree spirit; the hawk, aggression; the blue bird, happiness and enduring relationships; and the red bird, passion and impulsiveness.

bridge: Transition, change, new opportunity, or desire for continuity.

butterfly: Change, spiritual growth, and vulnerability.

candle: Truth, wisdom, and intelligence.

cavern: Mystery, desire to explore the unknown, or creativity.

chase: Escape, competitiveness, or vulnerability.

classroom: Opportunity, growth, or the desire to control or to be controlled.

color: Typically creativity; however, the particular color can have special significance. Red represents emotional intensity, anger, and urgency; pink, tenderness, femininity, and sensitivity; yellow, warmth and friendliness; green, virility, health, and wealth; light blue, peace and serenity; deep blue, the unknown and possible danger; orange, unpredictable circumstances; purple, mystery and spirituality; white, purity; gray, conservatism; black, unyielding or danger; and brown, practicality.

construction: A new beginning, new interests, changing relationships, or new projects.

conversation: Desire for social closeness, the need for acceptance.

crying: Guilt, insecurity, or the need to undo.

fire: Passion, a desire for vengeance, aggression, or a destroyed relationship.

firearm: Self-destruction, hostility, aggression, desperation, recklessness, or danger.

fish: Evasiveness, resistance, or the need to escape.

flood: Being overwhelmed, caught off-guard, unprepared, vulnerable.

flower: Serenity and pleasure. Specific flowers can convey a particular message or denote a specific characteristic or need. Roses are associated with affection and the expression of love; pansies, temporary but intense relationship; sweet pea, children or the desire to have children; carnation, a pensive, reflective state of mind; chrysanthemum, a gala affair; orchid, permanence and commitment; petunia, rugged endurance; daffodil, warmth or the restoration of a relationship; tulip, productivity; hyacinth, reflection and a time to nurture relationships; gardenia, sensuality, persuasive powers; goldenrod, abundance and security; violets, maturity and logic; and mixed flowers, balance and harmony within the self.

flying: Freedom or possibly an out-of-body experience.

fog: Uncertainty, unpreparedness, and procrastination. To be enveloped in fog suggests shortsightedness or danger.

fortress: The self's defense system; hence a crumbling fortress symbolizes vulnerability.

fruit: Productivity, the desire for children, or an intimate relationship.

holiday: Change, freedom, escape, or travel.

horse: Power or control.

house: Family and social relationships.

ice: A cold relationship, inflexibility, shallow emotions, unwise investments, or a stalemate.

infant: A new beginning, regression tendencies, or innocence.

injury: Vulnerability, traumatic experience, weakness, depleted power resources, threatened personal security, inferiority feelings, or arrested growth.

island: Refuge, safety, or security.

jewel/jewelry: Enrichment, good fortune, and certain characteristics of the self depending on the nature of the item: the diamond signifies commitment and resolution; the ruby, quality and depth; the topaz, sincerity and warmth; the pearl, moral and spiritual values; the amethyst, devotion; gold, integrity; and silver, maturity.

kissing: Desire for closeness, self-love, or erotic desire.

ladder: Desire to excel, ambition, or growth.

lantern: Self-orientation, skepticism, limited insight, or constricted interests.

laughter: Self-acceptance or self-satisfaction.

letter: Conscious or subconscious interaction, inner-attunement, forthcoming insight, or responsiveness to new knowledge.

light: A bright light signifies enlightenment and understanding. A flash of light symbolizes sudden insight.

metal: Metal objects can signify some unyielding aspect of the personality. Gold represents striving for either purity or wealth; silver represents excellence; and steel indicates fixed beliefs or inflexibility. Metal that becomes pliable in the dream suggests a willingness to modify one's position.

money: Material interests or financial concerns. A profitable financial venture is symbolized by finding money, whereas financial reversal is revealed by losing money. Large sums of money and counting money symbolize success.

monster: Inner fears, insecurities, struggle, or vulnerability.

moon: Romance, fantasy, mystery, strength, or sincerity.

mountain: Personal growth, obstacle, challenge, or struggle to achieve goals.

music: Harmony, balance, and inner peace.

nudity: Vulnerability, inferiority feelings, and inadequacy.

ocean: Typically, the ocean symbolizes the subconscious. A turbulent ocean suggests personal upheaval, inner struggle, discontent, and restlessness, whereas calm seas represent balance and harmony within the self.

painting: As a dream activity, painting represents an attempt to reverse some past action or to correct an adverse situation. Viewing a painting suggests passivity and possible voyeuristic impulses.

paralysis: Frustration, fear of failure, or hopelessness.

passageway: Transition, advancement, or escape.

people: Social interests or need for social acceptance. Strangers represent a new situation or the need to be cautious.

physical body: Sexual interests, narcissism when dreaming of one's own body, or concern for bodily functions and health.

race: Urgency, escape, or the need for patience.

railroad crossing: Caution or impending danger.

rainstorm: Unrequited love, unfulfilled desires, striving for excitement.

road: Journey, new discoveries, or an important transition.

rocket: Male sexuality, ambition, aggression, or virility concerns.

sanctuary: Safety, spiritual growth, or escape.

ship: Destiny. Steering a ship signifies being in control of destiny, whereas being a passenger suggests others are in control.

shoes: Material, earthly interests.

shopping: Efforts to nurture. Buying clothing represents strivings for acceptance and affiliation; buying shoes represents progress and advancement; buying food represents efforts to satisfy the needs of the inner self; and buying toiletries symbolizes erotic strivings.

singing: Happiness and fulfillment, spontaneity, genuineness, friendliness, or future gain.

skeleton: Impoverishment of personal resources; loss of power, reputation, or status.

skidding: Tendencies toward excessive risk-taking, altercation in a social relationship, or an impulsive confrontation.

snowstorm: Indecisiveness, unpreparedness, or vulnerability.

stairway: Transition, challenge, or struggle.

stone: A stone building symbolizes stability, whereas a stone landscape or boulder represents obstacles, adversity, and resistance.

struggle: Inner conflict, need for achievement, barriers to growth.

sunburn: Vulnerability to external influences, social pressures in particular.

sunrise: The beginning of a new and productive growth stage. A brilliant sunrise denotes unusual growth opportunities. Recurring dreams of a sunrise suggests self-confidence and a readiness to accommodate change and achieve new goals.

theater: Fantasy or escape needs.

tombstone: Gateway, death, or other life transition.

tower: Ambition, independence, self-reliance, male sexuality, strength, and purpose.

train: Spiritual growth, travel, or change.

tree: As a phallic symbol, virility, but when barren, sexual deficiency. A fallen tree can represent defeat, whereas a towering tree can signify aspiration.

uniform: Conformity, authority, or power.

walking: Patience, steady progress, or consistency.

SOURCES AND RECOMMENDED READING

Stephanie Clement and Terry Lee Rosen, *Dreams: Working Interactive* (includes CD-ROM with software program for journaling and interpretation) (Llewellyn, 2000).

Robert Gongloff, *Dream Exploration: A New Approach* (Llewellyn, 2006).

Migene Gonzalez-Wippler, *Dreams and What They Mean to You* (Llewellyn, 1990).

ESP Programs &
Psychic Empowerment

*The universe, by its very existence, demands exploration, contact,
and interaction. Unfortunately, we are all too often out of touch,
anesthetized by our limited awareness and fear of the unknown.
Through ESP, we become empowered to open new channels of experience
and knowledge. Only then do we become intimately connected
to the vast and wondrous powers of the universe. Equally important,
we become connected to the powers within ourselves.*

—JOE H. SLATE, *PSYCHIC PHENOMENA*

A cardinal principle of psychic empowerment holds that psychic potentials exist in everyone and can be developed through appropriate programs. Common to those programs are the following three essentials:

ESSENTIALS FOR DISCOVERY AND
DEVELOPMENT OF PSYCHIC POWERS

1. *Motivation.* The number one essential in developing your psychic potentials is motivation, the doorway to psychic power. Given motivation, you become goal oriented and focused in your pursuit of psychic empowerment. Without it, you are like a minnow in a shallow country stream, darting about without purpose or plan.

2. *Learning.* Through your exploration of various psychic concepts, exercises, and development programs, you will discover the knowledge that's essential to your psychic growth and development. You will also discover that knowledge is power, and knowledge of psychic origin is power in its highest form. You will find that the supreme personal psychic exists within your own being as an

essential part of yourself. It beckons your interaction and is constantly poised to enrich your life.

3. *Practice.* In developing your psychic potentials, there is no substitute for practice. Through practice using various exercises and programs, you will discover the tools and techniques that work best for you. Through continued practice, you will develop your psychic powers to their peaks.

Together, these three essentials provide the foundation for the discovery and development of your psychic powers, including ESP. Through motivation, learning, and practice, you will discover ways of using those powers to accelerate your growth and enrich the quality of your life. Beyond that, you will find effective ways of contributing to the greater good and making the world a better place.

CONSCIOUS VS. SUBCONSCIOUS

Our psychic potentials exist at all levels of consciousness, from the highest level of awareness, sometimes called the superconscious, to the deepest levels of the subconscious. Although many of our psychic experiences originate at the conscious level, others seem to originate in the subconscious and are then transferred to conscious awareness. For instance, telepathic sending is typically a function of the conscious mind, whereas telepathic receiving seems often to be a function of the subconscious, where the message is first received and then transferred to conscious awareness, at times in a form that includes emotions and intuitions related to the message. Similarly, clairvoyant and precognitive enlightenment seems often to be the product of advanced psychic faculties existing in the subconscious. Aside from psychic enlightenment that originates in the subconscious, the subconscious can function as a channel for enlightenment from external sources, including the spirit realm.

The subconscious at times transforms the message into symbolic form before relaying it to conscious awareness, often in the form of the dream experience. Symbolic manifestations seem to be particularly common for messages that are distressful or threatening. The subconscious use of symbolism tends to desensitize the message and make it more conducive to conscious awareness and analysis. For the psychic dream experience, recording your dreams in a journal can improve your recall of the dream while promoting your understanding of it.

GENERAL PSYCHIC DEVELOPMENT

Certain personal characteristics are known to accelerate human growth and development, to include all forms of psychic potentials. Among the most important traits are a positive self-concept and a success orientation. These two essentials together form the holy grail of psychic empowerment. Together, they can energize not only your psychic development, but your total growth as well. They can enrich the quality of your life—mentally, physically, and spiritually—and empower you with success in achieving your highest goals. Equipped with a positive self-concept and success orientation, you can effectively maximize your psychic potentials and successfully develop them to their fullest. Aside from that, you can develop other important potentials, including those required to solve problems, cope with stress, overcome setbacks, and add meaning to your life.

In the discussion that follows, we will first explore several important factors related to your general psychic growth and development. We will then examine the following three major categories of ESP: *telepathy*, which focuses on psychic communication, including sending and receiving thought messages as well as related emotions; *precognition* or the psychic awareness of the future; and *clairvoyance*, which includes the psychic perception of objects, conditions, situations, and events. For each of these categories, we will present practice exercises designed to promote psychic growth and personal empowerment.

THE X POSITION

The full actualization of your psychic potentials depends largely on your capacity not only to accept yourself, but to love yourself unconditionally. As a spiritual being, it is important to address your mind and body, and embrace them as expressions of who you are. Remind yourself that your body has a mind of its own and is receptive to your messages of better health, healing, rejuvenation, and balance, to list but a few.

Your body belongs to you and you alone. By loving your body as a divine creation, you have direct access to your growing brain and developing soul. The body thus becomes a partner that enriches your interaction not only with the external world but with your inner being and the spirit world as well. Loving your body empowers you to work "with your body" rather than "above it." The old view of "mind over body" has at last given way to a more enlightened view of "mind/body interaction."

The X Position is a simple, self-administered exercise that facilitates not only your acceptance of your physical body, but more importantly, an appreciation and love for it. It's based on the premise that you are a unique being of incomparable worth—mentally, physically, and spiritually. Here's the exercise:

Step 1. *The X Position:* While either standing or seated in an upright position, fold your arms to form an X over your chest. While holding the X position, feel the emerging sense of relaxation and balance throughout your body.

Step 2. *Body Embrace:* While retaining the X position, place your hands under your upper arms against your body and, with your palms resting upon your body, close your eyes and stroke your upper body gently, using upward and downward hand movements. As your palms continue to rest upon your body, affirm: *All my cares have rolled away. I am now at complete peace.*

Step 3. *Handclasp:* End the body embrace by bringing your hands together and affirming: *My body is the temple of both mind and spirit. Mentally, physically, and spiritually, I am worthy of love.*

Step 4. *Palm-engagement Cue:* You can initiate at any moment the full empowering effects of this exercise by simply bringing your palms together while affirming: *I am worthy of love.*

This simple self-administered exercise, with repeated use, is highly effective in building a positive self-image and promoting feelings of self-worth. It can banish feelings of inferiority, which are all too often at the core of anxiety and depression. A student struggling with feelings of inadequacy and inferiority reported, *"The X Position has been worth many hours of counseling. Through it, I discovered that my best therapist is within myself. The X Position put me in touch with that therapist."*

MIND/BODY INTERACTIONS

The mind and body are in a state of constant interaction, but understanding that interaction, and even more importantly managing it, can be a very difficult needle to thread. At a very basic level, the capacity of the conscious mind to engage in interaction with the physical body is clearly indicated by situations in which thought processes can stimulate such physical responses as hunger, sexual arousal, relaxation, and tension, to name but a few.

The capacity of mind/body interactions to influence complex biological functions can probably be best illustrated in the biofeedback lab setting. Examples include the raising or lowering of finger temperature, alterations in galvanic skin responses (GSR), and changes in brain-wave patterns through thought processes that interact with the physical body. Each of these alterations in physiology have significant health and fitness implications, such as the capacity of mind/body interactions to promote relaxation, alleviate anxiety, lower blood pressure, manage pain, facilitate rejuvenation, and accelerate recovery from illness.

Beyond the laboratory, the power of mind/body interactions is illustrated in a myriad of sports situations, such as boxing, wrestling, skating, gymnastics, and a wide range of team sports. A positive mental state with strong expectations of success can be the deciding factor that improves physical performance and increases the probability success. That same mental state can improve intellectual performance, social interactions, and career success. Aside from these, there is evidence that even mortality can be influenced by mind/body interactions. Terminally ill patients, for instance, have been known to extend their lives far beyond medical expectations in order to participate in an important life event, such as an anniversary, celebration, or holiday. Conversely, longevity seems also receptive to mental processes that in some instances actually target the date of death. That power of mind/body interactions seemed to have been dramatically illustrated by Mark Twain's "self-fulfilling prophecy" in which he accurately predicted the exact date of his death. Born at the appearance of Halley's Comet, he seemed to have actually programmed his body over the years by his expectations of death at the reappearance of the comet seventy-five years later. One could argue, of course, that his prediction of death could be the result of pre-cognitive insight and as such was unrelated to self-fulfilling prophecy. Nevertheless, these findings when taken together clearly suggest the capacity of mind/body inter-actions to influence physiology, either positively or negatively, a central concept in psychosomatic medicine.

Another interesting example of mind/body interactions is a form of ESP called *derma-optic perception,* or the capacity of the mind to receive information through touch, typically through the hands or fingers. That sensory/extrasensory phenom-enon was illustrated by our lab studies in which blindfolded subjects were given the task of perceiving the color of a stimulus, such as a sheet of paper, through touch alone. In one remarkable instance, the subject, a celebrated psychic, accurately identi-fied the color of ten sheets of construction paper, each of a different color, through touch alone. Another explanation of these phenomena, however, suggests that the message is first subconsciously perceived through clairvoyance and then communi-cated through touch to conscious awareness.

There is strong evidence that you can develop your derma-optic skills through certain practice exercises. Our studies included the use of ten colored jelly beans in which blindfolded subjects were given the task of identifying the color of each jelly bean through touch alone. Following sufficient practice, all subjects typically improved their performance in identifying the color of each bean. In another study, ten colored glass marbles were substituted for jelly beans with similar results. In yet another study, ten 2" x 2" samples of colored construction paper were used, also with similar results. Our lab studies further revealed that the development of your derma-optic potentials results in a powerful generalization effect that markedly stimulates the development of other ESP faculties. Repeatedly, performance on telepathy, clair-voyance, and precognition tasks using ESP cards appreciably improved following practice of derma-optic exercises.

The simplicity of the above experiments should not distract from the value of them and similar practices. The point is that they become truly supportive of develop-ing your psychic awareness, which modern culture—until recently—has largely sup-pressed. Take opportunities to guess what comes next on the daily news, who is call-ing on the telephone, whether the person you are calling answers the phone, when the gift you ordered will be delivered, etc. Paying attention to the "unknown" opens the doors of perception beyond the seeming certainty of the "here and now" physical world.

Yet another example of sensory/extrasensory interaction is *psychometry*, in which tangible objects, typically of a personal nature, are used to activate psychic functions through touch. In one celebrated case, a clairvoyant located a lost child through psychometry. While holding an article of the child's clothing, she accurately described a nearby wooded area with a towering tree situated near a stream. The child was found resting under the tree. In another instance, a seriously injured dog that took shelter in an abandoned building was located through psychometry using one of the dog's leashes. In our labs, a group of five students participating in a clairvoyant research project used a map of a shopping mall to locate a lost ring. By scanning the map with their fingers, the group accurately determined the ring's exact location—the dressing room of an upscale ladies' apparel shop.

Along a different line, there is a mountain of evidence supporting the possibility of physiological interactions with the spirit realm, or perhaps better stated, the capacity of the spirit realm to initiate an interaction with consciousness through physiological channels. That possibility has been repeatedly illustrated by the aroma of roses that signaled the presence of the opera singer Abigail, a recurring apparition observed over many years on the campus of Athens State University. The appearance of the apparition, often before large audiences in McCandless Auditorium, is typically preceded by the aroma of roses that is collectively experienced by the full audience.

Another example of physiological interactions with the spirit realm is "automatic writing," in which specific messages, from either the subconscious or directly from the spirit world, are received through spontaneous writing and then communicated to conscious awareness. In automatic writing, the hand holding a writing pen typically rests lightly upon a sheet of blank paper and is allowed to write spontaneously. Not infrequently, meaningless scribble will precede meaningful writing that becomes the channel between consciousness and the information source, which is often a personal spirit guide.

Taken together, the evidence is clear. Your mind and body are critical components of your evolvement as a soul being. Both are unique to you. By embracing them with unconditional love and acceptance, you can take a major step toward the full actualization of your total being, to include the development of your ESP powers. In the discussion that follows, we'll explore several simple exercises programs designed to promote that important process.

TELEPATHY, CLAIRVOYANCE, AND PRECOGNITION: EXERCISES FOR GROWTH

For many of us, telepathy, clairvoyance, and precognition routinely knock at the door of consciousness and invite our attention. By simply opening that door, we can increase our receptiveness to our ESP potentials and enrich our lives with expanded awareness and new knowledge. More specifically, we can improve our communication skills, increase our understanding of ourselves, and expand our awareness of distant realities, including the spirit realm. We can even get glimpses into the future, to include events that hold profound relevance to the present.

We can further stimulate our psychic growth by exercising our ESP potentials through simple practice exercises, including the use of a deck of playing cards. Begin by shuffling the cards, and then with the cards turned downward, draw a card at random from the deck and use your clairvoyance skills to identify it. Check the card to determine the accuracy of your response. Do it again several times. To exercise your precognitive skills, predict before drawing the card which card you will draw from the deck. Draw the card and check it to determine your accuracy. To practice your telepathic skills, have another person draw a card from the deck and attempt to telepathically send its identity. Check the accuracy of your responses. Repeat each of these exercises several times and record the accuracy of your response after each trial. You will probably note that the accuracy of your responses increases with practice. If you prefer, you can substitute a deck of ESP cards for these exercises.

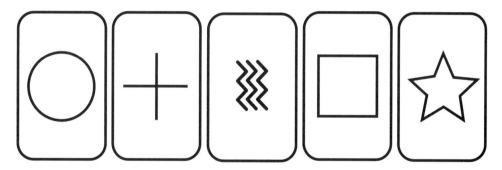

The Standard Zener Cards

Another interesting practice exercise is called "down-through-the-deck" in which the subject's task is to identify each card from the top to the bottom of the deck.

In our lab studies under highly controlled conditions, our subjects following appropriate practice typically improved their performance on a wide range of ESP tasks.

PSYCHIC BALANCE AND ATTUNEMENT TECHNIQUE

Psychic balance and attunement are important to all forms of psychic phenomena, whether a telepathic message from a friend, a clairvoyant image of a distant reality, precognitive awareness of a future event, or a psychic dream message. Beyond these, a state of psychic balance and attunement can enhance interdimensional interactions, such as communicating with spirit guides and the departed. The Psychic Balance and Attunement Technique is designed to increase your attentiveness to psychic experiences and to promote the full development of your psychic potentials. Here's the technique, which is recommended for use in a quiet, comfortable setting.

Step 1. *Connecting Mind, Body, and Spirit:* Settle back and begin with the affirmation, *Mentally, physically, and spiritually, I am committed to developing my ESP potentials.* Take a moment to sense the power of that affirmation flowing throughout your total being, energizing your mind, body, and spirit as they come into a state of oneness and balance. Repeat the affirmation and take plenty of time for it to resonate throughout your mind, body, and spirit.

Step 2. *Inner Point of Power:* With your eyes closed, center your attention on your solar plexus, that central region of your body rich in interconnected neurons. Picture that area as an inner center of power and the interactive exchange point for the mind, body, and spirit. Take a few moments for your attention to remained centered at that point, and you will sense the activation of your psychic powers. You can now take full command of those powers. You can send and receive mental messages by intent alone. You can target a distant reality and view it in full. You can tap into the future and acquire whatever information you need at the moment. You can experience the spirit realm, communicate with spirit guides, interact with various spiritual dimensions or planes of power, and draw from them whatever resources you need, including healing, rejuvenation, enlightenment, and enrichment, to list but a few.

Step 3. *Holistic Affirmation:* Infuse your total being with power by simply affirming: *My psychic powers are now at my command. I can use them at will to empower my life mentally, physically, and spiritually. With use, my psychic powers will become stronger and stronger.*

Step 4. *Conclusion:* Conclude the exercise by simply bringing together the tips of your fingers as a symbol of your resolve to develop your psychic potentials and use them, not only to empower your own life but to make the world a better place. You can use this simple gesture at any time to reactivate the full effects of this exercise.

The full development of your ESP powers depends largely on your ability to generate an inner state of mental, physical, and spiritual attunement and balance. This program puts your psychic potentials in a state of readiness that facilitates both their continuous development and spontaneous expression. When in that state, you have direct access to your telepathic, clairvoyant, and precognitive powers.

EMPOWERMENT-AT-ONCE PROCEDURE

The Empowerment-at-once Procedure energizes your psychic faculties and empowers you at once to tap into specific psychic functions and activate them on demand.

Paradoxically, the simplest, quickest exercise is often the most effective. The Empowerment-at-once procedure requires only seconds to implement, yet its empowering effects can be profound and long term. Here's the procedure.

Step 1. *Upward Palms:* Turn the palms of both hands upward and sense energy of the highest order permeating them. Remind yourself that your hands are your body's antennae to the universe and beyond. The sensation of tingling in your palms and fingers is typical at this important strep.

Step 2. *Temple Touch:* Touch your temples with your fingertips. You will immediately sense energy permeating your total being.

Step 3. *Affirmation:* Affirm: *I am energized and empowered mentally, physically, and spiritually.*

Step 4. *Empowerment-at-once Cue:* You can reactivate in seconds the full empowering effects of this procedure by simply touching your temples with your fingertips. It is important, however, to occasionally repeat the full procedure.

This simple procedure is one of the most effective ways known for generating in an instant a profound state of empowerment that is highly conducive to psychic expression. Aside from that application, this brief procedure can induce a state of relaxation, self-confidence, and security in even the most stressful of situations.

The Empowerment-at-once Procedure is an excellent motivational exercise when accompanied by additional relevant affirmations in Step 3 for such goals as breaking unwanted habits, losing weight, overcoming phobias, and building self-confidence. A former student, who was a participant in our development of this technique and is now a top manager in a large business firm, reports that she uses the technique regularly before important conferences and business meetings. She calls it her "career accelerant."

CONCLUSION

Everyone, rather than a privileged few, is psychic. Our psychic potentials, including ESP, are essential parts of our being—mentally, physically, and spiritually. But developing those potentials requires motivation, learning, and practice. Using the exercises presented in this chapter, you can develop your ESP potentials and apply them to enrich and empower your life. Beginning now, you can gain a deeper understanding of your existence—past, present, and future. You can transcend all self-imposed limits to your growth and discover a vast range of totally new possibilities. In other words, you can become *psychically empowered*.

As a concluding note, each of the programs and exercises presented in this chapter can be easily adapted for use by groups.

SOURCES AND RECOMMENDED READING

Ted Andrews, *How to Do Psychic Readings Through Touch* (Llewellyn, 2003).

Melita Denning and Osborne Phillips, *Practical Guide to Psychic Powers: Awaken Your Sixth Sense* (Llewellyn, 2000).

William Hewitt, *Psychic Development for Beginners: An Easy Guide to Releasing and Developing Your Psychic Abilities* (Llewellyn, 2002).

Debra Lynne Katz, *Extraordinary Psychic: Proven Techniques to Master Your Natural Psychic Abilities* (Llewellyn, 2008).

Joe H. Slate, *Psychic Phenomena* (McFarland, 1988).

Joe H. Slate, *Psychic Empowerment for Health & Happiness* (Llewellyn, 1996).

Joe H. Slate and Carl Llewellyn Weschcke, *Psychic Empowerment for Everyone: You Have the Power, Learn to Use It* (Llewellyn, 2009).

MAGIC, RITUAL & SHAMANISM
Ancient Practices of Psychic Empowerment

By all the power of Land and Sea.
By all the might of Moon and Sun.
What is my will—"So Mote it Be."
Then I do say—"It shall be done."

—A VARIATION OF THE *WITCHES' RUNE* BY GERALD GARDNER

RHYTHM AND PATTERN IN RITUAL

Rituals and patterns are everywhere. You can see them in the rituals of courtship and social interaction among insects, fish, birds, and animals, as well as humans. And you can see patterns throughout the world of nature and the movements and energy interactions of our own sun and moon, of planets and their satellites, of asteroids, comets, and even of artificial satellites.

Most people are personally familiar with rituals of one form or another—from school graduation ceremonies to various social rituals, from religious "coming of age" celebrations to marriages and funerals. Rituals are part of life, and most especially of civilized life. They mark transition points and establish new beginnings and endings, and even endings that are new beginnings.

Patterns of energy interaction form the background stage for all of life's adventures and the foundation of our individual and group interaction. Such patterns reappear in the background of all of our rituals.

Some rituals have also become commercial events while still retaining older traditional elements—adding entertainment and "shopping experiences" and newer elements that we see prominently in our celebrations of major holy/holidays, including Samhain/Halloween, Thanksgiving, Yule/Christmas, Imbolc, Valentine's Day, Ostara/Easter, Beltane, and various celebrations of Spring from spring cleaning to new wardrobes, Summer Solstice and summer vacations, Lammas and back-to-school shopping, Mabon and Fall shopping. Commerce is a fundamental part of civilized life, just as rituals are.

These rituals are all celebrations that express the natural rhythms of life and of the seasons. Without these rituals, we would lose attunement to the stages of life and of nature. Even where the rituals are masked behind the commerce of Santa Claus and trips to the mall, they still serve to align our personal energies with those of the Earth and cosmos. Each one of us *is* Humanity, and all of us *are* the Cosmic Family.

ESOTERIC RITUALS

The rituals we've discussed thus far could be called "exoteric" rituals. They range from the purely social to those intended to unite people into groups. They permeate the entire culture and, with minor variations, connect us globally. They unite us as humanity, and they unite humanity with the invisible global consciousness.

At the more esoteric level, some fewer people have experienced more involved rituals such as found in Masonry, the Magical Orders, Wiccan and Pagan groups, and other esoteric societies that celebrate the seasons, the lunar passages, and some even celebrate the daily tides. And, usually, there are particular rituals that identify individual members with the group's egregor and some celebrations that commemorate the founder and particular events and individuals unique to the group's history.

Still fewer people have experienced the deeper mysteries of ritual initiations that are supposed to transmit spiritual contacts through the intentional infusion of archetypal symbols and associations, and the arousal of particular energies. And there are some concerned with the evocation and direction of particular psychic powers—including Astral Projection, Remote Viewing, Past Life Reviews, Reading of Akashic Records, Local and Distant Healing, the Evocation (and sometimes Invocation) of Gods and Spirits, and such special powers as travel to Spirit Worlds, Fire Walking without injury, Body Piercing that leaves no wounds, and other demonstrations of transcendent skills.

It is these in particular—rituals to evoke and apply innate psychic powers—that interest us in this book.

HYPNOSIS

These particular rituals, whether simple or complex, whether involving large groups (including audience involvement) or just two people, all utilize hypnotic techniques directed by a single director or leader and, most commonly, one subject (the person being hypnotized). Sometimes there is group hypnosis, or serial hypnosis of several people, and sometimes the spontaneous hypnosis of a nonparticipating witness.

Of course, rarely does anyone apply the word "hypnosis" to these experiences, but analysis of the techniques involved will demonstrate the point.

Hypnosis, in these situations, proceeds along these lines:

HYPNOSIS IN RITUAL SETTINGS

1. The culminating energies from choral and/or audience singing, chanting, and group prayer, often including body movements of clapping, swaying, bowing, dancing, and even marching with focus toward a dedicated platform.

2. Focus of attention by the Subject upon the Director.

3. Further concentration of that focus through the Director's movements, use of the Subject's name, specific prayers in a loud sing-song manner.

4. A constant arousal of expectation, both in the group and in Subject, that something "big" is about to happen through intervention from some higher power channeled through the Director.

5. And the final culmination when the Director directs all that focused energy to the Subject, either by gesture or actual touch.

You can readily see the technique at work by watching the TV evangelists, who used to work in large tents and then in large auditoriums, and who now have huge mega-churches with immense auditoriums with special effects lighting and sound controls, colorful symbols, and architectural focus on the dedicated platform.

All that focused energy and the high expectations do often result in psychic healing, and sometimes in transformation of the Subject. Sometimes the healing effect is permanent and other times it is temporary—but the important thing is the realization of the technique itself and of the psychic power involved.

A question that might be asked: *Is that psychic power manifested from the Director or from the Subject, or is it—as presented—channeled from another source?* In any case, the point is that there was an effective demonstration of psychic power translated into a psychic skill.

In similar situations, but more often in secret magical orders or shamanic practices, the same techniques are used to induce the subject into a deep trance, and then the Director arouses a particular psychic power in the subject, bringing it up from the subconsciousness to be used under the control of the Director. The Subject may be directed to enter into a telepathic relationship with a similarly entranced subject at a distant location and serve the respective directors as a kind of occult telephone. The Subject may be directed to send his astral body to observe a particular event or person, and report back to the Director. Or he may be directed to harm, or heal, a distant person as victim or beneficiary. He may be directed to discover particular information and report it back to the Director.

In other words, the Director is employing the Subject as a kind of psychic probe or robot to accomplish particular missions of interest to the director regardless of the subject's interests, ethics, personal morality, or values.

Note: This use of hypnosis mostly leaves control in the hands of the hypnotist, whether a professional, a priest, or a group leader. As such, unless otherwise directed, it essentially leaves whatever psychic power was involved to return to the subconscious. Not only is the Subject generally unconscious of the experience, but his conscious mind is not expanded through the experience. He was just used, like "slave labor," for the benefit of others, often without knowledge of the intended purpose.

Conscious Participation in Group Rituals
In most group rituals, even those in the evangelical setting, there is a conscious participation by the members of the group, which range from audience involvement on up to scripted support roles by the officers and members of the group—be it a lodge, temple, coven, assembly, church, and even a political rally.

Watch and observe, and learn. Attending and participating in any of these group settings can become a lesson in applied hypnosis.

Self-Hypnosis
From what we learned above, you can readily see that such rituals—whether occurring in an evangelical setting or in a magical order—are powerful hypnotic formulae composed of carefully chosen power-words spoken in near poetic rhythmic cadence, in an environment of supporting symbols, sounds, lights, and colors, sometimes incenses, and supporting actors (including an audience).

Self-hypnosis also benefits from a similar formula of carefully chosen words in a crafted sequence. There may be a musical or sound background, and the environment should be dedicated to support the program. One major difference is that—in contrast to the group performance described previously—where the litany of sermons or ceremonial evocations may be long and sometimes boring—the self-hypnosis pre-prepared script must be as concise as possible. It is a condensed formula of a few words that can easily be memorized and repeated again and again.

Another characteristic that is shared with those of a magical lodge is the Oath of Secrecy—keeping magical rituals secret concentrates their power. The same principle applies to self-hypnosis: talking about it dissipates its power.

Another obvious difference is that the self-hypnotic ritual is self-directed by the most powerful priest/director of all—your Higher Self speaking through the Conscious Mind.

Self-hypnosis, including self-directed rituals developed as part of personal programming, can accomplish all that "hetero-hypnosis" (involving hypnotist and subject) does plus *conscious retention of those "extra" skills and memories.*

Our goal is not only to accomplish a particular mission—weight loss, for example—*but to expand our personal consciousness*—what we call the Conscious Mind, by making conscious selected natural psychic powers, and *links* to other levels, powers, and memories. With development and training, these powers are turned into reliable skills that can be applied to practical needs and everyday benefits, as well as to what we may call *"spiritual growth and development."*

Instead of a self-help mission of becoming a nonsmoker, losing weight, gaining self-confidence in public-speaking, etc., you can design your scripts to focus on bringing any of your natural psychic powers "up" from the Subconscious Mind to the Conscious Mind.

In addition to the direct use of self-hypnosis in this manner, the serious and conscious study and use of any of the psychic tools we will describe in the second part of this book can be scripted with simple rituals of mental focus aiding the actual learning process, memorization of information, and dexterity with the tools involved, while also calling on higher powers or spirit guides, surrounding yourself with visualized white light, etc.

After initial application, this can be continued by means of a prayer, as a purely silent internal procedure, or something that a client might join in.

PRAYER AND SPELLS

Prayers and spells, whether in group or solitary settings, should employ most of the same principles seen in hypnosis and self-hypnosis. The goals may be different, and the script may be different but—to be effective—a prayer or spell must call up energies from the Subconscious Mind to be directed by the Conscious Mind. The "power" is not in the words but as evoked by the mind.

THE MAGIC OF FAITH

Faith, or belief, is part of the technology we've been describing. But it is not always faith in something external and "above" the participant. Faith can be described as the "Calling Down" of a Higher Power which some interpret as mostly a call to your Higher Self. Belief, alternatively is a "Calling Up" of particular images and archetypes from the Subconscious Mind in unison with what we call the Collective Unconscious where all humanity's memories and *programming* is contained.

Belief is a somewhat different word than faith. While Belief serves the same fundamental purpose, it has generally developed from personal knowledge and experience.

You have faith in an external source, while you have belief in an internal source. Ultimately, the internal and external sources may be the same. Consciousness is universal and primal; Consciousness was there at the "Beginning," and being timeless, it is with us now.

EXTRA-CONSCIOUSNESS

The goal of Psychic Empowerment is the "raising" of natural psychic powers from the subconscious mind into the conscious mind as a developed skill. As such, they are "extra" and part of the process of mind expansion.

As innate powers are developed through training and practice, that which was formerly unconscious becomes conscious. And, through application, various experiences and new knowledge are retained as added skills—just as training in mathematics, sciences, and arts adds not only to particular skills but consciously retained memories of abilities and facts. We retain language and math skills, scientific facts and understanding, artistic abilities, and so on that are available on a daily basis for continuous self-improvement.

SHAMANIC TECHNIQUES AND EXPERIENCES, AND THE EIGHT PATHS TO THE CENTER IN WITCHCRAFT

Traditional Shamanism has existed for twenty thousand or more years and is found in most indigenous cultures in a nearly identical form. "Shaman" is a Turkic word of the language used in ancient Siberia, and it was the study of Siberian Shamanism that opened the academic world to a global awareness of these ecstatic techniques to be found among "primitive" people nearly everywhere.

Primarily through the work of Michael Harner, the New Age movement appropriated and combined ideas from traditional shamanism with beliefs and practices from Native American and Eastern cultures to create modern Pagan neoshamanism mostly around ecstatic dancing and ritual drumming, while variously including psychedelic substances, sweat lodges, and monotonous chanting, adopting ritual names and additional practices from older European, African, and Middle Eastern traditions, particularly those of their own ancestral cultures.

Nevertheless, it is the study of Gerald Gardner (from personal correspondence), who is properly credited as the "Father of Wicca" or modern Witchcraft, that sums up shamanic practices in the "Eightfold Path to the Center."

Gerald Gardner

THE EIGHTFOLD PATH TO THE CENTER

1. Concentration, Meditation, and Visualization.
2. The induction of trance states leading to Clairvoyance, Astral Projection, and "Etc." (We don't know all of what Gardner included under "Etc.")
3. Rites with a purpose, Chants, Spells, Runes, Charms, etc.
4. Drugs, Incense, Wine, etc. "Whatever is used to release the Spirit." The Dance and kindred practices.
5. The Dance, and kindred practices
6. Blood Control (the Cords), Breath Control, and kindred practices.
7. Scourging and ritual flagellation.
8. The Great Rite, i.e. ritual sex.

In addition to the Eight Paths, Gardner lists Five Essentials:

a. These are the ways, you may combine many of them into the one experience. *The more the better.* The most important is "Intention." You must know that you can and will succeed. It is essential in every operation.
b. Preparation. You must be properly prepared according to the Rules of the Art. Otherwise, you will never succeed.
c. The Circle must be properly formed and purified. Likewise all the operators.
d. You must be properly purified, several times if necessary, and this purification should be repeated several times during the rite.
e. You must have properly consecrated tools.

Gardner adds: *These Five Essentials and Eight Paths, or ways, cannot all be combined in one rite: Meditation and Dancing do not combine well, but Forming the Mental Image and the Dance may be well combined with Chants, Spells, etc. combined with No. 6 and No. 7 followed by No. 8 form a splendid combination. Meditation, followed by No. 7, combined with Nos. 3, 4, and 5 are also very good. For short cuts, No. 1 with Nos. 5, 6, 7, and 8 are excellent. The Five Essentials are essential in all experiments. If a chant is used to reinforce a work already begun, end with this:*

> *By all the power of Land and Sea.*
> *By all the might of Moon and Sun.*
> *What is my will—"So Mote it Be."*
> *Then I do say—"It shall be done."*

I'm afraid that The Eightfold Paths may seem to have little relevance to the average non-Wiccan reader, so some explanation is desirable. Before doing so, we need to have a better understanding of shamanism itself. As defined in *The Element Encyclopedia of the Psychic World* (Cheung, 2006):

> *The Shaman lives in two worlds: ordinary reality and a non-ordinary reality called the "shamanic state of consciousness" . . . believed to be a unique altered state of consciousness in which the shaman has access to three cosmologies: earth, sky and underworld. The shaman remains lucid throughout his altered state and . . . has access to information that is closed off during ordinary reality.*
>
> *This ability to enter the shamanic state at will is essential to the shaman. Techniques for doing so include drumming, chanting, dancing, fasting, sweat baths, staring into flames, visualization and isolating oneself in darkness. In some instances psychedelic drugs will be used for this purpose but they are not essential for the shamanic process. The shaman has the clairvoyant skills to see spirits and souls and the mediumistic ability to communicate with them. He is also able to take magical flights . . . through shape-shifting.*
>
> *The shaman's primary function is to heal and restore the connectedness of his people to the universe.*

The shaman, using several of these techniques, is able to contact and utilize the elemental powers of nature, bring clients into contact with their personal totem animal spirit guides, practice herbal medicine and spiritual healing, and communicate with spirits on behalf of his or her people or clients. Spirit communication is mainly in the form of séances, just like Western spiritual mediums, usually accompanied by paranormal phenomena including levitation of objects, rapping, handling of hot coals, and spirit voices.

What we should note in shamanism is that the shaman enters into an altered state in order to enter into or access an alternate reality. And we can readily note that the techniques for such access are basically hypnotic in nature. The shaman simply is accessing his own Subconscious Mind, and through that the Collective Unconscious or Universal Consciousness, wherein he finds spirits, brings his psychic powers under the control of the Conscious Mind, and uses his abilities on behalf of his people and clients.

Now let's go back and review Gardner's Eight Paths to the Center.

1. Meditation and Visualization. A note in Gardner's own words: "*This in practice means forming a mental image of what is desired, & forcing yourself to see that it is fulfilled, with the fierce belief & knowledge that it can & will be fulfilled, & that you will go on willing till you force it to be fulfilled. Called for short: Intent.*"

   Note this use of "intent" is identical with that of Lynne McTaggert and others writing about the applications of Quantum Theory to visualized accomplishment. In traditional self-help and magical practice, this is referred to as "Creative Visualization." It is not so much a conscious act as it taps into the Subconscious Mind by which "intent" is focused at the very basic universal creative level where change is possible.

2. Trance states leading to psychic powers. A trance state is a hypnotic state, whether induced through a group setting or a solitary practice. The use of drumming, chanting, spells, and rituals all bring the practitioner into access with the Subconscious Mind and bring its amazing power under conscious direction. Its purpose is to achieve personally established and affirmed goals.

3. Rites with a purpose. In other words, rituals—rather than ceremonies—are practiced to bring about a goal. Just another way to formulate a spell or a purposeful prayer. Such rituals are really self-hypnosis scripts, and in recognizing that, your prayers and spells can become much more powerful and effective.

4. Drugs, Incense, Wine, etc. "Whatever is used to release the Spirit." He adds a further admonition: "Note, One must be very careful about this. Incense is usually harmless but you must be careful, if it has bad after effects, reduce the amount used or the duration of the time it is inhaled. Drugs are very dangerous if taken to excess, but it must be remembered that there are drugs that are absolutely harmless though people talk of them with bated breath. But Hemp is especially dangerous because it unlocks the inner eye swiftly and easily, so one is tempted to use it more and more. If it is used at all, it must be with the strictest precautions, so that the person who uses it has no control over the supply—this should be doled out by some responsible person, and the supply strictly limited."

Wine and alcohol have a long tradition of use both in religious ceremonies and communal settings to "loosen things up," reducing normal conscious restraints. Incense, on the other hand, is a mood enhancer used in magical rituals tying the particular incense through "correspondences" to the function of the ritual. Symbols and colors are used similarly to reinforce the intent of the ritual. Group use of drugs is generally forbidden because of the unreliable effects they may have, possibly leading to violence, severe depression, suicide, and other irrational behavior.

5. The Dance and kindred practices. The dance can be anything from a somber movement within the Circle to wild ecstatic dancing, whether personally undertaken to induce altered states or experienced through participation in folk dancing. Most folk dances are derived from shamanic and ritual dancing.

6. Blood Control (the Cords), Breath Control, and kindred practices. Forms of "bondage" that involve restraint of movement, loss of circulation, and numbness in the limbs; forms of sensory deprivation using hoods or placement in an isolation chamber, or the swinging "Witches Cradle," are intended to bring focus to the other world rather than ordinary reality and to bring access to the Subconscious Mind and the Collective Unconscious.

7. Scourging and ritual flagellation. The controlled use of pain has a long history in shamanic practices that "leverage" the body to induce an altered state of consciousness. Numbers 5, 6, and 7 share this leveraging of the physical body to induce an altered and often ecstatic state of consciousness. All three, but especially numbers 6 and 7, must involve an experienced operator to avoid injury, both physical and psychological, demonstrating the greater safety and value to be found in the use of self-hypnosis.

8. The Great Rite, i.e. ritual sex. Deliberately controlled sex is part of Indian Tantra, Chinese sexual alchemy, and Western sex magick practices involving control or denial of male ejaculation to drive sexual excitement higher and higher, particularly to induce a sustained altered state of consciousness in the female, and sometimes—with the exchange of energies back and forth—in both female and male. Under the direction of the male priest or a third party, this energy combined with the altered state may be directed to a magical goal (a "magickal childe"). Sometimes the sexual fluids are exchanged and mixed together for Eucharistic consumption or used as a magickal ink to inscribe symbols or sigils on parchment as a talisman. In Wicca and some magickal orders, the Great Rite was also used within the initiation of the candidate as a High Priest or Priestess.

In all of these shamanic practices, whether in solitary practice or practices requiring two or more people, the intent is to induce an altered state. Sometimes it is purely a solitary mystical state as in Dervish dancing, other times it may be used to invoke a spirit or god into the body, as in Voudoun where the god "rides" the subject who is then called a "horse," and other times it is used to direct the subject's consciousness in using psychic powers for a particular goal.

Always, we can see hypnosis or self-hypnosis at work.

Programming for Self-Directed Rituals and Self-Hypnosis

Rituals are simply highly effective forms of hypnosis and self-hypnosis. As a technique of Psychic Empowerment it is exactly that: *a powerful self-directed program to involve natural psychic powers under conscious control.*

We will borrow from our book, *Self-Empowerment through Self-Hypnosis* (Slate and Weschcke, 2010) to provide sample self-hypnosis scripts to illustrate the process of ritual programming.

THE PRINCIPLES OF INDUCTION

Induction is the process that precedes the state of hypnosis, helping the subject to become receptive to new ideas and to change old habits and views. Induction *induces* the state of receptivity. Since we are emphasizing Self-Hypnosis for Self-Empowerment, the induction principles are simplified. You wouldn't be hypnotizing yourself if you had not already accepted the concept of hypnosis to bring about desired change and self-improvement and agreed to use it.

Belief and acceptance. One of the values of this book is to affirm with you the importance of both Self-Empowerment and Self-Hypnosis in bringing about desired changes and improvements in your life, and the even greater value of putting yourself in charge rather than being dependent upon external authority figures who at best have only secondhand knowledge of your needs and desires and little understanding of your concerns, values, and dreams.

Hypnosis is a science, but there is nothing difficult to learning it. Like any applied science, using hypnosis is an art that is personal to the user. The principles of induction are easy to understand and apply, and you will learn to adapt them in making them a normal part of your life. The use of Self-Hypnosis should become as constant to you as any other positive habit.

Induction aids. We know that you can put yourself into a hypnotic state, or trance. Some people use 'fascination' objects to help them enter a trance state, while others make use of special sound recordings. Neither, of course, is necessary but there is no reason not to make use of them to facilitate the process if you feel a need or desire to do so.

Among the more popular fascination objects are crystal balls (often made of glass), small pocket mirrors, black skrying "magic" mirrors, small pieces of polished black obsidian, spinning swirl discs, flickering candle flames, flickering or whirling lights, and pendulums. Or you can place a device above the head so that one must look up, a position that makes the eyes want to close.

In addition to fascination objects, other induction aids include sound recordings, counting backward (usually from ten to one), special visualizations including descending elevators or escalators, downward stairs, ocean waves rolling onto the beach, the setting sun descending to and below the horizon, retreating star fields, passing through doorways, scenes in which light is slowly replaced by darkness, etc.

In making the choice of any induction aid, simplicity is best. You don't want to become more interested in the device than in the process; you don't want to be *listening* to music; you don't want to worry about dripping wax or the danger of your candle setting things on fire. The induction aid is intended to help focus your attention inward, not on outward objects.

Security and confidence. It's up to you to set a location and situation that is secure against disturbance and disruption. Nearly any room with closed doors and windows will do, turning off the telephone and other appliances that could interrupt your session, and leaving instructions—if necessary—that you are not to be disturbed for an hour or other time period. As to confidence—of course you have confidence in yourself. You have no better friend, no better guardian, and no finer guide than yourself. If you feel the need for some form of psychic self-defense, we will provide for that as an option in your own induction process.

Relaxed body and calm mind. You are your own worst enemy and your own best friend. You are in charge of your own body and mind and it is you who can unstress your body and calm the chatter of your mind. Put aside any concerns; think 'blankly', free of wants, desires, worries; don't even think of your goals during this phase. Instruct yourself to hear only your inner voice unless there is a real emergency. (Your inner voice is exactly that: do not speak words, do not even mouth the words, but learn to hear the words in your head as if they were spoken in your own strong voice.)

Learn to think without words; instead think with feelings.

As you breathe, feel yourself doing what you would say with words—such as "sinking deeper and deeper." Feel that you are entering into your subconsciousness, where you have the power to bring your goals into manifestation. Know that your subconsciousness knows no barriers except those that you, in innocence and ignorance, or fear, self-impose. We will give you specific steps to cleanse the slate.

The right time. It is not your goal to fall asleep, hence it is important that you do not conduct your Self-Hypnosis sessions when you are fatigued and ready for sleep.

Sure, it is wonderful to go to sleep after the session, but do not use Self-Hypnosis to fall asleep unless your problem is insomnia. For this reason, it is preferable to conduct your session seated in a chair rather than lying in bed. A recliner may be acceptable, provided you are not too "laid back."

For many people the better times may be early morning or early evening. You want to be alert but not ready to hit a home run or feel disturbed by the morning or evening news. "Calm" and "alert" are your keywords in choosing the time.

THE KEY STEPS IN THE INDUCTION PROCESS

Identify. Before selecting a goal for your Self-Hypnosis program, it is important that you identify what it is that you really want. Meditate and ask your subconscious to give you some answers. Determine those psychic powers of interest, and select one. Perhaps it is astral projection, clairvoyance, or telepathy. Or perhaps it is greater skill in Tarot Reading, the Runes, use of the Pendulum, the Crystal Ball, etc. It is better to focus on a single goal at a time, or you can add two or three closely related subgoals to it. Make sure that the subgoals support the major goal.

Write it down. Write down your reasons for your choice. Build a solid case, and show the benefits. Be specific and justify the program. Convince yourself of the desirability of your goal. Why do you want to Astral Project? Why do you want to read the Tarot, or why do you want to become a better reader?

Write your expectations. Write down your expectations for results. Look into the future and see yourself accomplishing your goals, and see all that it involves.

Write an I AM sentence. Write a short, single sentence starting with "**I AM**" that expresses the successful outcome of the Self-Hypnosis you are about to undertake. Always keep the "I AM" in capital letters. This is a statement of the goal accomplished, of the new reality that has replaced the old.

Memorize it. Say it to yourself in a way that *feels* meaningful and powerful. Speak the words out loud and listen to them, and memorize the sound, the inflection, and the feeling. Then say it silently while hearing it in your head with the same feelings as when spoken out loud. Say it with energy. Say it with certainty that it already is. You will say it silently with your inner voice.

Visualize it. Close your eyes and visualize the sentence in white letters against a black background. As you see it, speak the sentence with your inner voice.

See it now. Build a picture of the future in which your goal is attained. See yourself already living in the new reality. See it, feel it, think it, believe it—you have accomplished your goal and all the benefits you expect from it. Write it down.

THE RELAXATION PROCESS

Comfort and security. Make yourself comfortable and arrange things so you will not be disturbed except for a genuine emergency. Sit either upright or partially reclining, but do not lie down unless that's a physical necessity for you. Dim the lights to a comfortable level. It is preferable that you do not have incense burning or background music. You want to avoid the distraction that these otherwise niceties can provide.

Relaxation. Do your regular relaxation to enter into meditation. One very powerful procedure is called "Tension and Release," made up of the following steps:

Tense all muscles. Take a deep breath and hold it while tensing all your muscles, from head to toe, including the facial muscles. Feel the muscle contraction in your jaw, around your eyes, even around your ears, feel it in your neck and shoulders, chest and arms, make fists, feel the contraction in your chest, abdomen, groin, upper thighs, knees, and calves, and point your toes. Hold your body with all the muscles in deep tensions until you have to let your breath out, and then relax as you breathe out completely, letting go of all tension, mind chatter, and emotional concerns.

> An alternative is called 'fractional relaxation' where you tense first your toes and then release, then your foot and release, progressing up the body all the way to the scalp. After you've done it a few times, you will be amazed at how fast and how completely you will relax the whole body.

Breathe fully and regularly. Breathe deeply, in and out, in and out, again and again. Feel and see the oxygen-rich air filled with life energy filling your lungs and spreading throughout your body. Then as you exhale, feel and see the out-breath carrying away waste products. Your body feels refreshed, healed, and deeply relaxed. Feel yourself fully cleansed, physically and mentally.

Finding the center. Continue the regular breathing, continue feeling cleansed and relaxed, and a moment will come when you feel yourself experiencing an inner awakening, opening like a flower into full receptivity. Continue enjoying this blissful state, feeling calmness, vitality, peacefulness, and strength, ready to receive your self-instruction.

INVOKING YOUR SUBCONSCIOUS MIND

See and hear your I AM sentence. When ready, see your memorized sentence in white letters against a black background in your mind's eye. Hold that vision for about two minutes while silently saying the sentence slowly with feeling and inflection. Do not count seconds and do not open your eyes to check the actual time. Just do it until you feel satisfied. Listen to your inner voice and hear it with your inner ears so it seems just as if you were hearing it aloud.

Image or Symbol. Now, silently ask your Subconscious Mind to produce a simple image or symbol to fully represent that sentence. If nothing comes to you, repeat daily until it does. There is a difference between an image and a symbol. A symbol is usually something already existing, often a three-dimensional object, with particular ideas and energies associated with it. Those ideas and energies must be in harmony with your I AM sentence to work effectively for you. An Image is usually a simple picture or visual pattern created by your subconscious to work with your "I AM" sentence. Memorize it, and draw it—no matter what your artistic skills are.

Memorize it. See your image or symbol in the same mental scene as your "I AM" sentence. Know that you now have the power to make your dream come true, the power to realize your goal, the power to make it your new reality replacing the old reality.

The New Reality. Remember that we are not merely leaving old habits behind but an old reality and replacing it with a new reality that is your own. Think about yourself in the future that will be after you have solved your problem, after you have fulfilled your goal. See yourself in this new reality as if it has already happened. Make this your future NOW. Feel yourself in the new reality, repeat your vision of the image and your "I AM" sentence together, and hear your inner voice say it. Tie all together so any time you repeat the sentence in your mind, you know that what is accomplished in the Inner World is manifesting in the physical world, and that your Body, Mind, and Spirit are working together to bring this about.

SCRIPT 1: DEVELOPING YOUR ESP AND PK POTENTIALS

This script is based on the premise that psychic potentials exist in everyone. Through appropriate practice and experience you can develop those potentials and apply them to achieve your goals and enrich your life. You can develop your Extra-Sensory-Perception (ESP) powers, which include *telepathy* or the ability to communicate mentally with others, *precognition* or the ability to perceive future events, and *clairvoyance* or the ability to mentally perceive conditions and distant events. You can develop your

Psycho-Kinetic (PK) powers or your ability to mentally influence happenings and pro-cesses. Through the script that follows, you can establish the essential conditions required to exercise each of these potentials and thus promote their full development.

Step 1. Goal Statement. Begin the script by stating in your own words your goal of developing your ESP and PK potentials.

Step 2. Focused Attention and Receptivity. Induce a state of focused atten-tion and receptivity to suggestion, either through self-hypnosis or if you prefer, through the use of a preferred meditation or deep relaxation program. Yet an-other highly effective option is the use of the drowsy state preceding sleep.

Step 3. Self-Empowerment Dialogue. While in the deeply receptive state, initiate positive self-dialogue related to your stated goal. Here are a few examples.

> *I am psychic by nature.*
>
> *My psychic potentials are essential to my personal evolvement. They are basic to my mental, physical, and spiritual existence.*
>
> *I am committed to developing my ESP and PK powers to their peaks.*
>
> *I will find ways of using my ESP and PK powers to enrich my life.*
>
> *By embracing my ESP powers, I expand the scope of my existence and give new meaning to my life.*
>
> *Day by day, I will use my psychic powers to enrich my life and bring forth de-sired change.*
>
> At this point, you may wish to present in your own words additional dia-logue specific to your personal goals and present life situation. Examples include dialogue related to social relationships, career success, problem solving, and personal improvement, to mention but a few. Such dialogue focuses your Self-Empowerment program to the Here and Now.

Step 4. Visualization. As you remain in the deeply focused and receptive state, draw and visualize a Triangle of Light* as a channel through which to experience your psychic powers. By centering your attention on the bright space within the triangle, you will become empowered to send and receive telepathic messages, allow images of precognitive significance to emerge, and view distant realities, both material and spiritual. You can use the triangle as a framework for exercising your PK power to influence events and conditions, including internal biological functions related to better health and wellness. Managing pain, promoting heal-

---

* The Triangle of Light is simply an equilateral triangle of light that you create in your imagina-tion as *you draw it with the index finger of your stronger hand.* The physical act of drawing it gives 'substance' to the visualization.

ing, and stimulating rejuvenation are all available to you through the Triangle of Light.

Step 5. Affirmation. Affirm in your own words that you are now empowered to exercise your psychic powers at will. Further affirm that you will use your ESP and PK powers to promote your personal evolvement while contributing to the good of others.

Step 6. Post-script Cue. Affirm that by simply visualizing the Triangle of Light, you will become empowered at any moment to activate the full effects of this script. This mental cue is applicable to any situation and its results are instant.

Step 7. Exit and Conclusion. Give yourself permission to exit the trance or other receptive state. End the script by taking a few moments to reflect on the relevance of this experience to your present life situation. You will further enable it by recording the entire experience in your journal.

You can accelerate the development of your ESP and PK skills through repeated use of this script along with practice in a variety of real-life situations. For instance, you can fine-tune your telepathic skills by working with others in sending and receiving telepathic messages. You can exercise your precognitive skills by visualizing future happenings, to include events ranging from personal relevance to widespread global significance. You can exercise your clairvoyant skills by such activities as locating a lost article or identifying the contents of package before opening it. You can practice your PK ability by such exercises as bringing a stationary object, such as a crumpled piece of paper, into motion. Use your creative powers to design practice exercises, and keep a journal of your progress.

With practice, you will note rapid development of your psychic skills,along with such spin-off benefits as increased feelings of competency and overall enrichment in the quality of your life. Clearly, developing your psychic powers is well worth your time and effort.

SCRIPT 2: INTERACTING WITH SPIRIT GUIDES

This script is based on the twofold concept that the spirit dimension exists and that you, as a spirit being, can interact with it. This script recognizes that you are more than mind and body, you are also spirit. Without the spirit, the mind and body would not exist. Even the physical universe at large is sustained by the spiritual force that underlies it.

This script recognizes that as a soul being, your existence is forever—from everlasting to everlasting. All things physical have a beginning and therefore an end. Difficult though it may be to comprehend, you as a soul existed forever before your first lifetime and you will exist forever beyond your last. Within that endless spectrum, you are inextricably linked to the spirit realm. You came from that realm, and you will return to it. Rather than a cold, distant inaccessible realm, it is a present though nonphysical dimension of power that is available to you at any moment. As a soul, you are in fact integrally connected to it.

Through your interactions with that dimension, you can become increasingly empowered to fulfill the basic purpose of your existence in this physical realm—to learn and grow while, at the same time, helping others. Spirit guides from the spirit realm are constantly poised to promote your fulfillment of that all-important purpose. This script is designed to promote empowering interactions with those spirit guides.

(This script makes no presumptions about the form that your Spirit Guide may assume in your consciousness, and neither should you. Spirit is multidimensional and nondimensional. Your guide will manifest as most beneficial to your needs—as a wise person, a loving animal, an angelic being, or a mere presences. You may experience your guide in vision, as a voice, or in just knowing. There may be dialogue or there may just be a flash of knowledge. Spirit knows no boundaries and your spirit, too, is without bounds.)

Step 1. Goal Statement. Begin the script by stating in your own words your goal of interacting with spirit guides. You may wish to include other specific goals related to that interaction, such as solving a particular personal problem, achieving career success, building self-esteem, or coping with a difficult life situation.

Step 2. Focused Attention and Receptivity. Induce a state of focused attention and receptivity to suggestion, either through self-hypnosis or another preferred option, such as meditation, deep relaxation, or the drowsy state preceding sleep.

Step 3. Self-Empowerment Dialogue. While in the deeply receptive state, initiate positive self-dialogue related to your stated goal. Here are a few examples:

I am more than mind and body, I am also spirit—the essential essence of my existence.

As a spirit being, I am intimately connected to the spirit realm and its wealth of empowerment resources.

I am at this moment empowered to engage the spirit realm and interact with spirit guides that make up that bright dimension.

My interactions with the spirit realm are essential to my growth as an evolving soul.

Step 4. Visualization. As you remain in the deeply focused and receptive state, visualize a beam of light connecting you to the spirit realm as a glowing dimension of unparalleled beauty. Rather than some distant, untouchable realm, think of it as spiritually present with spirit guides in clear view. Should you decide to do so, you can even reach out and touch that realm and embrace its spirit guides.

Step 5. Affirmation. Affirm your resolve to engage an on-going interaction with your personal spirit guides as sources of enlightenment, support, and fulfillment. As you continue the interaction, you can again state your personal goals and invite the support of spirit guides in achieving them. (At this step, a particular guide will sometimes come forward, and its name will become known.)

Step 6. Postscript Cue. Affirm that by simply visualizing the bright beam of light connecting you to the spirit dimension, you can instantly generate an interaction with your spirit guide(s) and activate the full empowering effects of this script.

Step 7. Exit and Conclusion. End the script by giving yourself permission to exit the trance or other receptive state. Take as long as you need to reflect on the experience and its empowering relevance.

The script now complete, reaffirm in your own words the spiritual essence of your existence and the supremacy of the spiritual over the physical. Express your appreciation of the guiding presence you came to know through this script. Take time to enjoy that presence as a source of comfort, power, and joy. Record it in your Journal.

SCRIPT 3: DEVELOPING YOUR MEDIUMISTIC POTENTIAL

The mediumistic potential is the capacity to directly communicate with entities in the spirit realm. The skilled medium is anyone who has developed that potential and applies it, often to initiate communication with a departed relative or friend. At another level, the skill can be applied to initiate interactions with highly advanced spirit beings who can be important sources of spiritual enlightenment and knowledge.

This script is based on the premise that the mediumistic potential exists to some degree in everyone. The best medium is, in fact, already a part of your innermost self. Through this script, that personal medium can become an invaluable source of spiritual insight and personal power. Mediumistic communications that utilize that inner medium can increase your feelings of self-worth, promote inner balance and attunement, and inspire you to reach your highest peak of spiritual growth. Here's the script.

Step 1. Goal Statement. Formulate your goal of developing your mediumistic potentials and using them to empower your life. In stating your goal, you may wish to specify the discovery of advanced spirit teachers who will facilitate your mediumistic development.

Step 2. Focused Attention and Receptivity. Induce a state of focused attention and receptivity to suggestion, either through self-hypnosis or some other referred option, such as meditation, deep relaxation, or the drowsy state preceding sleep.

Step 3. Self-Empowerment Dialogue. While in the deeply focused and receptive state, initiate positive self-dialogue related to the development and application of your mediumistic potentials. Here are a few examples.

> *I am a spiritual being, and my destiny is spiritual evolvement.*

> *By interacting with the spirit dimension, I am fulfilling that destiny and bringing deeper meaning into my life.*

> *By developing my mediumistic powers, I am becoming empowered to communicate and interact with spirit entities existing in the spirit dimension.*

> *My mediumistic interactions are critical to my understanding of myself and my destiny.*

> *I am committed to using my mediumistic powers to accelerate my spiritual evolvement while contributing to the greater good.*

Step 4. Visualization. Visualize a gateway to the spirit realm and imagine yourself opening it to reveal a dimension of indescribable beauty. Sense the peace and harmony flowing from that dimension permeating your total being. Notice the presence of others beyond the gate and the bright glow enveloping them. At this point, you may recognize certain departed loved ones, friends, and familiar spirit guides who have been with you in the past. Give yourself permission to communicate and interact with them. You will notice that beings on the other side can come and go through the gateway to interact with souls on this side. Clearly, it's a spiritual gateway of interaction, not separation. You too can briefly slip through that gate to interact with the spirit realm, should you decide to do so. Adding to the beauty of the spirit realm is the presence of animals and plant life—could it be heaven without them? To conclude this step, visualize yourself closing the gateway, thus ending your mediumistic interaction with the other side.

Step 5. Affirmation. Affirm your strong commitment to use your mediumistic powers to gain knowledge of spiritual relevance and use it as needed to promote your spiritual evolvement while contributing to the higher good.

Step 6. Postscript Cue. Give yourself the postscript cue that you can at any moment activate your mediumistic powers by simply visualizing the gateway to the spirit realm and yourself opening it.

Step 7. Exit and Conclusion. Conclude this script by giving yourself permission to exit the trance or other receptive state. Take time to reflect on the information gained during the experience and your sense of spiritual empowerment. Record your experience.

This script opens an exciting gateway to the spirit realm as an unlimited source of power and knowledge. Through repeated practice of the script, you will fine-tune your ability to use your mediumistic powers. You will discover ways of applying them at will to increase your understanding of your present and future existence. You will discover that the other side is a rich dimension of continued growth and fulfillment. You will see your present life as filled with wondrous opportunities for growth and fulfillment. You will see death, not as a sad closing of a door, but as a marvelous gateway to another dimension filled with limitless possibilities.

SCRIPT 4: DISCOVERING HIGHER PLANES OF POWER

The script is based on the premise that the spirit dimension consists of not only spirit beings but also many planes, each of a different power. Through this script, you will discover ways of interacting with different planes and accessing their unique powers. You will discover that the color of a given plane provides a valuable guide to its power attribute.

Interestingly, the significance of color in the spirit realm is not unlike that associated with the human aura. Radiant green, for instance, in the human and the spirit realm alike, is typically associated with healing, clear blue with serenity, and yellow with intelligence, to list but a few. Our lab studies found that through this script, *you can actually introduce new color into your aura with the associated skill by interacting with a higher plane of that color.* That finding suggests that higher planes are not simply lifeless or dormant repositories of color, but rather dynamic life force energies that are readily accessible to each of us to enrich and empower our lives. Here's the script.

Step 1. Goal Statement. State in your own words your goal of discovering higher planes of power and interacting with them to access their wide-ranging powers. You may wish to address specific concerns related to your present life situation, such as social relationships, finances, health and fitness, academic or career success, and rejuvenation, to mention but a few.

Step 2. Focused Attention and Receptivity. Induce a state of focused attention and receptivity to suggestion, either through self-hypnosis or if you prefer, through the use of a preferred meditation or deep relaxation program. Yet another highly effective option is the use of the drowsy state preceding sleep. For this script, it is important to relax your hands either in your lap or at your sides with the palms turned upward.

Step 3. Self-Empowerment Dialogue. While in the deeply focused and receptive state, initiate positive self-dialogue related to your goal of discovering and interacting with higher planes of power. Here are a few examples:

Life-force energy is essential to my existence as an evolving soul.

The higher planes of life-force energy are constantly available to me and receptive to my interest and interactions.

I am fully committed to developing my capacity to interact with higher planes of power.

By interacting with higher planes of power, I can achieve even my most difficult goals.

I am enriched mentally, physically, and spiritually through my interactions with higher planes of power.

Balance, attunement, and success are now available to me through my interactions with higher planes of power.

Note: You may wish at this point to include highly specific dialogue related to particular personal goals, such as better health, stress control, problem solving, or breaking an unwanted habit.

Step 4. Visualization. As you remain in a deeply receptive state, visualize the spirit realm with its myriad of colorful planes, each situated over the other like smooth layers of cirrus clouds stretched across the horizon. With your hands resting comfortably in your lap or at your sides and your palms turned upward, select a shimmering plane that stands out from the others and visualize a bright beam of light reaching from the plane to the palm of your hand. Think of your hands as your body's antennae to the universe as you sense the powerful infusion of the plane's energy, first in your hands and then throughout your body. Sense the attunement and balance that always accompany this experience. Once the infusion is complete, you can select other planes of color and interact with them one-by-one, depending on your preferences and needs. For goals related to health, fitness, and rejuvenation, interactions with iridescent planes of emerald are recommended. Planes of yellow are associated with enriched mental and social functions. Blue planes represent serenity, relaxation, and balance. For goals related to spirituality, interactions with planes of purple or indigo are recommended. An exceptionally radiant plane that commands your attention is typically appropriate for any pressing life situation.

5. Affirmation. In your own words, affirm the empowering effects of your interactions with higher planes. Further affirm that the multiple higher planes of power are constantly available and receptive to your interaction with them.

6. Postscript Cue. Affirm that you can at any moment activate the full empowering effects of this script by simply bringing your hands together to form the so-called *handclasp of power*. You can use that simple cue at will to generate an instant infusion of higher plane power related to the situation at hand.

7. Exit and Conclusion. To end the script, give yourself permission to exit the trance or other receptive state. Take plenty of time to reflect on the experience and ways of using it to more fully empower your life. Journal your experience.

This script is one of the most effective Self-Empowerment programs known—its limits, if they exist at all, are unknown. It has been used with success to instantly break the smoking habit, generate highly creative ideas, overcome persistent fear, lose weight, manage pain, retrieve past-life experiences, solve pressing problems, and even gain material wealth, to list only a few of the possibilities. Beginning now, you can use this script to empower your life as never before with enrichment, success, and happiness.

In this chapter, we have reviewed the use of Ritual, Prayer, Shamanic Practices, and Hypnotic Scripts as techniques to evoke innate psychic powers and develop them into functioning skills that can be used independently or in conjunction with various "tools" we will introduce in Part Two of this book.

It is our belief that all "power" comes from the *Source* within and does not reside in the words and gestures of ritual and action used in its evocation. Nevertheless, these words, gestures, tools, and techniques are all part of the time-proven esoteric technology passed down to us generation after generation. We literally "walk on the bones of our ancestors" and honor them for their Great Work through which we grow and *become more than we are.*

The Past has given us the Future, and the Future is our call to act with Vision and Wisdom to fulfill the Great Plan that has been with us from the Beginning.

SOURCES AND RECOMMENDED READING

Personal Correspondence between Carl Llewellyn Weschcke, Gerald B. Gardner, and Charles Clarke.

Teresa Cheung, *The Element Encyclopedia of the Psychic World* (HarperElement, 2006).

Lynne McTaggert, *The Intention Experiment: Using Your Thoughts to Change Your Life and the World* (Free Press, 2007).

Joe H. Slate and Carl Llewellyn Weschcke, *Self-Empowerment through Self-Hypnosis* (Llewellyn, 2010).

10

PRECOGNITION

Tomorrow as Probability

For I dipt into the future, far as human eye could see,
Saw the Vision of the world, and all the wonder that would be...

—ALFRED, LORD TENNYSON, *LOCKSLEY HALL*

In the above quotation from *Locksley Hall* (1835), Tennyson reflects on the human capacity to experience precognitively the future. Like other mental faculties, the ability to perceive the future independently of presently known predictive circumstances exists to some degree in everyone. Explaining that faculty, however, is a difficult needle to thread. One view holds that events yet to occur already exist in a fixed, unalterable form in the dimension we call the future. A related view assumes that while future events already exist, they exist in a flexible form that is subject to human intervention. A "middle-of-the road" explanation postulates that while some future events are unalterably fixed in time and cannot be influenced or changed, others exist in forms that are responsive to human intervention and shifting present conditions. A modification of that view holds that the future exists only in varying degrees of probabilities, ever dependent on past and present realities.

When the dots are finally connected, each view related to the fixedness of the future assumes the existence of time as an energy dimension within a continuum of the past, present, and future. From that perspective, personal consciousness, likewise an energy phenomenon, is endowed with the capacity to interact with that dimension to generate a *mind/future interaction* that not only perceives the future but influences it as well. In today's complex world, the precognitive challenge thus becomes twofold: to develop our precognitive powers to their peaks and use them to bring forth desired change.

By developing our capacity to interact with the continuum of time, we become empowered not only to access the future through precognition but also to dip into the past through retrocognition. While the past exists in unalterable or fixed form, increased knowledge of that dimension can alter our perceptions of the present and empower us to more effectively shape the future. For instance, personal growth blockages including phobias and conflicts of past-life origin can be resolved, often instantly, through the retrocognitive retrieval of relevant past-life experiences. On a broader scale, awareness of the sources of global problems ranging from disease to environmental pollution can be essential to the correction of causative conditions. Once you're attuned to the continuum of time, your retrocognitive and precognitive potentials will become activated to work hand-in-hand to empower you as never before to increase the quality of your life while contributing to a better world.

In addition to our retrocognitive and precognitive potentials are a host of other psychic faculties with relevance to the future. Among them are *clairvoyance* as the extrasensory ability to increase awareness of distant conditions, including those with important implications for the future, and *telepathy* with its capacity to send and receive thought messages, again to include messages with relevance to future happenings. Aside from these extrasensory faculties is our capacity to actually influence distant causative happenings through *psychokinesis* (PK). When we add to these the human capacity to tap into higher sources of knowledge and power through such programs as *interdimensional interaction*, the possibilities are expanded beyond all limits.

Like other forms of ESP, precognition can include both thought and mood elements. The mood element alone is often a critical precursor of the impending event, with the mood state directly proportional to the event. Unexplained changes in mood are particularly relevant with the anxious or depressed state foretelling adversity or misfortune, and the elated, optimistic state foretelling positive events. Several days prior to his tragic death in a plane crash, Ricky Nelson was reportedly despondent, a mood state reportedly highly uncharacteristic of the singer. Similarly, Clark Gable was reportedly agitated and depressed for several days prior to the death of the actress, Carol Lombard, also in a plane crash.

Future misfortunes that will exact a heavy toll on our lives tend to signal their impending occurrence either to prepare us for the imminent misfortune or to help us prevent it. That application was vividly illustrated by a nurse whose spontaneous precognitive impression may have prevented a serious auto accident. Upon nearing a busy intersection, she experienced the distinct impression of a car failing to yield the right of way. She applied her brakes only moments before a van suddenly appeared from a side street and skidded into her path. In a similar instance, a graduate student, upon approaching a sharp curve on a busy street, experienced a clear image of a stalled automobile just around the curve. He applied his brakes barely in time to avoid colliding with the vehicle.

Although reported instances of precognition involving adversity and misfortune are not uncommon, the typical precognitive experience concerns ordinary, non-threatening life situations which nevertheless hold significant relevance to the present. Even ill-defined impressions of future events can provide important information about the future that would be otherwise unavailable to us.

PRECOGNITION AND THE SUBCONSCIOUS

Although precognition can be explained simply as the extrasensory capacity of consciousness to perceive the future, there is powerful evidence that the subconscious can function as both a channel and a storehouse for precognitive knowledge. Once perceived at a subconscious level, precognitive awareness of a future happening can be retained in the subconscious to become a powerful motivator. On the other hand, it can be conveyed from there to conscious awareness, either directly or indirectly, through such mechanisms as dreams, déjà vu, and a host of challenging fragments such as slips of the tongue or pen, vague premonitions, and enigmatic emotions. Like a picture puzzle, these "precognitive bits and pieces," once assembled, can provide a coherent picture of a significant future event. Fortunately, programs are now available, as we will later see, to access precognitive knowledge existing within the subconscious and convey it from there to conscious awareness.

Based on the view that time exists as an energized continuum, the role of the subconscious in precognition can be summarized as a three-step phenomenon:

PRECOGNITIVE ROLE OF THE SUBCONSCIOUS

1. Subconscious energies interact with the continuum of time to gain extrasensory awareness of the future;

2. The subconscious interacts with consciousness to facilitate a direct or indirect transfer of precognitive information; and

3. The conscious/subconscious interaction becomes a motivational force that promotes the productive application of precognitive knowledge.

A related view of precognition explains the phenomenon as an energized linkage between the continuum of human consciousness and the continuum of time. The resultant interaction between consciousness and time embraces the infinite nature of both continuums, a phenomenon that could help explain the spiritual nature of our existence and our capacity as spiritual beings to tap into the future, including the afterlife, as a source of knowledge and power.

THE PRECOGNITIVE REALITY SLIP

A seemingly unrelated situational cue can precipitate a spontaneous but significant precognitive impression. Called a "precognitive reality slip," the cue becomes a signal that instantly activates the mind's precognitive faculty, particularly in danger-related situations. That possibility was illustrated by a supervisor at a chemical plant who experienced during an early afternoon thunderstorm a vivid image of an explosion in the plant's storage facility. He ordered an evacuation of the area shortly before the explosion occurred exactly as envisioned. The sudden burst of thunder provided a critical reality slip that may have saved many lives and prevented serious injuries.

In another instance of precognitive reality slippage, an accountant experienced over lunch a voice from a nearby table that he mistook to be that of his mother, who lived in a distant city. The experience lingered in his mind until late afternoon when he received an urgent call that his mother had just suffered a stroke. Yet another precognitive reality slip was reported by a couple who, upon leaving their home, mistook for a fire the unusually bright reflection of their car lights in a front window of their home. A few days later, the house was destroyed by fire. Rather than simply coincidental, such slips as these could be purposefully designed by the subconscious to command our attention and promote preparation or prevention of a future event. A key feature of such slips is that they tend to linger in the conscious mind, often in vivid detail, until either preventive measures are undertaken or the predicted event occurs.

Adding to its complexity, the precognitive reality slip occasionally occurs in antithetical form, particularly when it involves dreaming. A high school athlete's recurring dream of losing a scheduled football game actually predicted antithetically a winning game. Fortunately, antithetical precognitive reality slips are often accompanied by clues to their antithetical meanings. In the athlete's dream, the helmet he wore was that of the opposing team, a clue to the dream's antithetical significance. In another instance, a noted trial attorney vividly dreamed of a guilty verdict for his client, but there was a critical flaw in the dream: his client, a female, was depicted as a male, a clear signal of the dream's true antithetical message which later proved accurate—a not-guilty verdict for his client.

EMPOWERMENT AT ITS PEAK

Knowledge is by its intrinsic nature empowering, and precognitive knowledge is empowerment at its peak. We now know that our conscious and subconscious faculties work together to acquire new knowledge, including that of precognitive and retrocognitive origin. Assuming that time exists on an energized continuum consisting of past, present, and future, it's plausible that the energies of consciousness could conceivably interact with the energies of time to acquire the knowledge required to promote our personal growth while bringing forth desired change.

Precognition provides such an extensive range of information and insight that hardly an individual or organization could fail to benefit from the experience. Here's a summary of the empowering possibilities of precognitive knowledge:

PRECOGNITION AND PSYCHIC EMPOWERMENT

- Precognition can awaken and place in a state of readiness the inner faculties required to more effectively meet the demands of the present and future alike.

- Precognition can expand our awareness of the consequences of present actions and our capacity to shape the future by taking command of present situations. It can provide the lead time essential in preparing for disquieting or formidable events.

- Precognition along with retrocognition can attune us to the continuum of time and thereby manifest the continuity of our existence as evolving souls.

- Precognition and retrocognition together can generate a state of inner balance and self-enlightenment that empowers us to reach beyond the limitations of the present.

- Precognition can increase our sense of personal worth and well-being by connecting us to the psychic nature of our being.

- Precognition can expand our awareness of the afterlife and provide confirmation of our existence beyond death.

- Precognition can increase our effectiveness in making personal decisions, including but not limited to those related to careers, relationships, and finances.

- Precognition can stimulate problem solving and creativity.

- Precognitive awareness of future possibilities can build a powerful success-expectancy effect that increases motivation, generates self-confidence, and gives the winning edge to future performance.

- Precognition and retrocognition can together validate the expansive nature of consciousness and the bidirectional endlessness of our existence.

PRECOGNITIVE DEVELOPMENT

To deny our capacity to experience the future through precognition is to eliminate one of the most important gateways to new knowledge, growth, and power. Fortunately, procedures are now available to develop our precognitive capacities and apply them as personal empowerment resources.

As an enriched extension of sensory perception, precognition is an expression of our native tendency to perceive the future psychically. In its voluntarily induced form, precognitive awareness is activated deliberately through certain procedures and techniques, some of which were developed in the controlled laboratory setting. Almost without exception, programs designed to promote precognition resulted in a generalized effect that promoted the development of other psychic functions, including telepathy and clairvoyance. Here a few of the precognition programs developed in our labs at Athens State University under the auspices of the Parapsychology Research Institute and Foundation, which was established at the university specifically to explore psychic phenomena.

THE FUTURE PROBE PROGRAM

The Future Probe Program, a group procedure, is designed to promote development of the precognition potential which exists to some degree in everyone. The program begins with the formulation of a set of measurable precognitive objectives. For instance, the group may decide to precognitively identify future events that will be reported as news headlines in a local paper within a limited time period. The group then engages in a relaxation exercise presented verbally by a group leader as follows:

> As I prepare to probe the future, I am becoming more and more comfortable and relaxed. Every muscle and joint from my forehead to the tips of my toes is loose and limp. As I breathe slowly and rhythmically, time is slowing down. I am tranquil and serene, confident and secure. I am now ready to begin my probe of the future.

With eyes closed, the group is then instructed to form a mental image of a selected moving object—a bird in flight, a leaf in a breeze, a fluffy cloud, and so forth. The group stays with the moving object until a sense of the future is achieved. An open, receptive state of mind is maintained as precognitive impressions unfold. Results of the probe session are then recorded and researched to determine the accuracy of the predictions.

Given sufficient practice, future probe groups typically increase both the quantity and accuracy of their predictions.

THE FUTURE SCREEN PROGRAM

Another highly effective program designed to stimulate precognitive awareness is The Future Screen, a meditative approach that emphasizes the role of relaxation and imagery in exercising the precognitive faculty. To begin the program, close your eyes and induce a progressively relaxed state by slowing your breathing and mentally scanning your body from the head downward. Allow every muscle and joint to become loose and limp as relaxation soaks deeper and deeper into your body. With your body relaxed, clear your mind of all active thought and allow a passive, serene mental state to emerge slowly. Next, envision a blank screen upon which scenes of the future can be projected. Take a few moments to focus only on the blank screen, and then allow scenes from the future to appear spontaneously on the screen. Take plenty of time for meaningful images to form. To assume control over the future, generate images of desired developments or outcomes. Deliberately project them as clearly as possible upon the screen as precognitive images of the future. Conclude the procedure with positive affirmations that your precognitive powers are fully liberated.

THE DOORS TO THE FUTURE PROGRAM

The Doors to the Future Program is designed to literally open selected doors to the future to reveal future events related to certain specific concerns. Here's the procedure.

While in a relaxed, tranquil state, visualize a hallway with the word "Future" inscribed in bold letters over the entrance. Imagine yourself entering the hallway with its many doors on each side. Visualize doors of many colors and materials: gold, steel, wood, glass, silver, brass, and jade. Picture a word representing the future inscribed on each door: career, finances, relationships, family, and health; or more deeply personal inscriptions such as the names of persons and personal issues. The inscriptions can also be national or global in nature. Allow one door to remain without an inscription. Select a door and imagine yourself opening it. Allow a panoramic view of the future to emerge. You may choose to step inside the door and become an active participant in the unfolding events of the future. Select other doors and open them at will. The noninscribed door is reserved for accessing information about the future concerning nonspecified topics. The noninscribed door is useful in uncovering future events such as natural catastrophes, political developments, and international affairs. Conclude the program with affirmations of your power to use precognitive knowledge responsibly to either alter the future or to effectively accommodate the unalterable. *Note: This program can be effectively implemented during hypnosis following appropriate training that included the mastery of effective trance induction and management skills.*

PRECOGNITIVE REVIEW PROGRAM

Precognitive Review is a program designed to review future events related to a current situation until a particular outcome emerges as the most probable. Here's the program.

While in a tranquil, relaxed state, identify a situation for which precognitive information would be useful. Take plenty of time to form realistic images of the prevailing situation, giving attention to specific details. Mentally identify the potential outcomes of the present situation. Identify as many alternatives as possible. Review the potential outcomes, turning them over one by one in your mind. Permit images of other outcomes to unfold spontaneously. Allow the process to continue until one outcome emerges as the strongest and most probable. Following a brief resting period in which the mind is cleared, repeat the reviewing process, giving particular attention to any confirmation of the previous result. Continue the review process until a clear impression of the future unfolds.

Concerns regarding the future of personal relationships and careers seem particularly receptive to this procedure. College students have found this exercise useful as a source of information about graduate schools they will attend, geographic locations of their future employment, and career specialties they will pursue.

Hypnotic Age Progression

A highly promising program for developing your precognitive skills is *hypnotic age progression*, an innovative approach that has demonstrated unusual effectiveness in identifying future events of both personal and global significance. The program uses self-hypnosis to induce the trance state, during which awareness flows with ease along the time continuum until it is arrested either voluntarily or spontaneously to engage areas that command special attention. This approach is especially effective in identifying future happenings that can be either prevented or minimized through appropriate intervention measures. Crises related to business and personal concerns are particularly receptive to this approach. *Note: This approach requires specialized training in self-hypnosis, and should be practiced only under appropriately controlled conditions.*

CONCLUSION

Aside from its capacity to forecast specific future events, precognition as a gateway to the future can function as a continuing source of insight that promotes our overall growth and self-empowerment. The ever-increasing span of knowledge available through precognition empowers us to engage life with greater confidence and enthusiasm. While precognition can accurately identify the most highly probable of future happenings, it at the same time recognizes personal choice as the major force in shaping future events.

SOURCES AND RECOMMENDED READING

Larry Dossey, *The Power of Premonitions: How Knowing the Future Can Shape Our Lives* (Dutton, 2009).

Joe H. Slate and Carl Llewellyn Weschcke, *Self-Empowerment Through Self-Hypnosis* (Llewellyn Publications, 2010).

11

PSYCHOKINESIS: A HOLISTIC VIEW
Mind over Matter—Every Day

Nothing more vividly illustrates the far-reaching power of the mind than psychokinesis (PK). Psychokinesis, also known as telekinesis, is typically defined as the ability to mentally influence objects or conditions in the absence of intervening physical energy or intermediary instrumentation. Within this broad definition is the assumed capacity of the mind to generate and target energy to influence external situations and internal conditions as well.

Although PK is typically considered a singular mental phenomenon, the psychic empowerment perspective embraces a "holistic" view that reaches far beyond conventional explanations. While focusing on the relevance of thinking, feeling, and perceiving, the holistic view of PK embraces our capacity as energized beings to engage empowering interactions with other dimensions of reality as sources of energy and power. Aside from that, the holistic view recognizes the contributions of quantum mechanics, to include concepts related to the teleporting of tangible objects and the transmitting of matter to distant destinations (*The Futurist*, 2008). From a holistic perspective, it becomes increasing conceivable that the teleportation of materials and matter to distant destinations is a reasonable reality awaiting our discovery and poised for unfoldment.

Within our definition of PK is the assumed capacity of PK to influence not only external conditions but also physiology, to include critical systems and organ functions. The capacity of PK to intervene physiologically has been dramatically illustrated in the biofeedback setting, where increased awareness of biological processes led to the ability to mentally control them, including such functions as blood pressure, muscular tension, migraine and tension headaches, heart rate, and brain wave patterns. Given these powers of the mind over the body, PK interventions that promote wellness and healing become reasonable possibilities. Aside from these, our lab studies offered convincing evidence of the capacity of PK to slow the aging process, and in some instances to literally reverse the effects of aging (Slate, 2001).

Not unlike other paranormal phenomena, PK can be either spontaneous or deliberately induced. You may have, for instance, dropped a valuable vase or other object, and found yourself spontaneously reacting by catching your breath and assuming a tense physical state to mentally slow the fall and prevent damage to the object. Almost incredibly, in some instances it may have worked, with the fragile object perhaps bouncing instead of shattering. Similarly, in emergency situations, such as a near-accident involving a skidding automobile, you may have attempted mentally to bring the situation under control by perhaps catching your breath and tensing your muscles rather than passively awaiting a collision. As a passenger, you may have even pressed the floorboard as your brake substitute. From a nonpsychic perspective, these reactions could be seen as merely normal mental and physical responses to perceived danger, but psychically, they could reflect our innate tendency under certain circumstances to intervene mentally into the physical world to manage situations and bring forth desired outcomes.

The influences of mind over matter and motion are especially evident in a variety of sports-related situations in which the mental state of athletes and spectators alike appear to influence outcomes in competitive events. There's abundant evidence that a highly positive mental state with strong expectations of success asserts a powerful influence in any performance situation. In team sports, the positive energies of the team can generate a force that increases its physical capacities and sharpens its skills. Complementing that effect is the influence of supportive spectators whose energies can tilt the balance and determine which team wins. While we could call this phenomenon the "audience effect," it could more accurately be called the "interactive PK effect" in which the "pull" of the audience generates a powerful PK interaction that literally increases the team's performance powers. Perhaps not surprisingly, the larger the support group and the more focused its supportive energies, the greater its psychokinetic empowering effects. Similarly, in highly skilled activities such as ballet, karate, gymnastics, and figure skating, the mental state of the performer combined with the interactive PK effect can dramatically increase the quality of performance.

PK IN THE LABORATORY

The PK potential existing in everyone seems at times to have a mind of its own. We've yet to uncover the limits of this remarkable phenomenon. In the laboratory setting, it seeks validation of not only its existence, but its relevance as well. Outside the lab setting, it seeks a host of practical applications. More effective problem solving, better quality of life, greater success in achieving your personal goals, and of course, better health and fitness are all suggested by the capacity of mind to influence objects, conditions, and events.

That capacity has been repeatedly demonstrated in experiments at Athens State University designed to initiate motion in stationary objects. Among the studies was an experiment in which a group of ten volunteer subjects was instructed to induce movement in a pendulum suspended under a bell jar. With the bell jar and its suspended glass pendulum situated on a table before the group, the group was instructed simply to gaze at the pendulum in an effort to bring it into motion. Within moments, the pendulum began a slow turning movement, followed by a swinging motion that increased until the pendulum struck the sides of the bell jar. The students were then instructed to bring the pendulum to rest and, again within moments, the pendulum returned to its slow turning movement and then to complete rest.

Similar results were obtained with a second group of ten students with five seated at opposite sides of the bell jar. Using the so-called "push-pull technique" with a metronome pacing their efforts, one group pushed against the pendulum as the other group pulled the pendulum toward them. Again, within minutes, the pendulum began a slow swinging movement, whereupon the metronome was promptly stopped. Through their continued pushing against the pendulum as it moved away from them and pulling at it as it moved toward them, the group increased the pendulum's swinging motion until it struck the sides of the bell jar. The groups were then instructed to reverse their efforts by pushing against the pendulum as it moved toward them and pulling the pendulum toward them as it moved away. Within moments, the pendulum came to a complete rest.

In another experiment, conducted as a learning exercise in a classroom setting in which there was no breeze or airflow, a group of forty-three students was given the task of bringing into motion a sheet of paper crumpled into a spherical mass. With the crumpled mass situated at the center of a desk located in front of the class, the students were instructed to use their PK powers to move the mass across the desk. They were then given two-minute practice exercises with a one-minute rest period between them. On the third exercise, the crumpled mass began to move slowly toward the edge of the desk until it fell upon the floor.

REALITY PK

PK outside the lab is a goal-oriented phenomenon with a wide range of practical applications. It can provide personal enrichment, and in some instances, protection in times of danger. A teacher, for instance, used her PK powers to slow her fall down a flight of stairs. Upon losing her step at the top of the stairs, she caught her breath and thought, "Slow motion." She recalled, "I felt myself flowing with the fall until I firmly said, *Stop*."

She sustained only minor injuries in an accident that could have had serious consequences. In a similar instance, an engineer who had just purchased a car experienced a PK event that may have saved his life. While attempting to negotiate a sharp curve on an unfamiliar road, he lost control of the car as it began skidding toward a railing. With his foot on the brakes, the car continued to speed toward the railing until he commanded it to stop. It stopped immediately, as if in direct response to his command.

In another instance, a student with a history of migraine headaches discovered, while enrolled in a biofeedback class, that he could control the headaches by physically relaxing his body and deliberately altering the temperature of his fingers. Basic to biofeedback training is the concept of mind over body, or the capacity of mental processes to alter physiological functions in order to achieve a stated goal, yet another example of the empowering possibilities of PK.

THE DELIBERATE INDUCTION OF PK

When we consider the many manifestations of PK, whether spontaneous or deliberate, the empowering potential of this interactive phenomenon becomes increasing evident. When the dots are finally connected, PK could be considered an on-going mental phenomenon, constantly influencing both internal and external physical realities. Even though the complexities of PK are far from fully understood, the following four progressive stages tend to characterize the induced PK event that targets a specific goal:

STAGES OF INDUCED PK

Alert stage. At this stage, the inner PK potential enters a state of mental alertness and empowerment readiness. The following three essential conditions are effective in alerting the PK potential and placing it in a readiness mode: (1) formulating clear objectives; (2) envisioning desired results; and (3) generating positive expectations of success. A positive mental state invariably increases PK readiness, whereas doubt dilutes the PK potential.

Centering stage. This is a critical stage at which PK energies are generated, typically through concentration, and then mentally assembled into an appropriate image, such as a ray of bright energy or an orb with an enveloping glow.

Focusing stage. At this stage, the mind is cleared of distractions as the centered energies are mentally aimed at the target. For distant, unseen targets, the eyes are typically closed to form a clear mental image of the target.

Releasing stage. In this final stage, the focused energies are mentally released. Strong affirmations of success are crucial at this stage. For either seen or unseen targets, images of desired effects generated as brief affirmations are presented. Such direct, one-word statements as *move, heal, repair, correct, make whole,* and even *levitate*, when combined with relevant imagery, are effective, especially when presented verbally. *The sound of your own voice almost always increases the effectiveness of empowering affirmations.*

As with other psychic empowerment programs, practice is essential to the development of your PK potentials. Practice that exercises your PK powers can energize each of the progressive stages of PK as previously discussed. Beyond that, it can build your self-confidence and increase your expectations of success, both of which are critical to the development of your psychic skills. Among the simplest practice exercises is the PK Bombardment Drill. Developed in our labs, the simple drill is a coin-flipping exercise designed to influence the fall of a coin in an effort to determine which side is turned up when the coin comes to rest. Here's the exercise.

PK BOMBARDMENT DRILL

Step 1. While holding the selected coin prior to each toss, clear your mind, and with your eyes closed, visualize the designated outcome (heads or tails). Stroke the coin as you continue to visualize the designated outcome. Affirm: *I will influence the fall of this coin.*

Step 2. Toss the coin and assume firm control by focusing your attention upon it. Bombard the coin with clear imagery and verbal commands of the selected outcome.

Step 3. Continue bombarding the coin until it comes to rest.

Step 4. Repeat the drill and keep a record of your progress.

The PK Bombardment Drill can be easily adapted to other PK practice exercises, including the tossing of dice and bringing a pendulum into motion. It is also readily adaptable to the group setting. Group PK is based on the premise that the combined PK faculties of a group can be organized to produce a synergistic PK effect in which the PK power of the whole group is greater than the sum of its individual parts. *Critical to group PK are a positive and cooperative group interaction, consensus of purpose within the group, and a fusion of the group's psychic energies,* all of which can be facilitated by group participation in goal setting and practice in a variety of preliminary visualization exercises prior to the PK activity.

PK AND WELLNESS

Repeated observations of PK in both the laboratory setting and real-life situations suggest a phenomenon with near-unlimited empowerment possibilities. Given the capacity of PK to mentally influence external processes and conditions, it requires no quantum leap to assume the potential of PK to influence complex inner processes and conditions, including those related to our mental and physical health and well-being.

The capacity of mental factors to influence the physical body, as indicated earlier in our discussion of biofeedback, suggests profound empowering possibilities. Unfortunately, the same capacity of the mind, if misdirected, also suggests potentially disempowering consequences. Many physical and mental illnesses are associated with disempowering stress that chips away at our biological systems, depletes our psychological resources, and weakens our ability to adjust to the demands of daily life. Given time, excessive stress can lead to serious tissue damage, organ dysfunctions, and even death. Almost every major category of illness can, in fact, be affected by psychological factors.

If disempowering mental factors—stress, conflict, fear, inferiority, and inadequacy feelings, to list but a few—can contribute to the initiation or exacerbation of illness, it would follow that the alleviation of negative stress and disempowering mental states could promote tissue repair and normal physiological functioning. Even more exiting is the possibility of our actively intervening in ways that prevent illness and promote mental and physical well-being.

The mind and body are in a state of constant interaction. Wellness programs are designed to tap into that interaction and influence it in ways that meet the goals of health and fitness. The psychic concept of wellness is based on the twofold premise that inner wellness resources exist in a form that can be mentally accessed, and second, those resources are at a state of constant readiness to distribute wellness energies throughout the body.

MIND-BODY INTERACTION FOR WELLNESS

The Wellness Activation Program was designed at Athens State University to promote a mental and physical state conducive to wellness. Its central focus is the activation of the PK potential to infuse the body with wellness energy. Critical elements in the program are positive affirmations of personal well-being accompanied by related wellness imagery. The program requires a relaxed state and consists of six essential steps. Each step, however, can be altered to include additional affirmations required for specific wellness needs. Here's the program.

THE WELLNESS ACTIVATION PROGRAM

Step 1. Settle back into a comfortable position and with your eyes closed, slow your breathing, and let yourself become increasingly relaxed by mentally scanning your body from your head downward as you let all tension dissolve away. Once relaxed, affirm:

I am day by day becoming a more confident, secure person. I am becoming increasingly aware of my inner potential for wellness and well-being. The powers of my conscious mind are now merging with the hidden energies deep in my subconscious mind to influence my total being with vibrant health. I am now empowered with positive energy and new vigor.

Step 2. With your eyes remaining closed, envision a glowing wellness core as the empowerment generator situated in your body's central or solar plexus region. Affirm:

My potential for wellness centered at the luminous core of my being is now at its peak. I am fully permeated with the inner and outer glow of wellness.

Step 3. Further activate the wellness core by envisioning an expansive, luminous field of energy surrounding it as you affirm:

The empowering wellness core at the innermost part of my being is now saturated with brilliant, healthful energy, pulsating with potential and power.

Step 4. Mentally disperse wellness energy as rays of light throughout your body. Visualize your body enveloped in a glowing aura of wellness as you affirm:

My empowerment potential for wellness, now fully activated, is radiating powerful wellness energies through my total being. My mind and body are absorbing soothing, invigorating, and rejuvenating wellness. The glow of wellness now envelops my body as a brilliant aura of health and vitality.

Step 5. Imagine your circulatory system as a conveyor of powerful wellness energy. Mentally permeate the organs and systems of your body with the glow of wellness. Affirm:

I now direct wellness to each system, organ, and function of my body, strengthening and fortifying them with powerful energy.

Step 6. Conclude with the following affirmation:

By simply visualizing the luminous core of wellness energy within, I will become instantly empowered to disperse wellness throughout my total body and being.

The self-affirmations presented in this program are flexible and can be revised as needed to meet your personal preferences and specific applications. They can be presented silently, or if you prefer, audibly. Remember: *The sound of your own voice almost always increases the effectiveness of empowering affirmations.*

Wellness PK is a promising and developing field of personal empowerment. We now know that constricting PK to external conditions alone is both contradictory and limiting. Our personal empowerment rests largely on our commitment to liberate our thinking, eliminate constricted thinking, and embrace new possibilities, including those related to wellness and well-being.

PK AND REJUVENATION

Possibly no other human developmental phenomenon is more complex than aging and its counterpart, rejuvenation. Physical, social, cultural, environmental, psychological, and psychical factors all interact to influence both aging and rejuvenation. Within that intricate interaction, the empowered self can emerge to assume a central role with the capacity to intervene and direct the interaction.

The application of PK to rejuvenation suggests a state of empowered control over physiology, including systems typically considered autonomous. Through the appropriate direction of our inner PK faculty, we can alter crucial aging variables and activate our rejuvenating potentials, thus restoring the natural flow of youthful energy and, in some instances, literally reversing the aging process.

The term *rejuvenation*, as used in psychic self-empowerment, implies the deliberate restoration of youth and vigor through self-intervention into the aging process. Psychic rejuvenation recognizes the aging effects of an array of negative mental states, among them anxiety, depression, hostility, and insecurity. Even more importantly, psychic rejuvenation emphasizes the constructive effects of positive mental states, along with the empowering capacity of positive states to eliminate their negative opposites. Love, for instance, is one of the most empowering rejuvenation forces known. When present in the psyche, it neutralizes hate—its negative counterpart that is physically and mentally destructive and disempowering. Such positive states as self-confidence, self-esteem, and self-acceptance are both empowering and rejuvenating. They inject rejuvenating energies into the self system, eradicating those disempowering states that contribute to aging.

From the self-empowerment perspective, the application of PK to rejuvenation recognizes the following three important principles.

PK REJUVENATION PRINCIPLES

1. Aging is primarily a physical-mental interactive phenomenon. Any alteration of aging must engage the mind's power to influence physiology.

2. Aging is a complex process with many influencing factors. Some of those factors, such as genetic makeup and biological dispositions, resist intervention and direct alteration. Others are psychosocial and highly receptive to the empowered self, thus allowing their functions to be altered or extinguished altogether.

Equally important, new functions affecting aging can be introduced by the empowered self into the self system.

3. Any alteration of the psychosocial influences related to aging will invariably alter the underlying physiology associated with aging.

Together, these principles suggest several profound empowerment possibilities. First, the complex factors related to aging are clearly within reach of the empowered self. When we embrace the positive elements conducive to rejuvenation into the self system, the physical aging process is altered. Dominant aging forces are eliminated or minimized while dormant rejuvenating forces are activated and strengthened. As a result, the negative energies and interactions underlying accelerated aging are extinguished altogether.

REJUVENATION PK

The extension of PK to include rejuvenation suggests the possibility of living younger, longer, and better while literally reversing the physical signs of aging. An exercise called Rejuvenation PK is designed to activate the body's rejuvenation potentials and unblock the flow of rejuvenating energies from the inside out. Developed in our labs at Athens State University, the exercise is similar to PK wellness approaches in that it involves empowering imagery and affirmations. Through Rejuvenation PK, physical functions, including those considered autonomic or involuntary, are linked to mental functions in a positive rejuvenating interaction. The results are actual and observable changes in the physical body. Here's the exercise.

THE REJUVENATION PK PROGRAM

Step l. Relaxation. Physical relaxation sets the stage for PK intervention into the physical body's many functions. For this exercise, breathing is slowed and muscles are allowed to relax from the forehead downward as the following affirmation is presented:

I am now fully in charge of my physical body. I am empowered to influence every function, mental and physical. All the rejuvenating energy of my being is now at my command.

Step 2. Stress Expiation. Relaxation procedures are intended to reduce stress, but even when stress is reduced, the residual wear-and-tear effects of stress can linger. The goals of stress expiation are first, to extinguish stress and all its residual effects, and second, to infuse the physical body with positive, rejuvenating energy. To achieve these goals, the physical body's systems and organs are visualized and mentally energized. This energizing process is accomplished by centering your full awareness on various body regions and mentally bathing them with glowing energy accompanied by the following affirmation:

> *Youthful, invigorating energy is now flowing through my body. All organs, systems, and functions are now fully revitalized. The wear-and-tear of stress is now replaced by the flow of youth and vigor.*

Step 3. Attunement and Balance. The goal of this step is to establish a state of mental and physical attunement and balance, which is the most powerful rejuvenation force known. With the body physically relaxed and the effects of stress expiated, an empowering state of full attunement and balance is possible through the *Finger Engagement Procedure.* This procedure is based on the premise that the complex functions of the mind and body seek not only balance, but rejuvenation and efficiency as well. Beyond that, they seek simplicity. The Finger Engagement Procedure meets that goal. To implement the procedure, simply bring the tips of your fingers together and, with your eyes closed, imagine your hands as antennae for your brain. Imagine your left brain actively generating positive energy that flows into your right hand as the extension of that hemisphere. Next, imagine your right brain actively generating positive energy that flows into your left hand as the extension of that hemisphere. Allow the energies flowing into your hands and merging at your fingertips to engage in a powerful interaction that balances you mentally, physically, and spiritually. To end the exercise, disengage your finger tips and allow your hands to relax, palm sides up. Imagine your hands as your body's antennae to the universe as you affirm:

> *My total being is now fully balanced and attuned mentally, physically, and spiritually. The energies of youth are now unleashed to flow throughout my being. I am now at one, both within myself and with the universe.*

It is important to note that, although left- or right-hemisphere dominance in brain functions is considered normal, balancing the functions of the two hemispheres increases the efficiency of both without affecting their functional asymmetry.

Step 4. PK Illumination. At this final step in Rejuvenation PK, the rejuvenation process reaches its peak. PK illumination is initiated by viewing a photograph of yourself at your youthful prime. If no photo is available, you can create one mentally, which can be equally effective. Study the picture (either real or imagined), carefully noting your youthfulness, especially in your facial features. Now close your eyes and imagine yourself at your peak of youth standing, preferably nude, before a full-length mirror. Study your eyes and note the youthful gleam. Next, allow a colorful glow of rejuvenating energy to envelop your full body. While breathing slowly, soak in the colorful rejuvenating glow while affirming:

My inner powers of rejuvenation are now being unleashed to permeate my total being with the glow of youth and vigor. Every system within is now being revitalized with the infusion of rejuvenating power. Tired, worn tissue is being renewed with glowing youthfulness. Every function of my body is now fully infused as sparkling, youthful energy is absorbed into every cell and fiber. Surrounded by a colorful aura of rejuvenating energy, I am now secure in the present, bathed in vitality and the glow of youth. My inner rejuvenating powers are fully unleashed to flow freely throughout my total being. Each day, my mind and body will absorb the abundance of youthful energy that is constantly being unleashed within my being. Whenever I envision myself enveloped with the colorful glow of radiant energy, I will become instantly invigorated and fully empowered.

These affirmations, which can be recited either silently or audibly, can be revised to fit your personal preferences or needs. A small, self-adhesive star or dot of color consistent with the rejuvenation glow seen enveloping your body during the exercise can be strategically situated—on a mirror or computer for instance—as a cue to promote the inner flow of rejuvenating energy.

The complete PK Rejuvenation procedure can be practiced daily or as often as desired to maximize its rejuvenation effects. You can view the star or dot at frequent intervals throughout the day to instantly infuse your mind and body with rejuvenation. With practice of this exercise, you will discover that relevant imagery and accompanying affirmations become a natural, spontaneous, and continuous function of the psychically empowered self.

Together, positive affirmations and empowering imagery form a powerful two-component system of wellness and rejuvenation. In that system, PK assumes a critical role as the essential vehicle for physical change and well-being.

CONCLUSION

PK is psychic empowerment in its most basic and material form. It provides dramatic evidence of the power of the mind to intervene into the physical world of matter and movement. As an empowering phenomenon, PK meets the ultimate test: It enriches our lives and brings forth empowering change. Whether to promote wellness, stimulate healing, activate rejuvenation, or simply influence external conditions or events, the PK faculty existing in everyone spontaneously maintains a state of readiness that is responsive to our personal and situation needs. We can enrich the empowering potential of that faculty through practice and experience. The result is an abundance of positive energy that can be maintained and expended as needed.

SOURCES AND RECOMMENDED READING

Joanne Austin and Rosemary Guiley, *ESP, Psychokinesis, and Psychics: Mysteries, Legends, and Unexplained Phenomena* (Checkmark Books, 2008).

Department of Defense, *20th Century U.S.Military Defense and Intelligence Declassified Report: Soviet and Czechoslovakian Parapsychology Research, Telepathy, Energy Transfer, ... the Paranormal, Psychokinesis (PK),* (CD-ROM) (Progressive Management, 2004).

Department of Defense, *20th Century U.S. Military Defense and Intelligence Declassified Reports: Paraphysics, Controlled Offensive Behavior, and Parapsychology Research—Extrasensory ... Psychokinesis (PK), Levitation,* (CD-ROM), (Progressive Management, 2004).

The Futurist (2008).

William Hewitt, *Psychic Development for Beginners: An Easy Guide to Releasing and Developing Your Psychic Abilities* (Llewellyn, 1996).

Lynne McTaggart, *The Intention Experiment: Using Your Thoughts to Change Your Life and the World* (Free Press, 2008).

Joe H. Slate, *Psychic Empowerment for Health & Happiness* (Llewellyn, 1996).

Joe H. Slate, *Aura Energy for Health, Healing and Balance* (Llewellyn, 1999).

Joe H. Slate, *Rejuvenation: Strategies for Living Younger, Longer, and Better* (Llewellyn, 2001).

Joe H. Slate and Carl Llewellyn Weschcke, *Psychic Empowerment for Everyone: You Have the Power, Learn to Use It* (Llewellyn, 2009).

World Spaceflight News, *21st Century U.S. Military Documents, Teleportation Physics Study: Analysis for the Air Force Research Laboratory of Teleportation of Physical Objects, ... Psychokinesis (PK), Levitation* (CD-ROM) (Progressive Management, 2005).

12

REINCARNATION &
PAST-LIFE ENLIGHTENMENT

Our past-life experiences remain forever with us for a purpose. But rather than being automatically available to us at the beginning of each lifetime, they challenge us to retrieve them and discover their relevance for ourselves. Only then can we integrate them into our present lifetime. It's through concentrated effort and self-discovery that we learn and grow. It's then that knowledge of the past becomes power for the present. It's then that we uncover totally new potentials to be realized and enjoyed. Once we discover them, our past-life achievements in particular can build feelings of worth and well-being. We become less constricted in our self-identity and more at one with the universe.

—DR. JOE H. SLATE, *DOORS TO PAST LIVES*

INTRODUCTION

Can you imagine living in a world that is for the most part uncharted and undeveloped? Imagine the hidden resources and abundant possibilities existing beyond the limited zone of your present awareness. You could, of course, choose to live your lifetime in that familiar but constricted zone of that planet, or you could choose to boldly explore its unknown regions and uncover its hidden resources. As an explorer, you know, of course, that you could encounter the unexpected, but given what you already know about the planet, your confidence will only build as you uncover its hidden side and experience the rich rewards of your new discoveries.

Interestingly, such a largely unexplored planet does indeed exist, not at some distant, faraway place, but as an essential part of you. We call it your subconscious, that vast world of potentials and past experiences unknown to present conscious awareness. Among the major challenges of our existence is to discover this vast "undiscovered country" and develop its rich potentials. Only then can we become "all that we can be."

Also existing in the subconscious are many complex processes in dormant form that can be activated through our interactions with the subconscious. Examples include a host of learning functions that, once tapped into, can promote learning while generating exciting new potentials for growth. The realization of our inner potentials, whether conscious or subconscious, thus becomes a continuing growth process, with the development of one function contributing to the advancement of another, a phenomenon sometimes called "the positive transfer of learning." From that perspective, learning becomes a never-ending process of growth and self-discovery. You can promote that important process by clearly setting your personal goals and activating your inner potentials related to them, including those existing in dormant, subconscious form.

Aside from developing our potentials to their peaks, a major goal of our existence is to promote global progress by making the planet a better place for present and future populations. Solving global problems such as cultural deprivation, conflict, poverty, and disease become reasonable possibilities for a global population committed to positive change and the well-being of others. Past-life enlightenment is essential to that process. It can initiate a course of action that results in both global and personal progress and actualization.

THE MULTIPLE DIMENSIONS OF PERSONAL EXISTENCE

Although we do not know all there is to know about our existence as soul beings, the evidence points clearly to the possibility of multiple lifetimes as well as our existence between lifetimes. When we add to that our existence before our first lifetime and our existence after our last lifetime, our life span becomes endless, a concept called the *bidirectional endlessness of the soul*. When the dots are finally connected, the evidence including both laboratory and anecdotal records points convincingly to a dynamic, four-dimensional context of personal existence: (1) You existed before your first lifetime, (2) you existed during each of your lifetimes, (3) you existed between your lifetimes, and (4) you will exist after your last lifetime.

Although you may have lived many past lifetimes along with intervals between them, your soul identity or *spiritual genotype* remained unchanged. It's within that spiritual makeup that you learn and grow in each lifetime, as well as in between lifetimes. Although your existence in past lifetimes may have consisted of various cultural identities, orientations, and personalities, the makeup of your soul is forever fixed. Each lifetime is in a different body with a different genetic makeup while the soul identity remains forever the same from your early preexistence to afterlife and beyond.

Just as the span of your existence is without limits, so are the possibilities for your personal growth and enlightenment. As evolving souls, each lifetime along with each life between lifetimes, offers new opportunities to achieve higher levels of personal development while at the same time contributing to the good of others, a factor all too often overlooked. In recent years, we've seen an emerging body of evidence that contributing to the good of others is among the most powerful accelerants of personal growth and well-being. In fact, altruism is now known to be one of the major forces contributing to the quality of life and longevity as well. Interestingly, simply observing acts of kindness can generate a rejuvenating effect in the giver and receiver of the act as well as in the person observing the act, a phenomenon called the "observational longevity effect." Throughout our research on rejuvenation, a sense of humor combined with acts of kindness was found to be so important that we called it the "holy grail of rejuvenation."

Fortunately, the cumulative experiences of each lifetime and life between them remain forever with us as critical growth resources. They together provide the master key that unlocks our understanding of our past and our future as well. It would seem reasonable that those experiences that enriched our existence in each past lifetime would continue to enrich our existence in the present and afterlife alike. Although unfinished tasks and works in progress will accompany us to the other side, abundant afterlife resources are available to us at any moment to promote our growth and spiritual fulfillment. Among them are ministering guides, guardian entities, and growth specialists, including the same spiritual companions that enriched our existence in our past lifetimes.

Although all our past experiences remain forever with us as crucial growth resources, our transition to the afterlife realm at the end of each lifetime is characterized by a phenomenon called "the preservation of peak growth." Through that process, we instantly regain at our transition the highest peak of our past growth. That peak, regardless of when it occurs, like all growth experiences, is never lost. It can occur at any point in your development, but once achieved it remains a critical point in your spiritual growth. That preservation of your growth peak empowers you in afterlife to reach even higher levels of growth and fulfillment. Equipped with the highest peak of our past growth, we can embrace death, not as a sad ending, but rather a wondrous continuation of life in which our dreams are realized and works in progress are brought into fruition.

Your present lifetime could be your first embodiment on Earth or it could be only one of many past lives. It could be your last incarnation, or it could be one among others yet to come. It doesn't really matter how many lifetimes you've lived in the past or will live in the future; it's the quality of life in the present that counts. We're here at this time in this life to learn and grow. The experiences we gather at the moment will be with us forever. They become resources for our continued development in this lifetime as well as in our life beyond.

INTERACTING WITH THE SUBCONSCIOUS

Like the call of an unknown planet beckoning discovery, your subconscious beckons your interactions. It reveals its presence in a variety of ways, including such spontaneous channels as dreams, intuitive awareness, déjà vu, precognitive impressions, and flashes of insight and creativity. That "other country within" reaches forth with persistence in its efforts to enrich your life with expanded knowledge, insight, and power.

The spontaneous channels of subconscious enlightenment reflect the important relevance of the abundant growth resources existing in the subconscious. Through your interactions with the subconscious, you can expand your awareness of your past lives and generate a totally new growth process. You can generate healing interactions with the best of healers and therapists—those existing within the self. You can resolve deep-seated conflicts, extinguish phobias, and initiate totally new growth processes. Though it may seem too good to be true, you can generate a rejuvenating interaction with the subconscious that promotes better health and fitness, slows aging, and even erases the physical signs of aging. All of these possibilities and more are available to you when you tap into that vast country of resources existing in your subconscious.

While spontaneous channels often provide crucial glimpses into the subconscious, structured step-by-step programs are now available to facilitate that important process. Among them are hypnosis, sleep intervention programs, various meditation approaches, and a host of tools and techniques. It's through these programs that we can directly access the subconscious sources of knowledge and insight related to our personal growth and development.

SELF-HYPNOSIS AND PAST-LIFE REGRESSION

Nothing can adequately explain the fullness of our existence, but past-life enlightenment through self-hypnosis comes close. As the evidence continues to build, both in the controlled laboratory and in real life, it becomes increasingly clear that reincarnation and past-life enlightenment are essential, not only to our understanding of our existence but also to the fulfillment of our potential as evolving souls.

During hypnosis, a fully developed skill unknown to conscious awareness will occasionally emerge spontaneously, a phenomenon called hypnoproduction. Examples include highly advanced technical skills, breakthrough scientific concepts, and fluency in another language, possibly acquired in another lifetime. Unfortunately, hypnoproduction is sometimes short-lived with the skill remaining in subconscious inactive form following the trance state. Nevertheless, hypnoproduction illustrates the enormous possibilities of probing the subconscious mind through self-hypnosis.

Among the most effective self-hypnosis programs for past-life enlightenment is an adaptation of a procedure called Past-life Corridor, which uses a combination of age regression and past-life regression. The procedure introduces the concept of a Past-life Corridor of many doors, with each door representing a past lifetime. Approximately one hour in a relaxed, comfortable setting free of distractions is recommended for the full program. Throughout the procedure, which was developed in the labs at Athens State University, you alone remain in charge. To induce the trance state, you can use any self-induction procedure, including Eye Movement/ Reverse Counting (EM/RC), that combines certain controlled eye movements and reverse counting as detailed in *Beyond Reincarnation: Experience Your Past Lives and Lives Between Lives* by Slate (2008) and reproduced below.

PAST-LIFE REGRESSION SELF-HYPNOSIS PROCEDURES

Given the fact that your best personal hypnotist exists within yourself, it follows that the most effective hypnotic regression procedure would logically focus on that inner specialist. Two self-administered procedures were developed in the labs to activate that specialist. The first procedure, a self-hypnosis strategy known as EM/RC, incorporates eye movement (EM) and reverse counting (RC) into a procedure designed to induce a trance state conducive to past-life regression. This procedure accepts the premise that within each of us is not only a master hypnotist but also a master teacher, therapist, healer, and psychic, all of which are receptive to our probes. Our task is to find ways of getting in touch with those powers. EM/RC was designed to meet that challenge.

The second procedure, known as Past-life Corridor, was developed as a self-regression strategy for use in concert with EM/RC. The Past-life Corridor, as we will later see, contains doors representing each of your past lifetimes as well as your pre-existence and life between lifetimes. Each door is a living gateway to your past. When used together, EM/RC and Past-life Corridor provide the essentials for successful hypnosis and regression to your past life in its totality.

It is important to point out here that in our development and use of these procedures, no effort was made at any time to influence the beliefs of our research subjects, nor to shape in any way their regression experiences. Your past experiences are unique to you, and you have sole ownership of them. In our labs, Topic A was to develop workable tools for self-discovery of those experiences. It was our position that, once given the tools, you could explore for yourself the past-life experiences that are presently relevant to you. Once given that knowledge, you can draw your own conclusions independent of the opinions and influences of others.

In our labs, EM/RC and Past-life Corridor, when used together, were found to be the most effective strategy known for retrieving relevant past-life experiences.

Although they lack the bells and whistles of other approaches, these self-administered procedures typically extinguish any semblance of resistance, either to hypnosis or past-life regression. With the subject in command of the induction and regression process, the degree of satisfaction for this do-it-yourself approach was at a level far greater than that of any other known induction or regression strategy. The follow-on ratings by our subjects regarding the relevance of their regression experiences were likewise very high.

Specifically designed to induce a hypnotic state that facilitates past-life regression, the EM/RC procedure incorporates age regression to an early childhood experience, which then becomes the springboard for past-life regression using the Past-life Corridor. Later during the trance, the same childhood experience becomes the portal for reentry into your present lifetime. It is important to keep in mind that you are the keeper of that portal, and you can return to it at any time during the regression experience.

Both EM/RC and the Past-life Corridor, like all the strategies presented in this book, are self-administered throughout. They are based on a simple threefold premise: first, you know yourself better than anyone else; second, all your past experiences exist within yourself as an integral part of your being; and third, you are your own best hypnotist and past-life regression specialist. All the resources you need are within yourself and now accessible to you.

Together, EM/RC and the Past-life Corridor can put you in touch with that knowing, innermost part of yourself and safely guide your probes into your past. With practice, these procedures can empower you to discover whatever you need to know at the moment about your past. Beyond that, they can reveal the relevance of your past to your future. They provide an invaluable path to self-discovery with signposts to guide you all along the way.

Our past-life studies using these procedures suggested over and over again that there exists a higher—or dare I say it—divine intelligence that knows what exists behind each door. That intelligence can illuminate a particular door in the Past-life Corridor and draw your attention to it. That intelligence knows that out of a given past lifetime of experience, a certain experience can hold critical relevance for you at this moment in your life. It can reveal that segment, or it can present a past lifetime in its full scope. But best of all, that higher intelligence is within yourself—it is a part of you. It can point the way for you to go, but it's up to you to embark on the journey. It can illuminate a past-life door, but it's up to you to open it. It can reveal which past lifetime and which specific experience in that lifetime hold greatest relevance for you at this time in your life.

Guided by that higher intelligence within, you can experience through these procedures an overview of all your past lifetimes from which you can choose a particular lifetime to explore, either as a spectator or active participant. Once you've selected a particular lifetime, you can experience a small but relevant segment of it, or you can move backward or forward within that lifetime to experience it in its greater fullness. Upon returning to the corridor after a particular past-lifetime experience, you can, should you decide to do so, open the "between lifetimes" door at the corridor's end to discover relevant afterlife experiences for that particular lifetime. Later in this book, we will discuss the "between lifetimes" as well as the preexistence dimensions of your past life.

It is important to keep in mind that the Past-life Corridor with its many doors to an incredible wealth of experience is actually within yourself. With these procedures, you can open the doors of your choosing. You will discover that no aspect of your past is beyond your probe.

On a practical note, these procedures should be used only in a comfortable, safe, and quiet setting, completely free of distractions. They should never be used under conditions requiring alertness and vigilance, such as while driving or operating machinery. It is important to read both procedures in their entirety before starting. You will find them easy to follow, but practice is usually required to maximize their effectiveness. Here are the two procedures, which together require approximately one hour.

EM/RC AND PAST-LIFE CORRIDOR REGRESSION PROGRAM

Step 1. EM/RC Preliminaries

Begin the EM/RC procedure by settling back into a comfortable, reclining position with your legs uncrossed and your hands resting at your sides. As you become increasingly relaxed, take in several breaths, inhaling deeply and exhaling slowly. Develop a slow, rhythmic breathing pattern as you clear your mind of all active thought. Notice your sense of peace with yourself and the world.

At this early stage, give yourself permission to enter hypnosis and, while in the trance state, to travel into your past to retrieve whatever is relevant for you at the moment. Affirm that you will be in full and complete control throughout the trance experience. Further affirm that you can at any moment exit hypnosis by simply counting upward from one to five.

Step 2. Trance Induction

You are now ready to initiate the trance state using a combination of eye movement and reverse counting. Tell yourself that by shifting your eyes from side to side as you count backward from ten, you will enter the trance state. Further affirm that each count backward will take you deeper and deeper until you reach a successful trance state on the count of one.

As your eyes remain open, begin the procedure by slowly shifting your eyes upward and to your right, without turning your head, on the count of ten. Hold your eyes in that upper-right position until they begin to tire. Then slowly shift your eyes downward and then upward to your left on the count of nine and hold them in that upper-left position until they begin to tire. As you shift your eyes from side to side on each count, develop a rhythmic downward and then upward swinging movement, always holding your eyes in each upper position. You will notice your eyes becoming increasingly tired as you continue the rhythmic eye movement and reverse-counting combination. Upon reaching the count of one, slowly close your eyes while still holding them in the upper position. Once your eyes are closed, let them return to their normal position. With your eyes now comfortably closed and the muscles around them relaxed, let yourself slowly enter the trance state.

Step 3. Deepening the Trance

As your eyes remain closed, deepen the trance state by taking a few moments to envision a very peaceful scene and then letting yourself become progressively relaxed from your head downward. Notice first the relaxation around your eyes and then let it spread slowly over your face and then into your neck and shoulders. Let the relaxation then radiate into your arms, right through the tips of your fingers. Then notice the relaxation in your chest and let it spread deep into your abdomen. Let the relaxation extend slowly downward, soaking into your hips, thighs, lower legs, and finally right through the tips of your toes.

As you remain comfortable and deeply relaxed, envision again a very peaceful scene—either the one you pictured earlier or a totally new one. Notice the pleasing details of the mental image, and let yourself absorb the tranquility of the scene. You are now at complete peace with yourself and the world.

You can at this point reach an even deeper level of hypnosis, should you decide to do so, by focusing your full attention on the little finger of either hand, noticing its weight, tingling, warmth, and so forth, and then mentally replacing these sensations with numbness. As your finger remains numb, let yourself go deeper and deeper into hypnosis. When you reach the desired trance level, allow the feeling to return and then move your finger slightly as a signal of your success. Again remind yourself that you are in full and complete control of the trance state.

Note: With practice, you will find that the EM/RC procedure is a very flexible induction procedure that can be easily tailored to your own preferences and needs. Some subjects find that the rhythmic eye movement independent of reverse counting is sufficient to induce the trance state. Almost everyone will find that inserting such suggestions as "more and more relaxed" and "deeper and deeper" at times throughout the procedure facilitates the induction process. Should you enter a satisfactory trance state before completing the full EM/RC procedure, simply proceed to the next stage: regression to childhood.

Step 4. Regression to Childhood

Once you've reached a successful trance level, begin your regression to childhood by envisioning a pleasant childhood situation in which you participated in a festive occasion—perhaps a birthday party or holiday celebration. Take plenty of time to become a part of the childhood experience and give yourself permission to use it as a springboard for past-life regression. You are now ready to begin the past-life regression experience using the Past-life Corridor procedure.

Step 5. Past-life Corridor Preliminaries

While remaining in the trance state, give yourself permission to use the trance as a vehicle for past-life regression. Reaffirm that you will experience only those past-life events that are relevant and presently useful to you. Remind yourself that you can at any moment end the trance state and return safely to the present by simply counting upward from one to five.

Affirm that you will be protected and secure throughout the regression experience. You may decide at this point to invite a personal spirit guide to accompany you in your past-life probes.

Tell yourself that upon later exiting hypnosis, you will recall those past-life experiences that are important to you at this time. Affirm your ability to use past-life insight productively to enrich your present life and promote your future growth. Remind yourself that you will remain in full control throughout the regression experience.

Step 6. Entering the Past-life Corridor

You are now ready to enter the Past-life Corridor. Notice the brightly illuminated corridor stretching into the distance. Your personal past-life corridor is unique to you—it is unlike any other corridor. It can be of any combination of materials, colors, and shapes. It can, for instance, be of stone, marble, or gold. The colors can range from the boldest shades to the most delicate pastels.

On the sides of the corridor you will notice doors, one for each of your past lifetimes. If your present lifetime is your first, there will be no side doors. But if you have lived many lifetimes, there will, of course, be many doors. They, like the hallway itself, can be of a variety of materials, such as jade, amber, or glass. Their shapes can likewise vary, to include rectangular, round, heart-shaped, or oval forms, to list but a few of the possibilities.

Behind each door is a past lifetime, with the doors closest to the corridor's entrance representing your most recent lifetimes, and the doors in the distance representing your earlier lifetimes. By opening the door of your choosing, you can experience the events of that life which hold relevance for you at the moment.

At the far end of the bright corridor, you will notice a resplendent door representing your preexistence. Provided you have lived a previous lifetime, you will notice a second bright door situated to the right of the preexistence door. It represents your life between lifetimes in the spirit realm. Together, the two luminous side-by-side doors provide a gateway to the spirit realm as you experienced it in past life. You can at will open either door to gain the information you need concerning these important dimensions of your past. (In our studies, less than three percent of our subjects experienced no previous lifetimes upon entering the Past-life Corridor. For them, the corridor included only the preexistence door.)

Step 7. Experiencing Past Lifetimes

Upon entering the corridor, select the door that holds particular appeal for you at the moment. Almost always, it is the door that first commanded your attention, or the door that stands out as brightest among the others. Upon approaching the door, you may decide to open the door and view from the doorway the past life it represents, or you can step through the door and become an active participant in that past life.

As you experience the past lifetime you selected, either from the open door as a spectator or from beyond the door as an active participant, you can at will shift your awareness either forward or backward to experience it in as much scope and detail as you prefer. To shift forward, count 1, 2, 3; to shift backward, count 3, 2, 1.

Once regression to a particular past lifetime is complete, you can leave that lifetime by simply returning to the corridor and closing the door behind you. At this point, you may wish to explore another past lifetime by opening another past-lifetime door. To promote recall of the regression experience, it is recommended that no more than two past lifetimes be experienced during a particular regression session.

We should note here that should you wish to explore the afterlife that followed a given past lifetime, you can open the life-between-lifetimes door at the end of the corridor. Opening that afterlife door immediately following your regression to a particular past lifetime ensures that the afterlife depicted is the immediate follow-on to that lifetime. The next section explores in detail life between lifetimes as well as preexistence and ways of experiencing these important realms of your past.

Step 8. Conclusion

To exit the Past-life Corridor, give yourself permission to return first to the childhood situation you experienced earlier, and from there, into the present. Upon your

return to the present and before exiting the trance state, affirm that you will successfully recall the regression experience in as much detail as needed and that you will
understand its full relevance.

To end the trance state, count slowly from one to five with interjected suggestions
of alertness and well-being. On the count of five, open your eyes and take a few moments to reflect on the experience.

Many of our subjects found that upon opening a particular door, the past lifetime
it represented unfolded before them like a movie. The more highly relevant experiences of that lifetime often appeared in bright detail, thereby commanding attention
and inviting interaction.

Subjects who remain spectator observers during their regression often describe
their experiences as three-dimensional, in which relevant aspects of their past were
depicted in colorful detail. In these dramatizations, our regression subjects invariably
recognized themselves, even when they were pictured as the other gender or another
race.

In contrast to spectators, active participants who "stepped into" their past lifetime
experienced it close-up, as though they were actually there interacting with their surroundings and others exactly as they did in that past lifetime. Both spectators and
participants alike were typically aware of their past-life personal identity and life situation as well as the historical settings and geographical location of the past lifetime
depicted.

The EM/RC procedure can be supplemented as needed with a variety of trance
deepening techniques, or if you prefer, you can use a totally different induction approach, perhaps one you have already mastered. Although EM/RC is particularly
conducive to past-life regression, some subjects prefer alternative strategies, including the popular hand levitation technique. In this procedure, the hand at rest on
your thigh gently rises at your suggestion to touch your forehead, thereby inducing
the trance state. A second popular procedure is eye fixation, in which attention is
centered on a fixed object to facilitate the upward gaze and thus promote the trance
state. Both of these techniques use suggestions of drowsiness along with a variety of
other deepening strategies.

Regardless of the strategies used, you will find that, with practice, your ability
to enter hypnosis and regress to designated past lifetimes will improve. Given sufficient practice and experience, you may successfully master, like many of our subjects,
the highest form of trance induction known—the ability to enter hypnosis through
sheer intent alone.

Although EM/RC was developed in our labs as a self-induction procedure specifically for use in combination with Past-life Corridor, it can be easily adapted for other

uses, including such wide-ranging applications as losing weight, breaking unwanted habits, managing pain, improving memory, and even slowing aging.

As with EM/RC, you can revise the Past-life Corridor procedure to meet your personal preferences, or you can substitute a totally different regression strategy. Although Past-life Corridor has shown remarkable effectiveness with subjects of different backgrounds and experience, you may prefer an alternative procedure, such as the Blank Screen Technique, which was also developed in our labs. This technique uses imagery of a blank screen upon which appears scenes related to your past lifetimes. Once a scene appears, you can either view the unfolding images or actually enter the action of the scene to experience past-life happenings firsthand and in great detail. From there, you can either "fast-forward" by counting 1, 2, 3, or "fast-backward" by counting 3, 2, 1 to experience a particular past lifetime in greater scope and detail.

To maximize the effectiveness of your regression experiences, it is important to maintain a detailed journal of each session. Research your journal entries and take time to reflect upon them, keeping in mind that all experiences, past and present, are purposeful. You will eventually discover the relevance of your regression experiences to your present-life situation.

Whatever strategies you choose for inducing the trance state and experiencing your past life, don't rush it—take plenty of time to enjoy the regression experience and discover its relevance. It is important again to emphasize that the best specialist—whether for hypnosis or past-life regression—exists within yourself. After all, you know yourself better than anyone else, and all your past-life experiences remain a critical part of your growth history. By acquiring the skills to reconnect to them, you can discover for yourself all you need to know about your past and its relevance to you at this moment in your life.

In an interesting example of the past-life corridor program, a university professor with a strong interest in Egyptian culture viewed upon entering the corridor a bright door with a pyramid inscribed upon it. When he opened the door, a pharaoh sitting on a throne with a beautiful blond woman at his side appeared vividly before him. Puzzled by the experience, he later researched it and discovered that a pharaoh whose partner was blond did indeed briefly rule Egypt, a finding that is little known even among expert Egyptologists. The experience, in his opinion, suggested a past lifetime as an Egyptian pharaoh, a possibility later confirmed by the readings of two skilled psychics, one from England and the other from the Netherlands. The psychics, each unknown to the other, gave detailed descriptions of the pharaoh whose partner, a blond, was "always at his side." For the professor, the experience explained his strong interest in Egyptian history since early childhood. Note: The professor is one of your coauthors (Slate).

SLEEP INTERVENTION PROGRAM

The Sleep Intervention Program uses sleep as a gateway to relevant past-life experiences buried in the subconscious. This program, however, does more than simply uncover past-life experiences—it activates the empowering effects of the experience. This approach is especially effective in targeting experiences related to a particular striving or unresolved conflict. It is also effective in activating specific abilities and skills acquired in a past life but presently existing in the subconscious. The awakening of artistic potentials is particularly receptive to this approach. Similarly, the program is among the best known for accelerating mastery of new cognitive and performance skills that were acquired in a past life but are presently existing in a dormant subconscious state. Through this approach, learning can be rapidly accelerated and memory dramatically improved.

This program is especially effective in balancing the mind, body, and spirit. It can provide solutions to pressing problems and bring forth a therapeutic congruency within the self. It can effectively ventilate the build-up of stress and anxiety that can interrupt your daily life. Here's the program:

Step 1. Upon becoming drowsy, with your eyes closed, mentally specify your intent to interact with your subconscious and activate its powers as you sleep. Specify your goals and affirm your intent to experience the subconscious powers related to them.

Step 2. *Circle of Power.* Form a circle with your hands by first joining the tips of your index fingers and then the tips of your thumbs. While holding the circle, visualize it glowing with energy as you sense its calming effects. Allow plenty of time for your total being—mind, body, and spirit—to become attuned and balanced.

Step 3. *Sphere of Consciousness.* Relax your hands and visualize yourself fully enveloped in a sphere of glowing energy. Think of the center of that sphere as the center of your being as an evolving soul. Affirm that as you sleep, all the insight and power you need will become available to you.

Step 4. Relax your hands, briefly review your goals, and then let yourself drift into restful sleep.

Step 5. Upon awakening, take a few moments to reflect on your dream experiences and then record them in your sleep journal.

A college student who used the Sleep Intervention Program in her efforts to overcome her lifelong fears of enclosed places and darkness experienced during sleep an apparent past-life experience in which she, as a male, was a coal miner. While working deep in the mine, she became entrapped in darkness when the mine collapsed. Given that brief but vivid glimpse into the apparent sources of her fears, she, in her own words, "felt the fears dissolving away" as she continued to sleep. Upon awakening, the student knew with confidence that her fear of enclosed places and darkness had been fully extinguished. Enlightenment is power, and enlightenment related to the origin of fear is often sufficient to totally eradicate the fear and replace it with powerful feelings of security and well-being.

This student's experiences suggest that certain phobias and conflicts related to past-life experience are not always resolved in the afterlife, even with the counsel and guidance of spiritual helpers. While our experiences in the afterlife are critical to our evolvement as souls, another lifetime may be required to find complete resolution of certain conditions of past-life origin, including acquired phobias and conflicts. Nothing is more powerful and convincing than personal experience, and certain personal experiences during a lifetime on Earth can be equally or even more important to our spiritual growth than our experiences in the afterlife. That could be a major reason why we're here in this lifetime at this time—to experience growth opportunities not otherwise available to us in the afterlife. It thus becomes critically important that we take advantage of the abundant growth opportunities available to us in this lifetime.

Aside from such problem-solving functions as resolving conflicts and fears, our past-life interactions through the Sleep Intervention Program can add enrichment and instant meaning to our existence. The program can energize our lives and accelerate our progress in achieving our personal goals. A doctoral student who did not speak French reported a sleep intervention experience in which he spoke the language fluently. Since his degree required a reading proficiency in two languages, he arranged tutoring in French and within weeks acquired fluency in both speaking and reading the language. He later used the Past-life Corridor Program to discover that he had lived two past lifetimes in France. In his words, "The Sleep Intervention Program combined with the Past-life Corridor put me in touch with my past lives and the skills acquired in them."

Self-hypnosis and sleep intervention programs are only two of many approaches with potential for past-life enlightenment. Numerous other approaches as discussed elsewhere in this book can be easily adapted to access past-life knowledge and activate the skills acquired in our past lifetimes.

Your existence as an evolving soul is a continuous, never-ending process of growth and self-discovery. Past-life enlightenment can enrich that process with a deeper understanding of yourself and your existence in the here and now. Aside from that, it can accelerate your growth by awakening the dormant skills you acquired in your past lifetimes. You can overcome all barriers to your growth, including fear, anxiety, and uncertainty. Through past-life enlightenment, you can achieve your highest destiny and generate totally new possibilities in your life. Equipped with the concepts and programs presented in this chapter, you can now become empowered as never before.

PREEXISTENCE AND LIFE BETWEEN LIVES

As souls, we evolve within a life span that is from everlasting to everlasting. Growth without end is our destiny. We have already explored those very critical intervals known as our past lifetimes using the EM/RC and Past-life Corridor. We have focused particularly on the relevance of past lifetimes to our present existence. We have illustrated the enlightenment and healing potentials of our past-life experiences when integrated into our present lifetimes.

We will now examine two additional dimensions of our past existence: (1) our preexistence before our first lifetime and (2) our existence between lifetimes. In exploring these critical aspects of our past, it is again important to note that our existence is not only forever, it is forever forward.

Exploring Preexistence

Over the years, scores of subjects participating in our past-life regression studies volunteered to explore their preexistence. To uncover their past, they used the EM/RC and Past-life Corridor procedures as previously discussed to induce hypnosis and then enter the Past-life Corridor. To experience their preexistence, they opened the preexistence door at the end of the corridor and observed their preexistence as a spectator from the open doorway. From there, many of them chose to step through the doorway to become active participants in their preexistence as they knew it before their first lifetime on Earth. Our journey back to our preexistence is, of course, a journey within ourselves in which we discover anew the vastness of our past and how it relates to our present and future.

In preexistence, other souls were seen as bright beings with the capacity for growth and change. Every soul was seen as an excellent work in progress, arrayed in beauty and full of love. Our subjects, even as spectators, experienced their preexistence as a "fellowship of friends." Our subjects described their preexistence as without borders or the familiar constrictions of time and space.

Our subjects, upon stepping into their preexistence to become active participants, experienced an infusion of pure energy and a state of peace beyond anything they had experienced in their present lifetime. They experienced complete autonomy, along with harmony and equality with all other souls, a state many of them described as *collective oneness* within which they felt connected to all other souls, while at the same time maintaining their own individuality and personal soul identity.

In their preexistence (and as we will later see, in afterlife as well), all souls seem to experience no limits in their ability to relate to other souls. They found that all souls had a personality identity by which they were known. They recognized each other by their flaw-less cosmic makeup or spiritual genotype.

According to many of our subjects, the most impressive structural features of the preexistence realm were the so-called "celestial gardens," which included wondrous foun-tains and shimmering pools of what seemed to be the highest forms of energy. Situated among the many colorful planes, these gardens were seen by our subjects as "beautiful classrooms for the soul" in which they grew in wisdom and power before their first lifetime on Earth (and later, between lifetimes).

It was usually in these garden settings that our subjects interacted with master teachers and guides, some of whom had lived past lifetimes on Earth and, in some instances, past lifetimes on other planets as well. From these ministering teachers and guides, they learned of the potential value of life on Earth, along with the possible pitfalls and risks of embodiment. They examined the nature of mind, body, and spirit interaction. They studied the nature of the spiritual and physical worlds, to include ways in which they interacted with each other. Under the guidance of master teachers, their learning experiences included actual observations of Earth conditions and events, along with limited participation in Earth affairs.

Observing and interacting with incarnates on the earth plane were among the major growth activities of their preexistence. They concluded that our embodiment on earth (and other planets as well) promotes not only our own development, but the development of souls on the other side who observe and interact with us. The Earth, as it turns out, is a learning laboratory not only for incarnates, but for preincarnates and discarnates as well. It follows that our existence in each lifetime should facilitate our own evolution as well as the evolution of others, including souls on the other side.

Although our subjects found many highly evolved souls in the preexistence realm with no history of incarnation, they usually concluded that life on Earth could accelerate their evolution. Here are some examples of the specific benefits of the embodiment of souls as reported by our subjects immediately following their preexistence regression:

BENEFITS OF THE EMBODIMENT OF SOULS

- Each lifetime offers totally new mind, body, and spirit interactions that can pro-mote our evolution while contributing to the evolution of others.

- Each lifetime offers new opportunities to experience Earth-plane realities and to make the world a better place.

- Each lifetime can be a source of personal enlightenment and enrichment, in-cluding self-discovery and self-fulfillment.

- Each lifetime expands our opportunities to experience love, commitment, and understanding of others.

- Our Earth-plane existence can build feelings of worth and well-being that are essential to our continued development.

- Earth-plane interactions expand our perspective of life and our appreciation of diversity.

- Through our Earth-plane existence, we can learn to take responsibility for the consequences of our actions, attitudes, and beliefs.

- Each lifetime offers new opportunities to develop our nurturing, caring side.

- Each lifetime offers opportunities to discover the beauty and power of nature.

- Each lifetime presents new challenges that can include overcoming physical limitations, compensating for past actions, completing unfinished tasks, and setting new goals.

Without exception, our preexistence regression subjects reported that Earth-plane embodiment was by choice; it was never imposed. Although the subjects of our studies concluded that growth is best when it is self-directed, they welcomed the continuing support of their ministering guides and teachers.

Also without exception, our subjects concluded that their lifetimes on Earth were "developmental intervals" that included opportunities to accelerate their personal growth while contributing to the greater good. Achieving important personal and humanitarian goals, they concluded, was the major purpose of their embodiment—a purpose that could involve numerous lifetimes.

Here's a summary of some of our findings regarding preexistence based on the reports of scores of subjects of varying backgrounds and personal characteristics who volunteered for our studies:

- *Our existence as souls has neither seminal beginning nor final ending.* The life span of every soul is endless. Before our first embodiment, it extended forever into the past; following our last embodiment, it will extend forever into the future.

- *The progress of souls in preexistence is forever forward.* As in each lifetime, preexistence growth was continuous but uneven. There were periods of rapid growth and slow growth. Although growth plateaus and occasional downward spirals were observed, they were important because they prepared souls for major leaps forward. Growth of the soul was regulated by self-determination rather than by others.

- *All the resources required for our growth were available to us in our preexistence.* Included were the collective support and wisdom of teachers and guides.

- *Censure, punishment, and value judgments were absent in preexistence.* All souls were recognized as autonomous beings of incomparable worth and dignity.

- *During their preexistence, our subjects interacted with many souls, including some who had previously lived on Earth.*

- *During their preexistence, our subjects occasionally interacted with souls presently living on earth.* Occasionally, they intervened in Earth affairs to influence unfolding Earth events.

- *Many of our subjects who regressed to their preexistence experienced rewarding interactions with animals in the spirit world.*

LIFE BETWEEN LIFETIMES

All subjects who had participated in our preexistence studies volunteered to participate in our life-between-lifetimes studies. Typically, our subjects using EM/RC and the Past-life Corridor felt no reluctance in opening their life-between-lifetimes door at the corridor's end. From there, they viewed only briefly their between-lifetimes existence as spectators before stepping through the door to become active participants, always, it seemed, in the company of ministering guides. Following their regression experiences, they concluded without exception that the preexistence realm and the life-between-lifetimes realm are not two separate realms at all, but rather one and the same.

As in their preexistence, our subjects found that a host of helpers was always available to guide and facilitate their growth during their between-lifetimes intervals. They were able to retrieve whatever was presently relevant to them with the help of their spirit guides. They believed they were guided into the experiences that were important to their continued growth and self-fulfillment.

Our subjects during their between-lifetimes regression often interacted with other discarnates they had known during their past lifetimes, particularly their most recent past lifetime. During their regressed discarnate state, they could assume the gender and personality characteristics of their most recent past lifetime, or for that matter, of any previous lifetime. They interacted with discarnate family members, friends, teachers, and even casual acquaintances. Their interactions with discarnates and preincarnates alike were consistently positive and productive.

To experience the afterlife that followed a particular lifetime, our subjects first regressed to that past lifetime, after which they opened the between-lifetimes door.

Our regression studies consistently showed that each afterlife interval integrates the experiences of our most recent past lifetime into a growth pattern that maximizes our past lifetime experiences and prepares us for the next lifetime, should we choose to reincarnate. Following each lifetime, the growth process includes the integration of experiences that may have come beyond our developmental peak for that lifetime.

In preexistence and between-lifetimes alike, the focus is consistently on the perfection and potentials of souls rather than on faults and limitations. Fortunately, we do not have to wait until our transition to take command of our growth destiny. As souls, we are at present autonomous. We can initiate new growth processes, activate dormant powers, reverse downward spirals, and in the process, discover new meaning to our lives. As we develop our higher potentials, we move beyond a fixated state of existence to a dynamic evolvement of the spirit. We take responsibility for our lives and integrate our life experiences in ways that maximize our own growth potentials while contributing to the growth of others.

Our between-lifetimes regression subjects unanimously concluded that future lifetime events, while often predictable, are not predestined. But although we determine our own destiny as souls, a certain cosmic justice does seem to prevail. For instance, a given extremity in one lifetime is often followed by its opposite in another lifetime. A lifetime of wealth and affluence is often followed by a lifetime of impoverishment and deprivation. Similarly, a lifetime of exploitation of others is often followed by a lifetime of victimization. Such reversals in lifetimes could be explained by the cosmic principle of balance in which two extremes occurring in succession tend to moderate each other to induce a state of balance.

Past-life Regression and ESP

Throughout our past-life studies, a standard feature of our research was to study our subjects' backgrounds and assess their psychic abilities using a variety of evaluation methods, including case studies as well as objective ESP tests. The decision to include psychic assessment in our studies was based on the possibility that insight into our past life could influence our present psychic functions. Our studies confirmed that possibility. With repeated past-life regression, the performance of our subjects on controlled ESP tests for telepathy, clairvoyance, and precognition markedly improved. (As typically defined, telepathy is mind-to-mind communication, clairvoyance is the psychic awareness of existing but unseen realities, and precognition is the psychic awareness of future events.) Regression to preexistence particularly resulted in a dramatic increase in psychic performance in the laboratory. Given insight into their preexistence, several of our subjects demonstrated remarkable mediumistic and channeling powers, which they attributed to the attuning and balancing effects of their regression experiences.

SUMMARY AND CONCLUSIONS

Through EM/RC and the Past-life Corridor, we can reexperience our past existence in the spirit realm. The experiences of our past, once integrated into the soul, add meaning and direction to our lives. They provide a strong foundation for our future evolution.

The experiences of the preexistence realm seem to show a world remarkably like the "Paradise" common to all major scriptures—a world of beauty and love characterized by promise rather than conflict. But when the inhabitants leave Paradise—

incarnating in the physical body—they encounter Polarity (designated as "sin" in Biblical interpretation).

The experiences of the Lives-Between-Lives Realm in many ways are like the "Return to Paradise" found in many teachings.

We can refer to both these realms as the Spirit World, from which we move into incarnation and to which we return upon the death of the physical body.

We return to our "Home" to integrate our experiences and ponder the lessons learned. And then to prepare for our next growth opportunity through rebirth, by being "born again."

Why do we choose to leave the Paradise in which we experience so much Love and Beauty? Paradise is like a matrix of possibilities. By entering physical life, we have the opportunity to *actively* love and to *actively* beautify the earthly plane. Receiving love in Paradise shows us what love is and our incarnation enables us to give love. Seeing beauty in Paradise shows us what beauty is and our incarnation enables us to walk in beauty.

Much of our incarnate life actively centers around love and beauty. We seek to love one another, and we seek to add beauty to our life experience.

In Paradise, we learn what life can be, and in our incarnation we bring that potential into actuality. Through our action we grow in knowledge and power, which is why we're here. We transform earthly life by following a spiritual model. As we transform the world, we transform ourselves.

In our incarnate life we progress by having goals. Most of these goals are practical—to become more successful in our careers, to achieve wealth and prosperity, to own our own home, to win in the upcoming competition, and other smaller or larger goals that set our attainable targets. Those are parts of the picture, but they represent the larger picture of the *ideal* world we experienced in Paradise.

That "Real Ideal" is a fundamental part of our soul and lies behind the drive to incarnate and transform the world and in the process to ourselves become the living ideal that we are intended to be. We grow by doing, and to do that we have goals, and when we return to Paradise between lives we are refreshed and reminded of the Real Ideal for which all life is striving.

As we grow, we become. We grow in consciousness; we integrate that which has gone before with that which is now and becoming. We manifest more abilities and more powers—including psychic powers that are conceived in the Soul and intended to be manifested in the fullness of the Soul.

We grow and become more because that is who we are and what we are here to do. Through incarnation we fulfill the Plan, the Purpose, and we find the Meaning of our lives.

SOURCES AND RECOMMENDED READING

Joe H. Slate, *Beyond Reincarnation: Experience Your Past Lives and Lives Between Lives* (Llewellyn, 2008).

Joe H. Slate and Carl Llewellyn Weschcke, *Doors to Past Lives & Life Between Lives: Do-it-Yourself Regression & Self-Hypnosis* (Llewellyn, 2011).

13

SIGILS

Pictures that Work

*A **sigil** (lat. sigillum, diminutive of signum, "sign") is a symbol designed for a specific magical purpose. They are designed to represent a glyph, composed of a variety of symbols or concepts with the intent and inherent iconic meaning. Essentially, sigils are symbolic icons that are condensed representations of more complex ideas or information.*

—*THELEMAPEDIA: THE ENCYCLOPEDIA OF THELEMA & MAGICK*

A picture may be worth a thousand words as stated in an ancient Chinese proverb quoted again and again. A specifically created drawing of a particular thing or idea may be worth many thousands of words in clarifying our understanding of it. A sigil may be worth more than words because it is a magical formula charged with energy to do a certain kind of work.

As you will see, the "modern" form of sigil magick is very similar to the practice of self-hypnosis involving specific goals expressed in affirmation form. Both sigil magick and traditional self-hypnosis are a kind of "programming" to mobilize the resources of the subconscious mind to accomplish your objectives.

WHAT ARE SIGILS?

Wikipedia defines, "A **sigil** is a symbol created for a specific magical purpose. A sigil is usually made up of a complex combination of several specific symbols or geometric figures, each with a specific meaning or intent, and given spiritual 'power' through prayer, meditation, ceremonial magic, sex magic, or other methods."

Actually, a sigil is a different kind of symbol than our more traditional symbols, which often are powerful archetypal images representing gods, elemental forces, locality and geological/geographical energies, Qabalistic concepts, and long-established historic thought-forms. Both traditional and modern sigils have abstract forms usually resembling geometric patterns, almost like schematic drawings of electronic connections that function to focus, concentrate, and direct the flow of mental and esoteric energies.

In actuality, a symbol *represents* something—whether an idea or an object—while a sigil *describes* something in a particular way. The symbol represents the idea of something while a sigil describes the thing itself, but in a way that directs energy and consciousness to secure the thing.

The difference between traditional and most modern sigils is that the former are formulas for the *evocation* of universal forces while the modern sigil is an individual *invoking* of energies for personal goals.

The term *sigil* derives from the Hebrew word הלוגס (*segulah*, meaning a word, action, or item having a spiritual effect. There is also the Latin word *sigillum*, meaning a "seal" that expresses the more common idea in medieval magick of *sealing* the spirit within a container to control it.

In medieval ceremonial magick, sigils referred to occult signs that represented various angels (and demons) whom the magician might summon to do his bidding. Magical grimoires commonly included long lists of such sigils. One concept is that these sigils are the equivalent of the true name of the spirit, knowledge of which gives the magician a measure of control over these entities.

Sigils are common to Jewish mysticism and Kabbalistic philosophy, which make up the foundations of much of Western magick. Symbols and signs have always been important working tools of alchemists and magicians, and of some Witches and shamans, although the latter are more involved with the arousal and direction of physical (and etheric) body energies.

One of the most definitive forms of traditional sigils is the *yantras* found in Hindu Tantra. Other forms include Germanic and Norse bind runes, the Voudoun *veves* used to summon the *loa*, the hex signs seen in rural Pennsylvania, and the Chinese I Ching hexagrams.

Most traditional sigils are constructed using geometric patterns, such as magic squares or circles containing numbers and/or letters

It is important to note that the sigils that represent more abstract natural forces, like the I Ching hexagrams and the runes, serve in both divination and magick.

TRADITIONAL SIGILS

Traditional sigils are graphic symbols (also called "glyphs") that identify and represent spiritual beings and are used to summon and control the spirit represented to (generally) infuse its power into a specific object. In theory, the sigil is a graphic form of the spirit's name. By knowing the name, the magician controls the spirit, and manipulates the sigil through visualization.

Some of the most common sigils are derived from "Magick Squares" in which the columns and rows of numbers all add up to the same total—whether vertical, horizontal, or diagonal. Through correspondence with the Qabalah's Tree of Life (also represented as a glyph), the number of pockets or boxes (the small squares in the larger square that each contain a number) in each row or column identify the magick square with one of seven planetary forces.

Another well-known glyph is in the form of a "rose," with letters on each petal instead of numbers. Connecting the letters of a name forms the graphic image, or glyph, of a spiritual force.

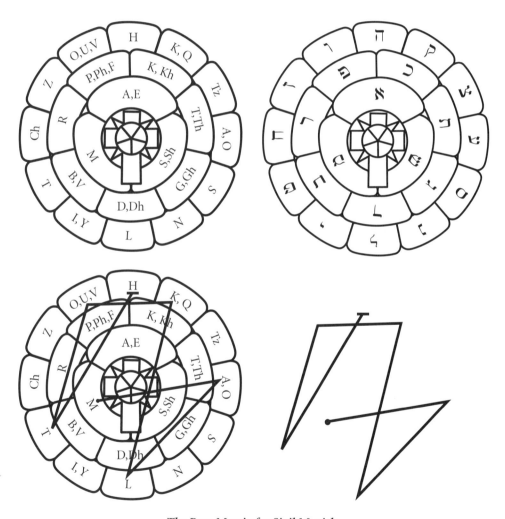

The Rose Matrix for Sigil Magick

Full instructions for the construction and use of these Magick Squares and Planetary Sigils are found in Israel Regardie's *Golden Dawn* and in Denning and Phillips' *Mysteria Magica*.

Using the illustrated Magick Squares, and other particular diagrams developed by the magical orders of Aurum Solis and the Golden Dawn, as templates, a sigil may be easily created by tracing the associated numbers and letters in relation to your own name or the goal of your operation.

These sigils are symbols used to create "reality" according to the will of the magician. These symbols have been used for thousands of years and provide a very powerful way to practice magick.

THE MODERN SIGIL

Unlike traditional sigils, whose creators made use of practices passed down over generations or those taken from ancient books, modern users often create sigils themselves for specifically personal needs and desires, and then "charge" them with invoked rather than evoked power.

The modern sigil was mostly popularized by the British artist and magician Austin Osman Spare (1886–1956) who developed a method, now known as sigilization, by which a personal intention is first expressed in a precise statement of a few words that is then reduced into an abstract design, thus becoming a symbolic instruction to direct the will. The resulting sigil is then charged with the will of the creator through deep meditation or sexual orgasm, and projected into the Unconscious or "Universal Spirit." Spare felt that the total absence of thought during orgasm eliminated any distraction from the intent embedded in the sigil.

> *Sigils are monograms of thought, for the government of energy ... a mathematical means of symbolizing desire and giving it form that has the virtue of preventing any thought and association on that particular desire (at the magical time), escaping the detection of the Ego, so that it does not restrain or attach such desire to its own transitory images, memories and worries, but allows it free passage to the sub-consciousness.*
>
> —A. O. SPARE, *THE BOOK OF PLEASURE*

SIGILS IN PRACTICAL MAGIC

Spare was primarily interested in "High" Magick—personal rituals and techniques for bridging to the Higher Self and the spiritual worlds—but his methods were quickly adapted to what some still call "Low" Magic (or magic without the "K") and most others call "Practical" magic. This involves rituals of varying simplicity to complexity focused on immediate material gain. In general, we prefer not to use the word "spell" for this work because many people have come to a simplistic belief that the "power" is in the words, in contrast to image and action.

Practical Sigil Magic is essentially very simple in construction but can become very complex in the detail, and in the method of charging with energy and projecting into the Unconscious, where all magical action ultimately takes place. The method is composed of the following steps:

STEPS IN PRACTICAL SIGIL MAGIC

Step 1. Using only capital letters, write out a concise sentence expressing the magical intention and desired goal, such as "IT IS MY DESIRE TO MAKE THIS BOOK A BESTSELLER." The statement must use only positive words stated without any ambiguity. There can be debate about the choice of the action word; some prefer it expressed in terms of emotion (desire) and others in terms of will. One definition of E-Motion is *energy in motion,* and magic does involve the movement of energy to bring the intention into reality.

Step 2. Break the sentence into its component parts:

- IT IS MY DESIRE

- TO MAKE THIS

- BOOK A BESTSELLER

Step 3. Cross out all repeating letters in each part, and then between the parts. By condensing and combining letters and reducing them to a single glyph we have our desire formed into a single image that can be visualized and focused on for charging.

- ITSMYDER

- TOMAKEHIS

- BOKAESTLR

  a. ITSMYDER

  b. OAKHS

  c. BL

Step 4. Using the condensed sentence parts, rearranging and omitting the letters as you wish, come up with a single word *mantra* that conveys the essence in sound, just as the sigil expresses it visually. An example might be *MAKEBSLR* (pronounced "makebslr").

Step 5. While treating each part separately—i.e. Upper, Middle, and Lower— make a single glyph with the remaining letters so that they appear unrecognizable to their original form (see figure on next page). Spare thought of sigils as "monograms of thought," and it is true that thoughts have both form and energy, and we are giving form to thought by expressing it in a glyph constructed of the essence of our sentence.

6. Stare at the sigil to deeply embed it in your visual imagination so that you see it in front of your eyes at will—even with your eyes open.

7. Build energy around the sigil, either through meditation or an ecstatic method such as orgasm, dancing, and music, or the *expressive chanting* we will describe below, "as the physical body is the instrument of action, so the subconscious is the instrument of desire."

8. Once this energy has reached its peak, release it while visualizing the sigil.

9. "Expressive Chanting." As an alternative to other energy arousal and release methods, we have developed the concept of using a single word mantra in Step 4 above in a style of chanting. While holding the visual sigil in your mind, silently and slowly chant the audible mantra, and then begin to chant it aloud building up both speed and loudness until releasing the image with a final shout. See the image as shooting away from you into the universe.

10. Try to forget about the sigil after this. Otherwise, the energy hasn't truly been let go for the magic to work.

11. Make a record of successes and failures in a magical diary in order to develop the best personal magical practice.

As mentioned earlier, the process of making and using a modern sigil is basically identical with the procedure followed in self-hypnosis:

1. Writing a concise and positively worded statement of your intent and goal.

2. Strongly affirm the goal through an image.

3. Enter a trance state in which the statement is repeated and the image reinforced.

4. Conclude and record.

The difference between the two is that with self-hypnosis the program is repeated, while in sigil magic the energy release culminates the process. In both cases, the consciously developed goal is implanted in the subconscious for accomplishment of the goal.

Is one procedure better than the other? Probably not, and which one you use is a matter of personal preference. Experimentation is always broadening.

SIGILS AND THOUGHT FORMS

Thought forms are a more complex form of Magick, but sigils may be used in this manner as well. However, it is too complex a subject to develop in this introductory chapter, other than to mention it for your further research.

PRINCIPLES OF SIGIL MAGIC

- A sigil is an abstract image you create, and then use to focus your subconscious to accomplish a specific task.

- In substance, you simplify and abstract the letters to become nearly unrecognizable, and add some artistic elements, just as a craftsperson does to personalize a common object.

- You empower (charge) the sigil by visualizing it as the body is intensely energized. This can be accomplished in a variety of *shamanic* ways involving orgasm, a quick sting of pain, exhaustive dancing, clear meditation ended with visualization of the sigil, chanting, etc. In other words, the image is charged with a burst of energy.

- The final act is to "let go" of the image and the thought of what it represents. *Forget it!* Unless you do so, **it is still here and not there**. It is in the conscious mind, but you want it in the subconscious mind, which connects to the Unconscious.

Magick in Theory

It's not our intention to complicate the matter, but we are all so conditioned to "Conscious Thinking" that we commonly act in ways that contradict "Magical Thinking."

Magical Theory recognizes that the *conscious mind inhibits magical action*. We must project our magical intent into the subconscious mind, through which our intention manifests in quantum-level actions—otherwise defined in terms of "astral" mechanics. Once implanted in the subconscious mind, results are brought about "unconsciously."

Magick uses the active imagination to tap into those unconscious archetypes that have become fundamental to mythology, religious symbolism, and the universal consciousness common to all humanity, and perhaps to all entities. In the broadest sense, not everything magical is called "magick"—artistic endeavors, religious ceremonies, shamanic action, emotional interaction, and many paranormal events are archetypal in their essence.

SOURCES AND RECOMMENDED READING

Melita Denning and Osborne Phillips, *Mysteria Magica: Fundamental Techniques of High Magick,* 3rd ed. (Llewellyn, 2004).

Patrick Dunn, *Magic, Power, Language, Symbol* (Llewellyn, 2008).

Israel Regardie, edited by Carl Llewellyn Weschcke, *The Golden Dawn: The Original Account of the Teachings, Rites & Ceremonies of the Hermetic Order,* 6th ed. (Llewellyn, 1989).

Joe H. Slate and Carl Llewellyn Weschcke, *Self-Empowerment through Self-Hypnosis* (Llewellyn, 2010).

Austin O. Spare, *The Book of Pleasure* (I-H-O Books, 2005).

U∴D∴, Frater, *Practical Sigil Magic: Creating Personal Symbols for Success* (Llewellyn, 1990).

14

TELEPATHY

The Power of Self-Talk in Self-Empowerment, Mind-to-Mind Messaging, & Global Communication

Telepathy was called "Mental Radio" in 1930 by the famous writer Upton Sinclair, and his positive research was complemented by Albert Einstein in his preface to the book. Since then, telepathy has been increasingly accepted as natural and common to all of us, but—like all other innate psychic powers—it can be developed and turned into a reliable psychic skill implemented by the conscious mind for personal success and global security.

Telepathy is communication without physical limitation. As a psychic sending and receiving phenomenon, it surpasses even the most advanced communication technology. It is a comprehensive phenomenon that can include not only the sending and receiving of thought messages but the emotions and motives underlying them. It can even include the transference of positive energy.

Thought is energy. In telepathy, positive thoughts generate positive energies that tend to open the telepathic communication channels. They are potentially empowering to sender and receiver alike. Any negative or deliberately damaging telepathic message, on the other hand, generates a self-contained, enfeebling state within the sender alone. Once unleashed, negative messages close down the communication process and return to the sender in a boomerang effect to disempower the sender only. Insecurity and low self-esteem are often the result of such negative thoughts as resentment and hostility toward others turned inward. Consequently, telepathy, perhaps more than any other extrasensory skill, requires careful reflection on purposes and desired outcomes.

Telepathic messages typically include both informational and emotional content. Positive psychic messages, including messages of love, will often induce a positive mood state, even when the specific informational content of the message remains consciously unknown to the receiver.

All social interactions include a spontaneous telepathic component. When positive, that component can promote productive interactions by enriching the communication process. Even when subconscious, the sender's motives, attitudes, and thoughts can influence the receiver's perceptions of the interaction. In the group setting, the communication process as well as the productiveness of the group can be strongly influenced by the telepathic interactions within the group. Perhaps not surprisingly, effective leaders are usually highly skilled at promoting positive group interactions. Almost always, exceptionally effective speakers readily admit their use of nonverbal telepathic components to generate an energized state of receptiveness in their audiences that increases the appeal of their communication.

Because they occur independently of limiting sensory channels, powerful telepathic messages could conceivably span the globe, or even be dispersed throughout the universe. Imagine the possibilities when widespread thoughts of peace and other humanitarian goals are sent forth to encircle the globe. Positive thoughts generate not only positive energy, they generate power as well. Thoughts of peace and love in sufficient measure can overcome all barriers to global advancement. We will later explore ways of telepathically achieving that important goal.

TELEPATHY EXPLAINED

Telepathy as a communication phenomenon has three essential components: the sender, the receiver, and the communication medium. As already noted, telepathic interactions can be conscious or subconscious as well as voluntary or involuntary. The sender in the communication system has two major functions: first, formulating the message in some appropriate encoded form, notably imagery, words, symbols, or a combination of these, and second, sending the encoded message. The receiver in the communication system likewise has two major functions: first, receiving the encoded message and second, decoding it. The remaining component, the communication medium, is the psychically engaged minds of both sender and receiver.

In the group situations involving telepathic sending and receiving between groups, the essential components remain the same, but in collective form. The collective psychic faculties of the sending group are organized to form and send the encoded message, while the collective psychic faculties of the receiving group function to receive and decode the message. In telepathy between groups, the communication medium is the combined psychically engaged minds of the two groups.

Among the several explanations of telepathy is the *thought-as-energy perspective*. This view holds that, once thought is generated, it exists in a meaningful energy form that can be transmitted and received telepathically. Critical to that energy transfer process is the sender who formulates a clear message in positive energy form and the receiver who deciphers the energy as a meaningful communication.

Another view of telepathy speculates that telepathy is essentially a spiritual phenomenon. According to this perspective, telepathy can transcend the purely physical nature of our being to engage an interaction on a nonphysical plane. This view holds that telepathy as mind-to-mind communication often activates the sending and receiving faculties of our spiritual being. This concept of telepathy suggests several empowering possibilities, including the capacity of higher consciousness to telepathically interact with departed entities along with other non-physical sources of enlightenment and power. Prayer, mediumship, psychic channeling, and other interactions with the discarnate realm are cited as examples of telepathic communication on that plane. Our research at Athens State University related to this view of telepathy as a manifestation of the spiritual nature of our being offers convincing evidence of the survival of consciousness and personal identity beyond death.

From a purely physiological perspective, it is possible that among the brain's legion of faculties there exists a psychic network that can engage an unlimited range of currently unknown or unexplained functions. Included is not only telepathy but also precognitive awareness of the future and the world around us, as well as the psychokinetic power of biologically based functions to influence matter, events, and minds. The resolution of global conflicts and the promotion of world peace thus become reasonable possibilities when the powers of the inner psychic network become fully engaged. On a more personal level, healing, rejuvenation, happiness, and success are all within the scope of possibilities when we activate the powers within.

A related view holds that cognitive psychic faculties, including telepathy and other forms of ESP, exist within the cognitive structure of the brain. Like global or general intelligence that embodies multiple mental faculties, our psychic makeup includes a host of psychic potentials that can be developed through practice and experience. According to this view, psychic growth and actualization require an organized educational approach that recognizes individual difference in potentials and motivation.

TELEPATHIC INITIATIVE

Common to the various explanations of telepathy is recognition of the phenomenon as an interactive communication process that can involve conscious and subconscious levels of awareness in both the sender and the receiver. Although the typical telepathic interaction probably includes both levels, the most efficient telepathic mechanisms seem to reside in the subconscious. Collectively, they are poised to work with us as we work with them. They challenge us to recognize them and master effective ways of using them. The Telepathic Initiative Program (Revised) was developed at

Athens State University as a personal empowerment exercise to meet that challenge. Here's the program, which is suitable for practice individually or with a group.

TELEPATHIC INITIATIVE PROGRAM

Step 1. Psychic Orientation. In a quiet, comfortable setting, remind yourself in your own words that you are by nature endowed with a host of psychic potentials, including telepathy. Next, affirm you are now committed to developing your telepathic potentials and using them in positive, productive ways. Here are examples:

I am endowed with telepathic potential.

I will develop that potential and use it responsibly for myself and others.

Telepathy expands my awareness and enriches my interactions with others.

It empowers me with new knowledge, insight, and understanding.

Step 2. Conscious/Subconscious Attunement. With your eyes closed, note the sense of oneness within. Remind yourself that you are *one person in one body in this one moment in time.* Notice the sense of attunement within as the energies of your being, both conscious and subconscious, merge. Affirm:

I am now balanced, attuned, and empowered.

My conscious and subconscious powers are now working with me as I work with them.

We are one.

Step 3. Telepathic Activation. As you remain in that state of attunement, form a specific telepathic goal with a specific message and designated recipient. It could be something as specific as sending forth a message of comfort to a person recovering from grief, or it could be as expansive as sending forth a message of hope to victims of a natural disaster. Where possible, follow up your telepathic message with action, perhaps an altruistic act of kindness or generosity.

Step 4. Telepathy in Daily Life. Let positive telepathy become a part of your daily life. Welcome ways of sending forth positive messages of peace and good will. Incorporate positive telepathy into your lifestyle. It will promote rejuvenation, better health, and quality of life. Beyond that, it will contribute to humanity's higher cause.

In our study of this program in the controlled lab setting, individuals as well as groups who practiced this step-by-step approach showed progressive improvement in laboratory telepathy tasks, including their ability to send and receive such simple telepathic messages as the identity of a playing card or the critical elements depicted in a picture. Interestingly, comparisons of the telepathic performances of men and women showed that women typically outperformed men in the morning hours whereas men typically outperformed women in the evening hours. No significant difference was noted between men and women in their performances during the afternoon hours. We've yet to explain that finding.

TELEPATHIC ACTIVATION

The Telepathic Activation Procedure is designed specifically to facilitate telepathic sending and receiving. Developed in our labs, the procedure requires a comfortable setting free of distractions.

TELEPATHIC ACTIVATION PROCEDURE

Step 1. For telepathic sending or receiving: With your eyes closed, clear your mind and relax your body. An excellent mind-clearing and relaxation exercise combines imagery of a clear, blue sky and the affirmation:

I am now becoming relaxed as my mind is cleared of all active thought.

The clearing and relaxation process is further facilitated by breathing slowly and mentally scanning your body from the head downward. Areas of tension are noted, and muscles are progressively relaxed.

Step 2. For telepathic sending: Formulate the message and related imagery. Visualize a vehicle, such as a beam of light or a transparent sphere, for transporting the thought message. Actively concentrate on the message and related imagery. Take in a deep breath and as you exhale, release the telepathic message to go forth to the envisioned target receiver.

Step 3. For telepathic receiving: Maintain a mentally passive state and allow the thought messages and images to emerge in conscious awareness.

The Telepathic Activation Program increases in effectiveness with practice, whether by individuals or groups. Except in a structured or controlled lab setting, we typically have no advance notice that we are the selected recipients of a telepathic communication. Our telepathic receiving under those circumstances is spontaneous, thus involving no receiving effort on our part. When we are aware of the sending effort, however, we can deliberately facilitate the receiving process through the Telepathic Activation Procedure.

TELEPATHY AS A TWO-PART PHENOMENON

The Two-Part Composite Procedure focuses on telepathy as a two-part phenomenon with clearly defined sending and receiving components. Developed in the laboratory setting, it identifies conducive conditions and specific procedures for activating each component. Finally, it interfaces the two components in ways that promote development of each component.

TWO-PART COMPOSITE TELEPATHIC PROCEDURE

Part One: Telepathic Sending

Step 1. Select the telepathic recipient and formulate the telepathic message.

Step 2. Become physically relaxed and mentally passive.

Step 3. Focus your full attention on the telepathic message. Simplify the message. If you use language, keep the content brief—complicated messages tend to become fragmented and distorted.

Step 4. With your eyes closed, supplement the message with appropriate mental imagery. Try to use visual symbols. For example, the message *I love you* can be accompanied by the image of a favorite flower or a heart with the word *Love* superimposed.

Step 5. With your eyes remaining closed, focus your full attention on the message and related imagery. Concentrate. Avoid any distraction that could weaken your concentration.

Step 6. As you continue to concentrate, mentally or audibly articulate the message while continuing to engage the related mental imagery. Allow the articulated message and related imagery to emerge as a powerful thought-form.

Step 7. Visualize the target receiver. Release the thought-form and mentally direct it to the envisioned target. Allow a few minutes for the thought transfer to occur. With experience, you will learn to sense when the message has been received.

Step 8. Close down your telepathic system by clearing your mind and relaxing your body.

Part Two: Telepathic Receiving

Step 1. Relax. Mentally scan your body, releasing all tension from your forehead to the tips of your toes. Develop a slow, rhythmic breathing pattern.

Step 2. With your eyes closed, extinguish all active thought. Clear your mind by imagining a mist or fog slowly moving in and closing off other images and thoughts.

Step 3. As your eyes remain closed, create a receptive state of mind. Allow new thoughts to emerge or new images to appear spontaneously against a white background. Be patient. Allow sufficient time for the telepathic message to form.

Step 4. Upon receiving the message, close down the receiving system by relaxing your body and clearing your mind.

The effectiveness of this procedure, like most telepathic exercises, will improve with practice in which a variety of telepathic materials and messages are used. Although practice with aids such as ESP or playing cards are usually productive, marked improvements in both sending and receiving skills are noted when highly meaningful messages and interesting materials are introduced into the practice sessions.

INNER-TELEPATHY

Telepathy is typically considered an interpersonal form of psychic communication between individuals or groups. It can, however, be experienced as an intrapsychic phenomenon in which the self or separate parts of the self function as both sender and receiver. This extension of conventional telepathy reflects the power of our mental and physical subsystems to engage in an empowering interaction that is fully autonomous and self-contained. Through this phenomenon, called *inner-telepathy*, empowering messages can be formulated and targeted to one's inner mental or physical functions. The results can be a profound state of self-initiated psychic empowerment.

Similar in some ways to self-hypnosis, inner-telepathy empowers us to take command of the complex, ongoing interactions within the self. One of the most common examples of inner-telepathy is *self-talk*, in which we generate thought messages that are subsequently dispersed either generally throughout the self-system or specifically to selected inner targets. For instance, we can build a positive state of self-esteem through such messages as *I am a person of worth; I am capable, self-confident, and secure; I am fully empowered.* When affirmed frequently and convincingly, positive self-messages can generate a powerful force within the self that empowers us to achieve even our most challenging personal goals. When combined with more specific messages, self-talk can empower us to achieve personal goals such as quitting smoking, losing weight, accelerating learning, improving memory, and succeeding in business. In fact, there are almost no limitations to the empowering possibilities of self-talk. It can activate dormant potentials and actually create new ones. If practiced consistently, it can generate a continuous state of personal empowerment.

Mental imagery is a critical component of positive self-talk. It can increase the power of self-talk a hundredfold. Given the vehicle of mental imagery, thoughts become powerful accelerators of growth and success. By giving substance to thought, mental imagery transports raw power to targeted destinations that include mental functions such as learning, creativity, and reasoning. Aside from these, positive mental imagery can empower biological organs and their functions in ways that promote better health, fitness, and rejuvenation. Athletes have used positive self-talk combined with relevant mental imagery to promote achievement and perfection in a variety of highly complex skills, including figure skating, skiing, swimming, and golf. It can generate a state of mental and physical well-being related to almost any personal goal.

Self-talk combined with mental imagery is especially effective in generating creative ideas. That application is illustrated by an accomplished artist who regularly envisions a blank canvas upon which new works slowly unfold as she affirms, *My artistic potentials are now unleashed.* Similarly, a composer reports that he routinely imagines a music staff upon which notes appear as he affirms: *My creative powers are now unfolding.* Such combinations of thought and imagery can generate a forceful message that is readily perceived by the psychic mind to awaken dormant potentials and creative ideas.

Inner-telepathy can activate a host of inner psychic faculties, including those existing in the subconscious mind. Clairvoyant and precognitive insights are often experienced first in the subconscious, and then conveyed to consciousness in either direct or disguised form. Inner-telepathy is the critical vehicle for the internal delivery of such insights. That vehicle can include direct and complete delivery of subconscious psychic insight to full conscious awareness, or it can promote spontaneous, indirect awareness through such channels as slips of the tongue, pen, and sight. Aside from these, it can provide awareness of a future event through emotional expressions related to the event. For instance, a dejected mental state can be the precursor of adversity, whereas an elated state can foretell good fortune.

Although the capacity of the mind to generate thought messages and disperse them telepathically within the self is among our most crucial empowerment resources, that same capacity if misdirected can disempower both mind and body. Negative self-talk, such as *I am unable to succeed; I am inferior to others; I am incapable of meeting the demands of this job;* and *My future is bleak* predispose both mind and body for failure. Fortunately, empowering thoughts are available to you right now. A positive thought will consistently extinguish its negative counterpart. You can choose empowerment over disempowerment even when faced with the most highly uncertain or adverse life situation.

GLOBAL TELEPATHY

The human mind is an amazing force. The more we explore its secrets, the more we come to appreciate its complexity and wondrous power. It is capable of thinking, reasoning, and remembering. It can also create, communicate, and empower. Conventional telepathy illustrates the power of the mind to interact psychically with others; whereas intrapsychic telepathy illustrates the power of the mind to interact with the self. Global telepathy illustrates the power of the mind to interact with the globe.

Global telepathy is based on the premise that we can psychically generate global interactions that affect global conditions and bring forth global change. Peace, for instance, can become the product of thoughts of peace generated on a massive scale. If thought is power, thoughts of peace become the energies of peace. It follows that thoughts of peace on a global scale could literally create global peace. If individually we can shape our own destinies, then collectively we can shape the destiny of the world.

CONCLUSION

All too often we are out of touch, not only with ourselves but with others and the universe as well. Telepathy can bridge the gaps that separate us. It can enrich our lives by expanding our capacity to communicate and interact. It can bring forth new insight that expands our understanding of ourselves and others. It can lift consciousness and empower each of us to achieve new levels of personal actualization. At a global level, it can make the world a better place for present and future generations.

SOURCES AND RECOMMENDED READING

Joe H. Slate and Carl Llewellyn Weschcke, *Psychic Empowerment for Everyone* (Llewellyn, 2009).

Joe H. Slate and Carl Llewellyn Weschcke, *Self-Empowerment & Your Subconscious Mind* (Llewellyn, 2010).

Joe H. Slate and Carl Llewellyn Weschcke, *Self-Empowerment & Self-Hypnosis* (Llewellyn, 2010).

15

VISUALIZATION

The Key to Empowering Your Imagination

Imagination is what makes our sensory experience meaningful, enabling us to interpret and make sense of it, whether from a conventional perspective or from a fresh, original, individual one. It is what makes perception more than the mere physical stimulation of sense organs. It also produces mental imagery, visual and otherwise, which is what makes it possible for us to think outside the confines of our present perceptual reality, to consider memories of the past and possibilities for the future, and to weigh alternatives against one another. Thus, imagination makes possible all our thinking about what is, what has been, and, perhaps most important, what might be.

—NIGEL J. T. THOMAS, WWW.IMAGERY–IMAGINATION.COM

To imagine is to create. The imagination (image-plus-action) is our faculty that puts an image into action. To act upon an image is to turn it into reality. An image may be a picture or representation of something remembered, seen currently, or dreamed of, but it may also be a picture created in the imagination as a representation of something not yet existent.

The image in the imagination was visualized—created wholly out of "mind stuff" which can become the seed or matrix or core of energy that becomes converted into matter to enter the world of reality. To enable that process to happen, the visualized image attracts energy and matter that becomes the thing visualized through any of a variety of processes.

When people are asked, *"Can you visualize?"* most people tend to answer in the negative—"No, I cannot," "Well, a little," "Sometimes, maybe," and other answers far from positive.

When people are asked, *"Do you see pictures in your dreams?"* most people answer in the positive. Many people also affirm that they dream in color, and a few affirm that they occasionally have "lucid" dreams in which everything is not only usually in color but has a boldness and vitality that seems "realer than real."

Many people also will experience vivid dreams after seeing an exciting and active motion picture—seeing images as clearly as they did in the theater. Most people, upon thinking about it, admit to seeing mental pictures as they carry on conversations, and when writing anything descriptive.

WHAT'S THE DIFFERENCE?

Most people do see images in their dreams, while conversing, and while doing descriptive writing. *Why do these same people say they can't visualize?*

Just as someone in an interview will say, "That's a very good question." *What is the difference, if any, between seeing pictures and visualizing?*

In part, the answer is that the people involved think that visualizing an image is different than seeing one. When we're told to look at a *flowering plant,* for example, and then close our eyes and visualize it in detail and answer questions about the size and quantity of leaves, we're faced with a task that would be difficult even with our eyes open looking at the real plant itself. Too often, visualization exercises are absurd and unrealistic. In theory, the claim is made that a visualized image should be as "real" as REAL. That may be the goal, but it's not necessarily realistic for the first exposure to developing the ability to visualize. Nor is it absolutely necessary for *creative visualization* which we will discuss shortly.

Let's change the scene and turn to a typical "creative" visualization example. You want a **new car.** You study the various models and research their safety, economy, and other specifications to fit your needs and desires, and your budget. You decide what you want and make a color choice. And certainly you visit a dealer and look at the real thing, you sit in it, and maybe are allowed to test drive it. But, honestly, you realize the price is really more than you can afford. You pick up a beautiful brochure with a picture of exactly what you want. It goes on your wish list.

You've familiarized yourself with that car, and you've looked at the picture many times. When you close your eyes, you can see it. When you are with friends, you talk about it and can describe it in detail. Perhaps you even see it in your dreams.

Yes, you really can visualize that car. You want it. You've made an emotional commitment to having it. It is on your wish list and you return to visualizing it again and again. You see yourself in the driver's seat again and again—but you still can't afford it.

Lo and behold, one day the dealer you visited calls and says the manufacturer is putting on a year-end clearance sale on that exact car, and now the price does fit your budget. You buy it and now you really are in the driver's seat.

CREATIVE VISUALIZATION

What is the difference between our two examples of the plant and the car? The easiest answer, and one that is essential for Creative Visualization, is *emotion.* You put a lot of feeling into the search for the car of your dreams, and in doing so, you easily focused on details and had a perfect picture that you "memorized" without effort.

Emotion is one technique for effective visualization, but it isn't the only one and it doesn't necessarily apply to all the situations in which visualization can be used.

THE POWER OF ATTRACTION

This example of creative visualization that created the opportunity to own the car of your desire is just one example of developing the "power of attraction" to activate opportunities to bring fulfillment to your desires and accomplish your goals in life.

Know what you want, be specific without limiting the opportunity to access the reality by which it can be accomplished, find the picture or symbol to represent your desire or goal, empower it with emotion, and see it in your imagination with you "in the driver's seat."

You not only want to create the opportunity to attain your desire, but you have to "put yourself in the picture" so that the opportunity comes to you.

And be careful to include the right details. In another book, we mentioned the example of a person who did visualize himself in the driver's seat of a Rolls Royce automobile. He got it, but he had forgotten to specify that it would be in running condition. Instead, it was up on blocks in his back yard, too costly to repair. And he died shortly after.

VISUALIZATION AS A TECHNIQUE

Visualization is an important technique used in conjunction with your imagination. Your ability to effectively visualize turns your imagination into a **psychic power tool** for use in psychic work as well as in all forms of magical application, active meditation, astral travel, Qabalistic pathworking, the development of clairvoyance, remote viewing, symbol "doorways" to access specific areas of the astral world, activating archetypal powers, the assumption of god-forms, entering mythic worlds, and much more.

Effective visualization is the key to empowering your imagination to "make real the unreal." Emotion, as used in creative visualization, is not always the answer, and sometimes it becomes an obstacle in other applications.

ARE THERE PRACTICAL APPLICATIONS?

To imagine and to visualize is to move from past into future, which becomes the present. "Present" in time, and a "present" (i.e. a gift) to you.

Are there practical applications of visualization other than Creative Visualization? The complete answer involves all the more occult applications mentioned previously, and some people might debate about how practical they are.

There is one famous example from recent history. The mechanical and electrical genius, Nikola Tesla, inventor of the alternating current, which was necessary for the long-distance transmission of electric power, induction motors, and much more, did his research and development entirely in his imagination.

> *Before I put a sketch on paper, the whole idea is worked out mentally. In my mind I change the construction, make improvements, and even operate the device. Without ever having drawn a sketch I can give the measurements of all parts to workmen, and when completed all these parts will fit, just as certainly as though I had made the actual drawings. It is immaterial to me whether I run my machine in my mind or test it in my shop. The inventions I have conceived in this way have always worked. In thirty years there has not been a single exception. My first electric motor, the vacuum wireless light, my turbine engine and many other devices have all been developed in exactly this way.*
>
> —NIKOLA TESLA, LUCIDCAFÉ: LIBRARY

Few of us have even dreamt that such a thing was possible. No doubt many people are actually doing nearly as much in their imagination without thinking of it as exceptional. But, just as in our first example of the visualized plant, had you such a powerful imagination, you could indeed have counted the leaves, measured their length, and probably have sensed when the plant needed water.

Other examples of practical application: Sculptors state that they are able to project a three-dimensional mental image onto a block of marble, and then chip away the marble to conform to the image; creative artists say much the same thing—they see their image as if projected onto the canvas, and paint the picture as if the image was printed on the canvas; illustrators have the same ability—projecting an image onto paper and then sketching the picture by following the image.

MAKING THE IMAGINED IMAGE AS "REAL" AS REAL

That's the "great secret" of Magick, and of Creation. That and reaching down into your Subconscious and through it to the Universal Consciousness to actually *energize* the image by your conscious intent to bring about the specific change in existing reality to that of your intended reality.

The "energy" is there, but the more energy you actually are able to *charge* your image with—by means of such adjuncts as chanting, burning incense, burning candles, bringing Qabalistic "correspondences" into play, ritual gestures, ecstatic dancing, and more—the better. In addition, you can draw upon your personal energy, called variously "the Power," Kundalini, Chi, Prana, and many other traditional names.

But, this all belongs to another subject, that of Magick, which we are not really discussing in this book on Psychic Development. Our concern here is simply with visualization.

CULTIVATING VISUALIZATION

As in all things, *practice makes perfect.* The simplest method is to utilize basic symbols in principal colors and practice what is called, in Tantric Yoga, *Tratak*—staring at a brightly lit image against a plain background until your eyes tear and you have to close them. In a few seconds you will see that image in its complementary colors floating in space in front of your brow, actually in the psychic space of *Ajna,* the Third Eye.

Subsequently, you can follow the same procedure of "burning the image into your retina" and then seeing it against a white background.

Among the best images to start with are the simple geometric Tattwa symbols of a Square, Inverse Triangle, Crescent, Circle, and Oval in their traditional colors of Yellow, White, Red, Blue, and Blue-Violet. You can refer to the chapter on Chakras for further details. In addition, the Tattwa symbols, in greater complexity, are available on Tattwa Cards.

As you develop your ability to hold the colored images in your imagination for longer periods of time, they can be used as "Astral Doorways" to access specific areas of the Astral World and, in the process, develop the associated psychic powers.

A more complex meditation can use the individual Tarot Cards in the same visualization technique, progressing through the Major Arcana, and then the Minor Arcana. Indeed, this is one of the best methods to learn the meanings of the cards. Eventually it will be possible for you to use the cards to travel the paths on the Tree of Life from one Sephiroth to another. This will be discussed further in a later chapter.

In this work, you are learning to use symbols and colors in very powerful meditations. Visualizing and "entering" into the astral world opened by a symbol key is a powerful method of learning the reality represented by the symbol. But the same visualization technique can open the hidden reality behind any thing or idea for your study and understanding—from a repair job to a business opportunity, from a personal challenge to financial success, from a mystery to its solution.

CONCLUSION

In this short chapter, we have outlined one of the most powerful techniques used in psychic development. As a fundamental technique, visualization can be employed with all other techniques and with all the tools to be described in Part Two of this book.

Visualization can be the subject of several much expanded books, but as is the case with all the techniques and tools described in this book, you are the one to— in essence—write those books through your own study and development. Once the basic information has been provided, you learn best by doing, not necessarily by more reading. Of course, further study in any of the areas touched on in this book will be beneficial, but not as beneficial as the actual practice. *We learn by doing.*

SOURCES AND RECOMMENDED READING

Melita Denning and Osborne Phillips, *Practical Guide to Creative Visualization* (Llewellyn, 2001).

Jonn Mumford, *A Chakra & Kundalini Workbook: Psycho-Spiritual Techniques for Health, Rejuvenation, Psychic Powers & Spiritual Realization* (Llewellyn, 1994).

Nikola Tesla, www.Lucidcafé : Library.com.

Nigel J. T. Thomas, www.imagery–imagination.com.

PART TWO
Awareness-Expanding Divinatory Tools
for Psychic Development

16

OBJECTOLOGY & PSYCHIC EMPOWERMENT

Objectology—the study of the psychic significance of inanimate objects—is among the most challenging fields of psychic exploration and discovery. Through our interactions with them, objects become more than tangible tools, they become energized forces that connect us to the boundless powers within ourselves and beyond. When charged either historically or deliberately by ritual, they can become power objects with national and international significance. Like flags of nations and historic landmarks, they can assume power as symbols of national and global significance. When viewed through the prism of objectology, even the moon, a certain planet, or a distant star can become a magnificent force that connects and attunes us to the great beyond.

—JOE H. SLATE

Psychic phenomena do not always lend themselves to direct activation. We therefore often seek indirect means to access our inner psychic potentials and promote their development. These methods can include psychic empowering programs that involve altered states such as hypnosis, self-hypnosis, meditation, and dreams, as well as the application of psychic tools, which typically are material objects purposefully applied to connect us to sources of psychic power within the self. We call the study of these tangible tools and the techniques associated with them "objectology." Among the frequently used tools in objectology are the pendulum, dowsing rods, quartz crystals, the pyramid, and various forms of ESP cards, to list but a few.

It is important to note that psychic empowerment tools and techniques are valuable, not only in stimulating our psychic functions and promoting their development, but also in research designed to explore and better understand the world of psychic phenomena. Through the use of tangible objects, we can develop techniques and assemble objective data that can be statistically analyzed for significance and relevance to the psychic experience. The application of dowsing rods, for example, can yield specific data regarding natural subterranean resources, which can be analyzed for accuracy. Likewise, the pendulum when appropriately applied can provide a wealth of data in a quantified form that can be treated statistically. ESP cards are often used by researchers to gather objective data related to various psychic faculties and provide comparisons of psychic abilities among individuals. Many of our conclusions concerning the nature of psychic phenomena are based on the results of studies that applied tangible objects under appropriately controlled, scientific conditions.

Paralleling the use of tangible objects in psychical research is the spontaneous though often unexplained role they play in real-life situations. Like the lyricist's grandfather's clock that "stopped short, never to run again when the old man died," some objects appear almost to have a mind—or an energy—of their own. They seem to function as mediators or conveyers of critical psychic information, particularly concerning individuals with whom they are closely associated. An attorney, for instance, reported that a bronze figure—a gift from his grandson—toppled mysteriously from a bookcase in his office at the very moment his grandson was seriously injured in a traffic accident. In another instance, a student reported that a plant—a birthday gift from her mother—fell from its place over a kitchen sink at the exact moment her mother suffered a heart attack. Although we could dismiss these phenomena as simply chance occurrences, the high frequency of such events illustrates an interesting possibility: In the psychic realm, tangible objects can spontaneously, yet purposefully, deliver critical psychic information.

The use of objects as communication tools in our daily lives is not uncommon. Trophies, certificates, and awards not only recognize accomplishments, they also satisfy certain needs for status and recognition. Objects, in fact, are often used deliberately to influence the perceptions of others or to compensate for one's own felt weaknesses. For instance, a highly successful contractor from a somewhat impoverished background occupies an unusually luxurious and pretentious office that, he observes, "leaves no doubt about my success." Along another vein, a businessman previously convicted of embezzlement conspicuously displays a Bible in his office as well as on the dashboard of his car because, in his words, "It sends a good message." An executive, who was a high-school dropout, prominently places the works of Shakespeare and the Greek classics on the shelves in his office. Even in higher education, a survey of college professors in a small, liberal-arts college revealed an inverse relationship between the number of books in a given professor's office and the number of articles he had published in scholarly journals—the greater the number of books, the fewer the number of articles published. It seems that the presence of many books, while possibly conveying scholarly concerns, can also be explained as an effort to compensate for perceived inadequacy.

Many objects, once vested with certain meanings or culturally ascribed with certain powers, can assert a significant influence in our lives. For instance, objects of religious significance such as the cross, holy water, eternal flame, or temple can signify deep devotion or a divine presence for many. The diamond, wedding band, anniversary gifts, and flowers have become important symbols of caring in our culture. Some objects, like flowers for a friend and Shakespeare's "sweets to the sweet," have assumed almost universal significance.

Because of the meanings we attribute to them, objects can be valued so highly that they become powerful, controlling forces in our lives. For instance, money has been empowered to signify status, success, and authority. Unfortunately, material wealth is often seen as a measure of human value. It can become so personally controlling that its loss can lead to tragic and devastating consequences. When equated with human worth, wealth, whether inherited or earned, becomes destructive and disempowering.

Emotions and attitudes as well as social interactions can be strongly influenced by our perceptions and associations related to material objects. The mere presence of a firearm in social situations can increase anxiety and promote aggressive behavior. Conversely, the presence of flowers and plants tends to promote a calm, serene state of mind. The badge, stethoscope, and uniform, all associated with professions, can influence not only our perceptions of the people wearing them, but our emotions and behaviors toward them as well. Our perceptions of objects and the meanings we assign them usually take into account other variables, including the characteristics of the setting in which they are found. Few objects retain a given significance independent of their surroundings. A quartz crystal, for instance, can be seen as simply a decorative object when displayed on a desk, but when worn as a pendant, it can be seen as a significant conveyer of energy.

Of particular interest in our study of psychic empowerment is the "power" or "energy" often attributed to objects as if inherent in the object itself. Although the effects of tangible objects are, for the most part, a function of the meanings we assign to them, some objects and certain physical settings do seem to be uniquely energized. Examples are religious shrines with the serenity they evoke; a cemetery that, by its sheer existence, calls forth a somber state of mind; memorials that connect us to those who gave their lives for an important cause; or a special, enchanted place—a secluded beach, meadow, or cove—that inspires faith and renews hope.

The great works of famous artists sometimes have powerful effects on our awareness and appreciation of beauty. This was illustrated by the author, Octave Mirbeau, who, after viewing Monet's series of Poplars, reportedly wrote to the impressionist, "In front of the series I experienced an emotion I cannot express, so profound that I wanted to hug you. Never did any artist render anything equal to it."

At another level, even something as mundane as a favorite article of clothing or a piece of jewelry can be endowed with special significance, and even power, that can go beyond the meanings we normally attribute to them. These special objects are often gifts with psychological attachments or associations that signify caring and love. An honor student reported that wearing a birthstone ring given to her by a friend consistently improved her performance on examinations—which she attributed to the ring's psychological significance as well as its special physical features. She believed the stone—an amethyst—generated a frequency of energy that synchronized her own energy system to result in the full activation of her intellectual powers.

In a similar instance, a pre-med student discovered that wearing a certain blue suit always generated a more positive mental state and brought good fortune into his life. He claimed the suit was consistently empowering, whether worn for course examinations or other important events. "Like an old and trusted friend," he insisted, "the suit never let me down." When the suit became too worn for further wear, he recycled it by cutting it into patches, which he sewed inside his other clothing. The result, he firmly holds, was a transfer of the suit's original power.

The empowerment potential of tangible objects was strikingly illustrated by the founder of a men's clothing firm who discovered early in his career that a tape measure draped around his neck increased his sales. He became so committed to the tape measure that it became a company trademark. He frequently challenged his employees, "If you see me without my tape measure, I will reward you with a new suit." In a similar instance, a famous film director found that his effectiveness on the set was at its peak when he occupied a certain chair. The chair soon assumed the highest respect of the studio and was reserved for the director alone. Other examples of objects that take on special meaning over time are an old but reliable automobile that becomes personalized as a trusted friend, or a home place with its treasury of memories, perhaps of childhood.

From the psychic perspective, tangible objects can at times assume a role of life-and-death significance. In a remarkable instance of that possibility, a simple scrap of paper may have saved the life of a young Wall Street stock broker who was about to board a subway train. He paused uncharacteristically to pick up a small piece of paper that had drifted by in the breeze and settled at his feet. His pause of only seconds was long enough for him to miss a train that moments later crashed in the tunnel. The insignificant object strangely commanded his attention and possibly saved his life.

SUMMARY

Although we cannot fully explain the complex roles of certain tangible objects as psychic empowerment tools, mastery of strategies that employ them could empower our lives and promote psychic growth. In the following chapters, we will explore the use of several objects in psychic empowerment with emphasis on possible explanations, workable techniques, and appropriate applications. Although numerous tools and techniques are considered, our steadfast focus throughout is upon a common goal: the full actualization of our psychic empowerment potentials through workable do-it-for-yourself programs.

17
ASCENDING THE PYRAMID

A UNIVERSAL SYMBOL OF POWER AND MYSTERY

For centuries, the pyramid has been a universal symbol of power and mystery. The Great Pyramid near Cairo is probably the best-known example of this ancient architectural wonder. Believed to have been built by Pharaoh Khufu (Cheops) during the 2600s BC, the Great Pyramid is thought by some Egyptologists to have been an astronomical observatory. Others argue that, because of the exactness and complexity of its design, it may have represented a meteorological standard. Still others find evidence that it served as a power source, using technology still not understood.

The Great Pyramid provides a permanent record of certain geometric facts: the ratio of the perimeter of its base to its height is almost exactly that of the radius of a circle to its circumference. With the original capstone in place, some theorize that the pyramid may even have served as an energy generator. It remains a source of wonder and mystery, and a stimulus to historical and esoteric speculation.

The fact that various forms of the pyramid were found in other ancient cultures—in China, Mexico, Italy, Greece, and Assyria—suggests an archetypal significance that could help explain the pyramid's contemporary appeal. Appearing on the reverse side of the Great Seal of the United States is a pyramid with the motto, "*annuit coeptis*" (He, meaning God, has smiled on our undertaking).

DIVISIONS OF HUMAN CONSCIOUSNESS

Today, the pyramid shape is often integrated into the architecture of structures ranging from residential dwellings to skyscrapers and is commonly associated with ideas suggestive of ancient wisdom and mysteries yet to be revealed. Inside the Great Pyramid are passageways and chambers historically used in mystical practices, while a schematic representation of the interior is used to describe divisions of human consciousness (Slate and Weschcke, 2010).

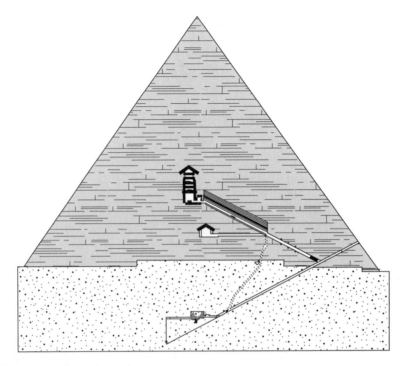

The Great Pyramid

BASIC GEOMETRIC SHAPES
FUNDAMENTAL TO THE UNIVERSE

The pyramid, along with the circle, square, triangle, etc. is one of the basic geometric shapes fundamental to the universe. Through our creative imagination it connects us to the energies of the material world, and as an archetypal symbol is used in Masonic and Esoteric programs to align the psyche with basic philosophical concepts.

Ascending the Pyramid, as later discussed, is a practical psychic empowerment meditation exercise to be discussed later in this chapter in relation to goal setting.

THE PYRAMID

Adding to the mystery of the pyramid and further reflecting its possible archetypal character are the contemporary beliefs regarding its empowerment properties. Energizing the self and balancing it with the cosmos are typically cited as examples of the pyramid's empowering capacities. These empowering functions do not seem to be related to either the construction material or the size of the pyramid. A small-scale replica in glass, plastic, wood, metal, or even cardboard seems equally as empowering as the Great Pyramid, provided its orientation and proportional design are exactly those of the Great Pyramid.

The effectiveness of the pyramid as an empowering tool is enhanced to some degree by a personal interest in the object. Although storing the pyramid in a box or displaying it on a shelf as an object of beauty could conceivably be empowering, the deliberate application of the pyramid as an empowerment tool enhances its empowering efficacy, particularly in goal-related situations. Setting personal goals and generating affirmations of success are, of course, empowering independently of any association with the pyramid; but linking goals to the pyramid and incorporating the pyramid into goal strivings can dramatically increase motivation and potential for success. Simply relating the pyramid to our goals gives concrete substance to goal strivings, which can be empowering, even in the absence of any intrinsic empowering function of the pyramid.

A popular view of pyramid power centers on the inherent empowering properties of the object itself. This view holds that the pyramid's physical design endows it with certain potential powers, including its inspiring, balancing, preserving, and rejuvenating properties. When the pyramid is oriented with one side accurately aligned to one of the four cardinal points of the compass, its positive potentials are believed to be activated. For most personal applications, the pyramid's empowerment potentials are admittedly expanded through appropriate affirmations and a belief in the pyramid's empowering properties.

The physical environment of the pyramid also seems to influence its empowering properties. To induce peaceful, restful sleep and productive dreaming, for example, the pyramid is usually placed under the bed—a placement that can also be effective in enhancing the sex drive. To improve intellectual functions, particularly memory, the pyramid is usually placed in the study area at eye level, if possible. A high-school history teacher noted a remarkable improvement in his students' test performance after he placed a pyramid in a classroom bookcase. In a work setting, the pyramid can be centrally located to promote productivity and harmony among employees, even when they are unaware of the pyramid's presence. Likewise, the pyramid, when strategically located in the home, tends to promote harmony and positive interactions. Some corporations reportedly have pyramids of metal encased in the foundations of their buildings to generate a constructive environment and promote corporate success.

POSSIBLE HEALING PROPERTIES

There is evidence to suggest that the pyramid may have healing properties as well. For example, a heart transplant patient, having placed a small cardboard pyramid under his hospital bed, experienced an extraordinarily rapid recovery. He believed the pyramid energized his body and induced a state of balance in his bodily systems that promoted acceptance of the organ. In a similar instance, a writer with high blood pressure showed a marked decrease in blood pressure after she placed a crystal pyramid on a bookshelf in her study. The sheer presence of the pyramid, she reported, produced a serene, peaceful environment for writing and research.

Some of the most dramatic empowering results associated with the pyramid are observed in sports and recreational settings. When the pyramid was introduced into training programs, rapid improvements were noted in activities such as body building, weight lifting, gymnastics, and wrestling. The reported benefits included better concentration, improved motor coordination, and greater endurance.

THE PYRAMID'S APPLICATIONS AS AN EMPOWERMENT TOOL

Here are a few other examples of the pyramid's wide-ranging applications as an empowerment tool:

- A college student experienced a marked improvement in her test performance after placing a small crystal pyramid under her desk during examinations.
- A high school physics teacher noted an increase in student motivation and more positive class interactions after she placed a glass pyramid among other geometric objects on her desk.
- A choral group reported dramatic improvements after a silver pyramid was introduced into the practice and performance sessions.
- A real estate broker attributed a significant increase in sales to a plastic pyramid positioned under a conference table in his office.
- A writer reported that a glass pyramid suspended from the ceiling over his computer improved his concentration and stimulated creative thinking.
- A musician found that holding his hands briefly over a pyramid immediately prior to a concert induced relaxation, enhanced concentration, and improved the quality of his performance.
- An experienced gambler attributed his success to a small plastic pyramid he placed at his feet during gambling.

One of the most valued applications of the pyramid is its apparent usefulness in promoting psychic functions. Some psychics report that the pyramid, when present for their psychic readings, sharpens their psychic skills and generates an environment more conducive to positive psychic interactions. It could be argued that such results are due largely, if not altogether, to the expectancy effects of believing the pyramid to be an empowering tool. Admittedly, recognition and acceptance of an object's empowering potentials, whether real or imagined, would logically increase its empowering effects; but the empowering benefits of the pyramid are also seen in situations where individuals are unaware of its presence. A real estate agency, for instance, reported that the comments of prospective buyers were typically more positive for a building when a pyramid—unknown to the potential buyer—had been strategically placed in the building. A boutique owner reported a sharp increase in sales after she placed a pyramid in a concealed box over the shop's entrance.

PYRAMIDAL STRATEGIES

There is some evidence to suggest that a simple mental image of a pyramid can produce strong empowering results. In the practice of hypnosis, for example, imagery of a pyramid as a post-hypnotic cue has been effective in achieving the goals of reducing stress, losing weight, and breaking habits such as smoking and nail biting. The effects of pyramidal imagery can be intensified through practice in meditation approaches that include empowering affirmations accompanied by images of the pyramid. When used in meditation, pyramidal imagery increases the effectiveness of empowering affirmations and promotes a positive mental state conducive to a variety of empowerment goals. In drug treatment programs, meditative approaches incorporating imagery of the pyramid have been successful in building motivation and a more positive self-image considered essential to such programs.

A highly effective meditation strategy called *Ascending the Pyramid* combines mental imagery of a pyramid and self-affirmations to progressively build a state of peak empowerment. The procedure developed in the lab setting at Athens State University is initiated by slowing breathing and, with the eyes closed, focusing on the image of a pyramid with ten steps leading to its apex. The ten steps, each with an inscription, are then visualized one by one, beginning with the first step and culminating at the pyramid's apex, as empowering affirmations are formed. Following are the ten steps with the inscriptions and suggested affirmations for each step:

ASCENDING THE PYRAMID MEDITATION STRATEGY

Step 1: Love

> *Love is basic to my life. It is the energizing foundation of my existence and the center of my being. In my capacity to love, I discover myself and other human beings. Love is the most powerful expression of my being.*

Step 2: Forgiveness

> *In forgiving myself and others, I release the flow of growth potential in my life. Forgiveness is the attitude that characterizes myself and my interactions with others. It is the transforming inner force that soars always upward toward harmony and peace.*

Step 3: Peace

Peace is the river that flows through my being. It is deep, abiding, and secure. Infused with inner peace, I can weather any storm that enters my life. Disappointments, misfortune, and uncertainties all yield to the quieting force of inner peace.

Step 4: Faith

Faith is the elevating, activating power in my life. It is my belief in the divine power within my own being. It is the essence of my existence in the universe. In adversity, faith sustains and upholds me. It reveals boundless possibilities in the present and larger dimensions of meaning in the future. Faith is the eternal substance of triumphant living.

Step 5: Choice

Each moment of my life, I am choosing. I choose to think or not to think, to act or not to act, to feel or not to feel. Because I choose, I am responsible for my thoughts, actions, and feelings. They are all mine, and I choose to own them. I am what I choose to be at any moment in time.

Step 6: Change

Change is the current of growth and progress. To become more vibrant, full of life, sincere, and compassionate are changes I value. Positive change carries me always forward to experience something new and vital about myself and the world each day.

Step 7: Awareness

Through expanded awareness, my life is enriched and the meaning of my existence clarified. As I become more aware of my inner self, I become more completely attuned to my being. I know myself best when I come face to face with the totality of my existence in the here and now.

Step 8: Knowledge

Knowledge is power. Through knowing my inner self, I gain power over my life and my destiny. Knowledge empowers me to function more productively in the present, and to engage more effectively the future. Given knowledge, whatever its source, I am empowered to bring about needed change in myself and the world.

Step 9: Balance

Balance in my life enables me to be spontaneous and free. My thoughts, feelings, and actions are integrated into a harmonious system that empowers me to adapt to life's demands and to liberate my highest potentials.

Step 10: Empowerment

In my capacity to love, forgive, experience peace, exercise faith, make choices, promote change, expand awareness, discover knowledge, and maintain balance, I am fully empowered each moment of my life.

The empowering effects of this procedure can be magnified by visualizing oneself pausing at the pyramid's apex and reflecting on the experience. During that reflective state, any of the affirmations can be reaffirmed, and additional affirmations, along with related imagery, can be introduced. The procedure is concluded with the simple affirmation:

I am empowered.

Practice significantly improves the effectiveness of this meditation exercise. Following repeated practice, imagery of the ten-step pyramid, independent of the inscriptions and affirmations, can be profoundly empowering. In competitive sports, meditation exercises incorporating imagery of the pyramid immediately prior to an event can dramatically improve the quality of the performance and reduce the number of technical glitches, particularly in activities such as figure skating and gymnastics. In archery, golf, tennis, and bowling, precision was noticeably improved with the introduction of pyramidal meditation, followed by pyramidal imagery at intervals during performance. Similar improvements were seen in sports such as basketball, soccer, and hockey, following team meditation incorporating pyramidal imagery. Performance in any activity requiring precision, coordination, and mental alertness could be improved appreciably through pyramidal meditation and imagery at strategic points during training and competition.

BENEFITS OF THE ASCENDING IMAGERY

In the academic setting, students who had practiced Ascending the Pyramid and used imagery of the pyramid immediately prior to course examinations consistently demonstrated improvements in test performance. Other reported benefits of pyramidal meditation in the academic setting are improved memory of course materials, increased accuracy in problem solving, and greater self-confidence. In courses requiring creativity, students practicing pyramidal meditation reported better instructor ratings of their work.

There is also evidence that pyramidal meditation can be applied to increase the quality of oral presentations. Students in a law program found that practice in pyramidal meditation and imagery resulted in a more relaxed, focused mental state, and greater effectiveness in arguing cases. In one instance, a law student reported rapid progress in overcoming stage fright through simple imagery of a pyramid accompanied by positive self-affirmations immediately prior to a presentation.

Most demonstrated personal empowering benefits associated with the pyramid follow considerable practice of pyramidal meditation strategies, such as Ascending the Pyramid, which are designed to empower through imagery and affirmation. In situations demanding immediate empowerment, just the presence of a pyramid, or a mental image of one, will often work.

CONCLUSION

Because of its proven effectiveness in evoking the mind's creative and psychic processes, the pyramid is recognized as a highly useful empowerment tool. Its appeal in the psychic realm is due in part to its capacity to stimulate our psychic faculties by its sheer presence. Its effectiveness in other areas of personal empowerment, however, seems to depend largely on meditation strategies that purposefully utilize this object. When incorporated into empowerment strategies, the pyramid, or images of it, can enrich not only our psychic faculties, but a host of important non-psychic functions as well. The pyramid thus becomes an essential addition to our repertoire of valuable empowerment tools.

SOURCES AND RECOMMENDED READING

John DeSalvo, *The Complete Pyramid Sourcebook* (First Books, 2003).

John DeSalvo, *Decoding the Pyramids: Exploring the World's Most Enigmatic Structures* (Metro Books [Sterling], 2008).

Robert M. Schoch, *Pyramid Quest: Secrets of the Great Pyramid and the Dawn of Civilization* (Tarcher, 2005).

Dr. Joe H. Slate and Carl Llewellyn Weschcke, *Self-Empowerment & Your Subconscious Mind* (Llewellyn, 2010).

Peter Tomkins, *Secrets of the Great Pyramid* (Harper & Row, 1971).

Colin Wilson, *From Atlantis to the Sphinx: Recovering the Lost Wisdom of the Ancient World* (Virgin Books, 2007).

18

CRYSTAL GAZING &
PSYCHIC AWARENESS

Crystal Gazing (aka skrying*) enables the discovery and*
transfer of specific knowledge found in the subconsciousness
to the conscious mind as needed or on demand, or as
required in certain telepathic communications.

STIMULATING PSYCHIC FUNCTIONS

Crystal gazing using the familiar crystal ball is one of the most widely known techniques designed to stimulate inner psychic functions and expand psychic awareness. Through the centuries, crystal gazing, or skrying, has been used to probe the unknown; and, in recent years, crystal gazing has been incorporated into a variety of self-empowerment strategies designed to open new vistas of psychic understanding and knowledge.

THE MIND'S IMAGERY AND CONCENTRATION POWERS

Traditionally, the goal of crystal gazing has been the activation of mental processes specific to various forms of ESP. In our controlled laboratory studies at Athens State University, the technique has proved appropriate, not only in stimulating ESP but also for achieving other critical self-empowerment goals. Of particular note is its effectiveness in reducing stress, promoting a serene, meditative state of mind, facilitating psychic receptiveness, and heightening the mind's imagery and concentration powers.

POSITIONING THE CRYSTAL BALL

In crystal gazing, the crystal ball is typically situated on a table to promote a slightly downward gaze from a comfortable distance of around one to two feet. Mutual crystal gazing can result in significantly higher levels of successful telepathy between individuals or groups. If strategically positioned between sender and receiver, the crystal ball can provide a functional point of focus considered highly conducive to the exchange of psychic information. With even limited practice in crystal gazing, telepathic subjects report dramatic improvements in their capacities to communicate mentally.

CRYSTAL GAZING FACILITATES TRANSFER FROM SUBCONSCIOUS TO CONSCIOUS AWARENESS

In clairvoyance, crystal gazing can stimulate the complex imagery processes that are essential to clairvoyant insight. Clairvoyance frequently appears to originate in the subconscious mind. With practice in crystal gazing, we can stimulate the inner psychic transfer of important clairvoyant information from subconscious levels to conscious awareness. Furthermore, crystal gazing can become an important vehicle for clairvoyantly connecting conscious awareness to spatially distant unseen realities. For this application, attention is usually focused on the center of the ball, a process facilitated by a crystal ball with an air bubble at its center.

THE FUNCTION OF FOCAL POINTS

For both precognition and retrocognition, crystal gazing functions in two important modes: forward and reverse. In its forward mode, the technique transports awareness into the future to target selected events, while in its reverse mode, it projects awareness to unknown past events or experiences. For precognition, attention is usually focused on the distant side of the ball; for retrocognition, focus is on the closer side. Both past and future psychic perceptions usually occur as mental images or thought-forms which, according to some experienced crystal gazers, are often visible as psychic projections either within or upon the crystal ball.

For telepathy, attention is usually focused on the ball's interior regions. Imagery of a channel of light linking the sender and receiver to the crystal ball seems to activate telepathy and increase the accuracy of telepathic communication. The crystal ball, in effect, assumes a functional role as the center of a psychic communication network.

CRYSTAL GAZING PROCEDURES

Because the crystal ball seems to be effective in stimulating our inner psychic functions and generating new psychic knowledge, two procedures were developed in our labs at Athens State University to build the basic skills required for productive crystal gazing. The first, called Crystal Focusing, is designed to stimulate various psychic functions while generating an empowered state of relaxation and personal well-being. The second procedure, the Focal Shift, is designed to target specific goals and unleash the resources required for achieving them. Both procedures are devised to build the basic skills required for productive crystal gazing.

Here's the Crystal Focusing procedure which requires, in addition to the crystal ball, two practice articles: a colorful picture and a tangible object. Approximately thirty minutes are required for the procedure, which is conducted in a comfortable setting free of distractions.

CRYSTAL GAZING FOCUSING PROCEDURE

Step 1. View the colorful picture, giving special attention to essential features such as color, design, shapes, forms, and background.

Step 2. With your eyes closed, generate a detailed mental image of the picture.

Step 3. View the tangible object, such as an article of jewelry or a flower. Focus your full attention on the object's shape and other characteristics.

Step 4. With your eyes closed and while holding the object, generate a detailed mental image of the object.

Step 5. Replace these practice articles with a crystal ball at a comfortable distance and focus your full attention first on its surface, and then on its interior regions. Note specifically such characteristics as reflections, variations in brightness, and impressions of color and depth. Continue the focusing process and allow a tranquil, relaxed state to emerge.

Step 6. Close your eyes and create a clear mental image of the crystal ball. Take as much time as you need for the image to take shape. Note any physical or emotional effects that may accompany the imagery process. As images continue to form, permit a more relaxed, passive state to emerge.

Step 7. Continue the relaxed, passive state as your psychic receptiveness expands and new images spontaneously unfold. Concentrate your attention on any image that appears relevant at the moment.

Step 8. Open your eyes and focus again on the crystal ball. Continue crystal gazing, intermittently closing your eyes as you increase your receptiveness to the emerging psychic images and impressions.

Aside from its relevance in stimulating various psychic functions, crystal gazing has been successfully applied as a stress management, meditation, and general self-empowerment technique. As a stress management procedure, crystal gazing, accompanied by positive affirmations of self-worth, induces relaxation and a peaceful state of mind. Continued gazing while creating relaxing images such as billowy clouds, a peaceful lake with a sailboat drifting gently in the breeze, or a moonlit landscape, tends to deepen the empowered, relaxed state.

CRYSTAL GAZING AS MEDITATION AID

As a meditation technique, crystal gazing will often produce profound personal insight as well as highly relevant psychic knowledge. A second crystal gazing technique called Focal Shift was developed in our labs to generate an empowered mental state conducive not only to increased psychic awareness but personal insight as well. Similar to Crystal Focusing as previously discussed, the Focal Shift technique usually requires several practice trials to maximize its effectiveness. Allow approximately thirty minutes for the procedure, which is administered in a quiet, comfortable setting.

CRYSTAL GAZING FOCAL SHIFT TECHNIQUE

Step 1. Focus your full attention on the crystal ball, and then center your attention on a specific area of the ball's surface, such as an area reflecting a point of light.

Step 2. While continuing your focus on a selected area of the crystal ball, gradually expand your peripheral vision to take in the full ball and as much of its surroundings as possible.

Step 3. As your peripheral vision remains expanded to its limits, allow your eyes to shift slightly out of focus. You will notice a whitish glow forming around the ball and throughout its surroundings.

Step 4. Return your focus to the crystal ball, and after a few moments of focusing, close your eyes and permit your body to completely relax as meaningful images and impressions take shape in your mind.

Step 5. As your eyes remain closed, form affirmations that focus upon your goals. For general self-empowerment, focus your attention on a relaxed, empowerment-readiness state through such general empowerment affirmations as:

> *I am capable and secure; peace and tranquility surround me; I have an abundance of inner resources; I am empowered with happiness and success.*

For more specific empowerment applications, form affirmations that target your specific goals. For instance, if your goal is business success, the following specific empowerment affirmations can build your resolve and promote your full success:

> *I have all the ability I need to succeed at business. I am fully committed to achieve my goal. All the resources I need are now available to me.*

These affirmations can be made even more effective through related imagery that symbolizes your success. Even the most powerful affirmations can be strengthened through related empowering imagery.

Step 6. Conclude the exercise with the simple affirmation: *Success is my destiny!*

The flexibility and effectiveness of crystal gazing as an empowerment strategy have been demonstrated in a variety of settings. The technique has been used in the academic setting to increase motivation and promote creative thinking. A college art instructor reported that crystal gazing, when introduced as an experimental exercise into her course in oil painting, resulted in marked improvements in the creative quality of her students' paintings. In a private industrial setting, an increased number of ideas was noted immediately after the introduction of crystal gazing into a management training program that included the use of brainstorming. In competitive sports, crystal gazing has been effective in accelerating the development of essential skills. When practiced immediately prior to a competitive event, marked improvement in performance was noted.

Taken together, the diverse applications of both Crystal Focusing and Focal Shift reflect the wide-ranging possibilities of crystal gazing. Whether in the academic or work setting, crystal gazing has shown remarkable empowerment potential.

LABORATORY BEAKER GAZING

In our laboratory studies at Athens State University, we found that a lab beaker filled with clear water could be equally as effective for crystal gazing as the crystal ball. Using either the Crystal Screen Procedure or the Focal Shift Procedure, the effectiveness of crystal gazing was essentially the same when the crystal beaker was substituted for the crystal ball. Perhaps not unexpectedly, the effects of gazing remained basically the same when a clear bowl of water was substituted for the beaker. The key factor to success in gazing seems to be our capacity to activate our inner potentials through our interactions with the object as a tool rather than in the physical nature of the object alone.

SUMMARY

Crystal gazing is important in psychic empowerment because of its capacity to engage and liberate the mind's psychic powers while promoting a state of general self-empowerment. The crystal ball becomes more than an object of beauty; it opens the channels of the mind and permits the free expression of our multiple inner faculties. The sheer pleasure of crystal gazing, along with the balancing, relaxing, and actualizing effects of the experience, is becoming increasingly recognized as important to personal empowerment. Crystal gazing is pertinent to the quest for empowerment because of its potential to promote not only psychic growth, but also personal well-being.

SOURCES AND RECOMMENDED READING

Ted Andrews, *Crystal Balls & Crystal Bowls: Tools for Ancient Skrying & Modern Seership* (Llewellyn, 2002).

Scott Cunningham, *Divination for Beginners: Reading the Past, Present & Future* (Llewellyn, 2003).

Donald Tyson, *Scrying for Beginners: Use Your Subconscious Mind to See Beyond the Senses* (Llewellyn, 1997).

19

Probing the Energy Field with Dowsing & the Pendulum

*Dowsing is the exercise of a human faculty, which allows one
to obtain information in a manner beyond the scope and power of the
standard human physical senses of sight, sound, touch, etc.*

—RAYMOND C. WILLEY, *MODERN DOWSING*

DOWSING IS A RESPECTED PROFESSION

Dowsing is a technology that has been in use for thousands of years. There are eight-thousand-year-old wall paintings in African caves of a man with a forked stick dowsing for water; four-thousand-year-old Chinese and Egyptian artwork shows dowsing with forked tools; the biblical Moses used a rod to locate water; dowsing was used to locate coal deposits in Europe's middle ages; and in seventeenth-century France, criminals were tracked by means of dowsing. Leonardo de Vinci, Robert Boyle, and Albert Einstein recognized dowsing as a genuine practice.

Today, there are an estimated thirty thousand dowsers in the United States and the American Society of Dowsers is a professional group founded in 1961. Engineer Raymond C. Willey, one of the society's founders, defined dowsing in his 1970 book *Modern Dowsing:* **"Dowsing is the exercise of a human faculty, which allows one to obtain information in a manner beyond the scope and power of the standard human physical senses of sight, sound, touch, etc."**

According to Lyall Watson in *Beyond Supernature*, "Every major water and pipeline company in the United States has a dowser on the payroll. The Canadian Ministry of Agriculture employs a permanent dowser. UNESCO has engaged a Dutch dowser and geologist to pursue investigations for them. Engineers from the US First and Third Marine divisions in Vietnam have been trained to use dowsing rods to locate booby traps and sunken mortar shells. The Czechoslovakian Army has a permanent corps of dowsers in a special unit."

DOWSING AND THE MAGNETIC FIELD

Watson also clarifies the question of tool vs. man. Even with very sophisticated and complex instruments, "experiments in all countries suggest that, whatever the dowsing force may be, it cannot work on the rod alone. A living being has to act as a 'middleman.' The Dutch geologist Solco Trump has shown that dowsers are unusually sensitive to the earth's magnetic field, and respond to changes in the field that can be verified with magnetometers. He has also discovered that a good dowser can detect an artificial field only one two-hundredth the strength of the earth field and that he can use his rod to chart its extent in an experimental room."

Still, the common perception is that dowsing (sometimes called "water witching") is an old folk practice only known in backwards rural areas. *Perhaps those old folk practices are a lot more sophisticated than they are "backwards."*

About that image of an old farmer guy looking for water with a forked stick—that's only one of the benefits of dowsing, and the forked stick is only one familiar tool of many that are used today to search for water, oil, minerals, gems, buried pipelines, pirate treasures, electrical wiring, archaeological sites and artifacts, and more. While the natural freshly cut forked stick is still preferred by some, many dowsers use Y-shaped and L-shaped *divining rods*—some as simple as bent coat hangers and others complicated devices of exotic metals and coiled springs. In addition, the same functional usage is accomplished with a simple pendulum for dowsing earth resources with maps, for finding sources of illness, locating lost objects, and even in forensic applications to trace the human history of objects pertinent to a crime scene. And some dowsers (sometimes called "hand tremblers") use only their unaided hands or their *entire body* as divining instruments. While there are many theories offered to explain the phenomena of dowsing, it all pales as you learn that the greatest value of dowsing with the pendulum is *communication between the subconscious mind and the conscious mind, and actually going beyond to the universal consciousness, in which all memories and all knowledge resides.*

Energy and Consciousness

We share energy and we share consciousness with the Earth and ourselves at both the physical and the more subtle levels—also known as the etheric and astral planes.

There are many kinds and variations of energy and of consciousness, and it is within our personal consciousness—our subconscious and conscious minds—that we can make the fine attunements that can channel specific information useful in practical and beneficial applications.

Test It Yourself

As an initial experiment, sit in a comfortable chair next to a table on which you have placed several small objects, relax your mind and body, and then hold either hand about six inches above one of those objects, and then another, and so on. Perhaps you won't detect anything at first, but you will as you continue your developmental exercise. Change hands, change objects, let your conscious change and slide into different modes.

As you continue your program, try other objects like something battery powered (such as a small clock), something connected to household current, and perhaps a cell phone. Adding a natural crystal, a small magnet, a small photograph, an old heirloom watch or piece of jewelry, perhaps a child's small favorite toy, and similar objects will expand the experience.

As you become more comfortable with the experiment, you will be extending your own energy field and awareness to comprehend the energy fields of these objects. At some point you will *feel* their radiant energy, and will be able to detect differences among the objects. You might label them, shuffle them about with your eyes closed, and, eyes still closed, see if you can identify each object by name and move it aside for the next. Note your results in a journal.

Extend the experiment still further, holding your hand above small household plants, and then outdoors over different flowers and small vegetable plants.

The whole purpose of our experiment is for you to actually experience your own unaided hand as a *sensitive instrument* detecting different energies, and perhaps—in the case of crystals and plants—different kinds of consciousness. With some personal objects, like a grandmother's ring or a grandfather's watch, you may get impressions of the person to whom the object belonged. While the ability to detect such impressions is the subject of a separate study called "Psychometry," the ability to use the physical body to detect invisible subtle energies is the same as used in Dowsing and working with the Pendulum.

You Have the Power

In both dowsing and pendulum work, we are simply adding a dedicated "tool" amplifying the body's own sensitivity to the subtle energies surrounding and radiating from all things—animate and nonanimate. We commonly refer to this as an "aura" or a "field." Remember that the "power" of any of these tools is an extension, amplification, or refinement of the natural power inherent to the human body *and psyche* that you are learning to use.

Just as a fancy power saw is a development of a simple hand saw, the real power or skill is in the hands and mind of the carpenter using these tools. And even though the carpenter may have shown a natural talent and interest in working with wood from an early age, he gained his skill through training and practice. He has the power, not the saw. You have the power, not the dowsing rod or the pendulum. In all cases, it is necessary to direct and apply the innate power with skill, intelligence, and focused attention.

This is an important point because we have become so used to using technological instruments and gadgets that we often forget that technology only extends, magnifies, or specifies human power and consciousness, and is not itself the source of either. And the most marvelous "gadgets"—computers, television, automobiles, airplanes, electronic gismos, and science instruments, etc.—are all just tools whose energy source is ourselves. They become part of ourselves in the same way that supplements such as eyeglasses and hearing aids do, and that "replacement parts"—like knee or shoulder joints, cataract lens, and prosthetic limbs—do, and the way that simple and complex tools are used as extensions of our own arms, legs, hands, eyes, and ears to involve ourselves in the world about us.

As these tools advance in powerful applications and extensions of human knowledge and perception, so must each one of us grow and extend our consciousness to comprehend more and more of the universe in and about us. And we must accept the moral and ethical responsibilities that are imposed by the greater personal power that technology provides.

We must be grateful that since the first two atomic weapons were used to end World War II, no one has since "pushed the nuclear button" that probably would—not could— lead to Armageddon.

It All Starts at the Beginning

Sometimes it is important to step back and regain perspective. There is a great deal of wisdom and understanding contained in mythology and the many different scriptures, and when we read without cultural or religious bias, we uncover or recover some essential truths repeated across the global spectrum.

Look at the Western Bible that says, "In the Beginning was the Word, and the Word was with God."

That says to this writer that *it all starts with the Word,* and to me, "the word" means "Consciousness" and it means "Instruction," or in modern parlance, a "Program." From this Start-up Program, after Consciousness comes Energy and Matter, so it is this *Trinity* made up of Consciousness, Energy, and Matter that is the source of all we experience in the universe. Notice that I used current, not past tense, for that Beginning is still with us, and created in God's image we have the potential of co-creators. We are consciousness, and consciousness is at the core of all things, but all things are also Energy and Matter—even the most subtle or "spiritual" of things has Consciousness, Energy, and Matter—even though it is of such a subtle nature as still not to be recognized by present-day physical sciences.

When we reach out with our *extended awareness* to sense the energy and consciousness of these objects that appear to us as material things, we are in contact with their energy and their consciousness. Acknowledging this allows us to speak of "Psychic Awareness" and "Psychic Empowerment." All the tools and techniques we discuss in this book are instruments of our personal psychic awareness, the use of which is the source of our psychic empowerment and self-empowerment.

DOWSING—AN ANCIENT PRACTICE IS RENEWED

While typically valued as a procedure for locating subterranean resources such as water, oil, and minerals, dowsing usually employs wood (elm, peach, or witch hazel) or metal rods as information-accessing tools, and it is becoming recognized as a psychic information gathering and communicating art. Even as the applications of dowsing have expanded to include modern arenas such as aerospace, ecology, and quality control, so do they also extend to methods of self-understanding, self-help, and self-development.

Many accomplished dowsers believe their skill is genetically inherited, other successful dowsers were trained in the technique by experienced dowsers, and today courses of instruction are given by professional dowsers. The dowsing potential exists to some degree in everyone, and almost everyone, given practice and experience, can become successful at dowsing.

As "antennae" of mind and body applied as psychic tools, dowsing instruments stimulate a host of sensory and extrasensory receptors for gathering a vast amount of information.

CHANNELS OF COMMUNICATION
ACCESSING SUBCONSCIOUS KNOWLEDGE

As a psychic phenomenon, the dowsing instruments function as channels of communication giving us indirect, but valuable, access to subconscious knowledge. Just as do pendulums—which we will discuss later—dowsing rods probe subconscious regions of the mind to function as retrieval devices.

From that viewpoint, dowsing rods and pendulums are simply external tools of the psychic mind. As the psychic mind develops, so does our capacity for dowsing, as well as using any and all other of the psychic empowerment tools we describe in this book.

In contrast to this psychic view, others believe that dowsing as a probe of external realities can be explained as a physical phenomenon in which the dowser and his rods act as electrodes and conductors to record subterranean activity or other charged environments. Since subterranean resources do have their own unique energy frequencies, dowsing rods, combined with a finely tuned human system, can respond to those frequencies, identifying resources, their locations, and characteristics.

Rather than a single ability involving a single set of dynamics, dowsing can be explained as multiple abilities involving multiple dynamics, which vary from situation to situation. Each dowsing specialty could engage only the abilities specific to that specialty, and the dynamics for each specialty likewise would vary.

Notwithstanding these differences in explanations of dowsing, basic dowsing skills can be acquired through simply basic training and practice. Mastery of the technique's many applications, however, requires practice and the feedback of results along with clearly formulated goals, some degree of motivation, and recognition of dowsing's empowering possibilities. Not everyone has reason to develop external dowsing skills, but everyone can benefit from using the pendulum in everyday circumstances and specific communications with the subconscious mind—whether to locate misplaced car keys or to answer personal questions relating to career, relationships, health, and other matters. And the pendulum should take its place alongside other sophisticated divinatory practices such as Tarot, Runes, Geomancy, etc. We will be exploring that later in this chapter.

HOW TO DOWSE WITH RODS AND STICKS

For many applications, experienced dowsers prefer L-shaped metal rods designed to be held parallel, one in each hand, with the longer segments of the rods pointing forward. Each rod is balanced along the hand or index finger to permit easy, unobstructed movement.

The rod's typical response movements are the downward-and-upward pull, side-to-side parallel movement, the spreading movement, the crossing movement, and a variety of vibratory signals. Although the interpretation of these responses will vary among dowsers, the downward pull of the rods is typically believed to signal a subterranean resource, with the degree of forcefulness indicating either distance or strength. The experienced dowser usually can gauge both distance and strength based on the nature of the pulling response.

A parallel movement, with both rods pulling to the right or left, signifies the location of a strong energy field or natural resource. The separation or pulling apart of the rods indicates the border of an energy source located nearby and ahead.

The crossing of the rods is usually associated with negative energies that are either repelling to or incompatible with the dowser's own energy system. Radiation, toxic substances, or contaminated conditions will typically induce a crossing movement in the rods.

Influences that push the rods apart are usually nonrepelling. Examples include water, oil, and most minerals. Vibrations in the rods, whether independent or in conjunction with other movements, typically indicate a powerful energy field.

Some accomplished dowsers prefer twig rods over metal rods. When twig rods are used, they are usually forked. The forked ends are held, one in each hand, with the stem pointing forward. The interpretation of the twig rod's movements is, with a few exceptions, like that of the metal rods: the downward pull signals a subterranean resource, and a left or right movement signifies the position of a resource. An upward pull on the rod indicates a repelling or toxic condition located in either a subterranean or forward position.

Skilled dowsers report different vibratory frequencies for different resources. Frequencies associated with coal are described as tremulous or erratic, while those for water are usually described as soft and flowing, and natural gas frequencies are typically described as disruptive to the rods. Radiation, like many contaminants, emits repelling frequencies that cross metal L-rods and pull upward on twig or Y-rods. Unlike other contaminants, radiation also tends to generate impressions of warmth in the rods.

DOWSING'S MANY PRACTICAL APPLICATIONS

As a technique for gathering information, dowsing has been successfully applied to science and technology, business and industry, forensics, and the military. Valuable subterranean resources including oil, coal, water, minerals, and natural gas have been located through dowsing. In industrial settings, dowsing has been effective in locating buried cables, water, gas lines, and valuable resources. Before excavating, some contractors routinely engage dowsers to determine certain geological characteristics of the site, including water sources, bedrock formations, and the existence of any hazardous conditions.

During World War II, dowsing was used to locate mine fields, thus saving the lives of many foot soldiers. Dowsing was also used in locating a treasure of old coins and other gold relics buried on an island off the mainland of Spanish Honduras. In this instance, before on-site dowsing was attempted, a pendulum held over a map of the island identified the general area to be searched.

Although metal detectors are sometimes used for locating objects such as lost coins, jewelry, and buried metal pipe lines or cables, dowsing is often preferred because of its higher sensitivity and effectiveness in locating metal and specific nonmetal materials from a greater distance.

In forensic settings, dowsing has been used successfully to facilitate the investigative effort. In one case, a skilled dowser in a small boat used the technique to locate a weapon that had been tossed into a lake. In another instance, a dowser successfully located a murder victim buried in a shallow grave. Prior to on-site dowsing in each instance, the pendulum was used to identify probable locations by scanning a detailed map of the search area.

DOWSING AS A DIAGNOSTIC AID

There is some evidence that dowsing may have valuable diagnostic potential when applied to the human body. An example of this application is the use of metal rods to scan the physical body to identify dysfunctional areas. The subject stands facing the dowser, as the rods, one on each side of the subject, are moved close to the body from the head downward. Any disruption in the frequencies emitted by the body and recorded by the rods signifies an area of stress, organ dysfunction, or damaged tissue. A dysfunction in the cardiovascular system, such as high blood pressure, will emit a continuous but mild disruptive frequency pattern over the total body; whereas a specific organ dysfunction will produce a localized but intense disruption in the area of the organ involved.

The pendulum has also been used to locate and diagnose health problems.

These applications suggest dowsing could activate psychic faculties such as clairvoyance to expand awareness and reveal important new information.

American Dowsing Society Website

Dowsing equipment and notice of conferences and courses may be found at the American Dowsing Society's website: www.dowsers.org. There are also many local chapters listed on the site.

DOWSING WITH THE PENDULUM

The pendulum—simply a small weight suspended by a chain or string—is an important psychic-empowerment tool primarily because of its capacity to gather highly objective information not available by nonpsychic means. In its empowerment applications, the pendulum, suspended from the hand, can be used to answer questions and convey meaningful information by its simple movements.

The advantage to the pendulum as an information-gathering tool is its capacity to respond to very mild energy stimuli. As an extension of the physical body when suspended from one's hand, the pendulum can amplify minute, involuntary muscle activity and thus function as a highly sensitive recording instrument.

THE PENDULUM

Whether accessing subconscious processes, or functioning as an antenna to gather incoming information, the pendulum is a valuable empowerment tool to explore unseen sources.

Many applications of the pendulum emphasize its role in communicating with the innermost part of the self. Within the self is a knowing superintelligence that seeks interaction with the conscious self, but must often rely on indirect means of communication. The pendulum engages that superpower of knowledge.

The hand-held pendulum's psychic empowerment role includes its capacity to probe sources of knowledge outside the self. In its clairvoyant application, the pendulum engages externally charged stimuli to assert a mild but significant influence on either the pendulum or our inner psychic faculties to produce meaningful movement—perhaps psychokinetically—in the pendulum.

DETECTING GENDER

Such an external influence may explain the pendulum's usefulness in detecting the gender of the unborn. Meaningful movements of the pendulum held over the expectant mother's abdomen may reflect a gender influence by directly inducing the pendulum's movement, or indirectly as instigated by an inner psychic faculty. This suggests that subconscious psychic awareness of the unborn child's gender could be processed mentally to induce motion in the pendulum. In this way, precognitive content existing in the subconscious is transferred indirectly to conscious awareness through the pendulum.

The pendulum is a valuable psychic tool for gathering information regarding personal concerns. For that purpose, the pendulum is usually suspended over one's own hand or, when applicable, that of another individual, as questions are posed regarding financial investments, relationships, career decisions, and other issues.

Center Pendulum Here

The Pendulum Alphabet Chart

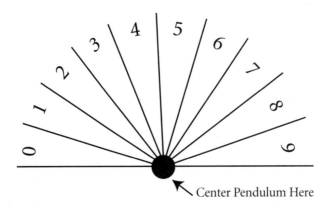

The Pendulum Number Chart

As both a precognitive and clairvoyant tool, the pendulum has demonstrated accuracy in gathering information on regional and world events. For this application, the pendulum is held over any relevant object, such as a map for national events or a globe for world affairs. The pendulum can also be used as a dowsing tool gathering archaeological data or researching historical artifacts, by suspending it over the object being studied.

The pendulum can provide highly specific and complex information when used with alphabet and number charts. Suspended from the hand and appropriately centered over the chart, the pendulum can spell out detailed messages regarding the past, present, and future.

As a simple information-gathering tool, the hand-held pendulum can accurately explore our inner motives, abilities, interests, and potentials. As a probe of external realities, the pendulum can tap distant sources of psychic insight and connect us to a vast wealth of empowering psychic knowledge.

PENDULUM PROSPECTING WITH MAPS

We see that the pendulum can be used as part of a dowsing program—especially by using the pendulum held over maps to locate targets for prospecting specific earth resources. We can start with large scale maps, and even aerial surveys, and then as target areas show up, we move on to aerial photos and local maps specific to those areas, preparing the way for field dowsing with L- or Y-rods.

Many operators using pendulums and dowsing rods often make use of "specimen samples" held in one hand or incorporated into compartments on the pendulum bob or handle area of a dowsing rod. The sample is of the material objective to the outer physical dowsing work—water, oil, gold, nickel, etc.—and functions as a *focus* for the inner, psychic part of the operation. Other operators simply keep the objective in mind during the mechanical process with either pendulum or dowsing rod.

PENDULUM POWER—PENDULUM MAGIC

In external field work, the entire body can become part of the dowsing instrument, while in internal pendulum work, the psychic and mental aspect is more clearly established. In either case, the real dynamic is psychic, with the focused awareness bridging between the subconscious mind and the conscious mind while involving the body as the contact instrument.

Perhaps the most important distinction to be made between dowsing and pendulum work is the opportunity the pendulum offers for two-way communication between the conscious and subconscious minds. And in this regard, the pendulum is an active partner in the program of personal self-help and growth, personal self-discovery and understanding, and personal psychic development and self-empowerment.

TAKING THE NEXT STEP

You can read all you want, but you have to take the next step of actual "doing" to achieve the benefits of any of the techniques and tools we discuss in this book.

In the case of dowsing, make or buy a dowsing instrument and use it. For a beginner, we really recommend that you make the first instrument yourself so that you have the hands-on involvement of the craftsperson. Other than cutting a Y-shaped branch from a living tree, the most simple starter instrument is a pair of L-rods easily made of two wire coat hangers. Simply cut each hanger as shown in the diagram, and then bend the short end at a right angle.

The short side should be about six inches long and the longer side between twelve and twenty inches.

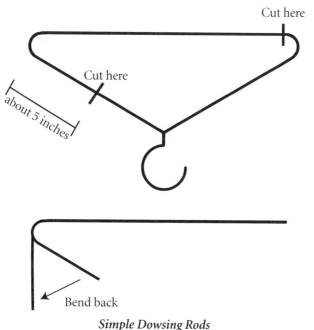

Simple Dowsing Rods

Unless you make a holder for the short side out of a hollowed wood dowel or plastic straws, simply hold the short end of the rods loosely in your fists, arms body-width apart, with the longer sections pointing straight ahead parallel to each other, so they can easily respond to the combined earth and human energies. This is the starting or "neutral" position. Refer back to the earlier section describing the movement of the L-rods.

Now, go for a walk and watch the L-rods for movement. It would be ideal to start with an area where you know the approximate location of underground resources—water lines, sewer lines, electric cables, and—of course—buried treasure. You can start, if you wish, inside a building on the ground floor. Your purpose is to "map" the resources underfoot, and to become familiar with the dowsing *feeling*.

As you develop your dowsing talent, expand your territory. If you live in an urban area, it will be simple to walk down the sidewalk and see and feel the response to gas, water, sewer, electric, and cable underground utilities. Sometimes you will pass over older abandoned utilities that will have a different reaction. Other times you may pass over actual underground streams, utility tunnels, and distinct geological formations. It may not be easy to verify these underground facilities unless you have a very cooperative public utilities department, but the experience alone will build not only your confidence but your psychic dowsing sensitivity.

Just as many people have a hobby of using a metal detector when on vacation visiting parks and beaches, so you can exercise your dowsing "hobby" until you want to move on toward more professional work.

However, it is not professional work that we're after, but the psychic development that dowsing affords. This becomes part of the structure of your personal, whole-person consciousness, establishing communications channels between the subconscious and conscious minds.

Working with the pendulum opens a different chapter in your psychic empowerment program because of the two-way nature it provides. You can easily make your own simple pendulum or adapt a watch chain or necklace to function as one. Or you can obtain a simple carpenter's bob from a hardware or building supply store or readily purchase a pendulum at a convenient metaphysical/New Age store. You will also find them available on the Llewellyn site, www.llewellyn.com.

Again, we do recommend you start with one you make yourself to directly inject your personal energies into the starter pendulum—even one as simple as a thread (the carrier) and a paper clip (the bob). You should also make a simple test pattern by drawing a circle divided into four segments by a vertical and a horizontal line.

Resting your elbow on a table, hold the carrier between thumb and first finger of your power hand (the one you normally use in writing), with the bob swinging freely over the test pattern. Now you can "program" the pendulum by first establishing one movement (such as the vertical line) as a "yes" answer and an alternate movement (horizontal line) as a "no" answer. The circular movement often indicates that a question has not been framed well for a yes-or-no answer.

You can start, if you wish, with a simple drawing of your own yard, over which you can trace with your finger or a hand-held pointer while watching the pendulum for movements to map underground utilities, just as we described for your starter dowsing program.

Then you can progress to direct conversation with the subconscious through carefully developed questions that can be answered yes or no. Record your questions and work in a personal journal, which can become a valuable part of your psychic and self-empowerment program.

Your questions can proceed in a process of self-discovery and understanding to those involving your career, relationships, subject interests, family history, the ownership history of personal and archaeological artifacts, and much more. There is no real limit to what can be accomplished via the pendulum as a means of communication with your subconscious mind and the universal consciousness.

Just as one example, let us assume you have an interest in Mayan history and mythology, and have questions about particular times, places, persons, or concepts. Frame questions to be answered yes or no to deepen your knowledge of the subject.

For another example, let us assume you are an astrologer and want to expand beyond textbook interpretations of the factors present in a client's horoscope. You can develop questions to check the accuracy of the reported birth time and place, to explore the nature of indicated relationships with parents and siblings, to pinpoint details about career potentials, and more.

A most unusual use of a "pendulum" was reported by one of Dr. Slate's students. Dr. Slate writes:

> I was reminded of a retired military pilot who took my class years ago and, by his report, used his plane as a pendulum to ensure a safe landing upon his return from a combat mission. The conditions were not good: a dark, foggy night with the plane either low or out of fuel, he used the plane's side-to-side tilting motions to provide the exact information required to determine specifically the best landing. He landed the plane safely and needless to say, became a firm believer in **pendulum power!**

Literally, a life was probably saved by this inspired use of the plane itself as a pendulum to channel information from subconscious to conscious mind.

What we have with pendulum work is a real objective/subjective opportunity for discussion with your subconscious, just as you could with a fellow student.

But it isn't just the direct practical value of such information and knowledge gained with dowsing and pendulum work—rather, it is the channeling process between the subconscious and conscious minds that builds structure and brings psychic power into objective and dependable reality for psychic empowerment.

The skills you learn become more than "accessories" and work as building blocks and scaffolding in the growth of the whole person, as you become more than you are.

SOURCES AND RECOMMENDED READING

Theresa Cheung, *The Element Encyclopedia of the Psychic Worlds* (HarperElement, 2006).

Joe H. Slate, *Psychic Empowerment: A 7-Day Plan for Self-Development* (Llewellyn, 1995).

Lyall Watson, *Supernature: An Unprecedented Look at Strange Phenomena and Their Place in Nature* (Anchor/Doubleday, 1973).

Lyall Watson, *Beyond Supernature: A New Natural History of the Supernatural* (Bantam, 1988).

Richard Webster, *Dowsing for Beginners: The Art of Discovering: Water, Treasure, Gold, Oil, Artifacts* (Llewellyn, 1996).

Richard Webster, *Pendulum Magic for Beginners: Power to Achieve All Goals, Tap Your Inner Wisdom, Find Lost Objects, Focus Energy for Self-Improvement* (Llewellyn, 2002).

Colin Wilson, *Strange Powers: Astral Projection, Reincarnation, Dowsing, Spirit Writing* (Random House, 1973).

20

GEOMANCY

What the Earth Tells You

AN EARTH-BASED DIVINATION SYSTEM

Factually, Geomancy is an *Earth*-based divination system. We don't often realize that different divinatory systems are structured in relation to our environment—mostly revolving about the four elements of Earth, Air, Sky, and Spirit.

Earth-based systems include dowsing, the pendulum, geomancy, tea-leaf reading, and, debatably, the I Ching (Yi King). Air-based (mental) systems include Tarot, aura reading, handwriting analysis, and, debatably, reading the runes. The sky above us, of course, relates to astrology which, today, is less a divinatory system than a psychological diagnostic system.

There probably are some Water-based systems, which do not include such things as shells or tea leaves, but might, debatably, include patterns left in the sand at low tide and, perhaps, using a glass of water like a crystal ball.

A *PICTURE* OF ENERGY INFLUENCES

An Earth-based system relates the Earth's energy system to a corresponding system within the physical body. Physically we are part of Earth, and understanding the mutual energetic relationship is important to various healing systems, including acupuncture, the role of megaliths, and such structures as Stonehenge and the Great Pyramid in the beneficial manipulation of those energies. The goal of an Earth-based divination, in particular geomancy, is to provide a *picture* of the immediate environmental influences on the question at hand.

TERRESTRIAL ASTROLOGY

Psychologist Carl Jung called Geomancy "terrestrial astrology," in which the astrological chart is recreated by counting pebbles and arriving at ones and twos to produce a chart read like a horoscope. Geomancy is most developed in Western Nigeria.

Many of the most familiar divinatory systems seem to have come to us from Egypt and the Middle East, where the dominant environment is divided between endless deserts and a sky that seems close enough to touch. Regardless, it is important to realize that all systems connect the Conscious Mind to the Subconscious and thence to the Universal Consciousness. Psychic empowerment depends on our abilities to consciously "channel" our questions to these *lower* realms and to use the answers in our *awakened consciousness* for their analysis and application.

Few of us have yet fully grasped these concepts of the Subconscious Mind and the Universal or Collective Unconscious, which is sometimes, as below, just called the "Unconscious." Nor do we fully grasp Consciousness itself, which is neither physical nor biological, nor limited to brain or body, nor—as our experiments in astral projection and remote viewing demonstrate—time and space.

> *It (the Unconscious) contains, beside an indeterminable number of subliminal perceptions, an immense fund of accumulated inheritance factors left by one generation of men after another, whose mere existence marks a step in the differentiation of the species. If it were permissible to personify the Unconscious, we might call it a collective human being combining the characteristics of both sexes, transcending youth and age, birth and death, and from having at his command a human experience of one or two million years, almost immortal. If such a being existed, he would be exalted above all temporal change; the present would mean neither more nor less to him than any year in the one hundredth century before Christ; he would be a dreamer of age-old dreams, and owing to his immeasurable experience, he would be an incomparable prognosticator. He would have lived countless times over the life of the individual, of the family, tribe, and people, and he would possess the living sense of the rhythms of growth, flowering and decay.*
>
> —CARL JUNG, *MODERN MAN IN SEARCH OF A SOUL*

COMMUNICATION DISGUISED
IN SYMBOLS AND STRANGE WORDS

We have learned that this Unconscious is able to "invent" the means to communicate with our conscious minds, often *disguised* in symbols and strange words that we must manipulate and interpret to gain answers to our questions and to discover the wisdom to make lives not merely meaningful, but also purposeful. Possibly, as we grow and develop, the communication becomes more direct as with great prophets, messengers, and seers—but still it is our own manipulation and interpretation that act as a bridge between a single person in the present time and this immortal and collective timeless being that we now call "Unconscious" and which in other times and places may have been called a god of many names.

An important point about divination was made by Israel Regardie in his *Practical Guide to Geomantic Divination* (1972):

> *The major contribution of (geomancy) is not so much slanted in the direction of prediction of what is yet to come, but to facilitate the growth and expression of this inner psycho-spiritual ability. To this extent, any and all systems of divination may be considered useful. Amongst the more commonly used methods are the Tarot cards, astrology, palmistry, graphology, and many others. The method to be described here, geomancy, is favored above all others because it is basically so simple to operate. One can use it quickly to obtain a simple 'yes' or 'no' answer. With sufficient practice, enough skill can be developed to provide considerable amplification of the first straight answer.*

GEOMANCY'S EVOLUTION FROM SIMPLE TO COMPLEX

Definitions of Geomancy show how it has evolved from very simple to rather complex divinatory systems.

> *A form of divination by interpreting the pattern of objects thrown on the ground. Gravel, small stones, sticks, seeds, or even jewels may be used. The practitioner holds the objects in cupped hands, concentrates on the divinatory request, and then allows the seeds or stones to drop. Interpretations are made intuitively on the basis of patterns on the ground.*
>
> — NEVILL DRURY, *THE DICTIONARY OF THE ESOTERIC*

> *A system of divination using the sixteen geomantic figures—patterns of four lines of dots, with either one or two dots in each line. These are essentially four-digit binary numbers; in divination, four such patterns are produced by a random process, and then combined with others according to traditional methods to produce a geomantic chart.*
>
> — JOHN MICHAEL GREER, *THE NEW ENCYCLOPEDIA OF THE OCCULT*

Geomancy is the art of divination through the earth and elemental forces. The word 'geomancy' derives from two Greek words: gaie (Earth) and manteia (divination).

Geomancy… uses randomly drawn dashes or dots, usually on the ground. These marks (frequently made ritually during trance) are reduced to a set number of broken or unbroken lines, or rows of one or two dots. In European geomancy, one dot (or unbroken line) represents positive nature (yang). Two dots (or a broken line) represent negative nature (yin).

The basic concepts of European geomancy derived primarily from ancient Arabic and Roman divination practices combined with astrology and the Greek doctrine of the four elements. In this system, the sixteen geomantic signs (made up of four rows of dots or lines) represent all possible basic combinations of the elements.… each of the seven planets is associated with two geomantic signs, the remaining two signs being associated with the nodes of the Moon (the point where the moon crosses the ecliptic). The Zodiacal symbols are assigned to the geomantic signs associated with the planets according to each planet's rulership of the Zodiac.

Because of the elemental basis, **geomancy is also used to determine and notate the flow of earth energies.**

— BILL WHITCOMB, *THE MAGICIAN'S COMPANION*

At its most fundamental and simple level, geomancy can be compared to playing in a miniature sandbox and letting your Unconscious do the talking. In this form, determine a question or concern you have, and then, using a pointed stick or stylus, make four lines of random dots in the sand—however many dots in each line that feels correct to you. Then count the number of dots in each line, and on a piece of paper record one dot if the total is odd, and two dots if the total is even.

In many ways it is better to complete one line at a time, and record it on a separate piece of paper, and then shake the sandbox to clear those dots away before starting the next line.

SIXTEEN TETRAGRAMS

When you have completed the four lines, you will have made one of the sixteen geomantic figures or *tetragrams*. Each figure is composed of four lines, each line containing either one or two points. Each line represents one of the four classical elements: from top to bottom, the lines represent fire, air, water, and earth. When a line has a single point, the element is said to be active; otherwise, with two points, the element is passive. Much of the art of geomantic interpretation rests on this simple construction.

FOUR MOTHERS

You need to repeat the whole process to produce four complete figures of four lines each. From these four "Mothers," you will create the next tetragrams in a further process we will clarify later. Subsequently, you need to refer to a table of geomantic signs to determine the ones you have created, and read the descriptive associations to find the answer to the question being asked.

A MAP OF THE UNCONSCIOUS AT THE MOMENT

This basic geomancy is shamanic in origin, and your divination can possibly benefit from the use of alcohol—like a natural beer—and by singing a monotonous song of spontaneous words reflecting your question. For the solitary practitioner, this form of geomancy provides a map of the Unconscious at that moment. While it can be used to gain some insight and alternative views of events, it will primarily relate to your personal state of awareness rather than the fully objective 'outside' world.

Note the quote marks in the last sentence above: we don't actually know the real outside world, but only our own conception of it, which constantly changes through our experience, interpretation, and understanding.

If pure sand isn't readily available to you, it can usually be purchased at a craft or garden store, a fish aquarium store, or a builder's store. The box shouldn't be too large—perhaps three inches deep and no more than twelve inches on each side. A wood "in" box from an office supply store would be excellent, or one might be cut from a cardboard box, or you could construct one out of a piece of plywood and four pieces of board glued together. A suitable stylus could be a wood pencil.

As you will see further along in this chapter, in some of the alternative techniques, dry dirt can be used instead of sand. The main point is to stay close to the Earth in all geomancy work—using sand, dirt, pebbles, chips of crystal, dried beans, seeds, jewels, and even metal (not plastic) coins.

However, sand is the most traditional as indicated by the Arabic term *'ilm al-raml*, or "the science of the sand," which was the original from which the Greek *geōmanteía* (foresight by earth) was derived. Other Arabic names include *khatt al-raml* (sand writing), and *darb al-raml* or *zarb al-raml* (striking the sand). This last name came from the practice of hitting the sand several times with a stick to read the patterns left behind.

NECESSITY OF A GEOMANTIC JOURNAL

As with all your psychic work, you should keep a geomantic journal of your questions and the results of your geomantic divination, returning at a later time to add later commentary. It is with this practice of later examination and comment that you learn and come to deeper understanding of the factors rising from the Subconscious and those revealed about the outside world. You are the point of intersection, and it is here that *action takes place*.

HISTORY AND ORIGINS

Geomancy was popularly practiced by people from all social classes throughout Africa and Europe during the Middle Ages and the Renaissance. Many people simply threw or dropped pebbles, dried beans, seeds, and even jewels within a circle or square marked off on the ground to get the required lines. Other methods included counting the "eyes" of a potato.

Many divinatory systems have mythological origins. Tarot (also called the *Book of Thoth*), for example, purports to be the ancient wisdom turned into a game of cards so that it would survive through the coming "Dark Ages." According to one Arabic story, Hermes Trismegistus dreamed of the angel Jibril and asked Jibril for enlightenment. The angel instructed him in geomancy. Hermes then revealed the secret art to an Indian king who wrote it all in a book, which was passed down to Khalaf al-Barbari. Al-Barbari was converted to Islam by the prophet Muhammad himself, who explained that by learning geomancy one could know all the prophets knew.

The oldest Arabic method consists of drawing sixteen random lines of dots in sand. This same system continues to this day in Arabic countries, and was introduced to Europe in the medieval era.

The Arabs brought geomancy to Africa, where one traditional form consists of throwing handfuls of dirt in the air and observing how the dirt falls. In West Africa, Ifá, one of the oldest forms of geomancy, uses the same sixteen geomantic figures but with different meanings and names reflecting cultural and environmental differences. In North Africa, another variation is called *vodou Fa*. In Madagascar, another is called *Sikidy*, while in India it is known as *Ramal Shastra*.

In China, the diviner may enter a trance and make markings on the ground that are interpreted by an associate (often a young or illiterate boy). Similar forms of geomancy include skrying involving the patterns seen in rocks or soil.

Geomancy arrived in Europe in the twelfth century, and scholars studied and wrote about it, including John Heydon and Christopher Cattan, and most famously Henry Cornelius Agrippa in his *Three Books of Occult Philosophy*. Other occultists, philosophers, and even theologians continued their studies into the seventeenth century, when most occult practices went out of popularity as science began to capture the imagination. One popular variation of geomancy was *Napoleon's Book of Fate*.

Christopher Cattan in *Geomancy* (c. 1558), wrote

> *Geomancy is to know and understand…*
> *all things uncertain, Present, Past, and To Come,*
> *And upon them to give counsel*
> *and take counsel in the examining of the figure…*

Geomancy made a revival in the nineteenth century, when renewed interest in the occult arose due to the works of Robert Thomas Cross and novelist Edward Bulwer-Lytton. Franz Hartmann published *The Principles of Astrological Geomancy*, which brought about further interest in the practice.

But it was the Hermetic Order of the Golden Dawn in the late nineteenth century that brought really serious new interest and development by including geomancy in its required curriculum. However, these Golden Dawn scholars somewhat simplified the old rituals and elaborate divinatory practices, including geomancy, losing much of the art in the process. Geomancy had become a complex art of interpretation requiring skill in recognizing patterns of paired figures and looking up the written answers.

Aleister Crowley revealed many of the "secrets" of the Golden Dawn through his publications. Now, in the twenty-first century, there is a further renewal through the works of John Michael Greer and other mainstream occultists.

Modern methods include dice, a coin (heads is one point, tails is two points) and special cards, each with a geomantic figure. Random number generators have also been used, and there are a number of software programs. *Is it really possible for an Earth-based system to remain meaningful with computer generations? Even if it does, hasn't it lost its fundamental identity with its earthen origins, and perhaps its validity—at least in relation to the earthy aspects of our personality?*

THE PRACTICE OF GEOMANCY

The starting point of all divination systems has to be *The Question*—the "Need to Know."

This is important! Divination is not a game undertaken for amusement. You should only undertake a divination because of true need for an answer. We ask the question when it become *imperative* to the questioner, so imperative that it will reverberate in your mind and cause an equal reverberation in the cosmos, leading to the answer given in the form of a traditional set of rules or code yet to be interpreted. Those rules will be given in *Techniques of Consultation* later in this chapter.

It is likewise important to make the question concise and clearly worded. There should be no ambiguity, and the question should confine itself to earthy, practical matters, unconcerned with issues of morality or judgment.

The best question is one that can be simply answered with either a "yes" or a "no." The simpler the question, the more precise the answer; the more serious the question, the more accurate the answer. Ideally the question is personal to the geomancer rather than one of worldly concern.

The question should always be written in your journal, and then also the results and your interpretation.

Yes, readings can be conducted on behalf of another person, but it's best that the person be present and directly involved, stating the question, which is then repeated or more concisely restated by the geomancer. Both the client and the geomancer concentrate upon it during the operation, and the client must wait until the casting and reading are both completed before asking additional questions or comments.

In the European tradition of geomancy, the person asking the question is called the "querent," and the matter being questioned about is called the "quested."

True to the original Arab practice of using a pointed stick punching into the surface of sand, draw the geomantic figures proceeding from *right to left*. A later development used a wax tablet and a stylus. Some simply make marks on paper, but others consider this as bordering too close to the possibility of conscious manipulation when the intention is to avoid any conscious intervention. Seeming random events, in this case the poking of the stick into the sand, are believed to be influenced by spiritual forces combined with the Subconscious Mind. For this reason, any divination should be preceded by a short ritual, prayer, or meditation—anything that establishes a psychic circle or "cone" around the operation.

Next the geomancer must create sixteen lines of random dots without counting while holding his or her question in mind. Once the lines are produced, the geomancer marks off the dots two by two until either one or two points remain in the line: one dot is odd and two dots are even. Taking them in groups of four, they form the first four geomantic figures, called the "Mothers," from which four additional tetragrams are generated and form the basis for the generation of the remaining figures.

THE SHIELD

The four Mothers are placed in the top row of a chart, called a "Shield." The first Mother is placed to the far right; the second Mother is placed to her left, and so on, *right to left*.

THE FOUR DAUGHTERS

The next four figures, called the "Daughters," are formed by taking the first line from the first Mother, then the second Mother, and so on (again moving from right to left) and assembling them to constitute the first Daughter. The second Daughter is formed the same way using the second line from each of the Mothers, and likewise for the third and fourth Daughters. These four Daughters are placed on the top row of the Shield next to the Mothers so that there are eight positions in total on the top row.

THE FOUR NIECES (OR NEPHEWS)

Beneath the top row of eight figures (four Mothers and four Daughters), we next form just four figures for the second line. In medieval sources these are named the four Nieces, but in modern books they are called Nephews. We will continue with the earlier tradition.

The first Niece (again moving from right to left) is formed by adding together the two Mothers above the first Niece; the third and forth Mothers are added together to form the second Niece; the first and second Daughters (positions five and six in the top line) are added together to form the third Niece, and the fourth Niece is formed by adding together the third and fourth Daughters.

Thus, if the top line of the first two Mothers consists of three dots, that will "reduce" to an odd number and so the top line in the first Niece will have one dot; if the second line of the first and second Mother consists of two dots, they add to an even number so the second line of the first Niece will have two dots, and so on to produce four lines. The same process is repeated with the third and fourth Mothers to produce the second Niece, and again the same process is followed with the first and second Daughters to produce the third Niece, and likewise the fourth Niece is produced from the third and fourth Daughters.

THE TWO WITNESSES

A similar process taking the first and second Nieces is used to form the Right Witness on the third line, and the Left Witness from the third and fourth Nieces.

THE JUDGE

From the two Witnesses, a third figure is placed in the middle of the bottom line—the Judge.

Sometimes a sixteenth figure is formed, called variously the Reconciler or the Superior Judge. However, two different processes are described in the literature: the first involves adding lines from the Judge and the First Mother; the second is more complex and involves adding the Judge to whatever figure corresponds to the subject of the question asked as found in the chart of the twelve houses that will be reproduced in the section on *Techniques of Consultation* below.

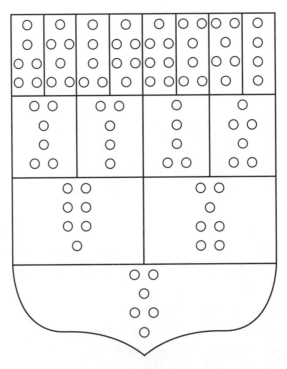

Geomantic Shield Chart

EXAMPLE OF A SHIELD CHART

Each tetragram has its own name, meaning, and personality. It is through their combinations and interactions that the querent sees the underlying pattern of the situation, past and present and future. In the example above, the Mothers are, right to left, Via, Acquisitio, Conjunctio, and Laetitia. The Daughters are Carcer, Cauda, Amisso, and Fortuna. The Right Witness is Fortuna Minor, and the Left Witness is Tristitia, and below is Acquisitio, the Judge. The Reconciler or Superior Judge, not pictured, would in this example be Amissio.

Sometimes, the first twelve tetragrams are placed in a square zodiacal chart for a more in-depth answer. See page 279 for an example and further details.

The figures are placed in the houses of the square zodiac with the first Mother from the Shield placed in the first House, the second Mother in the second House, and so on.

The houses are those of traditional astrology.

Geomantic House Meanings

Querent (person asking the question)

Money, moveable property

Siblings, neighbors, short trips

Father, home, real estate

Children, pleasure, gambling

Illness, servants, small animals

Marriage, romance, partners, open enemies

Death, inheritance

Higher education, long trips, spirituality

Career, government, reputation

Friends

Curses, secret enemies, imprisonment

In other operations, the Golden Dawn used the sixteen tetragrams as skrying symbols, as part of the Enochian magical system, and in creating geomantic sigils painted on talismans to attract particular energies.

It is perhaps of some interest to know the four lines of each figure allow for sixteen different combinations. Since each chart is generated from the four Mothers, 65,536 charts are possible.

TECHNIQUES OF CONSULTATION

The following tables and instruction have been excerpted from pages 526 to 539 of *The Golden Dawn,* sixth revised and corrected edition, by Israel Regardie.

GEOMANTIC HOUSE MEANINGS			
Sigil of Ruler	*Name of Ruler*	*Planet which rules Answer*	*Sign of Zodiac*
	Bartzabel	Mars ♂	♈ Aries
	Kedemel	Venus ♀	♉ Taurus
	Taphthartharath	Mercury ☿	♊ Gemini
	Chasmodai	Luna ☽	♋ Cancer
	Sorath	Sol ☉	♌ Leo
	Taphthartharath	Mercury ☿	♍ Virgo
	Kedemel	Venus ♀	♎ Libra
	Bartzabel	Mars ♂	♏ Scorpio
	Hismael	Jupiter ♃	♐ Sagittarius
	Zazel	Saturn ♄	♑ Capricorn
	Zazel	Saturn ♄	♒ Aquarius
	Hismael	Jupiter ♃	♓ Pisces
	Zazel and Bartzabel	Saturn ♄ and Mars ♂	☋ Cauda Draconis
	Hismael and Kedemel	Venus ♀ and Jupiter ♃	☊ Caput Draconis
	Sorath	Sol ☉	♌ Leo
	Chasmodai	Luna ☽	♋ Cancer

GEOMANTIC ATTRIBUTIONS		
Element	*Geomantic Figure*	*Name and Meaning of Figure*
Fire	O O O O O	PUER (a boy, yellow, beardless)
Earth	O O O O O O	AMISSIO (loss, comprehended without)
Air	O O O O O O O	ALBUS (white, fair)
Water	O O O O O O O O	POPULUS (people, congregation)
Fire	O O O O O O	FORTUNA MAJOR (greater fortune and aid, safeguard, entering)
Earth	O O O O O O	CONJUNCTO (assembly, conjunction)
Air	O O O O O	PUELLA (a girl, beautiful)
Water	O O O O O O O	RUBEUS (red, reddish)

Element	Geomantic Figure	Name and Meaning of Figure

Fire	O O
	  O
	O O
	  O
		ACQUISITIO (obtaining, comprehended within)

Earth	O O O O O O	CARCER (a prison, bound)
Air	O O O O O O O	TRISTITIA (sadness, damned, cross)
Water	O O O O O O O	LAETITIA (joy, laughing, healthy, bearded)
Fire	O O O O O	CAUDA DRACONIS (the lower threshold, going out)

Earth	O O
	  O
	  O
	  O
		CAPUT DRACONIS (heart, upper threshold, entering)

Fire	O O O O O O	FORTUNA MINOR (lesser fortune and aid, safeguard going out)
Water	O O O O	VIA (way, journey)

THE FOUR MOTHERS

4th West	3rd North	2nd East	1st South
O O	O O	O	O
O	O O	O O	O
O O	O	O	O O
O O	O	O O	O O
Rubeus	Fortuna Major	Amissio	Fortuna Minor

From these Four Mothers, four resulting figures called the *Four Daughters* are now to be derived, thus: The uppermost points of the First Mother will be the uppermost points of the First Daughter. The corresponding, that is the first line of, points of the Second Mother will be the second points of The First Daughter. The same line of points of the Third Mother will constitute the third points of the First Daughter. The same point of the Fourth Mother will be the fourth point of the First Daughter. The same rule applies to all the figures. The second line of points of the Four Mothers will comprise the Second Daughter. The third line of points of the Four Mothers will comprise the Third Daughter, and the fourth line of points of the Four Mothers will comprise the Fourth Daughter.

	Mothers			
	4th	3rd	2nd	1st
First Daughter, 4 uppermost points	O O	O O	O	O
Second Daughter, 4 next points	O	O O	O O	O
Third Daughter, 4 next points	O O	O	O	O O
Fourth Daughter, 4 next points	O O	O	O O	O O
	Rubeus	Fortuna Major	Amissio	Fortuna Minor

Applying the above rule throughout, the following will represent the Four Daughters. (Read right to left.)

4th	3rd	2nd	1st
O O	O O	O	O
O O	O	O O	O
O	O	O O	O O
O O	O O	O	O O
Albus	Conjuntio	Carcer	Fortuna Minor

These, again for the convenience of the beginner, are now to be placed on the left hand of the Four Mothers in a single line from right to left.

	Four Daughters				Four Mothers		
8th	7th	6th	5th	4th	3rd	2nd	1st
O O	O O	O	O	O O	O O	O	O
O O	O	O O	O	O	O O	O O	O
O	O	O O	O O	O O	O	O	O O
O O	O O	O	O O	O O	O	O O	O O
Albus	Conjuntio	Carcer	Fortuna Minor	Rubeus	Fortuna Major	Amissio	Fortuna Minor

From these eight figures, four others are now to be calculated, which may be called the *Four Resultants*, or the Four Nephews. These will be the ninth, tenth, eleventh and twelfth figures of the whole scheme. The ninth figure is formed from the points of the first and second figures compared together. The tenth from the third and fourth figures; the eleventh from the fifth and sixth. The twelfth from the seventh and eighth figures. The rule is to compare or add together the points of the corresponding lines. If, for instance, the first line of the First Mother consists of one point, and the first line of the Second Mother also consists of one point, these two are added together, and since they are an even number, two points are marked down for the first line of the Resultant. If the added points are odd, only one point is marked for the resulting figure. The Ninth figure is thus formed:

2nd	1st		
O	O	Uppermost points added equals 2	O O
O O	O	Second points added equals 3	O
O	O O	Third points added equals 3	O
O O	O O	Lowest points added equals 4	O O
Amissio	Fortuna Minor		Conjunctio

The other Resultants are calculated in precisely the same way:

	Four Daughters				Four Mothers		
8th	7th	6th	5th	4th	3rd	2nd	1st
O O	O O	O	O	O O	O O	O	O
O O	O	O O	O	O	O O	O O	O
O	O	O O	O O	O O	O	O	O O
O O	O O	O	O O	O O	O	O O	O O
Albus	Conjuntio	Carcer	Fortuna Minor	Rubeus	Fortuna Major	Amissio	Fortuna Minor

In this way are yielded the Four Resultants:

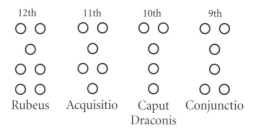

And thus the Twelve Principal Figures of the Geomantic scheme of Divination are completed. These again correspond to the Twelve Astrological Houses of Heaven, with which they will later on be compared.

For the greater assistance of the Diviner in forming a judgment upon the general condition of the scheme of twelve figures thus far obtained, it is usual to deduce from them three other subsidiary figures. These three are of less importance than the twelve previous figures, and are not to be considered at all in the light of component figures of the scheme, but only as aids to the general judgment. These other figures are known as the Right Witness, the Left Witness, and the Judge.

The two witnesses are without significance in the divination, except as they are the roots from which the figure known as the Judge is derived. The Right Witness is formed from the ninth and tenth figures by comparing the points in the manner before shown in the formation of the Resultants. That is, the corresponding lines of points in the two figures are compared together, and the addition, whether odd or even, comprises the points of the Witness. The Left Witness represents the combination in a similar manner of the eleventh and twelfth figures. The Judge again is formed in precisely the same way from the Two Witnesses, and is therefore a synthesis of the whole figure. If he be good, the figure is good and the judgment will be favorable; and vice versa. From the nature of the formation of the fifteenth figure, the Judge, it should always consist of an even number of points, and never of odd. That is, in adding together the four lines of points comprising the Judge, the result should be an even number. If the Judge were a figure of odd points, it would show that a mistake had been made somewhere in the calculations.

THE RECONCILER

The Reconciler is a sixteenth figure sometimes used for adding the Judgment by combining the Judge with the Figure in the Particular House signifying the thing demanded. Thus, in the preceding scheme, the Judge formed is Populus, and the Second Figure, being Amissio, their combination also yields Amissio.

In order to discover where the Part of Fortune will fall, add together all the points of the first twelve figures. Divide that number by twelve, and place the Part of Fortune with the figure answering to the remainder. If there is no remainder, it will fall on the twelfth figure. The Part of Fortune is a symbol of ready money, money in cash belonging to the Querent, and is of the greatest importance in all questions of money.

GEOMANTIC SIGNIFICATION
OF THE TWELVE HOUSES OF HEAVEN

First House (Ascendant): Life, health, querent.

Second House: Money, property, personal worth.

Third House: Brothers, sisters, news, short journeys.

Fourth House: Father, landed property, inheritance. The grave, the end of the matter.

Fifth House: Children, pleasure, feasts, speculation.

Sixth House: Servants, sickness, uncles and aunts, small animals.

Seventh House: Love, marriage, husband or wife. Partnerships and associations, public enemies, lawsuits.

Eighth House: Deaths, wills, legacies; pain, anxiety. Estate of deceased.

Ninth House: Long journeys, voyages. Science, religion, art, visions, and divinations.

Tenth House: Mother. Rank and honor, trade or profession, authority, employment, and worldly position generally.

Eleventh House: Friends, hopes and wishes.

Twelfth House: Sorrows, fears, punishments, enemies in secret, institutions, unseen dangers, restriction.

The Twelve Figures of the geomantic scheme are attributed to Twelve Houses.

The First figure goes with the Tenth House.

The Second figure goes with the First House.

The Third figure goes with the Fourth House.

The Fourth figure goes with the Seventh House.

The Fifth figure goes with the Eleventh House.

The Sixth figure goes with the Second House.

The Seventh figure goes with the Fifth House.

The Eighth figure goes with the Eighth House.

The Ninth figure goes with the Twelfth House.

The Tenth figure goes with the Third House.

The Eleventh figure goes with the Sixth House.

The Twelfth figure goes with the Ninth House.

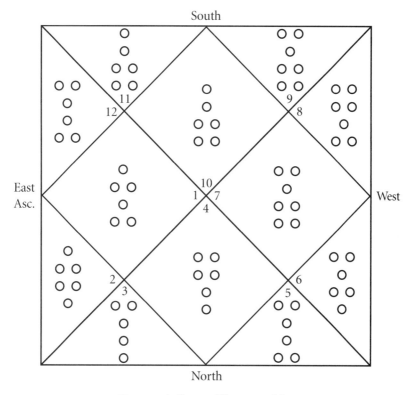

Geomantic Square Horoscope Map

Thus the figures derived by the calculations provided in the example given previously would occupy a Geomantic map as follows:

(Note: here I omit a series of interpretations based upon the use of the Two Witnesses and the Judge. I have found these most untrustworthy, giving answers in utter contradiction to the proper divination worked out by the readings which follow. The mediaeval origin of the present omission is clearly shown, and is not a credit to the system. The following facts, which should be very carefully studied, will provide the fundamental authoritative data to enable the student to divine correctly.—I. R.

GEOMANTIC HOUSE MEANINGS

Herein follows a set of general Tables of the sixteen figures in the Twelve Houses for the better convenience of forming a general judgment of the Scheme. Under the head of each figure separately is given its general effect in whatever House of the Map of the Heavens it may be located.

Thus, by taking the House signifying the end or result of the matter, the Fourth House, etc., and by noting what figures fall therein, the student may find by these tables the general effect in that position.

Acquisitio

Generally good for profit and gain.

Ascendant	Happy, success in all things.
Second House	Very prosperous.
Third House	Favour and riches.
Fourth House	Good fortune and success.
Fifth House	Good success.
Sixth House	Good—especially if it agree with the fifth.
Seventh House	Reasonably good.
Eighth House	Rather good, but not very. The sick shall die.
Ninth House	Good in all demands.
Tenth House	Good in suits. Very prosperous.
Eleventh House	Good in all.
Twelfth House	Evil, pain,and loss.

"Gain" is generally positive, especially for acquiring things, and can indicate travel and financial gain.

Amissio

Good for loss of substance and sometimes for love; but *very bad* for gain.

Ascendant	Ill in all things but for prisoners.
Second House	Very ill for money, but good for love.
Third House	Ill end—except for quarrels.
Fourth House	Ill in all.
Fifth House	Evil except for agriculture.
Sixth House	Rather evil for love.
Seventh House	Very good for love, otherwise evil.
Eighth House	Excellent in all questions.
Ninth House	Evil in all things.
Tenth House	Evil except for favor with women.
Eleventh House	Good for love, otherwise bad.
Twelfth House	Evil in all things.

"Loss" is generally negative except for love matters. It often represents something beyond one's grasp. It can be positive in situations where loss is desired.

Fortuna Major

Good for gain in all things where a person has hopes to win.

Ascendant	Good save in secrecy.
Second House	Good except in sad things.
Third House	Good in all.
Fourth House	Good in all, but melancholy.
Fifth House	Very good in all things.
Sixth House	Very good except for debauchery.
Seventh House	Good in all.
Eighth House	Moderately good.
Ninth House	Very good.
Tenth House	Exceedingly good. Go to superiors.
Eleventh House	Very good.
Twelfth House	Good in all.

"The Greater Fortune" is positive suggesting good fortune, especially in new beginnings. It also represents power, stability, and long-term success.

Fortuna Minor

Good in any matter in which a person wishes to proceed quickly.

Ascendant	Speed in victory and in love, but choleric.
Second House	Very good.
Third House	Good—but wrathful.
Fourth House	Haste; rather evil except for peace.
Fifth House	Good in all things.
Sixth House	Medium in all.
Seventh House	Evil except for war or love.
Eighth House	Evil generally.
Ninth House	Good, but choleric.
Tenth House	Good, except for peace.
Eleventh House	Good, especially for love.
Twelfth House	Good, except for alteration, or for suing another.

"The Lesser Fortune" suggests a weak or transient success that is dependent upon outside help in matters that should be resolved quickly, as it is subject to rapid change and instability.

Laetitia

Good for joy, present or to come.

Ascendant	Good, except in war.
Second House	Sickly.
Third House	Ill.
Fourth House	Mainly good.
Fifth House	Excellently good.
Sixth House	Evil generally.
Seventh House	Indifferent.
Eighth House	Evil generally.
Ninth House	Very good.
Tenth House	Good, rather in war than in peace.
Eleventh House	Good in all.
Twelfth House	Evil generally.

"Joy" is generally positive in all situations.

Tristitia

Evil in almost all things.

Ascendant	Medium, but good for treasure and fortifying.
Second House	Medium, but good to fortify.
Third House	Evil in all.
Fourth House	Evil in all.
Fifth House	Very evil.
Sixth House	Evil, except for debauchery.
Seventh House	Evil for inheritance and magic only.
Eighth House	Evil, but in secrecy good.
Ninth House	Evil except for magic.
Tenth House	Evil except for fortifications.
Eleventh House	Evil in all.
Twelfth House	Evil. But good for magic and treasure.

"Sorrow" is generally negative, suggesting pain, suffering, sadness, and even mourning.
It can be positive in matters relating to Earth itself.

Puella

Good in all demands, especially in those relating to women.

Ascendant	Good except in war.
Second House	Very good.
Third House	Good.
Fourth House	Indifferent.
Fifth House	Very good, but notice the aspects.
Sixth House	Good, but especially so for debauchery.
Seventh House	Good except for war.
Eighth House	Good.
Ninth House	Good for music. Otherwise only medium.
Tenth House	Good for peace.
Eleventh House	Good, and love of ladies.
Twelfth House	Good in all.

"The Girl" represents feminine sexuality, peace, and passivity. It can be either positive or negative, but is generally positive in situations involving women.

Puer

Evil in most demands, except in those relating to war or love.

Ascendant	Indifferent. Best in war.
Second House	Good, but with trouble.
Third House	Good fortune.
Fourth House	Evil, except in war and love.
Fifth House	Medium good.
Sixth House	Medium.
Seventh House	Evil, save in war.
Eighth House	Evil, save for love.
Ninth House	Evil except for war.
Tenth House	Rather evil. But good for love and war. Most other things medium.
Eleventh House	Medium; good favor.
Twelfth House	Very good in all.

"The Boy" symbolizes courage and initiative, the pioneering spirit, and entrepreneurship. It can represent a helpful young man or the important man in a relationship.

Rubeus

Evil in all that is good and good in all that is evil.

Ascendant	Destroy the figure if it falls here! It makes the judgment worthless.
Second House	Evil in all demands.
Third House	Evil except to let blood.
Fourth House	Evil except in war and fire.
Fifth House	Evil save for love, and sowing seed.
Sixth House	Evil except for blood-letting.
Seventh House	Evil except for war and fire.
Eighth House	Evil.
Ninth House	Very evil.
Tenth House	Dissolute. Love, fire.
Eleventh House	Evil, except to let blood.
Twelfth House	Evil in all things.

"Red" represents passion, often with violence, vice, deception, force, and destruction.

Albus

Good for profit and for entering into a place or undertaking.

Ascendant	Good for marriage. Mercurial. Peace.
Second House	Good in all.
Third House	Very good.
Fourth House	Very good except in war.
Fifth House	Good.
Sixth House	Good in all things.
Seventh House	Good except for war.
Eighth House	Good.
Ninth House	A messenger brings a letter.
Tenth House	Excellent in all.
Eleventh House	Very good.
Twelfth House	Marvelously good.

"White" is weakly positive in situations where careful planning is needed and may indicate profit. It represents wisdom and peace.

Conjunctio

Good with good, or evil with evil. Recovery of things lost.

Ascendant	Good with good, evil with evil.
Second House	Commonly good.
Third House	Good fortune.
Fourth House	Good save for health; see the eighth.
Fifth House	Medium.
Sixth House	Good for immorality only.
Seventh House	Rather good.
Eighth House	Evil; death.
Ninth House	Medium good.
Tenth House	For love, good. For sickness, evil.
Eleventh House	Good in all.
Twelfth House	Medium. Bad for prisoners.

"The Conjunction" is neutral, but positive with joining or recovery situations such as relationships and marriage.

Carcer

Generally evil. Delay, binding, bar, restriction.

Ascendant	Evil except to fortify a place.
Second House	Good in Saturnine questions; else evil.
Third House	Evil.
Fourth House	Good only for melancholy.
Fifth House	Receive a letter within three days. Evil.
Sixth House	Very evil.
Seventh House	Evil.
Eighth House	Very evil.
Ninth House	Evil in all.
Tenth House	Evil save for hidden treasure.
Eleventh House	Much anxiety.
Twelfth House	Rather good.

"The Prison" is generally negative and suggests delays, setbacks, or restriction, but can be positive in matters involving stability or security.

Caput Draconis

Good with good; evil with evil.

Ascendant	Good in all things.
Second House	Good.
Third House	Very good.
Fourth House	Good save in war.
Fifth House	Very good.
Sixth House	Good for immorality only.
Seventh House	Good, especially for peace.
Eighth House	Good.
Ninth House	Very Good.
Tenth House	Good in all.
Eleventh House	Good for the Church and ecclesiastical gain.
Twelfth House	Not very good.

"The Head of the Dragon" is generally neutral but positive in start-up situations and new beginnings. However, it gives strength to other figures—negative or positive.

Cauda Draconis

Good with evil, and evil with good. Good for loss, and for passing out of an affair.

Ascendant	Destroy figure if it falls here! Makes judgment worthless.
Second House	Very evil.
Third House	Evil in all.
Fourth House	Good, especially for conclusion of the matter.
Fifth House	Very evil.
Sixth House	Rather good.
Seventh House	Evil, war, and fire.
Eighth House	No good, except for magic.
Ninth House	Good for science only. Bad for journeys. Robbery.
Tenth House	Evil save in works of fire.
Eleventh House	Evil save for favors.
Twelfth House	Rather good.

"The Tail of the Dragon" is usually negative and reflects past-due obligations including karmic debts. Adverse emotional and spiritual forces operating against the querent.

Via

Injurious to the goodness of other figures generally, but good for journeys and voyages.

Ascendant	Evil except for prison.
Second House	Indifferent.
Third House	Very good in all.
Fourth House	Good in all save love.
Fifth House	Voyages good.
Sixth House	Evil.
Seventh House	Rather good, especially for voyages.
Eighth House	Evil.
Ninth House	Indifferent. Good for journeys.
Tenth House	Good.
Eleventh House	Very good.
Twelfth House	Excellent.

"The Way" represent planning and guidance, always in relation to set goals. It's always positive if the plans and instructions are complete and sound.

Populus

Sometimes good and sometimes bad; good with good, and evil with evil.

Ascendant	Good for marriage.
Second House	Medium good.
Third House	Rather good than bad.
Fourth House	Good in all but love.
Fifth House	Good in most things.
Sixth House	Good.
Seventh House	In war good; else medium.
Eighth House	Evil.
Ninth House	Look for letters.
Tenth House	Good.
Eleventh House	Good in all.
Twelfth House	Very evil.

"The People" represents the people involved in a situation and is generally neutral.

By essential dignity is meant the strength of a figure when found in a particular house. A figure is, therefore, *strongest* when in what is called its house, *very strong* when in its exaltation, *strong* in its triplicity, *very weak in* its Fall; *weakest* of all in its detriment. A figure is in its fall when in a House opposite to that of its exaltation, and in its *detriment* when opposite to its own house.

The Geomantic figures, being attributed to the Planets and Signs, are dignified according to the rules which obtain in Astrology.* That is to say they follow the dignities of their Ruling Planets, considering the Twelve Houses of the scheme as answering to the Twelve Signs. Thus, the Ascendant or First House answers to Aries, the Second House to Taurus, the Third House to Gemini, and so on to the Twelfth answering to Pisces. Therefore the figures of Mars will be strong in the First House, but weak in the Seventh House, and so forth.

GEOMANTIC-ASTROLOGICAL RULES OF PLANETS IN SIGNS						
Name of Sign	*Ruler*	*Element*	*Exaltation*	*Fall*	*Detriment*	*Strong*
Aries	Mars	Fire	Sol	Saturn	Venus	Jupiter
Taurus	Venus	Earth	Luna	—	Mars	Jupiter
Gemini	Mercury	Air	—	—	Jupiter	Saturn
Cancer	Luna	Water	Jupiter	Mars	Saturn	Mercury
Leo	Sol	Fire	—	—	Saturn	Mars
Virgo	Mercury	Earth	Mercury	Venus	Jupiter	Saturn
Libra	Venus	Air	Saturn	Sol	Mars	Jupiter
Scorpio	Mars	Water	—	Luna	Venus	Sun
Sagittarius	Jupiter	Fire	—	—	Mercury	Venus
Capricorn	Saturn	Earth	Mars	Jupiter	Luna	Mercury
Aquarius	Saturn	Air	—	—	Sol	—
Pisces	Jupiter	Water	Venus	Mercury	Mercury	—

Caput Draconis is strong in the dignities of Jupiter and Venus.

Cauda Draconis is strong in the dignities of Saturn and Mars.

Remember always that if the figures Rubeus or Cauda Draconis fall in the Ascendant, or First House, the figure is not fit for Judgment and should be destroyed without consideration. Another figure for the question should not be erected before at least two hours have elapsed.

Your figure being thoroughly arranged as on a map of the heavens, as previously shown, note first to what house the demand belongs. Then look for the Witnesses and the Judge, as to whether the latter is favorable or otherwise, and in what particular way. Put this down.

* Note: These geomantic rules are those of *classical* astrology. Thus, the recently discovered planets Uranus, Neptune, Pluto, Chiron, etc. should not be substituted for the classical rulerships. —C.L.W.

Note next what Figure falls in the House required. Also whether it passes or springs — that is whether it is also present in any other House or Houses. These should also be considered — as for example in a question of money stolen, if the figure in the Second House be also found in the Sixth House, it might also show that the thief was a servant in the house.

Then look in the Table of Figures in the Houses and see what the figure signifies in the special House under consideration. Put this down also. Then look in the Table for the strength of the figures in that House. Following this, apply the astrological rule of aspects between houses, noting what houses are Sextile, Quintile, Square, Trine, etc. Write the "Good" on one side and the "Evil" on the other, noting also whether these figures also are "strong" or "weak," "friendly" or "unfriendly" in nature to the figure in the House required. Note that in looking up the aspects between houses, there are two directions, Dexter and Sinister. The Dexter aspect is that which is *contrary* to the natural succession of the houses; the Sinister is the reverse. The Dexter aspect is more powerful than the Sinister.

Then add the meaning of the figure in the Fourth House, which will signify the end of the matter. It may also assist you to form a Reconciler Figure from the Figure in the house required and the Judge, noting what figure results and whether it harmonizes with either or both by nature. Now consider all you have written down, and according to the balance of "good" and "evil" therein form your final judgment.

Consider also in "money" matters where the Part of Fortune falls.

For example, let us consider the figure previously set up and form a judgment for "Loss of money in business" from there.

Populus is the Judge, and we find that in questions of money, which concern the Second House, it signifies "medium good." The question as a whole is of the nature of the Second House, where we find Carcer. We then discover that Carcer here is "evil," as showing obstacles and delays. The Part of Fortune is in the Ascendant with Amissio, signifying loss through the querent's own mistake, and loss through the querent's self.

The figure of Amissio springs into no other house, therefore this does not affect the question. "Carcer" in the Second House is neither "strong" nor "weak"; its strength for evil is medium. The figures Sextile and Trine of the Second are Conjunctio, Fortuna Major, Fortuna Minor, and Acquisitio, all "good" figures, helping the matter and "friendly" in nature. This signifies well intentioned help of friends. The figures square and opposition of the Second are Fortuna Minor, Conjunctio, and Albus, which are not hostile to Carcer, therefore showing "opposition not great."

The figure in the Fourth House is Fortuna Major, which shows a good end but with anxiety. Let us now form a Reconciler between the figure of the Second House, which is Carcer, and the Judge, Populus, which produces Carcer again, a sympathetic figure, but denoting delay—delay, but helping the querent's wishes. Now let us add all these together:

1. Medium

2. Evil and Obstacles, delay.

3. Loss through querent's self.

4. Strength for evil, medium only.

5. Well-intentioned aid of friends.

6. Not much opposition from enemies.

7. Ending—good; but with anxiety.

8. Delay, but helping querent's wishes.

And we can formulate the final judgment:

That the querent's loss in business has been principally the result of his own mismanagement. That he will have a long and hard struggle, but will meet with help from friends. That his obstacles will gradually give way, and that after much anxiety he will eventually recoup himself for his former losses.

GEOMANTIC STEPS IN DIVINATION

1. If Rubeus or Cauda Draconis in Ascendant, destroy the figure.

2. Note the House to which the question belongs. See if the figure there springs into another house.

3. Form the Judge from the two Witnesses.

4. Part of Fortune—that is, if a money question.

5. See if figure in House concerned is "strong" or "weak." If it pass or spring into any other house.

6. See figures Sextile and Trine, Square and Opposition.

7. Friendly or unfriendly.

8. Note the figure in Fourth House, signifying the end or outcome.

9. Form a Reconciler from Judge and the figure in House to which the demand appertains.

Note: Although this whole instruction of Geomancy describes the process as being performed throughout on paper with a pencil, yet it should be remembered that this description is but a makeshift for the convenience of the unenterprising student. By definition, Geomancy is a scheme of divination by and through the Element of Earth. Therefore the student with initiative, to whom this method appeals, should act accordingly. Let him therefore prepare a quantity of clean and dry black earth — or desert sand, if possible, but not that taken from the seashore—and also a tray or wooden box which is to be reserved solely for the purpose of housing this consecrated earth. The outside of the box might be decorated with sigils or symbolic paintings in harmony with the general idea, and painted in the four Malkuth colors. A small slender wand, pointed to make clean sharp holes or markings, should be prepared since it will be with this instrument that the sixteen lines of dots or holes in the earth will be made. When all has been duly prepared, the box of earth should be given a ceremonial consecration; the student who has studied the general formulae of consecration will know exactly what should be done.

In actual divinatory practice, the invoking Earth Pentagram enclosing the Sigil, and the sixteen rows of dots from which the Four Mothers will be formed, can be quickly marked on the earth with this special wand or pointer. Then, for convenience's sake, the student can transfer these four primary figures to paper, calculate the remaining eight figures to be placed on the map and proceed to judgment exactly as this instruction lays down. Experience shows that the actual use of earth as a means of forming the fundamental magical link between the initiated diviner and the Geomantic divinatory genii is psychologically more valid and effectual than with paper and pencil, besides yielding far more satisfactory results. (I. R.).

THE ART OF INTERPRETATION

We have moved from simplicity to complexity, and it is up to you which form of Geomancy you will use—from the intuitive reading of a simple casting of pebbles or formations in dirt or sand to the complex and sophisticated operations that have taken up most of this chapter.

Even though the more complex process results in a single figure that can be interpreted based on the nature of the question as determined by the house meaning as given on page 278, and the related readings for the final figure, there must always be an element of intuition in all divinatory work.

"Divination" is ultimately a referral to the Divine Source of all, and the art of interpretation ultimately invokes our intuition for the final understanding of the answer to the question.

RITUAL IN ASSOCIATION WITH GEOMANCY

Earlier in this chapter we mentioned the importance of some kind of ritual, prayers or meditation. A ritual need not be elaborate—what counts is a statement to your Self and to the Universe of your intention to ask a question and look for an answer. It can be as simple as that or as elaborate as you want—so long as the elaboration doesn't get in the way! That, unfortunately is the trouble with many rituals. Instead, remember the KISS principle: *Keep It Simple Sweetheart.*

The Hermetic Order of the Golden Dawn recommended a very simple but Qaba-listically based ritual consisting of three actions:

GEOMANTIC GOLDEN DAWN RITUAL OF OPERATION

Step 1. Invoking the God ruling the Earth Element, since Geomancy is Earth-based divination.

> (You may prefer to call upon a Pagan Earth deity, or the Universal God or Source of All, or working with the aspect of God attributed to *Malkuth* on the Tree of Life. That divine name is *Adonai ha Aretz,* Lord of the Earth. This is pronounced ah-doh-nye hah-ah-retz, and softy "vibrated" in a lower than usual to you tone with a vibrating movement in the back of the throat. The awareness should be of exaltation, connecting Self with the God.)

Step 2. Tracing the invoking Earth Pentagram.

> (The invoking Earth Pentagram, a five-pointed star of interlaced lines, single point upward, is illustrated in the following diagram showing the movement of the extended arm holding the stylus or pencil used in the divination, or using your pointed index finger in one continuous, unbroken movement (1) from the top point downward to the bottom left point, and then (2) up and over to the right cross point, (3) straight across from right to the left cross point, (4) down and over to the bottom right point, and (5) completing the connecting movement up to the top point again.

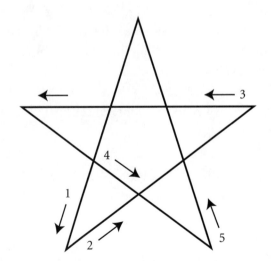

The Pentagram can be drawn either in the air before you, or circumscribed about the sandbox or work table where you are doing the divinatory work.)

Step 3. Summoning the appropriate power ruling the question being asked.

(The most difficult action involves determining which Power rules the nature of the question being asked. Refer to the table of Geomantic Attributions on pages 273–274, and from the meanings given for the Geomantic figures in the far right column select that which seems closest to the concern of your question. Then, on the same line, cross over to the two far left columns giving the Sigil and Name of the Ruler. The Sigil is to be inscribed in the center of the Pentagram while the Name of the Ruler is mentally vibrated several times.)

Just as you may utilize a simple form of Geomantic divination, so you may also keep your ritual simple. You can combine what you have learned in this chapter with a simple prayer or statement of your intent and appeal to the God and Power that you believe to be appropriate, or you can follow the Golden Dawn ritual described above. You are the Geomancer, and it is your choice.

SOURCES AND RECOMMENDED READING

Christopher Cattan, *Geomancy* (c. 1558).

Chic and Sandra Tabatha Cicero, *The Essential Golden Dawn* (Llewellyn, 2003).

Nevill Drury, *The Dictionary of the Esoteric* (Watkins, 2002).

John Michael Greer, *Earth Divination, Earth Magic: A Practical Guide to Geomancy* (Llewellyn, 1999).

John Michael Greer, *The New Encyclopedia of the Occult* (Llewellyn, 2003).

Carl Jung, *Modern Man in Search of a Soul* (Harcourt, 1933).

Israel Regardie, *Practical Guide to Geomantic Divination* (Aquarian, 1972).

Israel Regardie, *The Golden Dawn—the Original Account of the teachings, Rites & Ceremonies of the Hermetic Order,* 6th revised and corrected ed. (Llewellyn, 1989).

Priscilla Schwei and Ralph Pestka, *The Complete Book of Astrological Geomancy—The Master Divination System of Cornelius Agrippa* (Llewellyn, 1990).

Stephen Skinner, *Geomancy in Theory & Practice* (Golden Hoard, 2010).

Bill Whitcomb, *The Magician's Companion* (Llewellyn, 1993).

21

WHAT YOUR HANDWRITING SAYS ABOUT YOU

THE TWO POWERS OF DIVINATION

In an age when handwriting has all but been replaced by the computer and the smart phone, even among young children, you may well ask why we have a chapter on handwriting analysis (also called "graphology") in a book on psychic empowerment.

This section of the book is primarily concerned with the "tools" of divination which, for most people, mean ways to answer questions about past and future by means of Tarot cards, Runes, the I Ching, Dowsing, Geomancy, etc. These Tools complement the Techniques (Aura Reading, Dream Interpretation, Clairvoyance, etc.) of the first section, and often the tools "partner with" particular techniques. Certainly reading the Tarot invites and develops your Clairvoyant skills.

Throughout the book we've made two points:

THE TWO POWERS OF DIVINATION

1. The power of divination is not in the "tool" but in the different way in which each divinatory method calls upon the subconscious mind and organizes a segment of the conscious mind, building a semi-permanent "channel" between the two. This facilitates the process of Psychic Empowerment, and as such becomes Self-Empowerment.

2. Each system, and thus each tool, becomes a means to self-understanding, i.e. knowledge about Self, which in turn is creating a structure bringing Self into union with the Soul.

Sure, absolutely, divination is *also* a practical means to understanding the circumstances of the moment and from that determining a course of beneficial action for yourself, your family, your business, even for your community and your country. We don't call it "fortune telling," but for all practical purposes divination can become an important part of your "fortune *building*"—acting to improve your life in all aspects, including career, financial management, relationships, spiritual communication, and much more. But, your greatest fortune is in structuring and empowering the Whole Person to become fully integrated with the Soul.

This thought deserves some further development. Think of the Soul as an immense and preexistent entity that is the "super you," while the "familiar, everyday, you" is a temporary entity being structured and enlarged by the lessons and experiences of life after life to eventually become a suitable home for the Soul. Then, union is possible. There are many different names for this, including *Ascension, Becoming One, the Divine Marriage, Glorification, Grace,* etc.

HANDWRITING AS A METHOD OF COMMUNICATION AND RECORDING

As recently as a half-century ago, *Handwriting Analysis* was a scientific method of character study used to determine a candidate's suitability for a job, in psychological testing and analysis, for career guidance, as a forensic aid in criminal investigations, in considering relationship probabilities, in determining honesty in response to questions, and even in medical diagnostics.

Before the dominance of the computer in communication, children were taught penmanship and the art of writing. Even though most schools used the Palmer method of repetitive copying exercises, every child's handwriting was quickly seen to be a unique expression of individuality.

Even expert forgery can be detected by expert handwriting analysis.

Fast forward to today. Yes, children are still taught to write, but there is less emphasis on penmanship because we all know that it is no longer the pen that does the talking. Communication is facilitated by the use of keyboards of various sizes and degrees of mechanical or touch interaction. Some communication is facilitated by dictation software, translating speech into words on the screen and duplicating the action of the keyboard, and some devices translate words on the screen into audible speech to aid the sight-handicapped. Some e-book readers will read a book aloud if you choose.

In the final analysis, most communication, record keeping, data retention and storage, and everything related to information technology is digitalized and facilitated either by the "smart" phone in its various incarnations or the "electronic" keyboard.

HANDWRITING TODAY

While some personal identification techniques are by means of digitalized finger-prints and eyeball views, and other times by e-mail addresses and passwords, we still mostly sign checks, contracts, and reports with a handwritten signature. And we often make handwritten notes of conversations over the phone and during meetings. And, some people *doodle.* Also, many people write affirmative statements beginning with a strong "I."

In all of this, the signature, the handwritten "I," and the doodle remain as strong methods of self-identification and self-expression—and hence of *Self*-Analysis.

Analysis leads to understanding, and understanding provides an avenue for self-improvement. As humans, we have to accept that we are not *finished* products but are beings in the process of *becoming more than we are.* Self-improvement is our job and our obligation. Given Vision, Choice, and Will, we become partners in the continuing evolution of the human being, both as individual persons, as members of our human community, and of universal consciousness. We are not alone, but it is as the lone individual that we have the power to grow, and then "alone and together" we have the power to evolve.

This recognition has moved from the metaphysical to the scientific. Dennis Bushnell, NASA's chief research scientist at its Langley Center, has written: "Humans are now responsible for the evolution of nearly everything, including themselves… The ultimate impact of all this upon human society will be massive and could 'tip' in several directions" (speech at World Futurist Society's Annual Conference, July 8, 2010).

In addition to handwriting analysis, there is a more recent application called "Graphotherapy," in which deliberate changes made in handwriting are used to change attitude, behavior, and self-image, and even bring about physiological changes. Sentences structured around the personal pronoun "I" are not only positive affirmations energizing change, but also provide visual feedback of the changes affected over time.

It is not our intent to provide a full course in either handwriting analysis or graphotherapy as counseling techniques, but we do want to provide a basis for self-study and personal application.

We perceive our study of handwriting in five divisions.

THE MAIN ELEMENTS OF HANDWRITING ANALYSIS

1. The analysis of handwritten sentences and paragraphs, mainly in personal notes.

2. The analysis of handwritten signatures as commonly used to legally affirm a contract, transfer funds, and to confirm or acknowledge the details of a report.

3. The analysis of the energy embodied in the written pronoun "I" as in statements of affirmation, promise, and commitment, often used in self-hypnosis.

4. The analysis of handwritten affirmative statements as a baseline, and then the modification of particular elements to change mental, emotional, and physical states.

5. The analysis of hand-drawn shapes, figures, symbols, and patterns known as "doodles."

While the study of all these forms of handwriting has indeed developed in a scientific manner rather than as a psychic power, we also want to emphasize that the general rules of its practice conform to common sense to a greater extent than nearly any other form of divination, and in its present form it does call upon the subconscious mind and psychic perception.

It is a situation benefiting less from study and more from practice and observation than any other of our subjects. You, and you alone, are the best subject for this and our entire approach is toward your personal psychic empowerment, and hence self-empowerment.

If you want to study graphology further, there are references provided at the end of the chapter.

HANDWRITING ANALYSIS

First of all, handwriting refers only to *writing* and only rarely to hand *printing*. Your writing sample is most likely to be a note taken at a meeting or as a summary of a phone or other conversation; the more spontaneous it was, the better. Look at the whole sample like a picture in a frame; turn it sideways, upside down, from the back side, any way you want. Your analysis starts with simple observation and your impressions: *Is it orderly, neat, messy, unbalanced, heavy?* Write down your impressions. *Does the writing appear fluid or rigid, natural or stilted? Is it balanced and symmetrical? Is the use of white space harmonious? Does the writing feel rhythmic?* Write your impressions.

As you notice different factors that seem unusual, write the same thing yourself (even if you wrote the note originally) and see how it feels. Write your impressions.

Zones

Handwriting analysts break the handwriting into zones. We are not going to give you complete instructions, but there will be enough so that you will understand the process, and have enough both to apply common sense and to call upon your intuition for a complete impression. In all divinatory work, it is essential to write down the steps you have taken and note your observations and impressions. You will want to review them later so that you see the whole and are not swayed by the last few observations. Remember: you are your own best subject for study and your own best counselor for growth. You are your own best scientist, and the growth you yourself achieve contributes to universal consciousness.

Zones are the portions occupying the main area of the writing, and then those above and below, and are viewed symbolically for the energies expended in particular areas of the writer's life. All references are to uncapitalized letters.

All letters occupy the middle zone, while b, d, h, i, k, l, and t extend into the upper zone and g, j, p, q, y, and z extend into the lower zone; occupying two zones, these letters are called bizonal. The f is considered trizonal, occupying all three zones. Most capital letters are bizonal using the middle and upper zones except for J, Y, and Z which are trizonal.

It is essential to remind you that no matter how *objective* an analytical factor might seem, our observation of that factor is essentially *subjective.* In other words, don't get carried away by the seeming opportunity to micromeasure the extent a letter reaches into the upper or lower zone, the line or word spacing, the exact angle of a letter slant, or the depth of the writer's pressure upon the paper. Instead—and this applies equally to the analysis of your own writing and that of others—observe and *feel* what these things are saying to you.

Upper Zone identifies with the superconscious mind—the mental, spiritual, political, and intangible areas of life.

Middle Zone identifies with the conscious mind—the mundane matters of daily life, with social relationships, and conscious choices.

the more
of the US
in flocks

several things at the

Lower Zone identifies with the sub-conscious mind—the basic biological drives and desires, sex and sensuality, sports, and material matters of money and consumer comforts.

ything, work, play,
T, whatever you

Luckily,

outbursts

day has been going far

too long

In

an opportunity
people and

of my

going south

Now, just because a written sample has a lot of g's, j's, p's, q's, and y's, we do not have an indication of an extremely sexual person—after all, we are all sexual beings and our language is filled with these particular letters. However, the height, depth, pressure, and other factors may give us a *subjective* feeling about the person's sexual interests. But remember that all teenagers and younger adults are extremely interested in sex, and so let common sense enter into your analysis. By practicing with your own handwriting samples you will better appreciate the subtleties involved in analysis.

As the writer's b's, d's, h's, and other letters reach into the upper zone, we will again learn not to overreach in our analysis to declare the writer a mental genius or spiritual guru. Observe and note your feelings, and learn as you practice on your own writing samples.

Returning again to the *upper zone,* it is a concentration or emphasis or a lack of it that relates how the writer addresses those areas in his life. Extremes that show departures from the ordinary in writing style are reflected in the writer's actions, thoughts, and feelings about science, politics, spirituality, philosophy, etc., and indicate degrees of abstractness, imagination, creativity, and fantasy. Large, full, upper-zone letters generally indicate a thoughtful and imaginative approach to these interests.

Back to the *middle zone*—it is how the letters are written, accentuated, shaped, and placed that relates to the writer's mundane life. If they seem to carry more weight than letters in the upper and lower zones, it may indicate a particular interest and action in social relationships rather than in the "higher" intellectual and spiritual aspects or the "lower" material drives.

In contrast, smaller, less-accentuated letters (in relation to those in the upper or lower zones) suggests neglect of mundane matters (clothing, appearance, health, diet, home, etc.).

While the *lower zone* contains the lower extensions of bizonal letters, and "f," it is extremes in length or boldness of weight that may indicate that more attention is given to the biological drives. Extremes in pressure indicate the intensity of desire; extremes in the slant reflect the frequency of need; and in width the amount of thought involved.

Full, long, and wide lower loops signal an active imagination and probably a gregarious nature; possibly someone who likes being "seen," such as an actor, athlete, or news anchor. Unusual lower loop formations suggest eccentricity or repression. Very short lower loops suggest a disregard for basic drives and the material world.

Again, experiment. Try writing in these different ways and check your feelings. Ask others to let you see their notes of a conversation you've shared. Practice, and test your observations.

Baseline Slant

This reflects the writer's emotional state and the extremes of optimism or pessimism. If the writing sample runs parallel to the top and bottom of the paper, he is probably reliable, even tempered, in control of his emotions, and acts reasonably. When the baseline of the writing sample slants upward to the right, the writer is probably optimistic, joyful, invigorated, and feeling loved. When the baseline slants downward to the right, the writer probably feels pessimistic, fatigued, depressed, and may be feeling ill or unloved.

Yesterday was day. I had p I went farming

I've changed since

me to a stable and we
horse back riding.

is coming to
The weather is

Writing has both

Letter Slant

This relates to the writer's emotional direction and degree of emotional control. A vertical slant suggests the head controls the heart, and that the writer has a matter-of-fact approach to life and is able to control emotions in critical situations.

A moderate right slant shows confidence, extroversion, and affection, but an extreme right slant suggests a lack of self-control, impulsiveness, intensity, and super sensitivity.

A moderate left slant shows a reflective nature, one who is objective and independent, and perhaps is inhibited, choosy, and lacking in self-expression. Irregular slanting shows the writer to be unpredictable and uncommitted.

Letter Size

This projects the writer's self-importance and claim to space; vertical height shows striving for stature; horizontal shows the amount of "elbow room" needed. A tall letter suggests the writer is ambitious and farsighted. Wide letters may show lack of discipline, sociability, and tactfulness. Small letters show someone who is analytical, modest, thrifty, and meticulous. Narrow letters suggest restriction, conservatism, inhibition, timidity, and perhaps a suspicious nature. Irregularity in size reveals moodiness, unpredictability, and a vivacious and excitable nature.

*Insistance upon
coping with gray*

*Each meeting
in cyclic*

*family members
master my*

here is what we are doing

oriental culture.

I especially like

Pressure

This relates to the intensity and depth of feeling. Heavy pressure indicates an intense personality, strong determination, creative power, and strong libido and vitality. Extreme heavy pressure may reveal poorly channeled energy, pain, and lack of outlet. Lightness shows resistance to commitment, a desire to avoid friction, and a sensitive and tender nature.

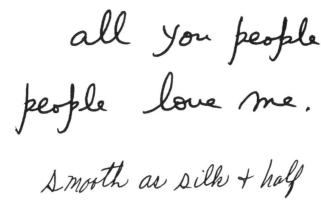

all you people
people love me.

Smooth as silk + half

Connecting Strokes

This reveals the writer's attitude toward others. There are four main types of connection:

THE FOUR MAIN TYPES OF CONNECTING STROKES

1. *Garland* is a rounded, cuplike connecting stroke. The deeper the garland cup, the more receptive the writer. The garland writer avoids conflict, and is adaptable, kind, and sympathetic—a good listener.

I feel like I'm
the air.

2. *Arcade* is like an umbrella—the more arched the stroke, the more artistic and protective the writer. The arcade writer places importance on appearance, lacks spontaneity, and is shy and reserved, formal and individualistic.

will be a short ceremony
warmth and love. I am

3. *Angular* suggests contraction and release. The angular writer is goal oriented and driven.

is on par with
with their feet.

4. *Thread* shows a writer's commitment to self with an intuitive capacity to attain a temporary identification with other people's feelings but more as a chameleon than genuine empathy.

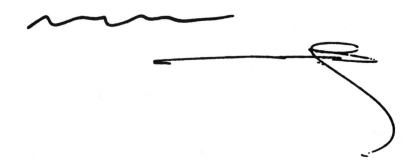

WHAT LETTER SPACING REVEALS

Letter Spacing

This reveals the writer's expression: introversion, extroversion, repression. Close spacing shows a writer who feels crowded and who is repressed, inhibited, scared, and resentful. Wide spacing shows a person who is sympathetic, extroverted, and understanding.

Word Spacing

This reveals the writer's degree of contact with the immediate environment. Small spaces show a desire to maintain close and constant relations with others. They show extroversion, impulsiveness, and spontaneity. Large spaces show a need for elbow room and are indicative of a critical and cautious nature, someone who is opinionated and isolationist and wants "to be left alone." Very large spaces show a person who is egotistical and inconsiderate.

Even spaces show a writer at ease with people, and who is reasonable, self-confident, well-balanced, and disinclined toward adventure. Uneven spaces reflect insecurity, difficulty with communications, and lacking spontaneity.

> Change is difficult.
> lose my cat last week.

> ane plant in my living
> the ceiling, so I guess

> The river is my
> home and I love it.

> Try to forget you're the
> yourself into the composer.

Line Spacing

This reveals the writer's sense of direction and order. Narrow spacing shows a person who is thrifty and frugal, who lacks reserve and makes decisions hastily. Even spacing shows a writer who is systematic, orderly, and a good planner. Wide spacing shows objectivity, good organization, and mental agility—but if too wide, there may be separation from reality. Overlapping lines show overinvolvement with activities and a lack of control.

THE MEANING OF MARGINS

Margins

This reveals the writer's relationship to the world as expressed in economy, consistency, tolerance, desire for esteem, and urge for acceptance.

Well-spaced margins show good organization and an intelligent arrangement of time and space.

Wide upper margins give a sense of formality and respect for the reader.

Narrow upper margins lack formality and indicate a lack of respect for the reader.

Widening left margins, going from top to bottom, show impatience, haste, enthusiasm, and impulsiveness.

Narrowing left margins show shyness and a lack of spontaneity. An even left margin shows self-discipline and good manners.

A wide left margin shows high standards, self-respect, and a sense of culture.

A narrow left margin shows familiarity, desire for popularity, economy, and practicality.

A narrowing right margin shows a decreasing shyness.

An even right margin suggests intolerance, conformity, rigidity, and anxiety.

A narrow right margin shows gregariousness, impulsiveness, the desire for close relationships, and a desire for acceptance.

A wide right margin shows one who is overly sensitive, unrealistic, aloof, wasteful, and fearful of the future.

Margins that are narrow on all sides suggest stinginess, tactlessness, and even morbidity, but also the potential for unlimited sympathy, hospitality, and kindness. (Sometimes you have to throw up your hands and say "Go figure," but there is always a problem with a "dictionary" of answers and always we need to call upon our subconscious mind to see what the situation really is.)

Margins that are wide on all sides show someone who is lonely, withdrawn, aloof, and secretive. Irregular margins on all sides show versatility and tolerance, and one who is disorganized, careless, and inattentive.

WHAT LETTER FORMATIONS REVEAL

Letter Formations

Individual letters can reflect considerable character tendencies, but vary considerably even within a single writing sample. The following are just a few examples that once again illustrate that applying common sense to the style and appearance of the writing sample can suggest very meaningful interpretation. The *writing* says it all, regardless of the message.

Upper case written as large lower case. Generally indicates modesty and the desire to simplify.

Upper case written narrow. Symbolically squeezed, suggests a shy, reserved, inhibited person.

Upper case "printed." Simple and unadorned, it signifies clear and straightforward thinking.

Sharp angles. Strokes that stop and change direction generally signify resentment or irresolution, often critical, rigid, and self-proclaimed as realistic and clever.

Fussy and ornate. Ostentatious and vulgar, hiding behind an elaborate façade.

Arc stroke back to left. Irresponsibility.

Tall and narrow. The stroke for lower-case letters reaches into the upper zone to indicate idealism.

Ovals open at top. Talkative and open about self.

Ovals that are closed. Secretive about self.

Ovals closed and tied to the left. Has trouble facing truth about self.

Upper loops large and full. Thoughtful and imaginative.

Pointed tops. Curious, probing.

Lower loops long and full. Gregarious and involved.

Lower loops that are triangular. Tension.

Retracing. Tension. Perhaps not sure.

Missing details—like undotted "i" or uncrossed "t." Wants to skip details in life.

Unfinished letters. Doesn't finish things.

Precise. Precise—just like it looks.

Printing, instead of writing. Independent.

Evenly balanced "f." Good organizer.

Rounded "s." Pushover.

Sharp peak "s." Stubborn.

Open oval on "e." Broadminded.

High, full loop on "p." Likes to argue.

WHAT THE HANDWRITTEN SIGNATURE HAS TO SAY

The signature is still commonly used to legally affirm a contract, transfer funds with a bank check, and to confirm or acknowledge the details of a report.

While most of the rules of handwriting analysis can be applied to the written signature, it is necessary to consider that the personal signature is often deliberately created as a public representation of the self. In some European cultures, the signature often resembles a "seal" as a symbolic representative of the identity and authority of the person. In other cases, the written name is condensed into a kind of sigil, almost like the writer's initials.

In most English and North American instances, the signature is a pretty straightforward writing of the person's name as they prefer to be known, including a middle name or middle initial. Other common cases combine the name or names and initial into a single ideogram surrounded by an upper and/or lower flourish or underline.

Once again, we have three zones and all the other factors of handwriting analysis to consider, but with an ever greater opportunity to call upon the imagination and the subconscious mind to clarify the picture.

Look at your own signature and ask yourself what you are saying about yourself. It is the public image that presents to the world legally, financially, and personally. Look at all the elements we discussed about Handwriting Analysis in previous paragraphs, and single them out and write them down.

Is your signature just your name, or is it more assertive than how you identify yourself on the telephone or in an e-mail? When you include a middle name, or a maiden name, in your signature, what are you saying that is beyond your simple identity? Do you surround your signature with protective flourishes, or assert it with a single stroke beneath? Instead of your entire name, do you abbreviate it with just the last name and the initials of your first name and perhaps middle name?

Write them all down and ask why you chose that as your signature, and then whether you still like it. You may not find it easy to change a signature without causing some confusion at your bank, or the IRS, or other organizations, but even without making official changes, recognize that your projected self-image may have changed over the years.

Generally speaking, you can apply the same technique to the analysis of another person's signature, while recognizing that while the signature may be frozen in time, the person is not.

There is one further area of handwriting analysis, often confined to just signatures, and that is examination of samples to determine the question of forgery. Because the signature is an emphatic presentation of self to the public, and is usually "frozen" for a lifetime, it does have minute details that can be measured and compared, and the opinion of a professional graphologist has legal standing. To become a professional takes study and certification, just like any other profession.

THE PERSONAL PRONOUN "I" AND THE PRIVATE YOU

Analysis of the Pronoun "I"

The written "I" is most commonly used in statements of affirmation, promise, and commitment, and often used in self-hypnosis. So let us take "the case of the Private I," because this use of the pronoun is not a presentation of the public you, but of the personal, private you.

You are now your own "Private I." Yes, of course the analysis can be applied to another person's "I" statements, but we start our study with you.

Write a positive affirmative sentence starting with "I" such as *I am an independent woman!* Now that sentence is making a strong statement about yourself, and the "I" really contains all the energy of your affirmation.

Now, let yourself feel what that "I" is really saying. Are you really saying that you are an independent woman, or are you saying that you want to become an independent woman? See if you can write two identical statements but each one expressing one or the other of these meanings, and then look carefully at the pronoun. There should be a difference, or perhaps you are not being honest with yourself.

Write a negative statement: *I am not your doormat!* That statement is also strongly independent, but the "I" feels different. Does it look different? Change the statement: *I am no longer your doormat!* Does that "I" look different, and did writing it feel different?

Now try a different kind of affirmation, and write: *I am a slim person at my perfect weight.* Note how the emphasis shifted a bit from the simple "I" to the more complex "I am" as used in self-hypnosis affirmations.

If you can, first write that sentence while feeling that you are actually overweight and feeling that the statement is a lie; then write it again while feeling that you are creating a new self-image of your ideal weight that is what you know you will become through continued self-affirmation. And, if you have experience with self-hypnosis, write that sentence while you repeat it as you slip into a trance.

With all these practice examples, you have enough experience to not only analyze your "Private I" but to use it in a therapeutic manner. As you noticed the differences in feeling while writing the same sentence, first with mild assertion and doubt, and then with determination and confidence, practice writing it every day with absolute determination that you are that person. Use that "I" as your personal talisman.

In Graphotherapy with the Pronoun "I"

What we have done is to start with a statement of affirmation as a baseline, and then modify particular elements to change mental, emotional, and physical states.

There are graphotherapists who can work with you, but you can be your own best therapist if you will combine your new analytic skills with determination to make desired changes. You can also combine what you have learned with self-hypnosis, which will be discussed in another chapter.

The Analysis of Doodles

The analysis of doodles is both too complex and too simple for development in this chapter. Doodles have been examined intensely by several therapeutic schools, and are a feature of association work. Sometimes it does take a second party, a therapist, to lead you to revealing the truths that may be hidden in those simple drawings in which we believe the subconscious was expressing some things perhaps hidden from the conscious mind. That is a job for a professional.

But most of the time, your doodle was done semiconsciously rather than unconsciously, and most of the time you know exactly what you were doing and what you meant. Perhaps you were bored in a meeting, and drew pictures of the other people. Perhaps you were daydreaming about a particular person of romantic interest. Some doodles are perfectly obvious, like dollar signs when you are thinking about money.

Understanding doodles is usually a matter of common sense. Nevertheless, they can reveal your concerns and desires. Seeing them for what they say brings the subconscious elements forward into consciousness, and they may tell you something you were not fully aware of.

Handwriting analysis, like every divinatory tool, can be your bridge between the mundane world and the secret world of meanings that can expand your consciousness and empower you to become the Whole Being you are intended to be.

Write? No, I mean Right!

SOURCES AND RECOMMENDED READING

Dennis Bushnell, speech at World Futurist Society Annual Conference, July 8, 2010.

Paul de Sainte Columbe, *Grapho-Therapeutics: Pen and Pencil Therapy* (Laurida Books, 1966).

Ruth Gardner, *A Graphology Student's Workbook: A Workbook for Group Instruction or Self Study* (Llewellyn, 1973, 1975).

Ruth Gardner, *Instant Handwriting Analysis: A Key to Personal Success* (Llewellyn, 1989, 1991).

Ruth Gardner, *The Truth About Graphology* (Llewellyn, 1991).

Jane Nugent Green, *You & Your Private I: Graphological Analysis focused on the Personal Pronoun I* (Llewellyn, 1975, 1983).

P. Scott Hollander, *Reading Between the Lines: The Basics of Handwriting Analysis* (Llewellyn, 1991).

22

THE I CHING

When the Moment Is Right

In all things, "timing is the key to success," and when the moment changes,
so will its nature. When the moment is right, the "rainbow bridge"
connects heaven and earth, placing the forces of Yin and Yang in perfect balance.
Such balance becomes the foundation for right action.

The Superior Man creates number and measure,
And examines the nature of Virtue and Correct Conduct.

—HEXAGRAM 60

What's the weather for tomorrow? Is it going to be a tough winter? Should I become a soldier in the Emperor's army? Should I accept the marriage proposal from the man my father has chosen for me? Will it be a good year? Will my husband return home?

Questions about the future occur early in humanity's growth and development. And each culture develops a unique approach to the invention (discovery, or gift from the gods) of a unique divinatory, and magical, methodology reflective of the culture's early history and concerns. While it is always recorded for us in the mythology—and sometimes in the religious tradition as well—of the culture, it usually has two stages of development. It moves from the discovery phase into a mature phase that becomes fully established and practiced by the society's political and religious leaders.

Chinese culture is ancient—one of the oldest, if not *the* oldest, civilization in the world. It is also amazing that as the most populous nation on Earth, the culture has extended to the farthest reaches of the land.

VIRTUE AND CORRECT CONDUCT

Every historical culture is dominated by particular themes that are part of daily life throughout all social classes, and it is these themes that are the primary focus of their divinatory and magical practices.

Chinese thought is concerned with Virtue and Correct Conduct, and divination is performed to determine the right course of action. The *I Ching* is not a fortune-telling system, but a way to examine the *nature of the moment* to determine right conduct.

"Correct Conduct" is not always the most personally beneficial action, but it is the *right thing to do*—ethically, practically, and "spiritually" in the cosmic scheme of things. But, as in all things, "timing is the key to success," and when the moment changes, so will its nature. *When the moment is right*, the "rainbow bridge" connects heaven and earth, placing the forces of Yin and Yang in perfect balance. Such balance becomes the foundation for right action.

The old adage that "Patience is a Virtue" is correct: Wait for the right moment to act. It's like a *Zen* moment: Be prepared, be ready, draw the arrow back from the bow—but wait until your inner sense says to let it fly to its target. Then, it and you will be "on target."

There are two different kinds of divination: one that *divines* for self-knowledge and the other that *divines* for self-action. One is to Know. The other is to Act. Behind each is the inner Divinity that is at the core of right understanding and right action.

As we will see, from Unity comes Duality—Yin and Yang—but Yin and Yang always manifest together as a Trinity, revealed in the *Trigram*. Within the duality there is always some contained *changing* movement, a *rhythm*—a rhythm that can be quickened into movement and manifestation through prayer and ritual. Our trigrams, again, function in duality as two trigrams become one *Hexagram*. The Hexagram is balanced by the element that is the Person for whom the I Ching is thrown to become a *reading* or mythic message.

Louis Culling considered the I Ching (also called Yi King) to be "the greatest Magick Oracle ever given to man." Even though it is Chinese in origin, and is found in some of the earliest myths and written histories, Culling strongly believed the I Ching was *beyond* "Chinese in thought, but is universal, ageless, and as 'modern' as today's English language." Some of this chapter is adapted from Culling's short classic, the *L.R.I. I Ching,* which he wrote in 1966 for Life Resources Institute, later purchased by Llewellyn Worldwide, Ltd.

Chinese civilization is one of the oldest where we've had deep scholarly study of myth and written history reaching back several thousand years. Chinese political thinking has explored all the issues of government and people that still occupy modern man, and Chinese studies of the human body—both physical and energetic—are among the most sophisticated and comprehensive in the history of medicine and the foundation of the various schools of traditional medicine and martial arts. Their studies of the natural foundations of relationships between man and woman, of families, of communities and government, and nearly every aspect of moral and ethical philosophy are still being explored.

The *I Ching* is an ancient Chinese oracle, and probably the oldest book in existence. The word "Ching" itself originally meant the warp of a fabric and came to symbolize the idea that written texts are *threads* composing guides to morality and right behavior. The famous ethical philosopher, Confucius, had profound praise for the I Ching. It is believed that actual experience with the I Ching was the source for both Confucianism and Taoism, and for many other schools of Eastern wisdom.

The I Ching began thousands of years ago (3322 BCE) with Fu-Hsi, a brilliant Chinese sage and scholar looked upon as practically a god because of his many innovative inventions and teachings. He is credited with originating a calendar, musical instruments, Chinese hieroglyphics, farming procedures, and instituting a patriarchal society to better meet the challenges of those times.

But most important, he made known the *eight Pa Kua*, the trigrams that are the very heart of the I Ching.

These linear figures held the golden keys to the mystery of divination. Two thousand years after Fu-Hsi, during the Chou Dynasty—a time of great developments in literature, agriculture, invention, education, industry, commerce, and culture—Wen Wang (1142 BCE) studied Fu-Hsi's eight Pau Kua and conditioned each trigram against each other trigram. Thus, he formulated the sixty-four Hexagrams into the "Book of Changes" that is the *I Ching* we know today, and which Lou Culling called "the oldest yet most modern and even futuristic in the world. Here is the ancient measure of personal 'physics' and abstract of changing nature, the modern key to 'programming' human intuition and insight and relating them to the flow of today's worldly events."

The premise of the I Ching is that all things on every level of existence—past, present, and future—are interrelated, and constantly changing and transforming. The past is in the present, for the past is the present's base and influence. The seeds of the future are in the present, and the future's roots are in the past. However, even though all things are constantly changing, a given moment in time may be isolated and its unique characteristics determined.

Carl Jung called this the "synchronistic concept" of the universe. Since the exact circumstances of a moment can occur only once, this becomes *legible* by means of the hexagram form. As the moment is, so do the thrown sticks or coins or dice or shuffled cards fall because they have the quality of that moment alone, a visible summation of all things past and present. The function of divination is to understand past and present in order to foresee the future, drawing from the unconscious to the conscious mind whatever is needed to understand the question asked and provide its solution.

But, *what is the purpose of the solution?*

The I Ching illuminates the conditions surrounding the seeker's question and the reading indicates the action desirable at that critical time. Out of the cycles of chance and changes of nature, the desired action is the querent's Correct Conduct. The purpose of divination is strictly personal. That is why the best person to do the divination is the person for whom it is intended. When you turn to a "professional" consultant, you are bypassing the most important role of your own subconscious mind—the one who knows all about you and who cares most for your well-being. *The object of all psychic development is self-empowerment: Self for Self.*

HOW IT WORKS!

The mechanism of the oracle is this: the eight basic trigrams symbolize all that is knowable to mankind, spiritually and physically. Because the trigrams are symbols of all that is in the midst of a state of change, the trigrams are true representations of life itself. Your trigram throw is yours alone, whether you use ancient yarrow sticks or alternative divinatory tools such as cards, coins, chess, or dice. (However, we believe that computerized throws are to be avoided and that *only* manual manipulation is productive.)

We also want to note that the throw with yarrow sticks is a slow, methodical, and somewhat tedious process leading to a kind of altered state of consciousness. This should be duplicated by slowly manipulating your chosen tools while mentally or vocally repeating the question several times, and doing the throw only when you feel "the moment is right."

As a modern student of the I Chin, you will learn the amazing discovery of the ancients based on the eight Pa Kua. You will learn the mastery of life's problems through divination. Your future *is* in your hands.

INSTRUCTIONS

The foundations of the I Ching cosmology are two great forces, the Yang and the Yin. In all Nature it is the interplay of Positive and Negative, Active and Passive, that is constant. Yin and Yang, Yang and Yin, these are the two co-equal cooperating complements operating in all Nature, animate and inanimate. The Yang starts and projects; the Yin nourishes and sustains. If either one did not exist, there would be no meaning for the other. Thus, each manifests its opposite. Below, the Yang and Yin are shown with their balancing opposites:

YIN AND YANG, AND BALANCING OPPOSITES	
YANG ———	*YIN* — —
Force of Sun	Nourishment of Earth
Lingam	Yoni
Male	Female
Projecting	Receiving
Active	Passive
Aspiration	Inspiration
Awake	Asleep
Beginning	Responding
Brilliance	Reflected Light
Centripetal Force	Centrifugal Force
Day	Night
Developing	Sustaining
Directed Will	Desire
Directing	Following
Extrovert	Introvert
Hard	Soft
Hot	Cold
Initiating	Sustaining and Completing
Leading	Following
Mid-day	Midnight
Point of Activity	Great Capacity
Salty, bitter	Sweet
Starting	Developing
Summer	Winter
Sun	Moon
Will	Emotion

Never are Yang and Yin to be regarded as antagonistic; they are co-equal and co-operating partners in the basic concept. There can be no manifestation without the union of the two Great Principles, just as there could be no offspring without the union of male and female.

Yang and Yin lines (— and — —) compose a trigram. Fu-Hsi based his eight Pa Kua trigrams on the triune principle of Body, Mind, and Soul. The bottom line is the body and automatic emotions. The middle line is the thinking man, mind, and intellect. The top line is the soul, spirit, and one's intuitive wisdom. The following table shows this in more detail:

TRIUNE PRINCIPLE OF BODY, MIND, AND SOUL
IN THE TRIGRAM

1. The Bottom Line Position: The physical body; the lower instinctive actions; the automatic or uncontrolled emotions. Also the drive to action.

2. Central Line Position: The Mind, or Thinking Man; Intelligence; the more or less consciously self-directing Mind. Conscious Will.

3. Top Line Position: Inspired direction, Wisdom. The highest inspiration, thinking, and action of Man.

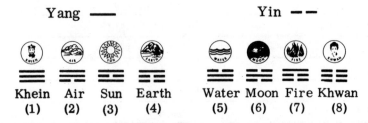

Diagram of the eight emanations (eight Pa Kua Trigrams) of Fu His from Tao-Teh

EIGHT EMANATIONS

Note how Yang dominates the first four trigrams, i.e. the top line is Yang, and then Yin gradually dominates in the second four.

Now the line positions of the Hexagram have added significance and correspondences, depending upon whether the lower or the upper trigram is being considered. The lower trigram is called 'the Inferior,' and the upper 'the Superior,' and this should be taken quite literally. The Superior trigram describes everything or every person which may be 'superior' to the consultant, while the Inferior trigram relates to any 'inferior' person or thing. For instance, any dealings with one's 'boss' relate to the upper trigram. Also, the Superior trigram often speaks of what the Chinese call 'The

Great One' or 'The Great Man', that is, one's Higher Self or a reflection of it in wisdom and direction.

There is one Great Key, and only one, to the interpretation of each of the sixty-four hexagrams in relation to any question or to any consultant. This Key is the right comprehension of the meaning of each of the eight trigrams, plus the special implications of the trigram's position in the hexagram, upper or lower. You should be able to deduce the meanings of the hexagrams as applied in any question that may be asked, simply by considering the nature of each trigram and the special meanings of its position in the hexagram.

By placing yourself in touch with the flow of universal energies through the random draw, you will find your place in the scheme of things—at this moment. The I Ching is not so much predictive as revealing of your circumstance if you continue to follow the path you are on. The interpretation will suggest ways to realign yourself with the deeper harmony.

THREE GREAT PRINCIPLES AND THE LINE POSITIONS

In Alchemy, we see three great principles called **Salt, Sulfur, and Mercury**. In the physical world, the three great principles are **Activity, Substance, and Form**: a carpenter (Activity) works upon wood (Substance) and produces a house (Form).

On the plane of living Nature, the Ego (top line position) works upon an organism or body (lower line) to produce an intelligent, thinking person (central line). This finally resolves down to these facts: the lower line position is the body and the automatic desires and emotions. The upper line position is the Superior Wisdom and the higher will, and the central line is the conscious, thinking man.

Two trigrams combine together in a six-line figure, the hexagram, and each trigram exerts an influence upon the other. Within the hexagram there is an Upper Trigram Position and a Lower Trigram Position.

Here are the Key Word meanings of each Trigram.

KEYWORDS OF EIGHT TRIGRAMS

#1 Khien.

The Great or higher will. Starting or initiating, projecting, masculine. It directs and leads and never follows. If in the upper trigram, it is "The Great One." If in the lower trigram, it does not easily accept an inferior position.

#2 Air.

Easily penetrating and easily penetrated. If in the upper trigram, it is the mind or mental concept, the dominant 'idea.' If in lower trigram, like air, it has no solid substance and is therefore, at times, insubstantial, small, and short lasting.

#3 Sun.

Brilliance, Realization, Capability, Union, Self-integrated Intelligence. In a general way, it is the best trigram. In the upper trigram, it is receptive to good and rejective to bad, but fair, amiable, and noble. In the lower trigram, there is a lack of intelligent guidance.

#4 Earth.

Body, Matter, Stable. In the upper trigram, it is good for consolidating things. In the lower trigram, it is fixed and immovable, materialistic, and stubborn.

#5 Water.

Placid still water: pleasure, satisfaction, complacency. In the upper trigram, there are no great demands, no forward push. In the lower trigram, it is self-indulgent, lacking ambition, and too easy-going.

#6 Moon.

A deep gorge of rushing water: hence danger or peril. Restriction, incapable, immature. Sometimes more ambition than good judgment. While generally an unfavorable oracle, it bodes well if one restricts ambitions to his capabilities or to the conditions.

#7 Fire.

Like #1 Khien, this is also will but not the "high" will of Khien. Often sudden motion, exciting energy, active will. If the upper trigram, it is generally fortunate. In the lower trigram, it is undirected and impulsive.

#8 Khwan

This is the "Great Womb" of Nature. Feminine: great capacity and containment, infinite desire. In the upper trigram, it nourishes and develops what has been started. In the lower trigram, it is too desirous, ruled by emotions. If for a woman questioner, it is best that the upper trigram is strong enough to "fill" her.

Here again are the eight Pa Kua restated as representing the divisions of the Earth's sphere:

The Eight Trigram Divisions of the Earth's Sphere

This diagram illustrates how to arrive at the hour and minute relationships of each of the sixty-four hexagrams.

Note: Position 3 is on the moon meridian and the point of summer solstice.

Position 6 is midnight and the winter solstice.

Position 1 is the eastern horizon at the theoretical sunrise and vernal equinox.

Position 8 is the western horizon at the theoretical sunset and autumnal equinox.

It is important to understand that there are no "hexagrams" but a composition of one ruling trigram in the upper position and a ruled trigram in the lower position. It is these compositions that make up the 64 "hexagrams."

TABLE OF QUALITIES OF UPPER & LOWER TRIGRAM POSITIONS	
Upper Trigram Position	Lower Trigram Position
The Greater	The Lesser
Initiative (or lack of it)	Response (or its lack)
Superior	Inferior or ordinary
Man	Woman
Active	Responsive (on higher plane)
Responsive	Active (on lower plane)
The Higher Will	The Lower Will
The Great Hidden	The Outward Person or manifested and objective
The Great One	The Man or Woman
Support from the Great	Support from the Ordinary
Spiritual Strength	Material Strength and Ability
The Thinking Mind	Impulses and Emotions

Upper and lower trigrams are determined when a question is asked about another person or thing in relation to oneself. The questioner determines the upper trigram by deciding who holds the superior position. For example, should the question involve one's boss, the upper trigram is obviously the boss.

In the answer, information will be given on how to handle the boss and yourself, what must be done and what must not be done. If the question involves yourself alone, then the upper trigram is your own "Spiritual" sanction and strength, and the lower trigram describes your material abilities and capabilities.

Putting the Question

When putting a question to the Oracle, you must be concise and coherent for the answer to be clear. Never ask the same question twice at a sitting.

You may, however, ask related questions for clarification. For example, you may first ask, "Will my boss grant me a certain favor?" Your second question could then be, "What is the best method of approaching my boss?" A third question might be, "What will happen to me concerning my job?"

Since answers to questions are key words in combination, the meanings must be evaluated in terms of the *positions* of the trigrams. The key words of the eight trigrams will guide you. Your guide is concise and complete. By combining the meanings of two trigrams in a hexagram, you should always seek added advice on a specified subject. Subsequent questions framed to bring out specific points are most effective in formulating a complete picture of each situation at hand.

As in all real divinations, the I Ching does not predict a thing irrevocably, but describes the existing conditions of the moment and suggests a course of attitudes and actions which will achieve the best for you. The difference between one system and another is the parameters being described. Those of each major system—Tarot, Runes, I Ching, Geomancy, Astrology, and so forth—establish different parameters to determine the surrounding forces for the question being asked. All work, but the wise diviner chooses his tools appropriately.

Within your grasp is an incredible power, the power of divination. Yes, it will take practice, but this is how your divination will develop your intuition and how you will become a truly superior person. This is the way to your psychic empowerment which, in turn, is the foundation of your Self-Empowerment.

CASTING THE YI HEXAGRAM I

Preparations

First determine what is to be represented by the upper and the lower trigrams. This will serve to protect you from wishful thinking when later interpreting the hexagram. Remember that the upper trigram always represents "The Great One." Its nature describes how your Higher Self will regard your question: strong, indifferent, or favorable. In addition to describing your superior self in relation to the subject, this trigram describes any other person or thing that is superior to yourself.

The Attitude

There should be a sense of reverence for the higher wisdom of the Oracle. A simple ritual is advised, such as saying, "I now invoke the wisdom of the Yi to communicate with my Intuition so that I am able to correctly interpret its message. May I correctly cast this oracle and correctly and inspirationally receive the answer."

The Cast

The traditional method of the I Ching was to use fifty yarrow sticks, but they're not readily available and are cumbersome to use. The querent tossed all fifty sticks, and then separated them into two arbitrary groups, picking them up separately and then counting by fours to come up with an odd or even count to make each line. The point that we need to take from this traditional method is (1) the role of Chance, and (2) the long-drawn-out process of line-building, giving the subconscious mind opportunity to influence the results.

We will describe several alternatives. Bear in mind that with the yarrow sticks the process was slow and deliberate. Whatever alternative you choose, imitate the slow and deliberate style of the traditional method.

One of Lou Culling's favorite methods was as follows:

> Start a slow regular walk in a small circle around the room. Continue until you have a "feeling" to stop in your stride; note which foot is forward. If the left foot is forward, it is Yin (broken line), if the right foot is forward, it is Yang (straight line). You have determined the bottom line. Write it down. Continue this procedure until all six lines have been made.

(Note: this has the advantage of full body involvement in the divination—which is valuable if you really understand the intricacies of the body's amazing energy systems and the extent of the body-mind-spirit connection—but it does reduce the freedom of chance of more traditional systems.)

Let us suppose that your cast hexagram is ䷑ and work through an example of an actual question and answer:

Question: "Will I really enjoy my visit to Mexico City?" Note that the question is clear, concise, and definite. Now determine the order of the trigrams. In this case ☴ (SUN) is the superior factor (the city) in the upper trigram, and ☴ (AIR) (the querent) is in the lower trigram. In other words, the city is the controlling factor and the querent is the recipient, the acted upon.

Refer to the "Master File Chart" on page 329. In the top row of upper trigrams, find Sun #3. In the left side row, find the Air trigram and move across that horizontal row to intersect with the vertical row descending from the Sun, and you will see the entire Hexagram, #18. Sun #3 means brilliance, realization, and integration for the city. Air #2 means the querent's mental concept of the visit and is *easily penetrated* by the *brilliance* of Sun #3. Now consult Hexagram #18. "A transmutation both for physical and spiritual blessings." Also, "There is no resistance or hard difficulties." All of this promises a marvelous time.

The querent may now have another question, "With what class of people should I associate in this city to get the best results indicated?" Assuming now that the cast hexagram is Khwan over Fire (#8 over #7), the hexagram is #63. Khwan indicates the "common people," but Fire indicates the fire of will, energy, and ambition. This is the class. Note too that #63 says that "A woman aids the man." The consultant planned to talk to a certain woman for making contacts. This was done with success.

CASTING BY COINS

There are two established methods for using coins. You can use a single, medium-sized coin, designating the head as Yang and the tails as Yin. Holding the coin in your cupped hands, first state the question, then shake your cupped hands until you are moved to cast. Record the order of your first casting as the bottom line of the lower trigram. Repeat for the next line up, and then the third to complete the first trigram. Draw it in your journal and repeat the process for the upper trigram. You now have the complete hexagram for the reading.

A second and more complex method involves three coins and the concept of a *changing* or *moving* line. With each toss of three coins, you have the following potential results:

THE THREE COIN TOSS WITH MOVING LINE RESULTS

COINS	RESULTS
3 Tails	— x — Yin (changing line)
2 Tails, 1 Heads	Yang
1 Tails, 2 Heads	Yin
3 Heads	— o — Yang (changing line)

As in other I Ching methods, you build each trigram from the bottom up. The theory is that the energy represented by a changing line is in the process of changing from Yin to Yang, or Yang to Yin. For more information on this approach we particularly recommend Mark McElroy's *I Ching for Beginners*.

THE I CHING SIXTY-FOUR CARD DECK

A printed deck of sixty-four Hexagram Cards (each card is one Hexagram) is a modern method combining much that is traditional, and one that adds a secondary element of representative artwork in the background, upon which the Hexagram is presented.

It is important to carefully develop your question, mindful of the energy forces involved with the upper and the lower trigrams. We suggest using your journal and writing down how the question is broken down between the two trigram positions, and keeping that in mind as you slowly and meditatively shuffle the deck. It is always desirable to let yourself slip into a light trance as you shuffle and then lay the cards out as follows:

Shuffle the deck and cut into two piles, and then place the second pile on top of the first. With the now reassembled deck, spread the cards out in a fan before you. Spread your hands, fingers fanned out, above the cards and hold them there for a moment while repeating the question aloud or silently. When the impulse comes, select cards and lay them out according to a spread chosen from the following four:

LAYOUTS USING THE SIXTY-FOUR I CHING CARDS

A—*The Pyramid Looks to the Future*

Lay out six cards, *face down*, vertically in the shape of a pyramid as shown in the diagram. Card #1 refers to the querent's starting situation. Cards #2 and #3 foretell the road to follow. Cards #4, #5, and #6 project that road into the future.

Turn each card over in the numerical sequence, and read them one by one, and then read them again line by line, i.e. read #2 and #3 together, and then #4, #5, and #6 together.

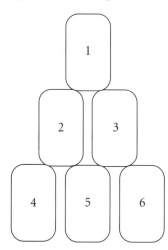

B—*General Picture of the Present*

Lay out nine cards, *face down*, in three rows of three cards each.

Turn them over in sequence, one row at a time, and read those three cards together as one presentation.

Cards #1, #2, and #3 present well-being, health, and amusement.

Cards #4, #5, and #6 present the economic, job, and social situation.

Cards #7, #8, and #9 present sentimental, love, and friendship situations.

C—For One Event, or One Time Period (Day, Week, Month)

Lay out three cards, *face down*, in a single row as shown.

Turn them over in sequence, and first read them one at a time, and then together as a single presentation.

D—The Star of Inner Evolution

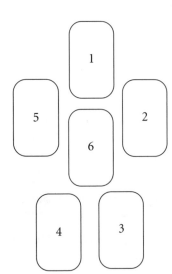

Lay out five cards in a star shape, and a sixth card in the center as shown. All cards should be face down.

Turn them over, one by one, in the same sequence as you laid them out.

The five cards around the center represent the querent's inner evolutionary path being followed, and the sixth represents the situation at the current moment.

The I Ching Cards are new, and their methodology and interpretation are still evolving. New layouts will be developed. The two decks available from Llewellyn/ Lo Scarabeo include individual instruction books with interpretations of each Hexagram particular to the general reading and the other to love and relationship reading. You will find them listed at the end of this chapter.

Remember that these are art cards. Each deck follows the artist's overall understanding, and within that, each card changes to represent the meaning of the Hexagram.

Following are some additional and astounding methods of divining the oracular message of the I Ching.

CHESS METHOD OF CASTING

Culling called this a secret method practiced by a small and ancient Japanese order devoted to the Yi for more than two thousand years. The method is based upon the correspondence between the meanings of the six line positions of the hexagram and the nature of the six different chess pieces.

Both the hexagrams and the chess squares are sixty-four in number. Beginning with the bottom line of the hexagram, we have the eight pawns—the weakest and most dispensable pieces on the board. The knight corresponds to the hexagram's second line, the bishop to the third line, the castle to the fourth line, the king to the fifth line, and the queen to the hexagram's sixth line, the top position.

This is not the place to teach the game of chess. There are many good introductory books available. When you purchase a chess set of a board and pieces, it will usually include a small but sufficient instruction booklet. The chess board has sixty-four squares and thirty-two pieces. Playing against yourself offers a voyage in self-discovery.

Look at the chess board. The lateral row where the major pieces are placed, if on the white side, are on the top hexagrams of the eight files on the Master File Chart (page 329): 1, 9, 17, 25, 33, 41, 49, and 57. The black major pieces are at the bottom of these major files: 8, 16, 24, 32, 40, 48, 56, and 64. The player first plays from the white side, then turning the board around, plays from the black side. The game continues until one of the kings is placed in checkmate. The square (hexagram number) that is held by the piece that has checkmated the king is the grand fortune hexagram, especially so if the subject matter is aggressive or calls for action. The number held by the checkmated king indicates the hexagram where one is most vulnerable, weak, or unfortunate. If the winner has not lost his queen, then the queen's hexagram number is significant toward final outcome and its satisfaction.

THE G∴B∴G∴ DICE SYSTEM

In the secret magickal order of the G∴B∴G∴, the Yi figures are correlated to the cube and die. The eight points to the cube correspond to the eight trigrams, the six faces correspond to the six lines of the hexagram, and the twelve edges correspond to the six Yang and the six Yin lines. Also of note: three edges converge on each of the eight points, this corresponding to the three lines of a trigram.

After a regular group ritual, the designated "King" and "Queen" advance to the altar where the two dice are kept. One die has the 6-spot facing up, the other has the 1-spot facing up. The King takes and turns one die over in his hand until impelled to stop. The number that is up when he stops, odd or even, determines the Yang or Yin for the first line. The Queen does the same for the second line. They alternate until the six lines have been cast. The dice are always in touch with the fingers, thus always under the control of the higher intelligence. The above method is also operable by one person, the right hand casting the first line, the left the second line, etc., until the six lines are completed.

HOW TO INTERPRET A HEXAGRAM ORACLE

To answer all possible questions in a written work would result in a compendious encyclopedia and even still be of small use. Book definitions are only "seeds" calling to your intuitive faculties.

First, however, we must explain the meaning of "The Great One" and "Crossing the Stream." In magickal orders such as the Golden Dawn, Aurum Solis, the G.B.G. and others, we find reference to "The Holy Guardian Angel." This is the "Great One," the Real Spiritual Identity or Higher Self. The upper Trigram is always this Great One. The nature of the upper trigram describes how your Higher Self regards your question, whether it is favorable to it, indifferent, complacent, weak, strong, or against it.

The upper trigram also describes any other person (or things) that are superior to yourself. Thus your "boss" would be the upper trigram, but if you are the boss then you are the upper trigram. The upper trigram is generally male while the lower is generally female; the upper is Yang, the lower is Yin; the upper is singular, the lower is many; the upper is the will, the lower the emotions and desires.

When a Hex says "consult the Great One," you had better do it! This means to seek inspired wisdom from your Higher Self. Now when the upper trigram is No. 6, Moon, we can hardly conceive that the "Great One" is so dangerous and undeveloped, but we can see that this is the "Higher" attitude regarding the question.

There are forty-five Hexagrams that mention either "progress and success" or "good fortune." This is *always* limited in scope to the nature of the particular hexagram and not to anything beyond its "rulership." For example, refer to Hex No. 41. "Good fortune" is implied but only within the scope of the Hex, i.e. if one combats "restriction and inability" with the firmness, will, and strength of the lower trigram No. 1. Now refer to No. 46, Moon doubled: it can be fortunate only if one refuses to "get involved" in what is described by the Moon trigram, most certainly not to "Cross the stream," which means 'new territory' or advancement into a new type of venture. Therefore stick to the familiar and be not venturesome.

There are enough "Keys" given in each Hexagram to invoke one's inspired intuition. To ask for more means that one does not understand the principles of divination. The *Interpretative Guide* that starts on page 329 may often seem obtuse, more symbolic than literary, but when applied to your real-life questions and situations, it will trigger deeper-level responses. Rarely are there quick and easy answers in real divinations and more than in real life. Write them in your journal along with your perceptions. Meditate and let your imagination "talk" with the Yi.

MASTER FILE CHART FOR DETERMINING
YOUR HEXAGRAM NUMBER

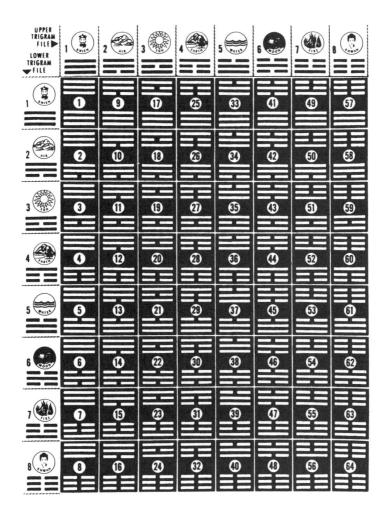

INSTRUCTIONS FOR DETERMINING A HEXAGRAM NUMBER

Use this Master File Chart to determine your hexagram number. Locate your upper trigram and lower trigram in the two master files. The point of focus at which they meet is your hexagram's location and number. For example, upper trigram file #3 and lower trigram file #1 point of focus yields hexagram #17.

INTERPRETIVE GUIDE TO THE SIXTY-FOUR HEXAGRAMS

Khien #1 is the upper trigram for the following eight trigrams, #1 to #8 Hexagrams.

Masculine. The Great One, or Higher Will. *Initiating and Projecting.* It leads and directs, and never follows. In the upper trigram, it always means "The Great One." In the lower, it does not give way easily.

Hexagram #1

Khien #1 over Khien #1. Masculine doubled! Great originating energy, but no Yin line to nourish and support it. A time to avoid excesses and to exercise much vigilance and self-discipline.

> *Restrain yourself. This is not the time for active doing.*

Hexagram #2

Khien #1 or over Air #2. Free and easy penetrating and being penetrated. Indicates success, or good, only in small things or the superficial. Not good for long attachments. It shows a female who is bold and strong.

> *Associate not for long.*

Hexagram #3

Khien #1 over Sun #3. The Brilliance and Realization of #3 is manifested in The greatness and Strength of #1. Good for uniting. There is neither difficulty nor obstruction: open for free and harmonious course of action. The best of the eight Hexagrams of the Khien file.

> *It will be advantageous to cross the great stream.*

Hexagram #4

Khien #1 over Earth #4. The Fixed Immobility of #4 is stubbornly asserted against the Greatness and Strength of #1. Small men, or the materialistic impulse, increase in power while the Great must retire while the good initiative is restricted. It is a good opportunity to *consolidate* anything such as material or physical resources.

> *No movement in any direction should be made.*

Hexagram #5

Khien #1 over Water #5. The Pleased Satisfaction of #5 is Strengthened by #1. The Chinese say, "Tread innocently on even the tiger's tail and he will not bite"—yet be humble and thankful, trusting in your pleasure. The Great One grants satisfaction even through difficulties.

> *Lucky even in hazardous circumstances.*

Hexagram #6

 Khien #1 over Moon #6. The peril of the weak or inept of #6, or restriction in attempt or contention with what is Great #1. The Moon #6 is never favorable. Restraint and caution, and no great ambition, is advised. At least it is right and good to seek the Great One for help.

It will not be advantageous to cross the great stream.

Hexagram #7

 Khien #1 over Fire #7. The Great Force and the Higher Will of #1 with the Energy, Motion, and Active Will of #7 results in a physical and determined will. There is danger that this may be too impetuous and therefore sincerity, earnestness, and self-regulation are advised. *Regulate* things.

This Hex indicates great progress and success, while there will be advantage in being firm and correct. If its subject and his action be not correct, he will fall into errors, and it will be advantageous for him to move in any direction, only if cautious.

Sincerity and self-control is advised.

Hexagram #8

 Khien #1 over Khwan #8. The Chinese say, "The Small has come; the Great has gone." But #8 is the feminine principle and is excellent for woman in relation to man. Excellent for receiving, but taking the initiative faces inordinate demands or desires.

Excellent for Receiving.

 Air #2 is the upper trigram of the following eight Hexagrams, #9 to #16
Easily penetrating and easily penetrated. It is the Mind, or mental concepts, i.e. "Ideas." When it is the lower trigram, it has no real substance and relates to small things that are not long-lasting.

Hexagram #9

 Air #2 over Khien #1. Mental ideas of image of #2. The Will or what is great. Penetrating and flexibility of #2 is given #1 Generating Strength. Quick success but not for long; it needs ultimate consolidation. Therefore it is said that there is "Small restraint."

Indicates that under its limitations there will be progress and success.

Hexagram #10

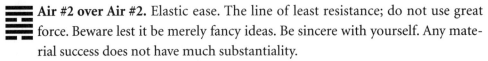 **Air #2 over Air #2.** Elastic ease. The line of least resistance; do not use great force. Beware lest it be merely fancy ideas. Be sincere with yourself. Any material success does not have much substantiality.

Caution: there's not a lot of substance to ideas.

Hexagram #11

Air #2 over Sun #3. Realization #3 of the mental image #2. This is a much better augury than indicated in the Yi texts. It is the modern concept of "Regulation," recognizing that some things will be (or should be) regulated in an orderly and intelligent manner. Proceed consistently and there will be realization. It is most advantageous that the mind be firm and correct.

The mental image must be firm and correct.

Hexagram #12

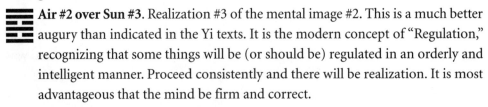 **Air #2 over Earth #4.** Fixedness #4 for consolidation of the mental ideas #2. There is a certain stolidness of #4 (or even stubbornness) which, if overcome, is fortunate to the penetrating quality of Air #2. It suggests the marriage of a young lady, and the good fortune attending it. This Hexagram is ordinarily applied gradually, with the idea of progress and advancement.

It is good for regulating and consolidating things.

Hexagram #13

Air #2 over Water #5. "Inmost Sincerity." Pleased Satisfaction #5 from the Mental concepts of #2. True imagination brings true response. Welcome everything and respond to what appears all right, for under sincerity and repose you can trust yourself. It denotes the highest quality of man, and gives its possessor power so that he prevails with spiritual beings, with other men, and with the lower creatures.

No really great gains or realization.

Hexagram #14

Air #2 over Moon #6. Restriction or Dispersion #6 of the mental ideas of #2. *Moon #6 is nearly always unfavorable.* It is descriptive primarily of men's minds alienated from what is right and good. Beware of dispersion and dissipation of the subject in question.

It is good to "disperse" some things.

Hexagram #15

Air #2 over Fire #7. The conscious will #7 easily penetrates the higher ideas of #2. The oracle is either good or bad according to the purpose and method. Good for laying plans for something brave and new, but not reckless. It indicates that there will be advantage in every movement that will be undertaken, even to cross the great stream.

When the moment is right, go with it!

Hexagram #16

Air #2 over Khwan #8. Good feminine principle of development and fulfillment. Full Expansion #8 of the mind #2. Contemplating and giving full course to the desire but not much activity of value yet. Ultimately, there is promised sustainment of the object of desires. It denotes showing and manifesting; in all other places it denotes contemplating, observing.

A woman's desires are a thing of beauty.

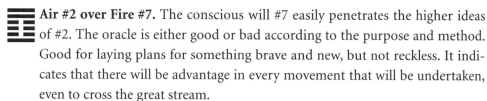 ***The Sun #3 is the upper trigram for the following eight Hexagrams, #17 through #24***

Brilliance. Realization. Capability. Union. Self-integrated. Intelligence. In a general way, it is the best of all trigrams. Realized position. Receptive to good and rejective to bad, but fair, amiable, and noble.

The upper trigram #3 Sun persists for the following eight Hexagrams, #17 to #24.

Hexagram #17

Sun #3 over Khien #1. The Great Creative #1 brings Realization and Brilliance #3. The Great One acting on the Realized Self and so uniting "All" and therefore called "Great Havings." Be satisfied and not greedy. Let the fire of your aspiration reach for the illumination and blessing of the Great One. It is very auspicious. Great "Paternal" relations.

There will be great progress and success.

Hexagram #18

Sun #3 over Air #2. "The Cauldron." The mental concept #2 in the sphere of Realization #3. An unusual Hex. It is a symbol of magical possibilities where there is a *transmutation* both for physical and spiritual blessings. Preparation processes, flexibility, "the Concubine." There is no resistance nor great difficulty.

It intimates great progress and success.

Hexagram #19

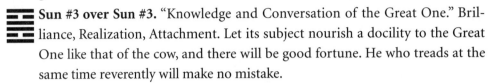 **Sun #3 over Sun #3.** "Knowledge and Conversation of the Great One." Brilliance, Realization, Attachment. Let its subject nourish a docility to the Great One like that of the cow, and there will be good fortune. He who treads at the same time reverently will make no mistake.

No new venture.

Hexagram #20

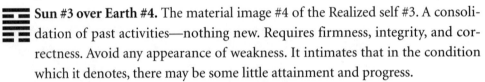 **Sun #3 over Earth #4.** The material image #4 of the Realized self #3. A consolidation of past activities—nothing new. Requires firmness, integrity, and correctness. Avoid any appearance of weakness. It intimates that in the condition which it denotes, there may be some little attainment and progress.

If the stranger or traveler be firm and correct as he ought to be,
there will be good fortune.

Hexagram #21

Sun #3 over Water #5. Pleased satisfaction #5 of the realized self #3. There is some small dissension or disagreement, but not much. Success only in small matters but no serious bad fortune. Should one meet with bad men, however, let him not shrink from them. Communication with them will be of benefit. His good may overcome their evil, and at least it will help silence their slanderous tongues.

Communication is always beneficial.

Hexagram #22

Sun #3 over Moon #6. Restriction and difficulty, incomplete success, foolish impulses. Struggles or desires for completeness start but do not develop well. Better for a woman than for a man. The successful accomplishment of whatever was in mind has not yet been realized. The vessel of the state has not been brought across the great and dangerous stream.

Patience is a virtue.

Hexagram #23

Sun #3 over Fire #7. "Gnawing at the obstruction." There is great movement and force directed to realization, but ability, self-restraint, and prudence are required. All else is futile "gnawing." Remove the obstacles to union, and high and low will come together in good understanding. *And how are those obstacles to be removed?* By force, if need be, within legal constraints. Then there is sure success.

Persistence is also a virtue.

Hexagram #24

Sun #3 over Khwan #8. Steady advance with increasing achievement and development. Expansion #8, and development of #3 Intelligence, and Union with the better. The Chinese text says, "Inferiors strive but cannot advance," but this is not true in modern classless society. Better for woman than man.

Education and ambition know no class.

Earth #4 is the upper trigram for the following eight Hexagrams, #25 to #32

Body, Matter, Stable. Good for consolidation of things. In the lower trigram, it is fixed and immovable: too materialistic and too stubborn.

Hexagram #25

Earth #4 over Khien #1. The Chinese say, "The Great accumulation," meaning that great creative energy #1 is applied to the material form of #4. If one guides, guards, and conserves this energy, then comes strength, volume, and stability. At times, some repression may be needed.

The accumulation to which all tends is that of virtue.

Hexagram #26

Earth #4 over Air #2. The movable #2 faces the immovable #4. The realistic and practical must take precedence: therefore it is said, "hard services to perform." One can be venturesome only in a practical way and with some mental or emotional restraint. There will be advantage in efforts like that of crossing the great stream. He should weigh well, however, the events of three days before the turning point, and those to be done three days after it.

Accomplishment is built upon practicality.

Hexagram #27

Earth #4 over Sun #3. "Adornment and Ornament." As there is ornament in nature, so should there be in society; but its place is secondary to what is substantial. The importance of certain material things—even its beauty—comes to the front. Free course and good, but unfavorable for much advancement.

Walk in beauty: Proper ornament leads to transformation.

Hexagram #28

Earth #4 over Earth #4. "Resting and Arresting." Active advancement is not advised. Arrange and consolidate everything at present. It denotes the mental characteristic of resting in what is right; especially resting, 'in principle,' that which is right, on the widest scale, and in the absolute conception of the mind; and that which is right in every different position in which a man can be placed.

A solid foundation supports the highest building.

Hexagram #29

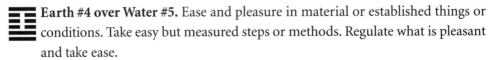 **Earth #4 over Water #5.** Ease and pleasure in material or established things or conditions. Take easy but measured steps or methods. Regulate what is pleasant and take ease.

Enjoy the moment!

Hexagram #30

Earth #4 over Moon #6. Youth, ignorance, inexperience, incapability, or downright bad augury. Better seek the counsel and blessing of the Great One and be sincere about it. Take no chances.

There will be advantage in being firm and correct.

Hexagram #31

Earth #4 over Fire #7. Strong, exciting movement of the will #7 toward what is stable and solid, the status quo of #4. This requires great ability or material force and calls for consolidation of things, even under force of law. It indicates that with firm correctness there will be good fortune in what is denoted by it. We must look at what we are seeking to nourish, and by the exercise of our thoughts seek for the proper sustenance.

Be strong in heart and soul.

Hexagram #32

Earth #4 over Khwan #8. The utmost expansion #8 of matter or the "solid and established" #4. The superior man seeks to strengthen those below in order to secure the stability of his position. It will not be advantageous to make a movement in any direction whatever, except to expand stability. Lay plans, but do not agitate.

A chain is only as strong as its weakest link.

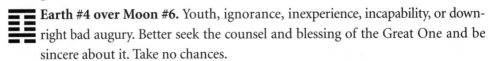 *Water #5 is the upper trigram, which continues for the following eight Hexagrams #33 to #40*

Placid still water represents pleasure, satisfaction, or complacency. In the upper trigram, there are no great demands upon the consultant. In the lower trigram, it is self-indulgent, lacking ambition, and too easy-going.

Hexagram #33

Water #5 over **Khien #1.** The Strong will and energy #1 brings pleased satisfaction #5, yet gently. This is the removal of old problems, restrictions, and that which has hindered pleasure and satisfaction. The result is not immediately apparent because #1 is initiating or starting, and not finishing.

What you no longer need or desire gets in the way of progress.

Hexagram #34

Water #5 over **Air #2.** This is called a "Weak bridge" because #2 the mental desire for #5 pleased satisfaction is strong enough to require carefulness, restraint, and ability. Beware of impulsiveness and also low or bad associations. Very extraordinary times require very extraordinary gifts. We have the symbolism of a decayed willow producing shoots, or an old husband and a young wife, or an old wife and a young husband. There will be occasion neither for blame nor for praise. There will be advantage in every way.

Does not guarantee long-term success.

Hexagram #35

Water #5 over **Sun #3**. The full Realization of brilliance #3 and pleasure and satisfaction #5. A great change or development, which is the forerunner of success.

Self-realization brings Self-Empowerment.

Hexagram #36

Water #5 over **Earth #4**. Called "Mutually influencing" because there is #4 the stability of "earth" and material resources (body) conjoined with #5 the easy fluidic "water" of pleased satisfaction. Good and correct aims bring effective pleased conditions and transformations. The symbolism is that of mutual influence, and that influence, correct in itself, and for correct ends, is sure to be effective. The subject of this hexagram may be given as perseverance in well doing, or in continuously acting out the law of one's being.

Persevere in expressing your true will.

Hexagram #37

Water #5 over **Water**. The great mirror. Just pleasure, satisfaction, and complacency.

Do not let complacency control you.

Hexagram #38

Water #5 over Moon #6. Moon #6 restricts the satisfaction of #5. Distressed. Not able to develop. Should restrain desires. In the condition denoted by this hexagram, there may yet be progress and success. For the firm and correct, the really great man, there will be good fortune. He will fall into no error but there is still lack of achievement. The character of this hexagram shows us the picture of a tree within an enclosure not allowed to spread its branches; a plant fading for want of room. This hexagram indicates a state of things in which the order and government that would be conducive to the well-being of the country can hardly get the development, which by skillful management on the part of "the great man" and others, is finally secured for them.

Success cannot be gained through constraint.

Hexagram #39

Water #5 over Fire #7. The strong force and energy of the will (Fire #7) to attain satisfaction #5. Conditions challenge complacency. Good for the superior to get a following and good for the inferior to follow. Progress and success if not too reckless or demanding. This hexagram indicates great progress and success is due to flexibility and applicability of it. Those following must be guided *by reference to what is proper and correct.*

Going beyond his own gate to find associates, he will achieve merit.

Hexagram #40

Water #5 over Khwan #8. The full expansion and development of #8 brings satisfaction of the desires to #5. Here is the great union, collecting together and cooperating in attaining full satisfaction. Meet the Great One.

It will be advantageous also to meet with the great man.

Moon #6 is the upper for the following eight Hexagrams, #41 to #48

The image is of "a deep gorge of rushing water," hence danger and peril. Restriction, lack of capability, immaturity. Sometimes more ambition than good judgment is evidenced. Though an unfavorable oracle generally, it bodes well if one restricts ambitions to his actual capabilities or to the conditions at hand.

Hexagram #41

Moon #6 over Khien #1. Restriction, weakness, or inability #6 limits the creative or initiative activity of #1. Strength and activity confronted by weakness or inadequacy. Do not risk the dubious. Wait until better signs.

Through firmness and correctness there will be good fortune.

Hexagram #42

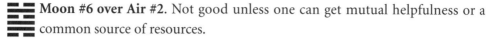**Moon #6 over Air #2.** Not good unless one can get mutual helpfulness or a common source of resources.

Strength can be found through cooperative effort.

Hexagram #43

Moon #6 over Sun #3. Realization or brilliance #3 is not likely unless help can be attained. The only good is to outshine a superior—also is good for a woman in relation to a man. It intimates progress and success in small matters. There will be advantage in being firm and correct. There has been good fortune in the beginning; there may be disorder in the end.

The past being completed, plan ahead but only for the short term.

Hexagram #44

Moon #6 over Earth #4. Fixed, unmovable, and stubborn #4 faces the #6 difficulty or incompetence in advancing. Some alternation between action and inaction may help. One needs much help for small successes. Three things seem to be required: attention to place, the presence of the great man, and the firm observance of correctness in order to cope successfully with the difficulties of the situation. Advancement on the part of its subject will lead to greater difficulties, while remaining stationary will afford ground for praise. The hexagram shows its subject struggling with the greatest difficulties, while friends are coming to help him.

A pause creates opportunity for support.

Hexagram #45

Moon #6 over Water #5. More desires and emotions than good judgment, should be repressed or avoided. Even requires great care in regulating the conditions. Also the subject of this hexagram is the regulations of government enacted for the guidance and control of the people.

Attempt no advance.

Hexagram #46

Moon #6 over Moon #6. Thoroughly inauspicious and difficult. The trigram exhibits a strong central line, between two divided lines. The central line represents the sincere honesty and goodness of the subject of the hexagram, whose mind was sharpened and made penetrating by contact with danger, and who acted in a manner worthy of his character. It is implied, though does not say it, that he would get out of the danger.

Stand still. Do not get involved.

Hexagram #47

Moon #6 over Fire #7. Energy and movement #7 amidst hazards and difficulty. Strivings of first stages that can not succeed unless by more favorable later development. Great will and patience and resignation is needed for a time. There will be great progress and success, and the advantage will come from being correct and firm. But any movement in advance should not be lightly undertaken.

Be patient while remaining correct and firm.

Hexagram #48

Moon #6 over Khwan #8. Nourishment and expansion #8 is restricted from above by #6. The "Superior" is difficult to find even in oneself—however, the person that is of quasi-superior position can seek and get help from the lower ones if there is a sincere attempt for harmony. A good woman can help a weak man if it is her desire. The idea of union between the different members and classes of a state, and how it can be secured, is the subject of the hexagram #48.

Sincerity of purpose can unite in common cause.

Fire #7 is the upper trigram in the following eight Hexagrams, #49 to #56

This is not the Higher Will of #1 Khien, rather it is the active, often unrestrained, lower will. It often brings sudden movement and excitement. In the upper trigram, it is more fortunate, but in the lower position, it is undirected impulsiveness.

Hexagram #49

Fire #7 over Khien #1. Here we have so much will, starting strength, vigor, and abundance that it could be self-destroying unless one is firm, correct, and self-reliant. Excellent, but only for starting something. Brook no outside interference. Use your intelligence. *Is strength alone enough for the conduct of affairs?* No. Strength should be held in subordination to the idea of right, and exerted only in harmony with it.

Hold energy and enthusiasm subordinate to intelligence and purpose.

Hexagram #50

Fire #7 over Air #2. The mind #2 assisting the material will of #7. There is successful progress if there is single-mindedness (and no vacillation) and perseverance in the aims, but mostly in just starting things. Movement in any direction whatever will be advantageous.

Avoid impulsiveness: use your mind.

Hexagram #51

Fire #7 over Sun #3. "Large, Abundant." Full realization #3 of the material will #7. However it is better to receive, consolidate, and maintain, rather than to make much advancing, but be active—and take initiative. The character of this hexagram is the symbol of being large and abundant, and denotes a condition of abundant prosperity. In the changes of human affairs, a condition of prosperity has often given place to one of an opposite character. The lesson of the hexagram is to show to rulers how they may preserve the prosperity of their state and people. The component trigrams have the attributes of intelligence and of motive force, and the second is under the direction of the first.

Consolidate and maintain, stay secure rather than overexpose.

Hexagram #52

Fire #7 over Earth #4. Consolidation #7 of the material with #4 is the best. Must not exceed except in small or materialistic things. There are only small divergences. Advised to save money and resources.

Hold on tight!

Hexagram #53

Fire #7 over Water #5. Too much exciting urge #7 for pleasure and satisfaction of #5. Do not act impulsively and watch out for the overly emotional ones. Fire your emotions, yes, but not in excess. It indicates that under such conditions action will be of small but good results and not evil.

Hold emotions in check and move forward slowly.

Hexagram #54

Fire #7 over Moon #6. Obstructions and complications must be untangled expediently. Quick action is necessary to avoid trouble or danger. Avoid the complications from low people—or from your own instability. It is the symbol of loosing, untying a knot or unraveling a complication; it denotes a condition in which the obstruction and difficulty have been removed. The object is to show how this new and better state is to be dealt with. If further operations be necessary, let them be carried through without delay.

Move quickly to avoid populist complications.

Hexagram #55

Fire #7 over Fire #6. The willful will. Such moving power requires caution and virtue. Be neither impulsive nor reckless. Not likely to develop and attain nourishment. This figure among the trigrams represents thunder and "the oldest son." The hexagram is formed of the trigram redoubled, and may be taken as representing the crash or peal of thunder; but we have seen that the attribute or virtue of the trigram is 'moving, exciting power;' and thence, symbolically, the character is indicative of movement taking place in society and the subject is the conduct to be pursued in a time of movement—such as insurrection or revolution—by the party promoting, and most interested in, the situation. It is shown how he ought to be aware of the dangers of the time, and how by precaution and the regulation of himself he may overcome them.

A controlled burn can tame a wild fire.

Hexagram #56

Fire #7 over Khwan #8. Full expansion of desires and will, and develops to success. Put the "many" in motion. Full harmony, contentment, and growth if not reckless nor greedy. Particularly good for the woman. Gather friends.

Let him not allow suspicions to enter his mind,
and thus friends will gather around him.

Khwan #8 is the upper trigram for the following eight Hexagrams, #57 to #64

Feminine. This is the "Great Womb" of Nature in which all things are nourished and developed of what has been previously started. It represents great capacity and containment, infinite desire. If for a woman questioner, it is best that the upper trigram is strong enough to "fill" her. In the lower trigrams, it is overcome with desire, ruled by emotions.

Hexagram #57

Khwan #8 over Khien #1. The Chinese say "The Great (#1) come: the small are gone." But this applies only to the material plane in a fashion. Great originating energy #1 dominates the great Nourisher #8. Both literally and metaphorically, it is a dominant wife and a nourishing and sustaining husband, but the Yi scholars did not see this. Harmony, contentment, and cooperation is assured if there is "correctness."

It indicates that there will be good fortune, with progress and success.

Hexagram #58

Khwan #8 over Air #2. "Advancing and ascending." Through the willingness and blessings of the "Great One," small things build to the high and great, according to the mental concept, and then success is assured. There, it denotes the advancement of a good officer to the highest pinnacle of distinction.

Supported from above, small things lead to great success.

Hexagram #59

Khwan #8 over Sun #3. Full realization of desire #3. Intelligence, brilliance, and status in some small danger of being hurt by weak superiors; however, self-integrity can prevail. The "Great One" will respond to one's good aspirations. It will be advantageous to realize the difficulty of the position and maintain firm correctness. In this hexagram we have the representation of a good and intelligent minister or officer going forward in the service of his country, notwithstanding the occupancy of the throne by a weak and unsympathetic sovereign. The good officer will be successful in his struggle; but let him not be overeager to put all things right at once.

Steady at the helm!

Hexagram #60

Khwan #8 over Earth #4. Humility and integrity are required for best results, and then there is success. Do not try to go beyond your own established status. Seek consolidation. Bountiful Mother Earth is in a nourishing and sustaining condition. Indicates progress and success. The superior man, being humble as it implies, will have a good issue to his undertakings.

Don't let ambition push you beyond your capabilities.

Hexagram #61

Khwan #8 over Water #5. Expansion #8 of Satisfaction #5. Free course to advancement and authority. Nourishment and support in easy satisfaction. Emotions excellent and can also be of value. Indicates that, under the conditions supposed in it, there will be great progress and success, while it will be advantageous to be firmly correct.

Hold to your convictions and gain support to move forward.

Hexagram #62

Khwan #8 over Moon #6. Emotional drive to be filled up with satisfaction, but the "low" or "multitudes" are in dominant command over the worthy. Bad for a man with a woman. Beware lest there be no ability, wisdom, and experience, for this is all that saves the condition from being completely bad. Indicates, in the case which it supposes, with firmness and correctness, and a leader of age and experience, there will be good fortune and no error; small men should not be employed in such positions.

Strong and experienced leadership is required.

Hexagram #63

Khwan #8 over Fire #7. The fire of the material #7 will get response from the nourisher and sustainer of #8. This is the returning of good conditions and gives advancement and free course—in whatever direction. The woman will aid the man. It symbolizes the idea of returning, coming back or over again. Change is the law of nature and society. When decay has reached its climax, recovery will begin to take place.

Credit and support are available.

Hexagram #64

Khwan #8 over Khwan #8. There is no Yang line (male initiative) in this Hex and therefore it is rather negative. Brings full production, capacity and growth, and full development to only that which has been started. Not good for advancing or starting anything. Typically a woman's hexagram. This hexagram represents what is great, penetrating, advantageous, correct, and having the firmness of a mare. If one rests in correctness and firmness, there will be good fortune.

The best of times.

We are challenged by the I Ching, and all divinatory systems, to reverse our basic perception of cause and effect. As Carl Jung wrote, "The science of the *I Ching,* indeed, is not based on the causality principle, but on a principle (hitherto unnamed because not met with among us) which I have tentatively called the synchronistic principle. My occupation with the psychology of unconscious processes long ago necessitated my casting around for another explanatory principle, because the causality principle seemed to me inadequate for the explanation of certain remarkable phenomena of the unconscious."

In the study of paranormal phenomena, Jung found "psychic parallelisms" that could not be related causally to one another but yet remained somehow connected together as events that happened together in time even though separated by distance.

In his study of astrology, he noted that the construction of a birth horoscope is not based on actual astronomical data but "upon an arbitrary, purely conceptual time-system," yet it produced really correct astrological diagnoses, establishing that "whatever is born or done in this moment of time has the quality of this moment of time."

He relates back to the I Ching: "This is also the basic formula for the use of the *I Ching.* One gains knowledge of the hexagram characterizing the moment by a method of manipulating yarrow stalks, or coins, a method depending on sheer chance. As the moment is, so do the runic stalks fall."

We experience two kinds of time: outer, physical reality, and inner "Linear Time," which is within consciousness where we can add psychic energy to our representations (archetypes) of the outer reality and actually change potentiality into new reality. That can be perceived as prediction or as magick. The archetypes are "engines" producing higher energies.

In our divinations, actual events are not predicted, but only the *quality of possible events.* The outer world is timeless, and what we perceive as the flow of time is our own inner perception imposed through the Collective Unconsciousness on the outer order to cause change.

We live in two different worlds: an outer reality and an inner reality. For the most part they coincide, but it does happen that sometimes the outer imposes on the inner, and other times it is the inner that imposes on the outer. Therein is the Great Mystery, and the Great Adventure that is our destiny and our challenge.

SOURCES AND RECOMMENDED READING

Raymond Buckland, *Coin Divination: Pocket Fortuneteller* (Llewellyn, 2000).

Louis T. Culling, *The LRI I Ching* (Llewellyn/Life Resources Institute, 1966).

Louis T. Culling, *The Incredible I Ching* (Helios Book Store, 1969).

Louis T. Culling and Carl Llewellyn Weschcke, *The Complete Magick Curriculum of the GBG*, Revised (Llewellyn, 2010).

Marie-Louise Von Franz, *On Divination and Synchronicity: The Psychology of Meaningful Chance* (Inner City Books, 1980).

Recommended Reading

Herbie Brennan, *The Magical I Ching* (Llewellyn, 2000).

Mark McElroy, *I Ching for Beginners: A Modern Interpretation of the Ancient Oracle* (Llewellyn, 2005).

Louis T. Culling and Carl Llewellyn Weschcke, *The Pristine Yi King* (forthcoming, Llewellyn).

Recommended Products

The I Ching deck of sixty-four numbered art cards, 2 5/8" x 4 ¾" with instruction booklet (Llewellyn/Lo Scarabeo, 2003).

The I Ching of Love deck of sixty-four numbered art cards, 2 5/8" x 4 ¾" with instruction booklet (Llewellyn/Lo Scarabeo, 2004).

Richard Wilhelm, *The I Ching or Book of Changes,* trans. Cary F. Baynes, with introduction by Carl Jung (Pantheon Books, 1967) (Bollengen Series).

H. Wilhelm, *Changes: Eight lectures on the I Ching,* trans. Cary F. Baynes (Pantheon Books, 1975) (Bollengen Series).

Richard Wilhelm and Carl Jung, *The Secret of the Golden Flower* (Harcourt Brace & World, 1962).

J. Legge, *I Ching—Book of Changes,* edited with introduction by Ch'u Chai with Winberg Chai (University Books, 1996).

23

SPIRIT COMMUNICATIONS
When the Spirit Moves

A LITTLE HISTORY

Spirits have been with us from the beginning of anything we know about humanity. Their presence is recorded in the sacred literature of all peoples and in their mythologies as well.

Spirits are part of the Jewish and Christian Bible, part of our familiar folklore, and more recently part of religious history studies and paranormal research. Spirits are likewise an intimate experience in the African-Spiritist-based religions of Santeria, Macumba, Voudoun, and others prominent in the African-American and Hispanic cultures of the United States, the Caribbean, and Latin America.

The advent of the modern renaissance started on March 31, 1848 in the Fox family home in Hydesville, located in upper New York State. Shortly after the family moved into this home, there was an outbreak of bangs and rapping on the walls. Of course, many older houses make noises as the seasons change and as the house settles into the ground. And, of course, there are often earth movements—mostly subtle and hardly noticed in themselves but having a cumulative effect on buildings—even in areas not known for earthquakes.

Before the family moved into the home, it already had a reputation for being haunted. Even the nearby neighbors of the Fox family admitted to similar phenomena, but what was different about March 31 is that two Fox sisters thought it would be interesting to ask questions of the rapping, *to which they started getting intelligent answers.* And the phenomenon was not limited to the two young girls, Maggie and Kate.

Neighbors were called in to witness the strange goings-on and likewise asked questions and received satisfactory answers. Because such a large group soon gathered, the girls and their mother left to sleep elsewhere that night—and the questions

347

and answers continued, *refuting later claims by doubters that it was the girls themselves producing the raps by cracking their finger and toe joints!*

The news of these nonvocal communications spread and soon the news media invaded the countryside. Among them were two people, Colonel Henry Olcott and Helena Blavatsky, who later, in 1875, founded the Theosophical Society in New York.

More rapping and communications followed, with the rapper claiming to have been murdered in the basement. Bones were indeed found buried under the basement floor, and in 1904 a complete human skeleton was found sealed in a basement wall.

This new interest in spirit communication spread from America to Great Britain, and then to Europe. The religion of Spiritualism was born with professional mediums serving as intermediaries between the living and those "on the other side." Famous scientists of the day investigated and some mediums were exposed as frauds, while others under close observation produced paranormal phenomena not explainable in purely materialistic terms standard at the time. While Spiritualism as a religion was far older than its new daughter (the Swedenborg church, for example, was founded in 1787), the new American Spiritualism rapidly became mainstream. Even President Lincoln consulted mediums in the White House, not merely to contact the spirit of his son Willie but on military matters. The news media of the day had a great time over that!

PARAPSYCHOLOGY AND METAPHYSICS

Truly the spirits have always been with us, and equally there has always been interest in the nonmaterial worlds. Priests and shamans, long before the Fox sisters and before Swedenborg, were communicating with spirits, and throughout the world there were nonreligious groups—sometimes organized into *Secret Initiatory Orders*—studying the larger universe beyond the purely physical world, just as there were scientists probing the heavens above despite repression and persecution by religious authorities.

What was new was the sudden popular awareness of these spiritual dimensions, leading to "uncontrolled" research and participation in these areas—once the exclusive domain of a special class of people operating within religious institutions.

We forget that it is only a few centuries ago that astronomers were burned at the stake for claiming that the Earth rotated about the Sun, and that Earth was not the center of a universe existing only for its inhabitants. We forget that it is only a few centuries ago that so-called Witches, otherwise known as herbalists and natural healers, were burned at the stake during the "Dark Ages" when knowledge outside the Church was proscribed.

What America brought to the world was not only freedom of religion but freedom from religion that claimed exclusivity of knowledge and the definition of what was "true." March 31, 1848 was truly the beginning of a New Age of spiritual and scientific freedom, and—even just as importantly—the birth of mass communication.

Today, knowledge once hidden away for fear of persecution and misunderstanding is widely available through our schools and universities, books, and the Internet, and is freely researched in laboratories and by ordinary people.

THE NEW AGE OF SPIRIT

Spirit communications—we've all experienced them in one form or another. They can be as subtle as a comforting impression of a spirit presence, or as bold as a materialization of a spirit entity. They can be spontaneous and unsolicited, or they can be deliberately prompted through structured programs and techniques. They can be cloaked in mystery or directly expressed in clear, meaningful ways. In whatever their forms, they invite us to experience them as invaluable sources of enlightenment and power.

In all their wide-ranging manifestations, spirit communications are consistently purposeful and empowerment driven. They can add enrichment and purpose to our lives while empowering us with the resources we need to achieve our highest goals. They can motivate us and give us the winning edge in our striving. As other-dimensional sources, they can provide insight into the nature of our existence as spiritual beings. They can expand our awareness of ourselves and offer insight into our past, present, and future as evolving souls. They can add happiness and a powerful sense of well-being to our lives. At times of adversity, sorrow, and disappointment, they can generate hope and positive expectations. They persistently invite us to acknowledge them as reassuring sources of comfort, knowledge, and power, while never imposing themselves upon us.

Note, however, how many of the previous paragraph's sentences say "can." Spirit resources, like any other, *can* be useful and helpful, but it is we who would make them so. We have to turn experience into understanding, and understanding into knowledge and practice that can be applied to the human situation. We have to become *active* partners in developing and applying new technology to the spiritual opportunity opened for us.

SPIRITUALITY IN THE LABORATORY

Even in the experimental laboratory, intervening manifestations of spiritual origin can occur, particularly in research with implications of spiritual relevance. That possibility was illustrated at Athens State University (founded in 1822, in northern

Alabama) in a highly controlled laboratory study designed to investigate electrophotographic recording of the human energy system surrounding the right index fingerpad. The fingerpad was chosen for analysis because the finger can be seen as the physical body's outermost antennae to other energy sources and dimensions, a concept illustrated by Michelangelo's Sistine Chapel painting of "The Creation of Adam," in which Adam's right index finger reaches forth to connect to the right index finger of God. Aside from that, it's with our hands and fingers that we often interact with environmental realities, including our interactions with persons, animals, musical instruments, machinery, computers, phones, and a host of recreational and career-related tools.

While our research revealed wide individual differences in the fingerpad photographs among the study's subjects, a strong stability was noted in the repeated photographs for individuals. That finding led to the labeling of the fingerpad pattern for each given subject as that person's unique "energy signature." Occasionally, the energy signature for a particular subject would include a remote image, typical in the form of a small glowing orb of energy found outside the normal range of the signature energy pattern. Our research subjects, upon first viewing the orb in their photographs, almost always concluded that it was the spiritual representation of a personal

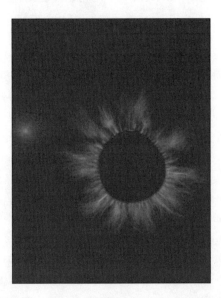

Electrophotographic Recording of Right Index Fingerpad with Remote Image

spirit guide, guardian, or other presence from the spirit realm. Not surprisingly, they felt an instant connection to that presence.

Many of our research subjects, upon viewing the photograph's remote image in the dark room where it was recorded, not only sensed the presence of a personal guide, they also engaged in a meaningful interaction with it. In one remarkable instance, the observation of a glowing orb in the photograph was accompanied by a much larger glowing orb silhouetted against the dark room's wall beyond the photographic station. The bright orb, which we called the "projected orb", was clearly visible to the researcher and the research subject alike. Lingering briefly before slowly fading into the darkness, the projected orb validated the subject's belief that a personal guardian presence had been with her since childhood. In the subject's own words, "The remote image in the photo, accompanied by the external glowing orb, gave clear evidence of my connection to the spirit realm." Other research subjects who experienced the remote image reported similar views. None of them concluded that the phenomenon was merely a chance happening.

A student assistant in the research project, upon noting the remote image in his own photograph, instantly associated it with his deceased father who was killed in the Iraq war. A few days after his father's death, the student, an only child, had been awakened in the night by the sound of his father's voice gently calling out to him by name. Suddenly, a glowing image of his father appeared before him, accompanied by the simple message, "All is well," which was a familiar saying of his father. As the image slowly faded, he felt, in his own words, "instant healing and resolution." The experience changed his view of his father's death and brought enduring assurance that his father was "safe on the other side."

Spirituality in the laboratory reflects the continuing presence of the spirit realm in our daily lives. It is a part of us and we are a part of it. Our personal interactions with it can range from peak experiences that change our views of the very nature of our existence to simply an abiding source of comfort, enrichment, and joy.

SPIRITUALITY AND THE OUT-OF-BODY EXPERIENCE

As spiritual beings, we are endowed with the capacity to disengage the physical body and consciously travel outside it to experience other realities. In that out-of-body state of awareness, we can travel to distant physical realities to observe and interact with them. In some instances, we can actually influence distant physical realities and initiate desired change in them, a phenomenon sometimes called *out-of-body psychokinesis* or simply *astral PK*. In our laboratory studies of this phenomenon, a research subject in the out-of-body state traveled to an art studio located in another campus building, where she accidently tipped over a container of paint brushes. A follow-up investigation of the reported incident validated her account. The container of brushes had spilled exactly as described by the subject.

Laboratory studies of out-of-body PK have reportedly demonstrated numerous espionage applications, including the observation of secretive situations, uncovering of classified documents, and even altering the sensitive settings of equipment. Although some of the applications of out-of-body PK clearly raise certain ethical concerns, the capacity of this extraordinary phenomenon to bring forth desired change far outweighs any hard evidence of its misapplication. There is, in fact, strong evidence of highly positive out-of-body PK interventions, including in situations involving danger or safety risks. A student who, due to a family emergency, drove overnight to her parent's residence in a distant state reported the intermittent awareness of her mother's presence throughout the long trip. According to the student, her mother's presence helped her stay awake and alert. Upon her arrival, her mother confirmed that she had periodically "visited" her daughter during the overnight drive out of concern for her safety.

Given the diverse examples of out-of-body PK, it is not surprising that the out-of-body experience can have important spiritual relevance. In fact, during the out-of-body state, awareness of a spirit presence along with meaningful interactions with the spirit realm is not uncommon. A familiar example is the near-death experience (NDE) in which life-changing interactions with the spirit realm often occur. A fashion designer reported an NDE associated with an auto accident in which she immediately ascended beyond her body to view the accident situation from overhead. She then traveled or, in her words, "glided" into the spirit realm and into the comforting presence of a familiar spirit guide. Once in the spirit realm, she interacted with other spirit beings as beautiful music emanated from a distant multicolored plane of indescribable beauty. She then experienced a comforting interaction with the gathering of warm, accepting souls. Suddenly, her departed mother appeared before her in a radiant garment of blue. They embraced, and during that "reunion of love," as she described it, she felt the healing energy of the spirit realm throughout her being. She then experienced a gently lifting sensation, after which she awakened in a hospital where her recovery was rapid and complete. Although the out-of-body experience was brief, it changed her perspective of not only death but life as well.

OUT-OF-ONE'S-OWN-BODY-AND-INTO-THE-BODY-OF-ANOTHER

Because of the numerous reports of meaningful out-of-body experiences, a research project was designed at Athens State University to explore the therapeutic potential of the out-of-body experience in partner relationships. The innovative program called *Out-of-One's-Own-Body-and-Into-the-Body-of-Another* was based on the concept that experiencing the body of one's partner from within could promote a deeper understanding of the partner and the relationship. Given a deeper understanding of each other, the relationship would become strengthened and empowered to more effectively meet the needs of both partners.

The research project was conducted in a controlled laboratory setting with the couple reclining in close proximity, but without physical contact. The partners, all having completed a college course in experimental parapsychology that included mastery of out-of-body travel techniques, were instructed while resting comfortably to give consent to each other to enter the out-of-body state, and to briefly occupy in astral form the physical body of the other partner. To end the experience, the couple together exited the partner's body and then briefly embraced while lingering together above their bodies before reengaging them.

The twelve couples who volunteered for the experiment all reported success in traveling out-of-body and briefly occupying their partner's body. In the return stage of the experiment, embracing each other while in the astral state was described as profoundly empowering. The couples described the experience as enlightening, and in most instances, sensuously rewarding.

It's important to note that the couples participating in this research found that practice was essential to their success. Given sufficient practice, they succeeded in each stage of the program while remaining in synchronization with their partner for the duration of the exercise.

Our follow-on studies of the experiment revealed highly positive results that included improvements in the overall quality of each relationship. Participants reported a greater understanding of each other and improved success in working productively together. The program proved particularly effective in increasing the sexual quality of the relationship.

THE NATURE OF SPIRITUAL COMMUNICATION

As spiritual beings, each of us is intimately connected to the spirit realm. It's a dimension from which we came and to which we will return. It was not only our home before our first lifetime; it was our home between lifetimes. In each lifetime, our ties to that realm, including our interactions with ministering guides, specialized helpers, guardian entities, and departed souls, offer both enlightenment and power. Through your interactions with the spirit dimension, you have constant access to its limitless powers. You can enrich your life and find solutions to the most difficult of personal problems.

But wait. Is there a downside to the other side? In the following discussion, we'll explore that possibility.

THE DOWNSIDE OF THE OTHER SIDE: FACT OR FICTION

The purpose of our existence in this lifetime is to learn and grow. As evolving souls, our destiny is greatness. In that context, greatness can be best defined as progress in actualizing our existing potentials while, at the same time, attaining new growth possibilities. The evolving of souls thus becomes a never-ending growth process. Even our mistakes, failures, setbacks, and other challenges can open new gateways to spiritual growth and progress. The deep valleys of our past can become challenges that push us upward and forward.

It should come then as no surprise that all the experiences of our past will remain forever with us as important growth resources. Beyond that, all the rich resources of the afterlife realm, including ministering guides and advanced growth specialists, will be available to us to promote our spiritual advancement. Fortunately, as earlier noted, we experience at the moment of our transition at death the restoration of the highest peak of our past growth as an evolving soul, a process we call *the preservation of peak growth.* The regaining of that peak can be explained as the result of disembodiment in which our spiritual genotype (makeup) triumphs over the mortal genotype with its imperfections and deficiencies. With the survival of the spirit over the body accompanied by the restoration of our past peak of spiritual growth, we become even better equipped in afterlife to achieve our destiny for greatness.

Given these enrichments in afterlife, could there possibly be a downside to the other side? Could there be negative barriers and perilous forces of spiritual origin bent on our destruction? Could there be noxious spirit energies poised to defeat us, or at least interrupt our progress? Even worse, could there be evil spirits intent on our total destruction? The answers to these unsettling questions lie in both reason and the findings of rigorous research in a controlled laboratory setting.

Over many years of our research at Athens State University into the nature of the afterlife, we've uncovered not a shred of evidence of dangerous, evil beings in the spirit world. Attributing evil to the afterlife is both irrational and ill-founded. At best, it's a projection of our fears of the unknown; at worst, it's a contradictory misconception of the basic nature of the spirit world. The spirit world is a benevolent, nurturing dimension with resources that are continuously available to us throughout our lives. Among them are personal spirit guides and growth facilitators who are with us in life and will be with us at our transition and beyond. Fears of malevolent spirits, evil spirit manipulators, and wicked possessions can only inhibit the empowering rewards of interacting with the spirit realm. Beyond that, fear of the afterlife can only thwart our search for a deeper understanding of our future destiny.

The popular concept of so-called "spirit attachments" that hinder our progress, or even worse, threaten our destruction is likewise without basis. It's contradictory and illogical to assume that nurturing guides from the spirit realm engage us to promote our progress, while at the same time threatening attachments, also from the spirit world, engage us to prevent our progress. As with other negative assumptions related to the afterlife, there exists no objective evidence of imposing attachments or any other negative force of spirit origin specifically designed to prevent our success as evolving souls. Unfortunately, these irrational assumptions, if accepted, can themselves become attachments that, like heavy baggage, slow our progress, and reduce the quality of our lives.

Now is the time to discard the misconceptions that interrupt our progress and reduce the quality of our lives. Logical optimism generates growth energy—irrational pessimism minimizes it. The spirit realm is a positive place of possibilities, not limitations. Rather than a distant inaccessible dimension, the spirit realm is a present reality that's constantly available to you. You can reach out and touch it right now! Its empowering and growth resources will never reject your probes.

THE MEDIUM WITHIN

Like your best personal psychic, therapist, and healer, your best personal medium exists within yourself as an essential part of your being. That medium is your personal link to the spirit realm with its abundance of empowering resources. When you connect to that medium, you will have full access to the spiritual enlightenment you need at the moment. Aside from that, you will interface the critical growth resources required for your spiritual fulfillment. While spiritual knowledge from any source is empowering, the spiritual growth available to you through the medium within is raw spiritual power that unleashes your latent growth processes and energizes you with the capacity to realize your present potentials while equipping you with totally new ones.

To interact with the medium within, one of the most effective approaches is the *Medium Activation Lift* that raises your awareness of that medium and connects you to its powers. With that connection, you have full access to all the spiritual resources you need at the moment, including those existing in the spirit realm. As a central part of yourself, your inner medium knows your past, present, and future. It's more than a tool to be used—it's your constant contact with the spirit realm. When you're attuned to that core of your being, enlightenment, power, and success are available to you.

To begin the Medium Activation Lift, find a quiet place and take a few moments to settle back and clear your mind of active thought. With your eyes closed, visualize the bright core at the center of your being. Let the brightness of that core expand to infuse your full being—mind, body, and spirit—with bright energy. Think of that brightness as the life force that sustains your existence as a soul being. Take plenty of time for that infusion to reach its peak. Sense the balance and attunement that always accompany the infusion process.

As you remain infused with bright energy, visualize the spirit realm as a bright energy source. Let that source take shape, possibly as a series of colorful planes of energy. As the shapes form, sense your connection to them and allow yourself to interact with them. You can facilitate that process by visualizing beams of energy connecting you to the energies of the spirit realm. At this stage of the exercise, you may experience your consciousness rising to embrace the spirit realm with its intelligent guides, helpers, growth specialists, and gathering of souls, some of whom will probably seem familiar to you. Among the gathering of souls, you may recognize certain of the departed, including significant others who welcome your presence. Not infrequently, certain entities will capture your attention and communicate important messages related to your present concerns or life situation. Impressions as well as specific spoken messages regarding the future can also emerge at this stage. Take plenty of time to linger at this stage and contemplate upon the messages that come forth.

When this stage of the program runs its course, shift your attention again to the inner medium situated at the innermost core of your being. Listen to the messages emerging from that knowing part of your inner self. At this stage, solutions to pressing problems, such as conflicts and difficult relationships, will often unfold.

TOOLS AND TECHNIQUES

Although our interactions with the spirit realm are often spontaneous and thus unplanned, a wide range of tools and techniques is now available to access that realm's abundant growth resources. The most powerful tools and techniques of spirit communications are those that balance and attune us to the spirit realm. While a particular technique can retrieve important bits and pieces of spiritual information, it is most effective when it brings us into a state of harmony within ourselves and with the spirit dimension. Equipped with spiritual insight through such programs as the séance, table tipping, and other mediumistic approaches, we can experience profound spiritual interactions that energize us with new insight and growth potential. You will find, however, that your interactions with the spirit dimension are unique to you—you have sole ownership of them. When integrated within, they become an essential part of you. In the final analysis, it becomes up to us individually to connect the dots and form our own conclusions. No one is better qualified for that task than you. The following tools and techniques of spiritual empowerment can facilitate that all-important process.

TABLE TIPPING

Table tipping, also called table tapping and table tilting, has in recent years gained popularity because of its purported usefulness in gathering highly meaningful information of spiritual origin. The technique is based on the concept that a tangible object, when used as an extension of the human energy system, can "tap into" sources of spiritual knowledge and power. In table tapping, that tangible object is usually a common card table, preferably with wooden legs. The procedure is typically initiated when a group of four persons is seated around the table with their fingertips (the body's antennae) resting lightly upon the table. Following a brief meditative state in which sources beyond are invited to communicate through the table, the group with hands resting on the table awaits a response that signals the presence of a spirit source.

Within moments, the table will typically signal a presence, first by subtle vibrations, followed by increased movement, and finally by the tilting of one side of the table as the group's hands continue to rest upon it. With the table in the tilted position, a member of the group invites the table to respond to the group's questions by tapping once upon the floor to signify a "yes" response and twice to signify "no." The table is further invited to tap thrice to questions to signal the unavailability of a "yes" or "no" answer. The table then typically retains the tilt position and awaits questions from the group. In table tipping, a permissive, nondemanding approach by the group throughout the program is essential to the success of the exercise.

The group's questions in table tipping can range from inquiries concerning the nature of the spirit realm to personal issues and concerns. They can include questions regarding future events, distant happenings, financial matters, career concerns, and the well-being of the departed. While departed souls are not "called up" or summoned, they are sometimes invited to communicate through the table if they choose to do so. Not infrequently, a departed friend or relative of a group member will come forth to communicate personally.

To end the table tilting session, the participants, with hands continuing to rest upon the table, express their gratitude for the opportunity to interact with the spirit realm and their appreciation for the spirit communications that emerged during the sessions. The table then typically returns to the rest position.

Table tipping is an excellent approach to activate the medium existing within oneself. Once a mediumistic connection is established, the possibilities reach far beyond the constricted information provided by the taps of the table. In table tipping, the mediumistic interaction, once activated, can add meaning to the experience that far exceeds the specific information provided through the table's tapping responses.

Table tipping has been effectively used by investigative psychics to gather specific information related to crime, including murder, in which the victim has been known to come forth through the table. While that information is not eligible for use in courts of law, it can provide critical knowledge, including specific clues that hold investigative significance. Psychics who use this technique often find that their clairvoyant powers related to the crime are activated. Detailed descriptions of the criminal act, crime scene, locations of lost weapons, and physical descriptions of the perpetrator(s) have been obtained by this simple technique. An investigative psychic and member of the Parapsychology Research Institute and Foundation regularly uses table tipping in her work. Her consultant services are in great demand, not only in Alabama, but throughout the Southeast. In her own words, "As a psychic, I use whatever resources are available to me, including table tipping."

Here are a few other applications of table tipping:

TABLE TIPPING APPLICATIONS

- Table tipping can promote attunement to the spirit realm.
- It offers opportunities to communicate with spiritual guides.
- It can provide information related to past lives, including the relevance of past-life experiences to the present.
- It can be used to gain important information related to lost articles.
- It can offer information related to personal concerns and relationships.
- It can address health issues, including those related to physical fitness and longevity.
- It can provide information regarding financial affairs, including investments and other financial management decisions.
- It can meet our needs to communicate with the departed and their needs to communicate with us.
- It can predict future happenings, including events of both personal and global relevance.
- It can identify career opportunities and provide specific information related to career success.

THE SÉANCE

The séance is a small group activity designed to communicate with a spirit source. It can include communications with the departed as well as such spiritual entities as guides and teachers. The séance group usually consists of at least three people who gather around a small round or oval table in a room free of distractions, typically with subdued lighting. At this stage, a medium among the group can be designated as the group's contact with the spirit realm, or if preferred, any member of the group can exercise the medium within, an alternative that recognizes the mediumistic potential existing in everyone.

To initiate the mediumistic interaction, the group with hands resting upon the table typically invites sources from the spirit realm to manifest their presence and communicate with the group. A focused state of receptiveness is then formed by the group by clearing the mind and, with eyes closed, mentally expressing openness to impressions and specific messages of spiritual origin. Advanced séance groups typically use a permissive approach that avoids summoning spirits in the belief that the sources appropriate for the situation at hand will voluntarily come forth.

Once contact is established with the spirit realm, mediumistic interactions with spirit beings are welcomed. The typical séance experience will include both informational and emotional exchanges, many of which can have significant empowering effects. Interactions with departed friends, family members, and personal spirit guides are common. Spontaneity within the group facilitates the interaction and adds to the relevance of the experience.

To end the séance, members of the group typically join hands and express gratitude for their interactions with spirits from the other side. The impressions and perceptions of group members are then shared and the empowering possibilities of the experience are explored with the full group. Special attention is focused on the empowering effects of the experience.

Almost always, the lingering presence of spirit entities, especially spirit guides, will continue well after the séance, a phenomenon we've labeled the *séance aftereffect*. Beyond that, the so-called *séance spin-off effect* can reach far beyond the séance situation to motivate and empower séance participants with success in achieving their personal goals. These two effects can be seen as a function of the inner medium existing in all of us. As such, they can be far more empowering than the brief interactions experienced during the formal séance session. Both effects reflect the importance of spontaneity over stilted adherence to procedural structure in the séance experience.

The modern séance, while recognizing the medium existing in everyone, is based on the synergistic concept that several mediums working together are more effective than one medium working alone. The effect of working together can overcome our personal limitations and tear down the walls that too often separate us from the other side. Although the spirit realm is a dimension that's as close as the air we breathe, we all too often erect artificial barriers that separate us from it. The séance as a group experience transcends those self-imposed partitions and brings us into a state of oneness with the spirit realm as our present source of power and our future destination as evolving souls.

The deeper our understanding of spirit communications, the deeper our understanding of ourselves and the spiritual nature of our existence. Although we are mind, body, and spirit, without the spirit we would not exist. Only the spirit is forever. It's the spirit that gives meaning to our existence and direction to our strivings as soul beings. Through our spirit communications, we become empowered to experience the spirit realm in all its beauty and power. Best of all, we can experience that realm for ourselves right now. We don't have to wait until the afterlife, nor do we have to depend on others. We have at this moment the best of spirit mediums—it exists within each of us. We furthermore have at this moment the best of spirit guides—they are our constant companions. There could be no better sources of enlightenment, fulfillment, and power!

Spirit Communication for Just One or Two

We've discussed the séance and table tipping—both of which tend to involve a group of people. While not necessary, generally the card table used in table tipping suggests the need for four people, while a séance may only involve two people but generally there are groups of three or more, and even rather large congregations or "audiences" of sometimes hundreds of people.

Other familiar tools that may be used include the Ouija board, accommodating two people, and the pendulum, easily used by a single person. You will find information on using the pendulum in Chapter Twenty-one, and the Ouija is so familiar that it hardly needs special instructions.

As always, what is important in all practice and research is a certain basic discipline—even when, as is often the situation, people at first engage with psychic tools for personal and party entertainment. To get results, here is a reminder of the basic rules of engagement:

1. Respect. Treat the tool and technology with respect—just as is desirable whether you are using a computer, driving a car, using a lawn mower, or even a shovel. Every tool is an extension of your whole physical and energetic body and you will always get better results through respect for the equipment.

2. Planning. Know what you need to do in the way of preparation, including:

   a. Physical relaxation—get rid of the tension that can stand between you and the subconscious and other consciousness. Relaxation clears the way.

   b. Preliminary ritual—it can be as formal or informal as you desire. It can be a prayer or simply a statement of your intention. The point is to set the stage and establish your expectations for success.

  c. Frame your questions—preferably in writing. It really is only when you put something on paper that it starts the process of physical manifestation.

3. Engage. Ask your questions and work with the chosen tool.

4. Thanks. Always express appreciation for the results. Again, be as formal or informal as you like. There is reason to believe that for every established tool or technique, there is a psychic entity formed that has grown with the practice and that works with your subconscious mind. Give it respect and appreciation.

5. Record your results. Even if your participation was entertaining, write down the answers to your questions accompanied by any observations and feelings.

6. Conclude. Return your tools to their container and place. Again, give them respect and protect them from casual handling.

Automatic Writing

Another well-recognized method of spirit and psychic communication is Automatic Writing, which may be experienced as a direct communication from a deceased person's spirit, or sometimes a higher spirit channeling through the writer, or as a communication from the personal subconscious. In most cases, it starts as a kind of involuntary process where the writer is unaware of the communication until it is completed.

As a psychic empowerment strategy, automatic writing is based on two important concepts: first, information existing in the subconscious regions of the mind persistently seeks manifestation in conscious awareness; and second, indirect channels, including automatic writing, can activate inner psychic faculties and access hidden sources of knowledge when more direct channels are either unavailable, or if available, are less efficient.

Automatic writing is a psychic accessing strategy in which spontaneous or involuntary writing is used to bring forth information from the subconscious mind. The technique is believed by some to tap into other sources of knowledge as well, including higher planes. Usually, the only materials required are a writing pen and paper. The pen is held in the writing position with the point resting lightly on the writing surface, as meaningful written messages are permitted to unfold.

A brief relaxation and mental-clearing exercise in which physical tension is released and active thought is minimized or banished altogether can increase the effectiveness of automatic writing.

The initial products in automatic writing are often illegible; but once meaningful writing emerges, the technique can provide important messages about the past, present, and future. Automatic writing can consist of a single significant word, sentence,

or phrase; and occasionally the technique will produce a drawing or other meaningful symbol. Although the technique often is used in an open-ended fashion, as
a completely spontaneous expression of the self, it can be used to gather answers to
specific questions or to find solutions to particular problems. At advanced levels, it
can access highly significant sources of psychic knowledge. For instance, a woman
who had been given up for adoption at birth used automatic writing to successfully
locate her biological brother. In another case, a writer used automatic writing to create the names for characters in a short story. Still other examples include a college
student who used automatic writing to develop major ideas for a research project; an
industrial firm that engaged a psychic consultant to explore the company's expansion
options; a consultant who identified an option which, once implemented, resulted in
a highly successful new product line; and a psychic consultant who used automatic
writing to gather critical information that led to the solution of a series of crimes.

Because of its capacity to tap into the psychic mind and channel messages, automatic writing, as a psychic accessing tool, has almost unlimited psychic applications.
Precognitively, the technique can tap into the future and provide information needed
for planning and decision making. At the advanced level of this technique's clairvoyant and precognitive applications, no reality can escape the penetrating probe of the
psychic pen.

As already noted, automatic writing as a psychic empowerment procedure is more
effective when preceded by a brief period of meditation, during which affirmations
are presented that are designed to prepare oneself for the exercise and to program the
technique to explore the psychic sources of knowledge. Here are a few examples.

*My psychic mind is now responsive to the probes of automatic writing. The infor-
mation I need will become available to me through this empowering technique.
Through automatic writing, I can activate my inner psychic faculties to endow
me with insight and expanded awareness. The one hundred billion cells of my
brain await the empowering intervention of automatic writing. Through automatic writing, the deepest recesses of my mind will yield their empowering secrets.*

These general empowering affirmations are usually followed by specific queries
designed to address an unlimited range of concerns.

*How can I increase my psychic powers? What investments should I consider at
this time? What do I need to know about my future? In what career field will I
find greatest satisfaction?*

When automatic writing is used to discover a specific answer, the question is usually written at the top of the page before beginning the process.

The effectiveness of automatic writing as a psychic tool is directly related to the spontaneity of the process. Any conscious intent to influence the process can negate its psychic significance. With conscious functions subdued and the physical body sufficiently relaxed, our psychic channels can be activated, and the sources of psychic insight accessed, through this empowering technique.

Through automatic writing, past experiences lost to conscious awareness are often brought forth. This phenomenon was illustrated by an armed robbery witness who used automatic writing to retrieve crucial information about the crime. Through the highly specific information produced by automatic writing, including a thorough description of the perpetrators and the getaway vehicle, investigators were successful in promptly solving the case.

One of the most important empowering applications of automatic writing is its therapeutic role in probing the subconscious for strivings, motives, and conflicts buried within the self. Knowledge and insight can be brought forth as a new surge of personal awareness and power. Note that the subconscious mind typically yields only the information we are prepared to accommodate at the time: A chemist who experienced frequent anxiety attacks used automatic writing to discover the hidden sources of her distress. A victim of sexual abuse in childhood, she had buried the painful experience in her subconscious mind. Unfortunately, repressed experiences, though outside conscious awareness, continue to assert their disempowering effects—typically in the form of either painful anxiety or some exaggerated defense mechanisms. Upon finally discovering the source of her anxiety through a series of automatic writings, the chemist was able to resolve the conflicts surrounding the abuse, and successfully overcome the anxiety that had plagued her for many years. This example of automatic writing reflects the advanced therapeutic skills of the subconscious mind. Through automatic writing, the therapeutic mind spontaneously yielded critical, but painful, information, while at the same time providing the coping resources essential to her recovery. Indeed, the model therapist exists within each of us. Automatic writing is but one of the many strategies that can connect us to that healing part of the inner self.

A major advantage of automatic writing over other psychic accessing strategies concerns the nature of the information the procedure can produce. The information yielded by some psychic tools is highly constricted, and in some instances limited to simple "yes" or "no" responses. Automatic writing, on the other hand, can address such concerns as what, when, where, why, and how. At its most advanced level, automatic writing is limited only by our willingness to yield to our subconscious faculties, and by the capacity of written language to communicate. Achieving that optimal level requires skill in consciously surrendering to the inner, knowing part of the self and allowing its written expression.

Because it is not subject to the screening and suppressive functions of consciousness, automatic writing, once mastered, offers a direct line to the vast powers of the subconscious mind. The super-intelligent part of our inner self is accessed and liberated, resulting in a full and free expression of our inner powers.

Automatic writing can overcome the language barriers that often thwart inner communication. Among its major functions is the translation of subconscious images into a meaningful conscious reality: the written word. Imagery is the native language of the subconscious mind, and as such, it is the most powerful language known. Imagery can convey an almost unlimited range of emotions and knowledge. Incipient imagery has been the embryo of major scientific inventions, new discoveries, and even global change. Seminal imagery can provide us with a challenging vision of our highest destiny, and empower us to achieve our loftiest goals. Through imagery we can get a glimpse of the vast regions of our inner world of awareness and stored experience. Automatic writing can tap into that inner powerhouse to permit direct, undisguised written expressions of empowering insight.

Automatic writing can enrich our psychic faculties and expand our capacity to actively communicate and interact with the inner self. Inner psychic communication channels—dreams, intuitions, and psychic impressions—can be supplemented and clarified. Many psychic communications occur in disguised or symbolic forms that require a concentrated effort to glean the essential substance of the message. Automatic writing is a powerful tool for disrobing the disguised figure of psychic communication. An impression of a rose can symbolize a developing romantic relationship, whereas a psychic impression of a whirlpool can represent a social relationship spinning out of control and overwhelming us. Automatic writing can be applied to glean the true meaning of these symbols from among the many possibilities.

Psychic messages, including many of our dream messages, can occur strangely in antithetical form—seeming the direct opposite of what really is intended. An impression of death can signify birth, and an impression of joy can signify sadness. Fortunately, the antithetical impression is usually accompanied by a clue that reveals its antithetical nature, such as an additional, but incongruent impression. Aside from antithesis, many psychic impressions are so general that deciphering their specific meanings can be very difficult. Automatic writing can be a useful tool for exploring the antithetical possibilities and true meanings of these disguised psychic signals. For this application of automatic writing, the sentence completion technique has been highly effective. Some examples of unfinished sentences are:

"My impression of danger means…"

"I need to concentrate on…"

"I will find happiness in…";

"My life is …";

"I can profit from …";

"I predict …";

"It is important that …"; and,

"My future …"

Automatic writing, as an adjunct to dream analysis, can follow each dream element to its root, and unleash empowering nutrients to permeate the self with new vigor and growth. A word-association method can help decipher the dream's symbolic meaning, using automatic writing to amplify and expound on the written dream symbol. Following are selected examples of dream symbols and their meanings as derived through automatic writing:

Dream Symbol	Meaning
Bridge	Change and opportunity
Earthquake	Loss of valued possession
Falling	Out of control
Fire	Anger that can be destructive
Fog	Go slowly, but don't give up
Letter	Listen to your inner self
Moon	Future romance
Ocean	Destiny
Sunrise	A new beginning

An expanded list of dream symbols and their meanings is found in the Appendix of Dream Symbols at the end of this book. Because a given dream symbol can have many interpretations, automatic writing is a useful tool for sorting through those possibilities and identifying those most relevant. The effectiveness of automatic writing in dream analysis requires practice and a willingness to explore the secret recesses of the mind. We are the best interpreters of our own dreams, and within each of us is an expert dream analyst who awaits our purposeful probes. Automatic writing equips us to engage that inner analyst in an empowerment interaction that can unleash an abundance of new insight and growth possibilities.

Aside from its complementary role in facilitating psychic processes, automatic writing can function independently of other psychic channels. It can directly probe the future, activate repressed faculties, initiate empowering dialogue, and generate new psychic knowledge and understanding. In its ultimate form, automatic writing can connect us to the central core of our existence; it can channel universal wisdom and manifest it materially as a visual, written message.

Any skill that unleashes our capacity for self-expression and discovery is essentially self-empowering. Automatic writing is valued as a psychic empowerment tool because it achieves that important goal. All the references to accessing the psychic faculties apply equally and more famously to automatic writing's use in spirit communication.

In addition, various books have been written, or claimed to have been written, while the authors were in trance with their hands guided by spiritual entities. Among the more famous are the writings of American Andrew Jackson Davis, including *The Principles of Nature, Her Divine Revelations, and a Voice to Mankind* published in 1847. Another is the "New Bible," *Oahspe,* by John Ballou Newbrough, published in 1882 and reported to have been written on a typewriter at enormous speeds.

While perhaps not the same as automatic writing, the receipt of information while in a trance state is, at least, similar. Two of the most important writers of dictated material are Alice Bailey and H. P. Blavatsky. Perhaps the most famous contemporary work that claimed to have been dictated by an inner voice is *The Course in Miracles*, published in 1976 with sales of over two million copies.

Prophets as Channels of God

It's easy to overlook the role that spirit communication has had in all the major religions. We tend to think that there was something special about the past that can't be duplicated in the present—and perhaps that is true. Nevertheless, it was human beings who received—*channeled*—the sacred teachings that are the foundation of at least the three major religions of the West.

Subsequent teachers—who were also prophets—are within the range of historic recording, but they themselves credited their own messages to divine sources—either to God or to archangels and spiritual intermediaries.

Why only in the distant past?

One answer is that our modern times are filled with distraction, with interference, and with "overload," making psychic and spiritual communication more difficult. Another answer is that, instead of turning within for guidance, we look to external experts and authorities for answers. Yet another answer is that we commonly "lack faith" that such direct experience is possible for people who have been conditioned to not only ignore the divinity within but to deny it. God is beyond, and even those who believe in a personal intermediary see that being as likewise distant. Religious practitioners are taught to *worship* rather than *communicate*. Even prayer is seen as impersonal—like the purchase of a lottery ticket that might be a winner, although we all know that's unlikely.

Spirits are a step away, on the "other side," and other beings—prophets, angels, archangels, etc.—are still more steps away, but there is no barrier between living people and the spiritual realities of this "other side."

Perhaps, like spirits of your loved ones, they are only waiting for you to reach toward them to make contact.

Spirits and Spirits

We often refer to the "departed" as spirits. We also refer to other entities as spirits. In different traditions, there are spirits of place, spirits of the natural elements, spirits of the animal species and of the natural world, and there are spirits of natural phenomena. Some of these are called "gods," and some are prayed to and petitioned for all those human desires of love, health, wealth, protection, special knowledge, blessings, and more.

Magicians often recognize two approaches to these other spirits: evocation and invocation. Evocation acts to bring a spirit to an external place outside of the magician's body for communication, while invocation brings a spirit *within* the magician.

Magicians may also recognize their own highest self—that portion of personal consciousness we call our Soul and the magician calls his *Holy Guardian Angel.* All the ceremonies and studies of "Magick" are steps toward identification with the Holy Guardian Angel, the same process referred to as "individuation" by Carl Jung—the bringing together of all the different functions we identify as the subconscious, conscious, and superconscious minds, getting rid of psychological baggage and conflict, and leaving the soul a fit vehicle for Divine inclusion.

Divination, whether through astrology, geomancy, or Tarot, or other methods, are all practices that develop the psychic powers innate to those who are themselves part of the total consciousness unified into the Whole Person expressing and glorifying the Divinity from within.

Spirit communication, no matter at what level or in what manner it is practiced, is filled with great potential. All the different tools and techniques are "bridges" to cross the divide that normally separates the material world from the greater spiritual worlds and dimensions. They are all steps toward your psychic empowerment, and every accomplishment is further progress in self-empowerment.

There are two ways to study Spirit communication: (1) to read about it, and (2) to do it. In this chapter we hope to have given you enough to read all the information you need to do it. We hope we have excited you sufficiently to take up any of the tools we've described and prepare you for an exciting and productive adventure.

SOURCES AND RECOMMENDED READING

Ted Andrews, *How to Meet & Work with Spirit Guides* (Llewellyn, 1992).

Raymond Buckland, *Buckland's Book of Spirit Communication* (Llewellyn, 2004).

Rose Vanden Eynden, *So You Want to be a Medium: A Down-to-Earth Guide* (Llewellyn, 2010).

Migene Gonzalez-Wippler, *What Happens After Death: Scientific & Personal Evidence for Survival* (Llewellyn, 1951).

Jon Klimo, *Channeling: Investigations on Receiving Information from Paranormal Sources* (Tarcher, 1987).

Konstantinos, *Speak with the Dead: Seven Methods for Spirit Communication* (Llewellyn, 2004).

Donald Michael Kraig, *The Truth About Evocation of Spirits* (Llewellyn, 1951).

Jodi Livon, *The Happy Medium: Awakening to Your Natural Intuition* (Llewellyn, 2009).

Patrick Mathews, *Never Say Goodbye: A Medium's Stories of Connecting with Your Loved Ones* (Llewellyn, 2003).

Edain McCoy, *How to Do Automatic Writing* (Llewellyn, 1994).

Elizabeth Owens, *How to Communicate with Spirits* (Llewellyn, 2001).

Elizabeth Owens, *Spiritualism & Clairvoyance for Beginners: Simple Techniques to Develop Your Psychic Abilities* (Llewellyn, 2005).

Troy Parkinson, *Bridge to the Afterlife: A Medium's Message of Hope & Healing* (Llewellyn, 2009).

Richard Webster, *Spirit Guides & Angel Guardians* (Llewellyn, 1998).

Colin Wilson, *After Life: Survival of the Soul* (Llewellyn, 2000).

Sara Wiseman, *Writing the Divine: How to Use Channeling for Soul Growth & Healing* (Llewellyn, 2009).

24

THE RUNES: FIRE & ICE
Our Northern Heritage

Note: We have gone into the subject of the Runes rather deeply in order to illustrate the apparent process in which a people's mythology, and the creation myth in particular, evolve, and lead first to the appearance of divinatory tools and then to the development of practical forms of magic. In the process, techniques of psychic development appear and lead to forms of a shamanic religion and then into "revealed religion."

Even after a later religion, Christianity, replaced the earlier, very rich Norse/ Germanic Paganism, and then modern culture and science in turn reduced the dominant role of religion in explaining "how things work," the roles of divination and magic remain and become more practical and applicable to personal growth and self-development.

Runic Divination and Runic Magick do work reliably, and reveal a well-structured cosmology and esoteric psychology comparable to that of the Kabbalah. However, it must be pointed out that the Northern Tradition's World Tree is not directly compatible with the Kabbalah's "Tree of Life." Each provides complex structures for organizing human experience and perceptions of the workings of the universe. Individual components of each system can find a correspondence in the other, but they are not always identical.

Because the myth is apparently Norse in origin, we have given preference to the Old Norse spellings for the names of the gods, with the German name in parentheses and the English and other spellings as alternatives. However, it is the German names for the Runes that have become the best known and it is those that we use in this chapter. It should not present any confusion, and hopefully will instead inspire further interest and study.

The Runes are well known but little understood images (originally wood carvings) used in both Divination and Magick. The word itself means "secret," and secret they are until personally activated by the user. Their origin is ancient and the lore is prehistoric, coming to us from undated verbal tradition, song, and poetry. They are part of the Nordic and Germanic pagan traditions, and like all ancient religions were ruthlessly suppressed by the Roman Catholic Church, and then further repressed and lost as modern culture denigrated the Pagan past.

Their use in divination and magick as signs and symbols precedes their evolvement as an alphabet called "Futhark," and then into a language. It is as symbols that the runes are significant. There is little understanding of the origin of *symbols* that embody meanings in contrast to *signs* that represent messages. A "STOP" sign is a specific message to stop a particular activity. A symbol—astrological, alchemical, religious, magical, and so forth—is "loaded" with meanings that are in turn specifically informative or that evoke feelings and awaken intuition.

Some symbols, such as the Christian cross, are historical in origin and deliberately associated with an event and as a "sign of affiliation," and have come to embody specific "magical powers" related to religious functions of blessings, exorcism, acceptance into the faith, consecration, spiritual cleansing, and so forth.

Other symbols originated as signs but have taken on many associations—such as that used to warn about nuclear radiation—that evoke feelings, remind us of historical events, represent arguments and debates about use in nuclear power, medicine, and weaponry.

There are other symbols that represent archetypal functions, perceptions, and events such as those in Tarot Cards, and yet others like those of the I Ching that represent the flow of life processes.

But there other symbols, like the Runes and the Tattwas, that have mythic origins and seem to actually embody Occult (psychic, magical, spiritual) powers, and energy processes and movement. To say that a symbol has a mythic origin merely reveals a mystery—we don't really know how or who or what was involved in its creation. It seems as if they were *self-evolved* or "channeled" from a higher consciousness. The creation myth we will relate later says that the Runes were discovered and recovered through a shamanic process by Odin (Wotan), the first god himself. In ancient practices, it was believed that it was the actual shape of the Rune (or the Tattwa) that excites and expresses (and projects) the specific power represented.

In the late nineteenth century, the revival of interest in Germanic and Nordic paganism led to the rediscovery of the Runes as more than ornament and an old "alphabet." Later, the German nationalists and then the Nazis adopted some of the Runes as symbols for their movement—fascinated by their occult powers and the grandeur of the warrior mythology and poetry.

In recent years, there was a literal explosion of interest in the Runes, and their lore and philosophy, through J. R. R. Tolkien's *The Lord of the Rings*. A broad revival of Northern Paganism in the United States has brought about a popular interest in runic divination and magical practice—although there is still little understanding of the fundamental power of the Runes themselves hidden beneath their popularity as a "fortune telling" system.

The Northern Tradition is essentially shamanic rather than religious—although modern devotees attempt to turn it into a religious movement with all the hierarchy and theological rigidity of Christianity, against which they have rebelled.

Michael Howard, in *The Magic of the Runes,* states this clearly:

The wizards who used the runes for magical purposes regarded themselves as blood kin to Odin, the Nordic god who was popularly accredited with inventing the runic alphabet. As we have seen, they were basically followers of the shamanistic tradition which is one of the oldest, if not the oldest, religious belief systems known to humanity…

Howard believes that the Runes are so ancient and so fundamental—*so loaded with intrinsic power*—that their modern usage will turn the user into a kind of shaman. The "father-god" of the Norse people was himself a shaman and everything about the Northern Tradition is shamanic. Their study will involve more than a "dictionary of meanings" and will require some immersion into the world of their gods and goddesses, into their practical magick, and a feeling for their poetry.

THE SOURCE OF DIVINATION AND MAGICK

With few possible exceptions, truly functional divinatory practices and magical systems derive from the creation myth of a particular land and people. It is this myth that reflects their worldview of our origins, how and why things happen, and how natural forces—inner and outer—can be altered for individual and group benefit.

I believe the Nordic/Germanic tradition is one of very few in which the creation myth specifically describes the origin of its divinatory and magical tools, the twenty-four Runes known as *Futhark.* In other traditions, there are subsequent stories or myths about their divinatory tools—of which the Tarot and the I Ching may be the best known.

The Runes themselves are symbols, or *occult formulae*, for the working Cosmic Forces as perceived by their shamanic discoverer. Rune Divination and Rune Magick are part of the complex cosmology of the peoples of northern Europe and Scandinavia.

Historically, this Nordic/Teutonic tradition and culture came into conflict with the Celtic tradition and culture of middle Europe. And then both these traditions came into historic conflict with that of southern Europe, mostly Greco-Roman, with the Roman Empire's subjugation of much of middle and northern Europe.

And the Roman Empire prepared the way for the Catholic Church and the various Christian offshoots to dominate, suppress, and convert the older Pagan traditions.

But the death of the Pagan religions did not wholly destroy the culture of the people, their art and their social perspectives formed by the beautiful and rugged environment. Nor did the imposition of Christianity and exposure to the broader European civilization alter their divinatory and magical perspectives or the many remnants of their folklore and folk practices that now contribute to our inner landscape and psychic world.

THE ROLE OF MYTH AND HISTORY

Ancient traditions come to us through myth and history.

There is no "real" history of humanity's earliest years. What we do have is scientific speculation based upon the discovery of ancient artifacts—bones, broken pottery, gravesites, indications of early settlements, cave paintings, petrified remains of cook fires and foods, shattered weapons, and finally—depending on the locations and the prevailing climate—larger artifacts and remnants of preserved foods, companion animals, jewelry and clothing, mummified bodies, art and statuary, and early indications of religion. And from these artifacts and remains, we try to understand the folklore and formative mythology to tell us about a particular people's movement and advancement in the world.

As humanity spread across the Earth, and as families evolved into tribes, and tribes united in larger units, becoming distinct cultures and eventually nations, there were first some individuals who gained understanding of the seasonal cycles and of the habits of those animals who were predators upon men, and those upon which men were the predators. As men gained further understanding of the signs of weather, and the nature of vegetation, and learned to distinguish plants that were beneficial and those that were harmful, members of a group began to specialize in distinct social functions.

Some became leaders of the hunt and eventually warriors defending family and tribe; others discovered and taught agricultural practices and became farmers and nomadic herders. Some developed abilities for making tools and weapons, and better and more individualized clothing distinguishing gender, position, and even occupation. Others became craftsmen, making dwellings and fortifications, and then simple furniture. Others expressed themselves through art and making jewelry, and began the all-important process of beautification of person and home.

As minimal as these early efforts may seem, we see that men have always been explorers, inventors, artisans, farmers, hunters, builders—always improving upon the efforts of earlier generations, always enlarging their habitat. Always "ever forward, ever upward."

Some looked upward and around, and speculated about the creation of the universe as they saw it, and about the origin of mankind. In seeking understanding, we have the beginnings of mythology, and then of technology, science, and religion.

Culture, technology, science, and religion all start with the particular creation myths of a people.

Creation myths reflect the natural environment in particular geographic areas. Is the local climate predominantly hot, cold, wet, or dry? Is it characterized by mountains or deserts, forests, or savannahs? Are there active volcanoes, frequent earth movement, devastating storms? What of the natural resources—is water plentiful or scarce, are there rivers across broad areas? Is the area seriously dependent on monsoons to supply needed water? Is the area rich in food and is that food vegetative, animal, or fish? Are there dangerous animals? And, what of human marauders—are they painfully recurrent?

The answers to these questions form the background of the creation myths. Myths are the stories that fill in the gaps between what we know and what we don't yet know. Myths make sense of the world of experience and provide structure upon which culture grows. Myths are created by the seekers of cosmological understanding about the origins of the universe and of man.

Whether through dreams and visions, intuition, or spirit's voices, the seekers formulated stories about creation and humankind's relationship to the forces and intelligence behind creation. These creation myths were peopled with supernatural beings fulfilling for the tribe and the culture those roles already familiar to the people: Father, Mother, Child, Friend, Foe, Predator, Defender, Healer, Leader, Arbiter. Those who communicated with spirits, interpreted dreams, and understood signs and omens, were the shamans as the cultures expanded and continued to evolve.

These supernatural beings became gods and goddesses "ruling" the various natural, biological, and social functions, and then the gods themselves sought additional specific knowledge and powers to help their "children," the people of the culture. And, nearly always, there was the person set apart from others who could travel the inner dimensions of time and space—the shaman who spoke with the deities and answered the people's questions about why things were as they were and how they could be changed.

BACKGROUND TO THE NORDIC CREATION MYTH

All creation myths have certain similarities, but each culture's mythology reflects the nature of reality as it is perceived by the people and, in particular, those "seekers" attempting to explain the nature of the world and the relationship of humanity to the forces of the universe and life.

The climate of the Northern world is mostly cold and wintery, and the land is rugged and more demanding than comfortably beneficent. Survival requires knowledge, planning, and strategy. It necessitates protection against the harsh winters, against predatory animals like wolves and bears, and likewise protection against marauders, both from nearby tribes and invaders coming from more distant cultures.

The Northern landscape is one of "Fire and Ice"—some of it frozen much of the year; some of it with active volcanoes and hot springs; much of it having mountains and long, rugged coasts with many rivers and deep valleys. While there were hunters and farmers, it was fishermen who characterized the culture. The people became seafarers of necessity, building large seaworthy vessels that they learned to navigate across great distances beyond visible land. In addition to fishing, they became marauders and then pirates. And they became explorers, pushing the boundaries of their known world to establish colonies in Iceland, Greenland, and then "Vineland," the outpost in North America that did not survive into modern times. Families were mostly clustered into small communities, often isolated from one another during the long winters. The long winters required careful preservation of food and fuel, and defense against attacks from those in need.

It is against this backdrop that the Northern Creation myth developed, and from which the Runes come alive in reading and deliver meaningful interpretations today.

THE MYTH: FIRE AND ICE

It is said that in the beginning was nothing, only a great void of chaotic forces known as *Ginnungagap*. Then a land of darkness, cold, mist, and ice appeared in the north called *Niflheim*, and in the south a land of fire, *Muspellsheim*. Twelve frigid rivers flowing from the north merged in Ginnungagap with rivers of fire and light from the south, creating *Eiter*—the fundamental substance that is the source of all life. From Eiter there arose the first being, the frost giant *Ymir*, a hermaphrodite giant in human shape, and *Audhumla*, the great cow, whose milk fed Ymir. From the sweat of Ymir's armpits came a son and daughter and from his legs came another son. Thus was born the race of evil frost giants.

Audhumla licked ice for sustenance and one day some hair emerged, the next day a head, and on the third day *Buri* emerged, fully formed. Buri, the primal precursor of man with neither father nor mother, self-begot a son, *Borr*, who married *Bestla*, daughter of the frost giant *Boltha* and produced the first of the Norse race of gods, *Odin* and his sons, *Ve* and *Villi*.

These three gods together slew the terrible Ymir, from whose body emerged a great sea of blood in which most of the giants drowned. The two survivors perpetuated the race of giants who became the constant enemies of the gods.

From Ymir's dead body, the gods made the Midgard, the earth. His bones became mountains, his hair trees, and his brains were strewn into the sky to become clouds. His flesh became dirt, and the maggots feasting on his decaying flesh became the race of dwarves living beneath the earth. Four great dwarves—*Norori* in the north, *Suori* in the south, *Austri* to the east, and *Vestri* to the west—hold up Ymir's skull to create the heavens. From the region of fire the gods took sparks to create the sun and moon, and the stars and planets. Then the gods created the first true man and woman, *Ask* and *Embla,* from an ash tree and a vine.

From the earth grew *Yggdrasil*, the great World Tree (an ash) that reaches through all time and space and whose branches support the universe, dividing heaven and earth. Yggdrasil has three roots, which support *Asgard,* home of the gods; *Jotnarheim,* land of the giants; and *Niflheim*, world of the dead.

In Niflheim there is the fountain called *Hvergelmir,* from which flow twelve northern rivers. Hvergelmir nourished the poisonous snake, *Nidhogge,* who gnaws at the roots of Yggdrasil. In Jotunheim is the fountain called *Mimir,* in whose sacred waters all the wisdom of the universe flows. In Asgard there is the fountain called *Urda,* a holy well where sit the three *Norns,* or fates—*Urda*, ruling the past; *Verdandi,* ruling the present; and *Skuld,* ruling the future. These three goddesses control the fate of men and of the gods, and are the source of strife from which arise the needs for divination and magick, and religion.

The gods established the days and the nights, and the seasons. The sun, *Sol,* daughter of *Mundilfari* and wife of *Glen,* daily rides through the sky in her chariot pulled by the two horses, *Arvakr* and *Alxvior.* Sol is forever chased by *Skoll,* the wolf who will eventually catch her and bring the world to its end. The moon, *Mani,* Sol's brother, is also chased by a wolf, *Hati Hroovitnisson.* When these wolves finally catch and destroy the sun and moon, the world will end in *Ragnarok,* only to be born anew.

The first man and woman received the gifts of sight, hearing, and intelligence from Ve and Villi. This was the beginning of the race of men who dwelled in *Midgard*, their fortress made secure from the evil giants by a great wall built from Ymir's great eyebrows. Around Midgard is an ocean where the serpent named *Jormungand* formed a ring around Midgard by putting his tail in his mouth.

Subsequent to their creation, men and gods struggle against evil forces, constantly striving to rid the world of corruption and cruelty. While never fully successful, they continue to persevere, demonstrating the heroism and valor characteristic of Norse and Germanic culture, and of all mankind that continues to this day. Odin—first of the gods—is the ruler of nature's forces through his magical skills and his knowledge of all secret things. It was Odin who sacrificed one eye at the fountain of Mimir to gain wisdom and thus became the wise lawgiver and eloquent speaker. He carries the dwarf-forged magick spear, *Gungnir,* which always finds its mark. Odin's heavenly palace is called *Valhalla,* where he presides over the heroes who fall in earthly battles. He walked the earth disguised as a road-stained traveler wearing a cloak and a broad-brimmed hat pulled low, hiding his empty eye socket. Two guardian wolves run at his side. Two crows fly before him to spy ahead.

In this creation myth we first see two opposing forces coming from opposite directions, and then their synthesis in the center. It was this that established the two basic principles of Duality and Trinity, which we will see permeate every aspect of the Northern Tradition. Later, in the three families of the Runes, we will see this same conflict between inner and outer forces, and then their synthesis in a third family. Such is the nature of the cosmos and the psyche—opposition and then synthesis—repeated again and again in higher levels of growth and development, of evolution and progress.

All the world's early traditions, subsequent to the original creative myth, became polytheistic, with the gods representing the creative—and hence magical—forces within nature and man. And even when the Church suppressed the Pagan traditions, many of the gods survived as angels and saints.

THE NATURE OF THE NORSE UNIVERSE

A simple outline is all that is needed to give perspective to portions of the mythology and the actions of the deities.

The universe has nine planes divided into three levels within Yggdrasil, the World Tree. In some sense the World Tree is like the Kabbalistic Tree of Life, for it is here that all the gods, forces, and their relations to manifested life and being are found and are open to our study and understanding.

YGGDRASIL—THE WORLD TREE—THE THREE LEVELS

The Upper Level consists of

Asgard: Home of the Aesir—gods of power and war; opponents of the Vanir.

Alfheim: Home of the elves.

Vanaheim: Home of the Vanir—gods of chaos, fertility, and cultivation; opponents of the Aesir.

The Middle Level consists of

Midgard: Home of humanity.

Jotunheim: The first created world, home of Mimir and the giants.

Svartalfaheim: Home of the dark-elves, trolls, and gnomes.

Nithavellir: Dark Field, home of the dwarves.

The Lower Level consists of

Muspelheim: Home to the fire demons.

Niflheim: Land of Mists and the Dead, ruled by Hel. It is the realm of the instincts, inertia, and the unconscious. Helgrind (Death Gate) separates the land of the living from the land of the dead.

Bifröst, the Rainbow Bridge from Heaven to Earth

The Gods built the rainbow bridge from Asgard (heaven) to Midgard (earth). The divine forces ride daily over the great bridge to mingle with men. As strong as Bifröst is, it will collapse when the frost giants ride out over it at Ragnarok. All is chaos when the gods and giants are at war.

RAGNAROK, END OF THE WORLD

The end of the world has long been prophesied in many traditions. When wise Mimir no longer guards his well, the World Tree's root will begin to rot, allowing the Nidhog serpent to finally gnaw through the root that ends at Hvergelmer well. The Norns will cry out at the yellowing of the World Tree's leaves and the pollution of the Urdu well.

Odin's sacrificed eye still lies in Mimir's well, revealing the coming of three years of endless winter, followed by Ragnarok. The days grow colder and the Urda well freezes solid. Storm and sleet will whip and pound Yggdrasil,; a broken branch falls upon Jormungand, the world serpent, causing it to let go of its tail. The Hel ship, Naglfar, will become visible through the mists. The wolves Skoll and Manegarm close in on the sun and moon, which they have chased for eons. The Fenrir wolf and the Hel-wolf Garm will break free of their chains and giants will release Loki from his. Nidhogge will leave the roots of Yggdrasil and move toward Asgard, followed by all the Giants. Heimdall will see all this, and will take up the Gjallarhorn to blow the final warning call to arms.

The gods were opposed by giants and demons, the irrational forces of the universe. At Ragnarok, the forces of evil and darkness attack the gods of goodness and light.

Loki leads the attack on the gods in the great battle of Ragnarok. Surt, the leader of the fire giants, will attack Freyr armed only with a deer's antler. Freyr will stick his deer horn through Surt's eye, but Surt will kill him with his flaming sword. Thor's son Magni will send a killing arrow toward Nidhogge's head. Side by side, Odin and Thor will fight Fenrir and Jormungand. Odin will put his spear in Fenrir's chest, but the wolf will crush Odin to the ground. Thor will kill Jormungand with his hammer, but then will take nine steps backwards and die, poisoned by the serpent's venom. Tyr will kill the wolf-dog Garm and Vidar will take revenge for Odin. Loki and Heimdall will simultaneously throw their spears at each other and both will die. Modi will be surrounded by giants, but Magni and Vidar will rescue him.

The winds will increase and blow from every direction until the great World-Tree falls, causing the dark Elves' forge to tip and set Yggdrasil on fire. The Bifrost Rainbow Bridge collapses, and one by one each of the worlds will fall. The remaining Aesir will escape in Freyr's ship, Skidbladnir. It will be almost overtaken by the Hel-ship Naglfar. Midgard will then be destroyed by fire and will sink into the sea.

The universe ends in a fire storm and a new cosmos will arise from the ashes of the old world. The earth reemerges from the sea. Seven sons of the dead Aesir will return to Asgard and rule the universe. A new generation of gods and humans will arise to dwell in harmony.

An alternative myth to the one previously quoted has it that, in the far distant past before human time began, the war of the gods was fought between the Aesir and the Vanir. The conflict began when Odin and Thor refused to recognize the Vanir as gods of equal stature. The Vanir sent a beautiful woman, Gullveig (meaning *gold-drink*), to seduce the Aesir. They tried to destroy her but she came back to life three times, and became the source of their corruption.

Neither god-family could be victorious over the other so they made a truce and exchanged hostages. The Vanir sent Njord and his son Freyr and daughter Freyja; the Aesir sent Mimir and Hoenir. The war ended with all the gods spitting into a bowl, creating a giant called Kvasir, to represent peace and harmony among the gods. Nevertheless, Kvasir was later sacrificed and from his blood they made mead, the nectar of the gods. Mead is potent ale brewed from honey and water, which inebriates gods and men alike, and gives inspiration to poets. When put in a drinking horn, it left a residue at the tip that turned into ergot, a hallucinogenic byproduct that probably led to their fanaticism in battle.

Baldur, son of Odin, was respected for his intelligence, piety, wisdom, and fair judgments. Baldur told Frigg, his mother, of a dream in which his life was threatened. Frigg then exacted an oath from all the earthly and godly beings and the elements themselves, never to harm Baldur. *All but one.*

Believing that he was immune, Baldur let himself be used as a target in games with the gods throwing darts and stones at him. When Loki, the trickster, saw this, he disguised himself as a woman and tricked Frigg into telling him that only mistletoe did not agree to the oath. Loki created arrows of mistletoe and gave them to Hoder, the blind brother of Baldur, and helped guide his arm so that he could participate in the game. When the mistletoe struck Baldur, he fell dead.

Because Baldur did not die as a heroic warrior in battle, he could not go to Valhalla but to Hel's World of the Dead. When Odin begged his release, Hel (Loki's daughter) agreed that if everything in the world, dead and alive, wept for Baldur, he could return to the Aesir. All agreed except Thokk (Loki in disguise), whose refusal kept Baldur in Hel's domain. The Aesir captured and punished Loki, chaining him beneath a serpent dripping venom, causing Loki terrible suffering.

You may ask if such mythology contains not only the secrets of the Beginning, but also of the Ending. Are we in the "End Times," or will there be a new beginning?

DISCOVERY OF THE RUNES

It was Odin who discovered the runes through a shamanic ritual of self-sacrifice. He slashed his body with the point of Gungnir, and then hung head down from Yggdrasil for nine long days with neither food nor water. Searching deep into the depths of all being, he saw the runes and reached down to bring them to the world of reality.

I trow that I hung on the windy tree,
Swing there nights all nine,
Gashed with a blade,
Bloodied for Odin,
Myself to sacrifice to myself –
Knotted to the tree,
No man knows
Whither the roots of it run.

None gave me bread,
None gave me drink,
Down to the depths
I peered
To snatch up runes
With a roaring scream
And fell in a dizzied swoon.

Well-being I won
And wisdom too,
I grew and joyed in my growth –
From a word to a word,
From a deed to another deed.

—From the *Havamal*, quoted in Tyson: *Rune Magic* (1988)

Thus the runes were *discovered*—not created—by the first god himself. They represent the secrets of universal forces and archetypes, and can be assembled in divinatory castings to show the destiny of the moment and then can be manipulated by magick to alter the probable future.

While Runes are used in both divination and magick, it begins with divination to ascertain the present situation of forces. Then we learn to do something to change those conditions to overcome the challenge. That's where we come to magick which will be discussed in greater detail later in this chapter.

We start, however, with a list of the Norse/German deities because of their role as supernatural personifications of the universal forces that apply to humankind and which are contained within the Runes.

THE NORSE DEITIES

We live in a universe of energies and "intelligences"—those archetypes in the Unconscious that embody Mother, Father, Priest, Lover, etc., found in the various pantheons of gods and goddesses and the forces behind human experience.

We will list those deities, along with their associated rune and powers, and later we will list the Runes along with their traditional meanings and associated deities. We will also describe some lesser supernatural beings and powers, and the Northern concept of the human soul and its various parts. And we will discuss Northern Magick and how the Runes are used as both tools of divination and of magickal power.

The gods are long lived, but not immortal. They are divided into two major families that represent the Duality principle mentioned earlier:

The Aesir are "Sky Gods" of power, wisdom, and war. Odin with his magical skills and wisdom is chief of the gods. Thor, the God of Thunder, with his magical hammer, presides over working men. Loki is Aesir by adoption only. He and Odin vowed the friendship of blood brothers, but Loki is forever a trickster, a troublemaker, and a shape-shifter.

The Vanir are the Gods of Earth and Sea, of wealth, fertility, and ever expanding life and productivity. The most important Gods of the Vanir are Njord, Freyr, Aegir, and Freyja.

It is through the magical world of supernatural forces that the runes function. The more you feel the myth and lore, absorbing the names and functions of the deities and of the runes into your consciousness, and studying their meaning, the more accurate will be your runic divination and the more effective will be your runic magick.

NORSE GODS, GODDESSES AND OTHER SUPERNATURAL BEINGS: THEIR LORE, POWERS & INFLUENCE

The names of the deities are in the old Norse language while the Rune names are in German for reasons previously explained.

(Note: Many of the correspondences given in the following section are adapted from D. J. Conway's *Norse Magic* and *Book of Gods & Goddesses*. Other major resources include Michael Howard's *The Magic of the Runes: Their Origins and Occult Power*, Lisa Peschel's *A Practical Guide to the Runes,* Jennifer Smith's *Runic Journey,* Edred Thorsson's *Northern Magic: Rune Mysteries and Shamanism, Runecaster's Handbook: At the Well of Wyrd,* and *A Handbook of Rune Magic,* and Donald Tyson's *Rune Magic.* Other sources on the Internet were important, as well as other texts that were consulted.)

Aegir, of the Vanir: The Ale-brewer and King of the Sea. Son of the giant, Fornjótr, and brother of Logi (fire, flame) and Kári (wind). He is a *jotunn* (giant nature spirit). Married to *Ran,* they had nine daughters (undines), each characterizing some aspect of ocean waves. Using a large cauldron given him by Thor, he and his daughters brew ale.

Correspondences:

Runes: Laguz, Naudiz

Color: Purple, turquoise

Day: Thursday

Incense: Cedar, rose

Plant: Oak, polybody (a leathery fern), rose

Rulership: Brewing, control of winds and waves, gold, prosperity, sailors, sunken treasure

Stone: Coral

Symbol: Dolphin, whale

Aesir, Asynur pl.: The Old Gods. The Old Gods are strong, beautiful, larger than humans and live longer than humans—but are not immortal. Each god has expertise in different categories. They generally are good, friendly, and helpful to humans. Those Vanir who have lived in Asgard for a long time are also considered as Aesir. The Aesir are the gods of consciousness and the sky, as opposed to the Vanir who are the gods of the earth, biological life, and the subconscious. The Aesir are direct descendants of Odin through the father, or are females who have married (male) Aesir.

Audhumla: The Great Cow. Nourisher. Primal shaping force of the universe.

Correspondences:

Runes: Hagalaz, Uruz

Astrological: Cancer

Color: Brown, green

Day: Monday

Incense: Jasmine, juniper, lotus

Plant: Birch, fir, hawthorn, mugwort, rose, willow

Rulership: Child-rearing, domestic crafts, motherhood

Stone: Copper, quartz crystal, topaz

Symbol: Cow

Baldur (German Phol), of the Aesir: The Bright One. His name means "Shining Day." Odin's second son, he is the God of Love, Light, Beauty, Loyalty, Innocence, and Rebirth. He is sacrificed at Midsummer by the dart of the mistletoe, and is reborn at Yule. He is married to the Goddess of Joy, Nanna, and is father to Forseti. He was slain by his blind brother Hodu, whose hand was guided by the evil Loki, and he will return after Ragnarok.

Correspondences:

Runes: Fehu, Raidho, Sowilo

Color: Gold, white

Day: Sunday

Incense: Cinnamon, frankincense

Plant: Ash, chamomile, marigold, St. John's wort

Rulership: Advice, beauty, gentleness, harmony, reconciliation, reincarnation

Stone: Gold, goldstone

Symbol: The sun

Bragi, of the Aesir: The Bard of the gods and the God of Eloquence, Poetry, and Wisdom. He is a son of Odin and Frigg, and husband to Idhunna.

Correspondences:

Runes: Dagaz, Gebo, Mannaz, Othala

Color: Orange, multicolored

Day: Wednesday

Incense: Sandalwood, storax

Plant: Beech, fern, lily of the valley

Rulership: Arts, music, poetry, song

Stone: Agate, carnelian

Symbol: Harp, book

Eir: A lesser known Goddess of Healing.

Forseti (German Forasizo), of the Aesir: His name means "Chairman." He is the God of Law and Justice. A son of Balder and Nanna, Nep's daughter. His hall had a silver ceiling, radiating light seen for a great distance.

Correspondences:

Runes: Ansuz, Ingwaz, Jera, Raidho, Sowilo

Astrological: Libra

Color: Yellow

Day: Friday

Incense: Cedar, rose

Plant: Mountain ash, yew, ivy, holly, nuts and cones

Rulership: Justice, law, mediation, peace, reconciliation, truth.

Stone: Amethyst, aquamarine, lapis lazuli, tin

Symbol: The scales of justice

Freyja (German Fricco), of the Vanir: She is the Great Goddess, second only to Frigg. Her name means "The Lady." The Goddess of the magic known as Seidhr (German Seith). which she taught to Odin, eroticism, and physical well-being. She is the Queen of the Valkyries who choose those to be slain in battle and carry them to Valhalla. She is daughter of Njord, and twin sister to Freyr. She is also a warrior goddess of great wisdom and magick. She wears the sacred necklace Brisingamen, which she paid for by spending the night with the dwarves. She is married to Odr and her children are Hnoos and Gersemi. Hers is the magic of reading runes, trance and astral travel, and casting spells. She owns a falcon cloak, takes dove form, rides in a chariot drawn by two cats, or rides a boar. She weeps tears of gold, which become amber, called "Freya's Tears."

Correspondences:

Runes: Fehu, Kaunaz, Tiwaz, Uruz

Astrological: Gemini

Color: Black (protection), green, red (sex), silver

Day: Friday

Incense: Mint, rose, sandalwood

Plant: Alder, apple, birch, bramble, elder, mugwort, rose, tansy, vervain, yarrow

Rulership: Beauty, cats, domestic crafts, death, enchantments, farming, fertility, flowers, foresight, horses, jewelry, love, luck, magic, the moon, passion, protection, romance, sex, trance, wealth, witchcraft

Stone: Amber, copper, emerald, jade, malachite, moonstone, silver,

Symbol: The boar, cat, full moon, necklace, number thirteen, five-pointed star

Freyr (German Fro), of the Vanir: His name means "Lord," and he is the lord of prosperity, eroticism, peace, and physical well-being. His weapon is a magickal sword and he has a magic ship that sails unguided to its destination. He is Freya's twin brother and is married to Gorda. Like the Celtic God Cernunnos, he is the horned God of fertility and King of the Elves. He is married to Gerd and is father to Fjolnir. His golden boar, Gullenbursti, is the dawn of day. He rules over Alfheim, the land of the Light Elves. He and Freyja are the archetypal Lord and Lady of Wicca/Witchcraft.

Correspondences:

Runes: Ansuz, Ingwaz, Jera, Raidho, Sowilo

Astrological: Gemini

Color: Gold, green, red

Day: Friday

Incense: Mint, rose, sandalwood

Plant: Ash, holly, ivy, mountain ash, nuts and cones, St. John's wort, yew

Rulership: Rain and sunshine and the fruits of the earth. Also abundance, boars, bravery, empowerment, harvest, horses, joy, plant growth, protection, sensual love, ships, success, wealth, weather

Stone: Brass, bronze, gold, goldstone, rose quartz

Symbol: Boar, the Sun

Frigg (German Frija, Fricka), of the Aesir: Her name means "Love." She is Odin's wife, and mother to Baldur and Hoor. She is the Goddess of Civilization and the true Mother of All and protector of children. She spins the sacred Distaff of Life, and is said to know the future, although she will not speak of it.

Correspondences:

Runes: Berkanan, Dagaz, Mannaz, Uruz

Astrological: Cancer

Color: Blue, silver

Day: Monday

Incense: Lily of the valley

Plant: Birch, fir, hawthorn

Rulership: Abundance, childbirth, children, creative arts, cunning, empowerment, enrichment, magical powers, marriage, physical love, and may be invoked by the childless. She teaches women all domestic crafts as well as farming.

Stone: Copper, crystal, moonstone, quartz, silver

Symbol: Crown

Gefion, of the Vanir: The Giver, Goddess of Virtue and unmarried women; a fertility goddess and a shape-shifter.

Correspondences:

Runes: Fehu, Gebo, Jera

Color: Gold, green

Day: Friday

Incense: Floral scents

Plant: Alder, corn, elder, hawthorn, thyme, wheat, yarrow

Rulership: Crops, fertility, good fortune, land, luck, magical arts, plowing, prosperity,

Stone: Amber, copper, malachite

Symbol: Corn, plow, wheat

Good Dwarves: The Master Smiths

Correspondences:

Color: Brown, dark green, gold, yellow

Incense: Cinnamon, ginger, milk and honey, spicy scents

Plant: Ferns, fir, juniper, pine

Rulership: Passiveness

Stone: Diamond, gold, goldstone, iron, pyrite, steel, zircon

Symbol: Anvil and hammer, jewelry, weapons

Gullveig, of the Vanir: The Gleaming One, Mistress of Magic. She came to live with the Aesir as a handmaiden to Freyja and a teacher of Seidhr. The Aesir tried to kill her, sparking the war with the Vanir.

Correspondences:

Runes: Dagaz, Ehwaz, Sowilo, Tiwaz

Color: Gold

Day: Sunday

Incense: Amber, cinnamon, frankincense

Plant: Ash, celandine, chamomile, marigold, mistletoe, St. John's wort

Rulership: Healing, magic, seer-ship, sorcery

Stone: Chrysolite, copper, gold, jacinth, topaz

Symbol: The sun

Heimdall (German Heimo), of the Vanir: The White God of Light and Guardianship. Born of nine maidens, all of whom were sisters, he is the handsome gold-
toothed guardian of Bifrost, the rainbow bridge leading to Asgard, the home of the
gods, and thus the connection between body and soul. As a child, Heimdall was
sent by the gods to teach humans to kindle the holy fire, to instruct them in runic
wisdom, to teach them workmanship and handicraft; he also organized their society, and originated and stabilized the three classes of men as spoken of in the Song
of Rig. He lived long as a man among men, and his rulership was a golden age of
peace and prosperity. Heimdall slept with three different women who bore the
ancestors of the three different classes: earls, farmers, and serfs. When he died as a
human, he returned to the gods, where he was stripped of his aged human shape,
regained his eternal youth, and was taken into Asgard. It is he who will sound the
signal horn to the Aesir that Ragnarok is beginning.

Correspondences:

Runes: Ehwaz, Ingwaz, Mannaz, Tiwaz

Astrological: Aquarius

Color: White, multicolor

Day: Thursday

Incense: Birch

Plant: Avens, oak, polypody, rose, verbena

Rulership: Beginnings and endings, defense against evil, guardian, morning light

Stone: Amethyst, aquamarine, bronze, copper, gold

Symbol: Horn, rainbow

Hel (German Holle, Hulda), of the Aesir: The Goddess of the Dead and the Afterlife,
she herself is half-dead, half-alive. The Vikings viewed her with considerable trepi-
dation. Nevertheless, the Germans saw her as Mother Holle: helpful in times of
need, but vengeful upon those who transgress natural law.

Correspondences:

Runes: Ehwaz, Hagalaz, Isa

Astrological: Scorpio

Color: Black

Day: Saturday

Incense: Myrrh, storax

Plant: Beech, elder, elm, ivy, juniper, mullein, willow, yew

Rulership: Dark magic, revenge

Stone: Black agate, jet, lead, obsidian, onyx

Symbol: Wolf

Hermod, of the Aesir: The Brave One. Son of Odin.
Correspondences:
Runes: Ehwaz, Ingwaz, Tiwaz

Color: Red

Day: Tuesday

Incense: Dragon's blood, pepper

Plant: Hawthorn, pine, thistle, woodruff, wormwood

Rulership: Bravery, honor

Stone: Bloodstone, garnet, iron, red agate, red topaz, ruby, steel

Symbol: Shield, sword

Hlin: Goddess of compassion and consolation, Frigga's second attendant. She kisses away the tears of mourners and relieves their grief. She listens to mortals' prayers and advises Frigga how best to answer them and give desired relief. She protects people whom Frigga wishes to save from danger.

Hodur, of the Aesir: The Blind God and the God of Blind Force. The son of Odin and Frigg who was tricked by Loki into killing his brother, Baldur.

Hoenir: The messenger of the Aesir. The Silent One.
Correspondences:
Runes: Ehwaz, Othala

Color: Red

Day: Tuesday

Incense: Pine

Plant: Hawthorn, pine, thistle, woodruff, wormwood

Rulership: Aggressiveness, bravery

Stone: Bloodstone, garnet, iron, red agate, red topaz, ruby, steel

Symbol: Helmet, shield

Holda: See Hel.

Idunna, of the Aesir: The Goddess of Immortality, Youth and Beauty.
Correspondences:
Runes: Ehwaz, Othala

Astrological: Taurus

Color: Green, silver

Day: Monday

Incense: Apple blossom

Plant: Birch, fir, hawthorn, mugwort, rose, willow

Rulership: Beauty, long life, responsibility, youth

Stone: Copper, crystal, quartz, smoky topaz

Symbol: Apple

Light Elves: The Little People. The Hidden People.

Correspondences:

Color: Blue, green, silver

Incense: Fir, floral scents, ginger, lily of the valley, milk and honey

Plant: Alder, ferns, fir, marigold, pine, thyme

Stone: Bronze, copper, moonstone quartz, rock crystal, silver

Symbol: Bow and arrow, horses, leaf, star, vine, wand

Lofn: A lesser-known Goddess of Indulgence. It is from her that permission may be secured for sexual indulgences and liaisons forbidden by custom and law.

Loki, neither an Aesir or a Vanir: Blood brother of Odin. The Father of Lies, Trickster, Shape-changer. Son of the giant Farbauti, he is of the race of Ettins (Elementals) and possesses some of their daemonic qualities. He is the Trickster and the God of Fire and Misfortune. He is both a helper and a foe of the Aesir, but it was he who spawned the monsters: the Fenris Wolf and the Midgard Wyrm, Jormurgandr. He is married to Sigyn and his other children include the goddess Hel and Sleipnir, Odin's eight-legged horse. He is the originator of deceit, the disgrace of all gods and men, and ultimately the Destroyer of all things. His wife is Sigyn, and their son is Nare, or Narfe.

Correspondences:

Runes: Kaunaz, Naudiz, Thurisaz

Astrological: Aries

Color: Black

Day: Saturday

Incense: Dragon's blood, pepper, yew

Plant: Beech, blackthorn, elder, elm, ivy, juniper, mullein, thistle, willow, yew

Rulership: Agility, cunning, dark magic, daring, death, deceit, destruction, earthquakes, evil, fires, lecherousness, lies, mischief, revenge, stealth, thieves, trickery, wit

Stone: Black agate, jet, lead, obsidian, onyx

Symbol: Snake

Mani: The moon.

Mimir, of the Aesir: The Wise One.

Correspondences:

Runes: Ansuz, Dagaz, Ehwaz, Laguz, Mannaz, Othala

Color: Yellow

Day: Sunday

Incense: Cinnamon

Plant: Ash, celandine, chamomile, marigold, mistletoe, St. John's wort

Rulership: The arts, inland lakes, knowledge, peace, pools, springs, teaching, wisdom

Stone: Chrysolite, copper, gold, jacinth, topaz

Symbol: Fountain, pool, well

Nanna, of the Vanir: She is married to Baldur and mother to Forseti. She is a Goddess of Love, Romance, and Fertility, also of Wealth and Prosperity.

Correspondences:

Runes: Berkanan, Uruz, Wunjo

Color: Pale green, silver

Day: Monday

Incense: Floral scents, jasmine, juniper, lotus

Plant: Birch, fir, hawthorn, mugwort, rose, willow

Rulership: Gentleness, love

Stone: Moonstone, quartz, silver

Symbol: Crescent moon

Nehallennia: Goddess of Plenty.

Correspondences:

Runes: Berkanan, Laguz, Uruz, Wunjo

Color: Green, yellow

Day: Friday

Incense: Floral scents, rose, sandalwood

Plant: Alder, birch, bramble, elder, feverfew, mugwort, rose, tansy, thyme, vervain, yarrow

Rulership: Fishing, fruitfulness, plenty, seafaring

Stone: Amber, bronze, copper, emerald, jade, malachite, moonstone, silver

Symbol: Cornucopia

Nerthus (German Hertha): She is Mother Earth and a Goddess of the Sea and of Rivers

Correspondences:

Runes: Berkanan, Dagaz, Ehwaz, Laguz, Raidho, Wunjo

Astrological: Pisces

Color: Light brown, green

Day: Monday

Incense: Jasmine, juniper, lotus

Plant: Birch, fir, hawthorn, loosestrife, mint, mugwort, rose, willow

Rulership: Fertility, groves, peace, purification, sea, Spring, wealth, witchcraft

Stone: Copper, crystal, quartz, smoky topaz

Symbol: Groves, the sea

Njord: God of the Oceans and River, Lord of Abundance and material well-being, and third among the Vanir. Married to the giantess Skadi, he begat two children: a son, Freyr, and a daughter, Freyja.

Correspondences:

Runes: Fehu, Ehwaz, Laguz, Mannaz, Othala

Astrological: Pisces

Color: Blue

Day: Thursday

Incense: Cedar, vervain

Plant: Avens, ferns, oak, oak moss, polypody, verbena

Rulership: Fire, fishing, guarantees oaths, lands, livestock, prosperity, sailors, sea, stubbornness, success, wind, wisdom

Stone: Amethyst, aquamarine, tin, turquoise

Symbol: Fish, the sea, ships

The Norns (Urda, Verdandi, and Skuld): The Norse equivalent of the Greek Fates. It is they who determine the destinies of the Gods and of Man, and who maintain the World Tree, Yggdrasill.

Odin (German Wotan), of the Aesir: Father of all the Gods and of men. The God of Magick, Ecstasy, Poetry, and man's consciousness of Inner Divinity; he brings knowledge, wisdom, ideas, and inspiration to help humankind. He is both the shaper of *Wyrd* (Fate: the past actions that continually affect and condition the future) and the bender of *Orlog* (Destiny: the future that affects the past), showing the interconnected nature of all actions. He is married to Frigg and father to Baldur and Hoor.

It is he who makes men mad, possessed of driving rage, and also the "madness" perceived of the warrior in battle, the seer in trance, the poet's creativity.

It is also he who sacrifices an eye at the well of Mimir to gain inner wisdom, and later hangs himself upon Yggdrasill to gain the knowledge and power of the Runes. He can travel to any realm within the nine Nordic worlds. He is pictured wearing a floppy hat and a blue-gray cloak and is accompanied by two ravens, *Hugginn* (thought) and *Munin* (memory), who daily fly over the world, reporting all that has happened.

Correspondences:

Runes: Ansuz, Dagaz, Ehwaz, Ingwaz, Jera, Lagaz, Othala, Wunjo

Astrological: Sagittarius

Color: Black (revenge, darkness), orange, red (healing, justice, weather)

Day: Wednesday, Saturday

Incense: Dragon's blood, pine, sandalwood

Plant: Beech, ferns, maidenhair, mandrake, marjoram, polypody, valerian, yew

Rulership: The arts, civilization, creativity, death and rebirth, divination, fate, healing, horses, initiation, inspiration, justice, knowledge, law, logic, love and romance, magic, medicine, music, poetry, prophecy, the runes, self-sacrifice, storms, thought, war, weapons, wild hunt, wisdom, words of power

Stone: Agate, carnelian, gold, jet, onyx, tin

Symbol: Blue cloak and floppy hat, eagle, raven, wolf

Ran, of the Vanir: The Ravager. She is married to Aegir, and is malicious and unpredictable.

Correspondences:

Runes: Kaunaz, Naudiz, Thurisaz

Astrological: Sagittarius

Color: Black

Day: Saturday

Incense: Dragon's blood, juniper, storax

Plant: Beech, buckthorn, elder, elm, ivy, juniper, mullein, willow, yew

Rulership: Drowning, great terror, sailors, the sea, storms

Stone: Black agate, jet, lead, obsidian, onyx

Symbol: Fish nets, stormy sea

Saga: A lesser known Goddess of Writing, Poetry, and Memory, and a prophet.

Sif (Sifa), of the Aesir: The Harvest Goddess. She is married to Thor, and mother to Pruor and Ullr.

Correspondences:

Runes: Berkanan, Gebo, Jera, Wunjo

Astrological: Virgo

Color: Gold, green

Day: Monday

Incense: Floral scents, jasmine

Plant: Birch, chamomile, fir, hawthorn, mugwort, rose, willow

Rulership: Beautiful hair, fruitfulness, generosity, harvest, plenty

Stone: Brass, bronze, copper, crystal, quartz, smoky topaz

Symbol: Loom, mirror

Sigyn: The Faithful. She is married to Loki, and mother to sons Nari and Vali.

Correspondences:

Runes: Sowilo, Uruz, Wunjo

Color: Brown, pink

Day: Monday

Incense: Floral scents

Plant: Birch, fir, hawthorn, mugwort, rose, willow

Rulership: Faithfulness, love, loyalty

Stone: Bronze, copper, crystal, quartz, smoky topaz

Symbol: Bowl

Sjofna: Goddess of Love who can turn anyone's thoughts to love.

Correspondences:

Runes: Gebo, Wunjo

Astrological: Capricorn

Color: Red

Day: Friday

Incense: Mint, rose, sandalwood

Plant: Alder, birch, elder, mugwort, rose, willow

Rulership: Dark magic, hunting, mountains, revenge, winter

Stone: Amber, copper, emerald, jade, malachite, moonstone, silver

Symbol: Heart

Skadi, of the Vanir: Mistress of Dark Magic and the Goddess of Winter and of the Hunt. She is married to Njord, the gloomy Sea God, noted for his beautiful bare feet, symbolic of fertility and attractive to Skadi. She may be invoked in cases of justice, vengeance, and righteous anger, and is the deity who sentenced Loki to be bound underground with a serpent dripping poison upon his face in punishment for his crimes. Skadi's character is found in two of Hans Christian Anderson's tales: "The Snow Queen" and "The Ice Princess."

Correspondences:

Runes: Ehwaz, Hagalaz, Isa, Kaunaz, Thurisaz

Astrological: Capricorn

Color: Black

Day: Saturday

Incense: Dragon's blood, myrrh, pepper

Plant: Beech, blackthorn, elder, elm, ivy, juniper, mullein, willow

Rulership: Dark magic, hunting, mountains, revenge, winter

Stone: Black agate, jet, obsidian, onyx, tin

Symbol: Mountains, new moon

Sunna: The Sun.

Thor (German Donnar), of the Aesir: The red-headed God of Thunder and weather in general, powerful Protection, Inspiration, Magical Power, and Personal Strength. Thor is a son of Odin, is the foremost of the Aesir, and rules over the realm called Thrudvang. He is the strongest of all gods and men, and is the protector of all Midgard. He wields the mighty hammer *Mjollnir*, which causes lightning flashes. His battle car is drawn by two goats. He is married to Sif, and father to Pruor and Ullr. The oak is sacred to Thor.

Correspondences:

Runes: Ansuz, Ehwaz, Ingwaz, Raidho, Thurisaz

Astrological: Leo

Color: Red

Day: Thursday

Incense: Dragon's blood, juniper, pine

Plant: Acorns, avens, oak, oak moss, thistle

Rulership: Courage, crops, defense, goats, law and order, oaks, storms, strength, thunder and lightning, trading voyages, trust, war, water, weather

Stone: Carnelian, iron, lodestone, red agate, steel

Symbol: Megingjardar (his magic belt that increases his strength), Mjollnir (his magic hammer, the destroyer)

Tyr (German Tiw), of the Aesir: Odin's son, Tyr is the God of Law and Justice, Rational Thought and Right Order, Protection, Divination, Astronomy, Strength, and Courage; he is the ancient God of War and the lawgiver of the gods. He sacrificed his hand so that the evil Fenris wolf may be bound. He may be invoked in all manners of Justice, Fair Play, and Right Action.

Correspondences:

Runes: Ehwaz, Ingwaz, Jera, Kaunaz, Thurisaz

Astrological: Libra

Color: Orange, yellow

Day: Tuesday

Incense: Juniper, pine

Plant: Blackthorn, juniper, oak, thistle, vervain

Rulership: Athletics, bravery, honor, integrity, justice, law, order, self-sacrifice, the sky, solemn oaths, victory, war

Stone: Bronze, gray agate, smoky topaz, steel

Symbol: Helmet, sword

Ullr, of the Aesir: The Magnificent, the Bow God, God of the Hunt. Ullr is a son of Sif and a stepson of Thor. Fair of face, he is a great warrior to be invoked by men in combat. He is the greatest archer, and the fastest skier.

Correspondences:

Runes: Ehwaz, Isa, Perth, Tiwaz

Astrological: Capricorn

Color: White, yellow

Day: Wednesday

Incense: Pine, sandalwood

Plant: Beech, fern, maidenhair, mandrake, marjoram, valerian

Rulership: Archery, beauty, single combat, hunting, magic, nobility

Stone: Agate, alloys, carnelian

Symbol: Bow, mountains, skis

Vidar, of the Aesir: A son of Odin who will survive Ragnarok, as will his brother Vali. He is the next strongest after Thor and helps all the gods in the hardest tasks.

Vali, of the Aesir: God of Vengeance, he is the avenger of Baldur. Vali is a son of Odin and Rindr. Daring in combat and a good shot, he and Vidar will survive Ragnarok.

Valkyries: Thirteen goddesses who choose slain warriors that will go to Valhalla.
Correspondences:
Rulership: Death, fearlessness, flying horses, war, wolves
Symbol: Helmets, spears crowned with flames

Vanic (not Vanir) are Mundilfari, Mundilfara, Mani, Sol; Freyr's servants: Byggvir, Beyla; Freya's Valkyries.

Vanir: The second race of gods, they are concerned with nature and with the functions of eroticism, fertility, and prosperity. Those gods and goddesses most concerned with family are Njord, Freyr, and Freyja. The Vanir are direct descendants of Holde, by way of the mother, or are males who have married (female) Vans. They are: Holde, Nerthus, Njord, Freya, Freyr, Odh, Hnoss, Aegir, Ran, Ullr, Ulla, Gerdh, Skirnir, Heimdallr, Idunna, Bragi, Siofyn, Gefjon, Skadhi, Erde, the Undines, Svol, Ostara, and Gullveig. Following the war with the Aesir, hostages were exchanged and those of the Vanir who came to the Aesir are called *Vanic* and have their own character. They are Mundilfari, Mundilfara, Mani, Sol; Freyr's servants: Byggvir, Beyla; Freya's Valkyries.

Correspondences:
Rulership: Fertility, magical powers, witchcraft

Vár: A lesser-known Goddess of Honesty who may be invoked to witness love-vows and other oaths and to punish those who break their oaths. Newly married couples call her name as they take each other's hands.

Weiland (Weyland): The Smith of the Gods.
Correspondences:
Runes: Ehwaz, Ingwaz, Perth, Tiwaz
Astrological: Taurus
Color: Yellow
Day: Wednesday
Incense: Juniper, thyme, vervain
Plant: Beech, ferns, juniper, marjoram, thyme, valerian
Rulership: Cunning, healing, horses, skill, magic, metalworking, strength

Stone: Agate, Bronze, carnelian, iron, jasper, steel

Symbol: Anvil and hammer, horseshoes

Ymir: The first Frost Giant. Brutal, evil, violent.

NORSE TRADITION, THE LESSER BEINGS

In addition to the Gods and Goddesses, there are **Dwarves, Elves**, and **Nature Spirits** that often appear like small and delicate humans. They are mostly night creatures that avoid men. There are also **Undines**, water spirits, usually female and humanlike ,who dwell in springs and rivers, and love to sit in the sun. There are **Forest Spirits** covered with moss, with faces like gnarled tree bark, who know the secrets of herbs and how to cure sickness. **Kobolds** are the familiar spirits of hearth and home that look like small old men with pointed hoods, sometimes living in the cellar or barn.

Bearers of Fate are entities attached to an individual and carry that individual's fate (ørlög), thus influencing his or her life and actions. Entities that belong to this group include the fetch (fylgja) and the lesser Norns (nornir), and sometime **Valkyries** and Dises.

Draugr: The undead (animated corpses), extremely strong and very dangerous; they kill with a strong slap to the head. Never look directly at them, as they steal vital life force from a person simply by gazing at them. Certain runes are carved on gravestones to prevent the dead from rising and walking among the living.

Dwarves: The Svartalfar are short, evil, greedy, miserly, grudging, and ill-tempered beings descended from maggots in Ymir's decaying body. Like **Goblins**, they fear the sun and live mostly in caves. They are talented smiths skillful in magic, forging both magical and regular treasures, including Freyja's necklace, Thor's magical hammer, Sif's golden hair, Freyr's ship, and more. They dwell in Svartalfheim, beneath Midgard's surface, where they hoard their gold and jewels. The Kobolds of the German mines may be classed as Svartalf, as may be the knocking spirits heard in subterranean works.

Elves are divided into three races: Ljosalfar, Dokkalfar, and Svartalfar, or Light Elves, Dark Elves, and Black Elves (also called Dwarves). All of the elves are wise magicians who will frequently take an interest in individual humans. They are very unpredictable, taking pleasure or offense at the slightest things; your attitude and manners are very important when dealing with them.

> **Light Elves** are good and Freyr is their leader. They are often beautiful, and live in Alfheim and in Andlang, the upper reaches of Midgard's atmosphere. The Ljøsalfar preserve and teach wisdom and are the source of earthly inspiration.
> **Dark Elves** live in mounds, hillocks, and rocks. They are great magicians and teachers of magic; the best time to approach them is at sunset, for they are

not fond of daylight. They appear as very beautiful, pale, and humanlike.

Black Elves are considered evil and are commonly thought to be the cause of sickness; their arrows (elf-shot) cause stroke and paralysis. They are skilled smiths and live in Svartalheim.

Fire Giants: The fire giants inhabit Muspellheim and are sworn enemies of the gods.

Frost Giants: Most of the frost giants drowned in Ymir's blood when the gods killed him, and their souls migrated down into the northernmost part of the Underworld, the dark and foggy Niflhel. A few of the youngest frost giants barely escaped, and crawled onto the beach of the northernmost part of the Earth called Jotunheimr.

Giants and Giantesses: All giants originally came from Ymir. They represent the raw forces of nature in their primitive form. They were usually beautiful and good, capable of intermarrying with humans. The greatest enemy of the giants is Thor, with his powerful hammer Mjollnir. Most giants live in Jotunheim. There are also fire giants who follow Surt in Muspelheim, and Rimthursar (Frost Giants), who came from the ice-cold Niflheim.

Huldru-folk: The "hidden folk," halfway between **Trolls** and **Landvaettir**, keepers of magical wisdom related to the lore of plants and healing. They can be both helpful and harmful to humans. They are people of the mound and forest who often try to capture mortals by tricks and magic.

Jormungand: The World Serpent, an extremely formidable but essential part of the world's structure. It is the offspring of Loki and the giant Angr-Boda and cannot be removed. Odin, fearing its evil intent, flung the serpent into the sea, where it grew to surround the earth, biting its own tail to form a barrier.

Jötun: The Jotuns are giants ranging from ghastly monsters to beautiful creatures that outshine even the gods. Some were welcomed as members of the Aesir, many of whom had affairs with Jotnar maidens. The Jotnars represent the forces of chaos, in contrast to the gods who struggle to keep the status quo. Ragnarok will be the final battle of these forces. Loki is of Jotnar heritage but was adopted as Odin's blood-brother. They live in **Jotunheim,** outside both Asgard and Midgard.

Kvaesir: A wise human created by the gods with spit in a truce between the Aesir and Vanir. He knew the answer to any question asked of him and traveled the world to teach his wisdom. On a visit to some dwarves he was killed, and his blood was brewed with honey to make the mead of ecstasy and poetry.

Landvaettir: Guardian earth sprites and lesser nature spirits that may be bound to rocks, streams, or trees to guard certain places. They are visible to psychic sight and to those traveling in the astral, and may appear in dreams.

Nykur: A Kelpie, a malignant water elemental, usually in the form of a horse.

Wight: A being or entity of any kind with some living quality.

NORSE TRADITION, ASPECTS OF SOUL AND PERSONALITY

This simple glossary of terms is intended to provide a basic understanding of the Norse vision of soul and psyche.

Fetch or **Fylgja** (also known as a "familiar"): An aspect of the soul attached to a person, though not actually part of the person. Its purpose is to assist the person in other realms. It appears to those with clairvoyant sight in a variety of forms: as an animal (fetch-deer) or the opposite sex (fetch-wife or fetch-man), and even in a purely geometrical shape. It can be developed over time to take on independent action; it can contain portions of a person's hughr and minni. The fylgja can also be used by the person to travel to one of the nine worlds. It can and often is passed along ancestral lines.

Hamingja: A part of the soul passed on from generation to generation, associated with the fylgja.

Hamr: A shape the soul may take when it leaves the body. Its appearance directly affects the appearance of the **lyke**, or physical body. The hamr joins with the wode upon death and will assist in forming the lyke in the next incarnation.

Hugauga: The mind's eye, the ajña chakra, or "third eye" in the forehead used in magical visualization.

Hughr: The conscious part of the soul that thinks. The hughr goes to Valhalla or Hel after physical death.

Hyde: The quasi-physical part of the soul that gives a person shape and form. It may be collected and reformed by magical power (hamingja) according to will (hughr).

Hyge: Thought, intuition.

Kinfylgja: Personification of inherited traits, usually dwelling within the head of the family, or else the most suitable member.

Lich: The physical part of the soul-body. Also called lyke or lik.

Megin: A personal force, distinct from physical power or strength, the possession of which assures success and good fortune.

Minni: The personal and transpersonal images from the deep past stored in the deep mind. It is the reflective part of the soul, the memory.

Mood: The emotional part of the soul, closely allied with the wode.

Need-fire: (1) Fire kindled directly from wood without flint but from the deep past by friction. (2) A person's intense driving motivation to achieve a desired end.

Odhr: "Inspired fury" or madness.

önd: The Energy of Life itself. Everything in the universe possesses önd. It is an active life-energy essential to both the material and magical worlds. In plants, it is the resident soul that gives medicinal powers; in foodstuffs, it is the vital essences making the child grow. It is an energy that can be lost, and that can degenerate or even be stolen by malicious magic; special rituals prevent this. In the natural world, it is often concentrated in special ways, making places of power where it may manifest in a variety of ways, some beneficial, some harmful. People can develop a special rapport with the place and the spiritual power within it.

Orlog: The cycle of "Fate," the past actions of an individual or the cosmos that shape present reality, which may be expected to come about as a result of what was. Orlog is the collective "wyrd" of the world as a whole, while wyrd applies to the individual.

Wode: An emotive part of the soul bringing various aspects together in a powerful and inspired way.

Wyrd: Corresponding roughly to "karma," the process in which past actions (ørlög) work through time to affect present reality. Although wyrd is mostly personal, it can be linked to whole families, tribes, and even races.

THE GERMANIC RUNES: THEIR MEANINGS AND CORRESPONDENCES

The Runes are in three "families" as the principle of Trinity mentioned earlier.

The Outer Life

The first Airt (Ætt) of Freya is primarily related to the Outer World of practical and mundane matters.

ᚠ **Fehu** (Norse Fe): Wealth, Fulfillment—Cattle, Nourishment, Possessions.
Alternate names: Faihu, Feh, Feoh
Correspondences:
Meaning: Positive: Success, abundance, good health, income, luck, fulfillment, property
Meaning: Negative: Failure, loss of credit and property, bondage, someone or something to be avoided
Deity: Primary—Freyr, Freyja, the Aesir; *Secondary*—Baldur, Gefion, Njord
Alphabet: F

Astrological: Aries

Color: Light red

Element: Fire and earth

Gemstone: Moss agate

Herb: Nettle

Magical Power: Primal energy—to attract, to progress, to increase, to protect, to send, to strengthen psychic power

Polarity: Female

Pronunciation: "fay-who"

Tarot Card: The Tower

Tree: Elder

ᚢ **Uruz** (Norse Ur): Strength—aurochs (a wild ox), Adulthood, Masculine Potency, Change, Desire

Alternate names: Ur, Urs, Urur.

Correspondences:

Meaning: Positive: Action, courage, energy, freedom, good fortune, health, potency, potential, strength

Meaning: Negative: Bad luck, brutality, domination, lust, obsession, rashness, sickness, violence

Deity: Primary—Thor, Urdl, the Vanir; *Secondary*—Audhumla, Freyja, Frigg, Nanna, Nehallennia, Sigyn

Alphabet: U V

Astrological: Taurus

Color: Dark green

Element: Earth

Gemstone: Carbuncle

Herb: Sphagnum moss

Magical Power: Manifestation—to change, to start, to heal

Polarity: Male

Pronunciation: "ooo-rooze"

Tarot Card: High Priestess

Tree: Birch

ᚦ **Thurisaz** (Norse Thurs): Thorn, Thorr's Hammer, giant, Non-Action. Reactive Force, Directed Force, Male Sexuality

Alternate names: Thorn, Thorunisaz, Thuith, Thurisa

Correspondences:

Meaning: Positive: Catharsis, comfort, good news, happiness, inner strength, journey over water, security, take great care in making decisions

Meaning: Negative: Betrayal, compulsion, conflict, danger, defenseless, delayed journey

Deity: Primary—Thor; *Secondary*—Loki, Ran, Skadi, Tyr

Alphabet: Th

Astrological: Mars

Color: Bright red

Element: Fire

Gemstone: Sapphire

Herb: Houseleek

Magical Power: Applied Power—to begin, to attract, to defend, to push

Polarity: Male

Pronunciation: "thoor-ee-saws"

Tarot Card: The Emperor

Tree: Oak

ᚨ **Ansuz** (Norse Ass): Odin, Sovereign Ancestor God. Messenger. Communication, Incantation, Information

Alternate names: Aesir, Ansur, Asa, Ass, Os, Oss.

Correspondences:

Meaning: Positive: Blessings, harmony, healing, insight, inspiration, new life-changing goals, revealing message, true vision, words of power

Meaning: Negative: Bad advice, delusion, manipulation, misunderstanding

Deity: Primary—Odin, Loki; *Secondary*—Forseti, Freyr, Mimir, Thor

Alphabet: A

Astrological: Mercury

Color: Dark blue

Element: Air

Gemstone: Emerald

Herb: Fly agaric

Magical Power: Communication—to convince, to know, to increase, to achieve

Polarity: Male

Pronunciation: "awn-sooze"

Tarot Card: Death

Tree: Ash

ᚱ **Raidho** or Raido (Norse Reid): Travel, Wagon—journey of life, the path to power.
  Disruption, Transportation, Law

Alternate names: Rad, Radh, Raidha, Raido, Reda, Reidh, Rit

Correspondences:

Meaning: Positive: Journey, getting to the truth, relocation, seeing past illusions.

Meaning: Negative: Disruption, inconvenience, irrationality, travel problems.

Deity: Primary—Forseti, Ing; *Secondary*—Baldur, Forseti, Freyr, Nerthus, Thor

Alphabet: R

Astrological: Sagittarius

Color: Bright red

Element: Air

Gemstone: Chrysophase

Herb: Mugwort

Polarity: Male

Magical Power: To bless, to obtain justice, to travel safely, to seek

Pronunciation: "rye-though"

Tarot Card: The Hierophant

Tree: Oak

ᚲ **Kenaz** or Kaunaz (Norse Kaunaz): Beacon, Enlightenment, Controlled Energy—
  boil, forge, hearth, pyre, sore, swelling. Revelation, Transformation

Alternate names: Cen, Chozma, Kano, Kaon, Kaun, Kaunaz, Ken

 Correspondences:

Meaning: Positive: Creativity, inspiration, new insights, new strength and energy,
  technical ability

Meaning: Negative: Bad judgment, false hope, confusion, hidden danger, instability

Deity: Primary—Freyja; *Secondary*—Ran, Skadi, Tyr

Alphabet: K

Astrological: Venus

Color: Light red

Element: Fire

Gemstone: Bloodstone

Magical Power: To banish, to restore self-confidence, to strengthen willpower

Polarity: Female

Pronunciation: "cane-awze"

Tarot Card: The Chariot

Tree: Pine

X **Gebo** (Norse Gyfu): Gift, Love, Exchange of Powers—blessing, generosity, hospitality, Partnership

Alternate names: Gifu, Gyfu, Gipt, Gyfu

Correspondences:

Meaning: Positive: Exchange of power between gods and humans, weddings, legacies, promotion, windfall

Meaning: Negative: Greed, loneliness, privation, someone close causes sadness

Deity: Primary—Odin, Freyja, Gefn; *Secondary*—Bragi, Gefion, Sif, Sjofna

Alphabet: G

Astrological: Scorpio

Color: Deep blue

Element: Air

Gemstone: Opal

Herb: Heartsease

Magical Power: To create harmony in partnerships, to integrate the energies of two people as in sex magick, to remove a curse

Polarity: Male and female

Pronunciation: "gay-boe"

Tarot Card: The Lovers

Tree: Ash, Elm

ᚹ **Wunjo** (Norse Wyn): Bliss, Joy—delight, gateway, glory, hope, mystery, pasture, pleasure, reward

Alternate names: Vend, Vin, Wunja, Wunju, Wunna, Wyn, Wynn

Correspondences:

Meaning: Positive: Comfort, happiness, success and recognition of worth

Meaning: Negative: Alienation, frenzy, needless self-sacrifice, strife

Deity: Primary—Freyr, Odin, the Elves; *Secondary*—Nanna, Nehallennia, Nerthus, Sif, Sigyn, Sjofna

Alphabet: W, V

Astrological: Leo

Color: Light blue

Element: Water

Gemstone: Diamond

Herb: Flax

Magical Power: To bring fulfillment, happiness, and spiritual transformation, to gain favor with superiors, to invoke fellowship

Polarity: Male

Pronunciation: "woon-yo"

Tarot Card: Strength

Tree: Ash

The Inner Life

The second airt, of Hagalaz, reflects the Inner World of emotional matters and the psychological conditions present within the individual

ᚺ **Hagalaz** (Norse Hagall): Ice, hail, snow, natural forces, disruption

Alternate names: Ghaegl, Haal, Haegl, Hagal, Hagall, Haglaz

Correspondences:

Meaning: Positive: Bringing opposites into harmony

Meaning: Negative: Crisis, delays, destruction, setbacks, situation beyond your control

Deity: Primary—Heimdall, Urd, Ymir; *Secondary*—Audhumla, Hel, Skadi

Alphabet: H

Astrological: Aquarius

Color: Light blue

Element: Water

Gemstone: Onyx

Herb: Lily of the valley

Magical Power: To attract positive influence, to bring luck, to gain mystical knowledge and experience

Polarity: Female

Pronunciation: "haw-gaw-laws"

Tarot Card: The World

Tree: Yew or Ash

ᚾ **Nauthiz** (Norse Nauthiz): Necessity—Need—Desire, Distress, constraint, survival.

Alternate names: Naud, Naut, Naudhr, Nauths, Nied, Nyd.

Correspondences:

Meaning: Positive: Caution is necessary, new strength, self-reliance

Meaning: Negative: Deprivation, impatience leads to disaster

Deity: Primary—Nornir, Skuld; *Secondary*—Loki, Ran

Alphabet: N

Astrological: Capricorn

Color: Black

Element: Fire

Gemstone: Lapis Lazuli

Herb: Bistort

Magical Power: To achieve long-term goals, to attract a lover, to develop spiritual power, to overcome stress

Polarity: Female

Pronunciation: "now-these"

Tarot Card: The Devil

Tree: Beech

Isa (Norse Is): Ice, Lack of Emotion, Contraction—Standstill. Psychological Blocks, Reinforcement

Alternative names: Eis, Icz, Is, Isar, Isaz, Iss

Correspondences:

Meaning: Positive: Patience, reinforcement, talk carefully

Meaning: Negative: Betrayal, hasty speech brings trouble, plots.

Deity: Primary—Rime-thurses; *Secondary*—Hel, Skadi

Alphabet: I

Astrological: Moon

Color: Black

Element: Water

Gemstone: Cat's eye

Herb: Henbane

Magical Power: To develop concentration and will, to halt unwanted forces, to make a situation "static"

Polarity: Female

Pronunciation: "ee-saw"

Tarot Card: The Hermit

Tree: Alder

Jera (Norse Ar): Spear, Cycles, Good Year, Good Season or Harvest. Earned Success.

Alternate names: Gaar, Jer, Jeran, Yer

Correspondences:

Meaning: Positive: Peace, progress, prosperity, time to reap rewards

Meaning: Negative: Bad timing, conflict, major change, no quick results

Deity: Primary—Freyr, Freyja; *Secondary*—Forseti, Gefion, Odin, Sif, Tyr

Alphabet: J or Y

Astrological: Sun

Color: Light blue

Element: Earth

Gemstone: Carnelian

Magical Power: To bring success in gardening and farming, to gain return on good investment and hard work, to help in legal matters

Polarity: Male and female

Pronunciation: "yare-awe"

Tarot Card: The Fool

Tree: Oak

ᛇ **Eihwaz** (Norse Eihwaz): Reliability, Strength, Trust

Alternative names: Eeoh, Eihwas, Ihwar, Ihwas, Iwar

Correspondences:

Meaning: Positive: Enlightenment, end of a matter or relationship, change

Meaning: Negative: Confusion, destruction, trouble from past situations

Deity: Primary—Odin, Ullr; *Secondary*—Gullveig, Heimdall, Hermod, Hoenir, Idunna, Njord, Thor, Tyr

Alphabet: E

Astrological: Scorpio

Color: Dark blue, magenta

Element: Earth, air, fire, water

Gemstone: Topaz

Magical Power: To banish, to communicate between levels of reality, to protect, to remove obstacles

Polarity: Male

Pronunciation: "eye-wawz"

Herb: Mandrake

Tarot Card: The Hanged Man

Tree: Yew

ᚲ **Perthro** (Norse Pertho): Chance, Evolutionary Force, Mystery, Science, Technology—Feminine Mysteries, Dice Cup, Fate, Occult, Secret, Sexuality, Vagina, Whisper

Alternate names: Pairthra, Pear, Peord, Perodh, Peorth, Perth, Perthrold

Correspondences:

Meaning: Positive: Initiation, knowledge of future, nice surprise, unexpected gain

Meaning: Negative: Addiction, hurtful secrets, malaise, stagnation

Deity: Freyr, Frigg, Elves

Alphabet: P

Astrological: Saturn

Color: Black

Element: Water

Gemstone: Aquamarine

Magical Power: To find lost things, to gain inner guidance, to protect against dark forces and the dead

Polarity: Female

Pronunciation: "pear-throw"

Herb: Aconite

Tarot Card: Wheel of Fortune

Tree: Nornir

ᛦ **Algiz** (Norse Yr): Elk, Protection, Opportunity—defense, refuge, stone axe, yew bow, Refuge

Alternate names: Elhaz, Eohl-secg, Aquizi, Ihwar, Yr

Correspondences:

Meaning: Positive: Channel energies, removal of blockage

Meaning: Negative: Hidden danger, people want to block you

Deity: Primary—Ymir, Heimdall; *Secondary*—Hermod, Hoenir, Idunna, Nerthus

Alphabet: Z or R

Astrological: Cancer

Color: Gold

Element: Air

Gemstone: Amethyst

Herb: Angelica

Magical Power: To communicate with other worlds, to defend, to promote luck, to protect, to strengthen the life force

Polarity: Male

Pronunciation: "all-geese"

Tarot Card: The Moon

Tree: Valkyr jur

⚡ **Sowilo,** or Sowelo (Norse Sunna): The Sun, a Sun-Wheel, Life-Energy, Revelation—Contact with the Higher Self, Wholeness

Alternate names: Saugil, Sighel, Sol, Sowelo, Sowelu, Sulhil, Sulu, Sunna, Sygel

Correspondences:

Meaning: Positive: Advancement, change of residence, power for change, time of renewal, turnaround, victory

Meaning: Negative: Bad advice, false goals, gullibility, retribution

Deity: Primary—Sol; *Secondary*—Baldur, Forseti, Freyr, Gullveig, Sigyn

Alphabet: S

Astrological: Sun

Color: White, silver

Element: Air

Gemstone: Ruby

Magical Power: To increase good health, vitality, and sexual powers, to strengthen psychic powers

Polarity: Male

Pronunciation: "soe-wee-low"

Tarot Card: The Sun

Tree: Juniper

Relationship and Synthesis

The third airt transcends the other two as it relates to relationships between people, and to the sexual side of life. Whereas the first airt deals largely with the outer world, the second mainly deals with the inner world, while the third airt synthesizes the inner and outer worlds. Most of the runes in the third airt contain a dual meaning involving both aspects.

↑ **Tiwaz** (Norse Tyr): Warrior—Sovereign order, the Sky God. Analysis, Authority, Honor, Rationality.

Alternate names: Teiwaz, Teiws, Tir, Tiu, tiw, Tyr, Tys.

Correspondences:

Meaning: Positive: Finding true strength, justice, law and order, victory and success, wisdom.

Meaning: Negative: Adversaries, deception, intrigue, mental stasis.

Deity: Primary—Tyr, Mani; *Secondary*—Freyja, Gullveig, Heimdall, Hermod

Alphabet: T

Astrological: Libra

Color: Bright red

Element: Air

Gemstone: Coral

Magical Power: To achieve victory over adversity, to bind an oath, to defend against known enemies, to fight, to make ardent love

Polarity: Male

Pronunciation: "tea-wawz"

Tarot Card: Justice

Tree: Oak

ᛒ Berkano, or Berkana (Norse Bjarkan): Growth, Fertility—Rebirth, spring growth. Personal Growth

Alternate names: Bairkan, Beorc, Berena, Berkana, Beroc, Birca

Correspondences:

Meaning: Positive: birth, creativity, desire, marriage, new beginnings.

Meaning: Negative: carelessness, divorce, miscarriage, stagnation.

Deity: Primary—Nerthus, Holda, Frigg; *Secondary*—Nanna, Nehallennia, Sif

Alphabet: B

Astrological: Virgo

Color: Dark green

Element: Earth

Gemstone: Moonstone

Herb: Lady's mantle

Magic Power: To conceal and protect, to heal, to nurture and love

Polarity: Female

Pronunciation: "bear-kawn-oh"

Tarot Card: The Empress

Tree: Birch

ᛖ Ehwaz, or Ehwo (Norse Eoh): Momentum, Trust, Cooperation—Horse, Stallion, War Horse. Partnership, Progress, Transportation

Alternate names: Aihws, Eh, Ehol, Ehw, Ehwo, Eoh, Eykur, Eys

Correspondences:

Meaning: Positive: Change for the better, new home, new goals, steady progress, teamwork

Meaning: Negative: Betrayal, mistrust, progress blocked, restless feelings

Deity: Primary—Freyja, Freyr; *Secondary*—Hel, Nerthus, Odin, Skadi, Tyr

Alphabet: E

Color: White

Element: Earth

Gemstone: Iceland spar

Herb: ragwort

Magical Power: To bring good luck, to call divine aid in time of trouble, to cause change, to facilitate astral travel, to travel safely

Polarity: Male and female

Pronunciation: "ay-wawz"

Tarot Card: The Lovers

Tree: Oak, ash

ᛗ **Mannaz** (Norse Madr): Man, and his connection to the Divine—Humanity, the Self, the World

Alternate names: Madhr, Madr, Man

Correspondences:

Meaning: Positive: expect help, forethought, man, lover, husband, new career opportunities, favors from the god

Meaning: Negative: Depression, expect no help, material loss

Deity: Primary—Heimdall, Odin, Frigg; *Secondary*—Bragi, Mimir, Njord

Alphabet: M

Astrological: Jupiter

Color: Deep red

Element: Air

Gemstone: Garnet

Herb: madder

Magical Power: To attract goodwill, to gain assistance from others, to increase memory and mental power, to know oneself

Polarity: Male and female

Pronunciation: "mawn-nawz"

Tarot Card: The Magician

Tree: Holly

ᛚ **Laguz** (Norse Logr): Water, Womb of the Great Mother—flow, lake, mysteries, organic growth, psychic matters, the source, the underworld

Alternate names: Laaz, Lagu, Lagur, Laukr, Laukz

Correspondences:

Meaning: Positive: Life energies, movement below surface, manifestation from other planes, renewal, success in travel

Meaning: Negative: Bad judgment, blockage behind the scenes, confusion, fear, obsession, a woman may be involved

Deity: Primary—Njord, Baldur; *Secondary*—Mimir, Nehallennia, Nerthus, Odin

Alphabet: L

Astrological: Moon

Color: Dark green

Element: Water

Gemstone: Pearl

Herb: Leek

Magical Power: To increase feminine life-force, to increase "magnetism," to manifest intuition and psychic power

Polarity: Female

Pronunciation: "law-gooze"

Tarot Card: The Star

Tree: Willow

ᛜ **Ingwaz** (Norse Inguz): Peace, Harmony—Tribe, Hero God, Fertility God. Male Fertility and Drive

Alternate names: Enguz, Iggus, Ing, Inguz, Ingvi, Ingwine

Correspondences:

Meaning: Positive: Common sense, family benefits, growth, inner wisdom

Meaning: Negative: Family burdens, impotence, spinning wheels

Deity: Primary—Inguz, Freyr; *Secondary*—Forseti, Heimdall, Hermod, Odin, Thor, Tyr

Alphabet: NG

Astrological: Cancer, New Moon

Color: Yellow

Element: Earth and Water

Gemstone: Amber

Herb: Self-heal

Magical Power: To fascinate and influence people, to "fix" the outcome, to gain influential position, to project energy in sex magic

Polarity: Male

Pronunciation: "eeeng-wawz"

Tarot Card: Judgment

Tree: Apple

ᛞ **Dagaz**(Norse Daeg): Transformation—Day or Dawn. Change, Growth, Release
Alternate names: Daaz, Dag, Dags, Dagr, Daeg
Correspondences:
Meaning: Positive: Awakening, breakthrough, clarity, new beginnings

Meaning: Negative: Coming full circle, completion, ending, hopelessness

Deity: Primary—Heimdall, Odin; *Secondary*—Bragi, Frigg, Gullveig, Mimir, Nerthus

Alphabet: D

Astrological: Increasing Moon

Color: Light blue

Element: Fire and Air

Gemstone: Chrysolite

Herb: Clary

Magical Power: To advance, to bring luck, to receive inspiration, to start over

Polarity: Male

Pronunciation: "thaw-gauze"

Tarot Card: Temperance

Tree: Spruce

ᛟ **Othala**, or Othila (Norse Odal): Family—Ancestral Property, Home, Spiritual Heritage. Fundamental Values, Inheritance
Alternate names: Ethel, Odal, Odhal, Otael, Othal, Othala, Othalaz, Othilia, Utal
Correspondences:
Meaning: Positive: Group order and prosperity, spiritual help, tangible possessions

Meaning: Negative: Clannishness, greed, illusions, lack of order, jealousy, greed, wasted effort

Deity: Primary—Odin, Thor; *Secondary*—Bragi, Hoenir, Idunna, Mimir, Njord

Alphabet: O

Astrological: Full Moon

Color: Deep yellow

Element: Earth

Gemstone: Spinel

Herb: Hawthorn

Magical Power: To call on ancestral powers and spirits, to charm a woman, to develop latent strengths and talents, to gain wealth and prosperity, to guard the family fortune, to protect the health of the elderly

Polarity: Male

Pronunciation: "oath-awe-law"

Tarot Card: The Moon

RUNIC DIVINATION

Techniques of Reading and Consultation

The runes originated in Norse mythology through Odin's shamanic act of self-sacrifice, and they remain inextricably bound to the creation myth and to the story of supernatural deities and forces described in the mythology and the writings of the runic era.

The essential key is to remember that the runes were *discovered*—not created—by the first god himself. They *embody* the secret universal forces and archetypes, and can be assembled in divinatory castings to show the destiny of the moment, and can then be manipulated by magick to alter the indicated future.

AN ALPHABETICAL LIST OF THE GERMAN RUNES

The following list is a quick reference to the basic meanings of the runes adapted from Edred Thorsson's *Runecaster's Handbook.*

ᛉ **Algiz:** Conclusion. Thing that needs attention. Way to the gods.

ᚨ **Ansuz:** Knowledge, inspiration, intellectual expression.

ᛒ **Berkanan:** New beginnings. Transformation. What provides growth and beauty?

ᛞ **Dagaz:** Area of unexpected synchronicity.

ᛖ **Ehwaz:** With what or whom you should work. Erotic relations.

ᛇ **Eihwaz:** Hidden influences, state of whole being. Relationship with the numinous environment.

ᚠ **Fehu:** Wealth, Money matters. Psychic energies.

ᚷ **Gebo:** What will be given to you?

ᚺ **Hagalaz:** Crisis leading to transformation.

ᛜ **Ingwaz:** What you should contemplate.

ᛁ **Isa:** Concentration. What is constraining you?

ᚼ **Jera:** Where rewards can be expected.? Relationship with the natural environment.

ᚲ **Kaunaz:** Creativity. Transformation. Erotic relationships.

ᛚ **Laguz:** Vital force. State of emotional balance. What will test you?

ᛗ **Mannaz:** Inner divinity. Overall psychic state. Attitude toward death.

ᚾ **Nauthiz:** Opposition. What resists you (psychically)? Source of discontent.

ᛟ **Othala:** Greater family matters. National or community issues.

ᛈ **Perthro:** How will you find joy.

ᚱ **Raidho:** Travels, inner or outer. Unexpected help. Rationality. Law and Justice.

ᛋ **Sowilo:** What will guide you? Hope. Higher Powers.

ᚦ **Thurisaz:** Opposition, crisis. What opposed you (perhaps physically)?

ᛏ **Tiwaz:** Loyalty. Cognitive state. Legal matters. Ideals.

ᚢ **Uruz:** Drive. Physical health. Vital energies.

ᚹ **Wunjo:** Relationships, friends. What will give you happiness?

RUNECASTING TECHNIQUES AND LAYOUTS, STEP-BY-STEP

Step 1. The most important step is to recognize that Runecasting, like all forms of Divination, is distinctly different from what we popularly call "fortune telling."

Oftentimes, the tools—playing cards, Tarot cards, Tattwa cards, Runes, I Ching Hexagrams, shells, stones—are used in similar ways, but the mindset of the operator is different. Many people are first exposed to these tools through fortune telling games and the results are considered fun and amusing, but rarely taken seriously.

And that is exactly the way it should be. Keep the two approaches separate. "Fun and Games" is for fortune telling, but *serious* questioning about the cosmic present and futures requires an entirely different state of consciousness and calls for preparation in regard to the tools to be used. Basically, the tools used are cultural and must be explored and understood through the cultural background.

For fortune telling, a "dictionary" of terms associated with each of the chosen tools is sufficient, but for serious divination the dictionary approach is at best a starting point. It is itself deceptively superficial and can be misleading when associated with others in a casting or throw or layout. A single number by itself clearly means something different than when grouped with others—even with duplicates. Thus "1" is one, but two ones in a group is "11" (eleven), and three ones is "111," and each of those signifies a vastly different quantity. When those numbers are associated with another signifier—cars, for example—the combined

THE RUNES: FIRE & ICE

meaning is far different. Add another signifier like *antique* for a more complex example, and the meaning is vastly different than would be another signifier like *new* for our example.

But this simple example neglects other important factors, starting with *you* if—as it should be—*you* are both the person doing the casting and the person for whom that casting is made. Are you a collector of antique cars, or a dealer in them? Are you buying new cars to expand your retail inventory, or do you have too many cars and need to liquidate your inventory? Still other factors may be represented by additional "signs"—the state of the economy, interest rates, consumer confidence, available credit, weather forecasts, trends and forecasts for the price of gasoline, and other factors that might be pertinent for one reading and not for another.

Serious divination is expected to provide an answer to a question, and that question needs to clearly recognize all the factors affecting the answer. Simple "canned" meanings associated with the signs (represented by the tools) will not provide the depth of meaning you need in your answer.

Step 2. It is necessary to immerse yourself sufficiently in the actual history of the culture and its "story"—in particular its *Creation Myth*—to understand how these people perceived the way things happen and the role of the person in the life of the universe.

The Runes were created to represent this understanding, and to interpret it within particular circumstances.

In the same way that Runes are effective in divination, they are used in Rune Magick to manipulate the universal forces in their specific connection to the person and the question asked.

Step 3. The actual technique of runecasting requires that one's entire conscious mind and unconscious mind (subconscious and the Collective Unconscious) be focused toward the question—and all the related factors—being asked. Both Ancient Wisdom and modern quantum theory recognize that "intention" will shape the selection of the signifiers.

The ancients were far more sophisticated in their understanding of "consciousness"—both individual and universal—than we give them credit for. Modern man tends to judge everything from the background of our technology and material sciences, believing that primitive technology means primitive psychology, and that the lack of advanced scientific instrumentation means a lack of understanding about "how things really work."

In more than one sense, today's science is still catching up with the "Ancient Wisdom," which expressed their understanding of the universe through myth and symbols. The single greatest difference is that the "old" wisdom was the property of the few and today we extend our knowledge to nearly any- and everyone. Modern education seeks to give everyone a basic knowledge of physical and psychological science, although there is a serious gap when it comes to spiritual science.

There is great difficulty because spirituality is thought to be the province of religion, and the institutions of religion limit themselves, and their adherents, to rigid theological interpretations of scriptures written down long ago within specific cultural environments vastly different than today. The result has been the building of vast empires that serve ambitious institutional managers but do not teach or apply spiritual science. The truth is that spirituality is not religion, but involves study of the higher levels of the psyche and an understanding of their role in the growth of the Whole Person and their beneficial applications to personal life and cosmic relationship.

The ancient philosophers had a remarkable understanding of the human psyche, the nature of cause and effect within the interconnectedness of all things, and the recognition that destiny is created by present actions that should be undertaken by each individual based on personal understanding and decision—not imposed by a religionist.

A "reading" examines the circumstances of the moment—those universal forces that are in constant play and interaction—in relation to the circumstances of the questioner and the question itself, and "forecasts" the likely outcome as a direct answer to the question. In doing so, there is also recognition that the likely outcome may be altered by changes in the circumstances controllable by the questioner himself. Making those changes is the subject of magick.

Step 4. It is necessary to secure a set of Runes, either by purchase or personal manufacture. A purchased set, often accompanied by a concise reference booklet, is a preferred way to start, and wood is recommended (the original material) over stone or plastic. The Lo Scarabeo/Llewellyn wood runes kit by Laura Tuan is our recommendation for its high quality and expert design.

Otherwise, a simple starter set can be created inexpensively by cutting cardboard squares approximately one inch per side, and copying the runes on to one side of the squares. More can be done in wood or with the use of painted poker chips. Place them in a small cloth bag or a box. If, at a later time, you wish to construct your own quality set, choose live fruitwood limbs and cut equal-sized round pieces, sand them smooth, carve the runes in straight lines with an Exacto knife, color the runes blood-red or use your own blood for the purpose, and then varnish the finished product.

Step 5. Seat yourself facing north—the location of the culture creating the mythology out of which the runes and their symbolism emerged. Place a squarish white cloth on the surface in front of you upon which to cast the runes.

Carefully form the question in your mind, specifically recognizing all the factors involved. Fix it in your consciousness by writing it down as concisely as possible. Keeping the question before you, relax and let what you know of the Old Norse culture flow through your consciousness.

While meditating, slowly mix the runes in the bag or box until you feel "compelled" to pick a rune and lay it face down on the cloth before you. Continue mixing and drawing runes until you have the number required for the layout you are using. Place the runes in position as you select them.

Step 6. Before you start your selection, you need to choose a "layout" suited to the purpose of your question.

Simple Cast. Simply stir the runes in your container, and then "grab a bunch" and cast them onto the cloth. Ignore any that fall face down.

Three-Rune Cast. Instead of a "bunch," draw one rune at a time for a total of three. Lay them face down. Turn them over one at a time, left to right. The first rune represents the past of the situation in question. The second indicates the present path of the questioner, and the third the likely outcome if he continues on the present path.

Nine-Rune Cast. Draw nine runes from your container, hold them in your hands as you focus on your question, and then scatter them on your cloth. Those that land face up represent the current situation and surrounding circumstances that led to it. Those in the center are more immediately pertinent while those at the edges are more general. Those close together or touching are seen to complement each other while those on opposite sides represent opposing influences.

Next, turn over the runes that were face down, but keep them in the same position. They will point to the possible future. Read everything in terms of relationship. (Adapted from *Runic Journey* by Jennifer Smith.)

Twenty-four Rune Cast. Cast all twenty-four runes at once and read those that land upright in the positions they land. Basically this calls upon your intuition, and your reading is a matter of inspiration without rules.

Five-Rune Layout, summarized from Peschel: *A Practical Guide to the Runes.*

This rune cast indicates future happenings, usually within a three-month time line. Draw five runes, one at a time, and lay them face down in the pattern illustrated on the next page.

The three horizontal runes represent your past, present, and future. Turn over the center rune (1) first. It represents the situation at the present time, and will

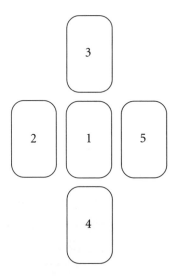

Five-Rune Layout

also reflect your current state of mind. A negative rune in this position that seems out-of-tune with the question may indicate that you are troubled.

The rune left of the center (2) signifies the past and what caused the present situation.

The rune above the center (3) indicates the help you can expect to receive. If it is a negative rune, it can indicate an unwillingness to accept the advice given by the runes or another person, or it can indicate delays or problems impeding resolution of the situation.

The rune below center (4) indicates aspects of the situation that must be accepted and cannot be changed. Positive runes here show a lack of troublesome influences and oppositions, while negative runes show the obstacles.

The rune to the right of center (5) indicates the final outcome, given the other factors in the runecast.

Seven-Rune Layout, summarized from Peschel: *A Practical Guide to the Runes.*

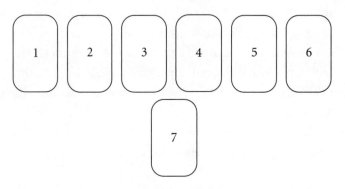

Seven-Rune Layout

The questions you can answer with this layout can be much broader in scope than with some others. It gives more detail and information on how to deal with your problem and on what led up to it. It covers a time line three months into the future and three into the past. If you wish to cover a longer time-span, concentrate on that as part of your question.

Select seven runes and lay them out in a row of six, with the final one below the row and centered as shown in the illustration. You will interpret two runes together as follows:

The first two runes define the problem.

Runes 3 and 4 show the factors in the past leading up to the problem.

Runes 5 and 6 represent advice. Their interpretation will call upon your intuition and will be shaped by your overall immersion in your runic study.

Rune 7 is the result position. A positive rune in this position will only be truly positive if the preceding runes indicate such a confirmation. Likewise, a negative rune will only be truly negative if the preceding runes indicate such a confirmation.

This is a very challenging runecast for advanced practitioners.

LIVING THE TRADITION

Can one live a tradition that is from another time and culture? Not really, although there are a number of groups attempting to do so—whether the Northern Tradition or others. Ancient traditions belong to history and were intrinsic to their time and place. It can be fun and adventurous to dress up as a Viking Warrior or Maiden, or as an Egyptian Priest or a Medieval Witch—but you can't really "go home again," you can't really turn back the clock and be someone you are not—even if you believe you once were in a past life.

But, there is another and far more valuable way to *live* a tradition and that is to see the divinatory symbols in your current life and environment. You will come across people who fit the role of the Tarot's Magician or High Priestess, and you can find images of the runes or the geomantic symbols in your daily life—and in doing so, they can help you understand your current situation and needs.

Lisa Peschel, in her forthcoming *Rune Workbook,* writes:

No matter which magickal system or type of divination you choose to employ on your personal path to a greater knowledge of yourself and the world around you, you will find that you will experience greater growth and more satisfying results if you find ways to work that system into your everyday life. By looking for magick, mystery, and inspiration in everyday sights and situations you will begin to experience the pleasure and the oneness that comes from being fully aware of yourself as you relate to your immediate environment as well as the universal currents of life and magick that surround us all. One really good way of doing this as a rune-user is to be mindful of the rune forms that you can see all around you as you go through your day.

Rune shapes can appear literally anywhere. I have seen them in sidewalk cracks, in frost patterns that form on windows, in the branches of trees, and on the ground in the form of broken sticks, grass, straws, and various types of other debris. Once you start looking, you will discover that you can find runes absolutely everywhere. One way for you to integrate these opportunistic rune sightings into your everyday practice is to carry a small pocket notebook with you.

The divinatory alphabet becomes part of your inner vocabulary and a means of communication between your conscious mind and your subconsciousness, and the consciousness everywhere about you, in which we all have our being. "Living the Runes" in this way is continuous and you are always connected with the "Secret World Within."

RUNIC MAGICK

How do we define Magick?

I'm not sure we can really define *magick* any more than we can actually define *consciousness* or *life itself,* or—for that matter—the *universe,* and certainly not whatever brought it all into being, no matter if we call it *God, the Source* or *Creative Force,* or something else.

Sure, there are "dictionary" definitions, but they exist only as reference points in our conversation and discussion. The Encarta Dictionary will tell you that life is *the quality that makes living animals and plants different from dead organisms and inorganic matter. Its functions include the ability to take in food, adapt to the environment, grow, and reproduce.* Does that really define "life" for you? Does it tell you what it feels like to be alive, what *your* life is all about, why you'd rather be alive than dead?

But you are aware of being alive, and so you *believe* you are alive; you *believe* in life. And likewise you believe in consciousness (it's so obvious!) and in the universe (even more obvious) even as you know that these all mean more to you than what the dictionary says.

You can define "magic" as the Encarta Dictionary does—"a supposed supernatural power that makes impossible things happen or gives somebody control over the forces of nature. Magic is used in many cultures for healing, keeping away evil, seeking the truth, and for vengeful purposes"—but that definition is meaningless if you *believe* in magick.

If you believe in magic, then the simple concept, "the ability to cause change through conscious intention," is all you need to have as a reference point for discussion. But, you also have to *believe in magick for it to work!* That's one good reason we have for spelling this Magick with a "K," to distinguish it from prestidigitation and legerdemain—trickery and sleight-of-hand for entertainment. Encarta Dictionary doesn't recognize "Magick," so obviously the editors don't believe in it.

Belief is essential, not only for Magick to work, but for anything you do to work effectively. Your lack of belief in the universe or life won't stop anything from working, but your lack of belief (or "faith") in what you are doing does affect the outcome. We do have an instinctive belief in Magick, but it is largely repressed both by institutional religion and modern scientific "belief," except for modern quantum physics, which demonstrates the actual positive effect of actions undertaken with *the intent to bring about change,* and even the act of observation brings about change at the sub-atomic level—and perhaps higher.

The magick used by our northern ancestors covered an amazing range of subjects and possibilities: Shape-shifting, runic divination, astral projection, weather control, defense magick, image magick, counter-magick, charms and spells, prophecy and second sight, herbalism, healing, mind control, curses, sexual magick, spirit communication, battle magick, and more.

Magick has been practiced in all cultures and times. People have cast spells and performed rituals for personal and social benefit for all of history, and longer. Cave people created wall paintings to gain control of the animals they would be hunting through "sympathetic" Magick. In later times, people used Magick to gain wealth, love, health, victory, peace, etc. Anything imagined can be the object of Magick, and indeed the ability to imagine is core to magical belief and practice.

Spells and rituals work through the agency of thought-forms. A thought-form is a mental and emotional construction on the astral plane made effective by your imagination. Whatever you think about and wish for with emotion creates a thought-form. With magick spells and rituals, thought-forms can be sent through time and space, and even beyond time and space, using spiritual beings to fulfill your wishes. The secret to magick is to cause change on the astral plane to bring change on the earth plane. *As above, so below.*

Thought-forms alone on the astral will not bring you what you want: you have to complete the equation by taking appropriate action on the physical plane. Again, *as above, so below.* You can't win the lottery unless you buy a ticket.

This one small part of a chapter on a broad subject cannot teach you how to do Magick, but we can give you some basics through a simple glossary of terms.

RUNE MAGICK GLOSSARY OF WORDS AND CONCEPTS

This section is intended to give you a background in Rune Magick so you can pursue it further, and also to provide some interesting lore that will build your feeling for the subject. The following terms are mostly adapted from Edred Thorsson's *Northern Magic*.

Ale Runes were used by men to block magical enchantments by strange women. They were written inside the cup from which the woman drank, and also on the back of the man's hand. The man would scratch the Nyd rune upon his fingernail as the final binding power.

Call: That part of a ritual in which the Gods or divine forces are invoked.

Drinking: That part of a ritual in which the liquid charged with divine forces is consumed.

Formali: A spoken formula loading ritual actions with magical intention.

Galdor: A form of magick using a magical incantation or rune-staves to objectify magical intention.

Galdor-stave: A magical sign to focus a magical operation.

Galdramyndur: A magical sigil, or sign, embodying magical intention.

Gand: A magical wand.

Giving: That part of a ritual in which any portion of the charged liquid not consumed is returned to the Divine realm, usually by pouring upon the soil, or burning.

Hallowing: That part of a ritual in which space is marked off to separate the holy from the profane.

Harrow: An outdoor altar.

Hex-sign: A round symbol painted with a magical symbol to function as an amulet or talisman, often placed on a barn.

Hugrúnar, Hugrunes: Mind-power runes by which one gains intelligence and mental brilliance. They are one of the most powerful and effective means of mind-consciousness. Traditionally they should be written upon the chest and 'secret parts.'

Leaving: Closing of a ritual.

Limrune: Runes used for healing. To get the best results, they should be carved on the south-facing bark or leaves of the corresponding tree. The rune Ul is a Lim-rune of great power, invoking Waldh.

Loading: That part of a ritual in which invoked power is channeled into the sacred drink.

Lot: A runic talisman (rune-tine) used for divinatory purposes.

Malrunes: Speech runes used in areas of life where words are important. A Malrune is a runic formula that is spoken, called, or sung to achieve the desired magical result. They can be used in legal actions to gain compensation against injuries. They should be written upon the walls of the place where the case is being tried. Malrunes are also used in the word magick of poetry and invocation.

Orúnar: Ale runes, by which one gains protection through higher consciousness and power.

Poetry: Poetry and rhyme have always been prominent in magical workings, and it was a particularly powerful technique for the northern magician; the majority of charms, spells, and incantations were in verse. Two possible meters (the rhythmic pattern of a poetic line) can be used for charms. The first, the incantation meter, is composed in the following manner. Lines one and three have four stresses, and are divided by a caesura (a pause in a line of verse dictated by sense or natural speech rhythm rather than by metrics) into two half-lines with two stresses in each. The first stressed syllable of the second half-line had to alliterate with either or both of the stresses in the first half-line. Lines two and four were not broken and contained only two or three stressed syllables, not four. Line five would be the same as line four, but with slight verbal variation in the content. The second form was chant meter. This varied from incantation meter only in that it did not use a fifth line, as described by Bernard King in *Elements of the Runes*. (See also: Galdor.)

Proving: This refers to the concept of magical initiation and to the runes being cut (inscribed) and the person doing the cutting. Knowledge taught and demonstrated has to be proven by its inward absorption. And any single inscription, once cut, would need to be proven before it would be of use to the runemaster and added to the corpus of knowledge that individual accumulated (King: *Elements of the Runes*).

Reading: (1) The part of a ritual in which a mythic-poetic text is recited in order to place the gathering into a mythic time/space, to engage in the mythic flow of timelessness. (2) A "psychic reading," or consulting for divination.

Rede: That part of a ritual in which the purpose of the working is stated.

Rune: The original meaning of the word "rune" is "secret" or "mystery." Every rune is made up of three elements: (1) a sound (song); (2) a shape (stave); (3) a rune (hidden lore). The sound or phonetic value of the rune is its vibratory quality in space, i.e. the magical and creative quality inherent in speech. This is a cosmic principle with which rune magicians work when they sing or speak the runes in acts of Galdor. The shape of the rune-stave is the spatial or visible quality of the rune, which can be deceptive because we put so much emphasis on what we see. The two-dimensional images we see are only approximations of those existing in a multidimensional world. The runes themselves are complex and multifaceted, and fit within a complex web of energies and information. No one definition of a rune is possible, for each rune is in and of itself infinite and without bounds. In practical terms, the rune is the sum total of lore and information stored in the image and the sound. "The song is the vibration, the stave is the image, and the rune is the lore needed to activate the magic" (Thorsson, *Northern Magic*).

Rune-craft: The use of magical knowledge to cause change in the real world.

Rune laying: An operation of runic divination in which the lots are not thrown, but rather laid in their steads of meaning.

Rune-stave: The physical shape of a runic character, or the physical object onto which the shape is carved (especially when carved in wood).

Rune-work: The process of self-transformation using runic methods.

Seidhr, Seid, Seidh: A particular form of magick used primarily by females. The **seidkona** (practitioner) enters a trance state and connects with the spirits, who then give her advice. Seidhr trance travel is comparable to shamanistic practices.

Sending: The magical technique of tracing rune-staves in the space before one and projecting their powers out of the self into the world to accomplish the magical intention.

Shape-shifting : A form of astral/etheric projection or out-of-body experience. While the magician's body is left unconscious, the practitioner assumes the form of a bird, beast, fish, or serpent and travels to distant places. Injuries to a shape-shifter often affect the physical body.

Signing: Magical signs or gestures made with motions of the hands to trace various magical symbols in the air around an object or person to be affected by their power.

Sigrúnar: Also called "Victory runes," they help to obtain victory in any kind of contest. They should be written upon the runemaster's clothing, instruments, tools, or weapons.

Sjónhverfing: A special subset of Seidhr magick involving hypnosis to create a magical delusion, or "deceiving of the sight," affecting the minds of others so that they cannot see things as they truly are. The role of Seidhr in illusion magick is particularly valuable in concealing a person from his pursuers.

Spae-craft: The craft of foreseeing, used by the Spåkonur in trance state.

Taufr: Talismanic magick and the talisman itself.

Tine: A talisman.

Tiver: A magically prepared coloring material used to stain runes. It can be made by grinding natural red ocher or rust. It can also be made from the root of the madder plant (*Rubia tinctorum*).

Troll Rune: (1) The troll-rune is Thurisaz, and its use was thought to evoke demons from the netherworld. The cutting of three Thurisaz staves perverts or inverts the meanings of those runes that follow it.

Útiseta: "Sitting-out magick." Trance-state magick practiced in Seidhr, where a person "sits out" under the stars to hear inner voices and commune with the nine worlds. The traditional rite of sitting-out is a trance of nonthinking, freeing body and mind, and making contact with your personal fetch or fylgja to gain an ongoing interaction with it. Both motionlessness and breath control are basics of Útiseta.

AFTER THE COMING OF CHRISTIANITY

Time did not cease. The oceans remain. The climate is still harsh and the land rugged. The people reflect their early history and beliefs.

But what of the gods? They are no longer worshiped as of old, but they are not dead, for all gods and goddesses are immortal, as are their creation myths. The Old Gods of every tradition still live, for we invented them to meet our needs and fulfill our desires. We may have forgotten them, but they still exist in the Unconscious and may still be reached through our subconscious mind. They are part of the tapestry of our ever-evolving consciousness that is the foundation of our now global civilization.

Do they sleep, awaiting the call of Ragnarok and the final battle against evil? Or do they still tirelessly watch over all of mankind and the world that we have not well stewarded?

And the Northern gods still may be called upon through the Runes to answer sincere questions, and their magick still may be worked. Look upon the Gods with respect, for they still live within you, and give them honor when you ask their assistance.

But know this, the Gods love us no matter the tradition, and we need to love the Divinity within for that is our source, and our future. We are One.

SOURCES AND RECOMMENDED READING

Freya Aswynn, *Northern Mysteries and Magick: Runes, Gods, and Feminine Powers* (Llewellyn, 2002).

D. J. Conway, *Magick of the Gods & Goddesses: How to Invoke Their Power* (Llewellyn, 1957).

D. J. Conway, *Norse Magic* (Llewellyn, 1993).

D. Jason Cooper, *Using the Runes* (Aquarian Press, 1987).

D. Jason Cooper, *Esoteric Rune Magic* (Llewellyn, 1994).

Michael Howard, *The Magic of the Runes: Their Origins and Occult Power* (Aquarian Press, 1986).

Lisa Peschel, *A Practical Guide to the Runes* (Llewellyn, 1991).

Jennifer Smith, *Raido: A Runic Journey* (Tara Hill Designs, n.d.).

Edred Thorsson, *Northern Magic: Rune Mysteries and Shamanism* (Llewellyn, 1992).

Edred Thorsson, *Runecaster's Handbook: At the Well of Wyrd* (Red Wheel/Weiser, 1999).

Edred Thorsson, *A Handbook of Rune Magic* (Weiser, 1984).

Laura Tuan, *Runes: The Gods' Magical Alphabet* (Lo Scarabeo/Llewellyn, n.d.).

Donald Tyson, *Rune Magic* (Llewellyn, 1988).

Website—Runes, Alphabet of Mystery: http://www.sunnyway.com/runes/

25

SAND READING

A Handprint Tells a Story

Lives of great men all remind us
We can make our lives sublime
And, departing, leave behind us
Footprints on the sands of time

—HENRY WADSWORTH LONGFELLOW, A *PSALM OF LIFE*

The "established" tools (Runes, the I Ching, Crystal Ball, etc.) we have considered thus far illustrate the effectiveness of tangible objects in facilitating psychic processes. Appropriate application of these objects can activate our inner psychic functions while promoting our overall psychic growth. Each of these objects exists in a stable, concrete form that is unaltered by its use as a psychic tool. Implied in that use, however, is the capacity of the object to directly or indirectly channel psychic knowledge to conscious awareness by initiating some kind of psychic interaction within the mind, or more specifically, between the mind and some superintelligent part of the inner self. When considered from a broader perspective, the interactions initiated by these tools could also involve some higher plane or spiritual dimension of knowledge and power.

Unlike these tools, some objects are effective as psychic instruments only when they have been deliberately acted upon and altered in some way; after which, they can provide a wealth of psychic information. Just as an artist's expressions on canvas can reveal important information about the artist, our use of these objects can reveal important information about ourselves, while at the same time promoting a deeper understanding of the nature of our existence—past, present, and future.

SAND READING

The notion of acting upon an object and altering it in some way to access psychic knowledge is the basis for a concept called "Extrasensory Apperception" (ESA). ESA is a complex phenomenon in which our sensory perceptions of changes produced in external objects are related to internal psychic functions. The result is the stimulation of our psychic potentials and the production of new psychic insight. Examples of this concept are sand reading, a technique practiced in various forms in Egypt for centuries, and the wrinkled sheet technique, a relatively new procedure developed in our labs at Athens State University (then College). ESA as a psychic technique always requires some alteration of an external, otherwise stable object. Sand reading, as discussed in a later chapter, requires making an imprint of the hand in a tray of sand, and the wrinkled sheet technique requires crumpling a blank sheet of paper into a mass. In both instances, the objects—a tray of sand and a sheet of paper—provide tangible materials for gathering psychic information only when they are acted upon or influenced in some way.

ALTERATIONS IN A PHYSICAL OBJECT
CONTAIN PSYCHIC IMPRESSIONS THAT CAN BE READ

You, like most of us, may have walked along a beach and noticed footprints in the sand, and you may have speculated about the individuals who left the footprints behind. In a sense, they left behind expressions of themselves: their energies had been captured by the sand to form unique foot-imprint signatures. You may have noted the distinctiveness of each imprint as a record in the sand that could never be exactly duplicated. The imprint could have evoked feelings or impressions about the individual who left it behind. Although laden with potential meaning, the imprint was temporary—it would soon be erased forever by an ocean wave or breeze.

Like footprints on a beach, a hand imprint formed in a tray of sand is a unique but temporary expression of the self. When considered psychically, it provides a personal recording that could yield valuable psychic insight. The past, present, and future often merge in a simple hand-imprint signature.

The only material required for sand reading is a small tray of sand sufficient in size to accommodate the hand in the spread position. Sand reading requires the subject, whether oneself or another individual, to form an imprint by pressing the hand, palm down, upon the smooth surface of the sand. Upon removal of the hand from the sand, the remaining imprint provides a valuable information source and essential stimulus for psychic insight to unfold. (Note: Sand that is slightly moist can provide a more detailed imprint. Following each reading, the edge of an index card can be used to effectively remove the imprint and smooth the sand's surface. A paper towel is usually provided to brush any residual sand from the hand.)

THE HAND IS A DIRECT INTERFACE BETWEEN PSYCHE AND ENVIRONMENT

Adding to the logical basis of sand reading is the fact that the hand is the antennae, not only for the physical body but for the psychic mind as well. It's with the hands that we often interact with our environment, from reaching forth to greet another person to operating machines and computers. Notwithstanding the advancements of science in recent years, there seems to be no substitute for hands-on interactions.

In sand reading, the hand interacts with sand to provide the substantive basis for objective observations and subjective impressions. These two essentials then interact in a logical ESA progression as follows:

Sensory Perception. First, the hand imprint and its specific features are objectively observed.

Apperception. Apperception is a conscious, deliberate process in which our objective observations of the hand imprint are associated with subjective, but not necessarily psychic, impressions.

Extrasensory Apperception. Our observations of the hand-imprint characteristics and our subjective impressions are associated with inner psychic elements to generate new psychic insight. At this stage, information gathered at various levels of awareness is integrated and psychically processed.

SAND READING IN THE LAB

The hand imprint on the sand's surface can provide considerable objective information about the subject that can, in turn, activate our psychic faculties. Awareness of research related to sand reading can facilitate that important process. For example, our research found that the hand imprints of stressed subjects usually have little or no space between the fingers. Although that scientifically based observation alone is important, it can give rise to critical psychic insight regarding the sources of stress, such as marital distress, a career crisis, or a health concern. Even more importantly, psychic impressions concerning solutions and coping strategies can then unfold as sand reading progresses.

Another important attribute of the hand imprint concerns its depth. Our studies found that men, on average, tend to press more firmly and to a greater depth in the sand than women; however, unemployed men tend to produce imprints of less depth. Interestingly, unemployment status among women does not appear to influence the depth of the imprint. More aggressive individuals tend to press the hand more firmly into the sand, producing imprints of greater-than-average depth. That pattern was particularly evident in hand imprints obtained from men and women prison inmates who had been convicted of violent crimes. Careful attention to depth can give rise to psychic impressions regarding the sources of destructive aggression, and effective means of coping with emotions such as hostility and frustration, which are often associated with aggressive behavior.

Very shallow imprints resulting from lightly touching the sand are usually associated with either passivity or frustration, and may suggest that more assertive behaviors are needed. Some subjects of sand reading will express dissatisfaction with the first hand imprint, and request a second or even third trial. This pattern typically indicates either insecurity or compulsive behavior.

Career interests and activities are frequently reflected in the hand imprint. Our analysis of the hand imprints of various career groups indicated that imprints in which the thumb digs into the sand are usually characteristic of individuals in skilled or semiskilled occupations. Imprints in which the little finger shows greater depth are associated with professional careers. It is important to note that correlations between imprint and occupations are not perfect—there are many exceptions. In sand reading, as with any psychic tool, flexibility and openness to alternate interpretations and other sources of information are essential. ESA recognizes both psychic and nonpsychic sources of insight, and the importance of balancing psychic or intuitive impressions with those based on logic and objective observation.

The orientation of the hand imprint in the tray also seems to reflect certain career characteristics. Our studies found that college students preparing for various careers tend to place the hand slightly to the right of the tray. Retirees, on the other hand, tend to orient the hand to the left of the tray. Individuals who are settled into their jobs tend to place the hand at the center of the tray. Interestingly, individuals who are dissatisfied with their careers tend to orient the hand non-perpendicularly, and with fingers pressed together.

Our observations of hand-imprint characteristics of certain occupational groups revealed wide differences among groups. For instance, comparisons of the hand imprints of dentists and plumbers showed greater variations in patterns among dentists. Dentists also showed, on average, greater depth in the imprints of the little finger, whereas plumbers tended to show greater depth in the thumb imprints. Dentists also showed less space between the fingers in their imprints, a finding that seemed to suggest that dentists were typically more stressed than plumbers.

Our analysis of the hand imprints of students revealed a strong relationship between imprint characteristics and emotional states. Hand imprints obtained immediately following meditation exercises that included progressive relaxation were typically characterized by a central orientation and considerable space between the fingers. Hand imprints of students under the potentially stressful condition of waiting to take a course examination revealed little or no space between the fingers, and imprints that were almost always not centrally oriented. In contrast, hand imprints obtained from the same students upon completion of the examination showed greater space between the fingers and a more central hand orientation. Hand imprints obtained under conditions such as watching a TV game show were typically characterized by space between the fingers, but with various orientations. When compared with psychological assessment results, hand imprints oriented to the left of the tray were associated with the need to please others and a reluctance to assume responsibility, whereas hand imprints oriented to the right of the tray were associated with high achievement needs and independence.

Systematic observations of hand imprints in the clinical setting have suggested possible diagnostic applications of this technique. Anxiety patients, as expected, tend to produce imprints with little or no space between their fingers. Their imprints are typically oriented to the left of the tray, and they frequently express dissatisfaction with the first imprint and request a second trial. Depressed patients tend to use very light pressure in forming their hand imprints, and their imprints are usually not perpendicularly oriented. Analysis of the hand imprints of patients undergoing treatment for substance abuse or substance dependency revealed imprints that were almost invariably placed at the bottom of the tray and oriented to the left.

Sand reading, when introduced into the clinical setting, can be applied as a projection tool similar to the inkblot to provide valuable psychodiagnostic information. In that context, the imprint is interpreted by the subject. In the therapy situation, sand reading can promote a positive therapeutic relationship, while acting as a self-exploration method that promotes self-awareness and insight.

SAND READING AND NUMEROLOGY

Sand reading as a psychic empowerment technique offers a unique opportunity for the introduction of numerology. If, indeed, the world is built on the power of numbers, as claimed by Pythagoras as early as 550 BC, a number we select at random could have significance for us at any given point in time. That is the basic premise underlying numerology in sand reading. For this application, first form a hand imprint in the sand and then arbitrarily select a number from one through nine. Having selected a number, write it with your fingertip anywhere in the sand, but without overlapping the hand imprint. The number is then interpreted in the light of certain numerologically assigned meanings.

For this application, spontaneity is essential. You can ensure the psychic significance of this exercise by selecting the first number that comes to mind, or simply placing your fingertip in the sand and allowing it to automatically form a number. The number you select is considered your present, though not necessarily permanent, *vibratory symbol*. It is considered a projection of your personal consciousness as well as a significant representation of the number's possible vibratory meanings. The following assigned numerological meanings are generalizations that are presented as suggestions only—there are many exceptions to these suggested meanings.

THE BASIC MEANINGS OF NUMBERS

The Number 1. This number reflects independence, self-reliance, and a strong achievement drive. As a universal number, it typifies purpose and action. This number is commonly selected by entrepreneurs and competitive sports figures. along with people who are strongly committed to a cause.

The Number 2. The vibration of this number signifies antithesis and balance. The subject who selects this number is usually flexible and easy-going, while sometimes unpredictable and inconsistent.

The Number 3. This number stands for versatility and talent. Individuals who select this number can usually do many things well, and do not give up easily. They are known to try their hand at many different projects, to frequently change jobs, and to be quite mobile.

The Number 4. Steadiness and solidity are symbolized by this number. People who select the number four are usually practical, trustworthy, and stable. In a crisis, they remain calm, cool, and collected. They are not usually talkative, but when they speak, people tend to listen. Unlike shallow brooks, this number is quiet and deep.

The Number 5. The number five represents adventure. People who write this number in the sand are usually impetuous and romantically involved, possibly with more than one person. They welcome excitement and even risk. Although their lives tend to be turbulent, they seem to thrive on new projects and relationships, and it is difficult for them to settle down and assume a routine existence. Entertainers, politicians, and actors often select this number.

The Number 6. This is the number of dependability. Individuals selecting this number are typically honest, optimistic, and socially competent; however, they are often stubborn. They have clarified their expectations of themselves, and they tend to impose those expectations on others. They value loyalty in social relationships, and they seek interactions with people who are, like themselves, dependable.

The Number 7. Mystery and knowledge are symbolized by the number seven. It is one of the numbers most frequently selected by psychics and scientists alike.

Analytical abilities and complexity are reflected by this number. People who select this number are often intelligent but impractical, independent but vulnerable, and multitalented but discontented. They are usually serious minded, but in social gatherings, they may become the life of the party.

The Number 8. This number stands for success. Individuals selecting this number are usually materialistic and strongly motivated. While typically financially secure, they are not highly satisfied with themselves, and their dissatisfaction often extends to others, particularly family members. Fathers who select this number are often in conflict with their children, particularly their teenage sons. The number eight man is typically self-indulgent, but restrictive with others. The number eight woman is usually forceful, and if married to a number eight man, in competition with him. Her relationships with children in the family are usually positive, however, due to her use of material rewards to reinforce their achievements, particularly academic success.

The Number 9. Nine is the number of achievement, but achievement as defined here does not necessarily signify material success. Individuals who select this number are interested in global conditions, and they usually express concern for issues such as world hunger and abuse of human rights. This number is often selected by individuals who are actively striving for self-actualization.

Although not included in the range of numbers presented to the subject in sand reading, the number zero will occasionally be selected. This number projects emptiness, loneliness, insecurity, and uncertainty. It is associated with depression, broken relationships, and financial adversity. When asked why they selected the number zero, subjects of sand reading will typically respond, "Because that is the way I feel."

When introduced as an adjunct to sand reading, numerology can become a highly useful empowerment technique. It can expand the interpretative possibilities of sand reading and further stimulate self-exploration and empowering new insight.

SAND READING AND PALMISTRY

A hand imprint recorded in a tray of slightly moist sand is often sufficiently detailed that the principles of palmistry can be applied to gather a wealth of additional information. With the features of the dominant palm detailed in the sand, interpretation of the palm's features can include a classification of the hand shape along with the significance of lines. The life line, head line, and heart line are often clearly visible along with the Sun line, Mercury line, fate line, and girdle of Venus. Other markings will sometimes appear in the imprint, among them stars, crosses, and triangles. Bumps in the hand will, of course, appear as indentations in the sand.

Once the palm of the dominant hand is read, the sand can be smoothed and an imprint of the other hand can be made and interpreted. When a large tray of sand is used, imprints of both hands can be recorded in the sand before reading begins.

A major advantage of so-called "sand-reading palmistry" is the objective, non-intrusive nature of the technique. Subjects of readings who express discomfort with physical touch and "firsthand" inspection of the palm by practicing palmists are typically more relaxed and comfortable with sand-reading palmistry. A disadvantage of this approach, however, is the occasional absence of fine lines in the sand, such as union and travel lines that are often short and faint. A tray of very fine sand will typical provide a more detailed palm imprint that often includes very fine lines. For this technique, one of your authors (Slate) uses a tray of very fine sand from the Great Pyramid, a gift from a former student.

SUMMARY

A simple surface of sand provides the essential condition for this potentially empowering technique. Like the potter's clay and the artist's canvas, the sand in sand reading awaits the touch of the hand and the interaction of the exploring mind. The result can be an extensive body of new information and insight. Sand reading offers yet another critical addition to our repertoire of psychic empowerment programs.

26

THE TAROT

Your Path to Good Fortune

The Tarot is more—much more—than the trite and familiar image of the "Fortune Telling Lady in her tent reading 'the cards.'" On the contrary, along with Astrology, the Tarot is one of the most important and powerful systems of Self-Empowerment in the Western Tradition, and indeed—like astrology—it has passed beyond cultural limitation and become global and universal in acceptance and application. However, unlike astrology, the Tarot is powered by the imagination to enable the user to soar beyond Earth and the Solar System to all the dimensions of the universe.

Nevertheless, we want to emphasize that astrology is a definitive technique and tool for self-knowledge and for anticipating the planetary energy cycles and managing your personal reaction and interaction with the cosmic patterns. Astrology is a foundation upon which to advance in your self-empowerment program. Active work with both astrology and the Tarot should be fundamental to all your empowerment work, regardless of your involvement with other esoteric, psychological, or religious/spiritual studies.

HISTORY AND MYTH

For such a powerful system, rich in beauty and tradition, there is a factual vacuum about its origin. There is only a limited history—and much of that is speculative—and there is a story that just barely qualifies as a myth, although it is often told as actual history.

We don't know if, historically, playing cards and Tarot cards are related, but Manly Palmer Hall writes that playing cards reached southern Europe from India by way of Arabia, and

> *It is probable that the Tarot cards were part of the magical and philosophical lore*
> *secured by the Knights Templars from the Saracens or one of the mystical sects*

435

*flourishing then in Syria. Returning to Europe, the Templars, to avoid persecu-
tion, concealed the arcane meaning of the symbols by introducing leaves of their
magical book ostensibly as a device for amusement and gambling.*

—MANLY PALMER HALL, *THE SECRET TEACHINGS OF ALL AGES*

Others believed that it may have been Gypsies who brought Tarot cards to Europe
and then used them in the profitable practice of fortune telling. The claim was made
that the Gypsy Tarot cards could be traced back to the religious symbolism of the
ancient Egyptians. One early authority wrote:

*When Gypsies originally arrived in England is very uncertain. They are first
noticed in our laws by several statutes against them in the reign of Henry VIII; in
which they are described as "an outlandish people, calling themselves Egyptians;
who do not profess any craft or trade, but go about in great numbers."*

—SAMUEL ROBERTS, *THE GYPSIES*

QUOTED IN HALL, *THE SECRET TEACHINGS OF ALL AGES*

Anthony Louis mentions that

*People used the early Tarot decks for card games and gambling. The earliest exist-
ing mention of Tarot cards occurs in the year 1332 when King Alfonse XI of Leon
and Castile issued a proclamation against their use. The Roman Catholic Church
also condemned the Tarot as a device of the devil and referred to the cards as "the
Devil's Bible" or "the Devil's Picture Book."*

— ANTHONY LOUIS, *TAROT PLAIN AND SIMPLE*

In addition to the cards' use in gambling and in a game called *Tarok* using special
decks called *tarocchi* (triumphs or trumps) documented as early as February 1442 in
Italy, there were several noble families who commissioned artists to produce glorious
artistic decks more or less in competition with one another.

In Germany there was a card game called *tarock,* and in sixteenth-century France
there were enough Tarot decks being produced that Parisian card makers called
themselves *tarotiers.*

Paul Foster Case notes that the oldest Tarot designs preserved in European museums date to around 1390. He also states his belief that the Tarot was actually invented
about 1200 CE by a group of adepts meeting in Fez, Morocco, who determined to
embody their secret doctrines in a *book of pictures,* which included the system of
numbers and Hebrew letters derived from the Kabbalistic tradition, in order to preserve the esoteric wisdom during the coming Dark Ages that they foresaw. These
"pictures" were the Tarot cards, to be used in seemingly innocent games in order to
escape censorship and persecution by religious authorities that ruled in those dark
times. Now, that's the story—the myth—that is told to students, but it is a *modern*

myth without known historical foundation. Therefore, we believe it is a myth developed *after the fact* to serve the purpose of giving a kind of legitimacy to the creative genius that took a common thing and adapted it to a higher purpose. It is such genius—of improving what already exists—that has marked the evolution of human consciousness from the very beginning, when men first took the fire from heaven—started by lightning—and thus made food safer and more edible, and added comfort to their caves and huts.

THE OCCULT REVIVAL

In *The Divine Arcana of the Aurum Solis*, Jean-Louis de Biasi writes:

> *The first occult interpretations of the Arcana were completed by Court de Gébelin and the Comte de Mellet in 1781. De Mellet published a short article about Tarot in the tome entitled* Le Monde Primitif *(The Origins of the World) organized by Court de Gébelin. It was in this text that he mentions a correspondence between Hebrew letters and the cards. Court de Gébelin reprised this idea briefly in his own book. To justify his affirmations, Court de Gébelin explained that the word Tarot comes from an Egyptian word meaning "the Science of Mercury" (Hermes, Thoth).*
>
> *The theories he developed about the magical character of this game were used by another Freemason named Etteilla (a pseudonym for Jean-François Alliette). He said that "Tarot is a book that came from Ancient Egypt whose pages contain the secret of a universal medicine, of the creation of the world and of the destiny of man. It originated in the year 2170 BCE when seventeen magicians met in a conclave chaired by Hermes Trismegistus. Several gold plates were engraved and put around the central fire of the Temple in Memphis. Finally, after various events, it was reproduced by inexperienced medieval engravers with a quantity of errors such that it was deprived of its original nature.*
>
> *Etteilla gave the name of "Book of Thoth" to the Tarot and changed a part of its iconography.*
>
> *It was Eliphas Lévi who uncovered the major errors of Etteilla by underlining as a fundamental and absolute fact the relationship between the 22 letters of the Hebrew alphabet and the 22 Major Arcana. For the first time he explicitly explained the connection between the Trumps and the 22 paths of the Qabalistic Tree of Life. He deduced this from the close relationship between the magical Qabalistic practices associated with the keys and their symbolic representations. Lévi became convinced that the Tarot did originate from pagan Egypt; he concluded it originated from Jewish Qabalistic Initiates and the biblical tradition. This relationship between the Tarot and the Hebrew Qabalah was never denied by later*

authorities on the subject, and there was a great deal of energy put into the task of verifying these associations.

De Biasi's reference to the identification of Mercury with Hermes and Thoth is worth noting, for this is where we get the attributions of the *Hermetic Tradition* and *The Book of Thoth.*

Lévi's inspired work was again improved by the adepts of the Hermetic Order of the Golden Dawn, leading to the publication of the most popular Tarot deck of the twentieth century, the *Rider-Waite-Smith Pictorial Tarot* in 1909.

It was this twentieth-century innovation of improving the existing Tarot deck by involving the underlying structure of the Kabbalistic Tree of Life with its numeric and alphabetic correspondences and then the addition of *art incorporating the appropriate archetypal imagery for all seventy-eight cards* that makes the Tarot the most dramatically powerful esoteric technology in the psychic and self-empowerment tool box.

It is not the purpose of this chapter to probe all the historic details surrounding the modern Tarot's origins, but to explain its modern usage and its superlative value in psychic empowerment.

OUR CHALLENGE

The Tarot is so rich in symbolism, imagery, and Kabbalistic correspondences that it is a challenge to introduce it concisely in a single chapter, and yet it is the very complexity of the system that enables us to do so by showing the comprehensive nature of the underlying structure. *Kabbalah* derives from the Hebrew word *QBLH* meaning "the oral tradition" in the sense that it was passed on by word of mouth from teacher to student. Some writers distinguish among the different spellings, using Kabbalah for the original Jewish version, Cabala for its Christian version, and Qabalah for the Hermetic version.

Today there are thousands of Tarot decks to choose from, and indeed there are decks to be chosen for specific applications in the same way that any professional must apply the correct tool to the nature of the work at hand. The Tarot has applications that include use in meditation for self-discovery and self-improvement, for guided meditation, or "journeys," for spiritual growth and enhancement, for the invocation of specific archetypal forces and consciousness, for particular magical applications including talismanic magic, for divinatory work for personal discovery, career and health guidance, love and romance questions, business matters, and for evoking answers to particular questions.

YOUR TRUE FORTUNE: THE LIFE YOU LIVE

In other words, the Tarot is *not* a "fortune telling" deck unless you change your very concept of what "fortune" means. Your real *fortune* is that of your entire life and whole being, that which you are in the process of becoming though self-directed growth and techniques of empowerment, and that which gives you "leverage" in the work of daily living. Your "fortune" is the life you live and not something you put in the bank to fund an extravagant lifestyle.

WHAT, REALLY, IS A TAROT DECK?

If you were simply to visit a large metaphysical specialty store and wander into the Tarot section, you could be nearly overwhelmed with hundreds if not thousands of different decks, along with as many books, running from showy art books and beginner texts to very advanced texts, along with more books on Kabbalah (also spelled Qabalah, Cabala, Cabbala, and even Quabala), Analytic Psychology, and Magic (both with and without a "K"). You may also find what are called *spread sheets* or *spread cloths,* charts, posters, handy reference sheets with basic divinatory meaning of the cards, fancy or plain bags and boxes for your decks, recommended incenses and oils, and even some spectacular Tarot-themed wall hangings, rugs, and so on.

The modern Tarot is not only a powerful psychic tool but has become an opportunity for creative artistic expression—sometimes with little or no understanding or attention paid to the deeper functions' potential in "real" Tarot decks. We will get further into that later in the chapter. It's just a warning for now that beauty is often only "skin deep" and the artwork may be just that and not have Tarot functionality other than simple divination.

If you can find the *Golden Dawn Magical Tarot* or the *Golden Dawn Ritual Tarot* (they're both the same deck) created by Sandra Tabatha Cicero, we believe it will be easier to understand all the elements represented in a good Tarot deck. We likewise recommend the book, *The Golden Dawn Ritual Tarot* by Chic Cicero and Sandra Tabatha Cicero, for the same reasons: all the essentials are presented logically and comprehensibly.

We don't mean that other Tarot decks and books are not as good or even excellent, but as we further explain Tarot methodology, you may understand the reasons for our recommendations. A good textbook is more precious than the finest jewels and, used well, it can be more valuable than a pot of gold.

At its simplest, a Tarot deck is made up of seventy-eight cards divided into two parts: twenty-two cards called the Major Arcana (sometimes called "trumps") and fifty-six cards called the Minor Arcana. "Arcana" just means *secrets* in the Latin language. *What secrets? Do the cards contain secret formulae hidden from noninitiates?*

ecret knowledge disguised in a format once used in games and gambling? Or, is it the function of the Tarot to reveal secrets about the world and about your own self?

The answer is "yes" to all these questions, as you will discover.

WHAT'S THIS ABOUT THE TREE OF LIFE, AND THE QABALAH?

In other chapters of this book, we've encountered the historical and the mythical origins of the technologies and tools of psychic development. In the case of the Tarot, we have a myth seemingly created after the fact as a justification for what has become perhaps the most evolved and dynamic system of divination and psychic empowerment in the Western Tradition, now becoming universal and global in acceptance and application.

We pointed out that it was in 1854 that Eliphas Lévi published his *Dogma and Ritual of Transcendental Magic,* which associated the twenty-two letters of the Hebrew alphabet to the twenty-two cards of the Tarot's Major Arcana, and launched the first steps in the Occult Renaissance that soon included Spiritualism, Theosophy, modern Masonry, Aurum Solis, and the Golden Dawn, along with most of what we now call New Thought, New Age, and the American Metaphysical religions, as well as modern psychology and parapsychology. And all of this further coincided with the advent of Quantum Physics (sometimes called Quantum Mechanics or Quantum Theory) and a revolution in our perception and understanding of the Cosmos and of Man that is nearly identical with that of the Ancient Wisdom, both East and West, when seen from an energetic rather than a mechanical viewpoint.

As noted, Lévi's inspired work was again improved by the adepts of the Hermetic Order of the Golden Dawn, leading to the publication of the most popular Tarot deck of all time, the Rider-Waite-Smith pictorial Tarot, in 1909.

Every major geographically distinct culture has produced a myth of the origins of the universe and of humanity, and at some level they are universal while at others there are distinct differences that have influenced the fundamental nature of each culture's development, its religions, its literature, and its sense of purpose. In modern times, that fundamental understanding of man and universe has inspired new directions in cultural civilization, political organization, economic thought, philosophy, and even the sciences, although we like to think of science as being absolute truth, culturally independent. And modern religions, while still drawing upon their ancient heritages, are also influenced by new directions in thought and an increasingly direct and personal experience of Divine Inspiration.

The Qabalah and its fundamental unifying symbol, the Tree of Life, are distinct to what we now call Western Culture, which—like it or not, politically correct or not—is rapidly evolving into the first truly global culture and civilization. Yes, there are still some underlying distinctions representative of the few major geographic groupings centered around China and Japan, India and Pakistan (despite religious differences), Russia and its Slavic satellites, Africa, Latin America—more and more centered about Brazil—and a Middle East in search of identity, but the nearly complete political and economic unity of North America and Europe has shaped most global economic and cultural institutions through underlying universally applied technologies and scientific perception, including the basic understanding of man and universe.

The Tree of Life is representational of our multidimensional universe that science is only beginning to perceive as more than just the physical cosmos. The Tree of Life is a time-proven schematic diagram of the Macrocosm (the universe in all its dimensions) and its complete correspondence in the Microcosm (the human entity).

The modern Tarot is crafted to incorporate this schema in a manipulatable mirror image adjusting to and interpreting each person's current and future needs.

Please refer to the sets of tables and charts for a fast visual presentation of the ways in which Tarot and Qabalah are interwoven. Indeed, a "picture is worth a thousand words" and charts and tables may substitute for many more thousands of words.

Each set of four numbered cards of the Minor Arcana is assigned to one of the Sephiroth (of which Sephirah is the singular): the Aces (ones) to Kether, the first or top Sephirah, the twos to Chokmah, etc. and the tens to Malkuth at the bottom, the physical world. In addition, the court cards are assigned to these particular Sephiroth: the four Kings to Number 2, Chokmah; the four Queens to Number 3, Binah; the four Princes to Number 6, Tiphareth, and the four Princesses to Number 10, Malkuth.

The twenty-two cards of the Major Arcana are assigned to the twenty-two paths connecting the Sephiroth. The Fool, Number 0 to the 11th path between Kether and Chokmah; the Magician, Number 1 to the 12th path between Kether and Binah, and so on. To complete the symbolical background, we are borrowing two tables from Israel Regardie's *The Golden Dawn*, with some slight modifications.

One of the most important innovations of the Golden Dawn researchers involves *color coding* in direct relation to the Sephiroth on the Tree of Life and the Four Worlds of manifestation. With these color codes, the images created trigger specific psychospiritual responses in Tarot card readers.

The following table consists of a classification of the scales of color in each of the Four Worlds. The numbers 1 to 10 refer to the Sephiroth, and those from 11 to 32 inclusive to the Paths.

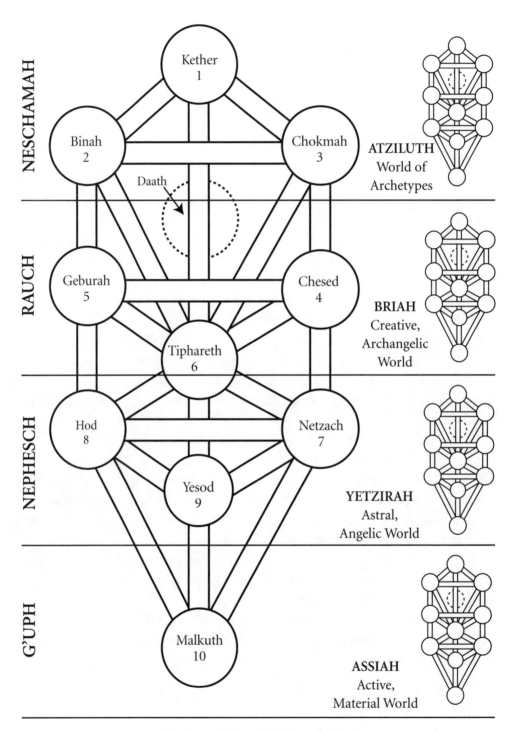

The Tree of Life and Division of Souls

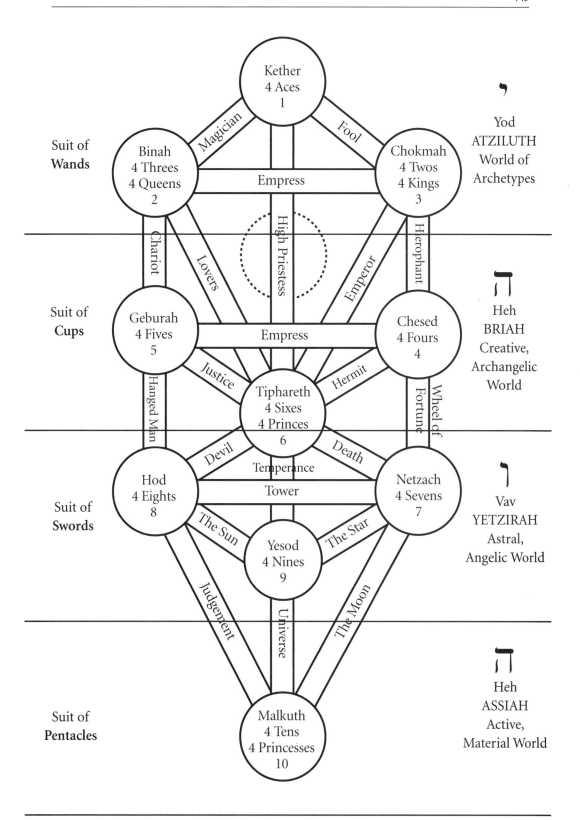

The Tree of Life and the Four Worlds

ATTRIBUTION OF THE TAROT TRUMPS					
Path	Number	Tarot Trump	Letter	Symbol	Meaning
11	0	The Foolish Man	א	△	Air
12	1	The Juggler	ב	☿	Mercury
13	2	The High Priestess	ג	☽	Moon
14	3	The Empress	ד	♀	Venus
15	4	The Emperor	ה	♈	Aries
16	5	The Hierophant	ו	♉	Taurus
17	6	The Lovers	ז	♊	Gemini
18	7	The Chairot	ח	♋	Cancer
19	8	Strength (Justice)	ט	♌	Leo
20	9	The Hermit	י	♍	Virgo
21	10	The Wheel of Fortune	כ	♃	Jupiter
22	11	Justice (Strength)	ל	♎	Libra
23	12	The Hanged Man	מ	▽	Water
24	13	Death	נ	♏	Scorpio
25	14	Temperance	ס	♐	Sagittarius
26	15	The Devil	ע	♑	Capricorn
27	16	Tower Struck by Lightning	פ	♂	Mars
28	17	The Star	צ	♒	Aquarius
29	18	The Moon	ק	♓	Pisces
30	19	The Sun	ר	☉	Sun
31	20	Last Judgment	ש	△	Fire
32	21	The Universe	ת	♄	Saturn

THE HEBREW ALPHABET					
Letter	Power	Value	Final Name	Outer Meaning	Inner Meaning*
א	A	1	Aleph	Ox	Father
ב	B, V	2	Beth	House	Mother
ג	G, Gh	3	Gimel	Camel	Nature
ד	D, Dh	4	Daleth	Door	Authority
ה	H	5	He	Window	Religion
ו	O, U, V	6	Vau	Pin or Hook	Liberty
ז	Z	7	Zayin	Sword or Armour	Ownership
ח	Ch	8	Cheth	Fence, Enclosure	Distribution
ט	T	9	Teth	Snake	Prudence
י	I, Y	10	Yod	Hand	Order
כ	K, Kh	20, 500	ך Kaph	Fist	Force
ל	L	30	Lamed	Ox Goad	Sacrifice
מ	M	40, 600	ם Mem	Water	Death
נ	N	50, 700	ן Nun	Fish	Reversibility
ס	S	60	Samekh	Prop	Universality
ע	Aa, Ngh	70	Ayin	Eye	Balance
פ	P, Ph	80, 800	ף Pe	Mouth	Immortality
צ	Tz	0, 900	ץ Tzaddi	Fishhook	Shadow
ק	Q	100	Qoph	Ear, Back of Head	Light
ר	R	200	Resh	Head	Recognition
ש	S, Sh	300	Shin	Tooth	Sacred Fire
ת	T, Th	400	Tau	Cross	Synthesis

* Adele Nozedar, *The Element Encyclopedia of Secret Signs and Symbols.*

THE FOUR COLOR SCALES

YOD—FIRE	HEH—WATER	VAU—AIR	HEH (final) EARTH
King Scale (Atsiluth) Wands	Queen Scale (Briah) Cups	Emperor or Prince (Yetsirah) Swords	Empress or Knave (Assiah) Pentacles
1 Brilliance	White Brilliance	White Brilliance	White flecked Gold
2 Soft Blue	Gray	Bluish mother of pearl	White flecked Red, Blue, Yellow
3 Crimson	Black	Dark Brown	Grey flecked pink
4 Deep Violet	Blue	Deep Purple	Deep Azure flecked Yellow
5 Orange	Scarlet Red	Bright Scarlet	Red flecked Black
6 Clear Pink rose	Yellow (gold)	Rich Salmon	Gold Amber
7 Amber	Emerald	Bright Yellow Green	Olive flecked Gold
8 Violet-Purple	Orange	Red Russet	Yellow-Brown flecked White
9 Indigo	Violet	Very Dark Purple	Citrine flecked Azure
10 Yellow	Citrine, olive, russet, Black	4 colors flecked Gold	Black rayed Yellow
11 Bright pale Yellow	Sky Blue	Blue-emerald Green	Emerald flecked Gold
12 Yellow	Purple	Gray	Indigo rayed Violet
13 Blue	Silver	Cold pale Blue	Silver-rayed Sky Blue
14 Emerald Green	Sky Blue	Early Spring Green	Bright Rose of Cerise rayed pale Yellow
15 Scarlet	Red	Brilliant Flame	Glowing Red
16 Red Orange	Deep Indigo	Deep warm olive	Rich Brown
17 Orange	Pale Mauve	New Yellow	Reddish-Gray inclined to Mauve
18 Amber	Maroon	Rich bright Russet	Dark greenish-Brown
19 Greenish-Yellow	Deep Purple	Gray	Reddish-amber
20 Yellowish-Green	Slate Gray	Green Gray	Plum color
21 Violet	Blue	Rich Purple	Bright Blue rayed Yellow
22 Emerald Green	Blue	Deep Blue Green	Pale Green
23 Deep Blue	Sea Green	Deep olive Green	White flecked Purple like mother of pearl
24 Green-Blue	Dull Brown	Very dark Brown	Livid Indigo Brown-Black-beetle

25 Blue	Yellow	Green	Dark vivid Blue
26 Indigo	Black	Blue Black	Cold-dark-Gray
27 Scarlet	Red	Venetian Red	Bright Red rayed Azure or Emerald
28 Violet	Sky blue	Bluish Mauve	White tinged Purple
29 Ultra Violet Crimson	Buff flecked Silver-White	Light translucent	Stone Color Pinkish Brown
30 Orange	Gold Yellow	Rich amber	Amber rayed Red
31 Glowing Scarlet-orange	Vermillion	Scarlet flecked gold	Vermillion flecked crimson and Emerald
32 Indigo	Black	Blue Black	Black rayed Blue
31 Citrine, olive, russet	Amber	Dark Brown	Black and Yellow Black
32 White, merging Gray	Deep Purple (nearly Black)	Seven prismatic colors, Blue Violet outside	White, Red, Yellow, Black (outside)
33 Lavender	Gray White	Pure Violet	Gray flecked Gold
(The table above is from page 99 of Regardie: *The Golden Dawn*.)			

We will discuss the divinatory and other uses for the Tarot later in this chapter, but we start with a description of the cards themselves.

THE MAJOR ARCANA

The twenty-two cards of the Major Arcana are the *glamour* cards so often seen on television or in movies involving "fortune telling," because their art *is* beautiful and they appear to have obvious meanings—like *Judgment, Death, Justice, the Lovers, Strength, Temperance*—and others that seem to be more challenging to understand—like *the Lightning Struck Tower, the Hanged Man, the Wheel of Fortune, the High Priestess,* and still others even more mysterious—like *the Hermit, the Moon, the (pregnant) Empress,* and *the Fool*.

Each card has intriguing elements that excite the imagination and beg for explanation. The Star, for example, in the Golden Dawn deck shows a nearly naked woman standing in water and holding two pitchers of water pouring into the water at her feet. In the water below are crystals and flowers; in the sky above are a single large star and seven smaller ones. On the shore we see a water bird nesting in a tree, and then opposite we see a living *Tree of Life*. Just as intriguing, there is some kind of energy flowing from the star above into the two pitchers that are pouring water.

On the card is the number seventeen, the astrological symbol for Aquarius, and the Hebrew letter *Tzaddi* whose meaning is "fishhook."

And what are we to make of the notorious card named *the Devil*, who is shown with the upper body of a man with a horned head and the lower body of a goat? He has batlike wings and stands upon a cubical altar or pillar to which are tethered dancing humanoid figures, seemingly in transformation into or evolving from animal shapes. In his left hand he holds a lighted torch pointed downward and in his right hand he holds aloft a horn of plenty, which we learn is filled with water.

When we turn to the Cicero's excellent book, *The New Golden Dawn Ritual Tarot*, we learn that the "Magickal Title of this card is The Lord of the Gates of Matter, the Child of the Forces of Time... The card is not to be viewed in Christian terms of evil. The Devil here is represented as the Ruler of manifested form... The Devil is an illusion, a veil. On this path (referring to a meditational exercise we will explore later), one must learn not to take what is seen in the material universe as truth. Our distorted perceptions of the world and what we call 'reality' is in fact a blind." We are told that this card's interpretation in a Tarot Reading is "Materiality. Material Force. Material Temptation; and sometimes obsession, especially if associated with the Lovers."

In summary, the Major Arcana consists of twenty-two cards, individually illustrated with allegorical, or *archetypal*, paintings, accompanied by name, number, astrological symbol, and Hebrew letter.

Why twenty-two cards? Because there are twenty-two letters in the Hebrew alphabet, and more importantly, there are twenty-two "Paths" on the Tree of Life that connect ten spheres (called *Sephiroth*, meaning "numerations"). But, when we go a little deeper into our study of the connection between the Tarot and the Tree of Life, we will find that these paths are numbered from eleven to thirty-two, while the ten spheres are numbered one through ten. This numerical system is important to remember.

BRIEF MEANINGS OF THE MAJOR ARCANA, ALSO CALLED THE TWENTY-TWO KEYS

Note: In the following, Qabalistic descriptions have been partly excerpted from the Cicero's *New Golden Dawn Ritual Tarot*; the Card Descriptions and Interpretations from Regardie's *The Golden Dawn*; and the Psychological Value from de Biasi's *The Divine Arcana of the Aurum Solis* and may be used in meditation. This is a lot of information, but combined with the charts and tables you will find that it all accumulates in your consciousness to provide a foundational background for Tarot reading, meditation, pathworking, magical talismans, and other applications that will continually grow in power for your psychic development and self-empowerment.

Read, but do not attempt to memorize. Let their logic slowly seep into your consciousness—because their relationship to the Tree of Life is carefully crafted to reflect the innate structure of the universe as a whole in all its dimensions, and likewise for human consciousness. Later, when you start using the cards in different applications) you will want to develop your own personal manual. That's how you truly learn.

BRIEF MEANINGS OF THE MAJOR ARCANA

O. The Fool (sometimes called The Foolish Man)

Qabalistic Description. The Zero Key, the 11th Path. The Magical Title of this card is the Spirit of Ether. The Path of the Fool connects Kether to Chokmah and is known as Fiery Intelligence. It is the first current of physical vibration. The Hebrew letter Aleph is attributed to this card, and means absolute unity, hence the number is 0.

Card Description. This card usually shows a man in a jester's costume striding along, heedless of a dog tearing at his garments and possibly threatening to attack him. In the GD pack, an effort is made to reveal the deeper meaning. A naked child giving the Sign of Silence sits beneath a rose-tree bearing yellow roses; while reaching up to the roses, the child also holds in leash a gray wolf—worldly wisdom held in check by perfect innocence. The colors are pale yellow, pale blue, greenish yellow—suggestive of the early dawn of a spring day.

Interpretation. Idea, thought, spirituality, that which seeks to rise above the material (that is, if the subject of enquiry is spiritual). However, if the divination regards a material event of ordinary life, this card is not positive, and may indicate folly, stupidity, eccentricity, and even mania, unless balanced with very good cards. It is too idealistic and unstable to be generally positive in material things.

Psychological Value. This card can be used whenever you are seeking to awaken, stir, and use the energetic forces of the universe. By reconnecting with these natural forces, it can enhance your creative energy and the vital principle tht is inside you. By fostering an open and quick mind, it helps you prepare for changes, challenges, and trips. (According to *The Divine Arcana of the Aurum Solis*)—Divinity: Ouranos; Greek Letter: Rho.)

I. The Magician (sometimes called the Juggler)

Qabalistic Description. The 1st Key, the 12th Path. The Magical title is the Magus of Power. The Path of the Magician connects Kether to Binah and is the beginning of material production. The letter Beth means house, and the Magician himself is the house in which the Divine Spirit dwells. He is the director of channeled energy.

Card Description. It represents the union and balance of the elemental powers controlled by mind. The Adept is dedicating the minor implements on the altar. The paths of Beth and Mercury link Kether, the Crown, with Binah. The Magician, therefore, is reflected in the Intellect which stores and gathers up knowledge and pours it into the House of Life, Binah. The number of the Path, 12, suggests the synthesis of the zodiac, as Mercury is the synthesis of the planets. The colors yellow, violet, gray, and indigo point to the mysterious astral light that surrounds the great Adept.

Interpretation. Skill, wisdom, adaptation, craft, cunning, etc. The exact application always depends on its dignity. Sometimes it refers to Occult Wisdom.

Psychological Value. This card may be used when you need to be focused to accomplish a single purpose or intention. The Magician develops acuteness, internal vision, and insight, and gives you the capacity to do something about the circumstances of your life to gain control over what is happening at any given moment.

This Arcanum represents your higher consciousness and the Power of the spoken Word. It can help you to develop your ability to express yourself in public, as well as the ability to think clearly. It helps you to develop your intellectual mind, your creativity, your writing ability, your love of science and books, and your effective use of memory. (According to *The Divine Arcana of the Aurum Solis*—Divinity: Hermes; Greek Letter: Epsilon.)

II. The High Priestess

Qabalistic Description. The 2nd Key, the 13th Path. The Priestess of the Silver Star. The Path of the High Priestess connects Kether to Tiphareth along the Middle Pillar, and functions as the purest root-essence of consciousness. It is the direct connection from the highest consciousness, across the Abyss, to the middle consciousness. The letter Gimel means camel, whose ability to store water enables the traveler to cross the Great Divide.

Card Description. The High Priestess rules the long path uniting Kether to Tiphareth, crossing the reciprocal Paths of Venus and Leo. She is the great feminine force controlling the very source of life, gathering into herself all the energizing forces and holding them in solution until the time of release. Her colors—pale blue deepening into sky blue, silvery white, and silver, relieved by touches of orange and flame—carry out these ideas.

Interpretation. Change, alteration, increase and decrease. Fluctuation—whether for good or evil is shown by cards connected with it. Compare with Death and the Moon.

Psychological Value. This Arcanum may be used when you are having difficulties in discerning the hidden elements of a problem or situation, or when you need to let go of certain emotions, entanglements, or situations you have been stuck in. It is especially useful when you are prone to periods of tension, anxiety, and selfishness. You can invoke this Arcanum when you are experiencing difficulties in achieving inner peace, are seeking serenity, or when you are trying to become most like your truest inner self. It can also be used when you need to receive inspiration, or develop and improve your skills of mediumship and psychometry. (According to *The Divine Arcana of the Aurum Solis*—Divinity: Pontos; Greek Letter: Delta.*)

III. The Empress

Qabalistic Description. The 3rd Key, the 14th Path. Daughter of the Mighty Ones, the Empress is the Universal Mother. The Path of the Empress connects Chokmah to Binah, Father to Mother. This is the Path of Unity, the union of Force and Form. The Empress is the root-essence of Emotion in its more pure form. Daleth is the door of the inner mysteries.

Card Description. The Empress is an aspect of Isis, suggesting the creative and positive side of Nature. She expresses the Egyptian trilogy of Isis, Hathor, and Nephthys. In the Tarot, the High Priestess, Hathor, is symbolized by the crescent or full moon; the Empress, Isis, is represented by either the crescent moon or Venus; Justice, Nephthys, is represented by the gibbous moon.

Isis, and Venus, gives the aspect of Love. Hathor is the Mystic, the full moon, reflecting the Sun of Tiphareth while in Yesod, transmitting the rays of the Sun in her path Gimel. In interpreting a practical Tarot, it is often admissible to regard the Empress as standing for Occultism, and the High Priestess for religion—the Church as distinguished from the Hermetic Order.

Interpretation. Beauty, happiness, pleasure, success, also luxury and sometimes dissipation, but only if with very evil cards.

Psychological Value. You may use this Arcanum when you feel alienated from the rest of the world, cut off from your environment. It can help you correct a feeling of inner isolation that has become an obstacle to your communication with others. You may also use this Arcanum when you want to disseminate your ideas in a convincing manner. It increases your capacity to adapt, as well as the reasoning power of your rational mind. (According to *The Divine Arcana of the Aurum Solis*—Divinity: Demeter; Greek Letter: Nu.)

---

* The Divine Tarot is rooted in the original Hermetic Tradition and the sources of these correspondences are demonstrated in the forthcoming book *The Divine Arcana of the Aurum Solis* by Jean-Louis de Biasi (Llewellyn).

IV. The Emperor

Qabalistic Description. The 4th Key, the 15th Path. The Son of Morning, Chief among the Mighty. This Path connects Chokmah (the Father) to Tiphareth (the Son), The Emperor takes the manifesting energy from the Empress and passes it down to the Higher Self of the individual. Together, the Emperor and Empress function almost as Animus and Anima. Heh is feminine energy balanced in masculine form.

Card Description. Here we have the great energizing forces as indicated by the varying shades of red. The red paths remain red ion all planes, varying only in shade. Thus Aries, the Emperor, the Pioneer, the General, is blood- and deep-crimson red, pure vermillion, or flowing fiery red. He is Ho Nike, the Conqueror, hot, passionate, impetuous, the apotheosis of Mars, whether in love or in war. He is the positive masculine as the Empress is the positive feminine.

Interpretation. War, conquest, victory, strife, ambition.

Psychological Value. This card can break you free from limiting beliefs; especially those that you feel trap you. It is possible to use this Arcanum to call upon a higher part of your being, to ask it to reject that part of your nature that belongs to the "old self" that you are trying to change. You can use this great power to help you to break free of whatever causes your difficulties.

This Arcanum is paradoxical. At first you may see it as a symbol of destruction, but in fact, it symbolizes the moment when old beliefs are broken to allow the transformation of your personality and life. It allows you to conquer the invisible kingdoms and defend yourself from negative attacks, and can defend you from your own internal devils as well as from external and real adversaries. These powers are veiled by darkness and are only accessible to those who can accept the neutrality of the Mars force.

This Arcanum represents the power of language, the power of the Word. (According to *The Divine Arcana of the Aurum Solis*—Divinity: Ares; Greek Letter: Omicron.)

V. The Hierophant (or the High Priest)

Qabalistic Description. The 5th Key, the 16th Path. Magus of the Eternal Gods. This Path connects Chesed (Mercy) with Chokmah (Wisdom). The primary function of the Hierophant is to tie together the Great Above to that which is Below. The Hierophant is also the Great Teacher of the Mysteries, bringing understanding as the link between sensory experience and inner illumination. Vav means "the nail," binding things together.

Card Description. The Hierophant as High Priest is the counterpart of the High Priestess. As Aries is the house of Mars and the exaltation of the Sun, so Taurus is the house of Venus and the exaltation of the Moon. He is the reflective or mystical aspect of the masculine. He is the thinker as the Emperor is the doer.

His colors, unlike those of the Emperor, vary considerably. Red, orange, maroon, deep brown, and chestnut brown, suggest veiled thought, interior power, endurance, contemplation and reconciliation. This card frequently indicates the hidden guardianship of the Masters.

Interpretation. Divine wisdom, occult wisdom, manifestation, explanation, teaching. The Hierophant differs from, though resembling in some respects, the meaning of the Magician, the Prophet, and the Lovers.

Psychological Value. You may use this Arcanum when you are eager to act, but have not yet figured out what your true heart's desire is, or when you are wasting your efforts on things you don't need, instead of focusing on your truest desires. It helps you develop generosity, sincerity, justice, tact, courtesy and refinement, as well as your sense of order and organization. It can help you to understand how to best present yourself socially. (According to *The Divine Arcana of the Aurum Solis*—Divinity: Zeus; Greek Letter: Upsilon.)

VI. The Lovers

Qabalistic Description. The 6th Key, the 17th Path. Children of the Voice Divine, Oracles of he Mighty Gods. This Path connects Tiphareth (the Solar Center of the Higher Self) to Binah (the Great Sea of Superconsciousness). This is the uniting of the Sun (male) and the Moon (female) energies within the initiate. Zayin means "sword," the weapon of the Will.

Card Description. The impact of inspiration on intuition, resulting in illumination and liberation—the sword striking off the fetters of habit and materialism. Perseus (acting as the Higher Self) rescues Andromeda (the Personality) from the Dragon of fear and the waters of stagnation. (Incidentally, note that this is the design of the Order card. Andromeda is shown manacled to a rock, the dragon rising from the waters at her feet. Perseus is depicted flying through the air to her assistance, with unsheathed sword. The design is wholly different from that of the Waite pack.—I.R.)

The colors are orange, violet, purplish gray, and pearl gray. The flashing color of orange gives deep vivid blue while the flashing color for violet is golden yellow. The flashing colors may always be introduced if they bring out the essential color meaning more clearly. In practice this card usually signifies sympathetic understanding.

Interpretation. Inspiration (passive and in some cases mediumistic, thus differing from that of the Hierophant, the Magician and the Prophet). Motive, power, and action, arising from Inspiration and Impulse.

Psychological Value. This Arcanum should be used when you feel the need to do some tidying up in your mind, to sort what is best among all the ideas you have stored there. It can help you make balanced choices that promote harmony. It also helps in developing acute intelligence and quick thinking. (According to *The Divine Arcana of the Aurum Solis*—Divinity: Apollo; Greek Letter: Kappa.)

VII. *The Chariot*

Qabalistic Description. The 7th Key, the 18th Path. Child of the Powers of the Waters, Lord of the Triumph of Light. This Path connects Binah (Understanding) to Geburah (Severity), the descent of Spirit into the lower manifest universe. The Chariot, having conquered the lower planes, is the first path to cross the Abyss from the lower Sephiroth. Cheth means a fence or enclosure, which is the Chariot itself enabling its driver, the Higher Self, to rise above limitations through the balance of opposites.

Card Description. Here we have a symbol of the spirit of man controlling the lower principles, soul and body, and thus passing triumphantly through the astral plane, rising above the clouds of illusion and penetrating to the higher spheres. The colors amber, silver-gray, blue-gray, and the deep blue violet of the night sky elucidate this symbol. It is the sublimation of the Psyche.

Interpretation. Triumph, victory, health. Success, although sometimes not stable and enduring.

Psychological Value. This Arcanum may be used to master episodes of manic delusions and uncontrollable fantasies. It helps you find a balanced, centered path, so that you may discover a personal expression for your spirituality. Thanks to this Arcanum, you can work on every aspect of your unconscious, and bring to light those elements that have been buried deep inside. It fosters gentleness and benevolence. This Arcanum is useful for assisting the Magus who wants to make spells, and it can also be used to resolve fantasies that get out of control. (According to *The Divine Arcana of the Aurum Solis*—Divinity: Poseidon; Greek Letter: Psi.)

VIII. *Strength (sometimes Justice, or Fortitude—see XI below)*

Qabalistic Description. The 8th Key, the 19th Path. Daughter of the Flaming Sword, Leader of the Lion. This Path connects Geburah to Chesed, Mercy tempering Severity. Just below the Abyss, it is a major path connecting the two great opposing forces of the Higher Self. Teth means a snake, or the serpent power guided by Will, that activates the body's energy centers.

Card Description. This card represents the mastery of the lower by the higher. It is the soul which holds in check the passions, although her feet are still planted on earth, and the dark veil still floats about her head and clings around her. The colors—pale greenish yellow, black, yellowish gray, and reddish amber—suggest the steadfast endurance and fortitude required, but the deep red rose, which is the flashing color to the greenish yellow, gives the motive power.

Interpretation. Eternal justice and balance; strength and force, but arrested as in the act of Judgment. Compare with XI—Fortitude. Also, in combination with other cards, legal proceedings, a court of law, a trial at law, etc.

Psychological Value. This Arcanum may be used to eliminate psychic blockages that you hold onto from your past experiences, and allow you to get rid of outmoded personality patterns. It can also be used to help you complete old projects that have failed to produce fruit. It can help increase your willpower and fighting spirit, and strengthen your capacity to work hard for long periods. (According to *The Divine Arcana of the Aurum Solis*—Divinity: Ares (2nd Aspect); Greek Letter: Sigma.)

IX. *The Hermit (sometimes the Prophet, or Prudence)*

Qabalistic Description. The 9th Key, the 20th Path. The Magus of the Voices of Light, the Prophet of the Gods. This Path leads from Tiphareth to Chesed, and represents communication between the Higher Self and the Spiritual Self. Yod means the hand reaching down to show the way to Hidden Knowledge. It is also the word of power that links the Lower Self to the Higher through vibration.

Card Description. Prudence. These three trumps should be collated in studying them for they represent the three stages of initiation. The man wrapped in hood and mantle, and carrying a lantern to illuminate the Path and a staff to support his footsteps, He is the eternal seeker, the Pilgrim soul. His hood and mantle are the brown of earth, and above him is the night sky. But the delicate yellow-greens and bluish-greens of spring are about him, and spring is in his heart.

Interpretation. Wisdom sought for and obtained from above. Divine Inspiration (but active as opposed to that of the Lovers). In the mystical titles, this card combines with the Hierophant and the Magician as the three Magi.

Psychological Value. You may use this Arcanum whenever you feel the need to re-establish contact with the inner- and uppermost parts of your being. It can help you complete something you have been hoping to accomplish; it does this by re-igniting the blazing force of inspiration, energy, and desire that led you to start it in the first place. It is basically an awakening and expanding force that supports the realization of your desires. (According to *The Divine Arcana of the Aurum Solis*—Divinity: Eros; Greek Letter: Pi.)

X. The Wheel of Fortune

Qabalistic Description. The 10th Key, the 21st Path. Lord of the Forces of Life. This Path connects Chesed and Netzach, conducting energy between the Higher Self and Lower Self, the Personality. Caph is a fist showing strength through the balance of opposites.

Card Description. In the Tree of Life, the Wheel is placed on the Pillar of Mercy, where it forms the principal column linking Netzach to Chesed, Victory to Mercy. It is the revolution of experience and progress, the steps of the zodiac, the revolving staircase, held in place by the counterchanging influence of Light and Darkness, Time and Eternity—presided over by the Plutonian cynocephalus below, and the Sphinx of Egypt above, the eternal riddle that can only be solved when we attain liberation. The basic colors of this trump are blue, violet, deep purple, and blue irradiated by yellow. But the zodiacal spokes of the wheel should be in the colors of the spectrum, while the Ape is in those of Malkuth, and the Sphinx in the primary colors and black.

Interpretation. Good fortune and happiness (within bounds), but sometimes also a species of intoxication with success, if the cards near it bear this out.

Psychological Value. This Arcanum will help you to develop better self-control and deeper understanding of yourself. You will find it easier to find the right words, to control your thoughts, and hence to achieve harmony between yourself and the world. It also helps you to develop your originality, imagination, and common sense, enabling you to discover what is most useful to you, in whatever is at hand. (According to *The Divine Arcana of the Aurum Solis*—Divinity: Hermes (2nd Aspect); Greek Letter: Lambda.)

XI. Justice (Sometimes Fortitude. At one time, VIII Justice and XI Fortitude were transposed)

Qabalistic Description. The 11th Key, the 22nd Path. The Daughter of the Lord of Truth, the Holder of the Balances. The Path of Justice runs between Tiphareth and Geburah. Lamed means an ox goad, a stick to prod the beast of burden forward. The Sword of Justice likewise prods us forward by keeping the field level through Truth and Justice.

Card Description. Nephthys, the third aspect of Luna, the twin sister of Isis. Justice as distinguished from love. Her emblems are the Sword and the Scales. Like her sister, she is clothed in green, but in a sharper, colder green than the pure emerald of Isis. Her subsidiary colors are blue, blue-green, and pale green. It is only by utilizing the flashing colors that we can find the hidden warmth and steadfastness.

Interpretation. Courage, strength, fortitude. Power not arrested as in the act of Judgment, but passing on to further action, sometimes obstinacy, etc. Compare with VIII—Justice.

Psychological Value. You can use this card to concentrate on problems and difficulties, making rational decisions about a proposed project or issues, grasping the complexity of a situation. It can also help you find practical solutions to restore balance and harmony after conflicts. It adds energy to your life, and helps you to become more active, energized, audacious; to develop your courage, combativeness, ambition, and a fighting spirit. (According to *The Divine Arcana of the Aurum Solis*—Divinity: Athena; Greek Letter: Beta.)

XII. The Hanged Man (sometimes called the Drowned Man)

Qabalistic Description. The 12th Key, the 23rd Path. The Spirit of the Mighty Waters. This Path runs between Hod and Geburah, the execution of judgment. It is also the self-sacrifice that leads to resurrection, the shamanic trance that leads to renewal, death that leads to rebirth. Mem means water, life consciousness.

Card Description. An elusive and profoundly significant symbol. It is sacrifice—the submergence of the higher in the lower in order to sublimate the lower. It is the descent of the Spirit into Matter, the incarnation of God in man, the submission to the bonds of matter so that the material may be transcended and transmuted. The colors are deep blue, white, and black intermingled but not merged, olive, green, and greenish fawn.

Interpretation. Enforced sacrifice. Punishment, Loss. Fatal and not voluntary. Suffering generally.

Psychological Value. This Arcanum can be used when you seek Divine Guidance and inspiration for some aspect of your life. It can sustain you in your efforts, especially during periods when you feel abandoned and lonely. It gives you a feeling of balance, and opens you up to higher aspirations by increasing your receptivity to the Divine. Artemis helps you to develop seriousness and purposefulness, as well as increased inner joy. Artemis helps you to understand philosophical and religious issues. (According to *The Divine Arcana of the Aurum Solis*—Divinity: Artemis; Greek Letter: Tau.)

XIII. Death

Qabalistic Description. The 13th Key, the 24th Path. The Final Equalizer. This path leads from Netzach to Tiphareth. It is the initiation in which the Personality willingly undergoes "death" to attain the knowledge of the Higher Self. The Personality is dismembered, reassembled, and absorbed into the Higher Self. It is death and resurrection through the voluntary self-sacrifice that is the transformation of mundane ideas into purified thoughts. Nun means a fish.

Card Description. The sign of transmutation and disintegration. The skeleton, which alone survives the destructive power of time, may be regarded as the foundation upon which the structure is built, the type that persists through the permutations of Time and Space, adaptable to the requirements of evolution and yet radically unchanged. The transmuting power of Nature working from below upwards, as the Hanged Man is the transmuting power of the spirit working from above downwards. The colors are blue-green, both dark and pale, the two dominant colors of the visible world, and the flashing colors of orange and red-orange.

Interpretation. Time, age, transformation. Change that is involuntary as opposed to the Moon, XIX. Sometimes death and destruction, but rarely the latter, and the former only if it is borne out by the cards with it. Compare also with the High Priestess, II.

Psychological Value. This card can help you understand your own past history, uncovering the unconscious origins of present problems. It also helps you to have a real effect on the "time element" of your life, as well as helping you learn how to manage time and understand its influence. This Arcanum can assist you in eliminating old outmoded habits that have become obstacles to progress.

This Arcanum can help you to develop sincerity, precision, and depth of analysis, as well. (According to *The Divine Arcana of the Aurum Solis*—Divinity: Kronos; Greek Letter: Omega.)

XIV. Temperance

Qabalistic Description. The 14th Key, the 25th Path. The Daughter of the Reconcilers, the Bringer Forth of Life. The path of Temperance connects Yesod to Tiphareth, and has been called "the Dark Night of the Soul" because it leads from the core of the Lower Self to the center of the Higher Self on the Middle Pillar. Samekh means a prop and shows that spiritual support is always available for the "path of return."

Card Description. This is the equilibrium not of the balance of Libra but of the impetus of the Arrow, Sagittarius, which cleaves its way through the air by the force imparted to it by the taut string of the Bow. It requires the counterchanged forces of Fire and Water, Shin and Qoph, held by the restraining power of Saturn, and concentrated by the energies of Mars to initiate this impetus. All these are summed up in the symbolism of the figure standing between Earth and Water, holding the two amphorae with their streams of living water, and with the volcano in the background. The colors are bright blue, blue-gray, slate blue, and lilac-gray.

Interpretation. Combination of forces. Realization. Action (material). Effect either for good or evil.

Psychological Value. This Arcanum may be used to free you from your passions and impulses, while at the same time helping you to understand their true origin. It helps you to be more grounded, while dealing with the realities of the material world. In practice, it is beneficial to use this Arcanum in conjunction with another Arcanum (of an opposite nature) in order to stabilize the corresponding trait. It can help you to be rid of intrusive fantasies. It can help you to have a wider perspective on problem situation) and assist you in transforming suffering into joy. This Arcanum is a major tool you can use to fight against the impression that you are living in a hostile world, full of hatred; therefore it corrects paranoid tendencies. It fosters seriousness, concentration, patience, willpower, and perseverance. (According to *The Divine Arcana of the Aurum Solis*—Divinity: Hestia; Greek Letter: Phi.)

XV. The Devil

Qabalistic Description. The 15th Key, the 26th Path. The Lord of the Gates of Matter, the Child of the Forces of Time. The path of the Devil runs between Hod (Intellect) and Tiphareth (Solar Consciousness). The Devil is an illusion, and it is necessary to see beyond apparent "reality" to reach and understand the Beauty of Tiphareth. Ayin means the eye, representing the need for inner vision rather than the limitation of physical eyesight to penetrate the mysteries.

Card Description. This card should be studied in conjunction with Death, XIII. They are the two great controlling forces of the Universe, the centrifugal and the centripetal, destructive and reproductive, dynamic and static. The lower nature of man fears and hates the transmuting process; hence the chains binding the lesser figures and the bestial forms of their lower limbs. Yet this very fear of change and disintegration is necessary to stabilize the life force and preserve continuity. The colors are indigo, livid brown, golden brown, and gray.

Interpretation. Materiality. Material Force. Material temptation; sometimes obsession, especially if associated with the Lovers.

Psychological Value. You may use this Arcanum to balance your inner being, and to treat others fairly, with the inspiration of your Higher Self. It helps you develop a sense of beauty, refinement and intuition, and social skills as well. (According to *The Divine Arcana of the Aurum Solis*—Divinity: Hephaestos; Greek Letter: Xi.)

XVI. *The Tower*

Qabalistic Description. The 16th Key, the 27th Path. The Lord of the Hosts of the Mighty. The path of the Tower equilibrates between Hod (Intellect) and Netzach (Emotion). The Tower symbolizes the beliefs of a lifetime that make up the Ego. The Lightning Flash that breaks the Tower is the sudden illumination that blasts away outmoded beliefs and perceived realities. Peh means mouth, the vehicle of transformative language and vibration.

Card Description. As always, red remains persistent throughout the four planes, although modified in tone. Thus we find vivid scarlet shading into deep somber red and vermillion shot with amber. The contrasting shades of green serve to throw the red into relief. The tremendous destructive influence of the lightning, rending asunder established forms to make way for new forms to emerge; revolution as distinguished from transmutation or sublimation; the destructive as opposed to the conservative; energy attacking inertia; the impetuous ejection of those who would enclose themselves in the walls of ease and tradition.

Interpretation. Ambition, fighting, war, courage. Compare with the Emperor, IV. In certain combinations, destruction, danger, fall, ruin.

Psychological Value. You may use this Arcanum when you feel yourself overcome by seemingly uncontrollable desires or impulses. It is particularly recommended that you use this Arcanum when you are feeling restless, or subject to multiple streams of conflicting thoughts. It can also be used when you need a quick boost in strength or energy, such as when you feel depressed and down. (According to *The Divine Arcana of the Aurum Solis*—Divinity: Zeus (2nd Aspect); Greek Letter: Mu.)

XVII. *The Star*

Qabalistic Description. The 17th Key, the 28th Path. The Daughter of the Firmament, the Dweller between the Waters. The path of the Star connects Yesod to Netzach, and is the path of meditation combining concentrated effort and will, knowledge, and imagination in search of the Divine Light. Tzaddi means the fishhook cast broadly into the waters of consciousness to seek the intuition needed to align the Lower Self with the Higher Self.

Card Description. This shows the seven-pointed Star of Venus shining above the Waters of Aquarius. The guiding force of Love in all its forms and aspects illuminates the soul during her immersion in Humanity, so that the bonds of Saturn are dissolved in the purified Waters of Baptism. The Dove of the Spirit hovers above the Tree of Knowledge giving the promise of ultimate attainment—and on the other side gleams o the Tree of Life.

Pale colors suggest dawn and the morning Star—amethyst, pale gray, fawn, dove-color, and white, with the pale yellow of the Star.

Interpretation. Hope, faith, unexpected help. But sometimes also dreaminess, hope deceived, etc.

Psychological Value. This card can help you plan and develop projects. It helps you manifest the authentic personal treasures that you carry within, which you sometimes have trouble accessing. She allows you to reveal the best and the most authentic part of you, and allows you to express your body more naturally, as well as your sensitivity and passion. She allows you to accept your true human nature and your natural bodily needs, and to enjoy the pleasure that results naturally from that acceptance. She allows you to understand and really assimilate the true nature of desire, and to understand the meaning and purpose of your incarnation.

This Arcanum allows you to develop sympathy, optimism, friendliness, and sociability. The Goddess of Love enables you to develop beauty, pleasure, elegance, and a love of luxury (in the positive sense). This Arcanum develops your love for poetry, music, song, and the arts.

This Arcanum is the representation of the Great Mother, Aphrodite, and Venus. She is the Mother of Nature, who contains all of the forms that will ever be born (unmanifest). She is therefore the representation of creative imagination, of this internal force that helps you to combine things in new ways to make solutions that help you to adapt to life and the world around you. As a female symbol, she symbolizes birth, reproduction and manifestation. She is the matrix that receives the sperm of your intention and germinates it until it grows to fruition. (According to *The Divine Arcana of the Aurum Solis*—Divinity: Aphrodite; Greek Letter: Eta.)

XVIII. The Moon

Qabalistic Description. The 18th Key, the 29th Path. The Ruler of Flux and Reflux, the Child of the Sons of the Mighty. The path of the Moon connects Netzach and Malkuth. Qoph means the back of the head, i.e. the Subconscious. It is the path of Corporeal Intelligence, making physical life possible, but also instigating the animal lusts and fantasies that must be relegated by the conscious mind.

Card Description. Here is a river of the troubled waters of Night, wherein is a crayfish, counterpart of the Scarab. From the water's edge winds the dark path of toil, effort, and possible failure. It is guarded by the threatening watchdogs, seeking to intimidate the wayfarers, while in the distance the barren hills are surmounted by the frowning fortresses still further guarding the way to attainment. It is the path of blood and tears in which fear, weakness, and fluctuation must be overcome. The colors are dark crimson, reddish brown, brownish crimson, and plum colors—but their somber hues are lightened by the translucent faint greens and yellows to be found in their counterparts.

Interpretation. Dissatisfaction, voluntary change (unlike that of the Death card, XIII). Error, lying, falsity, deception. The extent depends on this card's relationship to others in the spread.

Psychological Value. This card can be used to increase your power of reasoning and logic, and can enable you to change bad habits and to travel with ease. She helps you to be in touch with the feminine side that exists in every person, helping you to become well-adjusted to whatever society you live in. She helps you to become more creative, but also cautious and thrifty. She can help you change the circumstances that hold you back from realizing your goals.

This Arcanum represents the unconscious part of your psyche. The Moon corresponds to different divinities that are frequently linked to different phases. Thus, the Moon may be associated with both Artemis and Hecate. In her character, Hecate summarizes the characteristics of the Moon: the Earth, the subterranean, and the realm of shadows. She is associated with magic, mysteries, and occult powers. She is the original power present in your unconscious which creates all mental forms and brings the manifest world into existence.

She helps you to think about the relatedness of things; to move from one thing to the next and see the relationship among things, ideas, and places that sometimes seem far apart. Hecate is a symbol of your memory, the sum of your experiences in their entirety. This ability to remember is a source of wealth, but it can also immobilize you if you become stuck in the past. As a result of the fact that she represents both past and present in its entirety, she symbolizes the nourishing, maternal, and protective aspects of consciousness. The character of the Moon bypasses the use of logical analysis. She represents that knowledge that remains hidden from those whose heart is impure. (According to *The Divine Arcana of the Aurum Solis*—Divinity: Selene; Greek Letter: Alpha.)

XIX. The Sun

Qabalistic Description. The 19th Key, the 30th Path. The Lord of the Fire of the World. The path of the Sun runs from Yesod to Hod, thus from the Astral foundation of material forms to the seat of the Intellect. Resh means the head, revealing this path's function as the "Collecting Intelligence" of the Personality seeking to "become more than you are."

Card Description. The Watery Paths of trial and probation are counterbalanced by the fiery paths of Temptation, Judgment, and Decision. In violent contrast to the somber coloring of Aquarius and Pisces, we are confronted by the flaring hues of the Sun and Fire. The high-flying, too-aspiring Icarus may find his waxen wings of Ambition and Curiosity shriveled and melted by the fiery rays of the Sun and the heat of Fire, but approached with humility and reverence, the Sun becomes the beneficent source of life.

Protected by an enclosing wall, standing by the Waters of repentance, the Pilgrim may submit himself humbly but without fear to the searching Light and absorb warmth and vitality from it for the struggle before him. The colors are clear-orange, golden-yellow, amber shot with red, and the contrasting blue and purple.

Interpretation. Glory, Gain, Riches. Sometimes also arrogance. Display, Vanity, but only when combined with very evil cards.

Psychological Value. This card may be used when you are emotionally or physically exhausted and need to increase your ability to manifest the hidden powers of your personality. You may use this Arcanum to achieve balance in your life, or when you want to make progress on the Way of Return. (According to *The Divine Arcana of the Aurum Solis*—Divinity: Helios; Greek Letter: Iota.)

XX. Judgment (also, the Last Judgment)

Qabalistic Description. The 20th Key, the 31st Path. The Spirit of Primal Fire. This path connects Hod and Malkuth, and is the first path undertaken for conscious growth and psychic development. Shin means tooth, providing the physical energy needed for conscious development. It is judgment that enables conscious and willed action.

Card Description. The three trumps attributed to the Elemental Paths are perhaps the most difficult to understand. They represent the action of forces exterior to the experience of humanity, not the influence of the environment but the impact of the Supernals (Kether, Chockmah, and Binah) upon the sublunary (below Yesod).

In the air we have pure spirit holding in leash the lust of the flesh. In water, the sublimating power of sacrifice. Here, in Fire, we are shown the cosmic forces concentrating on the pilgrim from all sides. Judgment is pronounced upon him. He is not the judge nor does decision rest in his hands. Lazarus cannot emerge from the sepulcher until the voice cries out, "Come forth!" Nor can he cast aside the constricting grave clothes until the command, "Loose him!" is given. Man of himself is helpless. The impulse to ascend must come from above, but by its power he may transcend the sepulcher of environment and cast aside the trammels of desire. Here once more, the fiery energy of red burns through the planes. Fiery scarlet, glowing crimson, and burning red are emphasized by the passive greens.

Interpretation. Final decision. Judgment. Sentence. Determination of a matter without appeal on its plane.

Psychological Value. This Arcanum allows you to contact an upper reality located above the limitations of your reasoning mind. It helps you to develop your intuitive faculties during relaxation and sleep. You may also use this Arcanum if you want to enhance your ability to listen to others, as well as achieving a form of receptivity that is open onto every dimension of reality. It also allows you to develop your decisiveness and willpower. (According to *The Divine Arcana of the Aurum Solis*—Divinity: Aphrodite (2nd Aspect); Greek Letter: Zeta.)

XXI. *The Universe*

Qabalistic Description. The 21st Key, the 32nd Path. The Great One of the Night of Time. This path connects Yesod to Malkuth. Tau means cross and is the final letter in the Hebrew alphabet, just as Aleph (the 11th path) is the beginning. The Universe is the end of one journey and the beginning of another. The 32nd path is the portal from the physical world to the Astral, whence we begin our journey toward the Wholeness intended from the Beginning. We now have the Keys to the Universe, and must learn to use them wisely.

Card Description. This card represents the Universe, not the World. It should be remembered that to the ancients, Saturn represented the outer limit of the Solar system. They had no means of measuring either Uranus or Neptune. To them, therefore, Saturn passing through the spiral path of the zodiac, marked at its cardinal points by the symbols of the Cherubim forming the Cross, was a comprehensive glyph of the whole.

Thus, in this card we find a synthesis of the whole Taro or *Rota*. The central figure should be taken as Hathor, Athor, or Ator, rather than Isis, thus indicating the hidden anagram that may perhaps be translated thus: ORAT—man prays. ATOR—to the Great Mother. TARO—who turns. ROTA—the wheel of Life and Death.

The colors of the Wheel of Fortune include the colors of the spectrum and those of the elements, but they are placed against the indigo and black of Saturn, with the white gleam of the stars shining in the darkness and the misty figure of the Airnah Elohim in the midst. In the practical Tarot, this card is taken to signify the matter in hand that is the subject of any question that has been asked.

Interpretation. The matter itself. Synthesis. World. Kingdom. Usually denotes the actual subject of the question, and therefore depends entirely on the accompanying cards.

Psychological Value. This Arcanum may be used as a major aid for your meditation practices. It fosters both inner peace and concentration. It guides you toward truth, and may help you in finding your initiatic path or the esoteric school that is best suited to you. It fosters a trusting nature and sincerity. It helps create the best conditions for you to meet and make friends. (According to *The Divine Arcana of the Aurum Solis*—Divinity: Hera; Greek Letter: Khi.)

THE MINOR ARCANA AND THE TREE OF LIFE

The minors are made up of four suits represented by:

Wands for the element of Fire

Cups for the element of Water

Swords for the element of Air

Pentacles (sometimes represented by coins) for the element of Earth

The fourfold division by the natural elements (put aside what you know about the chemical elements and the periodic table—that's a different perspective—is familiar enough to most people with an interest in esoteric or psychic subjects, but there is another four fold division at work here as well, and that is the Four Worlds of the Qabalistic Tree of Life.

The four suits of the Minor Arcana reflect the four worlds described earlier:

1. **Atziluth:** The World of Archetypes is the domain of Primordial Fire and the Divine realm of pure Spirit and our higher consciousness. Here is the *Yod*-force of the Tetragrammaton (the four-letter name of God), that Great Masculine Power that begins life and sets everything in motion, activating the other three Worlds. The suit of wands represents great energy and dynamic power.

2. **Briah:** The World of Creation is the domain of Primordial Water and the level of the Archangels, the Divine realm of pure Intellect, the inventive Mind. Here is the *Heh*-force, that Great Feminine Power that is the form-building aspect of the driving force of Creation. The suit of cups represents creativity, productivity (and reproduction), and the enjoyment of pure pleasure.

3. **Yetzirah:** The World of Primordial Air and the Divine realm of pure Emotion approximate to the Astral Plane and the etheric framework behind the material universe, and our subconsciousness. Here is the *Vav*-force that is the "Son" (the first offspring of the union of Fire and Water) that is the Astral Plane. The

World of Formation is the domain of Primordial Air and the level of the Angels. The suit of swords represents intellect, communication, and the mind.

4. **Assiah:** The World of Primordial Earth and the Divine realm of action and our physical consciousness. Here is the *Heh* (final) force that is the "Daughter" of Fire and Water that is the active Material World, the level of the four elements of the physical universe where tangible action can take place. This is the Divine realm of pure sensation and the hidden properties of matter. The suit of pentacles represents material worldly matters including business, finance, labor, and natural resource extraction, development, and management.

While not trying to make the subject more complex than necessary, there is a further fourfold division of the Tree of Life that functions within the patterns of the Tarot—the Four Divisions of the Soul:

1. **Neschamah:** Our Immortal Divine Self, the source of our True Will and Highest Intuition. It is our urge to "become more than we are" and the place of our highest aspirations. It is the source of humanity's evolutionary drive that has been with us from "the Beginning." The "superego."

2. **Ruach:** Our Conscious Mind and reasoning power. The "ego."

3. **Nephesch:** Our Subconscious Mind and emotional power. The "lower self."

4. **G'uph:** Our physical consciousness inclusive of the autonomic nervous and other physical/etheric functions of the *whole* body. It actually is a lower level of the subconscious mind that provides the means to the body-mind connection in healing through techniques of self-hypnosis, etc.

The fifty-six cards of the Minor Arcana are further divided into four suits of ten numbered cards for each elemental force, plus each suit has four additional "court" cards. In the Golden Dawn decks, these sixteen court cards are named the king, queen, prince, or princess of wands, cups, pentacles, or swords, with the elemental symbol of the suit at the top of the card.

In the Golden Dawn deck, you will find each of the forty numbered cards showing their number one through ten, and the names of the suit as wands, cups, pentacles, or swords. In addition, the traditional elemental symbol is shown in the form of upright, reversed, or crossed triangles and the basic meaning of each card is expressed in just one or two words.

We want to point out that the information described about the Minors is not spelled out on most Tarot decks, but you will quickly find it quite easy to keep such information in the background of your consciousness (both the conscious and subconscious minds functioning together) as you become familiar with the cards. As mentioned earlier, all the information and meanings of the cards are logically related to one another through the Tree of Life.

In the Golden Dawn Tarot, all seventy-eight cards are individually illustrated. In some decks only the Major Arcana are individually illustrated while the Minors may have only a common elemental theme. This is, in our opinion, unfortunate, and it was the pioneering innovation of the Golden Dawn adepts and popularized in the Rider-Waite-Smith deck that every card was appropriately illustrated. We will get into that artistic detail later.

In summary, the Minor Arcana consists of four suits of ten numbered cards and four court cards. Each of the fourteen cards is identified with the indicated element, and it is the name or number and elemental significance that are the keys to each card's meaning. The artwork is equally significant in conveying that meaning to your subconscious mind and then bringing the whole into consciousness interaction with the Tarot applications you are employing.

The numbers relate the cards to the Sephiroth on the Tree of Life, and it is there that the basic meanings of each are established. You can think of the connection between the Tree and the cards as a code, and as your knowledge of the Tarot grows, so will your knowledge of the Tree, and vice versa.

More, much more, about all this later.

Here are very general meanings of court and numbered cards related to the Sephiroth based on the Golden Dawn studies. The information also includes the ruling planets and zodiacal decanates. This adds more symbolical depth to your understanding. You will note both a short descriptive phrase for quick reference, and then a longer descriptive paragraph to stimulate your more subjective interpretation.

The decan cards are always modified by the other symbols with which they are in contact. You will observe the word "dignity" mentioned, which refers to the relative strength of the cards in relation to one another within a divinatory spread.

Your Birthday Tarot Card

A very simple technique to help *personalize* your Tarot experience is to adopt your "birthday" card as a simple talisman that you can carry with you or even frame like a picture for your desk.

Refer to the "Decanates of the Zodiac" chart, and note the card identified with your astrological sun sign in the inner circle. Thus, if your Sun is in Virgo, your birthday card is the Eight of Pentacles, named "Prudence." You may or may not think the birthday card is a good fit—and, of course, your birth horoscope is far more complex that just your Sun sign—but it is part of your personality. Just take it as an opportunity to make the Tarot more familiar and part of your daily life.

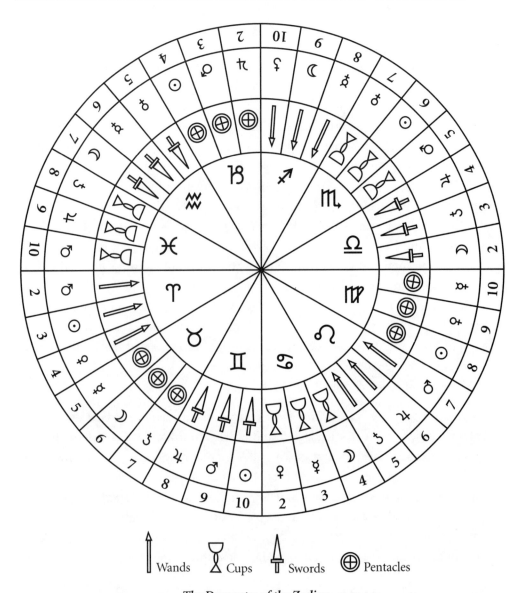

Wands   Cups   Swords   Pentacles

The Decanates of the Zodiac

♈ Aries   ♎ Libra
♉ Taurus   ♏ Scorpio
♊ Gemini   ♐ Sagittarius
♋ Cancer   ♑ Capricorn
♌ Leo   ♒ Aquarius
♍ Virgo   ♓ Pisces

THE MINOR ARCANA DESCRIBED BY SUIT AND NUMBER
Wands

The Ace of Wands—The root of the powers of Fire.
Masculine Fire.

This Ace symbolizes Fire, the masculine energy at the beginning of the universe. Here is the *Yod* of the Tetragrammaton, establishing Atziluth, the world of the archetypes.

The great and flaming torch symbolizes force, strength, rush, vigor, and energy, and it governs according to its nature various works and questions. It implies natural as opposed to invoked force.

2 of Wands—The Lord of Dominion. Chokmah of Yod. Mars in Aries, 1°–10°.
Influence over others. Authority, power, dominion.

Strength, dominion, harmony of rule and justice. Boldness, courage, fierceness, shamelessness, revenge, resolution, generous, proud, sensitive, ambitious, refined, restless, turbulent, sagacious withall, yet unforgiving and obstinate, according to dignity.

3 of Wands—The Lord of Established Strength. Binah of Yod. Sun in Aries, 10°–20°.
Pride, arrogance, and self-assertion.

Established force and strength. Realization of hope. Completion of labor, success of the struggle. Pride, nobility, wealth, power, conceit. Rude self-assumption and insolence. Generosity, obstinacy according to dignity.

4 of Wands—Lord of Perfected Work. Chesed of Yod. Venus in Aries, 20°–30°.
Settlement, arrangement, completion.

Perfection, completion of a thing built up with trouble and labor. Rest after labor. Subtlety, cleverness, beauty, mirth, success in completion. Reasoning faculty, conclusions drawn from previous knowledge. Lack of readiness, unreliable and unsteady, through over-anxiety and hurriedness of action. Graceful in manners. At times insincere, etc.

5 of Wands—The Lord of Strife. Geburah of Yod. Saturn in Leo, 1°–10°.
(This decan has its beginning from the Royal Star of Leo)
Quarreling and fighting.

Violent strife and contest, boldness, rashness, cruelty, violence, lust and desire, prodigality and generosity, depending on whether well- or ill-dignified.

6 of Wands—Lord of Victory. Tiphareth of Yod. Jupiter in Leo, 10°–20°.
Gain and success.

Victory after strife, success through energy and industry, love, pleasure gained by labor, carefulness, sociability and avoiding of strife, yet victory therein. Also insolence, pride of riches, and success, etc., the whole depending on dignity.

7 of Wands—Lord of Valor. Netzach of Yod. Mars in Leo, 20°–30°.
Opposition yet courage.
Possible victory, depending upon the energy and courage exercised; valor, opposition, obstacles, difficulties, yet courage to meet them; quarrelling, ignorance, pretense, wrangling and threatening; also victory in small and unimportant things, and influence over subordinates. Depending on dignity, as usual.

8 of Wands—The Lord of Swiftness. Hod of Yod. Mercury in Sagittarius, 1°–10°.
Hasty communication and messages. Swiftness.
Too much force applied too suddenly. Very rapid rush, but too quickly passed and expended. Violent but not lasting. Swiftness. Rapidity. Courage, boldness, confidence, freedom, warfare. Violence, love of open air, field sports, garden, meadows. Generous, subtle, eloquent, yet somewhat untrustworthy. Rapacious, insolent, oppressive. Theft and robbery, according to dignity.

9 of Wands—The Lord of Great Strength. Yesod of Yod. Moon in Sagittarius, 10°–20°.
Strength, power, health. Recovery from sickness.
Tremendous and steady force that cannot be shaken. Herculean strength, yet sometimes scientifically applied. Great success, but with strife and energy. Victory preceded by apprehension and fear. Health good and recovery, yet doubt. Generous, questioning, and curious, fond of external appearances, intractable, obstinate.

10 of Wands—The Lord of Oppression. Malkuth of Yod. Saturn in Sagittarius, 20°–30°.
Cruelty, malice, revenge, and injustice.
Cruel and overbearing force and energy, but applied only to selfish and material ends. Sometimes shows failure in a matter; the opposition too strong to be controlled, arising from the person's too great selfishness at the beginning. Ill will, levity, lying, malice, slander, envy, obstinacy, swiftness in evil, if ill-dignified. Also generosity, self-sacrifice, and disinterestedness when well-dignified.

King of Wands—King of the Spirits of Fire. The Lord of the Flame and Lightning. The YOD archetypal Force of Fire.
He is active, generous, fierce, sudden, and impetuous. If ill-dignified, he is evil-minded, cruel, bigoted, brutal. He rules the celestial heavens from above the 20th degree of Scorpio to the first two decans of Sagittarius, and this includes a part of the constellation Hercules (who also carries a club). Fire of Fire. King of the Salamanders.

Queen of Wands—Queen of the Thrones of Flame.
The HEH Creative Force of Fire.

Adaptability, steady force applied to an object. Steady rule; great attractive power, power of command, yet liked notwithstanding. Kind and generous when not opposed. If ill-dignified: obstinate, revengeful, domineering, tyrannical, and apt to turn suddenly against another without a cause. She rules the heavens from above the last decan of Pisces to above the twentieth degree of Aries, including a part of Andromeda. Water of Fire. Queen of the Salamanders or Salamandrines.

Prince of Wands—The Prince of the Chariot of Fire.
The VAU Astral force of Fire.

Swift, strong, hasty, rather violent, yet just and generous, noble and scorning meanness. If ill-dignified: cruel, intolerant, prejudiced, and ill-natured. He rules the heavens from above the last decan of Cancer to the second decan of Leo. Hence he includes most of Leo Minor. Air of Fire. Prince and Emperor of Salamanders.

Princess of Wands—Princess of the Shining Flame. The Rose of the Palace of Fire.
The HEH Active Material Force of Fire.

Brilliance, courage, beauty, force, sudden in anger or love, desire of power, enthusiasm, revenge. Ill-dignified: superficial, theatrical, cruel, unstable, domineering. She rules the heavens over one quadrant of the portion round the North Pole. Earth of Fire. Princess and Empress of the Salamanders. Throne of the Ace of Wands.

Cups

The Ace of Cups—The Root of the Powers of the Waters.
Feminine Water.

Here is the great letter *Heh* of the Tetragrammaton as the Supernal Mother establishing Briah, the Creative World Mind and Intellect. It represents the advent of Water. It symbolizes Fertility, Productiveness, Beauty, Pleasure, Happiness, etc.

2 of Cups—Lord of Love. Chokmah of Heh. Venus in Cancer, 1°–10°.
Marriage, home, pleasure.

Harmony of masculine and feminine united. Harmony, pleasure, mirth, subtlety, sometimes folly, dissipation, waste, and silly action, according to dignity.

3 of Cups—Lord of Abundance. Binah of Heh. Mercury in Cancer, 10°–20°.
Plenty, hospitality, eating and drinking, pleasure, dancing, new clothes, and merriment.

Abundance, plenty, success, pleasure, sensuality, passive success, good luck and fortune. Love, gladness, kindness and bounty. According to dignity.

4 of Cups—The Lord of Blended Pleasure. Chesed of Heh. Moon in Cancer, 20°–30°. Receiving pleasure, but some slight discomfort and anxieties therewith. Blended pleasure and success.

Success or pleasure, approaching their end. A stationary period in happiness, which may or may not continue. It does not show marriage and love so much as the previous symbol. It is too passive a symbol to represent perfectly complete happiness. Swiftness, hunting and pursuing. Acquisition by contention; injustice sometimes. Some drawbacks to pleasure implied.

5 of Cups—Lord of Loss in Pleasure. Geburah of Heh. Mars in Scorpio, 1°–10°. Disappointments in love, marriage broken off, unkindness from a friend, loss of friendship.

Death or end of pleasures. Disappointment. Sorrow and loss in those things from which pleasure is expected. Sadness, deceit, treachery, ill will, detraction, charity and kindness ill-requited. All kinds of anxieties and troubles from unexpected and unsuspected sources.

6 of Cups—Lord of Pleasure. Tiphareth of Heh. Sun in Scorpio, 10°–20°. Beginning of wish, happiness, success, or enjoyment.

Commencement of steady increase, gain, and pleasure, but commencement only. Also affront, defective knowledge, and in some instances, contention and strife, arising from unwarranted self-assertion and vanity. Sometimes thankless and presumptuous. Sometimes amiable and patient, according to dignity.

7 of Cups—Lord of Illusionary Success. Netzach of Heh. Venus in Scorpio, 20°–30°. Lying. Promises unfulfilled. Illusion. Error. Deception, slight success at outset, but want of energy to retain it.

Possibly victory, but neutralized by the supineness of the person. Illusionary success. Deception in the moment of apparent victory. Lying error, promises unfulfilled. Drunkenness, wrath, vanity, lust, fornication, violence against women. Selfish dissipation. Deception in love and friendship. Often success gained, but not followed up. Modified by dignity.

8 of Cups—The Lord of Abandoned Success. Hod of Heh. Saturn in Pisces, 1°–10°. Success abandoned, decline of interest in anything.

Temporary success, but without further result. Things thrown aside as soon as gained. No lasting even in the matter at hand. Indolence in success. Journeying from place to place. Misery and repining without cause. Seeking after riches. Instability according to dignity.

**9 of Cups—The Lord of Material Happiness. Yesod of Heh. Jupiter in Pisces, 10°
–20°.**

Complete success, pleasure, happiness, wish fulfilled.

Complete and perfect realization of pleasure and happiness almost perfect. Self-praise, vanity, conceit, much talking of self, yet kind and lovable, and may be self-denying therewith. High-minded, not easily satisfied with small and limited ideas. Apt to be maligned through too much self-assumption. A good, generous, but maybe foolish nature.

**10 of Cups—The Lord of Perfected Success. Malkuth of Heh. Mars in Pisces, 20°
–30°.**

Matters definitely arranged as wished, complete good fortune.

Permanent and lasting success, happiness because inspired from above. Not as sensual as the Nine of Cups, "The Lord of Material Happiness," yet almost more truly happy. Pleasure, dissipation, debauchery. Pity, quietness, peacemaking. Kindness, generosity, wantonness, waste, etc., according to dignity.

**King of Cups—Lord of the Waves and the Waters. King of the Hosts of the Sea.
The VOD Archetypal Force of Water.**

Graceful, poetic, Venusian, indolent, but enthusiastic if roused. Ill-dignified, he is sensual, idle, and untruthful. He rules the heavens from above 20° Aquarius to 20° Pisces, including the greater part of Pegasus. Fire of Water. King of Nymphs and Undines.

**Queen of Cups—Queen of the Thrones of the Waters.
The HEH Creative Force of Water.**

She is imaginative, poetic, kind, yet not willing to take much trouble for another. Coquettish, good-natured, underneath a dreamy appearance. Imagination stronger than feeling. Very much affected by other influences, and therefore more dependent upon good or ill-dignity than upon most other symbols. She rules from 20° Gemini to 20° Cancer. Water of Water. Queen of Nymphs and Undines.

**Prince of Cups—Prince of the Chariot of the Waters.
The VAU Astral Force of Water.**

He is subtle, violent, crafty, and artistic. A fierce nature with calm exterior. Powerful for good or evil, but more attracted by the evil, if allied with apparent Power or Wisdom. If ill-dignified, he is intensely evil and merciless. He rules from 20° Libra to 20° Scorpio. Air of Water. Prince and Emperor of Nymphs and Undines.

Princess of Cups—Princess of the Waters, Lotus of the Palace of the Floods.
The HEH Active Material Force of Water.

Sweetness, poetry, gentleness, and kindness. Imagination, dreamy, at times indolent, yet courageous if roused. Ill-dignified, she is selfish and luxurious. She rules a quadrant of the heavens around Kether. Earth of Water. Princess and Empress of Nymphs and Undines. Throne of the Ace of Cups.

Swords

Ace of Swords—The Root of the Powers of Air.
Masculine Air.

Here is the *Vav* of the Tetragrammaton that established the Astral World of Formation, Yetzirah, the essence of Air. This ace symbolizes masculine *Invoked Force* as contrasted with natural force; for it is the Invocation of the Sword, which is double-edged as mental power can be directed for good or evil. And it also represents whirling force and strength. It is the affirmation of justice, upholding divine authority.

2 of Swords—Lord of Peace Restored. Chokmah of Vay. Moon in Libra, 1°–10°
Quarrels made up, but still some tension in relationships. Actions sometimes selfish and sometimes unselfish.

Contradictory characteristics in the same nature: Strength through suffering, Pleasure after pain, Sacrifice and trouble yet strength arising therefrom, symbolized by the position of the rose, as though the pain itself had brought forth the beauty. Peace restored, truce, arrangement of differences, justice. Truth and untruth. Sorrow and sympathy for those in trouble, aid to the weak and oppressed, unselfishness. Also an inclination to repetition of affronts if once pardoned, asking questions of little moment, want of tact, often doing injury when meaning well. Talkative.

3 of Swords—Lord of Sorrow. Binah of Vau. Saturn in Libra, 10°–20°
Unhappiness, sorrow, tears.

Disruption, interruption, separation, quarrelling, sowing of discord and strife, mischief-making, sorrow, tears, yet mirth in evil pleasures, singing, faithfulness in promises, honesty in money transactions, selfish and dissipated, yet sometimes generous, deceitful in words and repetition. The whole according to dignity.

4 of Swords—The Lord of Rest from Strife. Chesed of Vay. Jupiter in Libra, 20°–30°
Convalescence, recovery from sickness, change for the better.

Rest from sorrow, yet after and through it. Peace from and after War. Relaxation of anxiety. Quietness, rest, ease, and plenty, yet after struggle. Goods of this life, abundance. Modified by the dignity as in the other cases.

5 of Swords—The Lord of Defeat. Geburah of Vay. Venus in Aquarius, 1°–10°.
Defeat, loss, malice, spite, slander, evil-speaking.
Contest finished, and decided against the person, failure, defeat, anxiety, trouble, poverty, avarice. Grieving after gain, laborious, unresting, loss, and vileness of nature. Malicious, slandering, lying, spiteful, and tale-bearing. A busybody and separator of friends, hating to see peace and love between others. Cruel yet cowardly, thankless, and unreliable. Clever and quick in thought and speech. Feelings of pity easily roused but unenduring. According to dignity.

6 of Swords—The Lord of Earned Success. Tiphareth of Vay. Mercury in Aquarius, 10°–20°.
Labor, work, journey by water.
Success after anxiety and trouble. Selfishness, beauty, conceit, but sometimes modesty therewith, dominion, patience, labor, etc., according to dignity.

7 of Swords—The Lord of Unstable Effort. Netzach of Vay. Moon in Aquarius, 20°–30°.
Journey by land, in character untrustworthy.
Partial success, yielding when victory is within grasp, as if the last reserves of strength were used up. Inclination to lose when on the point of gaining through not continuing the effort. Love of abundance, fascinated by display, given to compliments, affronts, and insolences, and to detect and spy on another. Inclined to betray confidences, not always intentional. Rather vacillating and unreliable, according to dignity as usual.

8 of Swords—Lord of Shortened Force. Hod of Vay. Jupiter in Gemini, 1°–10°
Narrow, restricted, petty, a prison.
Too much force applied to small things, too much attention to detail at expense of principle and more important points. If ill-dignified, these qualities produce malice, pettiness, and domineering qualities. Patience in detail of study, great ease in some things, counterbalanced by equal disorder in others. Impulsive, equally fond of giving or receiving money or presents.

Generous, clever, acute, selfish, and without strong feeling of affection. Admires wisdom, yet applies it to small and unworthy objects.

9 of Swords—The Lord of Despair and Cruelty. Yesod of Vay. Mars in Gemini, 10°–20°.
Illness, suffering, malice, cruelty, pain.
Despair, cruelty, pitilessness, malice, suffering, want, loss, misery. Burden, oppression, labor, subtlety and craft, lying, dishonesty, slander. Yet also obedience, faithfulness, patience, unselfishness, etc., according to dignity.

10 of Swords—Lord of Ruin. Malkuth of Vav. Sun in Gemini, 20°–30°.
Ruin, death, defeat, disruption.

(Almost a worse symbol than the Nine of Swords.) Undisciplined warring force, complete disruption and failure. Ruin of all plans and projects. Disdain, insolence, and impertinence, yet mirth and jolly therewith. An officious meddler, loving to overthrow the happiness of others, a repeater of things, given to much unprofitable speech, and of many words, yet clever, acute, and eloquent, etc., depending on dignity.

King of Swords—Lord of the Winds and Breezes. King of the Spirit of Air.
The YOD Archetypal Force of Air.

He is active, clever, subtle, fierce, delicate, courageous, skillful, but inclined to domineer. Also to overvalue small things, unless well-dignified. Ill-dignified: deceitful, tyrannical, and crafty. Rules from 20° Taurus to 20° Gemini. Fire of Air. King of Sylphs and Sylphides.

Queen of Swords—Queen of the Thrones of Air.
The HEH Creative Force of Air.

Intensely perceptive, keen observation, subtle, quick, confident, often perseveringly accurate in superficial things, graceful, fond of dancing and balancing. Ill-dignified: cruel, sly, deceitful, unreliable, though with a good exterior. Rules from 20° Virgo to 20° Libra. Water of Air. Queen of Sylphs and Sylphides.

Prince of Swords—Prince of the Chariots of the Winds.
The VAV Astral Force of Air.

Full of ideas and thoughts and designs, distrustful, suspicious, firm in friendship and enmity, careful, slow, overcautious. Symbolizes Alpha and Omega, the Giver of Death, who slays as fast as he creates. Ill-dignified: harsh, malicious, plotting, obstinate, yet hesitating and unreliable. Rulers from 20° Capricorn to 20° Aquarius. Air of Air. Prince and Emperor of Sylphs and Sylphides.

Princess of Swords—Princess of the Rushing Winds. Lotus of the Palace of Air.
The HEH Active Material Force of Air

Wisdom, strength, acuteness, subtleness in material things, grace and dexterity. If ill-dignified, she is frivolous and cunning. She rules a quadrant of the heavens around Kether. Earth of Air. Princess and Empress of Sylphs and Sylphides. Throne of the Ace of Swords.

Pentacles

Ace of Pentacles—The Root Powers of Earth.
Feminine Earth.

Here is the final *Heh* of the Tetragrammaton establishing Assiah, the active World of Matter. It is a feminine spirit guiding the powers of material manifestation. It represents materiality in all senses, good and evil, and is therefore in a sense illusionary. It shows material gain, labor, power, wealth, etc.

2 of Pentacles—Lord of Harmonious Change. Chokmah of Heh final. Jupiter in Capricorn, 1°–10°.
Pleasant change, visit to friends.

The harmony of change. Alternation of gain and loss, weakness and strength, ever varying occupation, wandering, discontented with any fixed condition of things; now elated, now melancholy, industrious yet unreliable, fortunate through prudence of management, yet sometimes unaccountably foolish. Alternately talkative and suspicious. Kind yet wavering and inconsistent. Fortunate in journeying. Argumentative.

3 of Pentacles—The Lord of Material Works. Binah of Heh final. Mars in Capricorn, 10°–20°.
Business, paid employment, commercial transactions.

Working and constructive force, building up, erection, creation, realization, increase of material things, gain in commercial transactions, rank, increase of substance, influence, cleverness in business, selfishness, commencement of matter to be established later. Narrow and prejudiced, keen in matters of gain. Modified by dignity. Sometimes given to seeking after the impossible.

4 of Pentacles—The Lord of Earthly Power. Chesed of Heh final. Sun in Capricorn, 20°–30°.
Gain of money or influence. A present.

Assured material gain, success, rank, dominion, earthly power completed, but leading to nothing beyond. Prejudiced, covetous, suspicious, careful and orderly, but discontented. Little enterprise or originality. Altered by dignity as usual.

5 of Pentacles—Lord of Material Trouble. Geburah of Heh final. Mercury in Taurus, 1°–10°.
Loss of profession, loss of money, monetary anxiety.

Loss of money or position. Trouble about material things. Toil, labor, land cultivation, building, knowledge and acuteness of earthly things, poverty, carefulness. Kindness, sometimes money regained after severe toil and labor. Unimaginative, harsh, stern, determined, obstinate.

6 of Pentacles—Lord of Material Success. Tiphareth of Heh final. Moon in Taurus, 10°–20°
Success in material things. Prosperity in business.
Success and gain in material undertakings, power, influence, rank, nobility, rule over the people. Fortunate, successful, just, and liberal. If ill-dignified, may be purse-proud, insolent from success, or prodigal.

7 of Pentacles—The Lord of Success Unfulfilled. Netzach of Heh. Saturn in Taurus, 20°–30°
Unprofitable speculation and employment. Little gain for much labor.
Promises of success unfulfilled. Loss of apparently promising fortune. Hopes deceived and crushed. Disappointment. Misery, slavery, necessity, and baseness. A cultivator of land, and yet a loser thereby. Sometimes it denotes slight and isolated gains with no fruits resulting therefrom, and of no further account, though seeming to promise well. According to dignity.

8 of Pentacles—Lord of Prudence. Hod of Heh. Sun in Virgo, 1°–10°
Skill, prudence, cunning.
Over-careful in small things at the expense of the great. Penny-wise and pound-foolish. Gain of ready money in small sums. Mean, avaricious. Industrious, cultivation of land, hoarding, lacking in enterprise.

9 of Pentacles—Lord of Material Gain. Yesod of Heh. Venus in Virgo, 10°–20°
Inheritance, much increase of goods.
Complete realization of material gain, inheritance, covetousness, treasuring of goods and sometimes theft, and knavery. All according to dignity.

10 of Pentacles—Lord of Wealth. Malkuth of Heh. Mercury in Virgo, 20°–30°
Riches and wealth.
Completion of material gain and fortune, but nothing beyond. As it were, at the very pinnacle of success. Old age, slothfulness, great wealth, yet sometimes loss in part, and later heaviness, dullness of mind, yet clever and prosperous in money transactions.

King of Pentacles—Lord of the Wild and Fertile Land. King of the Spirits of Earth. The YOD Archetypal Force of Earth.
Unless very well dignified, he is heavy, dull, and material. Laborious, clever, and patient in material matters. If ill-dignified, he is avaricious, grasping, dull, jealous, and not very courageous, unless assisted by other symbols. Rules from above 20° Leo to 20° Virgo. Fire of Earth. King of Gnomes.

Queen of Pentacles—Queen of the Thrones of Earth.
The HEH Creative Force of Earth.
She is impetuous, kind, timid, rather charming, great-hearted, intelligent, melancholy, truthful, yet of many moods. Ill-dignified, she is undecided, capricious, foolish, and changeable. Rules from 20° Sagittarius to 20° Capricorn. Water of Earth. Queen of Gnomes.

Prince of Pentacles—Prince of the Chariot of Earth.
The VAV Astral Force of Earth.
Increase of matter, increase of good and evil; solidifies, practically applies things, steady, reliable. If ill-dignified: animal, material, stupid. In either, slow to anger, but furious if roused. Rules from 20° Aries to 20° Taurus. Air of Earth. Prince and Emperor of the Gnomes.

Princess of Pentacles—Princess of the Echoing Hills. Rose of the Palace of Earth.
The HEH Active, Material Force of Earth.
She is generous, kind, diligent, benevolent, careful, courageous, preserving, pitiful. If ill-dignified, she is wasteful and prodigal. Rules over one quadrant of the heavens around the North Pole of the Ecliptic. Earth of Earth. Princess and Empress of Gnomes. Throne of the Ace of Pentacles.

There's more that will be said about the cards, about their artwork and the colors used, their relationship to the archetypes of the *Collective Unconscious*, about the symbols and other elements represented on the cards and in the artwork, and then how the cards can be used, and about their meanings. We will go into depth about their most popular use—*divination*—very soon, and then about those other even more interesting uses in *meditation, pathworking, astral travel, dream work, ritual magic,* and in the *Exploration of Alternative Realities.*

In one sense, these tables and charts give you all the information you need, both in the background of your mind and for ready reference. Yes, they are complex, but as a user you are not *subject* to the complexities even as you are *responsive* to them. They are challenges to the artists and designers of Tarot decks, but not to you as the beneficiary of their work, and the study and research of those pioneers in the Hermetic Order of the Golden Dawn who made the modern Tarot a living reality. It is to the Golden Dawn that all the world of Tarot owes appreciation.

In another sense, since you actually have read the material thus far, you have already opened the doors and windows of your personal consciousness to the glory and full potential offered by the Tarot. Trust your own self to slowly meld the information so that it is there for your use when needed—or, at worst, you will easily

know where in the pages read so far you can return to find what will flower to fulfill your needs.

You can study forever without actually learning anything, but you can instead take the next step by picking up your Tarot cards and starting to use them at the level that will lay a solid foundation for your future growth. We start with Divination.

DIVINATION: YOUR PATH TO THE FUTURE

Your cards are rich in symbols, the language of the Unconscious, and they are joined by pictures that have art created to express—through specified colors, images, and actions—archetypal powers derived from the Tree of Life. This is purposely true for the New Golden Dawn Ritual Tarot, but often equally true for many other purely art-driven Tarot decks drawn and painted by inspired artists and designers.

You may already have one or more Tarot decks, and perhaps one of them is the New Golden Dawn Ritual Tarot to which all the tables and information given here directly apply—but if you are using another deck, you will find that most of this information still applies. The Tarot is not actually based so much on specific physical formulae of the kind involved in chemical reactions but the more subtle kind of energy and emotional responses you experience with music and drama every day through television, movies, video, and actual life experiences.

In choosing a first deck, do make sure that all the cards are uniquely illustrated with actual pictures of people or entities in action. In addition to the New Golden Dawn Ritual Tarot, the Rider-Waite-Smith deck is of considerable value as a "beginner's" deck, simply because so many books use the deck in their instruction. See the end of this chapter for mention of a few other pictorial Tarot decks.

That a picture is "worth a thousand words" is a gross understatement. The colorful images "speak" directly to our emotional and mental selves. Even without the specific descriptions and interpretations that come later, you will find that you already "know" a great deal. It is better, initially, to "learn" by actually experiencing the cards in action.

The "secret" to all systems of divination starts with the establishment of rules and definitions to guide your interpretations of cards drawn in response to your well-defined questions. The first step is to define your question(s) as specifically as possible—even with questions asking for a "yes" or "no" answer—even though your answers will be much more extensive than that. With experience, your questions may become more general and expansive, while your answers will actually become more specific in application to your personal situation.

The cards of the Minor Arcana present to us the vibrations of Number, Color, and Element—that is, the plane on which number and color function. Thus, in the Ten of Pentacles we have the number ten and the tertiary colors: citrine, olive, and russet, working in Malkuth, the material plane. Whereas in the Ten of Wands, we have the number ten and the colors working in pure energy. In these cards, the Sephirah is indicated by the coloring of the clouds; the plane by the coloring of the symbols.

The following is a quick review of the cards as we prepare for our divinatory journey.

BRIEF MEANINGS OF THE NUMBERED CARDS

The Aces

First in order and appearance are the four Aces, representing the force of the Spirit acting in and binding together, the four scales of each element and answering to the Dominion of the letters of the name in the *Kether* of each. They represent the Root Force. The four aces are said to be placed on the North Pole of the Universe, wherein they revolve, governing its revolution, and ruling as the connecting link between Yetzirah and the Material Plane of Universe.

The Four Deuces

Relate to the second Sephirah. *Chokmah,* and generally represent the uniting and initiating powers of the King and Queen.

The Four Threes

Relate to the third Sephirah, *Binah,* and generally represent the realization of action owing to the Prince being produced and represented by the central symbol on each card. Action definitely commenced, for good or evil.

The Four Fours

Relate to the fourth Sephirah, *Chesed,* and generally represent perfection, realization, completion, making a matter settled and fixed.

The Four Fives

Relate to the fifth Sephirah, *Geburah,* and generally represent opposition, strife, and struggle; war, obstacle to the thing in hand. Ultimate success or failure is otherwise shown.

The Four Sixes

Relate to the sixth Sephirah, *Tiphareth,* and generally represent definite accomplishment and carrying out of a matter.

The Four Sevens

Relate to the seventh Sephirah, *Netzach*, and generally show a force transcending the material plane. The sevens then show a possible result that is dependent on the action then taken, as indicated by the symbols that accompany them.

The Four Eights

Relate to the eighth Sephirah, *Hod*, and generally show solitary success; i.e., success in the matter for the time being, but not leading to much result, apart from the thing itself.

The Four Nines

Relate to the ninth Sephirah, *Yesod*, and generally they show very great fundamental force. Executive power, because they rest on a firm basis—powerful for good or evil.

The Four Tens

Relate to the tenth Sephirah, *Malkuth*, and generally show fixed, culminated, and completed force, whether good or evil. The matter is thoroughly and definitely determined. Similar to the force of the nines, but finalizes it, carrying it out.

BRIEF MEANING OF THE THIRTY-SIX NUMBERED CARDS OF THE MINOR ARCANA

Wands

Two—Influence over another. Dominion.

Three—Pride and arrogance. Power sometimes.

Four—Settlement. Arrangement completed.

Five—Quarrelling. Fighting.

Six—Gain and success.

Seven—Opposition; sometimes courage therewith.

Eight—A hasty communication, letter, or message. Swiftness.

Nine—Strength. Power. Health. Energy.

Ten—Cruelty and malice toward others. Overbearing strength. Revenge. Injustice.

Cups

Two—Marriage, love, pleasure. Warm friendship.

Three—Plenty. Hospitality, eating, drinking. Pleasure, dancing, new clothes, and merriment.

Four—Receiving pleasures or kindness from others, yet some discomfort therewith.

Five—Disappointment in love. Marriage broken of. Unkindness from friends. (Whether deserved or not is shown by the cards with it, or counting from or to it.) Loss of friendship.

Six—Wish, happiness, success, enjoyment.

Seven—Lying, deceit, promises unfulfilled, illusion, deception. Error, slight success, but not enough energy to retain it.

Eight—Success abandoned, decline of interest in a thing. Ennui.

Nine—Complete success. Pleasure and happiness. Wishes fulfilled.

Ten—Matters definitely arranged and settled in accordance with one's wishes. Complete good fortune.

Swords

Two—Quarrel made up, and arranged. Peace restored, yet some tension in relations.

Three—Unhappiness, sorrow, tears.

Four—Convalescence, recovery from sickness, change for the better.

Five—Defeat, loss, malice. Slander, evil-speaking.

Six—Labor, work; journey, probably by water (shown by cards nearby).

Seven—In character untrustworthy, vacillation. Journey probably by land (shown by cards nearby).

Eight—Narrow or restricted. Petty. A prison.

Nine—Illness. Suffering. Malice. Cruelty. Pain.

Ten—Ruin. Death. Failure. Disaster.

Pentacles

Two—Pleasant change. Visit to friends, etc.

Three—Business, paid employment. Commercial transactions.

Four—Gain of money and influence. A present.

Five—Loss of profession. Loss of money. Monetary anxiety.

Six—Success in material things; prosperity in business.

Seven—Unprofitable speculations, employments; also honorary work undertaken for the love of it, and without desire of reward.

Eight—Skill, prudence, also artfulness, and cunning (depends on cards with it).

Nine—Inheritance. Much increase of money.

Ten—Riches and wealth.

BRIEF MEANINGS OF THE SIXTEEN COURT OR ROYAL CARDS

The four honors of each suit taken in their most abstract sense may be interpreted as:

Potential Power	The King
Brooding Power	The Queen
Power in action	The Prince
Reception and Transmission	The Princess

The Four Kings

They are mounted on Steeds and represent the Yod forces of the Name in each suit, the Radix, Father, and commencement of Material Forces. A Force in which all the others are implied and of which they form the development and completion. A force swift and violent in action, but whose effect soon passes away, and therefore symbolized by a figure on a steed riding swiftly, and clothed in complete armor.

Therefore is the knowledge of the scale of the King so necessary for the commencement of all magical working.

The Four Queens

They are seated upon Thrones, representing the Forces of *Heh* of the Name in each suit, the Mother, and bringer forth of material Force, a Force that develops and realizes the Force of the King. A force steady and unshaken, but not rapid though enduring. It is therefore symbolized by a figure seated upon a Throne but also clothed in armor.

The Four Princes

They are seated in Chariots, and thus borne forward. They represent the Vau Forces of the Name in each suit; the Mighty son of the King, and the Queen, who realizes the Influence of both scales of Force. A prince, the son of a King and Queen, yet a Prince of Princes, and a King of Kings. An Emperor, whose effect is at once rapid (though not so swift as that of a king) and enduring (though not as steadfast as that of a Queen). It is therefore symbolized by a figure borne in a chariot, and clothed with armor. Yet is his power illusionary, unless set in motion by his Father and Mother.

The Four Princesses

They are sometime named Knaves. The Four Princesses or figures of Amazons stand firmly by themselves, neither riding upon Horses, nor seated upon Thrones, nor borne on Chariots. They represent the forces of Heh final of the Name in each suit, completing the influences of the other scales. The mighty and potent daughter of a King and Queen: a Princess powerful and terrible. A Queen of Queens, an Empress, whose effect combines those of the King, Queen, and Prince. At once violent and permanent, she is therefore symbolized by a figure standing firmly by itself, only partially draped and having but little armor. Yet her power exists not save by reason of the others, and then indeed it is mighty and terrible materially, and is the Throne of the Forces of the Spirit. Woe unto whosoever shall make war upon her when thus established!

The Sphere of Influence of the Court Cards of the Tarot Pack

The Princesses rule over the four parts of the Celestial Heavens that lie around the North Pole, and above the respective Cherubic Signs of the Zodiac, and they form the Thrones of the Powers of the Four Aces.

The Twelve other Court Cards—four Kings, four Queens, and four Princes—rule the Dominions of the Celestial Heavens between the realm of the Four Princesses and the *Book "7"* Zodiac, as is hereafter shown. And they, as it were, link together the signs.

FIRST STEPS, AND RULES OF DIVINATION

Spreads

Spreads, or layouts, are intended to provide the foundation for your readings, but to start your experience we will use only the most simple and logical forms. More complex spreads and example readings can be found in Israel Regardie's *The Golden Dawn,* and in most other books on the Tarot. Some spreads are specific to the purpose of a divination and are based on extensive experience of authors who have been counseling people for years. Their wisdom should be respected.

Shuffling, Cutting, Dealing, and Examining

In shuffling, the mind of the enquirer should be earnestly fixed on the matter concerning which he desires information. If any cards fall in the process, they should be taken up without being noticed and the shuffling resumed. The shuffling being concluded and the pack placed upon the table, if any cards fall to the ground, or become turned in a different direction, the shuffling should be done again.

A cut should be clean and decisive. If any cards fall from the hand in the performance, the operation of shuffling should be repeated before they are again cut. In dealing, care should be taken not to invert the cards, and their relative order should be strictly observed. In examining a pack of cards, their relative order should be rigidly maintained, as without care in this respect, one may be easily pushed under or over another, which would of course have the effect of completely altering the counting in the Reading.

The Single Card Draw

Now, in the single card draw, you will have concentrated on a single question, such as what kind of day you can expect, or whether your important meeting will be successful. After shuffling as described, spread the cards out, face down, while continuing to think about your question, pause, and blindly select a single card. Lay that card face down in front of you, and repeat your question, either silently or aloud. Turn the card over and let it "talk" to you. We're not even going to provide an example with our interpretation. You are your own best instructor, and you are partnering with the cards in this experience.

> *Important! Record the date and time in a journal, state the question asked, and name the card drawn. Write your impressions about the card, and what you believe the answer to your question is.*

Repeat the single card draw many times before going on to more complex layouts, and always record the event in your journal.

The Three Card Spread

Most commonly, the three card spread is used in relation to questions involving the Past, the Present, and the Future of a single situation, which is the nature of the question being asked.

Formulate the question so that the answers involve understanding of the problem or situation in terms of the Past (what led up to the *crisis*—meaning the reason for asking the question), the Present (the nature of the *crisis*—what is important right now about it), and the Future (how the *crisis* will unfold, which may not be how the problem is solved).

Shuffle the entire deck as before, concentrate on the question, spread the deck out, face down, pause, and let your hands blindly select three cards. Lay the three cards, still face down, in a row in front of you and repeat your question, either silently or aloud. Turn the cards over one by one, and let each "talk" to you before turning the next one over.

Record the date and time in a journal, state the question asked, and name the cards drawn. Write your impressions about the three cards, and what you believe the answer to your question is.

MORE COMPLEX SPREADS FOR READINGS

These first two spreads are simple learning steps, and while most Tarot readings may be for your own needs, there will be more complex situations where it becomes important to understand who the *significant* person is. The Golden Dawn developed a set of rules for this purpose.

The Significicator

Of the Selection of the Significator, and of the Complexion assigned to the Court Cards:

Wands (generally)	fair and red-haired person
Cups (generally)	moderately fair
Swords (generally)	moderately dark
Pentacles (generally)	very dark
Kings	Men
Queens	Women
Princes	Young Men
Princesses (Knaves)	Young women

Therefore the Significators are to be thus selected. For example, a dark complexioned middle-aged man, King of Pentacles. A fair young woman, Princess (Knave) of Cups, etc.

In the actual reading of the cards, these descriptions can be modified by those which are on either side of them, thus: the Queen of Cups, which indicates a fair woman with golden-brown hair, if between cards of the suits of swords and pentacles, would show a woman with rather dark brown hair and dark eyes. As before stated, the Princes and Queens almost invariably represent actual men and women connected with the subject in hand.

But the Kings sometimes represent either the coming on or going off of a matter; arrival, or departure, according to the way in which they face. The Princesses (Knaves) show opinions, thoughts, or ideas, either in harmony with or opposed to the subject.

It is not our intention to provide detailed instruction in Tarot Divination in this short chapter, but to provide sufficient detail to get you started on learning for yourself *before* you turn to more advanced resources, of which there are several thousand advanced texts and reference books, as well as many good online courses and local instruction.

Before going on to other applications of the Tarot, we are going to give basic information about each card as defined by the Golden Dawn, continuing the rules as follows:

On the general Signification of the Majority of a particular suit and of the particular Signification of either three or four cards of a sort in a reading:

A majority of Wands—Energy, quarrelling, opposition.

A majority of Cups—Pleasure and merriment.

A majority of Swords—Trouble and sadness, sometimes sickness and even death.

A majority of Pentacles—Business, money, possessions, etc.

A majority of Keys (Major Arcana)—Forces of considerable strength, but beyond the enquirer's control.

A majority of court cards—Society, meeting with many persons.

A majority of Aces—Strength (generally); the aces are always strong cards.

4 Aces—Great power and force.

3 Aces—Riches and success.

Kings (generally) show news.

4 Kings—Great swiftness and rapidity.

3 Kings—Unexpected meetings.

4 Queens (generally)—Authority and influence.

3 Queens (generally)—Powerful and influential friends.

4 Princes or Knights—Meetings with the great.

3 Princes or Knights—Rank and honor.

4 Princesses (Knaves)—New ideas and plans.

3 Princesses (Knaves)—Society of the young.

4 Tens (generally)—Anxiety and responsibility.

3 Tens (generally)—Buying, selling, commercial transactions.

4 Nines (generally)—Added responsibility.

3 Nines (generally)—Much correspondence.

4 Eights (generally)—Much news.

3 Eights (generally)—Much journeying.

4 Sevens (generally)—Disappointments.

3 Sevens (generally)—Treaties and compacts.

4 Sixes (generally)—Pleasure.

3 Sixes (generally)—Gain and Success.

4 Fives (generally)—Order, regularity.

3 Fives (generally)—Quarrels, fights.

4 Fours (generally)—Rest and peace.

3 Fours (generally)—Industry.

4 Threes (generally)—Resolution and determination.

3 Threes (generally)—Deceit.

4 Deuces (generally)—Conference and conversations.

3 Deuces (generally)—Reorganization and recommencement of a thing. The Keys are *not* noticed as above, by threes and fours.

On the Signification and Dignity of the Cards

A card is strong or weak, well-dignified or ill-dignified, according to the cards that are next to it on either side. Cards of the same suit on either side strengthen it greatly, either for good or evil, according to their nature. Cards of the suits answering to its contrary element, on either side, *weaken* it greatly, for good or evil. Air and Earth are contraries, as also are Fire and Water. Air is friendly with Water and Fire, and Fire with Air and Earth.

If a card of the suit of Wands falls between a Cup and a Sword, the Sword modifies and connects the Wand with the Cup, so that it is not weakened by its vicinity, but is modified by the influence of both cards; therefore fairly strong. But if a card passes between two that are naturally contrary, it is not affected by either much, as a Wand between a Sword and a Pentacle which latter, being Air and Earth, are contrary and therefore weaken each other.

Here the question being of the Wand, this card is not to be noticed as forming a link between the Sword and Pentacle.

On Pairing the Cards together in Reading

On pairing the cards, each is to be taken as of equal force with the other. If, of opposite elements, they mutually weaken each other.

If, at the end of the pairing of the cards in a packet, one card remains over, it signifies the partial result of that particular part of the Divination only. If an evil card and the others good, it would modify the good.

If it be the Significator of the Enquirer, or of another person, it would show that matters would much depend on the line of action taken by the person represented. The reason for this importance of the single card is that it is alone, and not modified. If two cards are at the end instead of a single one, they are not of so much importance.

On the Exercise of Clairvoyance and Intuition

The Diviner should, in describing any person from a Significator in the actual reading, should endeavor, by Clairvoyance and using the card in question as a symbol, to see the person implied using the rules to aid, and restrict his vision. In describing an event from the cards in the reading, he should employ his intuition in the same manner. Personal descriptions are modified by the cards next them; e.g., the Knave of Wands usually represents a very fair girl, but if between cards of the suit of Pentacles, she might be even quite dark, though the Wands would still give a certain *brightness* to hair, eyes, and complexion.

WAIT—THERE'S MORE!

We wrote at the beginning of this chapter that there's much more than Divination to the Tarot. Here's what the Ciceros say in *The New Golden Dawn Ritual Tarot*:

> *Although many people think of divination as the primary use of Tarot cards, the Hermetic Order of the Golden Dawn considers it the least important of the Tarot's applications...*
>
> *The Tarot's greatest use is as a magickal implement which can bring spiritual attainment to one who studies it. This is because each Tarot card is an astral mirror of the human mind. Meditating on specific cards helps tune the student in to different aspects of his/her own mind establishing a communication link between the conscious and the subconscious...*
>
> *In this manner, imbalances in the personality, which may have gone unnoticed but have caused problems, can be brought to the individual's attention by studying a certain card. These problems can be consciously addressed and spiritual progress furthered.*
>
> *This brings us to the primary goal of the Magician who uses ritual objects such as wands, daggers, cups, pentacles, and mystical illustrations such as Tarot cards in magickal ceremonies. The Magician employs various techniques to ascend through the numerous inner levels of consciousness and reality...*
>
> *The Magician does this by exploring all the levels of reality experimentally— working his/her way up the Tree of Life by way of personal firsthand experience.*

We don't want to dismiss the value of divination, with the Tarot or otherwise. Divination is, for many people, and important first step in a program of psychic empowerment leading to the growth and development of their innate psychic powers, in turn leading to Wholeness and Self-Empowerment.

The very act of framing a question for divination as we've described initiates the process of communication between the conscious and subconscious mind, which is a step toward integration and expanded awareness.

Divination is not a "fortune telling *game*," although it is often used as party entertainment. Just because it can be so used doesn't mean that's the only use, any more than familiar newspaper and magazine horoscopes (based on your birth sign) are real astrology.

MAGICK VS. MAGIC

There is another very important point to be made: Magick (with a 'K') is not the same as Magic (without a 'K').

The word "magic" has become a common word in New Age circles, but primarily as an alternate for Spell Casting (or Making). In some circles, the distinction is made between low magick and high magick, and also a distinction between practical magic and spiritual magick.

We can play with words, but a simple approach is to distinguish between outer and inner goals. Practical magic is primarily concerned with outer-world goals of personal protection, health, financial gain, career advancement, love and relationships—in fact the very subjects often addressed in those magazine horoscopes.

Spell casting can have these practical applications and benefits—but these only address what we might call the physical personality, while ignoring the spiritual dimensions that are the real purpose of life. And it's not as if you have to choose between living a good material life and a spiritual one—we are many-dimensional beings and benefit from living fully at every level.

AND, ONE MORE IMPORTANT THING…

We've provided a depth of background information about the Tarot in the previous text and tables, but it is a fact that many people study only the Major Arcana, thinking that they are the really important cards. The fact is that they are using only half the deck, and working with only half the Tree of Life. The Major Arcana are the paths between the Sephiroth, while the Minor Arcana are the Sephiroth themselves.

The Tree is a schema for the Whole Universe and the Whole Person. To concentrate only on half the Tarot, half the Tree, is to miss the other half of reality—both personal and universal. Not only are both arcana important, but each and every card is equally important, and the phrase "playing with the whole deck" is deeply meaningful.

As we explore the other Paths of Tarot work, you will see that the whole deck is as involved in each as it is in the divinatory "Path to Good Fortune." We use the *whole* deck just as we must live *whole* lives—learning to use the *whole* of our consciousness and not limiting ourselves by the hereditary divisions. We are entering into a new age of evolutionary opportunity that is calling forth responses that once were relegated to "special studies" like shamans, priests, and other class distinctions. You have all the powers and abilities that enable you to function at a "whole" level—but you must develop those innate psychic powers that open the channels between conscious and subconscious minds, and thus enable what we call the "superconscious mind" that completes the structure we call "Self-Empowerment."

MEDITATION: YOUR PATH TO INNER WORLDS

Perhaps no word has been more bandied about in New Age discussions than has "meditation." It is a seemingly familiar word with a variety of applications ranging from physical relaxation to very deep explorations of nonphysical worlds and phenomena. It is used in connection with self-hypnosis, psychological self-examination, simple memory recall, forms of prayers, etc. In addition, there is a major difference in the meditative practices of East and West.

In Eastern traditions, more often meditation is approached as the cessation of mental activity—an emptying of the mind—often through repetition of a single word or phrase over and over again to block other mental activity. In the Western traditions, meditation is more often likely to concentrate on a single idea or image and, while excluding intruding thoughts, following out the implications and connecting thoughts, images, and *correspondences* to arrive at a deeper understanding and even new knowledge and insights.

In magical meditations, in particular Qabalistic practices, the goal is to use the thinking process as a vehicle to attain higher states of awareness. One such exercise that we will explore is called "Pathworking."

While most occultists recommend (some emphatically) that meditation and all other "psychic" work should be preceded by some form of psychic protection, it can be relatively simple: relax, consciously close your "mental" doors and windows to outside interruptions, and visualize an aura of white light surrounding you.

Serious magicians advocate the *Lesser Banishing Ritual of the Pentagram* (which can be found in the Ciceros's book, *The Golden Dawn,* or many others), which is a more complex program. We recommend it, but it is not part of this chapter. Likewise, they recommend performing a ritual of consecration when you obtain your Tarot deck or any other magical tool, which can also be found in the recommended books.

The following is the procedure outlined in the Ciceros's book.

TAROT CONSECRATION PROCEDURE

1. After preparing yourself for meditation, shuffle just the Major Arcana, and pick a single card at random. Place the card before you, observe the symbolism and colors, and every detail of the card.

2. Next, close your eyes and try to reproduce the card in your mind's eye, i.e. your imagination and power of visualization. Do this for about five minutes.

3. Now, reverse the process, and dismantle the card, detail by detail, as you would a jigsaw puzzle.

4. When your mind is clear of the image, maintain a state of *mental silence* for as long a period as you can afford to allow for spiritual information that may be transmitted to you.

5. Complete your meditation by recording your experience in a journal.

6. Repeat the process many times so that you experience all the Major Arcana in this manner.

Other visualization/meditation programs can be used to expand your psychic awareness as well as your Tarot communications. Some believe that the magical use of the Tarot has called into being a "Tarot Angel" that will be your inner helper in this work.

DREAM WORK

Sigmund Freud said that "The Dream is the royal road to the unconscious" (1900). Every dream is a transmittal from the subconscious mind, and because of that, the language of dreams is primarily that of symbols. But they are rarely the symbols we are familiar with from studies of mythology and magick. Often they are personal symbols with meaning only for you.

Sometimes dreams seem like straightforward stories or even forewarnings, but even when they are populated with friends and relatives, or celebrities and villains, their meaning is not straightforward. Dream studies have shown that what seems like the obvious message of a dream may actually be its opposite—like night and day are opposites. Yet, night and day are just two halves of the whole and our subconscious is part of our total consciousness. We need to bring the two halves together.

Dreams have a bad habit of seeming to slip away before you have much of a chance to capture their details. And because of that, we quickly forget what little we did remember and largely ignore dreams as having any importance in our daytime life.

But, people have learned that *when you pay attention to your dreams, dreams pay attention to you*. Dreams are messages about your life, and sometimes they are very important messages and even forewarnings about health, our children and other loved ones, work and career, and concerns about home.

Dreams have forewarned of major disasters—understood after the fact. Dreams commonly forewarn about health matters—understood after the fact and often too late to take corrective measures. Dreams can include predictions of winning horse races and lottery draws, and even stock market prices.

What good are they if you can't understand them in time to take advantage of this powerful resource from the subconscious mind?

There are many ways to study dreams and benefit from them, but our interest here is in the Tarot. Dreams work in symbols, the Tarot works in symbols. Dreams tell us stories and messages, the Tarot tells us stories. Dreams and the Tarot can work together to bring those messages and warnings from the subconscious into our conscious awareness and understanding.

The first step is to make use of a dream diary and learn to write down what you can remember of a dream immediately upon waking. Keep a note pad and jot a few words as clues for later expansion. You can even do that little bit in the dark so as not to wake your sleep partner. Again, as you pay attention to your dreams, your dreams will pay attention to you, and it will become easier to remember more of them.

Remember that the dream is a story, so with even a few clues you can try to create the missing parts of the story. And this is just one place where the Tarot can help. Glance through your deck, looking for one or more cards that seem to fit those clues. Even if clue and card don't match, one or more cards may trigger more memory of the dream. Give it time, and don't demand too much of the process right away. Just keep on doing it until you do get a result.

Another approach is to simply ask the Tarot, "What did that dream last night mean?" A similar method is to shuffle the deck and then go through it, card by card, and make note of those cards that give an emotional response or that start a story. Keep going, and that story may soon tell the tale.

Dream interpretation with the Tarot is more an art than a precise science, and it is an art that benefits from practice. Practice may take a while to "make it perfect," but every journey has a beginning, and this is one you can begin first thing tomorrow morning.

PATHWORKING: YOUR PATH TO INNER GROWTH

Pathworking is often practiced as a guided meditation involving a leader and one or more persons. In addition, audio recordings are available that include both voice and especially composed music. However, with the help of the Tarot, you can easily benefit from this technique by yourself. Ted Andrews calls pathworking a "process of self-initiation" as it

> ... contains specific elements that trigger archetypal responses; not only within us as individuals but within the environment. The pathworking sets in motion a force that manifests in situations and experiences in our day-to-day life that forces us to respond and grow ... through the forces of the meditation [we] encounter similar situations within our physical life so that we can more fully and more quickly learn the lesson associated with the path.
> —TED ANDREWS, SIMPLIFIED QABALA MAGIC

Referring back to the earlier tables and charts, and to the detailed descriptions of the Major Arcana, you will find basic information about the Major Arcana, the twenty-two numbered Paths between the ten Sephiroth which are the stations of the forty Minor Tarot, while the four court cards of each suit are assigned to Chokmah, Binah, Tiphareth, and Malkuth.

Pathworkings are journeys, almost like magical train trips, from one station through exotic landscapes to another station. The goal is to follow all the paths in reverse, starting with the 32nd, called "The Universe," which runs from the station named *Malkuth* to the one named *Yesod*. These magical trips on the paths—working in reverse—are progressive in training your mental skills (concentration, visualization, memory recall) and developing your psychic abilities (astral travel, clairvoyance, constructive imagination) while expanding and integrating your growing knowledge. And, like any journey, the more you travel each one, the more you will expand your horizons as you observe and experience the scenery and inner world inhabitants, gaining knowledge that can be turned to practical benefit.

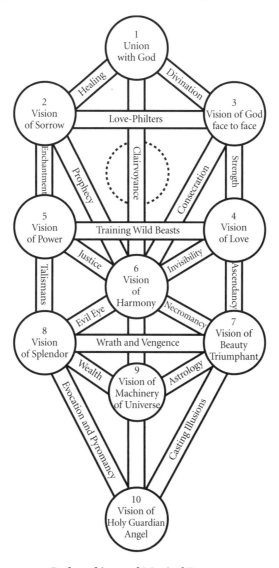

Pathworking and Magical Powers
From Ted Andrews' Simplified Qabala Magic

The pertinent cards of the Minor Arcana establish different "platforms" or levels for each station while the Major Arcana card assigned to the path is your ticket and passport for the particular journey.

The more you know about the Tree of Life and the correspondences to the Sephiroth and Paths, the richer your trip will be. It is like moving up from an economy class to higher luxury classes with better accommodations and more interesting traveling companions.

Rather than clutter this book with detailed instructions—which can be found in any of the several recommended books—I suggest that you simply familiarize yourself with the cards associated with Malkuth and Yesod, and the Universe card, and take your first imaginary trip. That's how it all starts—with your first step. As you become interested, you know where to go for more guidance.

ASTRAL TRAVEL: YOUR PATH TO INNER AWARENESS

There has been a special interest in using Tarot Cards as "an astral doorway" in a manner less complex than pathworking, but still based on the same concept that the card becomes a "key" to a specific area of the astral world. Rather than a journey from station to station, it is comparable to traveling to a single destination, and then passing through a doorway composed of the card, sightseeing at that single destination, and then turning around and exiting through that same door back to this world to come back home.

What is astral projection, or astral travel? That's a challenging question to answer because of the immense literature available—most of which is good and helpful—with somewhat different concepts ranging from the paranormal to the mystical, with stops in between for ritual magick, shamanism, religion, and more.

We start with the *Imagination*—the most misunderstood and underapplied power of the human mind. "It's only your imagination" has been inculcated into a child's mind for eons. Yes, it is appropriate to separate the imaginative reality from the reality of the material world, but that is not to say that what is created and experienced in the imagination isn't real, and that its reality does not influence material reality, and vice versa.

The trained imagination, which also means that it is controlled by the conscious mind, is *the creative power of the mind*. And that which is imagined is experienced in the astral world. Pathworking, astral doorways, and meditation are exercises of the creative imagination, just as are creative art, design, music, literature, inventions, scientific breakthroughs, and the ability to visualize.

Without the creative imagination, innovation would not happen. Without the creative imagination, humanity would exist only as animals on a planet on which the predator large animals would be the victors.

Pathworking, meditation, astral travel, and all magical and creative work are exercises of a controlled and guided imagination. Think about it, and pick a card to work with. Let it act as a doorway, but keep to the images and ideas that are associated specifically with that card. Record your experience and compare it with the information provided. The more you practice, the more rewarding will be your experience and your ability to employ the trained imagination in your material world as well as your astral world.

A further aspect of this can be found in your ability to "dream true"—solving problems through your dreams. See Chapter Seven.

RITUAL MAGICK: YOUR PATH TO POWER

Ritual Magick is a huge subject area, far beyond what we can cover with a few notes in a single chapter. We have, however, provided the "key" to magical power in our discussion of the trained imagination. The Tarot is a *dynamic key* that can make the complex world of ritual magick accessible to the person for whom group work is neither convenient nor attractive.

It should be understood that ritual magic is powerful, it is practical, and it is a means to psychic empowerment and thence to self-empowerment. Many books are available to help you in this regard, but we will mention two in particular as pertinent here in a chapter on Tarot: *Tarot Talismans* by the Ciceros and *Portable Magic* by Donald Tyson.

ALTERNATIVE REALITIES: YOUR PATH TO REVELATION

The skills you will learn with your Tarot work, and other techniques and tools of psychic empowerment, are steps toward your ability to actually experience what occultists refer to as the "Higher Planes" and scientists sometimes refer to as "Alternative Realities." The point being that the material universe is only a small aspect of the Greater Universe that opens to us as we *become more than we are* and fulfill more of the matrix of **the Whole Person we are destined to become.**

SOURCES AND RECOMMENDED READING

Ted Andrews, *Imagick: Qabalistic Pathworking for Imaginative Magicians* (Llewellyn, 1989).

Ted Andrews, *Simplified Qabala Magic* (Llewellyn, 2003).

Dolores Ashcroft-Nowicki, *Highways of the Mind: The Art and History of Pathworking* (Aquarian Press, 1987).

Paul Foster Case, *The Tarot: A Key to the Wisdom of the Ages* (Tarcher, 1947).

Chic Cicero and Sandra Tabatha Cicero, *The Golden Dawn Ritual Tarot* (Llewellyn, 1991).

Chic Cicero and Sandra Tabatha Cicero, *Experiencing the Kabbalah* (Llewellyn, 1997).

Chic Cicero and Sandra Tabatha Cicero, *Tarot Talismans: Invoke the Angels of the Tarot* (Llewellyn, 2006).

Sandra Tabatha Cicero, *The Golden Dawn Ritual Tarot* deck (Llewellyn, 1991) (or the same deck under name of *The Golden Dawn Magical Tarot*).

Jean-Louis de Biasi, *The Divine Arcana of the Aurum Solis* (Llewellyn, 2011).

Melita Denning and Osborne Phillips, *Magical States of Consciousness: Paths to Knowledge and Power* (Llewellyn, 1985).

Sigmund Freud, *The Interpretation of Dreams* (Macmillan, 3rd ed., 1913).

Julie Gillentine, *Tarot & Dream Interpretation* (Llewellyn, 2003).

Manly Palmer Hall, *The Secret Teachings of All Ages: An Encyclopedic Outline of Masonic, Hermetic, Qabbalistic, and Rosicrucian Symbolical Philosophy* (Philosophical Research Society, 1962).

Eliphas Lévi, *Transcendental Magic: Its Doctrine and Ritual* (Rider, 1923).

Anthony Louis, *Tarot Plain and Simple* (Llewellyn, 1996).

Adele Nozedar, *The Element Encyclopedia of Secret Signs and Symbols* (HarperElement, 2008).

The Papus, *Tarot of the Bohemians: The Most Ancient Book in the World* (Chapman and Hall, 1892).

Israel Regardie, edited by Carl Llewellyn Weschcke, *The Golden Dawn* (Llewellyn, 1994).

Israel Regardie, with new material by Chic Cicero and Sandra Tabatha Cicero. *A Garden of Pomegranates: Skrying on the Tree of Life* (Llewellyn, 1999).

Samuel Roberts, *The Gypsies* (London, 1842). Quoted in Hall: *Secret Teachings of All Ages.*

27
TEA LEAF & COFFEE GROUNDS
READING
May Your Cup Brimeth Over

A "FORTUNE" IN YOUR TEACUP

Tea Leaf Reading has been around for a long time and is technically called Tasseography or Tasseomancy, and sometimes Tassology. These words also refer to the interpretation of coffee grounds in the Middle East, which is discussed later in the chapter.

In this part of the chapter, we'll just call it Tea Leaf Reading, meaning finding patterns in the wet tea leaves in your cup and interpreting them as meaningful symbols.

While often associated with fortune-telling practices of wandering Gypsies, it has more ancient origins in Asia and was particularly popular in Victorian England and with Eastern European cultures. It is currently seeing a renaissance in North America because of the increase in tea drinking vs. coffee and the increase in tea shops and upscale restaurants serving afternoon "high tea."

Mostly Tea Leaf Reading is for fun and entertainment, and the always-hoped-for revelation showing the way to good fortune. However, the potential is much greater, and truly your simple teacup can "brimeth over" with information about your present situation and answers to your questions, if carefully phrased. *How is this possible?* Because everything is available in your subconscious mind and Tea Leaf Reading, like other forms of divination, can call up the exact information you need. But you must understand that the subconscious mind stores information in symbols rather than words, so we have to relate to those symbols in our reading.

TEA LEAVES AND MEANINGFUL IMAGES

As we will see, there are many "dictionary" approaches to the interpretation of tea leaf patterns and symbols, but they are best used as a "seed" to tap into the reader's subconscious mind.

The patterns found in the wet tea leaves often clearly show recognizable images and symbols, but other times we must use the imagination to "fill in the blanks" to arrive at a definable picture, and then create an individualized interpretation or solution to a posed question. As you progress as a reader, you will more often use the imagination to trigger the subconscious mind, rather than a dictionary definition.

It is this expansion of awareness, using the imagination calling to the subconscious mind and feeling the intuitive response, that helps open your psychic abilities. That's what we are really after—using this simple tool to bring you Psychic Empowerment.

To say it another way: when you seek to find and interpret "instant patterns" whether found in your tea or coffee cup, as sand or granules strewn on the ground (or stirred in a box), or even unconsciously drawn doodles, you are developing and employing a natural psychic power and turning it into a skill.

It isn't necessary to complete your study of this chapter before starting to read tea leaves. While we will give a short dictionary of common symbols (others will be found in the references at the end of the chapter), it's better not to depend upon dictionary definitions but to allow the meanings to come to you as you meditate on the patterns.

People use tea leaf reading to understand a current situation and to forecast the future, and the practice will help "train" your imagination to develop your psychic skills and intuition.

HOW DIVINATION WORKS

In some sense, avoiding technical details, the future already exists; but it is also important to know that your future is *not* fixed. Changes in your current situation can make changes in your future situation. At the same time, in terms of the bigger universe of which each of us is a minute part, small changes rarely have much impact on the future.

Nevertheless, it is *your* future we are talking about, without a lot of concern about the world around us. Always there are points of leverage that, if discovered and manipulated with willed intention, can make a difference. *But, that's magick, another subject altogether.*

Magick requires knowledge and understanding of your present circumstances and a firm belief in your goals. Simply stated, you must know where you are and where you want to go in order to find those points of leverage that will help you get to your destination.

YOUR AURA—AN INFORMATION INTERCHANGE

Most readings are not concerned with changing the future but with answering questions about the present and near future.

Please read the following few paragraphs carefully with your full attention.

Each person is surrounded by a field of energy called the "aura" that's powerful enough to be photographed with a "Kirlian" camera (named after its Russian inventor). Your own aura permeates your entire body and represents your feeling, your mind, and your spirit. It's all about you.

Every cell in your body contains all of the information about you—not only the present but the past and the probable future. Not only that, but every cell also contains a hologram of the universe; that is, all knowledge is resident within each one of us, and it is ours to retrieve if we know how.

Your aura further permeates your immediate surroundings—out to about three feet—and especially things you touch. Some substances more easily absorb the auric influence than others, and wet tea leaves are especially sensitive to this influence, serving as an ideal medium for our reading.

The minute particles, actually right down to the subatomic level, of the chosen "sensitive media"—the tea leaves, coffee grounds, sand, etc.—that we are using are responsive to your energy field, including the questions and concerns you have at the moment of the reading. The more often you practice this psychic talent, the more ably will your aura project the image-forming energy to the sensitive media.

As the tea is prepared, when it comes in contact with your hands and mouth as we will describe, and as your intention to read the leaves is present in your mind, all the necessary information is now recorded in the tea leaves and is available to us.

WHERE DOES INFORMATION COME FROM?

We say that "your simple teacup can 'brimeth over' with information about your present situation and answers to your questions" and that "everything is available in your subconscious mind." We also say that "divination can call up the exact information you need."

EVERY CELL OF YOUR BODY STORES
ALL YOUR PERSONAL INFORMATION

Yes, your personal information is actually recorded in every cell in your body, just as a small part of a hologram contains the whole of the hologram, but the reality is even more dynamic. Please understand that we use some words in an inclusive way rather than specific—so that sometimes we speak of the "unconscious" as meaning the same thing as the "subconscious mind," or we may mean that through the subconscious we access the unconscious or what we also call the "collective unconscious." Sometimes it is helpful to speak objectively about something that we experience only subjectively. At the same time, the worlds of the psyche and spirit are not perceived in definitive parts like the physical world is. You *can* have an "astral finger" just like a physical finger, but it's only as a *convenience* that we ourselves create it as a "thought-form" and give it such definition.

"CHANNELING" AND "TRANCE"

When the conscious mind derives information from the unconscious we are actually *channeling* it and to do so we must, to some degree, go into a trance. This is important to understand because, if you focus too much on the details of any image and depend on book definitions, you may miss part of the message.

Don't let the word "trance" confuse or scare you. Religionists and others have claimed that trance states will open you to "demonic" possession, loss of your personal identity, corruption of your soul, and other scary things that, in fact, are only true *to the extent that you believe them to be.* Many times they employ this kind of language for their own selfish purposes, which we may refer to as "power trips."

YOU ARE A FREE SPIRIT

You are a free spirit responsible for your own welfare. You do not need to be dependent upon others. They can be helpful to you, but don't let them think for you or control your life. You are not a sheep to be led about with a shepherd's crook. The ultimate goal of every chapter in this book is your ***self-empowerment.*** Incidentally, "self-empowerment" is the direct opposite of what is meant when we refer to another person's power trips, where their goal is to assert power, and control, over your *Self* and the Selves of many others.

THE EQUIPMENT YOU NEED

Tea Leaf Reading is an easily accessible psychic empowerment technique requiring only minimum tools and investment.

You do need to find an old-fashioned white porcelain cup and saucer. You can't use the more popular straight-sided mug but need the kind of cup that is larger at the top and smaller at the bottom. You will also need a kettle to boil the water, a small bowl to hold the drained water, and a paper napkin or paper towel for each reading.

And you need tea *leaves,* not powdered tea and not a tea bag. You can tear open a tea bag and use those leaves, but loose leaves are larger and better.

Place about a half teaspoon of leaves in the cup, pour in the hot water, and place the saucer over the cup while the tea is steeping, for as long as it takes to bring the temperature down to drinkable. *Do not add sugar or milk!*

AND HOW TO DO IT

Slowly drink about three-fourths of the tea while thinking of the problem or question you wish to answer. *Leave enough tea to cover the leaves.* Place the palm of your dominate hand over the top of the cup for about a minute to *charge* the cup and leaves with your aura as you think about what you are looking for in the reading. If you are reading for another person, have that person do the charging while thinking of the problem or question.

Put the saucer to one side and place a paper napkin or towel on it. You will use it to absorb excess water in a few minutes. Also have the small bowl handy.

The next step is important. It is necessary to *disperse* the leaves around the inside of the cup while getting rid of the remaining water. Hold the cup by the handle and, using your wrist motion, gently slosh the water around the entire inside of the cup. Some readers insist that you must hold the cup with your left, presumed *psychic*, hand during this process.

As you rotate and slosh the mixture, tip the cup sufficiently for small amounts of water to spill over the top and drip into the small bowl. Continue this until the water is gone and the tea leaves are dispersed around the inside of the cup. Don't worry if you lose a few leaves during the sloshing. It will take a little practice to get the motion right—if you go too slowly, the leaves will bunch into just one or a few large clumps; if you go too fast, the leaves won't stick to the sides of the cup.

Then turn the cup upside down and place it on the paper napkin or towel on the saucer you previously prepared. This will absorb the few remaining drops of tea water.

Set the cup, still upside down in the saucer, in front of the person for whom the reading is to be done.

Have the person rotate the cup three times in a clockwise direction. This accomplishes two things: it dislodges any remaining drops of water, and it gives the person's aura an additional chance to impregnate the leaves. (Note: some readers insist that this rotation should be done counterclockwise, but we—personally—prefer the clockwise rotation.)

Pick the cup up by the handle and turn it right side up. The cup may now be read.

ASKING THE QUESTION

In a reading to answer a question, it is desirable to have written the question on a piece of paper, and for the question to be broad enough to elicit an answer beyond a simple yes or no. For example, the question: *"Will I ever find a better job?"* provides little helpful information. The better question might be, *"What are my future career possibilities?"* With that you elicit helpful information.

You, or the person for whom the reading is intended, if present, should hold the paper in one hand while charging the cup with the dominant hand. Either concentrate on the question or speak it out loud.

What if the person for whom the reading is intended is not present? This is really an unsatisfactory process because there is no *direct* contact with the person's aura. If you must do it, prepare the cup as you would for yourself and then place your dominant hand over the cup and concentrate on the absent person. A good preparation for this is to write down that person's name, address, gender, age, and anything else that you know pertinent to the situation. Holding the paper in your other hand, state aloud that your intention is to permeate the tea leaves with that person's energy and what it is you want to know.

WHAT CAN YOU LEARN?

There are three primary functions for any divination: to read the present, the future, and the past. In reading the present, you are able to answer specific questions about your present circumstances, but *only one question per reading*. In reading for the future, you are engaging in "prophecy," mostly about your own probable future based on your present circumstances and the "path" you are on, but the reading is only meaningful for the more immediate future, so it may include 'world events' that will affect your present circumstances. In reading the past, this technique is poorly suited to the purpose and should be limited to simple personal questions in recent time. The better way to learn about past lives is through self-hypnosis and past-life regression.

But the most important lesson you can learn is of your own spiritual authority. Using the various techniques of psychic empowerment, it is your psyche that is being empowered, and using the tools we describe helps to channel information from the unconscious to your conscious mind. We want to make this a familiar pattern for you, regardless of the tools you choose to use.

PREPARING THE READING

Earlier we told you how to prepare the teacup for the reading.

After the final action of rotating the cup clockwise three times, pick it up by the handle and look at the leaves sticking on the inside. Using the handle as the focal point representing either you or the client, look not only for patterns (symbols) but their position.

Location, location, location. The cup should be read clockwise starting from the left side of the handle. The immediate left of the handle is NOW, the next position halfway up the left side (the first quarter) corresponds to three months from now, the position opposite the handle is six months from now, the three-quarter position is nine months, and the right side of the handle is one year into the future. From this you can easily subdivide each quarter into months.

Symbols near the rim represent early days of the month and those near the bottom, the end of the month. Symbols seen completely on the flat bottom apply as a background to the entire year ahead. Symbols touching both the side and the bottom apply from the end of the month for the remainder of the year. Make note of these positions. If you are reading to answer a specific question, time may not be a factor and can be ignored. If you insist on reading for the past, ignore timing even though some will argue for the same relationship backward as we have for forward—the first quarter being three months into the past, and so on.

Now, carefully study the whole interior of the cup, looking for symbols. Some will stand alone, others in groups, and some will overlap each other to be interpreted together.

What do you see? Even if the outline is vague but you *feel* that it is a duck, or a car, accept that as its identity. Don't let the vagueness of appearance interfere with your *feeling,* but don't necessarily accept the first idea that comes to you. It is a good idea to ruminate a bit and see if it continues to speak to you.

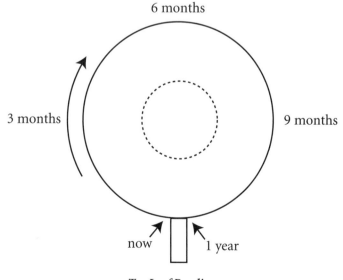

Tea Leaf Reading

A LITTLE TRANCE

Once you've given a name to each symbol, noted its position, and placed it in the whole revelation of patterns in the cup, it is time to let the *whole* cup tell the story, starting just left of the handle and moving clockwise around the circle that is established by the cup's brim.

Let yourself slide into a light trance and feel that each symbol tells part of the story. Sometimes each symbol has a specific message, other times it is groups of symbols, and in the end it is a comprehensive story bringing them all together. It's like chapters in a book—each one has a story to tell, but it's finally the whole book that completes the story and relates it to your life or that of your client.

It is a good idea to eventually write the whole story down with your notes of the symbols and their positions. At another time, note what actually happened for a better understanding of how the process works for you.

You can use a dictionary of symbols—and you will find such sources listed at the end of the chapter—but it is important to also build your own dictionary as you do numerous readings—not only of tea leaves but other tools. Don't let the symbol definitions in any dictionary *limit* your ideas in any way. At most, let them work as seeds that will flower in your imagination to become *your* definition for *this* reading. If the tea leaf pattern seems like a car, it is not so much a car as what a car does—it transports you. Likewise, an airplane transports you, but usually for a longer distance than a car. In other words, it is rarely the thing or person represented by the symbol but what they do.

There is one exception to this emphasis on what the object or person does and that would be when your question is specifically about that object or person—for example: *"When will I get my "dream car?"* or *"Will I marry John?"*

The other thing to remember about symbols is that their meaning is rarely limited to one thing, but rather they are part of the story completed by other symbols touching or close by as modifiers or adjectives. Read them in sequence as elements in the story. Always ask, *"Why this symbol at this time?"*

A SHORT DICTIONARY OF SYMBOLS

The following is just a short dictionary of the more common symbols you are likely to encounter in your early readings. Note that the symbol's meaning is not always limited to the object itself: an anvil is never an anvil. As you do more readings, you will experience more symbols, but their meanings should all come from the same source, channeled from your unconscious to your conscious mind. Some of the definitions given in any dictionary will seem totally wrong to you. If so, give them a chance and then see if your own definition seems more correct—at least for this particular reading. The one given here for *cat*—"signifies treachery against you"—will offend most cat lovers, but if they think about the nature of the cat as pretty much expressed as "feed me, pet me, or I will do something bad," you might understand the warning definition as given.

DICTIONARY OF COMMON TEA LEAF SYMBOLS

Airplane: An airplane probably indicates a trip, usually of a longer distance than a day's drive. If the airplane is by itself, the trip will be safe; if it is coupled with a negative symbol, the trip may be filled with minor discomforts or problems; if it is coupled with a positive symbol, the trip should be enjoyable. If the airplane looks to be crashing or falling apart, then it would be wise not to travel at this time.

Alligator or Crocodile: Use caution in new business or investment ventures.

Almonds: Good fortune at home and work.

Anchor: If the anchor appears to be "hanging loose" in midair it may indicate an unresolved situation. If, instead, it is coupled closely with another symbol, look to that to see what is not resolved. If the anchor lies across the bottom, it suggests that you have reached your goal.

Angel: This assures protection from all negative influences. It may also indicate a spiritual awakening at the time indicated in the cup. If the angel symbol is coupled with another, they should be interpreted together. For example, if coupled with a crashing airplane, you may have an accident while traveling, but will not be hurt.

Antelope: Indicates a new experience or new adventure. Commonly associated with other symbols to indicate their newness.

Anvil: An anvil indicates work, labor, or service, usually in relation to your job. If coupled with an antelope, it may mean a new job at the time indicated in the cup. If it is coupled with a bear, it may mean that you have to "bear up" under a heavy workload.

Apple: You may be faced with a major temptation at the time indicated in the cup. An apple commonly refers to cheating on your mate, stealing from your employer believing no one will ever know, spending money on something that you can't afford, or accepting a new job offer that may not be on the up-and-up. If the apple has a bite taken out of it, it will surely be harmful to you. A whole apple could be a good temptation. If the apple is coupled with another symbol, you must blend the meanings to get a more complete interpretation. The apple is never interpreted as just an apple.

Arm: An arm extending upward is an appeal for help, possibly searching for meaning in life. If extended straight out, it signifies assistance. If the arm has no hand on it or the hand is closed, you will give assistance. If the arm has an open hand, you will receive assistance. If hanging downward, it indicates that you will either feel helpless or actually be helpless. If coupled with some negative symbol, you will actually be helpless in the situation.

If coupled with a positive symbol, you will feel helpless, but the situation will turn out okay after you've gone through a period of deep concern.

Arrow: An arrow indicates that you will find the right direction in some aspect of your life. If the arrow points upward, things will be better than expected; if the arrow points across the cup, things will be about what you expected; if the arrow points downward, things will not be as good as expected.

Baby: A fresh start, another chance. A baby is always a good sign even when coupled with negative symbols. Negative symbols can indicate problems but the baby always indicates new, fresh, creative ideas and ventures.

Ball: A ball is never a ball, but indicates a time of smooth going and unimpeded progress in your life. It does not necessarily mean everything is good, only that whatever direction you are taking will go smoothly.

Barn: A barn indicates an abundance of food or other material goods, but not money.

Basket: If full, it indicates some kind of recognition; if empty, mental depression.

Bat: A bat is never just a flying mammal, but always indicates treachery by someone.

Beacon Light: Always indicates spiritual enlightenment.

Bear: A bear is never a bear. If it appears ferocious, it is a warning of loss, often of money. If it appears gentle, it indicates your personal strength. If it is appears playful, then you will receive help when needed.

Beaver: A time of constructive activity.

Bee: Always a negative symbol meaning gossip, whether you are doing it or it is about you.

Beehive: Indicates you will receive an important invitation.

Bell: Foretells of an announcement, the character of which is determined by related symbols. A monetary sign suggests a salary increase; a casket suggests a funeral announcement.

Bicycle: You're on the right path to reach your goal.

Birds: Good news, especially in business and marketing work.

Boat: Money, property, and valuables are coming your way through inheritance or winning the lottery. And, perhaps romance if it looks like a cruise ship.

Book: An open book signifies you are expanding your knowledge and growing as a person. A closed book, however, indicates secretiveness and limitation in your dealings with others that is hurtful to you.

Bowl: Material goods. If the bowl is full, you have plenty; if it is heaping full, you have more than you need and should share; if empty, you want more than you have.

Box: A surprise, or a gift, is coming your way.

Broom: A change of appearance and surroundings, perhaps new clothes, or a new home.

Buffalo: You need to act independently.

Bugs: Nasty influences around you, act with caution.

Camel: This means you must persevere.

Camera: Someone is watching you.

Cane: You will need assistance.

Canoe: A modest amount of money or property is coming your way.

Car: Travel, perhaps a day trip or a distance of between three hundred and a thousand miles.

Casket: A death, not your own, but which will affect you.

Cat: Signifies treachery against you.

Chair: If filled, a new person is coming into your life; if empty, someone is leaving your life.

Clover: Good luck.

Cobweb: You will be protected by someone.

Comb: You need to improve your appearance.

Cow: Multiplication in some sense. For a woman, it may mean many children; for a man, it may mean many jobs or multiple careers.

Cross: You will overcome whatever troubles you.

Deer: A timid person who could become a lifelong friend.

Desk: Always refers to your occupation.

Dice: A change in fortune.

Dirigible: A slow-moving event.

Dog: A faithful and true friend.

Door: An open door indicates your awareness of the new opportunities and possibilities, and you are working toward fulfilling them; a closed door means you are not fully aware of the possibilities before you.

Dragon: You are fooling yourself about something.

Duck: False gossip.

Eagle: A good symbol meaning you will soar over obstacles.

Ear: Good news is coming.

Egg: New beginnings. If unbroken, it indicates that your plans have been properly executed and your reward is coming; if broken, your plans are flawed and will not bring success.

Elephant: A positive sign assuring long life and endurance, and phenomenal resistance to disease and ill health.

Eye: Psychic sight. You need to use your psychic sight more often.

Face: If looking backward (to the left side of the handle), you dwell too much on the past; if looking forward (to the right), expect a life of achievement; if looking straight ahead, a life in balance.

Feather: Instability.

Fence: Limitation and restriction.

Ferry: Money or property is coming your way by inheritance or winnings, but you will be sharing with others.

Fire: Passion, emotion, love, hate, ecstasy.

Fireplace: Comfort, security, peace of mind.

Fish: An increase in wealth.

Fishing Pole: Fishing for information. If a line is on it, you are doing the fishing; if there is no line on it, you are being investigated.

Fist: Hold on tight. Hang tight. Be tenacious.

Forest: Your thinking is muddled and unclear.

Fork: Warning of a possible quarrel that can be avoided.

Frying Pan: You are going to get in trouble unless you make changes.

Gallows: Trouble.

Goat: You must be stubborn and push back against aggression.

Goose: A quarrelsome and difficult person you have to deal with.

Grapes, a bunch of: Abundant health for you.

Guitar: You have singing ability, perhaps as a solo performer.

Gun: Anger. You need to exercise control over your anger.

Hammer: Someone is hammering at you. You will be annoyed by a complaining person.

Hand: Friendly assistance.

Harp: Great joy.

Hat: A change of roles. You may change careers, get a new job, get married, etc.

Headstone: Troubles over a recent death.

Heart: The shape, not the organ: Love, affection, care.

Horse: A friend.

Horse Show: Good luck.

Iron, for Clothes: You have problems that must be "ironed out."

Jar: You will have a need to borrow unless you make changes now.

Jewelry, any kind: Good fortune.

Keg: You need to stock up on supplies.

Kettle: Guests are coming, probably overnight.

Key: Success. Your present path is leading to long-term success.

Ladder: You are climbing toward success.

Lamb: You need to act with gentleness and consideration.

Lamp: You will "see the light." You will receive guidance from another.

Lantern: You will be pioneering some cause or activity.

Leaf: Health.

Lemon or Lime: A grouchy, sour person.

Leopard: You will be facing difficulties and dangers.

Letter, alphabetic: Usually a single letter should be read as the abbreviation for someone's first name, or the name by which you usually identify him or her. Thus "G" could stand for someone you know as George, but could also be someone you always refer to by his last name, such as Garrison, or someone you always refer to as "Gorgeous."

Letter, mail: An important document is coming. The symbols associated with it, such as a dollar sign, will indicate what the subject is.

Lightning Bolt: A flash of insight. You will be exceptionally alert during the period indicated.

Lion: Fury. Look at the associated symbols. If someone is furious at you, this could be a warning of violence.

Lipstick: Vanity. You may be overly concerned with appearances.

Lizard: False fear. You don't need to be afraid of something.

Mailbox: Someone is expecting news from you.

Match: Someone hopes to impose on you.

Mirror: It's time for some self-examination.

Moon: A period of important change in your life.

Mountain: You are facing an important challenge.

Nail: You need to secure your possessions, to "nail them down."

Nets: You will be caught up in something.

Number: A number is a number is a number. What is associated with it?

Oars: You are progressing toward your goal.

Obelisk: You have to stand alone.

Olives and Olive Branch: Peace and happiness at home.

Owl: A good symbol meaning a wise person, perhaps a teacher, in your life.

Oyster: An aphrodisiac indicating "sexy times."

Padlock: Your troubles are coming to an end. They've been "locked down."

Pail: You need to "bail out" of some situation or relationship.

Palm Tree: A sign of good fortune and easy times.

Parrot: A negative symbol meaning someone is telling stories about you.

Penis: In a woman's reading, it means she is independent and does not allow herself to be intimidated by men.

Piano: You have the ability to write songs and music.

Pig: Greed. Get over it!

Plow: A time of struggle.

Pretzel: Complexities and confusion.

Pump: Someone will be asking a lot of questions, "pumping you" for information.

Purse: Your financial situation. Look at the associated symbols.

Pyramid: You are climbing to success.

Question Mark: Exactly what it signifies: a question.

Roadrunner (The bird): You will soon receive important news.

Rabbit: A carefree person. Also, a fertility symbol: pregnancy?

Ring: A ring is always connected to marriage.

Rocking Chair: Long life.

Rooster: A braggart not to be crossed.

Rowboat: An inheritance or winnings are coming your way, slowly because of some entanglements, probably legal.

Safe: Personal financial security.

Saw: Difficulties to "saw through."

Scissors: A major disappointment.

Shield: You have to defend yourself.

Ship: A large amount of money is coming your way. However, if a sailing ship, the money will likely come over a period of time.

Shoe: "If the shoe fits, wear it." You are in a comfortable position in life.

Shovel: Any occupation involving physical effort.

Sickle: Illness.

Skateboard: You are on your own.

Skeleton: You have a secret.

Skis: You are moving too fast.

Sled: A period of smooth sailing.

Snake: If coiled, treachery—someone is a "snake in the grass." If stretched out, a sign of wisdom and strength.

Spider: Good luck.

Squirrel: Saving. It's time to open a savings account. A time for budgeting.

Stairs: A sign of long-term success.

Star: Success.

Sun: Happiness and well-being.

Table: A favor, or favorable time.

Teapot: Deep friendship. There's someone you can trust with personal information.

Tent: A temporary situation.

Tornado: Emotional turbulence in your life.

Tree: Your family.

Truck: A period of hard work.

Turkey: Indicates a period of stupidity, either yours or someone else's.

Turtle: Move slowly and purposefully.

UFO: Always refers to your psychic ability.

Umbrella: Protection from harm.

Underwear, female: You are overly concerned about sex.

Vase: You have a secret admirer.

Vise: You will be squeezed hard.

Volcano: Unresolved problems will come to a head, and spill over.

Vulture: A negative symbol warning of deprivation or even poverty caused by someone working against you.

Wall: A period of misunderstanding between you and another.

Warship: An inheritance is coming but you will have to fight for it.

Wedge: Someone is "wedging their way" between you and someone or something you want.

Whale: A huge problem.

Wheel: You are generally indecisive.

Wheelbarrow: You will succeed through long, steady, hard work.

Window: You have the psychic ability to see through the wall separating one reality from another.

Wishbone: Unbroken, you will get your wish; broken, you won't.

Wolf Face: Someone is deceitful.

COFFEE GROUND READING

Coffee should be black as hell, strong as death, and sweet as love.

—TURKISH PROVERB

Coffee ground reading is a relatively new concept to the Western world, but an old practice still surviving in the Middle East and the countries surrounding the Mediterranean Sea. Even older is the concept of reading one's fortune from nearly any residual left from a liquid in a container. The Chinese found omens in the shapes found inside of used bells, and the shape of the Chinese teacup, when inverted, does indeed resemble a bell. The Romans read the lees (dregs) left by wine in their goblets, and no doubt our readers know of similar examples.

Coffee as a beverage seems to have originated in Ethiopia and then spread by Arab traders to the Middle East and into southern and eastern Europe before crossing to the Americas. Most of the lore about Coffee Reading involves heavy Turkish coffee, as it was the Turkish Ottoman Empire that was the cultural center of the area at this time.

Basically, reading coffee grounds is similar to tea leaf reading and starts with the preparation of a cup of coffee intended for reading. While most of the traditional instruction uses heavy Turkish coffee, many people now drinking various brews in Starbucks® and other coffee houses are experimenting with different coffees and brews, and variations of the traditional technique.

TO PREPARE TURKISH COFFEE

Everything is straightforward, but preparation is indeed a magical ritual and calls for your careful attention to each step in the process, for the simple reason that your focused awareness is part of the process that helps imbue a mechanical process with "magic." Even when preparing the coffee for another or for several people, this focus itself calls to elemental life forces and alerts your subconsciousness. For this reason, many readers prefer to involve every step in a ritual—starting with selecting the raw beans, roasting them, grinding them just for the reading, and the rest of the steps below. Some real aficionados will, for example, hold the beans in both hands while speaking the old traditional chant: *Out, tout, throughout and about; All good come in, all evil go out* (Sophia, 1999). Similarly, Sophia recommends psychic purification of the water to be used with this chant: *Pure as snow, pure as rain; pure as the sea, you be again.*

PREPARATION FOR COFFEE GROUND READING

Step 1. You will need some kind of coffee pot that you can heat on a stove or small electric or portable alcohol or oil burner at your table. Preferably you will want the same kind of slant-sided cups as used for tea, but traditional Turkish cups are acceptable. You also need a saucer for each cup.

Step 2. Use one cup of cold water for each cup you are making and then add an extra half cup of water "for the pot" for each four cups to be brewed. Add one tea-spoonful of ground Turkish coffee per cup in the water while it is still cold, and stir. The amount of coffee may be varied to taste, but remember that there should be a thick layer of coffee grounds left at the bottom of your cup with properly made Turkish coffee. If you need to add sugar you may do so now, not after the coffee has been poured into cups.

Step 3. Heat the pot as slowly as you can. The slower the heat, the better the flavor. Watch it so it doesn't boil over. This watching also is focused awareness, aiding the "secret" side of the process.

Step 4. When the water boils, pour some, but not all, of the coffee equally among the cups being served. You want to fill each cup about a quarter to a third of the way to get some of the foam forming on top of the pot, without which Turkish coffee loses much of its distinctive flavor. You can instead spoon some of the froth into the cup, but the careful pouring adds its own energy. Boil the remaining coffee again and distribute the rest of the coffee between the cups.

Since there is no filtering of coffee at any time during this process, you should wait for a few minutes before drinking your delicious Turkish coffee, so that the coffee grounds settle at the bottom of the cup.

Once again, you can interject a spell recommended by Sophia just before you pour the coffee by circling the cup clockwise with your left hand and chanting:

> *Force of fire, joy of water;*
> *Cup of Knowledge,*
> *Beans of earth;*
> *By steam and dream, give wisdom birth.*

Step 5. Drink slowly while meditating on your question or your current situation. When you have nearly finished your coffee so that there remains a little bit of coffee and lots of coffee grounds in your cup, turn the cup three times clockwise, put your saucer on top of your coffee cup, and then quickly turn the coffee cup and saucer upside down. This will slowly bring down the coffee grounds along the inside the coffee cup and on to the saucer while forming the patterns that you need to interpret about life needs and problems.

Step 6. Allow a few minutes for the coffee to settle and then pick up the cup for reading.

The general rules are somewhat different than those for tea leaf reading, reflecting the different cultural background of each tradition. Keep that in mind, even though you are reading for yourself or another within one culture. The source of the tradition may add a subtle accent to your interpretations.

The handle represents you, the "querent." Symbols positioned near the handle mean something is about to happen near your home. Symbols pointing to the handle from either side mean something or someone is approaching you. Symbols pointing away from the handle mean that someone or something will leave you.

Symbols near the rim of the cup are the future; midway down represents the present; and near the bottom IS the past. Any symbol on the actual bottom of the cup is interpreted as unlucky. Traditionally the querent is asked to crush a bottom symbol after it has been interpreted, to break the indicated bad-luck pattern.

Symbols are never interpreted in isolation. See the overall picture combining all the symbols in relation to each other while considering their size and position to give a meaningful reading.

At first you may not see anything in your coffee cup. The images may appear incomplete or blurry and meaningless. In this respect, coffee ground reading is more challenging than tea leaf reading. Relax, and scan the cup several times while tipping it toward you and then away from you while continuing to look at the coffee grounds. Here are some simple guidelines suggested in Sophia's book:

> *Many clustered specks may indicate movement.*
> *Clear lines show that plans must lead to a specific goal.*
> *Wavy lines show uncertainty.*
> *Poorly outlined things show indecision or obstacles.*

Soon you will make out one image and then another, and a picture will form in your imagination to tell the whole story. As you read more times, the subconscious mind will respond to the technique and your story will become richer and more detailed.

And that's important to remember—just as with tea leaf reading, you are telling a story based on your current situation as the starting point. You can ask a single question per reading, or you can see the situation in general.

The individual symbols are interpreted generally as those definitions given previously for tea leaf reading. Nevertheless, it can be very interesting to read those symbols while allowing your imagination to respect the Middle Eastern culture where coffee ground reading is more often practiced. In letting these cultural influences shape your imagination, you need to be careful not to let any personal prejudices you may have toward another culture actually dominate the process.

It's easy to assume that the appearance of an angel is beneficial, but the appearance of a bee has a different significance for a desert dweller than for one who lives in a modern city or in the rich farming areas that most Americans know. In the desert, a bee can mean water is nearby, and that can signify life over death.

In a traditional desert culture, the horse is as important as it was in the American cowboy west and symbolizes strength and independence. Trees mean changes for the better, and a wheel may mean that fortunes will change. In the Islamic world, the crescent moon may mean a religious calling.

SOURCES AND RECOMMENDED READING

Raymond Buckland, *Secrets of Gypsy Fortune Telling* (Llewellyn, 1988).

Carol Dow, *Tea Leaf Reading for Beginners* (Llewellyn, 2011).

William Hewitt, *Tea Leaf Reading* (Llewellyn, 1989).

Sophia, *Fortune in a Coffee Cup* (Llewellyn, 1999).

eHOW–"Fortune Telling with Turkish Coffee," http://www.ehow.com/ how_2251783_tell-fortunes-turkish-coffee.html.

eHOW–"How to Read Coffee Grounds," http://www.ehow.com/how_2121306_read-coffee-grounds.html.

28

THE WRINKLED SHEET

Anything Can Work Because the Power Is In You, Not the Thing

Like sand reading, the wrinkled sheet technique is a simple procedure with many empowering possibilities. Both sand reading and the wrinkled sheet as extrasensory apperception techniques (ESA) can be used together because they usually complement each other. Psychic impressions associated with the hand imprint can often be confirmed or supplemented by patterns appearing in the wrinkled sheet and vice versa. Frequently, the hand imprint will reveal aspects of the past and present, whereas the wrinkled sheet will probe the future.

ANY "THING," OLD OR NEW, CAN BE USED AS A TOOL IN PSYCHIC READING

The Wrinkled Sheet, like Sand Reading (Chapter 25), demonstrates an important point: the Psychic Tool need not be something with a long history and established lore about its use *because the "power" is not in the thing, i.e. the tool, but in the psyche of the reader.* Anything, old or new, simple or complex, inexpensive or expensive, natural or manufactured, etc. can be adapted for use in a psychic reading.

AN EXTENSION OF BODY AND PSYCHE

What is important is that the reader sees the "thing" to be a *tool* and remembers that a tool is an extension of the body, and of the psyche. In almost every situation involving a tool, the selected instrument is a "multiplier" of the physical or psychic strength of the user, just as is a hammer, shovel, pen, or computer.

RULES AND THE VOCABULARY OF INTERPRETATION

The key step is to establish some rules that will become the vocabulary of interpretation. Yes, it helps if there is a seemingly natural correlation between the defining rule and something about the object being used as a tool—such as, for example, the assignment of that generally most prominent line in the palm of the hand as the "life line"—but the real importance comes with the psychic (subconscious) feeling of correctness to the meanings so assigned.

In most cases, even with the arbitrary choice of the divinatory tool, we will see signs and symbols that resonate with long-established "intuitions," which will tell us that a heart-shaped image deals with love, and that one shaped like a clenched fist suggests anger. Those feelings are correct and should be respected.

Before a reading is undertaken, the important question should be carefully formulated and expressed.

A "CHARGE" OF ENERGY

Generally the "thing" is then given a charge of energy, preferably by the person for whom the reading is being given—cards are shuffled, dice are shaken, sand is carefully raked and smoothed, or the paper sheet is deliberately crumpled. With these principles and rules established, you can see how it is that "anything" can be substituted for the "real thing" in psychic divination. Just the same, those tools like the Tarot or Runes or the I Ching that do have a long history and established literature do have a kind of hereditary power that is truly valuable and helpful to the reader.

Sand Reading and the Wrinkled Sheet are valuable for contributing to your understanding of the principles involved, and your experimentation with them will enhance your psychic skills.

Developed at Athens State University in the early 1970s as a psychic empowerment tool, the wrinkled sheet technique (also known as the crumpled sheet) requires a blank sheet of 8-1/2 x 11-inch paper that is crumpled into a mass by the subject, as if to throw it away. The technique can be self-administered to gain information about oneself, or it can be used with others to gain important psychic information of past, present, and future relevance. When used for others, the subject is presented with the blank sheet and typically instructed as follows: "The wrinkled sheet technique is used as a psychic tool to explore the mind. It requires only a blank sheet of paper and a willingness to explore. Please write your name across the top of the page and then crumple it into a mass, just as you would if you were going to throw it away."

The crumpled sheet is then carefully unfolded and gently smoothed out with the name side up. The opened sheet is oriented with the subject's name at the top of the page, ready to provide the essential raw material for psychic analysis.

IT IS *PERSONAL ACTION* THAT SETS THE PSYCHIC IMPRINT

The interpretation of the wrinkled sheet begins with the crumpling process itself. A rapid, vigorous crumpling of the sheet, into a relatively small mass, is associated with assertiveness and independence. Men, on average, tend to crumple their sheets more rapidly than women, and their crumpled masses are typically smaller. However, in a study conducted by the author (Slate), women executives in a major southeastern corporation took less time to crumple their sheets, and produced masses similar in size to those of their male counterparts. At the top of the executive hierarchy, sex differences in the crumpled masses tended to disappear altogether. These findings suggest the usefulness of the technique, not only to identify the more successful businesswoman, but also to predict the probability of success for women in the business world.

THE CAPACITY OF THE OBJECT
TO ACTIVATE PSYCHIC INSIGHT

A major value of the wrinkled sheet technique is its capacity to generate psychic insight, particularly of clairvoyant and precognitive origin. Simply holding the crumpled mass in the hands will often activate the mind's psychic faculties. The energies expended in producing the mass are recorded in the mass itself, and, in a sense, function to hold its crumpled shape in place. Allowing the crumpled sheet to rest lightly in the cupped palm, while opening the mind to emerging psychic impressions, is of particular value in assessing current conditions or identifying pressing problems; but, by unfolding the wrinkled sheet and observing its intricate patterns of wrinkles, we can activate an array of other psychic faculties resulting in the production of totally new psychic insights. Briefly holding the unfolded sheet between the hands can further increase psychic awareness. Together, the unfolded wrinkled sheet and its counterpart, the unfolded psychic mind, provide the essential elements for a psychic interaction with near-unlimited empowerment possibilities.

SEEING THE WHOLE, AND THE PART

The application of the wrinkled sheet as a psychic empowerment tool is more effective when it combines both the "whole" and "part" methods of interpretation. The whole method emphasizes general impressions, and looks at overall patterns and the general distribution of wrinkles. The part method focuses on specific elements and targets unique features and small areas of line patterns. Together, these methods provide a comprehensive picture of past experiences, present conditions, and future events.

SEEING PATTERNS, WITH OPEN AWARENESS FOR THEIR POTENTIAL MEANINGS

Attention to patterns—both general and specific—and awareness of their potential meanings are essential to interpreting the wrinkled sheet. The variations in pattern for unfolded wrinkled sheets are extensive. No two wrinkled sheets, whether for the same individual or for different people, are ever identical; however, multiple wrinkled sheets produced by one individual do often reveal similar, distinguishable features in their overall distribution of lines, direction of lines, position of clusters, and presence of certain distinct characteristics, such as a well-formed star or circle.

Recurring similarities among patterns for a given individual suggest a stable influence or condition in the life of the subject. A recurring deep line across the sheet can indicate a strong resolve to achieve a particular goal, an unalterable course of events already set in motion, or an early traumatic experience with continuing adverse effects. The psychic mind must determine the relevance of each of these possibilities.

WRINKLED SHEET: PRINCIPLES OF PATTERN INTERPRETATION

Although a wide range of patterns can occur in the wrinkled sheet, certain patterns do seem to occur with greater frequency. Following are several suggestions for interpreting those patterns. As already noted, the orientation of the opened sheet is always with the subject's name at the top of the sheet.

Straight Lines

Straight lines appearing anywhere in the wrinkled sheet suggest a significant force or influence: the longer the line, the more significant its meaning. Diagonal lines from the lower left to the upper right of the page usually signify progress and future success, whereas diagonal lines from the upper left to the lower right usually signify struggle or a deterring influence. The wrinkled sheets of chemically dependent subjects will often show a strong line reaching from the upper left to the lower right of the sheet. Self-determining and forceful personalities, on the other hand, will frequently produce lines from the lower left to the upper right. A horizontal line can signify stability, determination, inflexibility, or conservative orientation. Vertical lines often indicate risk taking, adventurousness, and restlessness. The wrinkled sheets of compulsive gamblers nearly always show several vertical lines.

Clusters of Wrinkles

Clusters are produced by many intermeshing small wrinkles. Clusters can represent a complex such as inferiority, a talent that is musical or artistic, a turbulent mental state such as depression, or an entangled relationship. The psychic mind must sort through these and other possibilities to find the true significance of the pattern.

The *location* of the cluster can provide a clue to its meaning (See Quadrant Map and Interpretative Guide for Clusters in the Wrinkled Sheet). A cluster in the center of the sheet typically signifies a prominent concern. A series of wrinkled sheets for a young male executive consistently revealed a cluster at the center of the sheet. When it was pointed out that this pattern often signaled a current dilemma, he confided that his troubled marriage was threatened by divorce.

Clusters oriented toward the left side of the wrinkled sheet are typically associated with past influences and early experiences. When situated toward the right, clusters can reveal a significant future development. An attorney running for public office consistently produced a cluster in the lower right quadrant of the wrinkled sheet, suggesting highly tenuous circumstances. Although he vigorously continued his campaign, he was severely defeated. Conversely, a teacher planning a business venture produced a strong cluster in the upper right quadrant of her wrinkled sheet, a position favoring future success. She proceeded with her plans and successfully established a highly profitable business.

The quadrant location of a cluster in the wrinkled sheet reveals both time and intensity clues: The closer the cluster to the central vertical line, the closer to the present; the higher the cluster on the page, the more positive the influence.

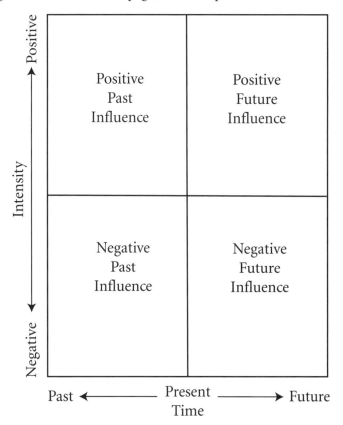

Quadrant Map and Interpretative Guide for Clusters in the Wrinkled Sheet

Crossed Lines

Two lines that cross are associated with strivings, conflict, and ambivalence. As with clusters, the position of the crossed lines provides critical time and intensity clues (See Quadrant Map and Interpretative Guide for Crossed Lines in the Wrinkled Sheet below). Crossed lines appearing on the left side of the page suggest unresolved past conflict, while crossed lines on the right side of the page predict future discord. Crossed lines at the center of the sheet reflect current strivings. A college student experiencing ambivalence regarding his future career consistently produced crossed lines in the central area of his wrinkled sheet. Highly anxious individuals will often produce wrinkled sheets with prominent crossed lines in the upper quadrants of the page. Crossed lines in the lower quadrants typically signify conditions of lesser intensity.

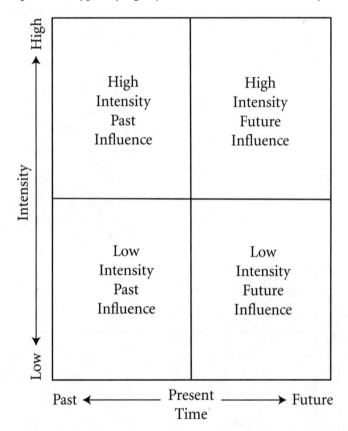

Quadrant Map and Interpretative Guide for Crossed Lines in the Wrinkled Sheet

The location of the crossed lines reveals both time and intensity clues: the closer the crossed lines to the central vertical line, the closer to the present; and the higher the crossed lines on the page, the more intense the influence.

Triangles

A triangle, appearing anywhere in the wrinkled sheet, is associated with a three-dimensional problem situation, with each side of the triangle representing one facet of the problem. These are usually asymmetrical, with the longer side of the triangle representing the dominant element or influence related to the problem.

Romantic triangles are often indicated by triangles appearing in the wrinkled sheet. A college student, torn between his fiancée and a new love interest, produced a wrinkled sheet with a prominent, asymmetrical triangle at the center. He interpreted the longer side of the triangle as representing himself and his vacillation in the triangle situation.

Circles

Good fortune is symbolized by circles appearing in the wrinkled sheet. Circles can predict career advancement, business success, and financial prosperity. Just prior to his appointment to a prestigious political post, a government official produced a wrinkled sheet with a large, near-perfect circle near the center of the sheet. Immediately before a job interview, a doctoral student's wrinkled sheet revealed a circle in the upper right quadrant of the page. He was soon notified that he was the successful candidate for a highly competitive position. Although the absence of a circle does not necessarily indicate misfortune, the presence of a circle is always considered a good omen.

Squares

Squares are usually considered foreboding when they occur anywhere in the wrinkled sheet. On the left side of the page, a square usually indicates negative influences that have already been activated, and in the absence of intervention, could culminate in adversity such as entrapment, betrayal, financial loss, or other misfortune. An investor's wrinkled sheet, just prior to a serious financial loss, revealed a clearly formed square of unusual symmetry near the center of the page. In a more tragic vein, a wealthy industrialist, whose daughter would later be diagnosed with a terminal illness, produced a wrinkled sheet with two large squares, one near the center and the other in the lower-right quadrant of the page. Typically, larger squares reflect more serious misfortune.

Hearts

Only rarely will a heart appear in the wrinkled sheet. Invariably, a heart symbolizes romance, although when it appears near the bottom of the page, it signifies a less than satisfying love relationship.

Stars

A star appearing anywhere in the wrinkled sheet symbolizes psychic giftedness. On her visit to northern Alabama, a highly gifted psychic from London produced a wrinkled sheet with four perfectly formed stars—one in each of the sheet's quadrants. A four-pointed star indicates rich but underdeveloped psychic potential, whereas a five-pointed star is associated with highly actualized psychic abilities.

Pyramids

The pyramid is the rarest of all patterns observed in the wrinkled sheet. It is usually formed by three or more triangles merging to produce a raised form. Even when the sheet has been smoothed out, the pyramid will retain its slight elevation. Like the star, the pyramid is a symbol of psychic giftedness. When it appears with a star, the pyramid signals extraordinary psychic power. The inverted pyramid, however, suggests a loss or deterioration of psychic power, or a denial of one's psychic potential.

Abundant Wrinkles and Clusters

These characteristics are usually observed in the wrinkled sheets of highly active and somewhat assertive individuals who are engaged in many activities. This pattern can indicate disorganization, impulsiveness, and scattered energies.

Parallel Lines

A pair of lines that are parallel to each other is associated with social interests and personal relationships. A high frequency of parallel lines suggests strong social interests. The isolated occurrence of a pair of lines symbolizes a specific personal relationship. The strength of a relationship can be gauged by the closeness of the two lines, with lines closer together signifying a stronger or more intimate relationship. The duration of the relationship can be gauged by the length of the lines: parallel lines that fade or separate toward the right side of the sheet suggest a future weakening of a relationship. When they appear near the top of the wrinkled sheet, parallel lines usually indicate a relationship that involves strong commitment or emotional investment. Parallel lines appearing in the lower half of the sheet suggest a more physical relationship, or a relationship based on practical considerations.

Intricate Patterns

Highly intricate patterns that include many complex clusters generously distributed throughout the sheet are associated with complicated life situations. Less intricate patterns and fewer clusters suggest a simpler life style. Individuals whose lives are highly structured and controlled will often produce a wrinkled sheet with very few intricate patterns.

Strong Creases

Wrinkles that form strong and sometimes raised creases are associated with assertiveness and independence. The wrinkled sheets of high-achieving men and women typically reveal strong creases generously distributed throughout the wrinkled sheet.

Tears

Occasionally a tear will appear in the wrinkled sheet. When it occurs at the sheet's edge, a tear suggests a tendency either to act on impulse or to rely on feelings rather than facts when making decisions. When the tear occurs elsewhere in the sheet, it reflects a potential crisis or traumatic event.

Although careful attention to detail is essential in interpreting the wrinkled sheet, more general or global impressions of the overall pattern can give rise to important psychic insight. When the apperception process is appropriately activated, each wrinkled sheet observation will trigger a function of the psychic mind to aid in the interpretation process.

It is important to emphasize that any given characteristic in the wrinkled sheet can have many potential meanings, and these can vary widely. A single pattern can signify a journey for one individual, a lifestyle for another, and goal-striving for yet another. A pattern of lines oriented diagonally from the lower left to the upper right can suggest financial success for one subject and self-fulfillment for another. A cluster of wrinkles can mean emotional upheaval for one individual and an organized plan of action for another. The answer lies in the psychic mind, and only when processed by the psychic mind can the wrinkled sheet fulfill its potential as an empowerment tool.

SUMMARY

The avenues for exploring the mind, like the mind itself, are endless. The wrinkled sheet technique, like sand reading, provides in symbolic form a representation of the innermost self. Its intricate complexity parallels the complexity of the human psyche, and when appropriately interpreted, provides yet another valuable source of psychic insight. In our continuing struggle for wisdom and understanding, the wrinkled sheet can offer the critical raw material for activating the creative, inquiring mind.

The exquisitely complex wrinkled sheet effectively engages its counterpart, the exquisitely complex mind, in an interaction that is both challenging and empowering. The greater our psychic skills, the more easily we can make that subjective leap into psychic space.

PART THREE
The Next Step in Self-Development

29

SELF-EMPOWERMENT
The Great Work

To bring together the World we live within
and the World that is within each of us
so that the forces of the Outer World
may be brought under the control of the Psyche.
Thus, and only thus, do we fulfill our destiny
and become the masters of our fate.

—DENNING AND PHILLIPS, *THE SWORD & THE SERPENT*

THE NEXT STEP
SELF-EMPOWERMENT
BEGINS WITH PSYCHIC EMPOWERMENT

It bears repeating: *Self-Empowerment does begin with Psychic Empowerment!* It is the "Next Step" in our evolutionary development, and is no less than bringing the innate psychic powers resident in the lower unconscious into the light of the conscious mind. It is the necessary *Next Step* in the integration of the Lower Self with the Higher Self in the Whole Person.

Self-Empowerment *empowers* the Whole Person to comprehend the world we live within, so that we may live intelligently and responsibly with our human family and other species in the home we all share. Psychic empowerment is not the only Next Step in our evolutionary journey being thrust upon us in the most critical moment in human history, but it is vital to our understanding the ramifications and necessity of other scientific, technological, economic, social, and medical innovations that must be made to adjust for new environmental and geopolitical realities that challenge our survival.

Only in recent years have we begun the serious exploration of the empowering nature of psychic phenomena, yet already we are struck with awe by the expanding body of convincing evidence. No longer can we dismiss the psychic event as merely an incredible, mystical phenomenon with little relevance to postmodern life. The more we probe the psychic world, the more we recognize its magnificent empowering possibilities.

Psychic empowerment goes beyond a simple belief in psychic phenomena: it involves a command of knowledge that justifies that belief and empowering skills that give it validity. Acquiring such knowledge and skills requires an accurate and critical assessment of the psychic experience and its empowering potential. When we evaluate the evidence, we come face to face with certain clear, inescapable conclusions:

THE EMPOWERING POTENTIALS
OF PSYCHIC EMPOWERMENT

1. The mind is unsurpassed in complexity and inexhaustible in potential. We have, at best, merely scratched the surface and tinkered at the borders.

2. The powers of the mind are, for the most part, underdeveloped. Among the mind's most neglected resources are the psychic potentials.

3. Our psychic potentials can be accessed, activated, and developed to empower our lives and bring forth global change.

4. A spark of divine power exists in everyone. Psychic empowerment fans that spark and brings it alive to illuminate our lives with a clearer awareness of our destiny for greatness and permanence in the universe.

These four conclusions, arrived at over several decades of *scientific* research involving ordinary people—not just people known for having psychic skills—are much more significant than you may realize. They actually show a *major shift* in the evolutionary scale of human consciousness of the same dimension as occurs when an adolescent enters adulthood.

Psychic powers are not new, but what we might consider their "availability" is. Since any historic recording began—including mythical and religious—certain select people have been able to exercise forms of psychic power: clairvoyance, far-seeing, astral projection, psychokinesis, telepathy, and precognition. These few people became priests and prophets, advisors to kings, and adored saints. They were separated from the general population, enjoying power and prestige, while establishing a hierarchy of students learning their "secrets" under strict controls that were ethical as well as "political."

In addition, certain people have demonstrated their ability to control normal body functions: fasting for extended periods, suspending breath and heartbeat, pain control, nearly instant healing of wounds and fractures, dramatic muscular power and fighting skills. Their methodology in Yoga and martial arts gradually became known and more readily accessible to potential students outside the ashrams and temples.

Over time we have thus become generally aware of the innate powers of both Mind and Body, and their Spiritual potentials.

Two factors are involved in this discussion:

1. Everyone has the potentials for what has been described.
2. Anyone can develop their potentials.

NO MORE SECRETS!

What is *new* is the universal access to the necessary knowledge for psychic development, knowledge that for millennia was restricted and kept secret from the general population so that the select few could maintain positions of power and prestige (always justified, of course, by claims that ordinary people would abuse the power or be injured by it). While even the present-day existence of such priestly powers can be debated, the point remains that today anyone can exercise and develop their innate psychic powers, and that such development is a vital part of our continued evolution.

UNLIMITED POWER WITHIN

Psychic self-empowerment is an endless process of growth, discovery, and change. Its hallmark is recognition of human worth, a firm commitment to truth, and a deep awareness of the illimitable Power within each of us. Ultimately, psychic empowerment brings us, individually and collectively, into oneness with that Power.

WINDOWS OF MIND, DOORS TO SOUL

Every practice described in the first two parts of this book, even when undertaken by the reader for nothing more than "entertainment," does open wider the windows of the mind and the doors to the soul. When they are undertaken with serious respect the result is not only expertise in any practice involved but expanding perspective of Spirit and insights into the wider dimensions of the universe within which we live and experience our very being.

In the third part, we add to the techniques and tools of the first two parts a program of systematic and integrative self-development. Psychic skills are as important to successful living as other physical and mental skills, and through the systemic integration programs of heightened conscious awareness, meditation, and self-hypnosis, your psychic powers become as "normal" and familiar as logical analysis, creative thinking, ethical judgment, and communal responsibility.

The "Lower Unconscious" is more than an alternative name for the Subconscious Mind, and yet all the names and descriptions we apply to divisions of consciousness, and indeed to just what those divisions are and what is actually divided and what those resulting parts are, is open to serious debate. You can't see a part of your consciousness the way you can see a body part. And even though we have mapped areas of the physical brain related to its functions of seeing, hearing, smelling, memory, speech, and even those areas *associated* with logical analysis and creative thinking, and can see changes in its energy patterns (the way areas "light up") during excitement, joy, meditation, etc., *we have very limited understanding of the full role of the physical brain as a "vehicle for personal consciousness."*

We know that we do think, that we do imagine, that we do dream, and that we do experience unaccountable insights into what we think of as "reality," but we also know that these do not *originate*—except reactively (fear, anger, etc.)—within the brain.

I am not the brain; the brain is not me.

The French philosopher DesCartes said "I think, therefore I am," but the most casual observation confirms that the *thinking mind* is only a part of personal consciousness that has no definitive boundaries. Psychologists tend to break personal consciousness into three parts: the Subconscious Mind, the Conscious Mind, and the Superconscious Mind (or Lower Unconscious, Conscious, and Higher Unconscious), but not all would recognize the superconscious mind as the Soul, or even agree that it is the same as still another descriptive phrase, the Higher Self.

In addition to the three parts of personal consciousness, we talk of the Collective Unconsciousness, which is also called the "Universal Consciousness," although that is sometimes considered as something greater yet—perhaps as "the Mind of God."

THE "HIGHER" UNCONSCIOUS

This coauthor (Weschcke) identifies the Lower Consciousness with that which *can* directly interact with the Collective Unconscious in order to *experience* universal (sometimes called "racial" as in the *Human* Race) memories, symbols, archetypes, and certain kinds of visions. When we receive inspiration that may seem to involve similar experiences, we may call this source the Higher Unconsciousness.

We accept that as we are presently constituted, we cannot know everything about consciousness any more than we can know everything about the physical universe, or even see all of it with the aid of the most powerful telescopes and microscopes. It may simply be that incarnate man cannot reach the level to comprehend the universe in totality.

SEEING THE BIGGER PICTURE

As scientists of the psyche—whether we are called psychologists, parapsychologists, or metaphysicians—we recognize that we can see only one part of the picture. Physical scientists, in particular physicists, biologists, and astronomers, see another part of the picture, while quantum physicists are beginning to see the unifying field where those parts come together in the big picture. As we work together, a more complete picture emerges and we learn that consciousness itself is pervasive in every dimension of the universe.

Yet, we are really just modern pioneers exploring "Creation." We can turn to ancient explorers for an alternative but not contradictory picture that offers opportunities that are practical and in use by other psychic explorers—magicians, shamans, yogis, practitioners of various traditions, and Kabbalists.

This view is commonly identified as "occult," simply meaning *hidden.* The occult universe is divided into "worlds" (or planes)—physical (which includes the etheric), astral, mental, and spiritual (which also includes several higher planes). Each plane has a vibratory range that is distinct to the "substance" of that world (See Chapter 2).

All things, living and nonliving, have counterparts in the astral and other worlds, so to confine the discussion to the human, we each have astral, mental, and spiritual bodies, and an in-between etheric body that is really the energy part of the physical body. It is within the etheric body that we locate the chakras, meridians, and other of the "esoteric" organs and energy pathways important in the alternative systems.

While the substance of each world and each body is distinctive, consciousness is pervasive and only requires an appropriate means of perception and expression in each world.

There is still a further variation in this discussion, for occultists and some parapsychologists refer to the astral body as the *emotional* body, and largely assign that to the realm of the subconscious mind. The etheric body relates to the autonomic nervous system and the mental body—no surprise—relates to the conscious mind while the spiritual body relates to the superconscious mind.

These are generalizations and more precise information can be found in many books, but one we recommend most highly in this regard is *The Sword & the Serpent* by Denning and Phillips. In particular, relating these divisions to the Qabalistic Tree of Life is helpful. The following charts are adapted from that text.

Again, as important as word definitions are, we have to accept that many of our modern psychological terms, and their concepts, are ill-defined, while certain words have become popular and at least approximately correct for general discussion—such as the "Subconscious Mind." In some ways, it is of no more importance than is "car" versus "automobile." A picture, or a chart, gives us a sensible understanding of the relationship of the parts to the whole, regardless of these word challenges.

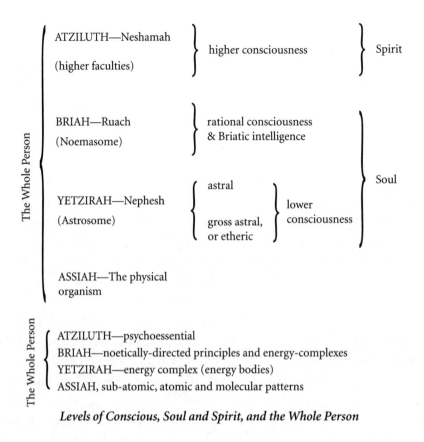

ATZILUTH—Neshamah
(higher faculties) } higher consciousness } Spirit

BRIAH—Ruach
(Noemasome) } rational consciousness
& Briatic intelligence

YETZIRAH—Nephesh
(Astrosome) { astral

gross astral,
or etheric } lower
consciousness } Soul

ASSIAH—The physical
organism

The Whole Person

The Whole Person {
ATZILUTH—psychoessential
BRIAH—noetically-directed principles and energy-complexes
YETZIRAH—energy complex (energy bodies)
ASSIAH, sub-atomic, atomic and molecular patterns

Levels of Conscious, Soul and Spirit, and the Whole Person

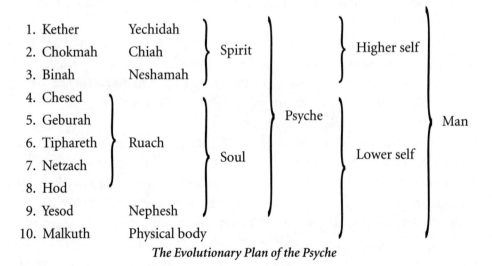

1. Kether　　　Yechidah
2. Chokmah　　Chiah　　　} Spirit
3. Binah　　　 Neshamah
4. Chesed
5. Geburah
6. Tiphareth　 } Ruach　　 } Soul
7. Netzach
8. Hod
9. Yesod　　　 Nephesh
10. Malkuth　　Physical body

} Psyche

} Higher self

} Lower self

} Man

The Evolutionary Plan of the Psyche

We offer these charts here simply as "challenges" for more study, as there is far more here than can be covered in a single chapter intended primarily to show the importance of Psychic Empowerment to the growth of the Whole Person and to suggest the critical importance of this "Next Step" at this historic time.

Humanity is on a journey, moving beyond the frontiers of past times, calling upon each and every one of us to individually move beyond past beliefs about personal limits to become more than we are, and to accept the greater responsibilities that our growth and development require. It's a journey comparable to that leading to the founding of the American republic and the first lunar landing. But it's a pioneering journey that only you can make—no government funding needed, no expensive equipment required, no strenuous physical preparation necessary. For you, it is not only a journey, it is also an adventure and it is personal development that benefits all of humanity.

RECOMMENDED READING

Melita Denning and Osborne Phillips, *The Sword & the Serpent: The Two-Fold Qabalistic Universe* (Llewellyn, 2005).

30
HYPNOSIS & SELF-HYPNOSIS

Although the definition of hypnosis varies among experts, *successful hypnosis* can best be described as a goal-related state of altered consciousness in which attention can be productively focused on specific goals. Among the many goals of hypnosis are habit control, pain management, weight loss, relaxation, and psychotherapy, to list but a few. In our labs, the study of hypnosis has been extended to include such quality of life goals as slowing aging, managing pain, increasing creativity, accelerating learning, improving memory, and promoting psychic development.

THE SUBCONSCIOUS AS A STOREHOUSE OF POWER

The primary goal of the professional hypnotist is to induce a state of successful hypnosis and apply it to achieve clearly defined goals. The induction process can range from a highly demanding, authoritative approach with such commands as "you will respond" to a more permissive approach with such suggestions as "let yourself respond." Although both approaches recognize the subconscious as a storehouse of power, the authoritative hypnotist takes greater command of the induction process and its outcomes. The permissive hypnotist, on the other hand, places greater emphasis on the subject as an interactive participant with power to choose. Perhaps not surprisingly, the most productive approach to successful hypnosis is typically subject-centered in which the hypnotist guides the interaction rather than controls it.

THE HYPNOTIST AS FACILITATOR

Let's face it. For either the authoritative or permissive approach, the professional hypnotist is, at best, merely a facilitator. In the final analysis, *all hypnosis is self-hypnosis.* There is a built-in hypnotist inside everyone. As that knowing part of you, it is your best potential hypnotist. It is poised at any moment to unleash the inner resources required for achieving your personal goals. Whether resolving deep-seated conflicts, overcoming fears, building self-confidence, or breaking unwanted habits, achieving career success, or even exploring your past lives, that invaluable hypnotist within is a most excellent coworker with full access to the powers required for your complete success. The goal of self-hypnosis is to put you in touch with that coworker.

THE BEST HYPNOTIST IS THE SELF-HYPNOTIST

Self-hypnosis puts you in touch not only with your best hypnotist, it also connects you to your best therapist, healer, teacher, and psychic—they also are a critical part of you. Together, they are the very core of your existence. Through self-hypnosis, you have direct access to their abundant powers.

SELF-HYPNOSIS ESSENTIALS

Numerous self-hypnosis programs are now available to empower you with success in achieving your stated goals while promoting your total growth—mentally, physically, and spiritually. In our development of these programs in our labs at Athens State University, certain essentials emerged as critical to the success of self-hypnosis. Here are a few of our findings:

- You alone know yourself best, including that part of you called "the hypnotist within."

- Through practice and experience, you can master the skills required to induce a state of successful self-hypnosis and use it to achieve your personal goals.

- Although susceptibility to self-hypnosis varies among individuals, successful self-hypnosis is possible for everyone.

- Your experience of self-hypnosis can differ markedly from that of others. Flexibility in the induction and application process thus becomes essential to successful self-hypnosis.

- Critical to the success of self-hypnosis are clear goal statements and positive expectations of success.

- The most effective application of self-hypnosis typically focuses on only one major goal for each session.

- Self-hypnosis can activate dormant potentials, a process called *hypnoproduction*, while generating totally new ones, a process called *hypnogenerativity*.

- Self-hypnosis can access past-life experiences and activate their empowering potentials.

- Through self-hypnosis, you can become connected to the best of healers, therapists, teachers, and psychics. They, like your inner hypnotist, are built-in parts of your being.

- Also built into your being is a personal rejuvenator that is constantly poised to slow aging and promote the quality of your life.

- The study of self-hypnosis is a science in progress—our understandings and applications of the experience continue to evolve.

FOUR ESSENTIALS FOR EFFECTIVE SELF-HYPNOSIS

The empowering effects of self-hypnosis depend largely on four essentials:

1. Clearly stated goals

2. Goal-related affirmations

3. Relevant visualizations

4. Post-hypnotic suggestions and cues

INDUCING AND APPLYING SELF-HYPNOSIS

Diversity among programs and techniques is critical to successful hypnosis—one approach does not fit all. Certain generalizations do, however, seem to apply across the board. For instance, you will likely find that the most effective approach focuses on possibilities, not limitations. In self-hypnosis, you will find that suggestions presented in the first person, either silently or out loud, are typically more effective. You may also discover that the sound of your voice increases the effectiveness of your suggestions. Throughout the session, addressing oneself as "I" rather than "you" typically facilitates successful hypnosis by more effectively engaging the subconscious. Likewise, the so-called "I am" approach tends to promote successful induction as well as application. Examples of that approach include: *I am now ready to enter self-hypnosis. I am receptive to each of my suggestions. I am now empowered to achieve my stated goal.*

The self-hypnosis programs that follow are not etched in stone. You can easily adapt them to fit your personal preferences and needs. Only through practice and experience can you discover the approaches that work best for you.

THE SOLAR PLEXUS PROGRAM

Our lab studies of various induction approaches found the solar plexus—that complex network of nerves located in the abdomen—is among the preferred starting points for promoting a relaxed state conducive to self-hypnosis. This approach, called the Solar Plexus Program, is easily mastered and especially effective for goals related to mind/body interactions. It is particularly useful for goals related to stress management, physical fitness, and rejuvenation. It is also effective in building feelings of security and well-being. The program requires approximately one hour.

Step 1. Formulate your personal goal in positive terms and state your firm intent to achieve it.

Step 2. In a comfortable setting free of distractions, settle back and free your mind of clutter. With your hands resting on your thighs or at your sides, state your goal in positive terms and affirm your commitment to achieve it.

Step 3. With your eyes closed, tense the muscles in your abdomen and hold them as the tension builds. When the tension nears its peak, slowly relax your solar plexus and sense relaxation flowing from there to permeate your full body. Affirm: *Relaxation is now soaking into every muscle, joint, and tendon of my body.* Visualize the glow or radiant energy in your solar plexus radiating throughout your body and enveloping you with a bright, healthful glow of energy.

Step 4. With relaxation flowing throughout your body, shift your attention to a peaceful, relaxing scene of your choice—a moonlit lake, golden meadow, nature trail, or waterfall. Visualize the scene, giving attention to each detail. With the image clear in your mind, affirm: "I am now ready to enter hypnosis by counting slowly backward from ten. Upon the count of one, I will be in successful hypnosis. I will be in full command of the trance experience. I can exit hypnosis at any moment by intent alone." As you count backward, you can accelerate the induction process through such interspersed suggestions as *going deeper, becoming more relaxed,* and *at peace.*

Step 5. Upon reaching a successful trance state, specify your goal and affirm: *I am now empowered to achieve this goal.* You can amplify that affirmation with such suggestions as: *Success is my destiny* and *Once I get started, nothing can stop me,* followed by the old standard: *I AM EMPOWERED.* Visualize your goal as a present reality as you sense the emotions accompanying your success.

Step 6. Formulate a post-hypnosis cue that seems appropriate for your goal, and affirm your ability to use it as needed to activate in an instant the full effects of this experience. An excellent all-purpose cue is the simple affirmation: *I AM EMPOWERED.*

Step 7. To exit the trance state, count slowly from one to five with suggestions of becoming fully alert.

Step 8. On the count of five, take a few moments to reflect upon the experience and its effects. Conclude with the affirmation: *I am now fully empowered to achieve my goal of* (state goal).

As noted, this program is especially effective for goals related to mind/body interactions. But rather than focusing on *mind over body*, it emphasizes *mind working with body*. For slowing aging and promoting longevity, imagine yourself at your youthful prime with your body enveloped in a healthful glow while affirming: *Time is slowing down. I am enveloped in and infused with the energies of youth and vitality.* For this application of the program, simply touching your solar plexus with the fingertips of either hand is an excellent post-hypnotic cue that instantly activates the program's effects.

For reducing stress in almost any situation, touching your forehead with the fingertips of either hand while taking in a deep breath and exhaling slowly can be an excellent cue that instantly expiates stress and replaces it with healthful relaxation. Accompanying this simple gesture with imagery of your body absorbing positive energy can greatly magnify its empowering effects. You will find that frequent use of this cue dramatically increases its effectiveness.

THE KNEE-PRESS PROGRAM

The Knee-press Program, also developed in our labs, is a progressive relaxation induction approach that begins by pressing the knees together and then slowly relaxing them to replace tension with relaxation throughout the body. Various techniques, including visualization and reverse counting, are then applied to induce a successful level of hypnosis.

This approach is especially effective for self-empowerment goals related to wellness, fitness, pain management, and breaking unwanted habits. It is also useful as an effective problem-solving technique. The trance state resulting from this approach is often accompanied by spontaneous insight into social interactions, including those related to romantic relationships. Here's the program, which requires approximately one hour in a comfortable setting free of distractions.

Step 1. Clearly formulate your personal goal in positive terms, and affirm your intent to achieve it. Visualize your goal as a reality poised for unfoldment.

Step 2. While in a comfortably seated position with your hands resting on your thighs, close your eyes and take in a few deep breaths, exhaling slowly. Develop a rhythmic breathing pattern and clear your mind of active thought as you affirm: "All my cares have rolled away. I am at peace with myself and the world around me."

Step 3. Press your knees together and hold the knee-press position until your legs begin to tire. Focus your full attention on your knees and the building tension in your legs. Take plenty of time for the tension to build above and below your knees.

Step 4. Very slowly relax your knees and let them return to their normal position as you sense relaxation spreading from your knees downward into your lower legs, right into the tips of your toes. With your lower legs and feet relaxed, sense the relaxation in your knees flowing upward into your thighs, hips, and abdomen. Finally, let the relaxation in your abdomen spread upward, soaking deeply into your shoulders, arms, and right into the tips of your fingers. Finally, sense the relaxation flowing from your shoulders into your neck and face, especially around your eyes and into the muscles of your forehead.

Step 5. Affirm in your own words the flow of deep relaxation throughout your body, from the tips of your toes to the top of your head. Note the feelings of peace and renewal accompanying relaxation.

Step 6. To increase your receptiveness to hypnosis, visualize a peaceful, relaxing scene, such as a tranquil moonlit cove, freshly fallen snow, mountains at a distance, fluffy clouds against a blue sky, sunset at sea, or city skyline. Let yourself soak in the tranquility of the scene.

Step 7. You are now ready to enter deep hypnosis by counting slowly from ten to one. Affirm that upon the count of one, you will be receptive to each of your suggestions. You can promote the effectiveness of reverse counting by interspersing such suggestions as "going deeper," "becoming even more relaxed," and "at complete peace." Should you experience a successful level of hypnosis before reaching the count of one, proceed to the next step.

Step 8. Once in the successful trance, state your goal and affirm your power to achieve it. Visualize your success in achieving your goal. For instance, if your goal is to lose weight, visualize yourself weighing the exact amount of your stated goal. If your goal is career advancement, visualize yourself in the desired career situation. Note the emotions accompanying your success. Use the "I am" approach by affirming *I am succeeding* as you visualize your goal, not as a distant possibility, but as a present reality.

Step 9. Give yourself the post-hypnotic suggestion that by bringing your knees together while affirming *I AM EMPOWERED*, you can activate in an instant the full empowering effects of this program.

Step 10. Conclude the program by simply counting slowly from one to five with accompanying suggestions of becoming fully alert.

With the session now ended, reflect on the experience and its empowering effects. You now can use the post-hypnotic cue at any time to instantly activate the subconscious powers related to your goal. Whether managing weight or building positive social relationships, simply pressing your knees together while affirming *I AM EMPOWERED* can instantly unleash the resources required for your success. If you prefer, however, you can designate during hypnosis a cue other than the knee press for use as needed.

THE PERIPHERAL GLOW PROGRAM

The Peripheral Glow Program is an excellent approach for building self-confidence and expectations of success, even against all odds. It is easily implemented and is especially recommended as a way to overcome barriers, including those encountered in academic and career situations. It has been very successful when used by students to overcome test anxiety and improve test performance. It's an excellent personal enrichment program that generates powerful expectations of success.

For this program, allow approximately one hour in a comfortable setting without distractions. A reclining position is preferred. Before beginning the session, situate a bright, stationary object such as a thumbtack on a wall or ceiling to facilitate a slightly upward gaze. It's important to limit the session to only one major goal.

Step 1. Begin the program by first formulating your goal and then settling back into a comfortable reclining position with your legs uncrossed and your hands resting at your sides.

Step 2. Center your gaze and focus your full attention on the bright, stationary object situated so as to accommodate a slightly upward gaze.

Step 3. As you continue to gaze at the object, slowly expand your peripheral vision by taking in the background above, below, and to each side of the object.

Step 4. With your peripheral vision expanded to its limits, let your eyes fall slightly out of focus and you will immediately see a bright glow called the *peripheral glow effect* enveloping the object.

Step 5. As you continue to focus on the object and the glow enveloping it, note the increasing tiredness in your eyes and give yourself permission to enter hypnosis by slowly closing them. Affirm your ability to exit hypnosis at any time during the experience by simply counting to five. Once your eyes are closed, note the relaxation around them and allow it to spread slowly downward throughout your body as you go deeper and deeper into hypnosis. You can go even deeper into hypnosis by counting slowly backward from ten while interjecting suggestions of increased relaxation and drowsiness.

Step 6. Once in the successful trance state, focus your full attention on your stated goal and, in your own words, affirm your complete success in achieving it. Visualize all barriers to your success slowly dissolving away. Form a clear image of your goal as a reality rather than a probability. Note the satisfying feelings accompanying the images of success.

Step 7. Give yourself the post-hypnotic cue that by simply bringing your hands together, you can instantly activate the empowering effects of this experience. Take full possession of the cue and think of it as yours to be used at will.

Step 8. To exit hypnosis, count slowly from one to five with suggestions of becoming fully awake upon the count of five.

Upon your completion of this program, reflecting on the experience can greatly increase its empowering effects.

Aside from its usefulness as a self-enrichment and anxiety management approach, the Peripheral Glow Program is an excellent past-life regression approach when used with the Past-life Corridor as described in the book, *Beyond Reincarnation* (Slate). Whether exploring past lifetimes, life between lifetimes, or preexistence, the two approaches seem to complement each other. According to our research subjects, the Past-Life Corridor with its array of doors typically takes on the same bright glow that characterizes the *peripheral glow effect* as observed in this program.

THE COSMIC POWER PROGRAM

The Cosmic Power Program is among the most advanced approaches known for inducing self-hypnosis. It is designed to generate a state of higher awareness that connects you not only to the spiritual part of your being, but also to the spirit realm with its empowering planes, guides, growth facilitators, and other advanced helpers. This program focuses on your unique spiritual identity—the "essential you" that's the totality of your existence as a soul being. The program recognizes the boundless power of the spirit realm from which you came and to which you will return. Once connected to that realm through self-hypnosis, you have full access to the unparalleled resources required to achieve your life's goals. Equally as important, you will experience in that state of spiritual oneness a foretaste of the wondrous joy that awaits your transition to that realm.

This induction approach, like the Peripheral Glow Program, requires focusing your attention on a visual target—in this case your hand extended at arm's length—and then slowly expanding your peripheral vision to generate a glow around your hand. That glow at first sight is considered essentially a visual phenomenon not unlike that seen around the bright object in the Peripheral Glow Program. In the Cosmic Power Program, however, the glow is the precursor of your personal aura with its patterns, colors, and other characteristics. Once your aura is in view, the Cosmic Power Program guides you into the trance state and from there connects you to the highest realms of power. Here's the program, which requires approximately one hour in a comfortable setting with soft, indirect lighting and free of distractions.

Step 1. While resting comfortably in a seated or semiprone position, formulate your goal and state your firm commitment to achieve it.

Step 2. Hold your hand, palm side forward, at arm's length, preferably against a neutral background. With your fingers in a spread position, focus your full attention on your middle finger.

Step 3. Slowly expand your peripheral vision to take in your full hand and its surroundings while continuing to focus on your middle finger.

Step 4. Once your peripheral vision has reached its limits, let your eyes fall out of focus and you will note a glow around your hand.

Step 5. Focus your attention on the glow, along with the patterns and colors that normally emerge during viewing, a phenomenon typically called the *human aura*.

Step 6. Close your eyes and visualize the glow with its distinguishing characteristics enveloping not only your hand but your full body as well. Take plenty of time to form a clear mental image of the colorful aura of energy enveloping your full body.

Step 7. Shift your attention to the tiredness in your hand and arm. Tell yourself that as you slowly relax your hand and arm and allow them to return to a position of rest, you will drift into the successful trance state.

Step 8. With your hand and arm now relaxed, you can enter a deeper state of hypnosis if needed by simply counting backward from ten with interjected suggestions of going deeper.

Step 9. Once in hypnosis, visualize the powerful center of energy in your solar plexus radiating bright energy that energizes your total being. Focus on that bright center as the energizing force underlying the aura enveloping your body. Focus on that energy center as a source of power required to achieve your stated goal. Visualize your goal enveloped in bright energy from that source as you affirm: *I am now empowered with success in achieving this goal.*

Step 10. Visualize distant cosmic planes of colorful energy and allow your own energy system to interact with them. Think of the energies enveloping your physical body as reaching upward and extending to infinity. Follow that with visualization of various distant planes of colorful energy also extending into infinity. Affirm your capacity to engage those planes, not simply as intangibles but as higher realities that are receptive to your interactions. Finally, visualize your own energies embracing and interacting with the energies of selected planes of bright color. Pay particular attention to planes that attract your special attention—their energies are typically appropriate for your life situation at the moment. It's at this stage that awareness of spiritual guides and helpers often emerges.

Step 11. Affirm that by simply visualizing distant cosmic planes of energy and your own energy system interacting with them, you can at any time access the power related to your goal.

Step 12. End the trance state by counting slowly from one to five with suggestions of becoming fully awake and alert.

Step 13. Conclude by reflecting on the experience and affirming its empowering effects.

EMPOWERING PROPERTIES THROUGH COLOR

Our studies found that visualizing your own energy system reaching forth and interacting with higher planes of energy can generate a state of mental, physical, and spiritual power appropriate for any goal. As noted, a specific cosmic plane that commands your special attention usually holds important relevance. During self-hypnosis, you can access that plane and its specialized powers. Here are a few examples of the empowering properties of various planes:

- Green—health, fitness, and rejuvenation
- Yellow or gold—intelligence, memory, learning, social enrichment
- Blue—serenity, attunement, peace
- Pink—love, affection
- Purple—spiritual balance, psychic enlightenment, conflict resolution
- Planes of mixed colors—a combination of the attributes of each color

An excellent post-hypnotic cue for instantly activating interactions with a particular plane of energy consists of simply visualizing the plane and your own energy system interacting with it.

Although the Cosmic Power Program may require practice, it is well worth your efforts. It is, in fact, one of the most effective programs known for tapping into the highest planes of power. Aside from that, it is an excellent aura-building strategy. It literally exercises the aura system and expands its powers.

CONCLUSION

Self-hypnosis is an indispensable gateway to self-empowerment. It provides ready access to the highest sources of power, both within you and beyond. Now equipped with the programs presented in this chapter, you can seize with confidence the splendor of the moment and the challenges of the future. Each built-in part of your being—psychic, healer, learner, therapist, creator, rejuvenator, and hypnotist—is now poised to ensure your destiny for endless greatness.

SOURCES AND RECOMMENDED READING

Bruce Goldberg, *New Age Hypnosis* (Llewellyn, 2002).

William Hewitt, *Hypnosis for Beginners: Reach New Levels of Awareness & Achievement* (Llewellyn, 2002).

William Hewitt, *Self-Hypnosis for a Better Life* (Llewellyn, 2002).

Marta Hiatt, *Mind Magic: Techniques for Transforming Your Life* (Llewellyn, 2001).

Ernest R. Hilgard, *The Experience of Hypnosis* (Harcourt, Brace, 1968).

Leslie M. LeCron, *Self-Hypnotism: The Technique and its Use in Daily Living* (Prentice-Hall, 1964).

Neville Goddard, *The Power of Awareness: Move from Desire to Wishes Fulfilled* (DeVorss, 1992).

Layton Park, *Get Out of Your Way: Unlocking the Power of Your Mind to Get What You Want* (Llewellyn, 2007).

Richard L. Shames and Chuck Sterin, *Healing with Mind Power: Living and Feeling the Way You Want to Through Guided Meditation and Self-Hypnosis* (Rodale, 1978).

Joe H. Slate, *Beyond Reincarnation* (LLewellyn, 2010).

Joe H. Slate and Carl Llewellyn Weschcke, *Self-Empowerment through Self-Hypnosis: Harnessing the Enormous Power of the Mind* (Llewellyn, 2010).

31

MEDITATION

From Body to Mind to Spirit

In this chapter, we will discuss meditation in various forms and also one with a particular perspective—the "Open Dialogue"—related to psychic empowerment that is not generally considered when various forms of meditation are practiced. However, to understand this additional perspective, we do need to provide an overview of meditation as it commonly practiced.

Hypnosis, self-hypnosis, and meditation are all associated with special mental states that facilitate positive personality changes and connect with higher dimensions of the psyche. In addition, those particular mind disciplines being used to achieve therapeutic results are receiving increasing professional and scientific attention.

Hypnosis is increasingly used with healing applications in all fields of medicine: to modulate pain, reduce certain side effects of medications, and accelerate healing during and after convalescence. It is also used to prepare patients for surgery, other hospital procedures, and childbirth, by reducing anxiety and instilling affirmative healing imagery. It should be understood that any discussion of hypnosis is inclusive of self-hypnosis, and it should also be understood that anything that can be accomplished through hypnosis can be accomplished through meditation, but we have to go beyond the common perceptions about meditation as just a state of soulful self-oblivion to understand the worldly practical applications.

Hypnosis has been called the most powerful nondrug physical relaxant available. In addition, it has the potential to reach beyond the neuromuscular system to involve the autonomic nervous system to positively influence the mechanisms of disease while integrating the healing process with the emotional system and the higher realms of the psyche.

Hypnosis, self-hypnosis, and meditation all progress from the relaxation of the physical body to remove or bypass emotional blockage and open the mind to possibilities beyond past restrictive conditioning. Meditation has a particular value in reduction of stress—considered by most health professionals as a genuine "killer" of older people because its physical damage is cumulative, as stress tends to become a habitual mental pattern.

This chapter focuses primarily on meditation used for personal health, psychological growth, and spiritual attainment. Meditation is the name given to many techniques bringing about harmonious control of the body, mind, and spirit through *relaxed focused attention* starting with modulation of the breath. Indeed, the word meditation comes from *med-*, meaning to measure, thus to measure the breath.

There are forms of meditation in every spiritual tradition, but meditation isn't limited to spiritual practices. Nor, we should interject, is hypnosis limited to non-spiritual applications.

One particular form of meditation involves the chakras, using the psychic development exercises already described in detail in Chapter 4.

Like self-hypnosis, meditation is mostly self-administered and can be applied entirely for physical, emotional, and mental benefits. From a Body/Mind perspective, meditation is a non-drug way to lower stress levels, relax any area of the body, reduce blood pressure levels, calm the emotions, and clear the mind.

BODY/MIND (BM) RELAXATION

To get started with Body/Mind meditation requires no training, just common sense. The keys to success are found in:

1. A comfortable posture, preferably seated in either a modest reclining or a spine upright position;

2. Deep but not exaggerated breathing at a comfortably slow pace;

3. An intentional stilling of the mind. While not a requirement, in most meditative traditions, the eyes are closed. In some traditions, different eye focus points have different effects, and points such as the "third eye," or gazing over the nose, help to lock the brain into a point of stillness. Different meditations may call for staring at a candle flame, or other object of focus (trataka meditation).

"EASIER SAID THAN DONE!"

Within a short time you may notice that there is tension in various muscle areas;perhaps you will note that you are constantly rubbing your hands, and your mind is wandering all over the place. You thought you could control your thoughts and feelings, but you're worried about things, and to stop worrying you start to fantasize various scenarios.

So, let's try "tension and release" to help our relaxation procedure.

TENSION AND RELEASE TO AID PHYSICAL RELAXATION

Start by pointing the toes of both feet like a ballet dancer, and hold them pointed for sixty seconds, and then relax. Next, spread the toes of both feet apart as hard as you can and hold them that way for sixty seconds, and release. You will feel mild warmth and relief. Repeat tensing, holding, and releasing with both ankles and calves. Then move upward, repeating for each muscle group: thighs, buttocks and groin, chest, upper arms, forearms and wrists, hands and fingers, neck and shoulders, mouth and facial muscles, brow and scalp.

Alternatively, you might prefer first working up the left leg, then the right, and similarly with the arms. Either way, *feel* the whole body as relaxed while restoring the breathing rhythm, slowly and deeply. Silently or quietly tell yourself, "Breathing deeply and evenly, I am more and more relaxed." Repeat to yourself, "breathing deeply and evenly" in a relaxed rhythm several times as you note that your mind is only involved with that one thought.

You may find yourself drifting off to sleep, or slipping into a mild trance. You might ask what the difference is between this rhythmically induced sleep and a rhythmically induced trance. Really, there's not a lot, except that in a trance you are not really asleep, but in a highly focused state of consciousness specifically receptive to your own carefully worded personal affirmations. *More on that later.*

Relaxation is not the same as meditation, but it is a necessary precondition. You will learn that you can meditate while walking, or doing repetitive mindless tasks, and can even meditate in the background while running, exercising, conversing, and writing. But, always, the body should be relaxed, your feelings calm, and your mind clear.

MANTRA MEDITATION

Mantra meditation is by far the best-known form of meditation, and you've already engaged in mantra meditation as you slowly repeated the phrase "breathing deeply and evenly" in a relaxed rhythm coordinated with your breath. Instead, in mantra meditation you can repeat other words, phrases, and short prayers in a similar fashion. Every tradition includes such mantras that may be used in the same way, but with effects that do reach into the spiritual dimension.

Each mantra, while having similar physical and mental effects, will also produce different emotional feelings and induce unique spiritual effects identified with the particular tradition and the words or names used. Phrases containing "god names" are especially powerful, as you would expect.

MEDITATION VS. SELF-HYPNOSIS

At this level of meditation (and we will be addressing other forms as we progress in this chapter) there are more similarities than differences between mantra meditation and self-hypnosis.

As noted earlier, self-hypnosis involves relaxation leading to an induced trance or highly focused state of consciousness receptive to your carefully worded *personal* affirmations intended to achieve generally short-term, beneficial "material" goals.

Mantra meditation, however, uses *traditional* words or names intended to achieve generally longer-term "spiritual" goals that are mostly unstated.

We need to examine the elements of both these statements.

In both cases, words are preceded by relaxation. It may not be an obvious proce-dure, but relaxation becomes an automatic function with habitual meditation. The same can happen with the regular practice of self-hypnosis.

"Personal" vs. "Traditional"

With the personal, you are responsible for developing a carefully worded affirmation that centers about "I AM" and states that you are *currently* benefiting from the goal, such as "I AM at my perfect weight" while you visualize yourself as you would then look. Nothing in the statement says anything that will contradict that the goal is al-ready accomplished.

With the traditional, you select from many long-used words that are part of an established spiritual tradition or religion, or related to your role in a magical order. One such example is the Tibetan Buddhist **Om Mani Padme Hum**, which is often translated as "Behold! The jewel in the lotus!" However, most authorities say it is untranslatable, but has another kind of meaning. The Dalai Lama writes "... the six syllables, **Om Mani Padme Hum**, mean that in dependence on the practice which is in indivisible union of method and wisdom, you can transform your impure body, speech, and mind into the pure body, speech, and mind of a Buddha." Thus a mantra is, or consists of, "power words" that are intended to have a *transforming effect* on the speaker.

"Trance" and a "Focused State of Consciousness"

They are pretty much the same thing, but accomplished differently. In self-hypno-sis, the induction process involves words with specific meaning, such as, "Breathing slowly and deeply, I am slipping into a deep hypnotic trance. Deeper and deeper. On the count of '1' I will be in a deep trance—10, 9, 8, 7, deeper and deeper, 6, 5, 4, deep, deep, 3, 2, 1. I am in a deep trance." In mantra meditation, it is the words themselves, repeated again and again while spoken in a rhythm inherent to them, which is indu-cive to the altered state.

The "Words"

In self-hypnosis, the words have objective meaning understood first by the conscious mind and then the subconscious mind. In mantra meditation, the objective meaning of the words is not important except for those that are centered about "god names" to be discussed later. The traditional mantra has been used for hundreds, sometimes thousands of years, and has built up an energy complex of transformative power greater than words can convey. It has also become an esoteric formula that brings the user into union with others and into communion with generations past.

The "Goal"

The goal state in hypnosis is stated in objectively understood words accompanied whenever possible with a realistic image of the material goal accomplished. The goal in mantra meditation is already part of the energy complex built up around the words, often including an image, uniting the user with the source behind the image—usually of Divinity—and transforming the user in various esoteric ways.

Words aside, meditation can be classified into three types according to their orientation, which in turn can be distinguished from each other by brainwave patterns.

Concentration is focused attention on a selected object, thought, image, sound, repetitive prayer, chant, mantra etc., while minimizing distractions and constantly bringing the mind back to concentrate on the chosen object.

Mindfulness requires a nonreactive monitoring of present experience: perception, thought, feelings, etc. The meditator centers awareness on an object *or* process—such as breath, sound, visualized image, mantra, or koan, or on a physical or mental exercise—while maintaining an "open" focus that may lead to insight or enlightenment. The meditator must passively observe without reaction.

Transcendent Mindfulness requires that the meditator is open to experiencing a *shift* in consciousness and even changes in the physical/etheric body, all the while focusing on a thought, image, or object to the point of identifying with it.

Meditation can be practiced while seated or standing in particular positions (called *asanas* in Yoga), but once you have broken habitual mental patterns that produce stress, you can be meditating while walking or doing simple repetitive tasks.

In a form of meditation using visualization, such as Chinese Qi Gong, the practitioner concentrates on flows of energy (qi) in the body, starting in the abdomen and then circulating through the body until dispersed.

Mantra meditation is the most familiar form of concentration, particularly when you expand the definition of "mantra" to include chants and prayers. Mantras are usually associated with Hinduism and Buddhism, but the word is generic and can apply to any tradition. Chants are commonly associated with Judaism and many neo-Pagan religions. Sometimes magical "spells" are chanted. Prayers are found in most religions, but are particularly associated with Christianity, Judaism, and Islam.

Rather than give an overview of the forms of meditation involved in all the major traditions, we are going to study only two—Hinduism, representative of most Eastern traditions, and Judaism, representative of most Western traditions, including Christianity

HINDUISM

One of the oldest sacred texts, **the *Brihadaranyaka Upanishad*, refers to the goal of meditation: "Having become calm and concentrated, one perceives the self (*ātman*) within oneself."**

When most people think of Hindu meditation, it is in connection with Yoga. The person most responsible for bringing Yoga to the West was Swami Vivekananda, who wrote: "The meditative state of mind is declared by the Yogis to be the highest state in which the mind exists. When the mind is studying the external object, it gets identified with it, loses itself."

The word "Yoga" comes from the Sanskrit *yuj*, meaning "to yoke," and refers to the practices of Yoga that help one to control the mind and senses so the ego can be transcended and the true self (*atman*) experienced, leading to *moksha* (liberation) where nondual consciousness is experienced throughout waking activities.

Yogic science teaches that man-tra ("man" meaning mind, "tra" to cut) helps "yoke" the mind to a more conscious and harmonious vibration. The repetitive use of mantras can aid meditation, clear the subconscious of unhealthy attachments, and break accumulated mental patterns.

MANTRAS IN HINDUISM AND BUDDHISM

Each tradition involves the use of its "native" language. However, certain languages are believed to be "sacred," with each letter and its sounds producing energetic transformative effects. These sacred languages include Sanskrit, Hebrew, Tibetan, Chinese, Greek, and Egyptian. *Sanskrit* was brought to India by the Aryans in about 1500 BCE with an alphabet of fifty letters of fixed pronunciation. While we list some of the best known Hindu or Buddhist mantras transliterated into English, we still need to provide a phonetic pronunciation guide.

SANSKRIT PRONUNCIATION GUIDE

a = *a* as in *sonata*   ai = *ai* as in *aisle*

ah = *a* as in *alms*   I = *I* as in *big*

ey = *ey* as in *they*   oh = *o* as in *no* ee = *ee* as in *reed*   u = *oo* as in *fool*

s (at the beginning of a word) = *ss* as in *Ssiva*

s or sh (in the middle of a word) = *sh* as in *she*

From *Words of Power* by Brian and Esther Crowley

We begin with the most well known of all mantras:

Om Symbol: The primal Sound

OM, OR AUM

Pronounced: *Aum,* or *Ah, Oo, Mm.* Note: The Ah can start at the solar plexus, moving up to the heart, and then to the throat. Repeat several times, and then the Ah should commence at the throat; then move up to the brow with the Oo; and up to the crown with the Mm. The full mantra should be extended out in vibratory fashion to *Ahuu-oooo-muummm,* feeling the vibrations as indicated.

Meaning: There is no meaning as this is said to be the primal sound that initiated the universe. Still, it can be considered in three parts: the "A" as in "the beginning," the "U" as the maintenance and preservation of what was created, and the "M" as transformational power. For another perspective, view the "A" as the Physical Plane, the "U" as the Astral and Mental Planes, and the "M" as Spirit.

OM MANI PADME HUM

Pronounced: *Aa-oo-mm Mah-nee-Pad-may Hoong.* Note: In extended meditative work, colors may be visualized with each syllable as follows:

Om—White, the world of the devas.

Ma—Green, the realms of spirits.

Ni—Yellow, the realm of human.

Pad—Blue, the realm of animals.

Me—Red, the realm of nature.

Hum—Gray, the realm of the underworld.

Meaning: "Hail to Him who is the Jewel in the Lotus." It is the Infinite bound within the Finite. It is used as a protective mantra, and as an attunement of person with the Divine.

ECK ONG KAR SAT NAM SIRI WHA GURU

Pronounced: *Ehk Ohng Karr Saht Nahm Ss-iree Whah Gu-ru.*
    Meanings: "The Supreme is One, His Names are Many."

SATYAM NASTI PARO DHARMA

Pronounced: *Saht-yam Nahs-tee Pah-roh D'hahr-mah.*
    This is the mantra of the Theosophical Society and means, "There is no religion higher than Truth."

OM TAT SAT

Pronounced: *Aum That Saht.*
    Meaning: "Thou are the Inexpressible Absolute Reality."

OM HRIM KRIM HUM SHRIM

This mantra is actually four mantras generally pronounced as one, but also separately. The "Four Great Goddess Mantras" bring about development and integration of the mind, body, and soul. Each governs primal forms of energy. (Frawley, 2011)

HRIM (pronounced *Hreem*) governs over the cosmic magnetic energy and the power of the soul and causal body. It is the prime mantra of the Great Goddess, ruler of the worlds, and holds all her creative and healing powers. HRIM awakens us at a soul or heart level, connecting us to divine forces of love and attraction, opening the lotus of the heart to the inner sun of consciousness.

KRIM (pronounced *Kreem*) governs over prana as lightning or electrical energy. KRIM grants all spiritual faculties and powers—from the arousing of kundalini to opening the third eye. It has a special power relative to the lower chakras, which it can both stimulate and transform. It helps awaken and purify the subtle body. It is the great mantra of Kali, the goddess of energy and transformation. KRIM carries the supreme life force.

HUM (pronounced *Hoom*) is a mantra of the inner fire. It represents the soul hidden in the body, the divine immanent in the world. It both calls the divine down into us and offers our soul upward to the divine for transformation in the sacred fire of awareness. It is used to destroy negativity and creates great passion and vitality.

SHRIM (pronounced *Shreem*) is a mantra of love, devotion, and beauty. SHRIM is a Lakshmi mantra, the goddess of beauty and divine grace. Yet SHRIM works at a deeper level than merely to give us the good things of life, including health. It takes us to the heart and gives faith and steadiness to our emotional nature.

Another group of mantras are used individually to stimulate the psychic centers, or *chakras.*

LANG (pronounced *LAM*)—Mooladhara: Root Center

VANG (pronounced *VAM*)—Swadhistana: Sex Center

RANG (pronounced *RAM*)—Manipura: Navel Center

YANG (pronounced *YAM*)—Anahata: Heart Center

HANG (pronounced *HAM*)—Vishuddhi: Throat Center

ONG (pronounced *OM*)—Ajna: Third Eye Center

Silence—Sahasrara: Crown Center

There are many more traditional Hindu and Buddhist mantras with various applications. As indicated above, some have specific transformational effects, while others are chanted or sung to produce feelings of peace, unity, and communion.

JUDAISM

The core of Jewish meditation disciplines are found in the Kabbalah, in which the ultimate purpose is to understand and cleave to the divine. Classic methods include mental visualization of the higher realms through which the soul navigates to achieve certain ends. One of the most well known in early Jewish mysticism was the work of the *Merkabah*, meaning "chariot" (of God), involving meditative techniques used to transcend to the spiritual worlds.

The basic belief is that through meditation one can separate the soul from the body and transcend to the upper universes. The Kabbalah serves as a map telling one how to prepare and where to go.

Meditation involves controlling one's thought process, blocking out the five senses and entering expanded consciousness. Without meditation, a person uses only three to five percent of his or her brain. Part of the brain receives signals of spirituality, but these signals are very sublime and are blocked out by the other five senses. When one clears the head of all thought, she or he can feel spirituality and eventually can transcend to the upper worlds.

Jewish meditations are, of course, in the native language of Hebrew, and the mantric words will be presented in transliterated English. Here is a phonetic pronunciation guide:

HEBREW PRONUNCIATION GUIDE

The Hebrew letter *chet* is pronounced "ch" as in the Scottish word *loch*.

The letter *zayin* = "dz" as in *adze*.

Kaph = "kh" as in *Khmer*.

Tzaddi = "tz" as the *ts* in *cats*.

Quf = the guttural "q" as in *Qoran*.

The proclaimed goal of Kabbalah meditation is to answer three of life's most critical questions: who we really are, where we came from, and why we are here. The answers provide the means to achieve true joy and a deep sense of accomplishment. You are able to experience life under the light of the Higher Being of your own realization.

The central focus of Kabbalah is on the Tree of Life, seen here as a unique diagram representing the Macrocosm and the Microcosm—that whole of that which is without and the whole of that which is within, the Universe and the Whole Person. Please refer to pages 442 and 443.

This Tree of Life and the wisdom of the Kabbalah are the foundation of Western metaphysics and, *invisibly*, of the whole of Western science and philosophy. With it, we have the means to understand and relate to the body of the Universe and of Man and the Soul of Man and of the Universe.

While there are individual Hebrew mantras, the premier form of meditation is found in the practices of "Pathworking," often in combination with individual cards from the Tarot. These are imaginative journeys or *guided meditations* following the twenty-two paths between the ten Sephiroth, which should be understood as the "God Forces" behind the universe.

From a psychic perspective, pathworking has been described as *the art of clairvoyantly investigating the Paths of the Tree of Life.* The technique was largely developed by adepts of the Golden Dawn and Aurum Solis but has become a comprehensive meditative system outside the magical orders. Once the meditator has passively followed the guided meditation, he should then attempt to retread the paths out-of-body following certain ritual techniques involving visualized symbols, performing certain gestures, and vibrating Divine Names.

Pathworking can be classified as a *Transcendent Mindfulness* form of meditation in which shifts in consciousness are the intended result. These are *astral* learning experiences that can be understood as "initiations."

Generally included in the visualized symbols used with each path are the related Tarot cards (major arcana) and/or the related Hebrew letter. Just as the individual Tarot arcanum communicates particular information and *energies,* so do the individual Hebrew letters.

Because pathworking is a visual exercise, it needs some sort of visual focus; the images of the Tarot trumps are the most convenient for this purpose, and often serve to frame the type of vision that ensues.

We can't go into even an overview of pathworking in a single chapter, so we refer the reader to *A Garden of Pomegranates—Skrying on the Tree of Life,* by Israel Regardie with Chic and Sandra Tabatha Cicero, for a full exposition.

To the Kabbalist, speech is the medium of revelation and hence language itself is sacred and an object of contemplation. The twenty-two letters of the Hebrew alphabet are profound realities embodying those primal spiritual forces that are, in effect, the "building blocks of Creation." Hebrew is called a "flame language" and each letter appears to be shaped out of *flames* that can channel forces connecting Heaven with Earth in special ways.

Because of the belief that these letters (the forces embodied therein) predated Creation, the letters themselves and the order and manner in which they are utilized are of crucial significance, and their properly pronounced sounds transformative. Hebrew chants (mantras) were designed as special formulae able to arouse spiritual forces.

As with Hindu mantras, the purification of the divine power within is attained through the correct and persistent vibration of the sacred sounds and can result in powerful effects of a physical and paranormal nature.

Dr. Philip Berg postulates (1984) that Hebrew may be a computer code for programming our bodies, i.e. "walking bio-computers," into "Superluminal Light Bodies" no longer requiring physical reincarnation. Similarly, Dr. James Hurtak (1976, Los Gatos CA, The Academy for Future Science) claims there is a biophysical connection linking the four letters of the Tetragrammaton (Holy Name of God) with the DNA-RNA matrix, and that, correctly intoned, the sacred name could reprogram the human body.

ACTIVE IMAGINATION

The preeminent psychologist, Carl Jung, developed a technique called "Active Imagination," which is similar to pathworking.

The meditator is instructed to choose a dream or fantasy image, and then concentrate on the image to fix it in the mind. Contemplating it serves to animate it, and the alterations that occur must be noted as they reflect the psychic processes occurring in the unconscious, which appear in the form of images of "conscious memory material," thus uniting conscious and unconscious.

Instead of merely observing events, the meditator participates as a real character in a drama that is taking place within his psyche. The goal is to assimilate lessons from the Unconscious into Consciousness in "Individuation"—the conscious process of psychic healing and integration of all parts of the psyche.

The importance of being involved in the vision rather than just being an observer is to integrate the statements of the unconscious and to assimilate their compensatory content—thereby producing a whole new meaning.

Jung observed in his own active imagination sessions two types of fantasies: one was related to images from his own past, but the others were mythological, archetypal, spiritual, and religious. He recognized these as symbols of basic drives common to every man throughout history—leading him to form the theory of the Collective Unconscious, perhaps his greatest achievement.

In pathworking, the meditator likewise must experience himself as a character fully participating in the vision he is experiencing. In addition, the symbolism of the Paths of the Tree of Life is likewise "mythological, archetypal, spiritual, and religious," and the Tarot arcana are direct representations of the archetypes. The pathworker has a set framework within which to explore the archetypes.

Likewise, we can compare the self-initiatory process of pathworking with the individuation process of Jung's Analytical Psychology.

HEBREW AND CHRISTIAN MANTRAS

There are many mantras of shared meanings between the Jewish and Christian traditions.

The four-lettered Name of God is known as the Tetragrammaton and appears 6,832 times in the Old Testament. Generally, the word is not spoken aloud because of its believed power, and the word *Adonai* ("my Lord") is substituted.

However, certain great masters have used the word. The creator of Hassidism, known as the *Baal Shem Tov* ("Master of the Good Name"), was reputed to have used the Name as described by a recent writer:

> *He was capable of using the Divine Name for purposes of changing things as they were, to what they ought to be, because there is always such a discrepancy between how things are and how they ought to be.*

—REB ZALMAN SCHACTER: *FRAGMENTS OF A FUTURE SCROLL*

Even if not spoken aloud, it is believed that considerable force can be generated in silent meditation. Aside from that, there is little common agreement about how the name of God is correctly pronounced. Instead, the four letters may be pronounced separately, thusly:

YOD HEY VAU HEY

(Yood—Hayi—Wau—Hayi)

*Name of God in Modern Hebrew Characters Ancient Hebrew circa 700 BCE,
uncovered in a burial cave twenty miles southwest of Jerusalem*

Name of God in Modern Hebrew Characters

In addition, there are twelve possible combinations of the four holy letters also used in meditation:

YHWH YHHW YWHH HWHY HWYH HHYW

WHHY WYHH WHYH HYHW HYWH HHWY

Familiar mantras used in blessings include:

SHALOM ALEICHEM

(Sha-lom A-laiy-chem)

Peace be with you

EL ELIYON

(El Eli-**yon**)

The Most High

EL SHADDAI

(El Sha-dhai)

The Almighty

ELI ELI

(Aye-li, Aye-li)

My God, my God

ADONAI
(Ad-o-**noy**)
Lord

BARUKH HA SHEM
(Ba-Rookh Ha Shem)
Blessed is the Name

RUACH ELOHIM
(Roo-**ach** El-o-**heem**)
Spirit of the Godhead

RIBONO SHEL OLAM
(Ri-bo-**no** Shel Oi-lam)
Lord of the Universe

THE MIDDLE PILLAR EXERCISE

Perhaps one of the most important magickal exercises based on the Kabbalah and given here in Hebrew was developed by the Golden Dawn, and I (Carl) urge anyone, no matter their other interests, to at least read *The Middle Pillar* by Israel Regardie (edited with new material by Chic and Sandra Tabatha Cicero).

Essentially, it is a meditational exercise intended to open and balance the five specific psychic centers (chakras) that correspond with the Sephiroth on the central pillar of the Tree of Life as visualized within the physical body.

While visualizing the Sephirothic Centers within the body as shown in the illustration, reach up to center above the head (Kether) with both hands, see the center fill with white light from the Cosmos above, then vibrate the holy name **AHIH** (Eh-he-yeh) three times, pausing in between each to take a deep breath. After the third vibration, inhale and bring your hands down to the throat center (Daath) while visualizing the light descending from the crown to the throat, and vibrate the holy name **YHVH ALHIM** (Ye-hoh-voh E-loh-heem) three times as done previously.

Continue on down the Middle Pillar in the same manner, vibrating **YHVH ALOAH ve-DAATH** (Ye-hoh-voh El-oah ve-Da-ath) at the heart, **SHADDAI AL CHAI** (Shah-dai El Chai) at the genital center, and then **ADNI HARTZ** (Ad-doh-nai ha-Ah-retz) at the earth center.

In review, you have brought light from above down the central column of the Tree and your spine, filling each center with that white light. Each center is pulsing

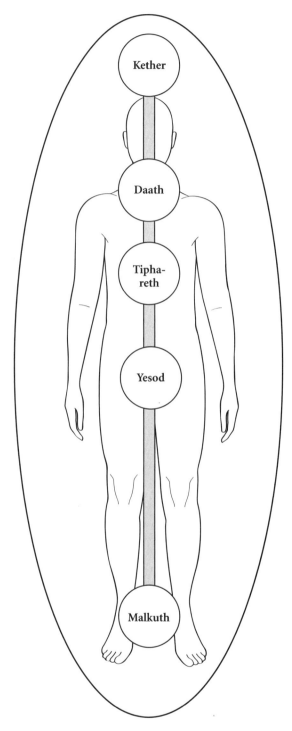

The Middle Pillar

with the light. Continue experiencing the light continuing down the central column, but now slowly bring your hands from their down position (just like in the illustration), up on each side while seeing and feeling Earth energy rising upward through the spinal column in your inhalation, and when you reach the crown, see and feel it fountain out and down, outside your body, to sweep back in at the feet. Now comes the more challenging part: with each inhalation, pull energy up the center column, and with each exhalation, let energy flow down the center column as well as outside the body in a complete and continuous full circulation of light and energy. It sounds more complex than it is. Continue this for several minutes, and then let it dissipate as you feel calmly energized in your body and aura.

What I've described is a minor variation from the traditional technique that I find very effective with daily use. It can be augmented with visualized colors, and you may even hear sounds like distant and very harmonious music.

CHRISTIAN MANTRAS AND PRAYERS

Some are given in English, others in Latin with the English translation.

To combat negativity from place or person:

IN THE NAME OF JESUS, JESUS, JESUS
Let that which cannot abide depart!
(Repeat three times)

The Hosanna Chant:

SANCTUS, SANCTUS, SANCTUS,
DOMINUS DEUS SABAOTH.
PLENI SUNT COELI, ET TERRA GLORIA TUA.
HOSANNA IN EXCELSIS.
Holy, holy, holy,
Lord God of Sabaoth.
Heaven and earth are full of thy glory!
Hosanna in the highest.

The Hail Mary:

AVE MARIA, GRATIA PLENA!
DOMINUS TECUM;
BENEDICTA TU IN MULIERIBUS,
ET BENEDICTUS FRUCTUS VENTRIS TUI, JESUS.
SANCTA MARIA, MATER DEI,
ORA PRO NOBIS PECCATORIBUS,
NUNC ET IN HORA MORTIS NOSTRAE. AMEN.
Hail Mary, full of grace!

The Lord is with thee;

Blessed art thou amongst women,

And blessed is the fruit of thy womb, Jesus.

Holy Mary, Mother of God,

Pray for us sinners,

Now and at the hour of our death. Amen.

The Gloria:

GLORIA PATRI,

ET FILIO,

ET SPIRITUI SANCTO.

SICUT ERAT IN PRINCIPIO,

ET NUNC ET SEMPER,

ET IN SAECULA SAECULORUM. AMEN.

Glory be to the Father,

And to the Son,

And to the Holy Ghost;

As it was in the beginning,

Is now, and ever shall be,

World without end. Amen!

THE OPEN DIALOGUE

There is one final principle regarding meditation we wish to cover. While we've touched on most meditative techniques and illustrated them as best we can in a single chapter devoted to psychic empowerment, there is one particular concept dear to writers and researchers alike—that of tapping into the Unconscious to secure answers to specific questions.

In the *Mindfulness Meditation*, there is focus on a single object or idea combined with openness to insight. In the "Open Dialogue," our focus is on a specific question while we are open to a variety of answers that might be specific to the question, but more often will be "clues" that can be noted and then become the object of further continued meditation, or taken up again at a later meditation.

In essence, we entrusting the Unconscious to come up with generally nonspecific answers to our specific question that may lead to further questions and further answers that are more cluelike than specific. It's a kind of inner brainstorming that can be continued over a period of time. And even though it is presented here in the chapter on meditation, the same process can be continued with the use of our Tarot cards, Tea Leaf Reading, the Pendulum, Dreaming, Crystal Gazing, Spirit Communication, etc.

The "Open Dialogue" is for Big Questions that may even be your Life Work, but more often are chapters in your "book of life."

AND, IN CLOSING...

For our final mantra, we remind the readers that the primary purpose of all meditation and all psychic work is to bring each person to union with the Divine:

SOHAM, HAMSA

(So-ham, Hahm-sa)

He am I; I am He.

SOURCES AND RECOMMENDED READING

Brian Crowley and Esther Crowley, *Words of Power: Sacred Sounds of East & West* (Llewellyn, 1991).

Philip Berg, "Extra-Terrestrial Life in Outer Space: Forces Behind the Future" (1984).

Melita Denning and Osborne Phillips, *Magical States of Consciousness* (Llewellyn, 1985).

Melita Denning and Osborne Phillips, *The Sword and the Serpent* Llewellyn, 1988).

David Frawley, "The Mantric Appoach of the Vedas." www.vedanet.com/index. php?option=com_content&task=view&id=26.

James Hurtak, *The Book of Knowledge: The Keys of Enoch* (The Academy for Future Science, 1976).

Israel Regardie, with Chic and Sandra Tabatha Cicero, *A Garden of Pomegranates: Skrying on the Tree of Life* (Llewellyn, 1999).

Israel Regardie, with Chic and Sandra Tabatha Cicero, *The Middle Pillar: The Balance Between Mind and Magic* (Llewellyn, 1998).

Israel Regardie, with Chic and Sandra Tabatha Cicero, *The Tree of Life: An Illustrated Study in Magic* (Llewellyn, 2001).

Reb Zaiman Schacter, *Fragments of a Future Scroll* (Leaves of Grass Press, 1975).

Donald Tyson, *The Power of the Word: The Secret Code of Creation* (Llewellyn, 1995).

APPENDIX A

JOURNEY OF A LIFETIME
A Program for Actualizing Your Psychic Powers

You are about to begin a Journey of a Lifetime. It's a journey for the rest of your life.

It's a journey designed to activate your psychic empowerment potentials and initiate a psychic-empowered lifestyle with totally new growth possibilities. It's a do-it-yourself journey based on the premise that the best psychic growth specialist exists within yourself—the journey empowers you to connect to that specialist. It organizes the concepts of psychic empowerment into a plan that progresses from positive self-affirmations to step-by-step psychic development techniques, all of which you can do for yourself. Included in the journey are totally new approaches that embrace the whole person in a growth process extending far beyond the completion of the step-by-step exercises presented in the program.

The journey recognizes the importance of considering new ideas and exploring new growth options. By remaining open to change in your perceptions and understandings of yourself and the world, you can introduce totally new possibilities into your life. You can dissolve growth barriers and open new doors for progress and change.

Because psychic development is a natural, continuous process, even sporadic intervention will yield positive results; but the full realization of your psychic potentials requires a more organized approach that recognizes your capacity to access your growth resources and fully activate them. The results are a mental, physical, and spiritual state of empowerment that transcends the demands of even the most difficult life situation.

The exercises that follow are designed to initiate a journey with life-changing possibilities for self-discovery, growth, and power. Through this Journey of a Lifetime, you will discover that the possibilities are unlimited when you tap into the powers within!

EXERCISE ONE: PROMOTING GROWTH READINESS
AND EXPECTATIONS OF SUCCESS

The psychic-empowerment goal for this introductory exercise is twofold: first, to generate a state of psychic growth readiness, and second, to promote powerful expectations of success. This exercise "packs your travel bags" with certain basic essentials you will need throughout your journey. These essentials function as both prerequisites and activators designed to ensure your complete success.

Among the most critical of those essentials is the recognition of your existence as a person of incomparable worth. Through positive self-affirmations of personal worth, you can establish an empowered state of mental, physical, and spiritual well-being within the self. The result is a motivated condition of growth readiness with firm expectations of success. Beginning upon awakening and continuing at frequent intervals throughout the day, empowering self-affirmations are presented, either out loud or mentally. You will discover that the most effective affirmations are presented in the first person and in the present tense. You can formulate affirmations that promote a state of general empowerment as well as affirmations that focus on a specific goal. For a specific goal, state the goal in positive terms and generate clear affirmations of success related to it. Here are a few examples:

I am willing to consider new ideas and embrace new opportunities for growth in my life.

I am a person of dignity and worth.

I am empowered to achieve the goals that are essential to my personal growth and development.

Success is my destiny.

I am empowered to meet the challenges of life.

I am in command of the forces that influence my life.

The solutions to my most difficult life situations exist within myself.

I am surrounded by boundless opportunities for growth and self-discovery.

I am resolved to enrich my life with new meaning and success while contributing to a better world.

I will succeed in achieving my stated goal of (state goal).

The best is yet to come!

You can increase the effectiveness of self-affirmations through the use of relevant gestures as post-affirmation cues. A simple gesture, once you've associated it with a stated affirmation, can later be used to activate the full effects of the affirmation. Such gestures as simply joining the tips of your fingers, touching your temple or forehead, and bringing your palms together in a handclasp can be excellent post-affirmation cues for such wide-ranging goals as breaking unwanted habits, increasing creativity, accelerating learning, and improving memory. Simply lifting a toe and pressing it against the top of your shoe can be a highly effective cue in promoting success related to almost any personal goal, from overcoming fear during a public presentation to building self-confidence. This so-called toe-lift cue can be used almost anytime and anywhere. Positive self-affirmations and relevant post-affirmation cues are so critical to psychic empowerment that we recommend them as daily components of the Journey of a Lifetime program.

EXERCISE TWO: PICTURE RECALL

The purpose of this second exercise, called Picture Recall, is to build the visualization skills required to access your inner potentials and apply them toward achieving your personal goals. Developed under controlled lab conditions at Athens State University, Picture Recall is designed to supplement self-affirmations and related cues with visualization that taps into your dormant inner resources. Visualization adds substance to empowering affirmation and builds the imagery skills required for your complete success. Given positive affirmations, relevant cues, and visualization, you have at your command the three critical skills required to unleash your highest psychic potentials. Even those psychic faculties residing in the deepest subconscious regions of your mind are at your command when you master these three essentials.

Picture Recall is among the most effective practice exercises known for building your visualization skills. The exercise requires first viewing a picture, preferably close-up, and then, with eyes closed, recalling in detail the picture's essential elements. For this exercise, a print or painting in color with numerous detailed features such as persons, animals, buildings, waterways, plants, and trees is recommended. Oil or watercolor paintings are especially effective but not essential for this exercise. Here's the exercise, which requires approximately thirty minutes in a quiet, comfortable setting:

Step 1. Select a colorful picture and view it, preferably close-up. Note the picture's essential features: objects, persons, actions, colors, and so forth. If possible, stroke the picture with your fingers.

Step 2. Close your eyes and form a detailed mental image of the picture. Focus again on the picture's essential features. As your eyes remained closed, scan the picture slowly from side to side and from top to bottom. You will note certain points of interest, such as a particular background or prominent foreground feature.

Step 3. Pay special attention to any emotional response that accompanies the scanning and visualization process. Note certain features of the picture that command special attention and arrest your scan.

Step 4. Open your eyes and again view the picture. Note the specific features you may have missed during the visualization process.

Step 5. Again, close your eyes and visualize the picture. Take plenty of time for the details of the picture to emerge as a clear mental image.

Step 6. Repeat the viewing/visualizing process until a highly detailed mental image of the picture emerges during visualization.

Step 7. To further master the visualization process, additional practice with other pictures, as well as tangible objects such as an article of jewelry, coin, or small rock is recommended. Picturesque nature scenes as well as specific objects of nature such as a flower, rock, or tree are highly effective when used to master this important skill.

You will discover through this exercise that a picture is indeed worth a thousand words. In fact, a stated goal, once visualized, could theoretically increase in power far beyond a mere thousandfold. Visualization takes your stated goals and infuses them with the energy and power required for their fulfillment.

EXERCISE THREE: THE BLANK SHEET

The Blank Sheet is designed to further exercise your visualization skills and empower you to use them to achieve your stated goals. This exercise is especially effective in activating your psychic faculties. The only material required for the exercise is a blank sheet of 8.5" x 11" white copy paper. For some subjects, relaxing background music in an otherwise quiet, comfortable setting can facilitate the exercise, which requires approximately thirty minutes.

Step 1. Formulate a specific goal and affirm your intent to achieve it.

Step 2. Take a few moments to view a blank sheet of paper. Focus your full attention on the paper, and then, with your eyes closed, allow a clear mental image of the blank sheet to emerge. Typically, the image will appear against a dark background.

Step 3. When the image fades, repeat the above step.

Step 4. With repeated practice, you'll find that the mental image of the blank sheet tends to linger for a longer period of time.

Step 5. With the image of the blank sheet lingering in your mind, restate your goal and allow images related to it to unfold upon the screen.

Step 6. Affirm your success in achieving your goal.

Step 7. To end the procedure, formulate a goal-related cue and affirm your intent to use it at will to reactivate the full effects of the exercise.

With repeated practice of this step-by-step exercise, you will discover that visualizing a blank screen upon which you can project images related to your stated goal becomes increasingly easy. For instance, if your goal is to write a book, you can visualize the finished book upon the screen as you affirm, "I am succeeding in achieving this goal." If your goal is an academic degree, you can visualize your diploma upon the screen as you affirm, "Achieving this goal is my destiny." If your goal is to lose weight, you can picture yourself weighing the exact amount of your goal projected upon the blank screen as you affirm, "This is the true me." If your goal is to slow aging and reverse the effects of aging, you can picture yourself at your youthful prime as you affirm, "The energies of youth are now flowing throughout my body." You can use these images and affirmations at will as post-procedure cues to activate on command the full empowering effects of this exercise. You can, however develop totally new cues, either mental or physical, for use as needed. Our studies found that among the most effective post-procedure cues for almost any goal is the word SUCCESS projected in bold, block letters upon the screen. By simply visualizing the word SUCCESS, you can, in an instant, access the inner resources required to achieve your goal.

SUCCESS

Spontaneous psychic impressions will often emerge during this exercise. Among the examples are insights related to past-life experiences, images of future events of both personal and global significance, and impressions of a spirit presence. Profound new insight and breakthrough solutions to difficult problems often accompany this exercise.

EXERCISE FOUR: BECOMING BALANCED AND ATTUNED

The goal of this exercise is to achieve an empowered state of mental, physical, and spiritual balance and attunement. Once you are wholly balanced and attuned, you are at your peak empowerment—nothing is beyond your reach. In that empowered state, you can achieve your loftiest goals. You can solve your most difficult problems and overcome all barriers to your success. When you are balanced and attuned, the complexities of life yield to the simplicity of oneness with the universe. You can fully achieve your destiny for greatness.

Each step in this exercise requires a physical gesture and a related affirmation, which is presented either mentally or out loud. You may find, however, that the sound of your voice in stating an affirmation adds to the empowering effects of the exercise.

Here's the four-part exercise, which requires approximately thirty minutes in a quiet, comfortable setting. It is important not to rush through the exercise—take plenty of time for each step to promote balance and attunement.

The fifth step consolidates and affirms all four of the previous steps.

Step 1. Handclasp of Power. With your eyes closed, slow your breathing and clear your mind of all active thought. Bring your hands together, palm against palm, and form a firm handclasp. Hold this so-called Handclasp of Power as you affirm: *I am physically balanced and attuned.*

Step 2. Temple Touch of Power. Relax your hands and touch your temples with your fingertips. Hold this so-called Temple Touch of Power as you affirm: *I am mentally balanced and attuned.*

Step 3. Palm Receivers of Power. Relax your hands and, with your palms turned upward, visualize streams of bright energy entering them and becoming dispersed throughout your total being. Affirm: *I am spiritually balanced and attuned.*

Step 4. Fingertip of Power. Brings your fingertips together and, while holding the so-called Fingertip of Power, affirm: *I am mentally, physically, and spiritually balanced and attuned.*

Step 5. Affirm: *I am now fully empowered. I can use the Fingertip of Power at any time to generate in an instant a complete state of mental, physical, and spiritual balance and attunement.*

With repeated practice of this exercise, you will find the effectiveness of each gesture dramatically increases. As noted in Step 5, you can use the Fingertip of Power at any time as a post-procedure cue to activate a state of complete balance and attunement.

EXERCISE FIVE: THE FOUR A'S OF PSYCHIC EMPOWERMENT

Everyone is psychic, but developing and effectively applying your psychic powers require recognition of your psychic potentials and a commitment to actualize them.

This exercise is based on the four A's of psychic empowerment: Awareness, Appreciation, Actualization, and Application. We now know that increased awareness and appreciation of your psychic abilities are essential, not only to their actualization but to the application of them as well. With these Four A's, your Journey of a Lifetime takes on new meaning and your potentials for growth rapidly increase.

Step 1. Awareness. Psychic enlightenment is knowledge in its purest form. A dream that came true; a mental message from a friend or relative; awareness of a spirit guide; and interactions with the afterlife—all reflect the psychic nature of our existence. You can increase your awareness of your psychic makeup and your possibilities for psychic enlightenment through the simple affirmation, "I am by nature psychic. I am endowed with psychic potentials and the capacity to develop them."

Step 2. Appreciation. Appreciation of your psychic potentials is essential to your development of them. By embracing your psychic makeup as a source of enlightenment and power, you will discover new meaning to your existence. Promoting that important process are the simple affirmations, "I value the psychic nature of my existence. I am at this moment receptive to knowledge of psychic origin."

Step 3. Actualization. Given awareness of your psychic potentials and appreciation of them, you can initiate a powerful psychic growth process by affirming: "I am committed to the full development of my psychic potentials. I will find ways of tapping into the sources of psychic enlightenment and power." You can use each of the exercises presented in this Journey of a Lifetime to promote your achievement of that goal.

Step 4. Application. Once equipped with workable psychic skills, you can effectively apply them to bring forth desired change, both in yourself and the world around you. Psychic insight has been the seminal inspiration for many groundbreaking inventions and technological advancements. It's conceivable that knowledge of psychic origin will provide solutions to complex global problems such as climate change, threatened and endangered species, and environmental pollution. The following affirmation recognizes the value of psychic knowledge and your ability to use it: "Through psychic knowledge, my life is enriched with new growth and power. Nothing is beyond my reach when I am psychically empowered."

Conclude the exercise by briefly reviewing each of the Four A's, and then affirming: "I am committed to developing my psychic potentials and using them to bring forth desired change."

EXERCISE SIX: BECOMING ALTRUISTICALLY EMPOWERED

Altruism is the pinnacle of mental, physical, and spiritual empowerment. Possibly nothing is more empowering than acts of kindness toward others, including persons and animals alike. Our studies found that altruistic acts of kindness, when expressed with no expectation of receiving something in return, promote the well-being of not only the receiver of the act but the contributor as well. Altruism was found to be the key to quality of life. Here are other conclusions based on our studies of altruism:

- **Rejuvenation.** Altruism literally slows the aging process. Frequent acts of kindness are among the common characteristics of persons aged ninety and older.

- **Positive Outlook.** Altruism is a major characteristic of persons whose outlook on life is hopeful and optimistic.

- **Quality of Life.** Ratings on quality of life are typically higher for individuals known for their altruistic contributions and support of such worthy causes as animal rights and environmental protection.

- **Career Success.** Altruism is associated with career success for a wide range of occupations. Measures of job satisfaction are typically much higher for persons known for their altruism.

- **Sense of Humor.** Altruism is typically accompanied by a strong sense of humor. In our studies, a sense of humor was so prevalent among persons aged ninety and older that we called it "the Holy Grail" of rejuvenation.

- **Health and Fitness.** Altruism is almost always associated with better health and fitness. Our subjects called it the best "health tonic" known. A positive self-concept along with problem-solving skills and effective stress management are characteristics common to individuals who value altruism.

- **Acceptance and Understanding of Others.** Prejudice, bigotry, discrimination, and disregard for the rights of others are characteristics incompatible with altruism.

Nothing seems to be more critical to the Journey of a Lifetime than altruistic acts of kindness that are selfless and motivated by the intrinsic need to help. Through such simple acts as coming to the aid of a person or animal in distress, caring for the environment, and sending positive thoughts, you can overcome growth blockages and accelerate your personal progress while activating totally new growth processes. Aside from that, you can make the world a much better place.

In our Journey of a Lifetime, altruistic empowerment seeks simplicity over complexity. The most effective program for empowerment through altruism is, simply stated: Performing at least one act of kindness daily. Through daily acts of kindness, you will discover for yourself the rewards of altruism. You will promote your personal growth along with that of others. You will discover that living younger, longer, and better is within your reach when you are committed to acts of generosity toward others. You will find new ways of making the world a better place. You will multiply many times over the unparalleled rewards that accompany your Journey of a Lifetime.

CONCLUSION

The Journey of a Lifetime is an endless adventure with unlimited possibilities for growth, self-discovery, and fulfillment. Although it is a journey with many twists and turns, it is forever onward and upward. It is a journey with an unmistakable destination: GREATNESS!

APPENDIX B
THE AUDIO CD
Supplementing the Power of Self-Hypnosis

Based on both scientific objectivity and subjective personal experience, the evidence is clear: *Your best personal hypnotist exists within yourself as a central part of your make-up.* Successful self-hypnosis connects you to that inner hypnotist and the resources required to achieve your personal goals. Once you are connected to that powerful built-in hypnotist, nothing is beyond your reach. You can build your resolve and unleash the power required to achieve even the most challenging personal goals. You can activate dormant potentials and even generate totally new ones, a phenomenon called *hypnogenerativity.*

You can uncover relevant past experiences, including those of past-life origin, and apply them to your present life situation. Even the highest realms of spiritual power are receptive to your probes. You can engage multiple planes and tap into their differential powers. You can interact with personal guides and other growth specialists of spiritual origin as sources of not only power but knowledge in its purest form.

SELF-HYPNOSIS: A BASIC SKILL

Mastering self-hypnosis demands practice and experience, not only to induce a successful trance state, but to use that state to unleash the powers required to achieve your stated goals. Successful self-hypnosis is a basic skill that focuses on that two-part process. Although a particular self-hypnosis approach may be highly effective for a particular goal, you may find it ineffective for other goals. Only through practice and experience can you discover the approaches that work best for you individually. Certain essentials, however, characterize all applications. These include a clear statement of goals, the use of imagery or visualization, positive affirmations, and relevant post-hypnotic suggestions or cues. You can easily apply these so-called "big four essentials" to fit your stated goal and empower you to achieve it.

THE FOUR BIG ESSENTIALS
FOR SUCCESSFUL SELF-HYPNOSIS

1. Form a Clear Statement of your goals.

2. Use Imagery or Visualization.

3. Make Positive Affirmations.

4. Apply relevant Post-hypnotic Suggestions or Cues.

Your mastery of a wide range of self-hypnosis skills and specific applications can be accelerated through the use of a basic audio CD that includes the "big four essentials."

THE BASIC "I AM" AUDIO PROGRAM

You can use the basic CD to supplement and in some instances replace your own personal script. The most effective basic CD recognizes the importance of the "I am" approach, in which suggestions and affirmations are presented in the first person/present tense. For instance, the affirmation, "I am succeeding," is far more effective than the affirmation, "You will succeed." The most effective CD will also provide sufficient time for you to repeat, either silently or out loud, the suggestions and affirmations presented on the CD. Although the sound of your own voice can be a powerful force in self-hypnosis, you may prefer the silent approach.

OTHER CD PROGRAMS UNDER DEVELOPMENT

The applications of audio CDs in self-empowerment can reach far beyond scripts designed to master self-hypnosis. Our research found, however, that mastery of self-hypnosis facilitates mastery of other important skills through appropriate CD programs. Highly specialized CD programs that focus on such topics as aura viewing, astral projection, developing your extrasensory powers, interacting with the spirit realm, connecting to nature, living longer and better, and retrieving past-life experiences have been researched and are projected for release by Llewellyn in the near future.

In your use of the audio CD or any other personal empowerment tool or technique, here are four guidelines that will accelerate your progress and keep you on course:

1. *Be flexible.* Explore different approaches. Find the tools and techniques that work best for you and your stated goals.

2. *Stay focused.* Clarify your objectives and commit yourself to achieve them.

3. *Be positive.* Keep in mind: Your destiny is *greatness.*

4. *Don't give up.* Once started, keep going!

UPON *YOUR* REQUEST

In Appendix C, you will find a simple survey or questionnaire asking for your input, including your preferences for new audio self-hypnosis programming. Each audio CD to be developed is specific to a single technique, and the script will be developed by Dr. Joe Slate in accompaniment with specially composed music backgrounds appropriate to the script.

Announcement of availability will be made on the Llewellyn website.

AVAILABLE NOW

SELF-EMPOWERMENT THROUGH SELF-HYPNOSIS MEDITATION CD COMPANION

SCRIPT BY DR. JOE H. SLATE, MUSIC AND PRODUCTION BY LARRY SMITH

This program introduces you to the best personal hypnotist, the one existing within. Through your inner hypnotist, you can achieve a focused state of self-hypnosis that empowers you to discover and use your subconscious potentials to achieve your highest goals. Through self-hypnosis, you can accelerate learning, improve memory, promote creativity, break unwanted habits, banish negative stress, extinguish phobias, overcome blockages to your growth, facilitate your career success, and enrich your social interactions. You can develop your psychic powers and use them to bring new knowledge, happiness, and success into your life. You can retrieve experiences lost to conscious awareness, including those related to your past lives. You can generate an attuned, empowered state of mind, body, and spirit that promotes health and fitness and even slows the aging process. *All of these, you can do for yourself through self-hypnosis.*

The script on this disk is carefully paced with step-by-step guidance and specially programmed music to induce the trance state and connect you to the subconscious powers related to your stated goal. The script is followed by an aura energy exercise that reinforces the effects of self-hypnosis and establishes a mental, physical, and spiritual state of personal empowerment that simply cannot fail.

HOW TO USE THIS AUDIO CD

Simply place the CD, label side up and shiny side down, in your player. Activate and adjust the volume. *Learn to really listen—even to the silence! While your attention is focused on the script, let your awareness expand to include every nuance, whether audible or silent. Listen to your own voice, whether spoken aloud or silently.*

For the typical session, set aside at least an hour in a quiet, comfortable setting, free of distractions. *Your willingness to respond to your own suggestions is the key to success using this program.* You may find that your receptiveness to hypnosis will vary depending on the time of day, with late afternoon and evening hours typically more conducive to self-hypnosis.

For best results, limit each self-hypnosis session to just one major goal. Before beginning the session, clearly formulate your goal in positive terms and write it down in a self-hypnosis journal using the first person. Begin with, "My goal is…" and if possible describe it in behavioral terms. After clearly formulating your goal, take a few moments to develop images and affirmations of success related to it. If your goal is to lose weight, specify your desired weight and visualize yourself standing before a mirror weighing that exact amount while affirming, "This is the true me." If your goal is career success, visualize yourself succeeding in your chosen career, while affirming, "I am empowered to achieve my career goal." If your goal is rejuvenation, visualize yourself at your youthful prime while affirming, "Time is now slowing down. Living younger, longer, and happier is my destiny." The use of creative visualization and relevant affirmations during self-hypnosis gives added substance to your stated goal and builds the commitment and confidence required to achieve it.

This program embraces the ***I Am Principle*** of self-empowerment that recognizes your power to induce the trance state and take charge of your destiny. Each suggestion in the script is presented in the first person and followed by sufficient time for you to repeat it, either silently or aloud as you prefer. Center your full attention on each suggestion and let yourself respond to it. The post-hypnotic cue presented near the end of the trance can be used on demand to trigger in an instant the full empowering effects of the session. With repeated practice, you will develop your ability to enter the trance state at will.

You can enhance your induction skills by using your imagination and focusing on images related to your suggestions. For instance, you can accompany your suggestions of relaxation with visualization of yourself in a relaxing natural setting, such as strolling along a serene nature trail or viewing a fluffy cloud drifting slowly against a clear blue sky. You can accompany your reverse counting with suggestions of "going deeper and deeper," combined with imagery of slowly descending a staircase step-by-step. You may find that simply visualizing each number in a favorite color against a blank background as you count downward can effectively deepen the trance state.

To begin the trance, settle back into a comfortably seated or reclining position with your legs uncrossed and your hands resting at your sides or on your thighs. With your eyes closed, listen carefully to each of the suggestions, and then repeat it either audibly or silently. You can repeat it exactly as presented, or if you prefer, you can revise it and state it in your own words. The pause following each suggestion allows plenty of time for you to repeat it at least once, and then to center your full attention upon it.

You can stabilize the empowering results of self-hypnosis by attuning and balancing your personal aura, that field of energy enveloping your physical body. Begin by simply turning your palms upward, and with your eyes closed, visualizing bright beams of energy from a distance entering your hands and then spreading throughout your body.

Think of your hands as your body's antennae to the universe with power to both send and receive energy. Allow the energy entering your hands to infuse your total being— mentally, physically, and spiritually. Visualize a bright glow of radiant energy enveloping your full body and reaching outward to infinity. Take a moment to sense your connection to the highest dimensions of energy and power.

With the infusion of new energy now at its peak, take a few minutes to attune and balance your aura system through the Aura Energy Massage. Begin the massage by first placing either hand, palm side down, a few inches from your solar plexus, the central core of your aura energy system. While carefully not touching your physical body, use small circular hand motions and gradually expand them. Almost instantly, you will sense the balancing and attuning effects of the massage throughout your aura system. Conclude the massage by bringing your hands together and affirming, "I am now balanced and attuned, mentally, physically, and spiritually." This simple massage is especially effective in activating the aura's rejuvenating powers. Through its regular use, you can take command of the aging process and, in some instances, literally reverse the effects of aging.

Finally, you can protect your aura energy system from the onslaught of stress or any other disempowering influence through the finger-interlock gesture. Begin the gesture by simply joining the tips of your thumb and middle finger of each hand to form two circles, and then bringing them together to form interlocking circles. While holding the finger-interlock gesture, affirm: "I am now fully empowered. Nothing is beyond my reach. Greatness is my destiny." Use this subtle gesture as needed to generate an instant state of mental, physical, and spiritual empowerment. You can use the gesture almost anywhere and anytime.

Conclude this program by further reflecting on the experience. Write a summary of the session in your self-hypnosis journal and periodically document your progress in achieving your personal goal. Keep in mind that *the power is within you. You are now in full command of it.*

Repeat each script at least once with your full attention upon it. You can repeat it as needed for other personal goals. You will find that, with repeated use, the script becomes increasingly effective.

You will find that there are no limits to the powers within yourself.

You may order this SELF-EMPOWERMENT THROUGH SELF-HYPNOSIS MEDITATION CD COMPAION from your favorite vendor or directly from Llewellyn.com (ISBN: 9780738726724).

APPENDIX C
WHAT DO YOU LIKE,
AND WHAT MORE DO YOU WANT?

SURVEY AND QUESTIONNAIRE

Llewellyn's Complete Book of Psychic Empowerment: Tools & Techniques has covered an important part of *your personal program* of psychic development and psychic empowerment—and Self-Empowerment. Yes, we considered additional subjects but decided to keep the book within limits while establishing principles—the most important of which is that it is you who must make a self-determined program into a *Journey of a Lifetime.*

That's not a small statement. We are used to being *taught,* used to being *instructed,* used to being *guided,* used to being *told what to do.* We've been through an Age of Kings, assembly lines, instruction manuals, teachers and gurus, and nonexpert authorities. Yet this New Age calls upon every individual to assume responsibilities and to secure from experts what is required for learning, growth, development, and empowerment. We look to authorities who are experts that we can respect for their knowledge and advice, authorities who teach to provide the resources for self-development, authorities who provide good management of individual talents and skills, authorities who *show the way* rather than command it and require that we merely follow it as sheep in a pasture, to be *processed for some goal beyond our control or understanding.*

This New Age is one of self-determination, self-discovery, self-understanding, self-help, and self-development; an age of self-expression and self-responsibility, of participation and spontaneous community, of informed citizens making informed choices and positive decisions for the common good. It's an age of "yes, we can," rather than "no, we won't."

It's called "the Information Age," in which you have the resources to discover, to learn, to grow and develop—but it is you who must make choices, who must choose to act, who must choose to participate in a community "of the willing" (without the politics), who must choose to govern without greed, who must develop rules for the common good (without subsidies and largesse for private benefit), who must choose to resolve conflict without war and destruction. It is you who have to turn away from a spectator role to become a participant. It is you who must learn to manage your own health and wealth. It is you who must find the Divine Within and refuse those who claim to speak for the Divine Without.

It is you who must *wake up* and learn to manage your own consciousness—turning unconscious powers into conscious skills and building the structure of your own super-consciousness.

We've prepared a simple Survey and Questionnaire so that we can better provide the resources to help you *become more than you are.* We've kept it simple and unencumbered with demographic mumbo-jumbo. We're not asking for opinions or commitment—*Just the Facts.*

JUST THE FACTS, PLEASE

Of the subjects covered in this book, please indicate which was most interesting to you, and which the least, and for which ones you would like to see Llewellyn produce an Advanced Book, an Audio Self-Hypnosis CD, or a University Level Course. Just fill in the boxes. You will find this same form online at www.llewellyn.com/carl/psychicsurvey. If you prefer, you can cut the pages out or make a photocopy and send to me directly at Carl Llewellyn Weschcke, Psychic Survey, 2143 Wooddale Drive, Woodbury, MN 55125-2989, USA.

Subject	Most interest	Least interest	Advanced book desired	Audio CD desired	Course desired
Ascending the Pyramid					
Astral Projection					
Auras					
Chakras					
Clairvoyance					
Coffee Ground Reading					
Consciousness					
Crystal Gazing					
Dictionary of Divination					
Dictionary of Dream Symbols					
Dictionary of Tea Leaf Symbols					
Dowsing and Pendulum					
Dreams					
ESP—Out of the Lab					
ESP and Psychic Development					
Geomancy					
Glossary					
Great Work					
Handwriting Analysis					
Hypnosis					
I Ching					
Journey of a Lifetime					

Subject	Most interest	Least interest	Advanced book desired	Audio CD desired	Course desired
Magic, Ritual, and Shamanism					
Meditation					
Objectology					
Psychic Empowerment					
Precognition					
Psychokinesis					
Reincarnation and Past-Lives Regression					
Remote Viewing					
Runes					
Sand Reading and Wrinkled Sheet					
Self-hypnosis					
Self-Empowerment					
Sigils					
Spirit Communication					
Tarot					
Tea Leaf Reading					
Telepathy					
Visualization					

If you wish to be notified of new products based on this survey, you may want to provide your name and address as follows:

Name: _____

Address: _____

City: _____ State or Province: _____

Zip or Postal Code: _____ Country: _____

E-mail address: _____

APPENDIX D
WHAT DO YOU KNOW?

Presumably you've just finished reading this book, or—at least—have read some of it and experimented with some of the tools and techniques.

Your coauthors worked very hard on this book for almost a year, and—quite honestly—we have high expectations for it. Not just for selling a lot of copies or getting good reviews, but for it to provide you with the resources for your personal growth, psychic development, and psychic empowerment.

Many readers do just read a book, and then move on to the next without really benefiting from what they've read. They think they've accomplished a lot simply by reading a lot of books—and, to some extent, they have. But we want to know: *What do you know now that you didn't know before?*

No, this really isn't a test. We're not asking questions about the word definitions used in a chapter, about the history or the names of people mentioned, or about how any of the tools we've described relate to others, or how any of the techniques relate to others.

But, how have you benefited from any one of the thirty-plus chapters, the nearly quarter million words in this book?

Let's just take a few examples:

Are you now successfully projecting your astral body? What have you learned about the astral world? Do you understand the differences between astral and etheric? How are you benefiting from this new skill? How has it transformed your perception and understanding of the world in which we live and have our being? Has it changed your belief in personal mortality, in life after death, and the possibility of reincarnation?

Are you now reading auras? Have you benefited by seeing your own? Have you been able to identify physical problems by examining the health aura? Have you found practical applications for your new skills? Have you gained new understanding of the role of color in your life?

What about the Tarot? Are you using it in daily divination? Are you using Tarot cards in meditation or as astral doorways? Do you see the potential to use the Tarot in talismanic magick? Are you able to integrate the Tarot into your other developmental programs?

Have you found handwriting analysis helpful in self-understanding? Have you given any thought to the potentials of making changes in your handwriting, or your signature, to make changes in your self-image or in the image you present to the public? Do you see a role in your writing the personal pronoun "I" in positive "I AM" affirmation statements?

Are you making use of the pendulum in dowsing practice, and in communication with your subconscious mind and in communication with spiritual entities?

Are you using self-hypnosis in positive self-help practices? Are you using self-hypnosis to explore past lives, and life between lives?

What of your experiments with precognition? Are you confident in making predictions of forthcoming events, next year's weather conditions, earth changes, political and economic forecasts? Would you be interested in registering your predictions with some independent agency to actually test your skills?

What of telepathy, psychokinesis, clairvoyance, and remote viewing? Have you moved beyond reading about these to developing and doing them?

Has your reading inspired you to adopt any of these tools and techniques into a personal program of psychic development? Could you write an essay about that and the values you see developing in you as a result? Perhaps you would want to write an article and submit it for publication in the Llewellyn Journal or elsewhere.

How has this book helped you? Why might you recommend it to others? Would you write a review of it for publication in your favorite journal or on Amazon, Barnes & Noble, Books-a-Million, or other sites?

Glossary and Dictionary of Divination

One goal of our glossary, as with our dictionary, is to confirm a vocabulary so that we communicate and exchange ideas without confusion. Because so much of Psychic Empowerment involves the use and techniques of Divination, we have made this dictionary quite extensive—ranging broadly into "exotic" territory in the hope of stimulating exploration and experimentation, and perhaps new discoveries.

A second goal in providing more than needed is to expand the parameters. Psychic powers are in no way limited to the experience of those who have gone before. It is our destiny to "walk upon the bones of our ancestors" and to build towering edifices from the resources they've left behind. We go "where no man has gone before"—sometimes to discover that others have indeed made this trip before, but even so, we add to the breadth of knowledge and prepare the way for others to venture even further.

We're scientists and mystics, visionaries and practical people, and dreamers with our feet firmly on *Terra Firma.* Our psychic journeys are great adventures, and we must record them well for those who follow in our footsteps.

Aeromancy: Divination by observation of atmospheric phenomena—clouds, winds, storms, etc., as well as sometimes related phenomena such as items carried by wind and rain, including birds in flight. In response to a yes/no question, winds that rise and blow to the north or west are favorable, those to the east and south unfavorable. If no wind rises within nine minutes of the asking, no answer is available. Whirlwinds and dust devils are unfavorable answers.

Cloud gazing in answer to a question involves perceiving images and symbols, and interpreting their seeming messages.

Affirmations: (Self-Hypnosis) As used in self-hypnosis, these are positive assertions of that which is desired *as if it is already realized.* This is vital to the involvement of the subconscious mind.

Age Progression: Hypnotic age progression is an innovative approach that has demonstrated unusual effectiveness in identifying future events of both personal and global significance. The program uses self-hypnosis to induce the trance state, during which

awareness flows with ease along the time continuum until it is arrested either voluntarily or spontaneously to engage areas that command special attention. This approach
is especially effective in identifying future happenings that can be either prevented or
minimized through appropriate intervention measures. Crises related to business and
personal concerns are particularly receptive to this approach.

Age Regression: A hypnotic state in which the subject experiences past events that
occurred in the present lifetime.

Akashic Records: The Collective Unconscious is a kind of group mind that is inherited
from all our ancestors, includes all the memories and knowledge acquired by humans,
and sometimes is called "the Akashic Records." It is believed to exist on the higher
astral and lower mental planes and to be accessible by the superconsciousness through
the subconscious mind in deep trance states induced through hypnosis, self-hypnosis,
meditation, and guided meditation.

It is a function of the Astral Light to retain all that has ever happened in thought
and deed; hence the Akashic Records are the enduring records of everything that has
ever happened and the repository of all knowledge and wisdom, and the files of every
personal memory.

Being able to call up infinite information and integrate it into your present life
needs is of enormous benefit—similar to, but beyond the capacity of, any present-day
Internet search engine. *See Chapter Twelve.*

Alectryomancy: Divination with roosters. A circle is created of small pieces of paper,
each marked with an alphabet letter. A kernel of corn is placed on top of each letter.
A white rooster is placed in the center of the circle, and those letters from which the
rooster pecks the corn are believed to form a message.

Aleuromancy: Divination using flour dough. Words and sentences are written on small
pieces of paper and rolled up in dough balls. Carefully mix up the dough balls nine
times, and then choose one to open and read the future. This is the probable origin of
the fortune cookie.

Alomancy: Divination with salt or dry sand. Pour the salt or sand into a square or rectangular tray to a depth of about three inches. Hold a pencil loosely in your hand, with
the point at the center of the substance. Relax, close your eyes, and state your question.
Let your hand move of its own accord until it stops—no longer than three minutes.
Open your eyes and look for symbols or letters among the markings.

Some common examples: "Y" for yes; "N" for no; "P" for perhaps; "X" for love. A
long line for a journey; a short line for a visitor. A large circle for misfortune; a small
circle for news; a triangle for success; a square for obstacles; a heart for love, a broken
heart for a parting. Read other symbols in relation to your question.

Alphitomancy: The use of wheat or barley bread to determine guilt. Suspects were gathered together and each made to repeat, "If I am deceiving you, may this bread act

upon me foul." The loaf was sometimes rubbed with vervain, and then a portion of bread was consumed by each suspect. The guilty person would suffer severe and painful indigestion while the innocent would not be affected.

Altered State of Consciousness (ASC): Wakefulness and sleep are the two most familiar states of consciousness. Others include dreaming, meditation, trance, hypnosis and self-hypnosis, hallucination, astral projection, etc. ASCs can be induced by sleep deprivation, chanting, fasting, ecstatic dancing, drumming, sex, psychedelic drugs, and conscious self-programming. Once you've been 'there,' it is easier to get there again.

Amniomancy: Examining the caul that sometimes covers a newborn's face is said to reveal the child's future.

Apparition: A projection of one's image that is seen by another. Unlike Astral Projection, the appearance is mostly spontaneous and does not involve the projector entering into a trance state. Apparitions are often connected with a personal crisis or intense interest in the other person. Sometimes the apparition is coincidental with the person's death.

Apperception: A phenomenon in which sensory perceptions are associated with inner, subjective impressions.

Apport: The appearance of an object as if moved from another location by psychic means. It is believed to involve the dematerialization and then rematerialization of the object.

Archetypes: A universal image and center of psychological function and energy mostly similar across nationalities, races, cultures, and historical times. Generally speaking, "Mom" is the same mom everywhere. Nevertheless, there may be some minor variation across long-established cultures as expressed in dominant religions, and personal variants may be the source of traumatic disturbances—as when a real-life mom fails to fulfill her archetypal stature.

The archetypes are the foundation of major mythologies, and correspond with gods, goddesses, and mythic heroes. They are found in the major arcana of the Tarot, may be seen and experienced through Qabalistic pathworking and shamanic trances, and are often met in dreams and projected onto real-life figures in times of crisis. One of the goals in every program of self-knowledge is to gain understanding of our particular interaction with them, and possibly change those interactions from a childish to a more mature level.

The archetypes may be the 'gods,' each charged with particular responsibilities in the natural world.

Ascending the Pyramid: A strategy combining imagery of a pyramid and self-affirmations to promote psychic empowerment. *See Chapter Seventeen.*

Ash Tree: In the Norse Tradition, the ash is greatest and best of all trees: its limbs spread over the entire world and reach above heaven. Three great roots of the tree uphold it: one is among the Æsir; another among the Rime-Giants where before time began was the Yawning Void; the third stands over Niflheim, and under that root is Hvergelmir, and Nídhöggr gnaws the root from below. *See Chapter Twenty-four.*

Astragalomancy: Letters, words, or symbols are written on each of a dozen "knuckle-bones" (an ancient form of dice), and then cast upon the ground. The future is determined by the symbols that fall face up, and by their relative position. See also cleromancy.

Astral Body: The third body or level of consciousness, also called the Desire or Emotional Body. In the process of incarnation, the astral body is composed of the planetary energies in their aspects to one another to form a matrix for the physical body. This matrix is, in a sense, the true horoscope guiding the structure of the body and defining karmic factors.

The astral body is the Lower Self of emotion, imagination, thinking, memory, and will—all the functions of the mind in response to sensory perception. It is the field of dreams and the subconscious mind. It is the vehicle for most psychic activities.

Yet, a distinction must be made: The physical body is the field of ordinary conscious mind and the Astral Body is that of the subconscious mind, and a doorway to the superconscious mind and the Collective Unconscious.

Astral Doorways: Meditation on certain objects may function (1) to induce an alternative state of consciousness or (2) to bring access to certain areas of the subconscious and astral plane. Among the first are fascination devices that focus awareness and induce trance—crystal balls, magick mirrors, swinging pendulums, pools of ink, etc.—allowing the user to receive impressions. Among the second are Tarot Cards, Rune Symbols, I Ching Hexagrams, Egyptian Hieroglyphs, Hebrew Letters, Tattwas, and Yantras, etc. used in meditation which open certain astral circuits and gain access to specific parts of the Astral Plane and to subjective states of consciousness.

Astral Excursion: An out-of-body induction procedure specifically designed to promote astral travel to the spirit realm.

Astral Flight: An imagery and relaxation procedure for inducing out-of-body travel.

Astral Light: The "substance" of the astral plane that responds to it is approximately equivalent to Ether, Mana, Vital Fluid, etc., holding the impressions of thought and emotion and feeling, forming memory. Suggested Reading—Regardie and the Ciceros: *The Tree of Life: An Illustrated Study of Magic.*

Astral Plane: The second plane, sometimes called the Inner Plane or subjective world, it is an alternate dimension both coincident to our physical world and extending beyond it. Some believe it extends to other planets and allows for astral travel between them.

It is that level of concrete consciousness between the physical/etheric, the sphere of ordinary consciousness, and the mental and spiritual levels. It is where dreams, vision-sand imagination are experienced and magical action shapes physical manifestation.

Astral Projection and Astral Travel: It's desirable to treat these two subjects together because of the confusion in terminology over the years. Astral projection is a particular state of consciousness in which the astral body separates from the physical and is able to travel on the astral plane, obtain information, communicate with other beings, and return to the physical with full memory. It is common that the astral body separates from the physical during sleep, but does not travel. Nonphysical movement in the familiar physical world is more likely to involve the *etheric* body than the astral. The etheric is the energy double of the physical body, able to function separately from the physical body while connected to it with the 'silver cord' that transfers energy and consciousness between the two.

The etheric body can travel anywhere in the physical world, moving with the speed of thought, and can interact with the physical in a limited manner.

The astral body does not leave the physical body because it is not really an independent body but is the subconscious mind and 'moves' within the field of consciousness without moving at all. Consciousness is everywhere, and in consciousness you can be anywhere. To the extent you want a body, you need to create a Body of Light in your imagination and then just imagine it doing what you want, going where you want.

But, the astral plane is not the physical world, and it lacks the 'solidity' of the physical plane, even though there is replication. However, things may appear on the astral that are not in the physical. *See Chapter Two.*

Astral World: Just as we can speak of the physical plane and the physical world, so can we speak of the astral plane and the astral world. A "plane" (like a "level") is descriptive of the characteristics of the things that make up a world—the substance, energies, laws, etc. A "world," in contrast, is descriptive of how the things are put together, hence the landscape, the life forms, the climates, and so forth.

The astral world has its own landscape, generally replicating the physical world, but is far more extensive, reaching wherever consciousness reaches. It has its own inhabitants, which include the astral bodies of the inhabitants of the physical world. Those astral inhabitants also include forms that have never incarnated into physical bodies as well as temporary inhabitants created by humans through the power of imagination, emotion, and fantasy.

It is also possible that some creatures, like certain paranormal entities such as UFOs, Aliens, and the Loch Ness and other 'monsters' that slip in and out of the physical world, have their origin in the astral, and that mythical beings like dragons also exist in the lower astral, close enough to the physical that they sometimes appear to the physical world inhabitants.

Astrology: Astronomy brought down to earth. It is the science that relates planetary patterns measured by positions in the sky and mapped in relation to the physical location and time of birth of a person or an event in a very long tradition of observation and interpretation to describe the character of the person or event.

While considered as an ancient form of divination, it is today used as a scientific approach to self-understanding and the forecasting of mundane events: weather and climate changes, earth movements, economic and political events, and cultural trends. The horoscope provides a 'map' of planetary energies at any specific time and as projected at a particular location. That map is correlated with the meanings of those planetary energies as established through thousands of years of observation and the now established principles of horoscopic analysis and interpretation.

A horoscope calculated for the exact moment and place of birth is like a photograph taken of the complex relationship of planetary forces as reflected in the astral body. Since the astral is formative to the physical, this photograph tells the tale of the physical incarnation and of the Personality. Solar return (birthday) horoscopes show the annual progression from the birth chart.

This scientific astrology has little to do with the simplistic 'birth sign' horoscopes found in popular media, which lump together approximately one-twelfth of the population as alike based purely on the position of the Sun in a particular zodiacal sign on their birthday. Thus, while there are some general similarities commonly shared by those of the same Sun sign, there are nearly as often powerful planetary factors involved providing a substantial deviation from some of the generalities. Suggested Reading—George: *Llewellyn's New A to Z Horoscope Maker & Interpreter, A Comprehensive Self-study Course*, and Riske: *Llewellyn's Complete Book of Astrology: The Easy Way to Learn Astrology.*

Attention: Focused awareness. Concentration. To "pay attention" is a conscious choice to limit perception and the work of consciousness to something specific.

Attraction: The principle involves believing yourself worthy and already in possession of those things you want. It functions best when used as a goal in our Self-Empowerment through Self-Hypnosis technique, which fully mobilizes your inner resources, leaving no doubt of your success.

Augur: One who performs divination.

Augury: Any kind of divination.

Aura: An egg-shaped sphere of energy extending as much as two to three feet beyond the physical body and viewed by clairvoyants in colorful layers that may be 'read' and interpreted. It includes layers outward from the physical: the etheric, astral, mental, and spiritual bodies. The aura is also known as the "magical mirror of the universe," in which our inner activities of thought and feeling are perceived in colors. It is also the matrix of planetary forces that shapes and sustains the physical body and the lower personality.

Clairvoyants may analyze the aura in relation to health, ethics, and spiritual development, and the aura can be shaped and its surface made to reflect psychic attacks back to their origin. *See Chapter Three.*

Aura Goggles: In 1908, Dr. Walter Kilner invented aura goggles involving a screen of dicyanin by which he could perceive the ultraviolet part of the field around the body which he termed "The Human Atmosphere" in a book of that title published in 1911.

Aura Photography: A procedure that photographs the aura. *See Kirlian Photography.*

Aura Reading: Clairvoyant 'reading' of the aura to determine the health, character, and spiritual development of the person (or animal) by the colors seen.

Aura self-massage: We can create powerful mind/body interaction to promote better health and fitness. Aura self-massage procedures can be adapted to many specific goals.

Aurum Solis: A magical order founded in England in 1897, claiming descent from the Ogdoadic Tradition of the Western Mystery Tradition. It is best known through the published works of two of its leaders, Melita Denning and Osborne Phillips, who wrote many books on different aspects of magical practice, such as *Astral Projection* and *Creative Visualization*, as well as their seminal work outlining the corpus of the Aurum Solis and the Ogdoadic Tradition, *The Magical Philosophy.*

Around 1971, Denning and Phillips began working with Carl Llewellyn Weschcke and moved to the United States in 1979. On July 8, 1987, Denning and Phillips retired from the Aurum Solis, and Weschcke became the Grand Master. Yet on June 23, 1988, both resumed office and returned to England in 1989. On June 14, 2003, Phillips retired as Grand Master and was replaced by Jean-Louis de Biasi, the current Grand Master, who issued a declaration emphasizing the scientific and Hermetic nature of the Order. More information can be found online. De Biasi's own works are being published by Llewellyn.

Auspices: Observation of the results of divination.

Austromancy: Divination from the winds.

Automatic Writing: A psychic strategy in which spontaneous or involuntary writing is used to bring forth information, typically from the subconscious mind or seemingly guided by spirits. A form of channeling in which a person, sometimes in trance, writes or even keyboards messages generally believed to originate with spiritual beings, or with aspects of the subconscious mind. *See Chapter Twenty-one.*

Awareness: Awareness is the focus of consciousness onto things, images, ideas, and sensations. Awareness is more than what we physically sense. We do have psychic impressions independent of the physical apparatus. We can focus our awareness on memories dredged up from the subconscious; we can focus on symbols and images and all the ideas, and memories, associated with them. We can turn our awareness to impressions from the astral and mental planes, and open ourselves to receiving information from other sources, from other planets, from other dimensions, and from other minds.

Awareness is how we use our consciousness. It is just as infinite as is consciousness, just as infinite as is the universe in all its dimensions and planes. When we speak of expanding or broadening our awareness, we are talking about paying attention to new impressions from new sources, and from other ways we can use our consciousness. Awareness is like the "operating system" that filters incoming information, sometimes blocking "what we don't believe in."

Awareness is something of a corollary to concentration. We are used to thinking of it as passive in sensory perception, but it changes dramatically when used actively. Your perceptions can be extended with expanded awareness, and what was invisible can become visible, or heard, or tasted, or sensed. To become more aware is to become enriched. And becoming aware is not limited to objects and people, but includes energies pulsing through and around objects, persons, and their environment.

Through extended awareness, we grow and develop our latent psychic powers into reliable skills.

Louis T. Culling wrote: "Surely one has seen the indispensable necessity for continual awareness in the trance practices. Awareness! Awareness! I would be tempted to say that 'awareness' is the most important word in Magick were it not for the fact that there is a dangerous hazard in being 'hung up' with one such category." Suggested Reading: Culling and Weschcke: *The Complete Magick Curriculum of the Secret Order G∴B∴G∴*.

Axinomancy: Divination with an axe. Toss it in the air in an open area. If it lands with the blade in the ground, note the direction in which the handle points for the answer to your question.

Backward-acting Influences: Richard Shoup of the Boundary Institute believes "we are surrounded by backward-acting influences, in which the future causes the present…they are often small and subtle…we are looking in the wrong places for them" (Larry Dossey, *The Power of Premonition).* We have to be attentive and expand our awareness, and above all we must want to know the future and give it a means to show itself through our psychic tools.

Become More than You Are! A phrase coined by Carl Llewellyn Weschcke to express the concept of self-directed evolution. You—we all—are a work-in-progress toward fulfilling the potential of the Whole Person already existent as a 'matrix' of consciousness into which we are evolving. To "become more than you are" is the goal of everyone who accepts the *opportunity* and *responsibility* of accelerated development and Self-Empowerment.

Belomancy: Divination with an arrow. Shoot the arrow straight up and note the direction of its flight and its position where it lands.

Beyond Dreaming: A technique developed by Joe H. Slate at Athens (Alabama) State University for "true dreaming," it specifies a certain goal and then focuses the dream experience upon it. Beyond Dreaming not only promotes psychic dreaming, it activates the subconscious resources required for successful achievement of your stated goals. Beyond Dreaming generates a powerful anticipation of success so essential to the achievement of both personal and career goals. Beyond that, the dream can literally unleash the subconscious resources required for your complete success.

Bibliomancy: A Bible or any other book may be opened at random, and the passage read indicates the answer.

Bidirectional Endlessness: From the reincarnation perspective, the continuum for individual existence is endless, with neither beginning nor end.

Bilocation: Instances where a person appears simultaneously in two separate locations, one of which is believed to be the physical body and the other the astral body.

Binary Response: A yes or no answer to your question.

Biofeedback: The use of instrumentation to measure the effects of various mental processes including imagery and suggestion on such biological functions as brainwave patterns, finger temperature, and galvanic skin response.

Body of Light: Sometimes used as an alternative for the astral body, but more correctly as an image created ritually out of the astral light through the power of imagination and used by a magician as a vehicle for conscious perception and action. Suggested Reading—Ashcroft-Nowicki and Brennan: *Magical Use of Thought-Forms: A Proven System of Mental & Spiritual Empowerment*.

Botanomancy: Divination with plants. As living things, plants have a stronger connection to human life than most divinatory tools. We will not discuss their visionary properties and uses. Some possibilities include:

- On the day of the full moon, plant the same type of flower seed one each in five small pots. Write five potential answers to your question and attach one to each pot. Treat all five pots the same, and note which plant first germinates for your answer.

- With a silver knife, peel an apple so that the peel comes off in one long unbroken strip. Ask your question and toss the peel over your left shoulder. The shape it takes on the floor behind you is your answer. If anything other than an "O" or "U," the answer is positive.

- Take a daisy and, as you remove each petal, say "yes" or "no." The last petal reveals the answer.

- There is a lot more lore regarding plants, including the famous finding of a lucky four-leaf clover. Seeing certain plants in blossom providesparticular messages: Holly indicates good luck, Laurel peace and goodwill, Myrtle good fortune, Nettle challenges ahead, Poppy not good, Rose for love, Wisteria your love is faithful.

Brain Waves: (Self-Hypnosis) The brain generates weak electrical impulses representative of its particular activities. As recorded by the electroencephalograph (EEG), they fall into particular levels assigned Greek letters. Beta, at 14 to 28 cycles per second, is our normal waking state including focused attention, concentration, thinking, etc. Alpha, 8 to 13 cycles, is the next level down, characteristic of relaxation, alert receptivity, meditation, and access to the subconscious mind. It is at 8 cycles per second, the border between alpha and theta, that trance occurs. Theta, 4 to 7, is lower yet and occurs just before (hypnopompic) or after (hypnagogic) sleep and is characteristic of light sleep, deep meditation, dreaming, vivid imagery, and high levels of inner awareness. Delta, 1 to 3, is characteristic of deep dreamless sleep, while 0 to 0.5 is the state of death or unconsciousness.

Captain of Your Own Ship: The personal commandment that each person should take full authority and responsibility for his or her being. Without question, it involves more than the modern perceptions of democratic government and capitalism, for it also makes demands upon both to provide each individual with certain basics of education, the rule of law, security of person, health, public services, etc.

To be "captain of your own ship" calls for a partnership between individual and government, with government guaranteeing both independence and opportunity for the individual in exchange for loyalty and tax payments.

The concept is developed as fundamental to "self-empowerment" in several books by Carl Llewellyn Weschcke and Joe H. Slate.

Capnomancy: Divination by smoke, also known as *Libanomancy* and *Thurifumia,* involves observation of smoke as it rises from a fire. While you can add your own complexities, generally smoke that rises straight up means that the answer is positive; if it instead hangs heavily over the fire, the answer is negative. Another method is to watch the smoke from extinguished candles. If smoke moves to the right, the answer is positive; if to the left, it is negative.

Catoptromancy: Divination with mirrors. There are two basic forms: One uses mirrors made from special metals associated with planetary lore, and the other uses special gazing mirrors, somewhat like crystal balls.

Sun Mirrors made of gold were consulted on Sundays to discover information concerning authority figures. Moon Mirrors were consulted on Mondays to help with dream interpretation. Mars Mirrors made of iron were consulted on Tuesdays in regard to lawsuits and arguments. Mercury Mirrors, glass globes filled with liquid mercury, were consulted on Wednesdays regarding business and money. The Venus Mirror made of copper is consulted on Fridays regarding questions of love. The Saturn Mirror, made of lead, is consulted on Saturdays to find lost objects and uncover secrets.

Consulting a reflective mirror means to focus on the question or matter of concern, asking specific questions if possible, and then letting yourself slide into a light trance to find the answers.

The other form of mirror is the Magick Mirror made of a concave clock glass painted black on the convex side. This mirror is sometimes placed on black velvet, or mounted in a convenient frame, allowing one to gaze at the unpainted side. The Magick Mirror is ideal to use as an aid in general clairvoyance.

Cartomancy: Divination with playing cards.

Causmomancy: Divination by fire, also known as *Pyromancy*. Fire is the most potent of the natural elements because it causes change, and is directly linked with the Sun, and hence with the earth and growing plants. Yet fire can also lead to disasters. Fire Gazing involves a light and spontaneous trance during which images and symbols may be seen in the fire. Fire Reading, in contrast, is more direct. After the fire has been lit, stir it, and if it burns brightly, a loved one far from home is safe; pale flames foretell bad weather; if the fire suddenly blazes up, a stranger will soon arrive; blue flames indicate a storm; showers of sparks foretell important news; buzzing sounds indicate storms at hand; sparks flying from the fire foretell a domestic dispute; difficulty in lighting the fire foretells hard work; if it lights quickly, visitors are expected; a very bright fire foretells rain; a sputtering fire foretells snow.

Ceroscopy: Divination with melted wax. Slowly pour the wax into cold water and look for images and symbols as the wax hardens in the water.

Chakras: Psychic centers located in the aura functioning through the etheric body that exchange particular energies between the physical body and the personality, and the higher sources of energy associated with the planets, the solar system, and the cosmos.

There are seven traditional "master" chakras and dozens of minor ones located in such places as the palms of the hands, soles of the feet, joints of arms and legs, and just about any place traditionally adorned with jewelry.

Chakras are whirling centers of energy associated with particular areas of the body. In the Hindu Tradition, *Muladhara* is located at the base of the spine and is the source of *kundalini* and the power used in sex magic. *Svadhisthna* is located at the sacrum. *Muladhara* and *Svadhisthana* are linked to the physical body. *Manipura* is located at the solar plexus. *Muladhara, Svadhisthana,* and *Manipura* are together associated as the personality, and their energies can be projected through the solar plexus in such psychic phenomena as rapping, ectoplasm, and the creation of familiars. *Manipura* is linked to the lower astral body. *Anahata* is located at the heart and is associated with group consciousness. *Vishuddha* is located at the throat and is associated with clairvoyance. *Anahata* and *Ajna* are linked to the higher astral body. *Ajna* is located at the brow and is associated with clairvoyance. *Sahasrara* is located at the crown and is associated with spiritual consciousness. *Anahata, Vishuddha,* and *Sahasrara* are together associated as the spiritual self. *See Chapter Four.*

Channels: (1) An alternate name for a medium, and (2) a specific connection similar to a television channel for astral and mental plane communications. Suggested Reading—Denning and Phillips: *Foundations of High Magick.*

Channeling: Receiving information from a discarnate entity or a higher spiritual being. It may also refer to communication with an aspect of one's own subconscious mind. It is similar to, but not necessarily the same as, the spirit communication of mediumship. In both, however, one person serves as a bridge between a spirit or spiritual intelligence and people of ordinary consciousness. In spirit communication, the medium is more often unaware of the communication; in channeling of spiritual intelligence, the channeler is more often aware and sometimes a participant.

Automatic Writing is a form of channeling in which a person, sometimes in trance, writes or even keyboards messages generally believed to originate with spiritual beings, or with aspects of the subconscious mind. Suggested Reading—Wiseman: *Writing the Divine: How to Use Channeling for Soul Growth & Healing.*

Channeling the Subconscious: While possibly related to "channeling" and "mediumship" in technique, the intention is to open the Conscious Mind to the Subconscious and experience the unity of consciousness as indeed there truly is.

Within that unity—just as there is in the ocean everywhere on planet Earth with its layers, currents, variations in temperature, etc.—there will often be practical barriers preventing the free flow of information from one to the other. Through our disciplines we must do the same kind of thing done with wireless communications technology: establish a channel of our own that is "interference free." We calm the mind through ritual, breath control, meditation, and routine. We isolate our channel from the noise of others and direct it toward known sources.

With either channeling or mediumship, it is what the practitioner does that 'powers up' the actual process; this is done with defined intention to establish the *channel* and then to clear it of all interference. The 'channel' may be the various tools, or the tools may only use the mentally created channel. Again, it is the practitioner's intention that matters.

The conscious mind can create the channel as an act of creative imagination in which a gate, door, natural stream, road of light, tunnel, etc., can serve as an "information highway," or it can just feel the intention itself, or that your own journal will itself serve as a channel (as in dream processing and in automatic writing). Find what has the strongest appeal to you, something that satisfies your sense of drama or propriety.

Clearing the channel of interference is commonly accomplished by keeping the whole operation secret, or revealed only to a group of supporters so that no expression of amusement, criticism, contrary images, or doubts interferes with your own sense of correctness.

The choice of either direct experience or of a divinatory or communication tool will, to some degree, shape the remaining elements of composition, transmittal, receiving, and interpretation.

Character Divination: Divination to determine a person's character.

Cheiromancy: *See Palmistry.*

Clairaudience: The psychic ability to hear things inaudible to most people, such as the voices of spirits, sometimes sounds of inanimate objects such as crystals, minerals, artifacts, etc.

Clairvoyance: Sometimes called "ESP," it is the psychic perception of objects, conditions, situations, or events invisible to most people, including auras, various health indicators, and spirits, as well as things at a distance in space or time. *See Chapter Five.*

Both clairaudience and clairvoyance, and other psychic skills, have been induced through hypnosis and self-hypnosis.

Clairvoyant Reversal: A rare phenomenon in which clairvoyant information is revealed in reverse form. Examples are reversed numbers and spellings.

Cleidomancy: Divination by means of a key suspended from a thread held between thumb and forefinger—actually a pendulum—lowered into a glass jar. After a question is asked, the key will knock against the glass—one knock for yes, two for no.

Cleromancy: Divination by the casting of lots, also called *sortilege,* or throwing dice. Actually the common flipping of a coin is a simple variation. An early form of dice was made from actual knucklebones of certain animals. Later forms were made of clay, ivory, wood, and plastic. A single die has six faces, and each face of the die has from one to six dots. In dice divination, three dice of the same size are shaken between your hands or in a cup while thinking of your question or problem, and the number of dots shown on the dice landing face up is interpreted.

> *Three:* foretells pleasant surprises
> *Four:* foretells unpleasantness
> *Five:* foretells good results
> *Six:* foretells a loss
> *Seven:* foretells money or business troubles, injurious gossip
> *Eight:* foretells criticism
> *Nine:* foretells a marriage or other union
> *Ten:* foretells a birth, either of a child or a project
> *Eleven:* foretells of a parting, which may be temporary
> *Twelve:* foretells of an important message
> *Thirteen:* foretells sorrow
> *Fourteen:* foretells of new friendship or help from a friend
> *Fifteen:* avoid starting anything new for three days

Sixteen: foretells of a pleasant journey

Seventeen: make a change in your plans

Eighteen: foretells success

Coffee Grounds Reading: A variation of Tasseography (also known as Tasseomancy, and sometimes Tassology), which encompasses Tea Leaf Reading. While the technology is somewhat different than for tea leaves, the basic principles are similar.

Cognitive Functions Perspective: The view that psychic faculties, including telepathy and other forms of ESP, exist within the cognitive structure of the brain.

Cognitive Relaxation: Inducing physical relaxation through intervention into the mental functions related to relaxation. Common examples are the use of visualization and suggestion to induce a peaceful, relaxed state.

Collective Clairvoyance: The combining of clairvoyant faculties of two or more persons to gather clairvoyant information.

Collective Unconscious: That function of the Personal Consciousness that bridges to the collective racial, cultural, mythic, even planetary memories and the world of archetypes of the Universal Consciousness, making them available to the Psyche mainly through the Subconscious Mind.

The memories of all of humanity—perhaps of more than humanity, and inclusive of the archetypes. The contents of the Collective Unconscious seem to progress from individual memories to universal memories as the person grows in his or her spiritual development and integration of the whole being. There is some suggestion that this progression also moves from individual memories through various groups or small collectives—family, tribe, race, and nation—so the character of each level is reflected in consciousness until the individual progresses to join in group consciousness with all humanity. This would seem to account for some of the variations of the universal archetypes each person encounters in life.

Composite Strategy for Telepathy: A two-component strategy for activating telepathic sending and receiving.

Conscious Mind: The 'middle' consciousness—the 'ordinary' consciousness, the 'objective' consciousness, the 'aware' consciousness—with which we exercise control and direction over our 'awake' lives.

With your Conscious Mind you can take charge of the great resource of the Subconscious Mind. Information is constantly coming in, more than you can take full cognizance of, and so much of it is automatically diverted to the Subconscious Mind. The Subconscious Mind is more that a passive collection of memories, it is also your personal connection to the Universal Consciousness containing all that is from the very beginning. Within this are all the potentials for all that you may become. This includes what we call "powers"—generally thought of as *psychic* powers. But before these powers are fully meaningful, they must be developed to become consciously directed *skills*.

But wait, as they say in television commercials, *there's more!* All that is the Conscious Mind—with its magnificent potentials for rational thinking, for creative development, for abstract analysis, for organization, for the use of imagination, for planning, and for all those skills that make it possible for the human being to manage the resources of the natural world—rose out of the Subconscious Mind. Outwardly, that's what we do; inwardly, we manage Consciousness, because that is what we are. In particular, the job of the Conscious Mind is to manage the Subconsciousness and develop its innate powers into skills that we can then deploy consciously with awareness and intention to work with the Great Plan of evolving life. In another sense, it is to make Conscious the Unconscious through careful management of its resources.

When you take deliberate charge of the subconscious, your life takes on a new dimension of both meaning and power. Rather than a risky existential leap into a dark cavern of the unknown, your probe of the subconscious is an "inward leap of power" that clarifies the nature of your existence and reaffirms your destiny for greatness and meaning. It's a leap of progress that not only accelerates your growth, but guides you toward greater happiness and fulfillment as well.

As we humans became more aware of ourselves as individuals and operated more in the Conscious Mind, developing personal memory, rationality, and new ways of thinking, we perceived ourselves in relationship to the natural world rather than as part of it. We learned to store knowledge in our memory rather than having immediate 'feeling' access to it. Rather than relating internally to the rhythms of Sun, Moon, and planets, we saw them externally and developed the sciences of astronomy, astrology, and agriculture. And we became aware of linear time.

Nature can show the ways to knowledge and understanding of her secret powers when you learn to listen. The Sun, the Moon, and the planets, too, have powers to share with humans in their wholeness.

As manager, it is the job of the Conscious Mind to know, understand, and direct all these resources. It's the most exciting, most gratifying, most rewarding, and grandest job you will ever have, and it's one that is yours forever! You can't be fired, nor can you abdicate.

Consciousness: Everything that is, out of which Energy and Matter manifest and Life evolves. Consciousness is the beginning of all things and part of the trinity of Consciousness, Energy, and Matter. "Consciousness just IS!" We can't really define consciousness because we are nothing but consciousness, and consciousness cannot really define itself. "I AM THAT I AM."

Our personal consciousness includes all states of awareness and our experiences of fear, love, hope, desire, happiness, sadness, depression, ecstasy, mystical union, etc. We experience connectedness through consciousness.

Consciousness is not a 'thing' nor is it a function of a 'thing' called the brain. Killing the brain doesn't kill consciousness, but it limits its expression in the familiar physical world. Consciousness is expressed through the brain, but it exists outside the brain. Consciousness acts upon the physical world, like a "force," as in telekinesis.

There are three levels of consciousness:

I for Instinct, a function of the lower subconscious

I for Intelligence, a function of the ordinary consciousness

I for Intuition, a function of the superconsciousness

Control: The spirit who acts as a kind of manager through which other spirits communicate to the medium during a séance.

Control Imagery: Meditation exercise designed to shape the future by generating images of desired developments or outcomes.

Countercheck: A second divination performed to check the correctness of the first one. Sort of like a second opinion in medical practices.

Creation Myth: Creation myths reflect the natural environment—in particular, geographic areas. Is the local climate predominantly hot, cold, wet, or dry? Is it characterized by mountains or deserts; forests or savannahs? Are there active volcanoes, frequent earth movement, devastating storms? What of the natural resources? Is water plentiful or scarce, are there rivers across broad areas? Is the area seriously dependent on monsoons to supply needed water? Is the area rich in food, and is that food vegetative, animal, or fish? Are there dangerous animals? And, what of human marauders—are they painfully recurrent?

The answers to these questions form the background of the creation myths. Myths are the stories that fill in the gaps between what we know and what we don't yet know. Myths make sense of the world of experience and provide structure upon which culture grows. Myths are created by the seekers of cosmological understanding about the origins of the universe and of man.

Whether through dreams and visions, or intuition, or the voices of spirit, the seekers formulated stories about creation and mankind's relationship to the forces and intelligence behind creation. These creation myths were peopled with supernatural beings fulfilling for the tribe and the culture those roles already familiar to the people: father, mother, child, friend, foe, predator, defender, healer, leader, arbiter. And those who communicated with spirits, interpreted dreams, and understood signs and omens, were the shamans as the cultures expanded and continued to evolve.

These supernatural beings became gods and goddesses "ruling" the various natural, biological, and social functions, and then the gods themselves sought additional specific knowledge and powers to help their "children," the people of the culture. And, nearly always, there was the person set apart from others who could travel the inner dimensions of time and space—the shaman who spoke with the deities and answered the people's questions about why things were as they were and how they could be changed.

All creation myths have certain similarities, but each culture's mythology reflects the nature of reality as it is perceived by the people and, in particular, those "seekers" attempting to explain the nature of the world and the relationship of humanity to the forces of the universe and life.

Critomancy: Baking a single symbolic object into one of many food items—cakes, pancakes, cookies, muffins, rolls, etc. The person who is served that piece containing the charm determines his or her future according to traditional meanings:

Rings foretell marriage

Silver coins foretell money

Walnuts foretell good health

Crystal Ball: A round ball of quartz crystal or glass used as a focal point in skrying. Gazing at the ball, one enters into a trancelike state where dreamlike scenes and symbols are seen and interpreted. Similar aids are the magick mirror, a pool of black ink, a piece of obsidian.

Crystal Gazing: Also known as *Crystallomancy,* a technique typically using a crystal ball to initiate psychic processes. *See Chapter Eighteen.*

Crystal Screen: A technique using various practice articles, along with the crystal ball, for building basic imagery skills required for activating specific forms of ESP.

Crystallomancy: Divination with a crystal ball. *See Chapter Nineteen.*

CyberSpace: The 'new' Astral Plane. The role of the Internet as a search engine duplicates the memory resources of the Akashic Records; the instant transfer of communications via e-mail duplicates mental telepathy; the social networking tools duplicates the astral body as a kind of magic mirrork; the role-playing avatar duplicates the projected Body of Light.

The expanding use of the Internet blends with similar functions on the astral plane to a degree that trains the user to function more directly, more *consciously,* in the subconscious mind, overcoming the barriers that previously existed.

Cyclomancy: Divination by means of letters and numbers painted on a turning wheel of fortune.

Dactylomancy: Divination by means of a ring, such as a wedding band, suspended from a thread held between thumb and forefinger—actually a pendulum—lowered into a glass jar. After a question is asked, the key will knock against the glass: one knock for yes, two for no.

Déjà vu: A phenomenon in which a new event appears familiar or as if it had been previously experienced.

Demystifying the Paranormal: One of the newer goals of paranormal research is to take the mystery out of the paranormal without loss of respect for the early pioneers and for the varieties of the subjects involved. Even where "scientific" understanding is still lacking, experiential evidence has its place.

The evolving body of evidence for psychic phenomena demands a careful reexamination of our thinking and a restructuring of our traditional views about human life and experience. The fact that the mind seems capable of experiencing realities beyond the known limits of sensory perception challenges our conventional belief systems and raises new questions about the nature of reality and human existence itself.

A major challenge facing us today is a riveting, demystifying probe of the so-called paranormal that will explain its nature and unleash its empowering potentials. The psychic experience, whether voluntary or involuntary, is always empowerment driven. Discovering its capacity for empowerment requires attention to the psychic event and understanding its significance.

Derma-optic Perception: The capacity of the mind to receive information through touch, typically through the hands or fingers. That sensory/extrasensory phenomenon has been illustrated in lab studies at Athens State University, under the guidance of Dr. Joe H. Slate, in which blindfolded subjects were given the task of perceiving the color of a stimulus, such as a sheet of paper, through touch alone. In one remarkable instance, the subject, a celebrated psychic, accurately identified the color of ten sheets of construction paper, each of a different color, through touch alone.

There is strong evidence that you can develop your derma-optic skills through certain practice exercises. ASU studies included the use of ten colored jelly beans in which blindfolded subjects were given the task of identifying the color of each jelly bean through touch alone. With sufficient practice, all subjects typically improved their performance in identifying the color of each bean. Similar results came from using ten colored glass marbles and ten 2" x 2" samples of colored construction paper.

Further ASU lab studies revealed that the development of your derma-optic potentials results in a powerful generalization effect that markedly stimulates the development of other ESP faculties. Repeatedly, performance on telepathy, clairvoyance, and precognition tasks using ESP cards appreciably improved following practice of derma-optic exercises.

Destination Control: A strategy utilizing sleep to induce out-of-body travel.

Direct Voice: When a medium allows a spirit to directly speak through her or him, it appears to be the voice of the deceased. *See Chapter Twenty-three.*

Distant, or Remote, Viewing: Non sensory knowledge of nonlocal events that are contemporaneous. *See Chapter Six.*

Discarnate Manifestation: Any of a myriad of manifestations of the discarnate realm, to include ghosts and hauntings.

Divination: The art or practice of "reading" particular *tools* or *natural phenomena* to gain information about the past, present, or future through the observation of certain rules and techniques to channel insights from the unconsciousness.

- By reading naturally produced signs ranging from the shape of clouds to the positions of planets (astrology).
- By reading artificially produced signs ranging from tea leaves to the throwing of dice or dominoes.
- By reading symbols such as the Tarot cards or the I Ching hexagrams.
- By reading visions as seen in Dreams or in Trance.

In each situation, something experienced is interpreted, usually by means of long-established rules justified by many years of observation across many cultures. In most cases, these interpretations are supplemented by psychic factors of impressions or intuition naturally arising in either conscious or subconscious (trance) states. Suggested Reading—Cunningham: *Divination for Beginners: Reading the Past, Present & Future.*

Divinatory Response: The answer to the question asked.

Diviner: The person using the divinatory system or practice.

Domino Divination: Divination with dominos according to certain rules and values assigned to individual dominos. Each domino is either blank or bears one to six dots. As a result, meanings are attached to each domino as follows:

Blank: the querent, or person asking the question or for whom a reading is done
One: travel or journey
Two: family and close friends
Three: love, relationship
Four: money, finances
Five: job, profession, career

Dominos are laid out, horizontally, in spreads. First, all dominos are laid face down, then a question is asked, the dominos are shuffled about, and then individual dominos are selected in the following techniques:

Triple Domino—Past, Present, and Future: Three dominos are chosen and laid end to end. The domino on the far left speaks of the past, the middle is the present, and the far right is the future.

Seven Veils: One domino is drawn and then returned to the group, which is re-shuffled, and a second domino is drawn, and so on for a total of seven times. Keep note, and read them as a story proceeding from past to future.

Future Fan: Thirteen dominos are selected and laid face up, end to end, and read in groups of three, in which the last domino of the first five becomes the first domino of the next five, and the last domino of the second five becomes the first domino for the last five. Again, a story is read proceeding from past to future.

Other spreads can be developed, always establishing rules and providing opportunity for the subconscious mind to both influence the dominos chosen and inspire the interpretation.

Doors: A precognitive strategy that emphasizes choice and self-determination.

Dowser: One who practices dowsing.

Dowsing: Psychic empathy with the natural world enabling the practitioner to locate water, ores, petroleum, ley lines, etc., usually aided by a device such as a forked stick, a pendulum, or a pair of L-shaped metal rods (as simple as coathanger wire), which will strongly respond in the dowser's hands when walking over the physical location. Some dowsers work with a pendulum and a large-scale map and obtain equally valid results. *See Chapter Nineteen.*

Dream Book, or Dream Journal: Record the elements of a dream immediately upon awakening (see Dream Recall Strategy below), but do not stop to interpret them. Later, you will also record your interpretation, and start a 'dictionary' of the symbols and other elements that seem meaningful to you, and what they seem to mean.

The dream experience is a personal gateway to the subconscious with its abundant empowering resources. Embraced by the subconscious mind, the dream experience becomes a powerful agent for growth and change. In that role, the dream can promote restful sleep while opening totally new channels for growth and self-discovery.

Aside from simply recalling the dream experience, a major task we face is unraveling its significance and developing our ability to use the dream experience as a channel for personal growth and empowerment. We now know that dreams don't do it *for* you; they instead work *with* you. Through your dreams, you can exercise your psychic skills, including your ability to see into the future and travel out-of-body to distant spatial realities. Beyond these, you can develop your ability to experience firsthand the spiritual realm with its advanced spirit guides and higher planes of spiritual power.

Dream Interpretation: An important factor in self-empowerment is the more complete utilization of lines of communication between levels of consciousness. While commercial dream dictionaries may have limited application, one that you compile yourself may be immensely helpful. Through the regular use of a Dream Journal, you become familiar with your own symbol meanings and can explore each further for more insight. When you actually pay attention to your dreams, they start to pay attention to you,and can deliver information and even guidance of immediate application. *See Chapter Seven.*

Dream Recall Strategy: An imagery practice exercise in which past dream experiences are visualized. The most important part of the process is to tell yourself to remember your dreams just before falling asleep, and that you will wake up from those dreams and immediately record the details you can remember. At this time, no effort is made to interpret the dream. Dream interpretation can wait for a day or more. If there is no immediate recall, then assume you did dream and just don't remember it. Lie there and ask yourself questions about the unremembered dream—*what was it about, were there people, what was the time period of the dream, were there messages in the dreams,* etc. If no dreams are recalled, ask one more question: *why can't I remember?* Record that answer.

Your recall, recording, and interpretation of dreams is part of an overall process of building lines of communication between the conscious mind and the subconscious, and ultimately with the superconsciousness. Part of the process of dream recall is developing your own personal dream dictionary to bring order to the chaos of forgotten memories and childish experiences. As you do so, you are also engaging in the 'house cleaning' necessary before total integration is attempted. (Don't presume that your dream dictionary is universal and offer it for publication! It is your dream dictionary, and no one else's.)

Dream Symbols Dictionary: *See Chapter Seven.*

Dream Time: In ordinary waking consciousness, we experience time as a linear flow from past through present to future. During dreams, these divisions are transcended and time is best understood as the "eternal now," thus allowing for dream premonitions or even deliberate programmed dreams to reveal specific future happenings.

Dreaming True: Programmed dreaming where a question or an intention is formulated before sleep, and left to the subconscious mind to respond with an answer or an action. It can also be effectively programmed with self-hypnosis.

Earthbound Spirits: The belief that some spirits, especially those dying in sudden and unexpected transitions, and children, cling to the earth experience they knew and fear moving on, and resist the natural process.

Ectoplasm: A mistlike substance emitted from various body orifices of the medium, believed to originate from the etheric body.

Ego: That function of the personal consciousness that *confronts* the outer world.

Elaeomancy: Water gazing. Seated with your back to the light in a somewhat darkened room, pour water into a blue bowl and ask your question. Let yourself slip into a light trance. The water may become cloudy and symbols or visions appear in the depths. Variations include having a candle's light reflected on the surface, or taking the bowl outside where the moon's image can be reflected on the surface of the water.

Electrophotography: Developed by the Russian scientists Semyon and Valentina Kirlian in 1939, electrophotography is a contact technique in which the object being photographed, such as a fingertip, is placed in direct contact with film placed on a metal plate charged with electricity of high voltage and frequency. Electrophotography was hailed by many parapsychologists as "a way to see the unseeable" and "a window on the unknown which could revolutionize our concept of self and the universe" (Ostrander and Schroeder). These authors concluded that the Kirlians had photographed the etheric or energy body and provided a new technique for "exploring the energy body of ESP." *See also Kirlian Photography.* Suggested Reading—Ostrander and Schroeder.: *Psychic Discoveries Behind the Iron Curtain.*

EM/RC Procedure: A trance induction procedure using certain controlled eye movements and reverse counting.

Emotion: "Energy in motion." Emotion is a dynamic and powerful response to something perceived that connects to universal human experience and archetypes. Emotion is the energy 'powering' most intentional psychic and magical operations, the energy responsible for many types of psychic phenomena, possibly including hauntings, poltergeists, rapping, etc., where there is potential for the emotion to have been 'recorded' in the woodwork of the building.

Empowering Imagery: Empowering imagery is second only to self-dialogue as an empowerment essential in activating the therapeutic powers of the subconscious. Once you've formulated your goals in positive terms, relevant imagery gives them the substance required for full embracement by the subconscious.

Goal-related imagery can be seen as a present manifestation of a future reality. For instance, if your goal is rejuvenation, imagery of your body at its youthful prime actually activates the subconscious processes related to rejuvenation. By visualizing yourself at your youthful prime while affirming, "I am now empowered with the energies of youth and vitality," you can take charge of the aging process and not only slow aging, you can actually reverse its effects. Living younger, healthier, and happier becomes your destiny.

Empowering Symbolism. The use of symbols related to your stated goals can efficiently activate at a moment's notice the subconscious faculties related to even highly complex goals. For instance, if your goal is financial success, simply visualizing a gold coin can increase your motivation and facilitate optimal decision making related to your financial success. Should you decide to do so, you can take that effect a step further by carrying on your person a gold coin and periodically stroking it.

ESA: *See Extrasensory Apperception.*

ESP: *See Extrasensory Perception.*

Ether: Identical with the Hindu *Akasha* and the fifth element in Western Magick, Spirit, which is believed to originate the other four: Earth, Water, Fire, and Air. Also called Astral Light, Qi, Odic Force, Orgone, Prana, Vril, the Force. It can be concentrated and directed by will, and intensified by breath.

Etheric Aura: The etheric aura is also called the "Health Aura" because it reflects the physical body's energy complex, and provides the perceiver with the means to determine the health status and even—for an experienced reader with medical training—a means for diagnosis and perception of progress or lack of progress in treatment of diseases.

For any medical practitioner, the ability to see *inside* the health factors revealed by the aura should be of immense value. This would be especially relevant in the case of energy work such as acupuncture, Reiki, chakra balancing, Rolfing, massage, etc., where seeing the immediate effect of the therapy could be extremely helpful.

Etheric Body: The second or energy body that is closest to the physical body. As with all the subtle bodies, it has two layers:

The first, sometimes called the "Etheric Double," is fully coincident with the physical body in health and extends about an inch beyond physical skin. It is the psycho-physical circuitry of the human body (the chakras, nadirs, and meridians) through which the life force flows under direction of the astral matrix. To clairvoyant vision, it is the health aura and appears as very fine needles of radiation—standing straight up in health and lying down in illness.

The second layer, along with the astral and mental bodies, forms the egg-shaped aura surrounding the human body. It is an interface between the individual and dynamic planetary energies and cosmic forces that sustain life.

The etheric body can be projected and can be molded by intense thought and thus shape the physical body. *See Etheric Projection.*

Etheric Double: *See Etheric Body.*

Etheric Plane: The Energy Plane between the physical and astral planes. Its energies are in constant movement, like tides and currents, ruled by the Moon, Sun, and planets and moving in cycles. In theory and practice, the etheric is considered to be the upper "layers" of the physical plane and consists of substance and energy not perceptible to the "hard" physical senses. However, its substance and energy permeates the physical plane and the physical body to provide the life force—mostly "regulated" by the Moon and planets—that enlivens all physical life.

Etheric Projection: A portion of the etheric body, sometimes along with other etheric material for added substance, can be formed as a vehicle for the operator's consciousness and projected to other physical locations. Being of near-physical substance and energy, it is sensitive to certain physical materials, like iron and silver. It can be injured, and such injuries will repercuss back to the physical body.

The etheric body can also be shaped to resemble other entities, and is a factor in the lore of werewolves and wereleopards.

Etheric Revenant: This is the foundation for vampire lore. As with the ancient Egyptian practice of mummification, the preserved body—hidden and protected from disturbance, including the effect of sunlight—provides a base for the continued use of the etheric body by the personality of a deceased person. The etheric body has to be nourished with substances rich with life energy, like blood.

Evolution: Unlike the Darwinian concept focusing primarily on the physical form, esotericism extends that concept of evolutionary change to every aspect of life and consciousness including the Soul, and sees a constant movement of growth and development throughout the Cosmos, both visible and invisible. Evolution is not a thing of the past but continues, both in physical response to the environment but also in fulfillment of a primal program set forth at the "Beginning."

For the human being, the evolutionary process is primarily in the fulfillment of the potentials of the Personal Consciousness, in particular in the fulfillment of the Whole Person and the growth and development of the Superconscious Mind.

Dennis Bushnell, NASA's chief research scientist at its Langley Center, has written: **"Humans are now responsible for the evolution of nearly everything, including themselves... The ultimate impacts of all this upon human society will be massive and could 'tip' in several directions."** (Bushnell, 2010, op. cit.)

Many in the esoteric community believe that the beginning of the New Age in the 1960s—whether or not coincident with the influx of Aquarian Age energies—brought an expansion of awareness and an actual change in consciousness that is having an increasing effect on personal and social development.

In the personal area, this is having an immediate effect in the developing of innate unconscious psychic powers into conscious psychic skills. In the social area, it is expected to translate into world government and global economy, law, and human rights.

As a factor in human consciousness, the evolutionary impulse is not limited by the physical structure but rather can mold it as needed by the emergent psychic faculties.

"... a divine purpose, a great plan... evolution, but not of form alone. [It is] a process which is dual in its operation, spiritual as well as material, directed rather than purely natural... The process is understood to consist of a continuous development of form accompanied by a complimentary and parallel unfolding of consciousness within the form" (F. Hodson: *The Kingdom of the Gods,* Madras, India: Theosophical Pub. House, 1953).

Expectancy Effect: The effect of expectation on the future, to include personal performance and outcomes, with expectations of success typically facilitating success.

Extispicy: Divination by observing the entrails of an animal sacrificed for that purpose.

Extrasensory Apperception (ESA): A phenomenon in which sensory perceptions of changes produced in external objects are related to internal psychic elements or faculties to reveal new psychic knowledge. Examples are sand reading and the wrinkled-sheet technique.

Extrasensory Perception (ESP): The knowledge of, awareness of, or response to events, conditions, and situations, whether past, present, or future, independently of our known sensory mechanisms or processes. Among the common forms are *telepathy, clairvoyance, precognition,* and *retrocognition,* each of which can expand our world of awareness. Telepathy can expand our communication capacities, promote productive interactions, and provide information, often from a great distance, that's otherwise unavailable to us.

Clairvoyance can dramatically expand our world of awareness and perception of spatially distant realities, and uncover critical sources of new knowledge and power. Precognition can provide advanced awareness, allowing us to prepare for future events and sometimes influence or prevent them altogether. While some future events seem to be unalterable destinies, others may be probabilities subject to our intervention. Through precognition, we are empowered to eliminate negative probabilities while accentuating the positive. Given precognitive knowledge, we can generate a powerful expectancy of success that literally transforms probabilities into realities. We *can* literally create the future of our choice.

Dr. Joe H. Slate, working at Athens (Alabama) State University, shows an emerging body of evidence that ESP, rather than an unexplained extension of sensory perception, is a fine-tuned manifestation of the nonbiological or spiritual nature of our being, and includes interactions with the spirit realm. *See Chapter One.*

Eye Blink Procedure: A procedure that incorporates eye blinks to induce both remote viewing and astral projection.

Fascination devices: Crystal balls (often made of glass), crystals, cut glass, mirrors, magick mirrors (black glass), swinging pendants, crystal bowls, painted eyes, icons and images painted in flashing colors (complimentary colors placed together), spinning disks, and other devices that focus the attention but tire the vision. Sometimes a small focal object is placed above ye level, forcing one to soon close the eyes. Combined with either a hetero or an internal dialogue, their use can be very effective in hypnotic induction. Suggested Reading—Andrews: *Crystal Balls & Crystal Bowls: Tools for Ancient Scrying & Modern Seership,* and Cunningham: *Divination for Beginners: Reading the Past, Present & Future.*

Field: The First Thing, the field of manifestation. Consciousness, from which first energy and then matter arose as Energy/Matter packets that manifest as waves or particles. The Field is the source for all that follows—today as yesterday and as tomorrow. The Field can be accessed through deliberate thought and responds to emotion expressed with intention.

Through the Field we can change 'reality,' hence it is the field of magick, phenomena, and miraculous things that matter. Suggested Reading—McTaggart: *The Field: The Quest for the Secret Force of the Universe,* and McTaggart: *The Intention Experiment: Using Your Thoughts to Change Your Life and the World.*

Fingerpad Engagement Procedure: A balancing technique in which the fingerpads of both hands are joined as psychic empowering affirmations are presented.

Finger Interlocking Technique: A three-step strategy designed to induce physical relaxation and inner balance.

Finger Spread Technique: A procedure requiring a spreading of the fingers of either hand and a brief holding of the spread position as empowering affirmations are presented, followed by a slow relaxing of the fingers. The technique is useful as a hypnotic induction strategy as well as a sleep arrest strategy.

Focal Shift: A crystal-gazing procedure designed to generate a mental state conducive to ESP.

Focusing tools: Like Fascination Devices, these aid by attracting either the visual or the auditory senses and are used to calm the mind during induction.

Forecast: Any kind of prediction of future trends or happenings.

Forgotten Memories: Are retained in the subconscious and may be recalled using various techniques including word association, asking questions, dialogue, and 'sleeping on it.' Nothing is truly forgotten, but things may have been insignificant at the time, painful and thus repressed, overshadowed by larger events, etc. Memories can be recovered if you know what you are looking for and if you know they are pertinent. Sometimes, events will remind you and otherwise tell you that something significant is missing.

Future Probe Technique: A group procedure designed to access precognitive data.

Future Screen: A precognitive activating strategy emphasizing physical relaxation and imagery.

Gas Discharge Visualization (GDV): A form of aura photography developed by Russian scientist, Dr. Konstantin Korotkov, using glass electrodes creating a pulsed electrical field to detect stress levels in preventative medicine. This technology led to the creation of the Gas Discharge Visualization (GDV) camera to photograph energy fields at the quantum level, enabling the user to observe the real-time effectiveness of medical treatments. The GDV camera is now certified as a medical instrument and is used in Russian hospitals and among medical professionals. One of the particular uses has been to identify plants and flowers useful in treating human health needs.

As a result of GDV technology, there is a new perception of the body as a web of energies that also extend beyond its borders to intercommunicate with its environment, including other human, plant, animal, and planetary energy fields. In addition, Dr. Korotkov and his associates experimentally confirmed the esoteric concept that there is a kind of collective intelligence or spirit relating to a garden of vegetation, a forest grove or garden, and even of humanity as a whole and of the Earth Being (Interview of Dr. Korotkov by Paula Peterson, *Spirit of Maat*, Vol. 3, No. 1).

Generalized Empowerment Self-talk: The use of self-talk to target empowerment to general goals or collective inner functions.

Geomancy: Primary divination by means of randomly made dots in sand. *See Chapter Twenty-one.* Also by studying cracks made in dried mud, and by the noises and movements of the earth in areas prone to earth changes. *See Chapter Twenty.*

Ghosts: (1) Earthbound spirits 'haunting' a particular location. (2) A psychic 'recording' of emotional energy released during traumatic experiences of suicide, murder, accidental death, and painful dying. As a psychic recording, it can be reproduced and experienced by psychically sensitive people, and almost always at night when nothing competes with the reception. These experiences are often accompanied by fear, which then reinforces the initial energy. Like other kinds of recording, the original energy can often be released or erased by 'overwriting' with other strong releases of emotion such as a ritual exorcism, happy children, shamanic practices, and even loud music. Suggested Reading—Danelek: *The Case for Ghosts: An Objective Look at the Paranormal*, and Wilder: *House of Spirits and Whispers: The True Story of a Haunted House.*

Global Civilization: The belief, fostered by Carl Llewellyn Weschcke among others, that humanity in the twentieth century struggled to create the first global civilization based on a commonality of Hollywood-centered entertainment, international political organizations growing out of World War II and the Cold War, the European Union, a world economy, a common currency, universal education, universal human law, and free trade.

Global Empowerment: Global empowerment must begin somewhere. Becoming personally empowered can be seen as the first step toward empowering the globe and making the world a better place for present and future generations. The starting point is personal empowerment, and grows person by person as psychic development leads from personal growth and development to the continued evolution of humanity as a whole in partnership with planetary consciousness.

Global Telepathy: The psychic engagement of a global interaction for such purposes as bringing forth global peace.

Golden Dawn, Hermetic Order of the: Founded in England in 1888, this magical order provided the impetus and source for magical study and practice within the Western Esoteric Tradition. Suggested Reading—Israel Regardie's *The Golden Dawn* is an encyclopedic resource for the rituals and knowledge lectures of the GD, while his *The Tree of Life: The Middle Pillar* and *A Garden of Pomegranates* provide in-depth exposition of the GD's magical system.

See also: Christopher: *Kabbalah, Magic and the Great Work of Self-Transformation*— based on the Order of the Golden Dawn, a step-by-step program towards spiritual attainment. Cicero: *Essential Golden Dawn: An Introduction to High Magic*—explores the origins of Hermeticism and the Western Esoteric Tradition, the Laws of magick and magical philosophy, and different areas of magical knowledge. Cicero: *Self-Initiation into the Golden Dawn*—become a practicing Golden Dawn magician with essential knowledge of Qabalah, Astrology, Tarot, Geomancy, and Spiritual Alchemy. Denning and Phillips: *The Sword & the Serpent: The Two-fold Qabalistic Universe*—the philosophy of ceremonial magic and its relationship to the Qabalah.

Got Psi?: Website has tests for psi ability (www.gotpsi.org).

Graphotherapy: Changing handwriting for self-improvement.

Great Plan, the: Some esoteric groups believe that there is a plan guiding the evolution of human consciousness to its eventual reunion with the ultimate Source. They further believe that humanity has a role to play as co-creators able to accelerate the plan in its application to human consciousness. *See also Divine Plan.*

Great Work, the: The path of self-directed spiritual growth and development. This is the object of your incarnation and the meaning of your life. The Great Work is the program of growth to become all that you can be—which is the realization that you are a 'god in the making.' Within your being there is the seed of Divinity, and your job is to grow that into the Whole Person that is a "Son of God." It is a process that has continued from 'the Beginning' and may have no ending, but it is your purpose in life. It is that which gives meaning to your being.

In this new age, you are both teacher and student and you must accept responsibility for your own destiny. *Time is of the essence!* Older methods give way to new ones because the entire process of growth and self-development has to be accelerated. Humanity has created a *time bomb* that's ticking away, and only our own higher consciousness can save us from self-destruction. But—have faith and do the Great Work, for it is all part of a Great Plan.

The Great Work is not denial and restriction but fulfillment. There's not just one narrow path, but many paths—one for each of us. Suggested Reading—Denning and Phillips: *Foundations of High Magick.*

Guided Imagery: The use of suggestion and visualization to guide thought processes, typically to promote a positive state of physical relaxation and personal well-being. Guided imagery can, however, be used to induce a trance state or as a goal-oriented technique for managing stress or pain, overcoming fear, breaking unwanted habits, slowing aging, and promoting wellness, to mention but a few of the possibilities.

Guided Meditation: A meditation led by an experienced guide following established inner pathways to access particular iconic collections of knowledge and experience. A typical example would be found in Kabbalistic pathworkings progressing on the Path from one Sphere to another on the Tree of Life. Suggested Reading—Lorenzo-Fuentes: *Meditation*; Clayton: *Transformative Meditation: Personal & Group Practice to*

Access Realms of Consciousness; and Mumford: *Yoga Nidra Meditation: Chakra Theory & Visualization* (Audio CD).

Handwring Interpretation: Also known as *Graphology. See Chapter Twenty-one.*

Hauntings: See "ghosts." Hauntings are confined to specific physical spaces and are associated with such experiences as 'bad vibes' and uncomfortable feelings, strange and scary sounds, and sights of swirling mists and of deceased people. The phenomena almost always occurs at night when there is no competition for the experience ,and most often in locations that are rarely disturbed such as abandoned houses and churches, old cemeteries, ancient religious sites, etc. There are claims that haunting experiences fluctuate with the phases of the Moon. Suggested Reading—Belanger: *Haunting Experiences: Encounters with the Otherworldly,* and Goodwyn: *Ghost Worlds: A Guide to Poltergeists, Portals, Ecto-mist & Spirit Behavior.*

Healing through Self-hypnosis: Based on the premise that a supreme healing force exists in everyone, healing through self-hypnosis accesses that force and focuses in on specific goals related to healing, both mental and physical. This concept also recognizes the existence of healing dimensions beyond the self and our capacity through self-hypnosis to tap into them.

Hypnosis is increasingly used with healing applications in all fields of medicine: to modulate pain, to reduce certain side effects of medications, and to accelerate healing during and after convalescence. It is also used to prepare patients for surgery, hospital procedures, and childbirth by reducing anxiety and instilling affirmative healing imagery. It should be understood that any discussion of hypnosis is inclusive of self-hypnosis, and it should also be understood that anything that can be accomplished through hypnosis can be accomplished through meditation, but we have to see beyond the common perceptions about meditation as just a state of soulful self-oblivion to understand the worldly practical applications.

Hypnosis has been called the most powerful nondrug physical relaxant available. It has the potential to reach beyond the neuromuscular system to involve the autonomic nervous system to positively influence the mechanisms of disease while integrating the healing process with the emotional system and the higher realms of the psyche.

Hypnosis, self-hypnosis, and meditation all progress from the relaxation of the physical body to remove or bypass emotional blockage and open the mind to possibilities beyond past restrictive conditioning. Meditation has a particular value in reduction of stress—considered by most health professionals as a genuine "killer" of older people because it is cumulative in physical damage and tends to become a habitual mental pattern. Suggested Reading—Slate and Weschcke: *Self-Empowerment through Self-Hypnosis.*

Health Aura: *See Etheric Aura.*

Health Diagnosis through Self-hypnosis: (Self-Hypnosis) This concept is based on the premise that you alone know yourself best. Through self-hypnosis, you can not only identify the conditions relevant to your health, you can intervene directly in ways that promote healing. Various techniques are employed, but the most common includes a visual (inner) survey of the body itself with the expectation that the subconscious mind will seize the opportunity to call attention to areas of the body with need for medical intervention. Suggested Reading—Slate and Weschcke: *Self-Empowerment through Self-Hypnosis.*

Higher planes: (1) A general reference to levels above the physical—generally meaning Etheric, Astral, Mental and Spiritual. (2) A reference to levels above that being discussed, and generally meaning planes above the Spiritual, or that are commonly grouped into the Spiritual Plane. Planes refer to (a) levels of manifestation and (b) levels of the Whole Person—as 'bodies.'

Higher Self: The third aspect of personal consciousness, also known as the Superconscious Mind. As the Middle Self, or Conscious Mind, takes conscious control of the Lower Self, or Subconscious Mind, the Higher Self becomes more directly involved in the functioning of the Personal Consciousness.

Even though the Higher Self is also known here as the Holy Guardian Angel, there is value in using a more easily comprehended psychological term. Words are words and there are often many names for the same thing. But each gives a particular shape or color or tone to the thing named, to expand our understanding comprehension when we are relating to larger concepts.

Qabalistically, it is the Superconscious Mind in Tiphareth that mediates between the Divine Self and the Lower Personality.

Hippomancy: Divination with horses. If, on leaving the stables, a war horse's left forefoot was the first to step outside, a planned attack would not be successful.

Hunch: Intuition. A 'feeling' expressing the 'truth' of a situation.

Hydromancy: Divination with water. Outside, at night, a large bowl was filled with water. Torches were placed around the bowl and incantations were made. A chaste boy or pregnant woman was seated to gaze into the water to see visions of the future.

Hypnogenerativity: Self-hypnosis brings together a host of subconscious processes in ways that generate totally new resources and growth possibilities.

Hypnagogic and **Hypnopompic:** These are the states between being awake and falling asleep, and being asleep and waking up. It is also called the 'Borderland Consciousness.' It is during this state of consciousness when we are most receptive to images, symbols, impressions, sounds, ideas, and feelings. It is also a state very receptive to Intuition.

Hypnagogic Arrest Strategy: A procedure that uses the hypnagogic stage of sleep to induce out-of-body travel. Suggested Reading—Slate: *Beyond Reincarnation*.

Hypnoproduction: A trance state in which totally new abilities and highly developed skills may emerge through self-hypnosis, including instantaneous command of a new language and sudden mastery of an artistic or scientific skill, each of which could be explained as the retrieval of skills acquired in a past life.

Hypnosis: An altered state of consciousness that provides a bridge to the subconscious mind by which conscious suggestions mobilize subconscious resources, including current and past-life memories, and exercise certain control over physical body responses to external stimuli and internal functions, access areas of the Collective Unconscious, and channel communication between astral and mental levels and the physical level. The hypnotic trance has been associated with various psychic abilities. *See also Self-hypnosis.*

As the historical and scientific advancements in hypnosis continue, interest in hypnosis has slowly expanded to include self-hypnosis and its applications, particularly toward *self-development and personal empowerment.* That trend is due in large part to the recognition that hypnosis, to be effective, depends not only on the skill of the hypnotist, but even more importantly, on the receptivity of the participant. That recognition places the participant, rather than the hypnotist, at the center of the induction process. The result is a moving away from an authoritative, often dramatic, induction approach that *commanded* the participant to respond toward a more permissive, person-centered approach that *permitted* the participant to respond. That change is based on the premise that *hypnotic suggestions become effective only when accepted and integrated by the cooperative participant. See Chapter Thirty.*

Hypnotic Age Progression: An innovative approach demonstrating unusual effectiveness in identifying future events of both personal and global significance. The program uses self-hypnosis to induce the trance state, during which awareness flows with ease along the time continuum until it is arrested either voluntarily or spontaneously, to engage areas that command special attention. This approach is especially effective in identifying future happenings that can be either prevented or minimized through appropriate intervention measures. Crises related to business and personal concerns are particularly receptive to this approach. *Note: This approach requires specialized training in self-hypnosis, and should be practiced only under appropriately controlled conditions.* See Slate and Weschcke: *Self Empowerment through Self Hypnosis.*

Hypnotic induction: (Self-Hypnosis) The procedures preliminary to the actual hypnosis session, starting with relaxation of the body and calmness of mind, focus on the established intention of the session, and the development of a concise statement of that intention as accomplished.

I AM: This phrase invokes the higher self in a powerful self-affirmation (in self-hypnosis).

I Ching: (Also Yi King) A Chinese divinatory system of sixty-four hexagrams that express the dynamic flow of energies into their physical manifestation. Like most divination, it is a manipulative system calling forth the practitioner's psychic abilities. The hexagrams are all the possible combinations of pairs of eight trigrams—which are blocks of three parallel lines either broken in the center or unbroken.

Louis Culling considered the Yi King to be the greatest Magick Oracle ever given to man. The pristine Yi is not Chinese in thought, but is universal, ageless, and as 'modern' as today's English language.

The trigrams which, doubled, compose the hexagrams are made up of combinations of Yang and Yin lines. The Yang is customarily represented by an unbroken line, and the Yin by a divided or broken line. One should become well acquainted with these elements of structure and commit to memory the eight original Pa Kua or trigrams with something of their basic meanings. *See Chapter Twenty-two.*

Images: It is through symbols and images, and icons, that we open the doors of our inner perception. The great secrets of magicians, shamans, and modern scientists are in the associations they attach to such icons, and in the power of certain signs and formulae to function as circuits and pathways—not in the brain but in consciousness.

Imagination: The ability to form and visualize images and ideas in the mind, especially of things never seen or experienced directly. The imagination is an amazing and powerful part of our consciousness because it empowers our creativity—the actual ability to create. On the Tree of Life, imagination is found in Tiphareth as part of Ruach, the Conscious Self.

Imagination is the making of images, and magick is accomplished by making images and their movement real. Some of that reality comes in the process of charging those images with energy, but more comes by the acceptance of their reality on the astral plane. As images are charged in the astral world, they can be drawn into the physical world, or have an effect on the physical plane.

Incarnate Preparation: A process of preparation in the spirit realm for embodiment on the earth plane. Suggested Reading—Slate and Weschcke: *Doors to Past Lives & Life Between Lives.*

Inner Bodies: "… the seven bodies or principles of man, beginning with the most dense, are stated to be the physical body, vehicle of thought, feeling, awareness, and action in the physical world; the etheric double, the connecting link between the inner and the outer man and the container of the vital energy or *prana* received physically from the sun and superphysically from the spiritual sun; the emotional or astral body, vehicle of desire; the mental body, vehicle of the formal mind and instrument of concrete thought; the higher mental or Causal Body, vehicle of the level of abstract mind of the threefold Spiritual Self, called by the Greeks the Augoiedes and frequently referred to as the Ego; the Buddhic Body, vehicle of spiritual intuitiveness; and the Atmic Body, vehicle of the spiritual will. Overshadowing and empowering the whole sevenfold man is the Dweller in the Innermost, the Monad or Divine Spark." (Geoffrey Hodson, *The Kingdom of the Gods*, Madras India, Theosophical Pub. House, 1953).

Inner Clairvoyance: Whether spontaneous or deliberately activated, clairvoyance is always purposeful and empowerment driven. When focused outward, clairvoyance can reveal important physical realities not otherwise available to conscious awareness. When focused inward, clairvoyance can reveal important nonphysical realities that are also hidden from conscious awareness. It can discover growth blockages and reveal ways of dissolving them. It can target subconscious conflicts and repressions and alleviate the anxiety generated by them. Inner clairvoyance is, in fact, among the self's most powerful therapeutic techniques. We now know that the best therapist, like the best psychic, exists within the developing self. Inner clairvoyance is among that therapist's most effective tools. Major therapeutic breakthroughs are almost always inner-clairvoyantly driven.

Inner clairvoyance can access the vast subconscious storehouse of past experience, including that of distant past-life origin. In that role, clairvoyance remains, by definition, the perception of distant realities not otherwise available to sensory awareness. Furthermore, it includes, as with other forms of clairvoyance, the attentive organization and practical application of those realities. Given past-life enlightenment through inner clairvoyance, you can awaken past-life memories and energize them with empowerment possibilities.

Through inner-clairvoyance, past-life baggage becomes a present-life growth resource.

Inner Dialogue: Positive inner dialogue is self-empowerment at its peak. It can be defined simply as *the empowering messages you send to yourself.* Once you've formulated your personal goals, inner dialogue can activate the resources required to achieve them. Think of your dialogue as personal affirmations of power, which you can present either audibly or silently as thought messages. You will probably find, however, that silent messages become even more powerful when supplemented by the sound of your own voice.

Positive inner dialogue is essential to self-empowerment because it provides instant and direct access to the unlimited powers of the subconscious. It includes all the positive messages we send to ourselves through a variety of channels, which include not only our verbal expressions but also our beliefs, orientations, aspirations, values, expectations, perceptions, and attitudes. A major advantage of inner dialogue is that it can be used almost any time or place.

Among the most effective forms of inner dialogue are the positive "I am" messages we send to ourselves. Examples are: *I am empowered to succeed. I am destined for greatness,* and *I am a person of worth,* each of which can build powerful feeling of self-confidence and well-being. Even when not directly targeted to the subconscious mind, inner dialogue will nonetheless be registered there.

Inner Therapist: Your best therapist, like your best hypnotist and healer, exists within yourself as a functional, advanced part of your subconscious. It is your direct link to the resources required to advance your growth and enrich the quality of your life. As a fundamental part of your being, it recognizes your basic nature as a person of dignity and incomparable worth.

Inspiration: Usually a sequence of ideas suggesting particular actions, originating at the psychic level. It is often associated with 'brainstorming,' and is especially productive in a group setting. *See Brainstorming.*'Suggested Reading—McElroy: *The Bright Idea Deck,* and McElroy: *Putting the Tarot to Work.*

Integration: Integration is more than a bringing together: it the uniting of parts into a new whole. It is used to describe the goal of psychological development in Jungian psychology, culminating in the person actually becoming the Higher Self rather than the personality.

It is a difficult concept because it is a change of identity from the "I" of the personality into a new "I" that incorporates the transformed elements of the old personality into a new Whole Person centered on the Higher Self.

"Who am I?" requires a new answer.

Intelligence: (1) The rational and cognitive powers of mind. On the Tree of Life, intelligence is found in Hod as part of Ruach, the Conscious Self. (2) An independent, nonhuman entity capable of communication across space or dimension.

Intention: Acting with a goal in mind. However, "Intention" has become a key word in applied Quantum Theory, where it is demonstrated that directed thought and image can effect changes in the Universal Field at the foundation of physical reality.

Interactive PK Effect: The influences of mind over matter and motion are evident in a variety of sports-related situations, in which the mental states of athletes and spectators alike appear to influence outcomes in competitive events. Evidence indicates that a highly positive mental state with strong expectations of success asserts a powerful influence in any performance situation. In team sports, the positive energies of the team can generate a force that increases its physical capacities and sharpens its skills. Complementing that effect is the influence of supportive spectators whose energies can tilt the balance and determine which team wins. The "pull" of the audience generates a powerful PK interaction that literally increases the team's performance powers.

Interfacing: A group procedure designed to merge the physical realm with the spiritual without the involvement of a spiritual medium. Suggested Reading—Slate: *Beyond Reincarnation.*

International Parapsychology Research Foundation (IPRF): Established at Athens State University in 1970 by Joe H. Slate, Ph.D., this foundation is committed to the study of parapsychology and related topics. It has conducted extensive research and established student scholarships in perpetuity at Athens State University and the University of Alabama. The president of the foundation is District Judge Sam Masdon of Montgomery, Alabama. For more information, contact Joe H. Slate, Ph.D. at JHSlate@aol.com.

Interdimensional Interaction Program: Nothing more clearly illustrates our spiritual essence than our capacity to interact with the spirit dimension. Our awareness of spirit guides and, in some instances, the departed, illustrates our capacity as spiritual beings to interact with the spiritual realm. To explore that interaction and its empowering potentials, the Interdimensional Interaction Program was formed at Athens State University under the auspices of the IPRF. A major objective of the program was to determine the relevance of self-hypnosis to spirituality, to include mediumistic communications.

Intuition: Instinctive knowing without actual knowledge and sensory validation. "Our central nervous system automatically responds to events that have not yet happened and of which we are unaware in the present." (Research by Dean Radin of the Institute of Noetic Sciences quoted in Larry Dossey, *The Power of Premonitions,* New York: Dutton, 2009).

Jungian Psychology: Also called Analytic Psychology—the system developed by Carl Jung. After studying with Freud, he advanced a more spiritual approach to psychotherapy evolving out of his studies of occult traditions and practices including, in particular, alchemy, astrology, dream interpretation, the I Ching, the Tarot, and spiritualism.

For Jung, the whole range of occult and religious phenomena has evolved out of the relationship between the individual consciousness and the Collective Unconscious. While the personal unconscious or subconscious mind is the 'lower' part of the individual consciousness, it is through it that we also experience and have experience of the elements of the Collective Uunconscious—most importantly the archetypes' role.

The archetypes are 'collectives' of images and energies relating to (1) role-specific functional, formative, and universal experiences such as Mother, Father, Lover, Judge, Hero, etc. (2) those that are more personal with karmic content including the Shadow (repressions), the Anima (expressions of the feminine in men), the Animus (expressions of the masculine in women), and (3) the Self (the evolving Whole Person that overshadows the personality).

Kabbalah: (also spelled Qabalah, Cabala, Cabbala, and even Quabala) A complete system of knowledge about all the dimensions of the universe and of the human psyche organized into the Tree of Life diagram, showing the inner construction and the connections between levels and forms of consciousness, energy, and matter. It provides a resource for understanding and applying the principles of Magick, for understanding the dynamics of the psyche, and for interpreting human history and action. The present-day Tarot specifically relates to the Tree of Life.

Suggested Reading—Christopher: *Kabbalah, Magic, and the Great Work of Self-Transformation: A Complete Course*; Dennis: *Encyclopedia of Jewish Myth, Magic and Mysticism*; Godwin: *Godwin's Cabalistic Encyclopedia: A Complete Guide to Cabalistic Magick*; Gonzalez-Wippler: *Kabbalah for the Modern World*; Gonzalez-Wippler: *Keys to the Kingdom: Jesus and the Mystic Kabbalah*; Malachi: *Gnosis of the Cosmic Christ: A Gnostic Christian Kabbalah*; Regardie and Ciceros: *A Garden of Pomegranates: Skrying on the Tree of Life*; Regardie and Ciceros: *The Middle Pillar: The Balance Between Mind & Magic*; Stavish: *Kabbalah for Health and Wellness*; Trobe: *Magic of Qabalah: Visions of the Tree of Life*.

Kirlian Photography: *See Electrophotography.* A method for photographing the etheric aura (electromagnetic field) around plant and animal parts. In 1939, Semyon Kirlian, a Russian scientist, developed Kirlian photography, which reveals an energy discharge around fingers, plant leaves, or other living forms. Rather than photographing the actual aura, the Kirlian photograph shows a corona discharge occurring when the subject is placed on a film upon a metal plate charged with high-voltage electricity. Suggested Reading—Krippner and Rubin: *The Kirlian Aura: Photographing the Galaxies of Life.*

Kundalini: The Life Force rising from the base of the spine, the *Muladhara* chakra, and animating the body, our sexuality, and the etheric body, and passing through the chakras to join with its opposite force, descending through the *Sahasrara* chakra, to open our higher consciousness.

Kundalini manifests as a transforming force centered in the Base Chakra and operating within the body, and driving evolution, desire, sex drive, growth, and individual development. It exists on all planes in seven degrees of force.

Bringing astral experiences into conscious (physical brain) awareness requires some arousal of Kundalini and its movement through other chakras, whether deliberately or spontaneously.

Suggested Reading—Mumford: *A Chakra & Kundalini Workbook: Psycho-Spiritual Techniques for Health, Rejuvenation, Psychic Powers & Spiritual Realization*; Paulson: *Kundalini and the Chakras: Evolution in this Lifetime—A Practical Guide.*

L-Field, or Life Field: A weak electrical field surrounding every living organism, which acts like a 'matrix' to guide its development. It is the etheric body.

Lampadomancy: Divination by flickering torches. Watching the torch flame, ask your question. If the flame forms into a single point, the answer is favorable; if into two points, the answer is unfavorable; if into three points, the answer is very favorable. If the flame bends, illness is coming. If the flame ias suddenly extinguished for no apparent reason, disaster is coming.

Levitation: Nonsupported elevation of physical objects and persons. (1) Partial elevation is common to 'table tipping,' in which the attendees place fingers lightly on a table and ask questions of supposed spirit presences. The table responds by lifting two or three of the four legs and taps answers. In some cases, the entire table has elevated. (2) During spiritual séances, various objects are elevated and move about the séance room. (3) During séances, the medium has actually been elevated and even moved outside the room through one window and returned through another. (4) During meditation and prayer, some people 'bounce,' and in other cases fully levitate.

Life-before-life: One's existence before one's first incarnation. *See Preexistence.* Suggested Reading—Slate: *Beyond Reincarnation.*

Life-between-lifetimes: One's existence in the spirit realm between one's lifetimes in physical incarnation. It is believed there is a period between the previous life and the next life during which the past life is reviewed and the next life planned. Suggested Reading—Newton: *Destiny of Souls: New Case Studies of Life Between Lives*; Newton: *Journey of Souls, Case Studies of Life Between Lives*; Newton: *Life Between Lives: Hypnotherapy for Spiritual Regression*; Newton: *Memories of the Afterlife: Life-Between Lives, Stories of Personal Transformation*; Slate: *Beyond Reincarnation.*

Life-between-lifetimes Regression: A trance state in which one experiences one's existence in the spirit realm between lifetimes.

Suggested Reading—Newton: *Destiny of Souls: New Case Studies of Life Between Lives*; Newton: *Journey of Souls: Case Studies of Life Between Lives*; Newton: *Life Between Lives: Hypnotherapy for Spiritual Regression*; Newton: *Memories of the Afterlife: Life Between Lives Stories of Personal Transformation*; Slate: *Beyond Reincarnation.*

Life Journey: The 'journey' through life that each person makes. It is the 'story' of one single lifetime.

Life Purpose: We are here to grow, to become more than we are. Each of us has the ability to apply our inherent powers and our emerging skills to the challenge of accelerating personal growth.

Lithomancy: Divination with polished stones by gazing into the surface. The preferred stone is black obsidian.

Loading: Associating an I AM sentence and symbol with a full description and image of that which is desired. Then the sentence and symbol are vehicles for the entire operation and are used in self-hypnosis to convey the desired goal to the subconscious.

Love: *In giving and receiving, there is love.* Love is one of the great mysteries. We *feel* love. Love is both something we project toward another, and then something that holds things together. It is an 'attractor force' and a 'binding force.' As humans, we yearn to give love and to receive love, and we speaking of 'making' love. As observers, we see the same phenomena 'out there' in the world—not only in living things but in nonorganic things, right down to the smallest particles. We think of love as an emotion, but it is unlike other emotions like fear and anger. We speak of "God's Love" but we don't speak of "God's Fear." Love is such a unique and powerful force that it almost takes on a physical dimension, right along with the force of gravity—and perhaps it is love that is the unifying force Einstein was searching for.

It is "love" that holds all the many parts together in a functional unity. Love brings people together in relationships, but it is also love that holds all the cells and organs and parts of the body together, and which holds all the many 'bodies' (physical, psychic, emotional, mental, spiritual, and even extraspiritual) together in the person each of us is. And it is love that allows us relationships with other dimensional beings and with our Divine origin. There is no limit to love, as it is the creative force of the Cosmos.

You can give this love other names if you prefer: attraction, gravity, magnetism, nuclear force, or others, but 'love' is something we know. We experience the power of attraction, and we experience the yearning to love. We want to receive love and we want to give love. Through love, we seek expansion, to go beyond ourselves, to reach out toward union with the beloved, and through union we go beyond present limitations.

Lower Self: The conscious mind and the subconscious mind, together, are the Lower Self.

Lucid Dream: A particularly vivid dream in which the dreamer himself appears. It is believed to be a form of astral projection, and if the dreamer can take conscious control of the dream, it then becomes a full out-of-body experience. Suggested Reading— McElroy: *Lucid Dreaming for Beginners*.

Macrocosm and Microcosm: The Cosmos and the individual person reflecting each in the other: "As above, so below."

Mind and Consciousness: Quotes from famous people—taken from Larry Dossey's *The Power of Premonitions*:

"I venture to call it (the mind) indestructible since it has a peculiar time-table, namely mind is always *now*. There is really no before and after for the mind." Erwin Schrodinger, physicist and Nobel Prize winner.

"We can admittedly find nothing in physics or chemistry that has even a remote bearing on consciousness. [We] know that there is such a thing as consciousness...we have it ourselves. Hence consciousness must be part of nature, or, more generally, of reality." Niels Bohr, physicist.

"There is evidence... that the universe as a whole is hospitable to the growth of mind...it is reasonable to believe in the existence of... a mental component of the universe. If we believe in this mental component...we can say that we are small pieces of God's mental apparatus." Freeman Dyson, physicist.

" [...physical reality] is in essence the same for all... [This] oneness of the all implies the universality of mind... each individual is part of God or part of the Universal

Mind… [which] has no need for memory, since all things and processes—past, present, and future—are open to its grasp." Henry Margenau, physicist.

"Deep down the consciousness of mankind is one. This is a virtual certainty… Ultimately all the moments are really one… therefore now is eternity…Everything is alive." David Bohm, physicist.

"Mind, rather than emerging as a late outgrowth in the evolution of life, has existed always… the source and condition of physical reality." George Wald, biologist.

"[T]he stuff of the world is mind-stuff." Sir Arthur Eddington, astronomer, physicist, mathematician.

"The individual mind is immanent not only in the body… [but] also in the pathways and messages outside the body; and there is a larger Mind of which the individual mind is only a sub-system. This larger Mind is comparable to God and is perhaps what some people mean by 'God,' but it is still immanent in the total interconnected social system and planetary ecology." Gregory Bateson, anthropologist.

Magick Mirror: A device, similar to the crystal ball, to focus attention in a process of self-hypnosis to open a channel to the astral world, i.e. the subconscious mind.

Magical Mirror of the Universe: The Hermetic Order of the Golden Dawn described the aura as "an etheric structure filled with astral energies" and serving as the "magical mirror of the universe," in which all objects of perception and all inner activities of thought and feeling are reflected. In his most comprehensive book, *Aura Energy for Health, Healing & Balance,* Dr. Joe Slate outlined the multiple roles of the aura system:

- It is a highly complex system that generates energy and sustains us mentally, physically, and spiritually.

- It is a sensitive yet dynamic force that encodes the totality of our individuality and connects us to the cosmic origins of our existence.

- It is an evolving chronicle of our past, present, and future.

- It is an interactive link between our innermost self and the external environment, including the aura systems of others.

- It is a repository of abundant resources with potential to enrich our lives.

- It is an interactive phenomenon receptive to our intervention and empowerment efforts.

- At any given moment, it is a weathervane of our personal development.

- The more we learn about the aura, the better we understand ourselves.

In summary, the aura is your own personal mirror, not only of health but of character, emotional strength, mentality, and spirituality. The aura can be strengthened, massaged, healed, enlarged, shaped, and charged with specific energies and energy forms for direct interaction with other entities.

Mantra: A word or phrase, usually in Sanskrit, Hebrew, or Latin, repeated or chanted repeatedly as a way to still the mind in meditation, and/or to instill a particular feeling or to invoke a special state of consciousness. Mantras are usually associated with particular images, which may be visualized during meditation and chanted for increased effect. Some of the mantras are god names, and the associated images are of the deities. *See Chapter Thirty-one.*

Materialization: When something appears as from nowhere. Apports reappear after being dematerialized. It is also associated with poltergeist-like activity, as when stones appear in midair to fall on a house. Materializations of human forms or just of limbs and hands sometimes occur in séances, and wax impressions have been made of them.

Matrix: The background framework for all and any manifestation. It is a union of consciousness in the Universal Field of primary energy/matter potentials. The universal matrix is the pattern for the evolving universe and all within it. The individual matrix is the pattern of energy/matter guiding the development and function of each life form. It is mostly a function of the mental, astral, and etheric levels of consciousness guided by an intention expressed at the Soul level. It functions as the Etheric Body. Suggested Reading—Bradden: *The Divine Matrix: Bridging Time, Space, Miracles, and Belief*

Meditation: (1) An emptying of the mind of all thoughts and 'chatter,' often by concentration only on the slow inhalation and exhalation of breath and characterized by slow alpha and theta waves. It induces relaxation and a 'clean slate' preparatory to receiving psychic impressions. (2) A careful thinking about a particular subject in a manner that brings access to physical memories as well as astral and mental level associations of knowledge about that subject. (3) A state of consciousness characterized by relaxed alertness reducing sensory impressions with increased receptivity to inner plane communications.

Meditation, hypnosis, and self-hypnosis are all associated with special mental states that facilitate positive personality changes and connect with higher dimensions of the psyche. In addition, those particular mind disciplines being used to achieve particular therapeutic results are receiving increasing professional and scientific attention. *See Chapter Thirty-one.*

Medium: *See also Channel.* Most mediums enter a trance state and then—often through the agency of a control or guide, enable communication with a discarnate person. Often the control speaks for the Spirit seeking communication. Suggested Reading— Mathews: *Never Say Goodbye: A Medium's Stories of Connecting with Your Loved Ones.*

Medium within: The belief that each person has the inner psychic ability to function as a personal spiritual medium.

Mediumship: The study and development of the skill necessary to function as a spiritual medium facilitating communication between the worlds of spirit and the living. *See* *also Spiritualism.* Suggesting Reading—Vanden Eynden: *So You Want to be a Medium? A Down-to-Earth Guide.*

Mental Body: The fourth body. The mental body "thinks" in abstract rather than emotional form. The lower mental body unites with the astral and etheric bodies as the personality for the current incarnation. The higher mental body is home to the Soul between incarnations.

Mental Imagery: The ability to visualize specific images is an acquired cognitive skill. Mental images are the language of the subconscious mind. Combining imagery with self-talk, you can successfully interact with your subconscious resources and even expand them. You can awaken your dormant resources and exercise them in ways that enrich your life with new potentials for growth and success. With the powers of your subconscious mind at your command through a combination of self-talk and imagery, literally nothing is impossible for you.

Through self-talk and mental imagery, you can energize your biological systems and even influence brain activity to rejuvenate and recreate yourself. You can increase the length and quality of your life by protecting and fortifying your innermost energy system.

Mental Plane: The third plane up from the physical/etheric, between the astral and the spiritual planes. It is the plane of abstract consciousness, where we find meaning, patterns, the laws of nature and mathematics, number and form. It is the plane where all thought is shared. It is the upper home for the Akashic Records, shared with the astral.

Mental Telepathy: Mind to mind communication by nonphysical means. Usually, an image of the intended receiver is held in mind while a simple message, such as "Call me," is projected. Once the message is sent, it is important to "let go" of it rather than doing constant repetition. *See also Telepathy, Chapter Fourteen.*

Middle Pillar Exercise: A very powerful and effective daily ritual/exercise for activating the five psychic centers of the Middle Pillar in the body. In some ways, it resembles the arousing of chakras, but follows the Kabbalistic pattern, and the concept of Light descending and then circulating. Each center is visualized as a sphere of colored light about six inches across, one at a time, and then its god name is vibrated four times. After all five centers are established, then currents of energy are visualized rising internally from the base and then descending externally to enter again to energize the aura.

It is one of the most dynamic forms of meditation in the Western Tradition, actually building the psychic structure. *See Chapters Four and Thirty-one.*

Mind-body Connection: It is only recently that science has recognized that there is somewhat of a two-way street between Mind and Body. Both are far more complex than earlier perceived and more intimately connected through energy and hormonal exchanges.

With this recognition, we have the beginning of 'mental healing' where visual images are found to influence the body. And, with meditation or hypnosis (and self-hypnosis, of course), imagined exercises and movements were found to result in muscular developments.

Equally interesting, with Reichian Therapy, deep massage and certain exercises involving specific muscle groups were found to release emotional traumas and bring memories of their origins to the conscious awareness. Suggested Reading—W. Reich: *Character Analysis.*

Mind-brain Connection: Understanding that the brain does not produce consciousness but receives it, filters it, and modifies it based its own conditioning. The physical brain is readily modified through its environment and cultural conditioning—including education, religious, and social teachings to deny the paranormal experience.

Mind-out-of Body: Understanding that consciousness is not a function of the brain, but separate and not dependent on it. Contrary to nineteenth-century beliefs, consciousness does not arise out of the brain but preexists it and survives it, and functions outside and beyond it.

Molybdomancy: Divination with melted lead quickly poured into cold water or onto the ground and interpreting the shapes.

Monad: The fifth or spiritual body that is separate from the personality and is a function of the Soul.

Mortal Soul: The astral body temporarily housing the soul after death of the physical body.

NDE: *See Near-Death Experience.*

Near-Death Experience (NDE): People near death, and sometimes those who have been resuscitated after dying, report common experiences of peacefulness followed by separation from the body. At first there is darkness, then seeing a source of light and moving into the light, sometimes through a tunnel. At this point, many turn or are turned to move back into the body. Sometimes they see family and friends, and other times a 'presence,' who all advise that it is not yet the time for the person to pass over. Other times, there may be a review of the lifetime and a decision made by the person to return to complete unfinished business. It is nearly always a very positive and transformative experience, giving the person a much greater appreciation of life.

New Age: A phrase adapted by certain writers to describe (1) A belief in a new level of consciousness coincident with the Aquarian Age. (2) A social movement of diverse spiritual and political elements directed toward the transformation of individuals and society through heightened spiritual awareness obtained through practices of meditation, yoga, ritual, and channeling. (3) A cultural phenomenon often associated with the psychedelic and mind-altering substances widely available in the 1960s.

It is an ideal of harmony and progress that includes feminist, ecological, holistic and organic principles expressed through an alternative lifestyle that developed its own music, fashions, communal living, open sexuality, and political activism.

It became a commercial category, particularly in the book trade, which brought together subjects related to self-understanding, self-transformation, and self-development including acupuncture, alchemy, ancient civilizations, angels, anthroposophy, aromatherapy, astral projection, astrology, Atlantis, auras, biofeedback, Buddhism, channeling, chanting, chakras, Chinese medicine, complementary healing, creative visualization, crystals, divination, dream interpretation, Egyptology, energy healing, ESP, extraterrestrial life, ghosts, Gnosticism, handwriting analysis, herbalism, hypnosis, Kabbalah, magick, martial arts, meditation, natural foods, numerology, occultism, organic gardening, Paganism, palmistry, paranormal phenomena, past lives, psychic healing, psychic powers, Reiki, reincarnation, runes, self-hypnosis, sex magick, shamanism, spiritual healing, Spiritualism, Tantra, Tarot, Theosophy, UFOs, Wicca, witchcraft, yoga, Zen, etc.

The New Age movement is inclusive of a resurgent paganism and rejection of formalistic religion in favor of Nature Mysticism and personal spirituality. While it generally includes roles for ministers and spiritual counselors, along with those for priest and priestess as in Wicca, the religious aspect is participatory rather than hierarchical, ecstatic rather than puritanical, initiatory rather than theological, and inner-directed rather than outer. Divinity is found both within the person and in Nature, directly experienced rather than requiring an intermediary, and self-responsible rather than authoritarian.

New Consciousness: In just the last few decades, there has been a whole new perception of the subconscious mind as a resource of considerable power, and a realization that "consciousness" itself is bigger, older, and more fundamental than previously perceived.

Consciousness is even more elemental than energy and matter and extends throughout time and space. Modern science, and in particular quantum physics and what we now dare to call 'new age psychology,' along with paranormal studies, have restored balance to our cosmology. We see life and consciousness as universal and limitless.

We are evolving into a new relationship between different levels of personal and extended consciousness, with the conscious mind as manager able to call upon the resources of the extended range of consciousness to tap into memories, knowledge, and perceptions. The new relationship is a two-way communication, with the conscious mind calling up specified content from the subconscious, the Collective Unconscious, and the greater universal consciousness, and using nearly forgotten psychic powers to expand awareness beyond the limitations of the physical senses.

The divisions between the conscious mind and the subconscious mind are becoming less substantial and are merging towards Wholeness, with the conscious mind functioning more like a managing director and the subconscious as a director of resources. While the conscious mind is still the functional director, the relationship to the subconscious is becoming more one of interactive teamwork than previously.

Evolution for humanity is continuing and accelerating. It is driven by purpose and meaning, and not only by chance and Darwinian natural selection. Evolution is not founded in biology but in consciousness, and continues to build upon a long-ago 'programming' for which no end is in sight.

New Man: A belief, sometimes associated with the "New Age" (which see), that human evolution continues and is in the process of producing a new species with expanded awareness, various spiritual powers, more immune to common diseases, longer lived, more altruistic, and consciousness-sharing. The New Man is less dependent upon governments, does not identify himself with race or nationality, is free of gender bias, is mostly vegetarian, and is self-supportive.

Nonlocal: Infinite, everywhere, omnipresent. Nonlocal events are eternal, immediate, timeless, and unmitigated by time or distance.

Noosphere: The network of human thought surrounding the Earth. *See also Collective Unconscious.*

Norse Gods and Goddesses: *See Chapter Twenty-four.*

Numerology: The study of the psychic significance of numbers, often based on numerical values assigned to the letters of a name or to the birthdate. In-depth numerology can be studied in the Kabbalah.

OBE: *See Out-of-Body Experience.*

OBE Conditioning Procedure: A five-step procedure for stimulating out-of-body travel during sleep.

Objectology: The study of tangible objects, including psychic tools, and their relationships to psychic events and processes.

Oinomancy: Divination with wine. Pour a glass of wine. Place it in front of a lighted candle and ask your question. Gaze into the illuminated wine and watch for symbols to appear.

Omen: A sign of the future interpreted through observed, mostly natural, seemingly spontaneous phenomena—such as the actions of bird and animals, the shapes of clouds, the shape of accidentally dropped multiple items, like kitchen flatware, marbles, etc. There are probably few rules, but rather spontaneous unconscious reactions to the event.

Onychomancy: Divination by gazing into highly polished fingernails.

Oomantia: Divination through the inspection of egg whites.

Oracle: Sometimes a reference to a divinatory system other than Tarot; other times to an established place or even a person such as the "Oracle of Delphi."

Ornithomancy: Divination by bird observation. Because they fly, birds are thought to be messengers of the gods. Omens are perceived from their sudden appearance and the direction in which they fly, their numbers, how they settle to the ground and move on the ground, and the sounds they make. Some cultures designate specific birds—such as eagles, crows, ravens, and vultures—for their divinatory symbolism.

Rules for interpretation are mostly geographic and culture driven. Some birds considered fortunate in one area may not be in another, or be so rare as not to be pertinent. It really is a matter of choice—set down what your own rules will be: an even number of birds may mean one thing, an odd number the opposite; four birds flying from the right may be favorable, three birds from the left unfavorable; the number of bird calls heard after a question is asked could indicate the answers—such as two calls for yes, one or three for no; the height at which they fly can be indicative, and so forth.

Common American birds include:

Blackbird: fortunate

Bluebird: fortunate, happiness

Crow: unfortunate

Dove: fortunate, love, happiness

Duck: fortunate, stable relationships

Eagle: mostly unfortunate, but also symbols of strength and power that may be pertinent to your question

Gull: fortunate, may indicate travel

Heron: unfortunate

Hummingbird: very fortunate, may indicate love, marriage, pregnancy

Lark: fortunate for love and health

Magpie: one brings misfortune; two, happiness and marriage; three, good travel; four, good news; five, friends to visit; more than five are unfavorable

Oriole: fortunate

Owl: generally considered unfortunate, even indicating death or disaster, but also may indicate wisdom

Quail: fortunate, a peaceful household

Raven: fortunate, but their appearance may foretell something prophetic

Robin: fortunate, harmony

Sparrow: fortunate, domestic tranquility

Swallow: fortunate

Stork: fortunate, children may be involved

Swallow: fortunate, love, luck

Wren: luckiest of all birds

Ouija™ Board: A simple board with the alphabet printed on it along with 'yes' and 'no,' and a planchette or easily moveable device used to communicate with spirits. The users, usually two people of opposite gender, rest fingers on the planchette, which slides quickly to the various letters to spell out answers to questions.

Out-of-Body Experience (OBE): A state of awareness in which the locus of perception shifts to result in a conscious sense of being in a spatial location away from the physical body.

Out-of-Body PK: The human capacity to influence matter or motion while in the out-of-body state. *See Psychokinesis.*

Out-of-One's-Own-Body-and-Into-the-Body-of-Another: An experimental program undertaken at Athens State University in Alabama in which partners in an established relationship were able while out-of-body to enter into and share the body of the opposite partner.

Ovomancy: Divination with egg whites, also known as *ovoscopy* and *oomantia.* You will need a tall and clear glass filled with water. Take an ordinary chicken egg, make a pin hole in the small end, and let the egg white drip into the water. Ask your question, watch the shapes and symbols formed in the water, and call upon your intuition to interpret the images.

Pain Management: Pain Management is one of the greatest personal challenges. Too often we meet that challenge by the use of medications that sometimes become addictive, other times have adverse side effects, and still other times are withdrawn from use because of demonstrated harm.

   Pain can also be managed by diverting awareness away from the painful area of the body or away from thoughts of the emotional source of pain. While this can be a simple focus of attention elsewhere—absorption in a good novel or other entertainment, mental exercises of visualization, repetition of prayer or mantra, inner dialogues, etc.—other times may require a greater depth of subconscious management accomplished through meditation or self-hypnosis. Suggested Reading—Slate and Weschcke: *Self-Empowerment through Self-Hypnosis.*

Pa Kua: Eight trigrams, the eight signs that form the basis of I Ching, and from which the sixty-four hexagrams are constructed.

Palm Memory Exercise: An imagery skill-building exercise in which the palm is visualized.

Palm Viewing Exercise: Developed by Joe H. Slate at Athens State University, the technique combines mental imagery and self-talk to communicate with the subconscious mind.

Palmistry: Also called *cheirognomy* and *cheiromancy,* palmistry is the science of reading character and other particulars involving health, relationships, etc. from the lines and shapes found in the palm, on the knuckles, and in the shape and length of the palm and the fingers, including the nails, and other details. While it is not a psychic art, the analysis and interpretation is aided by the psychic faculties.

Parakinesis: The movement of a far-too-heavy object by a person in a high emotional state who otherwise could not accomplish such a feat. The example is that of a mother lifting a heavy automobile to save her child from being crushed.

Paranormal: It literally means "apart from normal" or "parallel to the normal" or the older "not understood in terms of scientific knowledge." It applies to phenomena not easily explained in terms of a "Newtonian" worldview, but now understood within the Quantum realm of the subatomic interplay of consciousness, energy, and matter.

Parapsychology: Also called PSI, the broad category that includes such subjects as paranormal phenomena, clairvoyance, distant or remote viewing, out-of-body experience, precognition, psychokinesis (PK), telepathy, and others—all involving nonsensory perception.

Past-life Corridor: A strategy used to explore one's past lifetimes, including preexistence and life-between-lifetimes.

Past-life Illumination: An increase in the brightness of aura images obtained photographically during past-life regression. Suggested Reading—Slate: *Beyond Reincarnation*

Past Lives Regression: A technique involving hypnosis, self-hypnosis, or meditation to reexperience past-life events in order to resolve traumatic reactions, recover lost memories and skills, and resolve certain recurring problems. *See Chapter Twelve.*

Past-Lifetime Chart: A chart formulated to determine the number of past lifetimes one has lived. Suggested Reading—Slate: *Beyond Reincarnation*

Pathworking. A guided visualization meditation between two Sephiroth on the Tree of Life. *See Chapter Thirty-one.*

Pegomancy: Divination by listening to the sounds and appearance of water flowing from a fountain into a pool or pond.

Pendulum: Simply a weight on the end of a string somewhat shorter than the length of the forearm. The string is held by the fingers so that the weight can freely swing over a simple chart or map, or sometimes an object, and revealing by the direction of the swing answers to specific questionss framed mostly for a yes/no response. Bypassing conscious control, the subconscious provides the answers. Some people believe that spirits may move the pendulum, similar to the movement of the planchette on the Ouija™ board. Pendulums are also used in dowsing, often over a map with a sample of ore held in one hand or in a hollow cavity in the pendulum that serves as a 'witness' to find a body of the same ore in the geographic location indicated by the pendulum over the map. *See Chapter Nineteen.*

Peripheral Glow Procedure: A relaxation and ESP-conditioning exercise requiring eye fixation and expanded peripheral vision.

Personal Consciousness: Your personal consciousness that was once part of the Universal Consciousness remains forever connected to it. It is created in the image of God—its matrix is "the anatomy of the Body of God." *Lower, Middle,* and *Higher* Consciousness. Subconscious mind, Conscious Mind, and Superconscious Mind. We are born with a 'matrix' to be filled in by experience. Look at the pyramid (see diagram, p. 234) as the entirety of personal consciousness and think of this idea that it represents as the anatomy of the Body of God, *which is our own body of consciousness shaping our world of physical, emotional, mental, and spiritual experience.*

Personality: The immediate vehicle of personal consciousness we believe to be ourselves. It is a temporary complex drawn from the etheric, astral, and mental bodies containing current life memories, the current operating system, "*the totality of somebody's attitudes, interests, behavioral patterns, emotional responses, social roles, and other individual traits that endure over long periods of time*" (Encarta on-line dictionary, http://encarta.msn.com).

Pessomancy: Collect thirteen white and thirteen black small stones. Place them in a bag or bowl. While asking a yes/no question, shake them, and repeat the question two more times. With eyes closed, reach into the bag or bowl for a handful of stones. Count the number of each color of stones. If more white than black, the answer is yes; if more black than white, the answer is no; if an equal number of white and black, no answer at this time.

Another form of stone divination calls for thirteen stones of equal size. With white paint, mark each stone with one of the words in the list below. To use the stones, draw a circle one foot in diameter. Shake the stones in a bag and then throw them over the circle. Discard the stones that land blank-sideup and those that fall outside the circle. Stones next to each other are read together. Read the remaining stones according to the words you painted:

Sun: illumination, great activity

Moon: dreams, fantasies, healing, secrets, change

Mercury: think about it

Venus: love, beauty, compassion

Mars: danger, fights, arguments, energy

Jupiter: money, employment, business

Saturn: possible health problems, old age, durability challenges

Home: family relations, the house itself

Love: marriage, relationships. If near Mars or Saturn, there may be separation or divorce.

Money: increased income, bills, jobs, business, security

News: messages

Travel: trips

Health: healing or sickness

Phantasm: An apparition of a living person, probably an astral projection.

Phantom: An apparition of a dead person, possibly the etheric/astral bodies after leaving the physical body.

Physical/Etheric Body: When awake, the physical and etheric bodies are inseparable, although an adept is able to project parts of the etheric body in magical operations. Asleep, it is possible to partially separate the etheric body from the physical for travel on the physical plane.

Physical Plane: The material plane of matter and energy as objective reality, and the end product of creation.

Physiognomy: Character divination from the appearance and features of the body, especially of the head.

PK: *See Psychokinesis.*

PK Bombardment: A PK procedure that targets mental energies in an effort to influence the fall of a coin.

PK Illumination: An imagery procedure designed to unleash inner rejuvenating energy.

Planes: Different levels of existence and of consciousness. While there is debate on the total number and classification on the planes, the most common is that of the five planes as used in this book. From highest to lowest:

> Spiritual (sometimes considered as consisting of two additional planes)
> Mental (commonly divided into Lower and Higher)
> Astral (commonly divided into Lower and Higher)
> Etheric (sometimes considered as two layers, one always attached to the physical and the other always to the astral)
> Physical (sometimes with the lower part of the etheric attached)

Poltergeist: Literally, a mischievous spirit. A presence or energy, sometimes confined to a single room but more often associated with a particular person, that creates unintentional disturbances such as knocking over vases, clocks, mirrors, knick-knacks, and other small but generally favorite objects. At one time, it was believed that the activity was the result of unstable emotional energies, often repressed, and unconsciously projected by adolescents during puberty. Suggested Reading—Righi: *Ghosts, Apparitions and Poltergeists: An Exploration of the Supernatural Through History.*

Possession: The temporary displacement of the self by a spirit entity. Possession can be voluntary, as when a medium surrenders her/his body to a spirit or involuntary when the entity takes over. In Voudoun, the god takes possession and 'rides' the person like a horse. While the person is possessed, the body is often capable of physical feats beyond the normal ability of the person.

A somewhat different situation arises when the control is involuntary. It becomes a state of possession in which a spirit or other entity, such as a "Loa" in the Voudoun religion, seems to push your consciousness to one side and their consciousness takes over your body and personality.

Post-Hypnotic Cue: A word, thought, image, or gesture presented during hypnosis, usually near the end of the trance, as a signal for later use to activate the full or certain specific empowering effects of the trance on demand. Synonym: post-hypnotic suggestion.

Post-Hypnotic Suggestion: A suggestion given during hypnotic trance for action to be taken after the subject returns to normal consciousness, often intended to change one negative habit to a positive one.

Postscript Cue: A word, thought, image, or gesture presented during a script, typically near the end, for later use as a signal, typically to activate the full or certain specific empowering effects of the script on demand. Synonym: post-cue suggestion.

Power, The: Qhi, Prana, life force, Kundalini. It refers in particular to the direction of personal energy combined with emotional force and conscious direction to bring about magical change.

Powers: The innate particular complexes of the etheric, astral, and mental bodies that manifest in conscious perceptions and actions sometimes called occult, paranormal, supernatural, or spiritual.

Power Objects: Physical objects, whether natural or manufactured, that have either become naturally *charged* with emotional and mental energies, or deliberately so by means of ritual actions. By example, the statute of a deity—particularly if located in a place of worship—may become charged with particular energies through prayer and devotion, which in turn inspire or stimulate devotees. A different example might be an amulet deliberately created out of material selected for its traditional association with particular energies (protection, strength, success, etc.) and then shaped and inscribed with symbols similarly associated with the desired energies. Finally, certain natural objects—such as meteorite, fossil, lava stone—that have become historically associated with particular energies and emotions may become a source of power to people in contact with it.

Prana: Chi, the Force, the Power. The universal life force flowing throughout the universe, and locally emanating from the sun as vitality absorbed from the air we breathe and the food we eat. It can be visualized as flowing into the body as you inhale, and then distributed throughout the body as you exhale.

Prana is also considered as one of the "seven elements": Prana, Manas (mind), Ether, Fire, Air, Water, and Earth, corresponding to seven regions of the universe. In Hebrew Kabbalism, Nephesh (the Psyche) is Prana combined with Kama (Love), together making the vital spark that is the "breath of life."

Prayer: (1) A mantralike series of words addressed to deity to seek particular benevolence and blessing. (2) An emotionally laden plea to deity to meet a personal or collective need. (3) A form of affirmation used in meditation, ritual, or self-hypnosis to invoke the power of the subconscious mind to bring about change in personal circumstances. Suggested Reading—Bradden: *Secrets of the Lost Mode of Prayer*.

Precognition: The psychic awareness of the future, including knowledge of events, trends, and conditions. Like other mental faculties, the ability to perceive the future independently of presently known predictive circumstances exists to some degree in everyone.

Some believe that events yet to occur already exist in a fixed, unalterable form. Another view assumes that the future exists only in varying degrees of probabilities, ever dependent on past and present realities including human intervention.

Each view related to the fixedness of the future assumes the existence of time as an energy dimension within a continuum of the past, present, and future. From that perspective, personal consciousness, likewise an energy phenomenon, is endowed with the capacity to interact with that dimension to generate a *mind/future interaction* that not only perceives the future but influences it as well. In today's complex world, the precognitive challenge thus becomes twofold: to develop our precognitive powers to their peaks and use them to bring forth desired change.

By developing our capacity to interact with the continuum of time, we become empowered not only to access the future through precognition but also to dip into the past through retrocognition. While the past exists in unalterable or fixed form, increased knowledge of that dimension can alter our perceptions of the present and empower us to more effectively shape the future.

Dr. Joe Slate writes: "For instance, personal growth blockages including phobias and conflicts of past-life origin can be resolved, often instantly, through the retrocognitive retrieval of relevant past-life experiences. On a broader scale, awareness of the sources of global problems ranging from disease to environmental pollution can be essential to the correction of causative conditions. Once you're attuned to the continuum of time, your retrocognitive and precognitive potentials will become activated to work hand-in-hand to empower you as never before to increase the quality your life while contributing to a better world" (Slate and Weschcke, *Llewellyn's Complete Book of Psychic Empowerment*).

Accepting this interdependent view of time opens considerable speculation regarding *nterdimensional interaction* through our psychic faculties such as *telepathy* with its capacity to send and receive thought messages with relevance to future hap-penings. An event more challenging possibility is the capacity to actually influence distant causative happenings through *psychokinesis* (PK).

Precognition, as an enriched extension of sensory perception, is an expression of our innate ability to perceive the future psychically. In its voluntarily induced form, precognitive awareness is activated deliberately through certain procedures and techniques, some of which were developed in the controlled laboratory setting at Athens State University under the auspices of the International Parapsychology Research Foundation. *See Chapter Ten.*

Precognitive Reality Slip: A spontaneous cue that becomes a signal instantly activating the mind's precognitive faculty, particularly in danger-related situations. Rather than simple coincidences, such slips as these seem to be designed by the subconscious to command our attention and promote preparation for or prevention of a future event. A key feature of such slips is that they tend to linger in the conscious mind, often in vivid detail, until either preventive measures are undertaken or the predicted event occurs.

Precognitive Review: A five-step procedure designed to develop precognitive faculties.

Preexistence: One's existence before one's first embodiment on Earth. Suggested Reading—Slate: *Beyond Reincarnation.*

Preexistence Regression: Regression to one's existence prior to one's first embodiment. Suggested Reading—Slate: *Beyond Reincarnation*

Premonition: Knowledge of the future not explained by prior information or experience, usually *felt* as a forewarning that something unpleasant is about to happen.

Presage: A divined sign of the future.

Pre-Sleep Intervention: The "Pre-sleep Intervention Program" is based on the premise that consciousness and subconsciousness, rather than simply categories or content areas, are complex mental processes that exist on a continuum that is receptive to our intervention.

Through pre-sleep intervention, you can tap into that continuum in ways that in-fluence those processes. As a result, you access dormant potentials and activate them to achieve your personal goals. Beyond that, you can actually generate totally new po-tentials by taking command of the resources within. By perceiving consciousness and subconsciousness as a continuum, we are activating the Whole Person rather than see-ing division and separation. In the program, the most important step is before the beginning—that you really know what your goal is, or what your goals are. Only work with one at a time, but know that it is a vitally important goal and truly *feel* its impor-tance and value. Be willing to say to yourself that you are wholeheartedly *praying* for its realization.

Pre-sleep Suggestion: A strategy in which a suggestion designed to influence dreaming is presented immediately prior to sleep.

Probable Future: Based on better understanding of the quantum world, the future is not seen as either fixed or unknowable, but in terms of probabilities that can be changed either by unexpected events or deliberate human action.

Prophecy: It usually means a message (prophecy) from God through an intermediary (the prophet) to humanity or a chosen people. The message may be moral instruction, a warning to change behavior, and/or it may include prediction about the future.

The prophecy is usually communicated through the chosen messenger while in a state of ecstasy, sometimes induced through various shamanic techniques.

Generally, to be called 'prophetic,' the message must be evolutionary, leading to progressive or revolutionary changes such as the founding of a new religion or a new political movement. There is then the question as to whether the prophecy is responding to a need of the people, or does it instead leapfrog ahead to create a new situation or condition to which the people respond in an evolutionary way?

Prophet: The person channeling a prophecy.

PSI: Psychic phenomena.

Psyche: That function of the Personal Consciousness that *expresses* the feeling of self-hood.

Psychic, A: A person receiving extraphysical communication without the use of tools.

Psychic Antithesis: A phenomenon in which psychic materials represent their opposites or direct contrasts.

Psychic Body: Generally conceived as the Etheric and Astral bodies together.

Psychic Development Exercises: We can easily stimulate our psychic growth by exercising our ESP potentials through simple practice exercises, including the use of a deck of playing cards. Begin by shuffling the cards, and then with the cards turned downward, draw a card at random from the deck and use your clairvoyance skills to identify it. Check the card to determine the accuracy of your response. Do it again several times. To exercise your precognitive skills, predict before drawing the card which card you will draw from the deck. Draw the card and check it to determine your accuracy. To practice your telepathic skills, have another person draw a card from the deck and attempt to telepathically send its identity. Check the accuracy of your responses. Repeat each of these exercises several times and record the accuracy of your response after each trial. You will probably note that the accuracy of your responses increases with practice. If you prefer, you can substitute a deck of ESP cards for these exercises. Another interesting practice exercise is called "down-through-the-deck" in which the subject's task is to identify each card from the top to the bottom of the deck.

Psychic Empowerment: Generally the following of a specific plan or program, sometimes involving self-hypnosis and meditation, for the development of innate psychic powers into dependable skills. With empowerment, the psychic or spiritual bodies can be integrated into the Whole Person.

Psychic empowerment, rather than a theoretical possibility, is a measurable though complex process of personal evolvement. Using the traditional and newer tools and techniques, you can accelerate that process by accessing your dormant inner potentials and activate them to enrich the quality of your life. Beyond that, you can become the master builder of an endless *tower of power* to the great beyond, a tower that connects you to the far reaches of the cosmos and the entire powers underlying it. Built of the finest materials—those found in your own being—the tower of power can become your empowerment connection to the boundless resources of the great beyond. It's a tower that brings you into balance and constant attunement to the universe. Suggested Reading—Slate and Weschcke: *Psychic Empowerment for Everyone*

Psychic Empowerment Self-talk: The use of self-talk to initiate a self-contained state of psychic empowerment.

Psychic Guide: *See Spirit Guide.*

Psychic Powers: All the abilities, especially as trained skills, associated with the paranormal, including Astral Projection, Aura Reading, Channeling, Clairaudience, Clairvoyance, Extrasensory Perception, Mediumship, Mental Telepathy, Psychokinesis, Remote Viewing, Spirit Communication, Spiritual Healing, Telekinesis, Teleportation, etc.

Psychic Star: In the wrinkled-sheet technique, a star appearing among the patterns. This characteristic is often found in the wrinkled sheets of gifted psychics.

Psychic Vampires: Some people, usually unknowingly, extract energy—not blood—from living people around them. In most cases, such as politicians and entertainers working with crowds, this goes unnoticed, but between individuals this can be devastating. Suggested Reading—Slate: *Psychic Vampires: Protection from Energy Predators and Parasites.*

Psychokinesis (PK): The ability of the mind to influence objects, events, and processes in the apparent absence of intervening physical energy or intermediary instrumentation. An extended definition of PK includes its capacity to influence internal biological systems. *See Chapter Eleven.*

Psychometry: The use of tangible objects, typically of a personal nature, to activate psychic functions, particularly clairvoyance. The reading of emotional and psychic energies impressed on an object such as a watch, jewelry, etc. to reveal its history and ownership. Suggested Reading—Andrews: *How to Do Psychic Readings Through Touch.*

Qabala: There are various alternative spelling of the word, *Qabala* and *Qabalistic*. The most common is "Kabbalah" and "Kabalistic"; another is "Kabala," and then "Cabala" and "Cabalistic." All are transliterations of the Hebrew word QBLH meaning "an unwritten tradition transmitted orally from teacher to student." "Kabbalah" and "Kabala" generally refer to the original Jewish version, "Cabala" refers to the Christian version, and "Qabala" and "Qabalah" to the magical or Hermetic version.

The Kabbalah—no matter how spelled—is probably the most complete purview of the world as perceived and experienced through spiritual vision that we have. It is a systematic organization of spiritual reality into a manageable formula for human study along with a methodology of "correspondences" to organize all of human knowledge.

It is a treasure trove for practicing magicians and the most expert self-study program of progressive meditation the world has ever seen.

Suggested Reading—Andrews: *Simplified Qabala Magic*, easy-to-follow techniques for utilizing the transformative energies of the Qabala, including meditation, pathworking, the Qabalist Cross and Middle Pillar, and more.

Qabalistic pathworking: Generally, a progressive system of guided meditations following the connecting paths on the Sephiroth of the Tree of Life. Through systematic 'travel', the student builds pathways in the Subconscious Mind providing structure for the developing Superconscious Mind.

The Tree of Life is described as a 'filing cabinet' organizing all of life's experiences, memories, and knowledge into sets of 'correspondences' such that new experiences automatically reveal their 'inner secrets' and integrate their powers.

Quantum Theory: The new science of Quantum Theory tells us that the beginning *is* (not just was *but still is*) the Universal Field of Possibilities that manifests first as Energy/Matter under the guidance of packets of information/instruction. Thus we can see an analogy with a computer with its operating program and its application programs.

Querent: In Geomancy and in Tarot, the person asking the question.

Quested: In Geomancy, the matter being questioned.

Radionics: The study of the radiations sensed by dowsers, and further developed to measure radiations from the physical/etheric body.

Raps and Rapping: Noises produced during a séance, seeming to come from the surface of tables, walls, ceilings, floors. They seem to be some kind of energy materialization produced by a spirit to announce its presence and sometimes as a means of communication.

Reading: The act of interpreting a divination.

Reality Slip: A situational cue that precipitates a precognitive impression.

Recurring Dream: The repetition of a specific dream without significant change or variation in content.

Reduction: In the practice of numerology, larger numbers are, for the most part, *reduced* to single digit numbers. Thus 12 becomes $1 + 2 = 3$.

Regression: The recovery of past memories through hypnosis or meditation. To generate the regressed state, we use suggestions of traveling back in time to a stage of youthful prime. The program found that lingering in that regressed state of peak youthfulness tends to be rejuvenating.

Regressive Imagery Procedure: An imagery practice strategy in which past experiences are visualized.

Reincarnation: The belief that the Soul experiences multiple lives through newly born physical bodies and personalities. Upon death of the physical body, the personality withdraws to the astral and then mental plane while the essential lessons of that incarnation are abstracted to the Soul. *See Chapter Twelve.*

Rejuvenation: The condition of becoming youthful again, or the process of making the persona young or youthful again. Suggested Reading—Slate: *Rejuvenation: Strategies for Living Younger, Longer & Better* (book with audio CD).

Rejuvenation PK: A PK procedure for activating the physical body's rejuvenation potential.

Remote Viewing: Viewing at a distance by psychic means. The debate continues whether this is a form of Astral Projection, or simple Clairvoyance. *See Chapter Six.*

Retrocognition: Extrasensory awareness of the past.

Rhabdomancy: Another name for Dowsing.

Rhapsodomancy: Divination with a book of poetry opened at random; the first passage that meets the eye contains clues to the future.

Runes: The ancient alphabet of the Germanic and Scandinavian peoples, used for both divinatory and magical purposes. *See Chapter Twenty-four.*

Sand Reading: A procedure using a hand imprint in a tray of sand to facilitate psychic functions. *See Chapter Twenty-five.*

Scrying: *See Skrying.*

Séance: A group, usually gathered together as a circle, to give energy support to a person functioning as a 'medium' to serve as an intermediary in communication between the world of spirits of the deceased and living people. *See Chapter Twenty-Three.*

Seer: A psychic.

"Self": We distinguish between a little self (small 's') and a big Self (large 'S'). The small self is that of the personality, the person we think we are, and in fact are until we identify with the big Self that is also the 'Higher Self,' the permanent Self existing between incarnations.

Self-confidence: Self-reliance. Belief in the ability of self to solve problems.

Self-development: The work, also called 'the Great Work,' of developing the little self into the big Self.

Self-discovery: The discovery that there is a big Self that is different from the little self.

Self-Empowerment: A state of personal power originating within the self. Its goal is the fulfillment of the innate potentials leading to the Whole Person. Through the use of self-hypnosis, it condenses traditional esoteric programs by activating the subconscious mind and drawing upon the collective unconscious.

The self-empowerment perspective recognizes the subconscious as an interactive phenomenon in which various subconscious processes work in concert with each other to promote our personal empowerment. The self-empowerment perspective focuses on your capacity alone to experience the subconscious, activate its powers, and focus them on self-designed goals. That's what self-empowerment is all about!

It follows that our personal empowerment depends largely on our capacity to interact with the subconscious. Therapeutic techniques based on this view include hypnosis, dream analysis, free association, and various forms of meditation that focus on specific subconscious processes.

The self-empowerment view recognizes the subconscious as a storehouse of knowledge not yet manifest to conscious awareness. As we dive deeper into the subconscious, the more we learn about ourselves and the more empowered and balanced we become. Amazing though it may seem, complex bodies of new knowledge have been accessed and transferred to conscious awareness through appropriate empowerment programs, including hypnosis.

Self-Hypnosis: "Self-hypnosis can be best defined as a self-induced state of altered consciousness that gives direct access to the vast reserve of resources and underdeveloped potential existing in everyone. It's a strategy based on the premise that you alone are your best personal hypnotist and growth specialist" (from Slate and Weschcke: *Psychic Empowerment for Everyone*).

The self-induction of hypnotic trance and the *catalytic power* of direct self-programming through simple but carefully developed affirmations mostly expressed as already accomplished "I AM" conditions, such as "I AM slim." *See Chapter Thirty.*

Self-improvement: We can always change for the better; we can improve ourselves physically, mentally, and spiritually; and no matter what the challenges may be, we can try to meet them on our own terms. Self-improvement starts with knowing where we are now and understanding how our current situation limits us. Then comes examination of where we can go from the current position and what steps we can make to move forward. And, finally, the decisions to be made and the costs to be assumed.

Self-knowledge: Self-knowledge means knowing just who you are—free of the gloss of what other people say and think, free of the bounds of family and place, and aware of the role of education and environment in your current conditioning.

Self-programming: We make many programming choices, and the more understanding we have of the external programming placed upon us and knowing the opportunities we have to choose new programming, the greater our freedom to become more than we are.

Self-talk, Self-dialogue: Discussion with your self as if you are several people—which you are. Through such dialogue you isolate those different personae—masks—from one another until you know who you are and how you can make use of those different personae in your relationships with the outer world. You are the director and producer of the drama that is your life, and you are also all the main characters in the drama. They are the different personae that you can become at will as you gain knowledge and understanding.

The effectiveness of self-talk can be dramatically increased through practice in which you listen to your own voice messages and allow them to be absorbed within. Keep in mind that the sound of your own voice is a convincing, energizing force. Although positive self-talk can be initiated at almost any time or place, a quiet, peaceful state of mind can increase the effectiveness of the technique. Before falling asleep and immediately upon awakening are excellent times to practice self-talk.

Self-understanding: Self-understanding is different from self-knowledge. Knowing who you are is different from understanding who you are. Understanding involves "why" you are who you are—the karma leading up to now, the planetary factors in your horoscope, and the impact of your environment on who you are. Self-understanding also brings understanding of the choices you have before you actually evolve.

Sequential Imagery Technique: An imagery practice strategy in which pictures or scenes are mentally recreated.

Serial Clairvoyant Dream: A series of clairvoyant dreams that guides the dreamer, often symbolically, around a central theme.

Serial Dream: A series of dreams in which sequences of information, often precognitive in nature, are set forth.

Shamanic Practices: The projection of conscious awareness into the astral world accomplished through trance induction by methods of physical stress including fasting, sleep deprivation, ecstatic dancing, flagellation, prolonged bondage, sensory deprivation, sensory overload, drumming, and the use of hallucinogenic and psychoactive substances. *See Chapter Nine.*

Shape Shifting: The projection of the Etheric Body molded in the shape of an animal, or sometimes another person, to serve as a temporary vehicle for the lower self. *See Etheric Projection and Etheric Revenants.*

Shield: The map that is constructed in Geomancy.

Show Stone: Sometimes called a Shew Stone. A crystal ball or a polished black obsidian stone.

Sideromancy: Divination with straws. Prepare a hot skillet. Scatter several straws (stems of wheat, oat, or barley) on the hot surface. Watch the straws dance about as they burn and discover the future.

Sigil: (1) The seal or abstract symbol evoking a spirit; (2) A personal ideogram condensing a written affirmation used to magically accomplish a particular objective. (3) A composition of English letter or geometric shapes symbolizing the magical goal upon which the magician concentrates during sexual orgasm to bring it into materialization. *See Chapter Thirteen.*

Silver Cord: The support mechanism connecting the physical body to its astral counterpart during astral projection.

Skrying: Sometimes spelled 'Scrying.' The psychic techniques of reaching into the subconscious mind by means of fascination devices such as crystal balls, magick mirrors, pendulums, etc., and focusing devices such as dowsing rods, shells, oracular dreaming, Ouija™ boards, aura reading, and psychometry, as an aid to concentration to allow visions and automatic writing and speaking, etc. Suggested Reading—Tyson: *Scrying for Beginners, Tapping into the Supersensory Powers of Your Subconscious.*

Sleep Arrest Strategy: A procedure in which sleep is either delayed or arrested in its earliest stages, as suggestions or affirmations are presented.

Spark of Divinity: We have a spark of Divinity that gives us, in our consciousness, the power to shape the future and even to change the present. We will earn that power through the techniques of Self-Empowerment and the Self-Improvement programs presented in books on Self-Empowerment by Dr. Joe H. Slate and Carl Llewellyn Weschcke.

Specific Self-talk: The use of self-talk to target empowerment to specific goals or particular psychic faculties.

Speculum: A mirror or other object using a focus during gazing.

Sphere of Sensation: The human aura, in particular the *etheric* aura.

Spirit: Used variously: (1) to identify the Spiritual Body, or Soul; (2) the essence of the deceased person in communication with the living or appearing as a 'ghost;' (3) the 'collective' of etheric, astral, mental, and spirit bodies other than the physical; (4)entities from other dimensions or planets channeling to humans; (5) nonhuman inhabitants of the astral plane; (6) a collective term for nonindividual spiritual power and intelligence, probably an aspect of the Collective Unconscious or Universal Consciousness; (7) the fifth element from which the lower four—Fire, Air, Water, and Earth—are derived. In addition, there is the 'Holy Spirit, which may be the Primal Consciousness or Matrix that can be activated by prayer or other affirmative thoughts.

Spirit Body: In the hierarchy of subtle bodies, Spirit is higher than mental, astral, etheric and physical. There is a lack of a specific definition, but it could be that the Spirit Body is first in the process of the descent of the Soul into physical incarnation. In this scheme, the Soul creates the Spirit Body, which then serves as a kind of matrix for the Mental Body formed of mental 'substance,' then the Astral Body of astral substance, etc.

Spirit Communication: Generally, the communication between living people and the spirits of the deceased. Also may include communication with other spiritual entities—guides, angels, masters, etc. *See Chapter Twenty-three.*

Spirit Guide: An entity manifesting on the astral or mental plane exhibiting high intelligence and wisdom with a personal interest in the welfare of the individual experiencing the more or less constant presence of the Guide. Suggested Reading—Andrews: *How to Meet and Work with Spirit Guides* and Webster: *Spirit Guides & Angel Guardians, Contact Your Invisible Helpers.*

Spirit World: The nonphysical world. The subconscious is, in fact, in continuous interaction with the higher realms of power to meet your empowerment needs, including protection in time of danger, comfort in times of grief, and hope in times of despair. Through your connection to the spirit realm, you will experience the full beauty and power of your existence—past, present, and future—as an evolving soul.

Spiritual Body: The highest aspect and consciousness of the human being. *See Spirit Body.*

Spiritual Genotype: The individual's unique spiritual or cosmic makeup that remains unchanged from lifetime to lifetime. *See also Cosmic Genotype.* Suggested Reading—Slate: *Beyond Reincarnation.*

Spiritual Plane: The highest level of creative being from which the lower planes are derived.

Spiritual Worldview: A view of reality that emphasizes the spiritual over the secular.

Spiritualism: Generally the practice and the religion associated with spirit mediumship and communication, and the belief in the survival of the individual after physical death as Spirit. Suggested Reading—Owens: *Spiritualism & Clairvoyance for Beginners: Simple Techniques to Develop Your Psychic Abilities.*

Spiritualist: We are using this term not to identify persons interested in the practice or the religion of Spiritualism,but rather persons interested in exploring spirituality and the spiritual nature of the person, of humanity, and of the Cosmos itself.

Spirituality: The study and exploration of the spiritual nature of the person, of humanity, and of the Cosmos itself. The study includes the foundations and nature of religion, the nature of man in relation to the Creator, and the connections of Spirituality with metaphysical subjects.

Spontaneous Future Imagery: A meditation exercise designed to access the future by envisioning a mental screen upon which future events unfold.

Stargate Project: A project of the Cold War involving remote viewing as a means of psychic spying on the Soviet Union. The program was based on work by Ingo Swann and Hal Puthoff, and others, at the Stanford Research Institute in the 1970s, funded first by the CIA and then continued with funding from the Parapsychology Foundation and the Institute of Noetic Sciences.

At SRI, Ingo Swann and Hal Puthoff developed a remote-viewing training program meant to enable any individual with a suitable background to produce useful data. A number of military officers and civilians were trained and formed a military remote viewing unit based at Fort Meade, Maryland.

At its peak, the Stargate Project was a twenty-million-dollar program before it was terminated in 1995.

Strategic Telepathic Procedure: A procedure designed to promote telepathy through instruction, practice, and guided learning.

Subatomic Field: Also called simply 'the Field,' in which primal/universal energy and matter appear as waves and then as particles when observed. It is the foundation for the study of Quantum Physics (also called Quantum Mechanics and Quantum Theory). Packets of energy/matter are called Quanta.

Subconscious: The vast inner region of experiences not ordinarily available to the conscious awareness. It is believed to be the repository of all past-life experiences.

Subconsciousness: Also called 'the Unconscious.' It is the *lower* part of the personality containing forgotten and repressed feelings and memories, and the fundamental belief or operating system that filters reality, that collection of guilt feelings called the 'Shadow,' the 'Anima' or 'Animus' collection of feelings representing our idealization or fear and hatred of the opposite gender, the various archetypes and mythic images formed though the history of human experience, all of which can operate as door-ways or gates to the astral world and connect to the higher or superconsciousness. The subconscious is also home to our instincts and the autonomic system that cares for the body and its operation. The subconscious mind is accessed by various techniques including hypnosis, prayer, and ritual, and during sleep.

Subconscious Mind: The subconsciousness—never asleep, always aware. The *Nephesh*. That part of the mind below the threshold of consciousness. Normally unavailable to the conscious mind, it can be accessed through hypnosis and self-hypnosis, medita-tion, automatic writing, etc.

"The subconscious is not only a content domain but a dynamic constellation of processes and powers. It recognizes that the wealth of our subconscious resources is complementary to consciousness rather than counteractive. It's a powerful compo-nent of who we are and how we function" (from Slate and Weschcke: *Psychic Empow-erment for Everyone*).

The Subconscious mind has no ethics or morals; it is your conscious mind that must make choices and impose order on chaos, develop distinct channels to reliable resources, and otherwise understand and learn that your Subonscious Mind is your key to the infinite resources of the Universe. Helping you to build the relationship between the Subconscious Mind and the Conscious Mind is the purpose of *Self-Em-powerment & Your Subconscious Mind,* by Weschcke and Slate.

But the major message we want to give you is that the Subconscious mind is an unlimited resource, not only of memories and information but also of powers and skills. It the foundation and matrix to all we are and all that we will become. Our per-sonal unit of consciousness is part of the Universal Consciousness, so we have unlim-ited potential and have yet to discover any limits to our capacity or ability to use that potential. Our goal is to become *adept* at calling upon these powers and resources to match our needs and interests, and to keep "pushing the envelope" toward yet greater capacity and ability.

Aside from the integrative process, there's evidence suggesting that the subcon-scious can literally generate new potentials and growth energies independent of our conscious interactions through processes not yet fully understood, possibly through the synergistic or holistic results of the integrative process alone. What we need to understand is that the Subconscious Mind is not a passive bystander, but always aware and always active. As you grow in consciousness and integrate more of your psychic and other powers into your Whole Person, the Subconscious Mind grows and contrib-utes more to the Whole Person you are becoming.

Understanding these creative processes of the subconscious mind is among our greatest challenges, with potentials for enormous benefit. The point here, as elsewhere, is always that the greater our understanding, the greater the benefit, *but even as we face the continual challenges, the very attempt at understanding stimulates positive developments.*

Contrary to some views, the subconscious is "the essential you," the essence of your being as an evolving soul. Without the subconscious, you would not exist at all. It's the vast totality of your existence: the 'old you' of the past, the 'dynamic you' of the present and the 'infinite you' of the future.

According to the self-empowerment perspective, the subconscious never sleeps—it's in continuous interaction with consciousness. It embraces the physical, spiritual, and psychical nature of our existence. Awareness of future events, telepathic communications, and clairvoyant insight are all among its powers. The subconscious welcomes our probes and challenges us to use its powers.

Subconscious Resources: The subconscious, with communication to the Collective Unconscious and the Superconsciousness has very nearly unlimited resources available to you through your Guide.

Substance: Everything is made of "substance," even thoughts and feelings, but there are many levels of substance existing at different rates of vibration. There is physical substance, etheric substance, astral, mental, spiritual, etc. Every level of existence has substance, energy, and consciousness. The human psyche is able to operate on many but not all levels.

Superconscious Mind: Your subconscious mind is mostly conditioned by the past, and your conscious mind by the present. But you were born with a basic purpose, with some specific learning goals for this lifetime. The Superconscious Mind is your doorway to and from the future. The Superconscious Mind is the higher self and the source of your inspiration, ideals, ethical behavior, and heroic action, and the very essence that is "the Light of Men," as it was in the beginning and as it is now and as it will always be…

The Superconscious Mind is the *higher* level of personal consciousness with access to the universal of Collective Unconscious. It is where the 'gods' or powerful archetypes and spirit guides can be found, and where the Akashic Records are accessed.

Supernatural: Literally, beyond the natural, used to describe psychic and spiritual experience. Since we don't believe anything can be not natural, we extend our science to gain understanding of such phenomena.

Swedenborg, Emanual: A Swedish scientist and theologian who had a prolific career as an inventor and scientist (1688–1772). In 1741, at the age of fifty-three, he entered into a spiritual phase in which he eventually began to experience dreams and visions that culminated in a spiritual awakening, where he claimed he was appointed by the Lord to write a heavenly doctrine to reform Christianity. He claimed that the Lord had opened his eyes, so that from then on he could freely visit heaven and hell, and talk with angels, demons, and other spirits. During the remaining twenty-eight years of his life, he wrote and published eighteen theological works, of which the best known was *Heaven and Hell* (1758).

Swedenborgian Church: A Christian church founded on the spiritual teachings and experiences of Emanual Swedenborg (1699-1772). The Church believes that people are spirits clothed with material bodies. At death the material body is put aside and the spirit continues living in the spiritual world in an inner, spiritual body, according to the kind of life we have chosen while here on Earth.

Symbolic Response: Divinatory answers to posed questions that appear as symbols.

Symbolisms: "… These symbolisms work out in a very odd way, though nobody has even been able to explain how it comes about. You meditate on a set of symbols which make up a formula and soon they begin to express themselves in your life." (Dion Fortune, *The Winged Bull* (Society of the Inner Light, 1935).

Symbols: The Unconscious is able to "invent" the means to communicate with our conscious minds, often *disguised* in symbols and strange words that we must manipulate and interpret to gain answers to our questions and to discover the wisdom to make lives not merely meaningful but also purposeful. It is through symbols, images, and icons that we open the doors of our inner perception. The great secrets of magicians, shamans, and modern scientists are in the associations they attach to such icons, and in the power of certain signs and formulae to function as circuits and pathways — not in the brain but in consciousness.

Table Tilting: A group procedure that employs a small table to access psychic knowledge. The partial or complete lifting of a table in a séance setting used in communication (most in response to yes/no questions with one tilt or two) with spirits. *See Chapter Twenty-three.*

Tarot: A vast system of archetypal knowledge condensed into a system of seventy-eight images on cards that can be finger-manipulated and then laid out in systematic patterns to answer specific questions or provide guidance to the solution of problems. While it is a form of divination, it is one of the most sophisticated and carefully developed systems of images and relationships following the structure of the Kabbalah's Tree of Life. Going beyond divination, it is also a system to access the Unconscious, and to structure magical ritual. It's a powerful Western esoteric system comparable to the Eastern I Ching.

The concepts of the Tarot cards have kept pace with the evolution of advancing knowledge, with the concepts and psychology of the European peoples. This is a very important point, for it is fairly unique among occult divinatory systems for such evolution to take place. While interpretations of such systems as the I Ching will have some evolutionary change, the system and its physical representation in the sixty-four hexagrams has remained static. The Tarot, in contrast, has changed, been modified, and evolved in physical form and structure, and in interpretation and application.

There is also an interchange between the Tarot deck and the person using the deck, facilitated by the artwork that—in my opinion—provides a positive aspect no other system has. The reader is *invited* to communicate with the cards, and that's one among many reasons that there are so many Tarot decks—over a thousand—to choose from. *See Chapter Twenty-six.*

Tasseography: Divination with tea leaves. *See Chapter Twenty-seven.*

Tea Leaf Reading: Also called Tasseography (or Tasseomancy, and sometimes Tassology) which includes coffee ground reading—which is treated separately (which see). While often associated with fortune-telling practices of wandering Gypsies, it has more ancient origins in Asia and was particularly popular in Victorian England and with Eastern European cultures. It is currently seeing a renaissance in North America because of the increase in tea drinking vs. coffee and the increase in tea shops and upscale restaurants serving afternoon "high tea."

Tea Leaf Reading is most often practiced for entertainment, and the hoped-for revelation of good fortune. However, your simple teacup can provide information about your present situation and answers to your questions if carefully phrased. *How is this possible?* Because everything is available in your subconscious mind and Tea Leaf Reading, like other forms of divination, can call up the exact information you need. But you must understand that the subconscious mind stores information in symbols rather than words. *See Chapter Twenty-seven.*

Technique: As used in this book, any "psychic practice" not involving "tools" but instead using natural psychic faculties or abilities such as Astral Projection, Aura Reading, etc.

Telekinesis: The psychic skill to move the location or change the shape of a physical object. *See Psychokinesis.*

Telepathic Activation Procedure (TAP): A three-step procedure for activating telepathic sending and receiving. *See Chapter Fourteen.*

Telepathy: *See also Mental Telepathy.* Mind-to-mind communication of thoughts, ideas, images, feelings, and messages through psychic means and generally categorized within extrasensory perception. The communication may take the form of a mental image, voices, dreams, feelings of anxiety, or thoughts "out of the blue."

Telepathy is commonly recognized as a natural ability that can be developed through training and practice. Some people—as is the case with any natural ability—have a greater natural skill than others. Sometimes a temporary increase in ability is associated with shamanic practices and spiritualist phenomena. In other cases,telepathy is spontaneous in times of crisis.

Telepathic communication can be deliberately induced under hypnosis (Telepathic Hypnosis), and Russian scientists, including L. L. Vasiliev in the mid-1920s, investigated manipulating behavior at a distance in persons through post-hypnotic suggestion *and* telepathic communication between hypnotist and subject. Through both hypnosis and self-hypnosis, telepathic ability and sensitivity is experienced during trance, and likewise in other trance experiences in séances and meditation.

There is some evidence that telepathic ability improves with age, with caffeine, and when the physical senses are impaired. *See Chapter Fourteen.*

Teleportation: The dematerialization of a person and rematerialization at a different location.

Terrestrial Astrology: Carl Jung's description of geomancy (which see), particularly as practiced in Western Nigeria, in which the astrological chart is recreated by counting pebbles and arriving at ones and twos to produce a chart read like a horoscope.

Therapeutic Relaxation Induction Procedure (TRIP): A progressive relaxation strategy designed to reduce excessive stress and evoke a state of generalized empowerment.

Third Eye: A mental faculty associated with clairvoyance, connected to the sixth chakra, located at the center of the forehead.

Thought-form: (1) An astral image created by concentrated thought intended to accomplish a specified objective. When reinforced with emotion and charged with etheric energy, it will become physically manifest. (2) A spontaneous image created in the imagination that is charged with emotional energy. Either is perceived by a clairvoyant and is felt by ordinary people with some degree of psychic sensitivity. A carefully constructed mental image that is charged with emotional energy can become a manipulative tool used in product marketing, political action, and religious domination. Suggested Reading—Ashcroft-Nowicki and Brennan: *Magical Use of Thought Forms: A Proven System of Mental & Spiritual Empowerment*

Tiromancy: Divination with cheese. Cut a thick slice from a wheel of Swiss cheese. Count the holes on one side only. If they total an odd number, the coming year will be unfavorable; if an even number, it will be favorable.

Toe Lift Technique: A three-step strategy designed to induce physical relaxation.

Tool: As used in this book, any of the items used in divination—cards, stones, runes, dominos, dice, etc.

Trance: A state of consciousness in which awareness is concentrated, focused, and turned inward to the subconscious mind, either unconsciously through repetitive stimuli or consciously induced in a similar technique in hypnosis, meditation, or religious or shamanic practice. During a trance state, carefully designed programs of suggestion and affirmation can lead to dramatic changes in conscious behavior and perceptions.

Trance Psychic: A psychic who engages in the trance state during readings.

Transmuted: To be *transmuted* is to be changed in an evolutionary manner. Just as the alchemist sought to transmute base metal into gold, the goal of the Great Work is to transmute the lower self into the higher.

Tree of Life: (Qabalah) In Qabalah a diagram with ten spheres and twenty-two connecting paths that functions as a kind of interdimensional 'cross-indexing filing cabinet' for you to relate corresponding facts and experiences with others of the same nature, along with the information similarly experienced and related by millions of other students over hundreds of years.

Triangle of Light: The Triangle of Light is simply an equilateral triangle of light that you create in your imagination *as you draw it with the index finger of your stronger hand.* The physical act of drawing it gives 'substance' to the visualization.

Triangle of Power: A physical gesture used to generate a triangle with the hands by joining the thumbs to form its base and the right index fingers to form its peak. It is a multi-purposeful gesture that can be use to facilitate induction of self-hypnosis as well as to view the human aura, including that of oneself and others alike. It can also be used as a post-hypnotic or post-script cue.

Trigrams: A trigram is a block of three parallel straight lines, each line being either complete (unbroken) or broken. See Pa Kua and I Ching for more details.

TRIP: *See Therapeutic Relaxation Induction Procedure.*

Two-component Disengagement Principle: The concept that out-of-body experiences occur in the disengagement of two systems, one biological and the other astral or extrabiological.

Unconscious: (1) A lack of consciousness. (2) An alternate word for the subconscious mind. (3) A particular reference to the *personal* Unconscious region of the mind where suppressed desires, memories, and feelings reside. In common usage, the personal unconscious is somewhat lesser than the subconscious mind. Some theoreticians believe that at least some psychic phenomena rise from these areas of the personality as *quanta* of energy/matter packets manifesting in poltergeist-like phenomena.

Unconscious Premonitions: Premonitions below our conscious awareness that yet affect our behavior. Sometimes called "gut feelings."

Universal Consciousness: "In the Beginning is the Word." But before the manifestation of the physical cosmos, there was the emanation of Consciousness and the Great Plan that first guided the formation of Spirit and then of Space/Time and Energy/Matter, leading into the Big Bang of physical creation. With physical creation we have Universal Consciousness (or the Unconscious, or the Great Unconscious) functioning in the background of all there is, and permeating every life, visible and invisible, and every thing visible and invisible.

Universal Field of Possibilities: The Universal Field of Possibilities manifests first as Energy/Matter under the guidance of packets of information/instruction. Thus we can see an analogy with a computer with its operating and application programs.

Vibration: Everything that exists "vibrates," and our perceptions are uniquely *tuned in* to specific ranges of vibration that we sense with our appropriate organs—physical as well as psychic, although these psychic organs are different in structure and nature than the physical ones. Nevertheless, some psychic perceptions combine the physical organ with one of the chakras—which we can call "psychic" or etheric organs.

"Vibration" refers to movement and "vibrations" are measured by their frequency per second. Touch, sound, odor, taste, and sight are each characterized by particular ranges of vibrations and all phenomena perceived by these senses occur within defined ranges of vibration. *See Chapter Two.*

Visualization: (1) Create a vivid image in your mind, before your closed eyes, or whatever is called for—a pictured object, person, word, symbol, alphabetical letter, deity, etc., make it glow, and then retain that image as you open your eyes. (2) Using the imagination to create vivid images of desired conditions or objects to attract those goals. 'Creative Visualization' is a practical system for personal success. *See Chapter Fifteen.*

Visualizing scenes: The same process as above, but creating images of actual scenes rather than single objects. The scenes may be static or in motion depending upon the need.

Vital Body: Same as the Etheric Body, which see.

Waking Trance: Whenever you pay close attention to an idea, to a conversation, to an object, and to your imagination, you are in an awake trance. The greater your depth of attention, the focus of your awareness, the deeper is your trance. The deeper is your trance, the more you are directing your consciousness to the object of your attention.

Wellness Activation Strategy: A strategy designed to activate the PK potential to generate and distribute wellness throughout the physical body.

Whole-body Knowing: Experiments at the HeartMath Research Center in 2004 conclude that the heart may register future events before the brain does. "The body's perceptual apparatus is continuously scanning the future. [T]he heart is directly involved in processing information about a future emotional stimulus seconds before the body actually experiences the stimulus…" (Larry Dossey, *The Power of Premonitions*).

Whole Person: An expression to represent the entirety of our potential and inclusive of all the subtle bodies. In "becoming more than you are," you are fulfilling the innate potentials that you have. You are born a potentially whole and complete person, with undeveloped powers. The meaning of life is found in developing those powers, turning them into skills, and fulfilling all your potentials. That will make you a Whole Person and serve the purpose of Creation as we can know it.

Wrinkled Sheet Technique: A technique utilizing a crumpled sheet of paper to facilitate psychic processes. *See Chapter Twenty-eight.*

Xylomancy: Divination with wood. While walking in a wooded area, ask your question. Pieces of wood found in your path are interpreted according to their size, shape, variety, and condition.

Yi King: *See I Ching.*

***You're the Captain of Your Own Ship!*:** Magick is generally perceived as a group function, but like the journey of the Fool in the Tarot deck, the esoteric path is ultimately personal and solitary.

On the solitary path, you are the one in charge, you are the one responsible, and you are the lone actor on the stage of life, even though it is the same path and the same stage we all eventually traverse. You don't have a teacher to lean on, you are not apprenticed to a 'master,' and your only true guide is your own Higher Self—*your own Holy Guardian Angel!*

Of course you have resources—books, courses, lectures, and online information—to draw upon that were previously unavailable to sincere students. There was a time when only the teacher/student relationship was the reliable way to go, but that is no longer true.

There are hazards you will encounter, and you alone will meet and defeat the challenges to your success. Even with the help and guidance of others, you alone must crown yourself, just as Napoleon crowned himself Emperor of the French Empire.

INDEX

197, 237, 250, 297, 317, 327, 339, 347, 349, 362, 365, 374–375, 379, 386, 437, 441, 449, 464, 466, 469–470, 472, 490, 494, 535, 545, 557, 567, 570, 580, 597, 602–603, 612, 616, 620, 630, 640, 643, 651, 655

Belief, lxxvi, 25, 32–33, 47, 53, 63, 83, 141–142, 145, 147, 159, 207, 235, 238, 351, 359, 371, 421, 436, 500, 532, 559, 561, 587, 606, 609, 615, 628, 630, 632, 644–645, 649

Benefits of Preexistence Regression, 196

Berg, Phillip, 561, 568

"Best is yet to come," lxxiv, 2, 330, 333, 570

Beyond Dreaming, 21, 597, 626, 640

Bija, 74, 77, 79–80, 82, 88–90

Biological Mechanism, 61

Blavatsky, H. P., 348, 366

Body/Mind Relaxation, 552

Body, Mind & Spirit, lxvii, 8, 17–19, 29–31, 60, 118, 129–130, 134, 144, 151, 153, 193, 196, 318, 360, 501, 532–533, 535, 551–552, 592, 599, 606, 628, 647

Book of Thoth, 266, 436–438

Boomerang-effect, 211

Brain, 16, 23, 25, 28, 31, 35, 69, 71, 73, 75–76, 78, 81, 129, 169, 178, 213, 262, 362, 534, 552, 559, 598, 602, 604, 620, 624, 629–630, 652, 656

Brain Waves, 28, 598

Briah, 30, 446, 465, 471

Brow Chakra, 38–39, 48–49, 52, 55–56, 72, 76, 82–84, 88, 90, 92, 110

Bruce, Robert, 48, 53, 64

Buddhic Body, 30, 620

Buddhic Plane, 30

Buddhism, 555–556, 631

Building Blocks of Creation, 561

Bulwer-Lytton, Edward267

Bushnell, Dennis, 612

Business, 109, 116, 135, 168, 217, 225, 244–245, 253, 289–290, 295, 438, 466, 477–478, 483, 488, 507–508, 521, 523, 525, 590, 598, 601, 619, 630, 636–637

Canadian Ministry of Agriculture, 247

Career, 1, 12, 16, 21, 49, 62, 95, 118, 120, 130, 135, 152, 154, 157, 167–168, 232, 252, 255, 259, 271, 296, 357–358, 362, 410, 429–430, 438, 491, 493, 504, 524–525, 540, 544–545, 575, 579–580, 597, 607, 651

Casting by Coins, 324, 344

Casting the Yi Hexagram, 322, 326

Catholic Church, 370, 372, 436

Cattan, Christopher, 266

Causal Body, 30, 558, 620

Celtic Tradition, 371

Chakra Balancing, 49, 85–86, 611

Chakra Color, 49, 52, 55–57, 66–67, 71–74, 76–86, 88–90

Chakra Correspondences, 72–73, 76–85, 88–89

Chakra Development Exercises, 85–86

Chakra Location, 55–57, 66–67, 71–86, 88–89, 100, 110

Chakra names, colors, associated planets and Tattwas, 55

Chakra System, 26, 47, 55, 64–68, 71–72, 74–79, 84–86, 94, 654

Chakras, lxix, 27, 55, 58, 65–68, 70–72, 79, 84, 86, 88–91, 94, 110, 225, 535, 552, 558–559, 564, 585, 599, 611, 624, 629, 631, 656

Chamberlain, Gene, 42

Changing, 6, 8, 123, 314–316, 324, 501, 562, 616

Channeling, 82, 199, 213, 260, 361, 368, 502, 595, 600, 630–631, 641–642, 648

Chanting, 32, 90, 139, 142, 144–145, 208–209, 225, 515, 591, 631

Chants, 143–144, 555, 561

Charge, 147–148, 177, 185, 206, 209, 225, 503, 520, 580, 602–603, 610, 657

Chariot, 375, 383, 402, 454, 471, 473, 479, 484, 559

Chesed, 31, 82, 452, 454–456, 469, 472, 474, 477, 481

Chess Method of Casting, 326

Chiah, 31

Chokmah, 31, 55, 84, 441, 449, 451–452, 469, 471, 474, 477, 481, 494

Christianity, 369, 371–372, 425, 556, 651

CIA, 103–105, 649

Cicero, Chic, 439, 498, 568

Cicero, Sandra Tabatha, 439, 498, 568

GET MORE AT LLEWELLYN.COM

Visit us online to browse hundreds of our books and decks, plus sign up to receive our e-newsletters and exclusive online offers.

- Free tarot readings • Spell-a-Day • Moon phases
- Recipes, spells, and tips • Blogs • Encyclopedia
- Author interviews, articles, and upcoming events

GET SOCIAL WITH LLEWELLYN

Find us on

www.Facebook.com/LlewellynBooks

Follow us on

www.Twitter.com/Llewellynbooks

GET BOOKS AT LLEWELLYN

LLEWELLYN ORDERING INFORMATION

Order online: Visit our website at www.llewellyn.com to select your books and place an order on our secure server.

Order by phone:
- Call toll free within the U.S. at 1-877-NEW-WRLD (1-877-639-9753)
- Call toll free within Canada at 1-866-NEW-WRLD (1-866-639-9753)
- We accept VISA, MasterCard, and American Express

Order by mail:
Send the full price of your order (MN residents add 6.875% sales tax) in U.S. funds, plus postage and handling to: Llewellyn Worldwide, 2143 Wooddale Drive Woodbury, MN 55125-2989

POSTAGE AND HANDLING

STANDARD (U.S. & Canada):
(Please allow 12 business days)
$25.00 and under, add $4.00.
$25.01 and over, FREE SHIPPING.

INTERNATIONAL ORDERS (airmail only):
$16.00 for one book, plus $3.00 for each additional book.

Visit us online for more shipping options. Prices subject to change.

Psychic Empowerment for Everyone
You Have the Power, Learn How to Use It
CARL LLEWELLYN WESCHCKE
JOE H. SLATE PhD

Surging within us all is a limitless wellspring of psychic power. Open yourself to spiritual enlightenment, personal enrichment, and lifelong empowerment by tapping into this incredible resource.

Llewellyn's own Carl Llewellyn Weschcke has teamed up with parapsychologist Joe H. Slate to write this comprehensive guide to the psychic realm. Exploring the link between psychic phenomena and the paranormal, they map inner and outer psychic dimensions and explain how to access them. Easy techniques in self-hypnosis and dream work demonstrate how to expand your consciousness, navigate psychic planes, and communicate with the spirit realm and your higher self. Featuring a seven-day psychic empowerment plan, this exciting path to self-discovery will help you develop vast psychic skills to enrich your relationships, enhance your career, grow spiritually, fulfill your life purpose, and prepare for 2012.

978-0-7387-1893-4, 264 pp., 6 x 9   **$15.95**

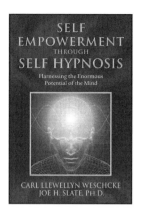

Self-Empowerment through Self-Hypnosis
Harnessing the Enormous Potential of the Mind
Carl Llewellyn Weschcke
Joe H. Slate, Ph.D.

Take charge of your life. Realize your full potential. Discover the limitless opportunities of self-hypnosis.

Carl Llewellyn Weschcke, chairman of Llewellyn Worldwide, and Joe H. Slate, a licensed psychologist and experienced hypnotist, can help you tap into the unlimited power of your subconscious. Follow helpful scripts and practice easy techniques—involving trance, meditation, and sleep—to transform into the empowered person you're meant to be. Once you've learned how to access your subconscious, anything is possible: changing your appearance, quitting bad habits, elevating your consciousness, and evolving into your higher self.

978-0-7387-1928-3, 264 pp., 6 x 9 $15.95